β

USING
ECONOMETRICS

SEVENTH EDITION

β

USING ECONOMETRICS
A PRACTICAL GUIDE

A. H. Studenmund
Occidental College

with the assistance of
Bruce K. Johnson
Centre College

PEARSON

Boston   Columbus   Indianapolis   New York   San Francisco

Amsterdam   Cape Town   Dubai   London   Madrid   Milan   Munich   Paris   Montreal   Toronto

Delhi   Mexico City   Sao Paulo   Sydney   Hong Kong   Seoul   Singapore   Taipei   Tokyo

Vice President, Business Publishing:
    Donna Battista
Editor-in-Chief: Adrienne D'Ambrosio
Senior Acquisitions Editor: Christina Masturzo
Acquisitions Editor/Program Manager:
    Neeraj Bhalla
Editorial Assistant: Diana Tetterton
Vice President, Product Marketing:
    Maggie Moylan
Director of Marketing, Digital Services and
    Products: Jeanette Koskinas
Field Marketing Manager: Ramona Elmer
Product Marketing Assistant: Jessica Quazza
Team Lead, Program Management:
    Ashley Santora
Team Lead, Project Management: Jeff Holcomb
Project Manager: Liz Napolitano
Operations Specialist: Carol Melville
Creative Director: Blair Brown

Art Director: Jon Boylan
Vice President, Director of Digital Strategy
    and Assessment: Paul Gentile
Manager of Learning Applications:
    Paul DeLuca
Digital Editor: Denise Clinton
Director, Digital Studio: Sacha Laustsen
Digital Studio Manager: Diane Lombardo
Digital Studio Project Manager: Melissa Honig
Digital Studio Project Manager: Robin Lazrus
Digital Content Team Lead: Noel Lotz
Digital Content Project Lead: Courtney Kamauf
Full-Service Project Management and
    Composition: Cenveo® Publisher Services
Interior Designer: Cenveo® Publisher Services
Cover Designer: Jon Boylan
Printer/Binder: Edwards Brothers
Cover Printer: Phoenix Color/Hagerstown

Dedicated to the memory of

Green Beret

Staff Sergeant

Scott Studenmund

Killed in action in Afghanistan on June 9, 2014

The Pearson Series in Economics

Keat/Young/Erfle
Managerial Economics

Klein
Mathematical Methods for Economics

Krugman/Obstfeld/Melitz
International Economics: Theory & Policy*

Laidler
The Demand for Money

Leeds/von Allmen
The Economics of Sports

Leeds/von Allmen/Schiming
Economics*

Lynn
Economic Development: Theory and Practice for a Divided World

Miller
Economics Today*

Understanding Modern Economics

Miller/Benjamin
The Economics of Macro Issues

Miller/Benjamin/North
The Economics of Public Issues

Mills/Hamilton
Urban Economics

Mishkin
The Economics of Money, Banking, and Financial Markets*

The Economics of Money, Banking, and Financial Markets, Business School Edition*

Macroeconomics: Policy and Practice*

Murray
Econometrics: A Modern Introduction

O'Sullivan/Sheffrin/Perez
Economics: Principles, Applications and Tools*

Parkin
Economics*

Perloff
Microeconomics*

Microeconomics: Theory and Applications with Calculus*

Perloff/Brander
Managerial Economics and Strategy*

Phelps
Health Economics

Pindyck/Rubinfeld
Microeconomics*

Riddell/Shackelford/Stamos/Schneider
Economics: A Tool for Critically Understanding Society

Roberts
The Choice: A Fable of Free Trade and Protection

Rohlf
Introduction to Economic Reasoning

Roland
Development Economics

Scherer
Industry Structure, Strategy, and Public Policy

Schiller
The Economics of Poverty and Discrimination

Sherman
Market Regulation

Stock/Watson
Introduction to Econometrics

Studenmund
Using Econometrics: A Practical Guide

Tietenberg/Lewis
Environmental and Natural Resource Economics
Environmental Economics and Policy

Todaro/Smith
Economic Development

Waldman/Jensen
Industrial Organization: Theory and Practice

Walters/Walters/Appel/Callahan/Centanni/ Maex/O'Neill
Econversations: Today's Students Discuss Today's Issues

Weil
Economic Growth

Williamson
Macroeconomics

CONTENTS

PREFACE

*Econometric education is a lot like learning to fly a plane; you learn
more from actually doing it than you learn from reading about it.*

Using Econometrics represents an innovative approach to the understanding of elementary econometrics. It covers the topic of single-equation linear regression analysis in an easily understandable format that emphasizes real-world examples and exercises. As the subtitle *A Practical Guide* implies, the book is aimed not only at beginning econometrics students but also at regression users looking for a refresher and at experienced practitioners who want a convenient reference.

What's New in the Seventh Edition?

Using Econometrics has been praised as "one of the most important new texts of the last 30 years," so we've retained the clarity and practicality of previous editions. However, we're delighted to have made a number of substantial improvements in the text.

The most exciting upgrades are:

1. **Econometric Labs**: These new and innovative learning tools are optional appendices that give students hands-on opportunities to better understand the econometric principles that they're reading about in the chapters. The labs originally were designed to be assigned in a classroom setting, but they also have turned out to be extremely valuable for readers who are not in a class or for individual students in classes where the labs aren't assigned. Hints on how best to use these econometric labs and answers to the lab questions are available in the instructor's manual on the *Using Econometrics* Web site.

2. **The Use of Stata throughout the Text:** In our opinion, Stata has become the econometric software package of choice among economic researchers. As a result, we have estimated all the text examples and exercises with Stata and have included a short appendix to help students get started with Stata. Beyond this, we have added a complete guide to *Using Stata* to our Web site. This guide, written by John Perry of Centre College, explains in detail all the Stata commands needed to replicate the text's equations and answer the text's exercises. However, even though we use Stata extensively, *Using Econometrics* is not tied to

Stata or any other econometric software, so the text works well with all standard regression packages.

3. **Expanded Econometric Content:** We have added coverage of a number of econometric tests and procedures, for example the Breusch-Pagan test and the Prais–Winsten approach to Generalized Least Squares. In addition, we have expanded the coverage of even more topics, for example the *F*-test, confidence intervals, the Lagrange Multiplier test, and the Dickey–Fuller test. Finally, we have simplified the notation and improved the clarity of the explanations in Chapters 12–16, particularly in topics like dynamic equations, dummy dependent variables, instrumental variables, and panel data.

4. **Answers to Many More Exercises:** In response to requests from instructors and students, we have more than tripled the number of exercises that are answered in the text's appendix. These answers will allow students to learn on their own, because students will be able to attempt an exercise and then check their answers against those in the back of the book without having to involve their professors. In order to continue to provide good exercises for professors to include in problem sets and exams, we have expanded the number of exercises contained in the text's Web site.

5. **Dramatically Improved PowerPoint Slides:** We recognize the importance of PowerPoint slides to instructors with large classes, so we have dramatically improved the quality of the text's PowerPoints. The slides replicate each chapter's main equations and examples, and also provide chapter summaries and lists of the key concepts in each chapter. The PowerPoint slides can be downloaded from the text's Web site, and they're designed to be easily edited and individualized.

6. **An Expanded and Improved Web Site:** We believe that this edition's Web site is the best we've produced. As you'd expect, the Web site includes all the text's data sets, in easily downloadable Stata, EViews, Excel, and ASCII formats, but we have gone far beyond that. We have added *Using Stata*, a complete guide to the Stata commands needed to estimate the book's equations; we have dramatically improved the PowerPoint slides; and we have added answers to the new econometric labs and instructions on how best to use these labs in a classroom setting. In addition, the Web site also includes an instructor's manual, additional exercises, extra interactive regression learning exercises, and additional data sets. But why take our word for it? Take a look for yourself at http://www.pearsonhighered.com/studenmund

Features

1. Our approach to the learning of econometrics is simple, intuitive, and easy to understand. We do not use matrix algebra, and we relegate proofs and calculus to the footnotes or exercises.

2. We include numerous examples and example-based exercises. We feel that the best way to get a solid grasp of applied econometrics is through an example-oriented approach.

3. Although most of this book is at a simpler level than other econometrics texts, Chapters 6 and 7 on specification choice are among the most complete in the field. We think that an understanding of specification issues is vital for regression users.

4. We use a unique kind of learning tool called an *interactive regression learning exercise* to help students simulate econometric analysis by giving them feedback on various kinds of decisions without relying on computer time or much instructor supervision.

5. We're delighted to introduce a new innovative learning tool called an *econometric lab*. These econometric labs, developed by Bruce Johnson of Centre College and tested successfully at two other institutions, are optional appendices aimed at giving students hands-on experience with the econometric procedures they're reading about. Students who complete these econometric labs will be much better prepared to undertake econometric research on their own.

The formal prerequisites for using this book are few. Readers are assumed to have been exposed to some microeconomic and macroeconomic theory, basic mathematical functions, and elementary statistics (even if they have forgotten most if it). Students with little statistical background are encouraged to begin their study of econometrics by reading Chapter 17, "Statistical Principles," on the text's Web site.

Because the prerequisites are few and the statistics material is self-contained, *Using Econometrics* can be used not only in undergraduate courses but also in MBA-level courses in quantitative methods. We also have been told that the book is a helpful supplement for graduate-level econometrics courses.

The Stata and EViews Options

We're delighted to be able to offer our readers the chance to purchase the student version of Stata or EViews at discounted prices when bundled with the textbook. Stata and EViews are two of the best econometric software programs available, so it's a real advantage to be able to buy them at substantial savings.

We urge professors to make these options available to their students even if Stata or EViews aren't used in class. The advantages to students of owning their own regression software are many. They can run regressions when they're off-campus, they will add a marketable skill to their résumé if they learn Stata or EViews, and they'll own a software package that will allow them to run regressions after the class is over if they choose the EViews option.

Acknowledgments

This edition of *Using Econometrics* has been blessed by superb contributions from Ron Michener of the University of Virginia and Bruce Johnson of Centre College. Ron was the lead reviewer, and in that role he commented on every section and virtually every equation in the book, creating a 132-page *magnum opus* of textbook reviewing that may never be surpassed in length or quality.

Just as importantly, Ron introduced us to Bruce Johnson. Bruce wrote the first drafts of the econometric labs and three other sections, made insightful comments on the entire revision, helped increase the role of Stata in the book, and proofread the manuscript. Because of Bruce's professional expertise, clear writing style, and infectious enthusiasm for econometrics, we're happy to announce that he will be a coauthor of the 8th and subsequent editions of *Using Econometrics*.

This book's spiritual parents were Henry Cassidy and Carolyn Summers. Henry co-authored the first edition of *Using Econometrics* as an expansion of his own work of the same name, and Carolyn was the text's editorial consultant, proofreader, and indexer for four straight editions. Other important professional contributors to previous editions were the late Peter Kennedy, Nobel Prize winner Rob Engle of New York University, Gary Smith of Pomona College, Doug Steigerwald of the University of California at Santa Barbara, and Susan Averett of Lafayette College.

In addition, this edition benefitted from the evaluations of a talented group of professional reviewers:

Lesley Chiou, Occidental College
Dylan Conger, George Washington University
Leila Farivar, Ohio State University
Abbass Grammy, California State University, Bakersfield

Jason Hecht, Ramapo College
Jin Man Lee, University of Illinois at Chicago
Noelwah Netusl, Reed College
Robert Parks, Washington University in St. Louis
David Phillips, Hope College
John Perry, Centre College
Robert Shapiro, Columbia University
Phanindra Wunnava, Middlebury College

Invaluable in the editorial and production process were Jean Bermingham, Neeraj Bhalla, Adrienne D'Ambrosio, Marguerite Dessornes, Christina Masturzo, Liz Napolitano, Bill Rising, and Kathy Smith. Providing crucial emotional support during an extremely difficult time were Sarah Newhall, Barbara Passerelle, Barbara and David Studenmund, and my immediate family, Jaynie and Connell Studenmund and Brent Morse. Finally, I'd like to thank my wonderful Occidental College colleagues and students for their feedback and encouragement. These particularly included Lesley Chiou, Jack Gephart, Jorge Gonzalez, Andy Jalil, Kate Johnstone, Mary Lopez, Jessica May, Cole Moniz, Robby Moore, Kyle Yee, and, especially, Koby Deitz.

A. H. Studenmund

Chapter 1

An Overview of Regression Analysis

1.1 What Is Econometrics?

"Econometrics is too mathematical; it's the reason my best friend isn't majoring in economics."

"There are two things you are better off not watching in the making: sausages and econometric estimates."[1]

"Econometrics may be defined as the quantitative analysis of actual economic phenomena."[2]

"It's my experience that 'economy-tricks' is usually nothing more than a justification of what the author believed before the research was begun."

Obviously, econometrics means different things to different people. To beginning students, it may seem as if econometrics is an overly complex obstacle to an otherwise useful education. To skeptical observers, econometric

---

1. Ed Leamer, "Let's take the Con out of Econometrics," *American Economic Review*, Vol. 73, No. 1, p. 37.

2. Paul A. Samuelson, T. C. Koopmans, and J. R. Stone, "Report of the Evaluative Committee for *Econometrica*," *Econometrica*, 1954, p. 141.

results should be trusted only when the steps that produced those results are completely known. To professionals in the field, econometrics is a fascinating set of techniques that allows the measurement and analysis of economic phenomena and the prediction of future economic trends.

You're probably thinking that such diverse points of view sound like the statements of blind people trying to describe an elephant based on which part they happen to be touching, and you're partially right. Econometrics has both a formal definition and a larger context. Although you can easily memorize the formal definition, you'll get the complete picture only by understanding the many uses of and alternative approaches to econometrics.

That said, we need a formal definition. **Econometrics**—literally, "economic measurement"—is the quantitative measurement and analysis of actual economic and business phenomena. It attempts to quantify economic reality and bridge the gap between the abstract world of economic theory and the real world of human activity. To many students, these worlds may seem far apart. On the one hand, economists theorize equilibrium prices based on carefully conceived marginal costs and marginal revenues; on the other, many firms seem to operate as though they have never heard of such concepts. Econometrics allows us to examine data and to quantify the actions of firms, consumers, and governments. Such measurements have a number of different uses, and an examination of these uses is the first step to understanding econometrics.

Uses of Econometrics

Econometrics has three major uses:

1. describing economic reality
2. testing hypotheses about economic theory and policy
3. forecasting future economic activity

The simplest use of econometrics is description. We can use econometrics to quantify economic activity and measure marginal effects because econometrics allows us to estimate numbers and put them in equations that previously contained only abstract symbols. For example, consumer demand for a particular product often can be thought of as a relationship between the quantity demanded (Q) and the product's price (P), the price of a substitute (P_s), and disposable income (Yd). For most goods, the relationship between consumption and disposable income is expected to be positive, because an increase in disposable income will be associated with an increase in the consumption of the product. Econometrics actually allows us to estimate that relationship based upon past consumption, income, and prices. In other words, a general and purely theoretical functional relationship like:

$$Q = \beta_0 + \beta_1 P + \beta_2 P_S + \beta_1 Yd \qquad (1.1)$$

can become explicit:

$$Q = 27.7 - 0.11P + 0.03P_S + 0.23Yd \qquad (1.2)$$

This technique gives a much more specific and descriptive picture of the function.[3] Let's compare Equations 1.1 and 1.2. Instead of expecting consumption merely to "increase" if there is an increase in disposable income, Equation 1.2 allows us to expect an increase of a specific amount (0.23 units for each unit of increased disposable income). The number 0.23 is called an estimated regression coefficient, and it is the ability to estimate these coefficients that makes econometrics valuable.

The second use of econometrics is hypothesis testing, the evaluation of alternative theories with quantitative evidence. Much of economics involves building theoretical models and testing them against evidence, and hypothesis testing is vital to that scientific approach. For example, you could test the hypothesis that the product in Equation 1.1 is what economists call a normal good (one for which the quantity demanded increases when disposable income increases). You could do this by applying various statistical tests to the estimated coefficient (0.23) of disposable income (Yd) in Equation 1.2. At first glance, the evidence would seem to support this hypothesis, because the coefficient's sign is positive, but the "statistical significance" of that estimate would have to be investigated before such a conclusion could be justified. Even though the estimated coefficient is positive, as expected, it may not be sufficiently different from zero to convince us that the true coefficient is indeed positive.

The third and most difficult use of econometrics is to forecast or predict what is likely to happen next quarter, next year, or further into the future, based on what has happened in the past. For example, economists use econometric models to make forecasts of variables like sales, profits, Gross Domestic Product (GDP), and the inflation rate. The accuracy of such forecasts depends in large measure on the degree to which the past is a good guide to the future. Business leaders and politicians tend to be especially interested in this use of

---

3. It's of course naïve to build a model of sales (demand) without taking supply into consideration. Unfortunately, it's very difficult to learn how to estimate a system of simultaneous equations until you've learned how to estimate a single equation. As a result, we will postpone our discussion of the econometrics of simultaneous equations until Chapter 14. Until then, you should be aware that we sometimes will encounter right-hand-side variables that are not truly "independent" from a theoretical point of view.

econometrics because they need to make decisions about the future, and the penalty for being wrong (bankruptcy for the entrepreneur and political defeat for the candidate) is high. To the extent that econometrics can shed light on the impact of their policies, business and government leaders will be better equipped to make decisions. For example, if the president of a company that sold the product modeled in Equation 1.1 wanted to decide whether to increase prices, forecasts of sales with and without the price increase could be calculated and compared to help make such a decision.

Alternative Econometric Approaches

There are many different approaches to quantitative work. For example, the fields of biology, psychology, and physics all face quantitative questions similar to those faced in economics and business. However, these fields tend to use somewhat different techniques for analysis because the problems they face aren't the same. For example, economics typically is an observational discipline rather than an experimental one. "We need a special field called econometrics, and textbooks about it, because it is generally accepted that economic data possess certain properties that are not considered in standard statistics texts or are not sufficiently emphasized there for use by economists."[4]

Different approaches also make sense within the field of economics. A model built solely for descriptive purposes might be different from a forecasting model, for example.

To get a better picture of these approaches, let's look at the steps used in nonexperimental quantitative research:

1. specifying the models or relationships to be studied
2. collecting the data needed to quantify the models
3. quantifying the models with the data

The specifications used in step 1 and the techniques used in step 3 differ widely between and within disciplines. Choosing the best specification for a given model is a theory-based skill that is often referred to as the "art" of econometrics. There are many alternative approaches to quantifying the same equation, and each approach may produce somewhat different results. The choice of approach is left to the individual econometrician (the researcher using econometrics), but each researcher should be able to justify that choice.

---

4. Clive Granger, "A Review of Some Recent Textbooks of Econometrics," *Journal of Economic Literature*, Vol. 32, No. 1, p. 117.

This book will focus primarily on one particular econometric approach: *single-equation linear regression analysis.* The majority of this book will thus concentrate on regression analysis, but it is important for every econometrician to remember that regression is only one of many approaches to econometric quantification.

The importance of critical evaluation cannot be stressed enough; a good econometrician can diagnose faults in a particular approach and figure out how to repair them. The limitations of the regression analysis approach must be fully perceived and appreciated by anyone attempting to use regression analysis or its findings. The possibility of missing or inaccurate data, incorrectly formulated relationships, poorly chosen estimating techniques, or improper statistical testing procedures implies that the results from regression analyses always should be viewed with some caution.

1.2 What Is Regression Analysis?

Econometricians use regression analysis to make quantitative estimates of economic relationships that previously have been completely theoretical in nature. After all, anybody can claim that the quantity of iPhones demanded will increase if the price of those phones decreases (holding everything else constant), but not many people can put specific numbers into an equation and estimate *by how many* iPhones the quantity demanded will increase for each dollar that price decreases. To predict the *direction* of the change, you need a knowledge of economic theory and the general characteristics of the product in question. To predict the *amount* of the change, though, you need a sample of data, and you need a way to estimate the relationship. The most frequently used method to estimate such a relationship in econometrics is regression analysis.

Dependent Variables, Independent Variables, and Causality

Regression analysis is a statistical technique that attempts to "explain" movements in one variable, the **dependent variable**, as a function of movements in a set of other variables, called the **independent** (or **explanatory**) **variables**, through the quantification of one or more equations. For example, in Equation 1.1:

$$Q = \beta_0 + \beta_1 P + \beta_2 P_S + \beta_1 Yd \qquad (1.1)$$

Q is the dependent variable and P, P_S, and Yd are the independent variables. Regression analysis is a natural tool for economists because most (though not all) economic propositions can be stated in such equations. For example, the quantity demanded (dependent variable) is a function of price, the prices of substitutes, and income (independent variables).

Much of economics and business is concerned with cause-and-effect propositions. If the price of a good increases by one unit, then the quantity demanded decreases on average by a certain amount, depending on the price elasticity of demand (defined as the percentage change in the quantity demanded that is caused by a one percent increase in price). Similarly, if the quantity of capital employed increases by one unit, then output increases by a certain amount, called the marginal productivity of capital. Propositions such as these pose an if-then, or causal, relationship that logically postulates that a dependent variable's movements are determined by movements in a number of specific independent variables.

> Don't be deceived by the words "dependent" and "independent," however. Although many economic relationships are causal by their very nature, a regression result, no matter how statistically significant, cannot prove causality. All regression analysis can do is test whether a significant quantitative relationship exists. Judgments as to causality must also include a healthy dose of economic theory and common sense. For example, the fact that the bell on the door of a flower shop rings just before a customer enters and purchases some flowers by no means implies that the bell causes purchases! If events A and B are related statistically, it may be that A causes B, that B causes A, that some omitted factor causes both, or that a chance correlation exists between the two.

The cause-and-effect relationship often is so subtle that it fools even the most prominent economists. For example, in the late nineteenth century, English economist Stanley Jevons hypothesized that sunspots caused an increase in economic activity. To test this theory, he collected data on national output (the dependent variable) and sunspot activity (the independent variable) and showed that a significant positive relationship existed. This result led him, and some others, to jump to the conclusion that sunspots did indeed cause output to rise. Such a conclusion was unjustified because regression analysis cannot confirm causality; it can only test the strength and direction of the quantitative relationships involved.

Single-Equation Linear Models

The simplest single-equation regression model is:

$$Y = \beta_0 + \beta_1 X \tag{1.3}$$

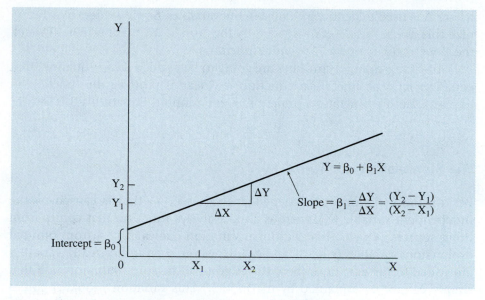

Figure 1.1 Graphical Representation of the Coefficients of the Regression Line

The graph of the equation $Y = \beta_0 + \beta_1 X$ is linear with a constant slope equal to $\beta_1 = \Delta Y / \Delta X$.

Equation 1.3 states that Y, the dependent variable, is a single-equation linear function of X, the independent variable. The model is a single-equation model because it's the only equation specified. The model is linear because if you were to plot Equation 1.3 it would be a straight line rather than a curve.

The βs are the coefficients that determine the coordinates of the straight line at any point. β_0 is the **constant** or **intercept** term; it indicates the value of Y when X equals zero. β_1 is the **slope coefficient**, and it indicates the amount that Y will change when X increases by one unit. The line in Figure 1.1 illustrates the relationship between the coefficients and the graphical meaning of the regression equation. As can be seen from the diagram, Equation 1.3 is indeed linear.

The slope coefficient, β_1, shows the response of Y to a one-unit increase in X. Much of the emphasis in regression analysis is on slope coefficients such as β_1. In Figure 1.1 for example, if X were to increase by one from X_1 to X_2 (ΔX), the value of Y in Equation 1.3 would increase from Y_1 to Y_2 (ΔY). For linear (i.e., straight-line) regression models, the response in the predicted value of Y due to a change in X is constant and equal to the slope coefficient β_1:

$$\frac{(Y_2 - Y_1)}{(X_2 - X_1)} = \frac{\Delta Y}{\Delta X} = \beta_1$$

where Δ is used to denote a change in the variables. Some readers may recognize this as the "rise" (ΔY) divided by the "run" (ΔX). For a linear model, the slope is constant over the entire function.

If linear regression techniques are going to be applied to an equation, that equation *must* be linear. An equation is **linear** if plotting the function in terms of X and Y generates a straight line; for example, Equation 1.3 is linear.[5]

$$Y = \beta_0 + \beta_1 X \qquad (1.3)$$

The Stochastic Error Term

Besides the variation in the dependent variable (Y) that is caused by the independent variable (X), there is almost always variation that comes from other sources as well. This additional variation comes in part from omitted explanatory variables (e.g., X_2 and X_3). However, even if these extra variables are added to the equation, there still is going to be some variation in Y that simply cannot be explained by the model.[6] This variation probably comes from sources such as omitted influences, measurement error, incorrect functional form, or purely random and totally unpredictable occurrences. By *random* we mean something that has its value determined entirely by chance.

Econometricians admit the existence of such inherent unexplained variation ("error") by explicitly including a stochastic (or random) error term in their regression models. A **stochastic error term** is a term that is added to a regression equation to introduce all of the variation in Y that cannot be explained by the included Xs. It is, in effect, a symbol of the econometrician's ignorance or inability to model all the movements of the dependent variable. The error term (sometimes called a disturbance term) usually is referred to with the symbol epsilon (ϵ), although other symbols (like u or v) sometimes are used.

---

5. Technically, as you will learn in Chapter 7, this equation is linear in the coefficients β_0 and β_1 and linear in the variables Y and X. The application of regression analysis to equations that are nonlinear in the variables is covered in Chapter 7. The application of regression techniques to equations that are nonlinear in the coefficients, however, is much more difficult.

6. The exception would be the extremely rare case where the data can be explained by some sort of physical law and are measured perfectly. Here, continued variation would point to an omitted independent variable. A similar kind of problem is often encountered in astronomy, where planets can be discovered by noting that the orbits of known planets exhibit variations that can be caused only by the gravitational pull of another heavenly body. Absent these kinds of physical laws, researchers in economics and business would be foolhardy to believe that *all* variation in Y can be explained by a regression model because there are always elements of error in any attempt to measure a behavioral relationship.

The addition of a stochastic error term (ϵ) to Equation 1.3 results in a typical regression equation:

$$Y = \beta_0 + \beta_1 X + \epsilon \qquad (1.4)$$

Equation 1.4 can be thought of as having two components, the *deterministic* component and the *stochastic*, or random, component. The expression $\beta_0 + \beta_1 X$ is called the *deterministic* component of the regression equation because it indicates the value of Y that is determined by a given value of X, which is assumed to be nonstochastic. This deterministic component can also be thought of as the **expected value** of Y given X, the mean value of the Ys associated with a particular value of X. For example, if the average height of all 13-year-old girls is 5 feet, then 5 feet is the expected value of a girl's height given that she is 13. The deterministic part of the equation may be written:

$$E(Y|X) = \beta_0 + \beta_1 X \qquad (1.5)$$

which states that the expected value of Y given X, denoted as $E(Y|X)$, is a linear function of the independent variable (or variables if there are more than one).

Unfortunately, the value of Y observed in the real world is unlikely to be exactly equal to the deterministic expected value $E(Y|X)$. After all, not all 13-year-old girls are 5 feet tall. As a result, the stochastic element (ϵ) must be added to the equation:

$$Y = E(Y|X) + \epsilon = \beta_0 + \beta_1 X + \epsilon \qquad (1.6)$$

The stochastic error term must be present in a regression equation because there are at least four sources of variation in Y other than the variation in the included Xs:

1. Many minor influences on Y are *omitted* from the equation (for example, because data are unavailable).

2. It is virtually impossible to avoid some sort of *measurement error* in the dependent variable.

3. The underlying theoretical equation might have a *different functional form* (or shape) than the one chosen for the regression. For example, the underlying equation might be nonlinear.

4. All attempts to generalize human behavior must contain at least some amount of unpredictable or *purely random* variation.

To get a better feeling for these components of the stochastic error term, let's think about a consumption function (aggregate consumption as a function of aggregate disposable income). First, consumption in a particular year may have been less than it would have been because of uncertainty over the future course of the economy. Since this uncertainty is hard to measure, there might be no variable measuring consumer uncertainty in the equation. In such a case, the impact of the omitted variable (consumer uncertainty) would likely end up in the stochastic error term. Second, the observed amount of consumption may have been different from the actual level of consumption in a particular year due to an error (such as a sampling error) in the measurement of consumption in the National Income Accounts. Third, the underlying consumption function may be nonlinear, but a linear consumption function might be estimated. (To see how this incorrect functional form would cause errors, see Figure 1.2.) Fourth, the consumption function

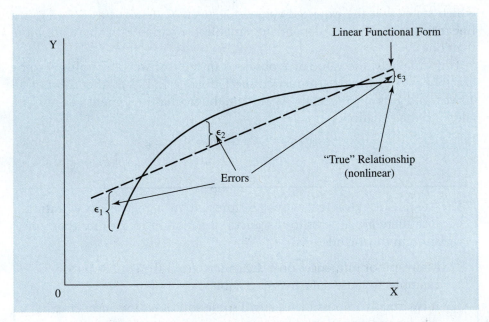

Figure 1.2 Errors Caused by Using a Linear Functional Form to Model a Nonlinear Relationship

One source of stochastic error is the use of an incorrect functional form. For example, if a linear functional form is used when the underlying relationship is nonlinear, systematic errors (the ϵs) will occur. These nonlinearities are just one component of the stochastic error term. The others are omitted variables, measurement error, and purely random variation.

attempts to portray the behavior of people, and there is always an element of unpredictability in human behavior. At any given time, some random event might increase or decrease aggregate consumption in a way that might never be repeated and couldn't be anticipated.

These possibilities explain the existence of a difference between the observed values of Y and the values expected from the deterministic component of the equation, $E(Y|X)$. These sources of error will be covered in more detail in the following chapters, but for now it is enough to recognize that in econometric research there will always be some stochastic or random element, and, for this reason, an error term must be added to all regression equations.

Extending the Notation

Our regression notation needs to be extended to allow the possibility of more than one independent variable and to include reference to the number of observations. A typical observation (or unit of analysis) is an individual person, year, or country. For example, a series of annual observations starting in 1985 would have $Y_1 = Y$ for 1985, Y_2 for 1986, etc. If we include a specific reference to the observations, the single-equation linear regression model may be written as:

$$Y_i = \beta_0 + \beta_1 X_i + \epsilon_i \qquad (i = 1, 2, \ldots, N) \qquad (1.7)$$

where: Y_i = the ith observation of the dependent variable
X_i = the ith observation of the independent variable
ϵ_i = the ith observation of the stochastic error term
β_0, β_1 = the regression coefficients
N = the number of observations

This equation is actually N equations, one for each of the N observations:

$$Y_1 = \beta_0 + \beta_1 X_1 + \epsilon_1$$
$$Y_2 = \beta_0 + \beta_1 X_2 + \epsilon_2$$
$$Y_3 = \beta_0 + \beta_1 X_3 + \epsilon_3$$
$$\vdots$$
$$Y_N = \beta_0 + \beta_1 X_N + \epsilon_N$$

That is, the regression model is assumed to hold for each observation. The coefficients do not change from observation to observation, but the values of Y, X, and ϵ do.

A second notational addition allows for more than one independent variable. Since more than one independent variable is likely to have an effect on the dependent variable, our notation should allow these additional explanatory Xs to be added. If we define:

X_{1i} = the ith observation of the first independent variable
X_{2i} = the ith observation of the second independent variable
X_{3i} = the ith observation of the third independent variable

then all three variables can be expressed as determinants of Y.

The resulting equation is called a **multivariate** (more than one independent variable) linear **regression model:**

$$Y_i = \beta_0 + \beta_1 X_{1i} + \beta_2 X_{2i} + \beta_3 X_{3i} + \epsilon_i \qquad (1.8)$$

The *meaning of the regression coefficient* β_1 in this equation is the impact of a one-unit increase in X_1 on the dependent variable Y, *holding constant* X_2 and X_3. Similarly, β_2 gives the impact of a one-unit increase in X_2 on Y, holding X_1 and X_3 constant.

These *multivariate regression coefficients* (which are parallel in nature to partial derivatives in calculus) serve to isolate the impact on Y of a change in one variable from the impact on Y of changes in the other variables. This is possible because multivariate regression takes the movements of X_2 and X_3 into account when it estimates the coefficient of X_1. The result is quite similar to what we would obtain if we were capable of conducting controlled laboratory experiments in which only one variable at a time was changed.

In the real world, though, it is very difficult to run controlled economic experiments,[7] because many economic factors change simultaneously, often in opposite directions. Thus the ability of regression analysis to measure the impact of one variable on the dependent variable, *holding constant the influence of the other variables in the equation,* is a tremendous advantage. Note that if a variable is not included in an equation, then its impact is *not* held constant in the estimation of the regression coefficients. This will be discussed further in Chapter 6.

---

7. Such experiments are difficult but not impossible. See Section 16.1.

This material is pretty abstract, so let's look at two examples. As a first example, consider an equation with only one independent variable, a model of a person's weight as a function of their height. The theory behind this equation is that, other things being equal, the taller a person is the more they tend to weigh.

The dependent variable in such an equation would be the weight of the person, while the independent variable would be that person's height:

$$Weight_i = \beta_0 + \beta_1 Height_i + \epsilon_i \qquad (1.9)$$

What exactly do the "i" subscripts mean in Equation 1.9? Each value of i refers to a different person in the sample, so another way to think about the subscripts is that:

$$Weight_{woody} = \beta_0 + \beta_1 Height_{woody} + \epsilon_{woody}$$
$$Weight_{lesley} = \beta_0 + \beta_1 Height_{lesley} + \epsilon_{lesley}$$
$$Weight_{bruce} = \beta_0 + \beta_1 Height_{bruce} + \epsilon_{bruce}$$
$$Weight_{mary} = \beta_0 + \beta_1 Height_{mary} + \epsilon_{mary}$$

Take a look at these equations. Each person (observation) in the sample has their own individual weight and height; that makes sense. But why does each person have their own value for ϵ, the stochastic error term? The answer is that random events (like those expressed by ϵ) impact people differently, so each person needs to have their own value of ϵ in order to reflect these differences. In contrast, note that the subscripts of the regression coefficients (the βs) don't change from person to person but instead apply to the entire sample. We'll learn more about this equation in Section 1.4.

As a second example, let's look at an equation with more than one independent variable. Suppose we want to understand how wages are determined in a particular field, perhaps because we think that there might be discrimination in that field. The wage of a worker would be the dependent variable (WAGE), but what would be good independent variables? What variables would influence a person's wage in a given field? Well, there are literally dozens of reasonable possibilities, but three of the most common are the work experience (EXP), education (EDU), and gender (GEND) of the worker, so let's use these. To create a regression equation with these variables, we'd redefine the variables in Equation 1.8 to meet our definitions:

Y = WAGE = the wage of the worker
X_1 = EXP = the years of work experience of the worker
X_2 = EDU = the years of education beyond high school of the worker
X_3 = GEND = the gender of the worker (1 = male and 0 = female)

The last variable, GEND, is unusual in that it can take on only two values, 0 and 1; this kind of variable is called a dummy variable, and it's extremely useful when we want to quantify a concept that is inherently qualitative (like gender). We'll discuss dummy variables in more depth in Sections 3.3 and 7.4.

If we substitute these definitions into Equation 1.8, we get:

$$WAGE_i = \beta_0 + \beta_1 EXP_i + \beta_2 EDU_i + \beta_3 GEND_i + \epsilon_i \qquad (1.10)$$

Equation 1.10 specifies that a worker's wage is a function of the experience, education, and gender of that worker. In such an equation, what would the meaning of β_1 be? Some readers will guess that β_1 measures the amount by which the average wage increases for an additional year of experience, but such a guess would miss the fact that there are two other independent variables in the equation that also explain wages. The correct answer is that β_1 gives us the impact on wages of a one-year increase in experience, *holding constant* education and gender. This is a significant difference, because it allows researchers to control for specific complicating factors without running controlled experiments.

Before we conclude this section, it's worth noting that the general multivariate regression model with K independent variables is written as:

$$Y_i = \beta_0 + \beta_1 X_{1i} + \beta_2 X_{2i} + \cdots + \beta_K X_{Ki} + \epsilon_i \qquad (1.11)$$

where i goes from 1 to N and indicates the observation number.

If the sample consists of a series of years or months (called a time series), then the subscript i is usually replaced with a t to denote time.[8]

1.3   The Estimated Regression Equation

Once a specific equation has been decided upon, it must be quantified. This quantified version of the theoretical regression equation is called the **estimated regression equation** and is obtained from a sample of data for actual Xs and Ys. Although the theoretical equation is purely abstract in nature:

$$Y_i = \beta_0 + \beta_1 X_i + \epsilon_i \qquad (1.12)$$

---

8. The order of the subscripts doesn't matter as long as the appropriate definitions are presented. We prefer to list the variable number first (X_{1i}) because we think it's easier for a beginning econometrician to understand. However, as the reader moves on to matrix algebra and computer spreadsheets, it will become common to list the observation number first, as in X_{i1}. Often the observational subscript is deleted, and the reader is expected to understand that the equation holds for each observation in the sample.

the estimated regression equation has actual numbers in it:

$$\hat{Y}_i = 103.40 + 6.38X_i \tag{1.13}$$

The observed, real-world values of X and Y are used to calculate the coefficient estimates 103.40 and 6.38. These estimates are used to determine $\hat{Y}$ (read as "Y-hat"), the *estimated* or *fitted* value of Y.

Let's look at the differences between a theoretical regression equation and an estimated regression equation. First, the theoretical regression coefficients β_0 and β_1 in Equation 1.12 have been replaced with *estimates* of those coefficients like 103.40 and 6.38 in Equation 1.13. We can't actually observe the values of the true[9] regression coefficients, so instead we calculate estimates of those coefficients from the data. The estimated regression coefficients, more generally denoted by $\hat{\beta}_0$ and $\hat{\beta}_1$ (read as "beta-hats"), are empirical best guesses of the true regression coefficients and are obtained from data from a sample of the Ys and Xs. The expression

$$\hat{Y}_i = \hat{\beta}_0 + \hat{\beta}_1 X_i \tag{1.14}$$

is the empirical counterpart of the theoretical regression Equation 1.12. The calculated estimates in Equation 1.13 are examples of the estimated regression coefficients $\hat{\beta}_0$ and $\hat{\beta}_1$. For each sample we calculate a different set of estimated regression coefficients.

$\hat{Y}_i$ is the *estimated value* of Y_i, and it represents the value of Y calculated from the estimated regression equation for the *i*th observation. As such, $\hat{Y}_i$ is our prediction of $E(Y_i|X_i)$ from the regression equation. The closer these $\hat{Y}$s are to the Ys in the sample, the better the fit of the equation. (The word *fit* is used here much as it would be used to describe how well clothes fit.)

The difference between the estimated value of the dependent variable ($\hat{Y}_i$) and the actual value of the dependent variable (Y_i) is defined as the **residual** (e_i):

$$e_i = Y_i - \hat{Y}_i \tag{1.15}$$

---

9. Our use of the word "true" throughout the text should be taken with a grain of salt. Many philosophers argue that the concept of truth is useful only relative to the scientific research program in question. Many economists agree, pointing out that what is true for one generation may well be false for another. To us, the true coefficient is the one that you'd obtain if you could run a regression on the entire relevant population. Thus, readers who so desire can substitute the phrase "population coefficient" for "true coefficient" with no loss in meaning.

Note the distinction between the residual in Equation 1.15 and the error term:

$$\epsilon_i = Y_i - E(Y_i|X_i) \tag{1.16}$$

The *residual* is the difference between the observed Y and the estimated regression line ($\hat{Y}$), while the *error term* is the difference between the observed Y and the true regression equation (the expected value of Y). Note that the error term is a theoretical concept that can never be observed, but the residual is a real-world value that is calculated for each observation every time a regression is run. The residual can be thought of as an estimate of the error term, and e could have been denoted as $\hat{\epsilon}$. Most regression techniques not only calculate the residuals but also attempt to compute values of $\hat{\beta}_0$ and $\hat{\beta}_1$ that keep the residuals as low as possible. The smaller the residuals, the better the fit, and the closer the $\hat{Y}$s will be to the Ys.

All these concepts are shown in Figure 1.3. The (X, Y) pairs are shown as points on the diagram, and both the true regression equation (which

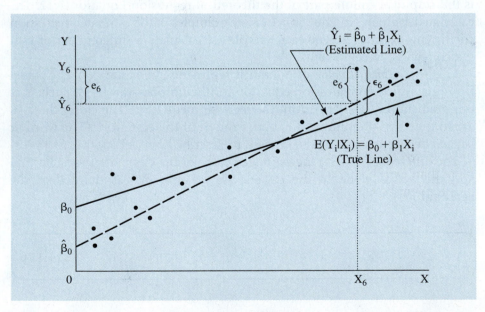

Figure 1.3 True and Estimated Regression Lines

The true relationship between X and Y (the solid line) typically cannot be observed, but the estimated regression line (the dashed line) can. The difference between an observed data point (for example, $i = 6$) and the true line is the value of the stochastic error term (ϵ_6). The difference between the observed Y_6 and the estimated value from the regression line ($\hat{Y}_6$) is the value of the residual for this observation, e_6.

cannot be seen in real applications) and an estimated regression equation are included. Notice that the estimated equation is close to but not equivalent to the true line. This is a typical result.

In Figure 1.3, $\hat{Y}_6$, the computed value of Y for the sixth observation, lies on the estimated (dashed) line, and it differs from Y_6, the actual observed value of Y for the sixth observation. The difference between the observed and estimated values is the residual, denoted by e_6. In addition, although we usually would not be able to see an observation of the error term, we have drawn the assumed true regression line here (the solid line) to see the sixth observation of the error term, ϵ_6, which is the difference between the true line and the observed value of Y, Y_6.

The following table summarizes the notation used in the true and estimated regression equations:

True Regression Equation	Estimated Regression Equation
β_0	$\hat{\beta}_0$
β_1	$\hat{\beta}_1$
ϵ_i	e_i

The estimated regression model can be extended to more than one independent variable by adding the additional Xs to the right side of the equation. The multivariate estimated regression counterpart of Equation 1.14 is:

$$\hat{Y}_i = \hat{\beta}_0 + \hat{\beta}_1 X_{1i} + \hat{\beta}_2 X_{2i} + \cdots + \hat{\beta}_K X_{Ki} \tag{1.17}$$

Diagrams of such multivariate equations, by the way, are not possible for more than two independent variables and are quite awkward for exactly two independent variables.

1.4 A Simple Example of Regression Analysis

Let's look at a fairly simple example of regression analysis. Suppose you've accepted a summer job as a weight guesser at the local amusement park, Magic Hill. Customers pay two dollars each, which you get to keep if you guess their weight within 10 pounds. If you miss by more than 10 pounds, then you have to return the two dollars and give the customer a small prize that you buy from Magic Hill for three dollars each. Luckily, the friendly managers of Magic Hill have arranged a number of marks on the wall behind the customer so that you are capable of measuring the customer's height accurately. Unfortunately, there is a five-foot wall between you and the customer, so you can tell little about the person except for height and (usually) gender.

On your first day on the job, you do so poorly that you work all day and somehow manage to lose two dollars, so on the second day you decide to collect data to run a regression to estimate the relationship between weight and height. Since most of the participants are male, you decide to limit your sample to males. You hypothesize the following theoretical relationship:

$$\overset{+}{}$$
$$Y_i = \beta_0 + \beta_1 X_i + \epsilon_i \qquad (1.18)$$

where: Y_i = the weight (in pounds) of the ith customer
X_i = the height (in inches above 5 feet) of the ith customer
ϵ_i = the value of the stochastic error term for the ith customer

In this case, the sign of the theoretical relationship between height and weight is believed to be positive (signified by the positive sign above β_1 in the general theoretical equation), but you must quantify that relationship in order to estimate weights when given heights. To do this, you need to collect a data set, and you need to apply regression analysis to the data.

The next day you collect the data summarized in Table 1.1 and run your regression on the Magic Hill computer, obtaining the following estimates:

$$\hat{\beta}_0 = 103.40 \qquad \hat{\beta}_1 = 6.38$$

This means that the equation

Estimated weight $= 103.40 + 6.38 \cdot$ Height (inches above five feet)   (1.19)

is worth trying as an alternative to just guessing the weights of your customers. Such an equation estimates weight with a constant base of 103.40 pounds and adds 6.38 pounds for every inch of height over 5 feet. Note that the sign of $\hat{\beta}_1$ is positive, as you expected.

How well does the equation work? To answer this question, you need to calculate the residuals (Y_i minus $\hat{Y}_i$) from Equation 1.19 to see how many were greater than ten. As can be seen in the last column in Table 1.1, if you had applied the equation to these 20 people, you wouldn't exactly have gotten rich, but at least you would have earned $25.00 instead of losing $2.00. Figure 1.4 shows not only Equation 1.19 but also the weight and height data for all 20 customers used as the sample. With a different group of people, the results would of course be different.

Equation 1.19 would probably help a beginning weight guesser, but it could be improved by adding other variables or by collecting a larger sample.

Table 1.1 Data for and Results of the Weight-Guessing Equation

Observation i (1)	Height Above 5' X_i (2)	Weight Y_i (3)	Predicted Weight $\hat{Y}_i$ (4)	Residual e_i (5)	$ Gain or Loss (6)
1	5.0	140.0	135.3	4.7	+2.00
2	9.0	157.0	160.8	−3.8	+2.00
3	13.0	205.0	186.3	18.7	−3.00
4	12.0	198.0	179.9	18.1	−3.00
5	10.0	162.0	167.2	−5.2	+2.00
6	11.0	174.0	173.6	0.4	+2.00
7	8.0	150.0	154.4	−4.4	+2.00
8	9.0	165.0	160.8	4.2	+2.00
9	10.0	170.0	167.2	2.8	+2.00
10	12.0	180.0	179.9	0.1	+2.00
11	11.0	170.0	173.6	−3.6	+2.00
12	9.0	162.0	160.8	1.2	+2.00
13	10.0	165.0	167.2	−2.2	+2.00
14	12.0	180.0	179.9	0.1	+2.00
15	8.0	160.0	154.4	5.6	+2.00
16	9.0	155.0	160.8	−5.8	+2.00
17	10.0	165.0	167.2	−2.2	+2.00
18	15.0	190.0	199.1	−9.1	+2.00
19	13.0	185.0	186.3	−1.3	+2.00
20	11.0	155.0	173.6	−18.6	−3.00
				TOTAL	= $25.00

Note: This data set, and every other data set in the text, is available on the text's website in four formats. Datafile = HTWT1

Such an equation is realistic, though, because it's likely that every successful weight guesser uses an equation like this without consciously thinking about that concept.

Our goal with this equation was to quantify the theoretical weight/height equation, Equation 1.18, by collecting data (Table 1.1) and calculating an estimated regression, Equation 1.19. Although the true equation, like observations of the stochastic error term, can never be known, we were able to come up with an estimated equation that had the sign we expected for $\hat{\beta}_1$ and that helped us in our job. Before you decide to quit school or your job and try to make your living guessing weights at Magic Hill, there is quite a bit more to learn about regression analysis, so we'd better move on.

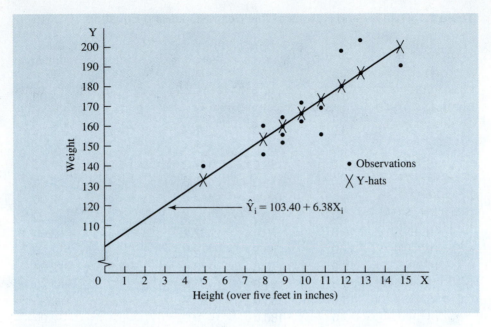

Figure 1.4 A Weight-Guessing Equation

If we plot the data from the weight-guessing example and include the estimated regression line, we can see that the estimated Ŷs come fairly close to the observed Ys for all but three observations. Find a male friend's height and weight on the graph. How well does the regression equation work?

1.5 Using Regression to Explain Housing Prices

As much fun as guessing weights at an amusement park might be, it's hardly a typical example of the use of regression analysis. For every regression run on such an off-the-wall topic, there are literally hundreds run to *describe* the reaction of GDP to an increase in the money supply, to *test* an economic theory with new data, or to *forecast* the effect of a price change on a firm's sales.

As a more realistic example, let's look at a model of housing prices. The purchase of a house is probably the most important financial decision in an individual's life, and one of the key elements in that decision is an appraisal of the house's value. If you overvalue the house, you can lose thousands of dollars by paying too much; if you undervalue the house, someone might outbid you.

All this wouldn't be much of a problem if houses were homogeneous products, like corn or gold, that have generally known market prices with which to compare a particular asking price. Such is hardly the case in the real estate market. Consequently, an important element of every housing purchase is an appraisal of the market value of the house, and many real estate appraisers use regression analysis to help them in their work.

Suppose your family is about to buy a house, but you're convinced that the owner is asking too much money. The owner says that the asking price of $230,000 is fair because a larger house next door sold for $230,000 about a year ago. You're not sure it's reasonable to compare the prices of different-sized houses that were purchased at different times. What can you do to help decide whether to pay the $230,000?

Since you're taking an econometrics class, you decide to collect data on all local houses that were sold within the last few weeks and to build a regression model of the sales prices of the houses as a function of their sizes.[10] Such a data set is called **cross-sectional** because all of the observations are from the same point in time and represent different individual economic entities (like countries or, in this case, houses) from that same point in time.

To measure the impact of size on price, you include the size of the house as an independent variable in a regression equation that has the price of that house as the dependent variable. You expect a positive sign for the coefficient of size, since big houses cost more to build and tend to be more desirable than small ones. Thus the theoretical model is:

$$\overset{+}{\text{PRICE}_i} = \beta_0 + \beta_1 \text{SIZE}_i + \epsilon_i \tag{1.20}$$

where: PRICE_i = the price (in thousands of $) of the ith house
SIZE_i = the size (in square feet) of that house
ϵ_i = the value of the stochastic error term for that house

You collect the records of all recent real estate transactions, find that 43 local houses were sold within the last 4 weeks, and estimate the following regression of those 43 observations:

$$\widehat{\text{PRICE}_i} = 40.0 + 0.138\text{SIZE}_i \tag{1.21}$$

What do these estimated coefficients mean? The most important coefficient is $\hat{\beta}_1 = 0.138$, since the reason for the regression is to find out the impact of size on price. This coefficient means that if size increases by 1 square foot,

---

10. It's unusual for an economist to build a model of price without including some measure of quantity on the right-hand side. Such models of the price of a good as a function of the attributes of that good are called *hedonic* models and will be discussed in greater depth in Section 11.8. The interested reader is encouraged to skim the first few paragraphs of that section before continuing on with this example.

price will increase by 0.138 thousand dollars ($138). $\hat{\beta}_1$ thus measures the change in $PRICE_i$ associated with a one-unit increase in $SIZE_i$. It's the slope of the regression line in a graph like Figure 1.5.

What does $\hat{\beta}_0 = 40.0$ mean? $\hat{\beta}_0$ is the estimate of the constant or intercept term. In our equation, it means that price equals 40.0 when size equals zero. As can be seen in Figure 1.5, the estimated regression line intersects the price axis at 40.0. While it might be tempting to say that the average price of a vacant lot is $40,000, such a conclusion would be unjustified for a number of reasons, which will be discussed in Section 7.1. It's much safer either to interpret $\hat{\beta}_0 = 40.0$ as nothing more than the value of the estimated regression when $S_i = 0$, or to not interpret $\hat{\beta}_0$ at all.

What does $\hat{\beta}_1 = 0.138$ mean? $\hat{\beta}_1$ is the estimate of the coefficient of SIZE in Equation 1.20, and as such it's also an estimate of the slope of the line in Figure 1.5. It implies that an increase in the size of a house by one square foot will cause the estimated price of the house to go up by 0.138 thousand dollars or $138. It's a good habit to analyze estimated slope coefficients to see whether they make sense. The positive sign of $\hat{\beta}_1$ certainly is what we expected, but what about the magnitude of the coefficient? Whenever you interpret a coefficient, be sure to take the units of measurement into consideration. In this case, is $138 per square foot a plausible number? Well, it's

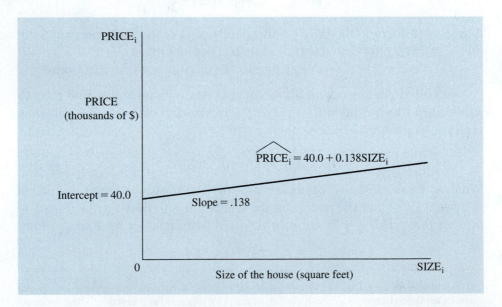

Figure 1.5 A Cross-Sectional Model of Housing Prices

A regression equation that has the price of a house as a function of the size of that house has an intercept of 40.0 and a slope of 0.138, using Equation 1.21.

hard to know for sure, but it certainly is a lot more reasonable than $1.38 per square foot or $13,800 per square foot!

How can you use this estimated regression to help decide whether to pay $230,000 for the house? If you calculate a $\hat{Y}$ (predicted price) for a house that is the same size (1,600 square feet) as the one you're thinking of buying, you can then compare this $\hat{Y}$ with the asking price of $230,000. To do this, substitute 1600 for $SIZE_i$ in Equation 1.21, obtaining:

$$\widehat{PRICE}_i = 40.0 + 0.138(1600) = 40.0 + 220.8 = 260.8$$

The house seems to be a good deal. The owner is asking "only" $230,000 for a house when the size implies a price of $260,800! Perhaps your original feeling that the price was too high was a reaction to steep housing prices in general and not a reflection of this specific price.

On the other hand, perhaps the price of a house is influenced by more than just the size of the house. Such multivariate models are the heart of econometrics, and we'll add more independent variables to Equation 1.21 when we return to this housing price example in Section 11.8.

1.6 Summary

1. Econometrics—literally, "economic measurement"—is a branch of economics that attempts to quantify theoretical relationships. Regression analysis is only one of the techniques used in econometrics, but it is by far the most frequently used.

2. The major uses of econometrics are description, hypothesis testing, and forecasting. The specific econometric techniques employed may vary depending on the use of the research.

3. While regression analysis specifies that a dependent variable is a function of one or more independent variables, regression analysis alone cannot prove or even imply causality.

4. A stochastic error term must be added to all regression equations to account for variations in the dependent variable that are not explained completely by the independent variables. The components of this error term include:
   a. omitted or left-out variables
   b. measurement errors in the data
   c. an underlying theoretical equation that has a different functional form (shape) than the regression equation
   d. purely random and unpredictable events

5. An estimated regression equation is an approximation of the true equation that is obtained by using data from a sample of actual Ys and Xs. Since we can never know the true equation, econometric analysis focuses on this estimated regression equation and the estimates of the regression coefficients. The difference between a particular observation of the dependent variable and the value estimated from the regression equation is called the residual.

EXERCISES

(The answers to the even-numbered exercises are in Appendix A.)

1. Write the meaning of each of the following terms without referring to the book (or your notes), and compare your definition with the version in the text for each:
    a. constant or intercept (p. 7)
    b. cross-sectional (p. 21)
    c. dependent variable (p. 5)
    d. estimated regression equation (p. 14)
    e. expected value (p. 9)
    f. independent (or explanatory) variable (p. 5)
    g. linear (p. 8)
    h. multivariate regression model (p. 12)
    i. regression analysis (p. 5)
    j. residual (p. 15)
    k. slope coefficient (p. 7)
    l. stochastic error term (p. 8)

2. Use your own computer's regression software and the weight (Y) and height (X) data from Table 1.1 to see if you can reproduce the estimates in Equation 1.19. There are two ways to load the data: You can type in the data yourself or you can download datafile HTWT1 (in Stata, EViews, Excel, or ASCII formats) from the text's website: http://www.pearsonhighered.com/studenmund. Once the datafile is loaded, run $Y = f(X)$, and your results should match Equation 1.19. Different programs require different commands to run a regression. For help in how to do this with Stata or EViews, either see the answer to this question in Appendix A or read Appendix 1.7.

3. Not all regression coefficients have positive expected signs. For example, a *Sports Illustrated* article by Jaime Diaz reported on a study of golfing putts of various lengths on the Professional Golfers' Association (PGA) Tour.[11] The article included data on the percentage of putts made (P_i) as a function of the length of the putt in feet (L_i). Since the longer the putt, the less likely even a professional is to make it, we'd expect L_i to have a negative coefficient in an equation explaining P_i. Sure enough, if you estimate an equation on the data in the article, you obtain:

$$\hat{P}_i = 83.6 - 4.1L_i \tag{1.22}$$

   a. Carefully write out the exact meaning of the coefficient of L_i.
   b. Suppose someone else took the data from the article and estimated:

$$P_i = 83.6 - 4.1L_i + e_i$$

   Is this the same result as that of Equation 1.22? If so, what definition do you need to use to convert this equation back to Equation 1.22?
   c. Use Equation 1.22 to determine the percent of the time you'd expect a PGA golfer to make a 10-foot putt. Does this seem realistic? How about a 1-foot putt or a 25-foot putt? Do these seem as realistic?
   d. Your answer to part c should suggest that there's a problem in applying a linear regression to these data. What is that problem?

4. Return to the housing price model of Section 1.5 and consider the following equation:

$$\widehat{SIZE}_i = -290 + 3.62\ PRICE_i \tag{1.23}$$

   where: $SIZE_i$ = the size (in square feet) of the *i*th house
   $PRICE_i$ = the price (in thousands of \$) of that house

   a. Carefully explain the meaning of each of the estimated regression coefficients.
   b. Suppose you're told that this equation explains a significant portion (more than 80 percent) of the variation in the size of a house. Have we shown that high housing prices cause houses to be large? If not, what have we shown?
   c. What do you think would happen to the estimated coefficients of this equation if we had measured the price variable in dollars instead of in thousands of dollars? Be specific.

---

11. Jaime Diaz, "Perils of Putting," *Sports Illustrated*, April 3, 1989, pp. 76–79.

5. If an equation has more than one independent variable, we have to be careful when we interpret the regression coefficients of that equation. Think, for example, about how you might build an equation to explain the amount of money that different states spend per pupil on public education. The more income a state has, the more they probably spend on public schools, but the faster enrollment is growing, the less there would be to spend on each pupil. Thus, a reasonable equation for per pupil spending would include at least two variables: income and enrollment growth:

$$S_i = \beta_0 + \beta_1 Y_i + \beta_2 G_i + \epsilon_i \qquad (1.24)$$

where: S_i = educational dollars spent per public school student in the ith state
    Y_i = per capita income in the ith state (in dollars)
    G_i = the percent growth of public school enrollment in the ith state

a. State the economic meaning of the coefficients of Y and G. (*Hint:* Remember to hold the impact of the other variable constant.)
b. If we were to estimate Equation 1.24, what signs would you expect the coefficients of Y and G to have? Why?
c. Silva and Sonstelie estimated a cross-sectional model of per student spending by state that is very similar to Equation 1.24:[12]

$$\hat{S}_i = -183 + 0.1422Y_i - 5926G_i \qquad (1.25)$$
$$N = 49$$

Do these estimated coefficients correspond to your expectations? Explain Equation 1.25 in common sense terms.
d. The authors measured G as a decimal, so if a state had a 10 percent growth in enrollment, then G equaled .10. What would Equation 1.25 have looked like if the authors had measured G in percentage points, so that if a state had 10 percent growth, then G would have equaled 10? (*Hint:* Write out the actual numbers for the estimated coefficients.)

6. Your friend has an on-campus job making telephone calls to alumni asking for donations to your college's annual fund, and she wonders

---

12. Fabio Silva and Jon Sonstelie, "Did Serrano Cause a Decline in School Spending?" *National Tax Review,* Vol. 48, No. 2, pp. 199–215. The authors also included the tax price for spending per pupil in the ith state as a variable.

whether her calling is making any difference. In an attempt to measure the impact of student calls on fund raising, she collects data from 50 alums and estimates the following equation:

$$\widehat{GIFT_i} = 2.29 + 0.001INCOME_i + 4.62CALLS_i \qquad (1.26)$$

where: $GIFT_i$ = the 2016 annual fund donation (in dollars) from the ith alum

$INCOME_i$ = the 2016 estimated income (in dollars) of the ith alum

$CALLS_i$ = the # of calls to the ith alum asking for a donation in 2016

a. Carefully explain the meaning of each estimated coefficient. Are the estimated signs what you expected?

b. Why is the left-hand variable in your friend's equation $\widehat{GIFT_i}$ and not $GIFT_i$?

c. Your friend didn't include the stochastic error term in the estimated equation. Was this a mistake? Why or why not?

d. Suppose that your friend decides to change the units of INCOME from "dollars" to "thousands of dollars." What will happen to the estimated coefficients of the equation? Be specific.

e. If you could add one more variable to this equation, what would it be? Explain.

7. Let's return to the wage determination example of Section 1.2. In that example, we built a model of the wage of the ith worker in a particular field as a function of the work experience, education, and gender of that worker:

$$WAGE_i = \beta_0 + \beta_1 EXP_i + \beta_2 EDU_i + \beta_3 GEND_i + \epsilon_i \qquad (1.10)$$

where: Y_i = $WAGE_i$ = the wage of the ith worker

X_{1i} = EXP_i = the years of work experience of the ith worker

X_{2i} = EDU_i = the years of education beyond high school of the ith worker

X_{3i} = $GEND_i$ = the gender of the ith worker (1 = male and 0 = female)

a. What is the real-world meaning of β_2? (*Hint:* If you're unsure where to start, review Section 1.2.)

b. What is the real-world meaning of β_3? (*Hint:* Remember that GEND is a dummy variable.)

c. Suppose that you wanted to add a variable to this equation to measure whether there might be discrimination against people of color. How would you define such a variable? Be specific.

d. Suppose that you had the opportunity to add another variable to the equation. Which of the following possibilities would seem best? Explain your answer.

    i. the age of the ith worker

    ii. the number of jobs in this field

    iii. the average wage in this field

    iv. the number of "employee of the month" awards won by the ith worker

    v. the number of children of the ith worker

8. Have you heard of "RateMyProfessors.com"? On this website, students evaluate a professor's overall teaching ability and a variety of other attributes. The website then summarizes these student-submitted ratings for the benefit of any student considering taking a class from the professor.

   Two of the most interesting attributes that the website tracks are how "easy" the professor is (in terms of workload and grading), and how "hot" the professor is (presumably in terms of physical attractiveness). An article by Otto and colleagues[13] indicates that being "hot" improves a professor's rating more than being "easy." To investigate these ideas ourselves, we created the following equation for RateMyProfessors.com:

$$RATING_i = \beta_0 + \beta_1 EASE_i + \beta_2 HOT_i + \epsilon_i \tag{1.27}$$

where: $RATING_i$ = the overall rating (5 = best) of the ith professor

         $EASE_i$ = the easiness rating (5 = easiest) of the ith professor

         HOT_i = 1 if the ith professor is considered "hot," 0 otherwise

To estimate Equation 1.27, we need data, and Table 1.2 contains data for these variables from 25 randomly chosen professors on RateMyProfessors.com. If we estimate Equation 1.27 with the data in Table 1.2, we obtain:

$$\widehat{RATING_i} = 3.23 + 0.01 EASE_i + 0.59 HOT_i \tag{1.28}$$

---

13. James Otto, Douglas Sanford, and Douglas Ross, "Does RateMyProfessors.com Really Rate My Professor?" *Assessment and Evaluation in Higher Education,* August 2008, pp. 355–368.

Table 1.2 RateMyProfessors.com Ratings

Observation	RATING	EASE	HOT
1	2.8	3.7	0
2	4.3	4.1	1
3	4.0	2.8	1
4	3.0	3.0	0
5	4.3	2.4	0
6	2.7	2.7	0
7	3.0	3.3	0
8	3.7	2.7	0
9	3.9	3.0	1
10	2.7	3.2	0
11	4.2	1.9	1
12	1.9	4.8	0
13	3.5	2.4	1
14	2.1	2.5	0
15	2.0	2.7	1
16	3.8	1.6	0
17	4.1	2.4	0
18	5.0	3.1	1
19	1.2	1.6	0
20	3.7	3.1	0
21	3.6	3.0	0
22	3.3	2.1	0
23	3.2	2.5	0
24	4.8	3.3	0
25	4.6	3.0	0

Datafile = RATE1

a. Take a look at Equation 1.28. Do the estimated coefficients support our expectations? Explain.

b. See if you can reproduce the results in Equation 1.28 on your own. To do this, take the data in Table 1.2 and use Stata or your own regression program to estimate the coefficients from these data. If you do everything correctly, you should be able to verify the estimates in Equation 1.28. (If you're not sure how to get started on this question, either take a look at the answer to Exercise 2 in Appendix A or read Appendix 1.7.)

c. This model includes two independent variables. Does it make sense to think that the teaching rating of a professor depends on just these two variables? What other variable(s) do you think might be important?

d. Suppose that you were able to add your suggested variable(s) to Equation 1.28. What do you think would happen to the coefficients of EASE and HOT when you added the variable(s)? Would you expect them to change? Would you expect them to remain the same? Explain.

e. (optional) Go to the RateMyProfessors.com website, choose 25 observations at random, and estimate your own version of Equation 1.27. Now compare your regression results to those in Equation 1.28. Do your estimated coefficients have the same signs as those in Equation 1.28? Are your estimated coefficients exactly the same as those in Equation 1.28? Why or why not?

1.7 Appendix: Using Stata

Using Econometrics is about, well, using econometrics, and it doesn't take long to realize that using econometrics requires software. The powerful and user-friendly econometric software package referred to in the text is Stata[14], and the purpose of this appendix[15] is to give you a brief introduction to Stata.

For most people (including me!), learning new computer software involves some pain. Our goal in this Appendix is to take away as much of that pain as possible. We hope to give you a head start with Stata and also convince you that it's worth your time to check out the complete "Using Stata" document found online at the *Using Econometrics* student companion website (http://www.pearsonhighered.com/studenmund). That free document (yes, free!) is designed to get you up and running in Stata with as little pain as possible. It shows in plain English and clear pictures how to use all the econometric techniques you'll encounter in the text (and more!)

How do you get Stata? There are a number of ways. Your college or university may provide Stata access in official computer labs. If it doesn't (or if you want a personal copy), you can buy and download Stata directly (http://www.stata.com). Fortunately, reasonable student pricing is available.

---

14. Other econometric software programs that you might encounter include EViews, SAS, R, and SPSS.

15. Written by John Perry, Centre College. Used with permission.

With access to Stata, go ahead and "open" it as you would any program on your computer (like Word, Excel, etc.). When you open Stata on a PC, you should see something like this:

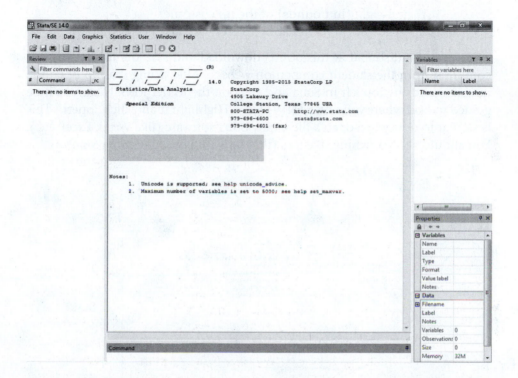

Stata also runs on a Mac, and while it looks slightly different, the commands and functionality are almost the same as on a PC.

Let's talk about what you see. There are five "windows" within Stata. The biggest one, squarely in the middle of the screen, is the "Results" window. Nicely, it shows you the results of what you tell Stata to do.

At the top left is the "Review" window. This window shows a history of all the commands you have given Stata. The top right is where the variables in your dataset will show up and the bottom right is where you'll see properties of the variables.

The bottom, center window is the "Command" window. As the name suggests, this is where you tell Stata what to do, where you actually "program." (Don't panic! You can work in Stata by typing commands one at a time or you can roll all your comments up into a single program—called in Stata language a "do-file." The full "Using Stata" document covers do-files.)

With Stata open, we should move along and open a dataset. In Section 1.4, you met a dataset from Magic Hill amusement park named HTWT1.dta (".dta" is the format of a Stata dataset much like "docx" is the format for a Microsoft Word document). It contained the height and weight of 20 people where:

Y_i = weight (in pounds) of the ith customer
X_i = height (in inches above 5 feet) of the ith customer

You can (and should at this point) download and save the dataset to your computer from the student companion website. After doing that, to open the dataset, go to the top left in Stata and click on the folder icon. Next, you'll be guided to find where you saved HTWT1.dta. Highlight it and click "open." This is similar to how you'd open a file in any other software (like Word, Excel, etc.). You should see something like this (this time we used Stata on a Mac):

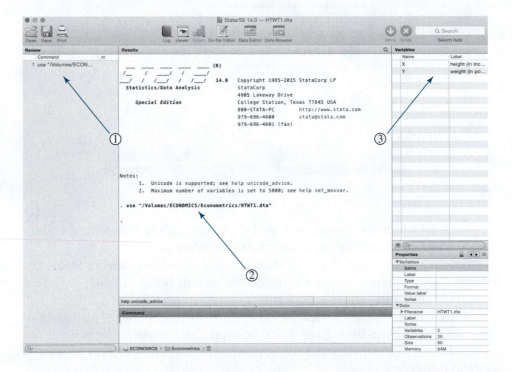

Notice that what you commanded Stata to do—to open HTWT1.dta—is recorded in the Results window (indicated by arrow 1). In Stata, "use" means open. The "use" statement is followed by the pathname (in quotes) where the file is saved on your computer (in my case "/Volumes/ECONOMICS/

Econometrics/HTWT1.dta"). This command is also recorded in the Review window and indicated by arrow 2.

At the top right, signaled by arrow 3, you see that you have two variables in your Variables window (X and Y). This means you now have data in Stata.

Things are about to get exciting! With our data open in Stata we're now in a position to replicate Equation 1.19. To do so, type "reg Y X" into the Command window in Stata and hit enter.

The "reg" command, which is short for "regress," tells Stata to perform a regression. Directly after "reg," insert the dependent variable (Y in our case). The dependent variable is followed by the model's independent variables. Equation 1.19 has one independent variable named X. Note that Stata is case sensitive. If you type "y" when the variable's name is "Y," Stata will yell.

After giving the "reg Y X" command, you should see something like this:

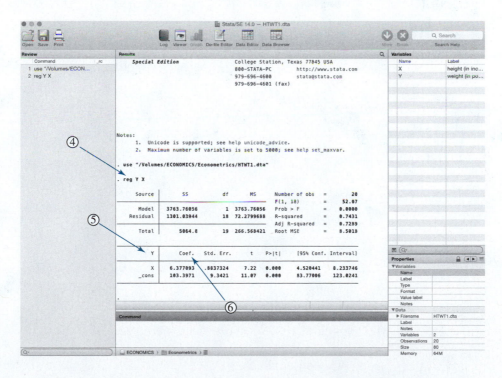

What you see in the Results window above could easily overwhelm a person. For now, focus on where the three arrows direct. Arrow 4 points to the command that had Stata produce the estimation. Arrow 5 points to the column that lists the variables in the regression: Y, X, and something called "_cons". That "something" is the model's intercept term, otherwise known as β_0.

Arrow 6 points to the "Coef." column, which reports the estimated coefficients. The first number in the Coef. column is 6.377093. That is $\hat{\beta}_1$, the coefficient estimate for X, and matches the 6.38 (rounded) of Equation 1.19. Moving down the Coef. column and next to the _cons is 103.3971. That is $\hat{\beta}_0$, the estimate of the intercept, which rounds to 103.40.

And with that, you've estimated your first regression in Stata! Keep in mind, however, that this short appendix is meant only to help get you started in Stata. The full "Using Stata" document will show you much more—while trying to minimize the pain.

Chapter 2

Ordinary Least Squares

2.1 **Estimating Single-Independent-Variable Models with OLS**

2.2 **Estimating Multivariate Regression Models with OLS**

2.3 **Evaluating the Quality of a Regression Equation**

2.4 **Describing the Overall Fit of the Estimated Model**

2.5 **An Example of the Misuse of $\overline{R}^2$**

2.6 **Summary and Exercises**

2.7 **Appendix: Econometric Lab #1**

The bread and butter of regression analysis is the estimation of the coefficients of econometric models using a technique called Ordinary Least Squares (OLS). The first two sections of this chapter summarize the reasoning behind and the mechanics of OLS. Regression users rely on computers to do the actual OLS calculations, so the emphasis here is on understanding what OLS attempts to do and how it goes about doing it.

How can you tell a good equation from a bad one once it has been estimated? There are a number of useful criteria, including the extent to which the estimated equation fits the actual data. A focus on fit is not without perils, however, so we share an example of the misuse of this criterion.

The chapter concludes with a new kind of learning tool that we call an econometric lab.

2.1 Estimating Single-Independent-Variable Models with OLS

The purpose of regression analysis is to take a purely theoretical equation like:

$$Y_i = \beta_0 + \beta_1 X_i + \epsilon_i \qquad (2.1)$$

and use a set of data to create an estimated equation like:

$$\hat{Y}_i = \hat{\beta}_0 + \hat{\beta}_1 X_i \tag{2.2}$$

where each "hat" indicates a sample estimate of the true population value. (In the case of Y, the "true population value" is $E[Y|X]$.) The purpose of the estimation technique is to obtain numerical values for the coefficients of an otherwise completely theoretical regression equation.

The most widely used method of obtaining these estimates is Ordinary Least Squares (OLS), which has become so standard that its estimates are presented as a point of reference even when results from other estimation techniques are used. **Ordinary Least Squares (OLS)** is a regression estimation technique that calculates the $\hat{\beta}$s so as to minimize the sum of the squared residuals, thus:[1]

$$\text{OLS minimizes } \sum_{i=1}^{N} e_i^2 \quad (i = 1, 2, \ldots, N) \tag{2.3}$$

Since these residuals (e_is) are the differences between the actual Ys and the estimated Ys produced by the regression (the $\hat{Y}$s in Equation 2.2), Equation 2.3 is equivalent to saying that OLS minimizes $\sum (Y_i - \hat{Y}_i)^2$.

Why Use Ordinary Least Squares?

Although OLS is the most-used regression estimation technique, it's not the only one. Indeed, econometricians have developed what seem like zillions of different estimation techniques, a number of which we'll discuss later in this text.

There are at least three important reasons for using OLS to estimate regression models:

1. OLS is relatively easy to use.
2. The goal of minimizing $\sum e_i^2$ is quite appropriate from a theoretical point of view.
3. OLS estimates have a number of useful characteristics.

---

1. The summation symbol, $\sum$, indicates that all terms to its right should be added (or summed) over the range of the i values attached to the bottom and top of the symbol. In Equation 2.3, for example, this would mean adding up e_i^2 for all integer values between 1 and N:

$$\sum_{i=1}^{N} e_i^2 = e_1^2 + e_2^2 + \cdots + e_N^2$$

Often the $\sum$ notation is simply written as $\sum_i$, and it is assumed that the summation is over all observations from $i = 1$ to $i = N$. Sometimes, the i is omitted entirely and the same assumption is made implicitly.

The first reason for using OLS is that it's the simplest of all econometric estimation techniques. Most other techniques involve complicated nonlinear formulas or iterative procedures, many of which are extensions of OLS itself. In contrast, OLS estimates are simple enough that, if you had to, you could calculate them without using a computer or a calculator (for a single-independent-variable model). Indeed, in the "dark ages" before computers and calculators, econometricians calculated OLS estimates by hand!

The second reason for using OLS is that minimizing the summed, squared residuals is a reasonable goal for an estimation technique. To see this, recall that the residual measures how close the estimated regression equation comes to the actual observed data:

$$e_i = Y_i - \hat{Y}_i \qquad (i = 1, 2, \ldots, N) \qquad (1.15)$$

Since it's reasonable to want our estimated regression equation to be as close as possible to the observed data, you might think that you'd want to minimize these residuals. The main problem with simply totaling the residuals is that e_i can be negative as well as positive. Thus, negative and positive residuals might cancel each other out, allowing a wildly inaccurate equation to have a very low $\sum e_i$. For example, if $Y = 100,000$ for two consecutive observations and if your equation predicts 1.1 million and $-900,000$, respectively, your residuals will be $+1$ million and -1 million, which add up to zero!

We could get around this problem by minimizing the sum of the absolute values of the residuals, but absolute values are difficult to work with mathematically. Luckily, minimizing the summed squared residuals does the job. Squared functions pose no unusual mathematical difficulties in terms of manipulations, and the technique avoids canceling positive and negative residuals because squared terms are always positive.

The final reason for using OLS is that its estimates have at least two useful properties:[2]

1. The sum of the residuals is exactly zero.
2. OLS can be shown to be the "best" estimator possible under a set of specific assumptions. We'll define "best" in Chapter 4.

An **estimator** is a mathematical technique that is applied to a sample of data to produce a real-world numerical **estimate** of the true population regression coefficient (or other parameters). Thus, OLS is an estimator, and a $\hat{\beta}$ produced by OLS is an estimate.

---

2. These properties, and indeed all the properties of OLS that we discuss in this book, are true as long as a constant term is included in the regression equation. For more on this, see Section 7.1.

How Does OLS Work?

How would OLS estimate a single-independent-variable regression model like Equation 2.1?

$$Y_i = \beta_0 + \beta_1 X_i + \epsilon_i \tag{2.1}$$

OLS selects those estimates of β_0 and β_1 that minimize the squared residuals, summed over all the sample data points.

For an equation with just one independent variable, these coefficients are:[3]

$$\hat{\beta}_1 = \frac{\sum_{i=1}^{N} [\,(X_i - \overline{X})\,(Y_i - \overline{Y})\,]}{\sum_{i=1}^{N} (X_i - \overline{X})^2} \tag{2.4}$$

and, given this estimate of β_1,

$$\hat{\beta}_0 = \overline{Y} - \hat{\beta}_1 \overline{X} \tag{2.5}$$

where $\overline{X}$ = the mean of X, or $\sum X_i / N$, and $\overline{Y}$ = the mean of Y, or $\sum Y_i / N$. Note that for each different data set, we'll get different estimates of β_1 and β_0, depending on the sample.

---

3. Since

$$\sum_{i=1}^{N} e_i^2 = \sum_{i=1}^{N} (Y_i - \hat{Y}_i)^2$$

and $\hat{Y}_i = \hat{\beta}_0 + \hat{\beta} X_{1i}$, OLS actually minimizes

$$\sum_i e_i^2 = \sum_i (Y_i - \hat{\beta}_0 - \hat{\beta}_1 X_i)^2$$

by choosing the $\hat{\beta}$s that do so. For those with a moderate grasp of calculus and algebra, the derivation of these equations is informative.

An Illustration of OLS Estimation

The equations for calculating regression coefficients might seem a little forbidding, but it's not hard to apply them yourself to data sets that have only a few observations and independent variables. Although you'll usually want to use regression software packages to do your estimation, you'll understand OLS better if you work through the following illustration.

To keep things simple, let's attempt to estimate the regression coefficients of the height and weight data given in Section 1.4. For your convenience in following this illustration, the original data are reproduced in Table 2.1. As was noted previously, the formulas for OLS estimation for a regression equation with one independent variable are Equations 2.4 and 2.5:

$$\hat{\beta}_1 = \frac{\sum_{i=1}^{N} [(X_i - \overline{X})(Y_i - \overline{Y})]}{\sum_{i=1}^{N} (X_i - \overline{X})^2} \tag{2.4}$$

$$\hat{\beta}_0 = \overline{Y} - \hat{\beta}_1 \overline{X} \tag{2.5}$$

If we undertake the calculations outlined in Table 2.1 and substitute them into Equations 2.4 and 2.5, we obtain these values:

$$\hat{\beta}_1 = \frac{590.20}{92.50} = 6.38$$

$$\hat{\beta}_0 = 169.4 - (6.38 \cdot 10.35) = 103.4$$

or

$$\hat{Y}_i = 103.4 + 6.38X_i \tag{2.6}$$

If you compare these estimates, you'll find that the manually calculated coefficient estimates are the same as the computer regression results summarized in Section 1.4.

As can be seen in Table 2.1, the sum of the $\hat{Y}$s (column 8) equals the sum of the Ys (column 2), so the sum of the residuals (column 9) does indeed equal zero (except for rounding errors).

Table 2.1 The Calculation of Estimated Regression Coefficients for the Weight/Height Example

	Raw Data					Required Intermediate Calculations			
i (1)	Y_i (2)	X_i (3)	$(Y_i - \bar{Y})$ (4)	$(X_i - \bar{X})$ (5)	$(X_i - \bar{X})^2$ (6)	$(X_i - \bar{X})(Y_i - \bar{Y})$ (7)	$\hat{Y}_i$ (8)	$e_i = Y_i - \hat{Y}_i$ (9)
1	140	5	−29.40	−5.35	28.62	157.29	135.3	4.7
2	157	9	−12.40	−1.35	1.82	16.74	160.8	−3.8
3	205	13	35.60	2.65	7.02	94.34	186.3	18.7
4	198	12	28.60	1.65	2.72	47.19	179.9	18.1
5	162	10	−7.40	−0.35	0.12	2.59	167.2	−5.2
6	174	11	4.60	0.65	0.42	2.99	173.5	0.5
7	150	8	−19.40	−2.35	5.52	45.59	154.4	−4.4
8	165	9	−4.40	−1.35	1.82	5.94	160.8	4.2
9	170	10	0.60	−0.35	0.12	−0.21	167.2	2.8
10	180	12	10.60	1.65	2.72	17.49	179.9	0.1
11	170	11	0.60	0.65	0.42	0.39	173.5	−3.5
12	162	9	−7.40	−1.35	1.82	9.99	160.8	1.2
13	165	10	−4.40	−0.35	0.12	1.54	167.2	−2.2
14	180	12	10.60	1.65	2.72	17.49	179.9	0.1
15	160	8	−9.40	−2.35	5.52	22.09	154.4	5.6
16	155	9	−14.40	−1.35	1.82	19.44	160.8	−5.8
17	165	10	−4.40	−0.35	0.12	1.54	167.2	−2.2
18	190	15	20.60	4.65	21.62	95.79	199.1	−9.1
19	185	13	15.60	2.65	7.02	41.34	186.3	−1.3
20	155	11	−14.40	0.65	0.42	−9.36	173.5	−18.5
Sum	3388	207	0.0	0.0	92.50	590.20	3388.0	−0.0
Mean	169.4	10.35	0.0	0.0			169.4	0.0

2.2 Estimating Multivariate Regression Models with OLS

Let's face it: only a few dependent variables can be explained fully by a single independent variable. A person's weight, for example, is influenced by more than just that person's height. What about bone structure, percent body fat, exercise habits, or diet?

As important as additional explanatory variables might seem to the height/weight example, there's even more reason to include a variety of independent variables in economic and business applications. Although the per capita quantity consumed of a product is certainly affected by price, that's not the whole story. Advertising, per capita income, the prices of substitutes, the influence of foreign markets, the quality of customer service, possible fads, and changing tastes all are important in real-world models. As a result, it's vital to move from single-independent-variable regressions to *multivariate regression models*, or equations with more than one independent variable.

The Meaning of Multivariate Regression Coefficients

The general multivariate regression model with K independent variables can be represented by Equation 1.11:

$$Y_i = \beta_0 + \beta_1 X_{1i} + \beta_2 X_{2i} + \cdots + \beta_K X_{Ki} + \epsilon_i \qquad (1.11)$$

where i, as before, goes from 1 to N and indicates the observation number. Thus, X_{1i} indicates the *i*th observation of independent variable X_1, while X_{2i} indicates the *i*th observation of another independent variable, X_2.

The biggest difference between a single-independent-variable regression model and a multivariate regression model is in the interpretation of the latter's slope coefficients. These coefficients, often called *partial* regression coefficients, are defined to allow a researcher to distinguish the impact of one variable from that of other independent variables.

> Specifically, a **multivariate regression coefficient** indicates the change in the dependent variable associated with a one-unit increase in the independent variable in question, *holding constant the other independent variables in the equation.*

This last italicized phrase is a key to understanding multiple regression (as multivariate regression is often called). The coefficient β_1 measures the impact on Y of a one-unit increase in X_1, holding constant X_2, X_3, . . . and X_K but *not* holding constant any relevant variables that might have been omitted from the equation (e.g., X_{K+1}). The coefficient β_0 is the value of Y when all the Xs and the error term equal zero. As you'll learn in Section 7.1, you should always include a constant term in a regression equation, but you should not rely on estimates of β_0 for inference.

As an example, let's consider the following annual model of the per capita consumption of beef in the United States:

$$\widehat{CB}_t = 37.54 - 0.88 P_t + 11.9 Yd_t \qquad (2.7)$$

where: CB_t = the per capita consumption of beef in year t (in pounds per person)

$\quad\quad\quad P_t$ = the price of beef in year t (in cents per pound)

$\quad\quad\quad Yd_t$ = the per capita disposable income in year t (in thousands of dollars)

The estimated coefficient of income, 11.9, tells us that beef consumption will increase by 11.9 pounds per person if per capita disposable income goes up by $1,000, holding constant the price of beef. The ability to hold price constant is crucial because we'd expect such a large increase in per capita income to stimulate demand, therefore pushing up prices and making it hard to distinguish the effect of the income increase from the effect of the price increase. The multivariate regression estimate allows us to focus on the impact of the income variable by holding the price variable constant. Note, however, that the equation does not hold constant other possible variables (like the price of a substitute) because these variables are not included in Equation 2.7.

Before we move on to the next section, let's take the time to analyze the estimated coefficients of Equation 2.7 in a bit more depth. First, the coefficient of P tells us the impact of a one-cent increase in the price of beef on the per capita consumption of beef, holding constant per capita income. Do you agree that the estimated coefficient has the sign that economic theory would predict? Second, think about how the estimated coefficients would change if we were to change the units of disposable income from "thousands of dollars" to "dollars." The estimated equation would remain the same except that the coefficient of Yd would decrease from 11.9 to 0.0119.

OLS Estimation of Multivariate Regression Models

The application of OLS to an equation with more than one independent variable is quite similar to its application to a single-independent-variable model. To see this, consider the estimation of the simplest possible multivariate model, one with just two independent variables:

$$Y_i = \beta_0 + \beta_1 X_{1i} + \beta_2 X_{2i} + \epsilon_i \tag{2.8}$$

The goal of OLS is to choose those $\hat{\beta}$s that minimize the summed squared residuals. These residuals are now from a multivariate model, but they can be minimized using the same mathematical approach used in Section 2.1. Thus the OLS estimation of multivariate models is identical in general approach to the OLS estimation of models with just one independent variable. The equations themselves are more cumbersome,[4] but the underlying principle of estimating $\hat{\beta}$s that minimize the summed squared residuals remains the same.

Luckily, user-friendly computer packages can calculate estimates with these unwieldy equations in less than a second of computer time. Indeed, only someone lost in time or stranded on a desert island would bother estimating a multivariate regression model without a computer. The rest of us will use Stata, EViews, SPSS, SAS, or any of the other commercially available regression packages.

An Example of a Multivariate Regression Model

As an example of multivariate regression, let's take a look at a model of financial aid awards at a liberal arts college. The dependent variable in such a study would be the amount, in dollars, awarded to a particular financial aid applicant:

$$\text{FINAID}_i = \text{the financial aid (measured in dollars of grant per year)}$$
$$\text{awarded to the } i\text{th applicant}$$

What kinds of independent variables might influence the amount of financial aid received by a given student? Well, most aid is either need-based or merit-based, so it makes sense to consider a model that includes at least these two attributes:

$$\overset{-}{}\qquad\overset{+}{}$$
$$\text{FINAID}_i = \beta_0 + \beta_1\text{PARENT}_i + \beta_2\text{HSRANK}_i + \epsilon_i \qquad (2.9)$$

where: $\text{PARENT}_i = $ the amount (in dollars per year) that the parents of the ith student are judged able to contribute to college expenses

         $\text{HSRANK}_i = $ the ith student's GPA rank in high school, measured as a percentage (ranging from a low of 0 to a high of 100)

---

4. For Equation 2.8, the estimated coefficients are:

$$\hat{\beta}_1 = \frac{\left(\sum yx_1\right)\left(\sum x_2^2\right) - \left(\sum yx_2\right)\left(\sum x_1x_2\right)}{\left(\sum x_1^2\right)\left(\sum x_2^2\right) - \left(\sum x_1x_2\right)^2}$$

$$\hat{\beta}_2 = \frac{\left(\sum yx_2\right)\left(\sum x_1^2\right) - \left(\sum yx_1\right)\left(\sum x_1x_2\right)}{\left(\sum x_1^2\right)\left(\sum x_2^2\right) - \left(\sum x_1x_2\right)^2}$$

$$\hat{\beta}_0 = \overline{Y} - \hat{\beta}_1\overline{X}_1 - \hat{\beta}_2\overline{X}_2$$

where lowercase variables indicate deviations from the mean, as in $y = Y_i - \overline{Y}$; $x_1 = X_{1i} - \overline{X}_1$; and $x_2 = X_{2i} - \overline{X}_2$.

Note from the signs over the coefficients in Equation 2.9 that we anticipate that the more parents can contribute to their child's education, the less the financial aid award will be. Similarly, we expect that the higher the student's rank in high school, the higher the financial aid award will be. Do you agree with these expectations?

If we estimate Equation 2.9 using OLS and the data[5] in Table 2.2, we get:

$$\widehat{FINAID_i} = 8927 - 0.36PARENT_i + 87.4HSRANK_i \qquad (2.10)$$

What do these coefficients mean? Well, the -0.36 means that the model implies that the ith student's financial aid grant will fall by \$0.36 for every dollar increase in his or her parents' ability to pay, holding constant high school rank. Does the sign of the estimated coefficient meet our expectations? Yes. Does the size of the coefficient make sense? Yes.

To be sure that you understand this concept, take the time to write down the meaning of the coefficient of HSRANK in Equation 2.10. Do you agree that the model implies that the ith student's financial aid grant will increase by \$87.40 for each percentage point increase in high school rank, holding constant parents' ability to pay? Does this estimated coefficient seem reasonable?

Let's analyze Equation 2.10. Suppose someone told you that they believed that HSRANK is the most important variable in the model because its coefficient, 87.4, is much larger than the coefficient of FINAID. Would you agree? Before you answer, consider what Equation 2.10 would look like if the units of measurement of PARENT had been thousands of dollars instead of dollars:

$$\widehat{FINAID} = 8927 - 357PARENT + 87.4HSRANK \qquad (2.11)$$

Whoops! That puts things in a different light. Now the coefficient of PARENT is much larger than the coefficient of HSRANK. Since the size of a coefficient clearly depends on the units of measurement of the variable, we can't use coefficient size alone to make judgments about the importance of a variable. For more on this issue, see Section 5.4.

Take a look at Figures 2.1 and 2.2. These figures contain two different views of Equation 2.10. Figure 2.1 is a diagram of the effect of PARENT on FINAID, holding HSRANK constant, and Figure 2.2 shows the effect of HSRANK on FINAID, holding PARENT constant. These two figures are graphical representations of multivariate regression coefficients, since they measure the impact

---

5. These data are from an unpublished analysis of financial aid awards at Occidental College. The fourth variable in Table 2.2 is $MALE_i$, which equals 1 if the ith student is male and 0 otherwise.

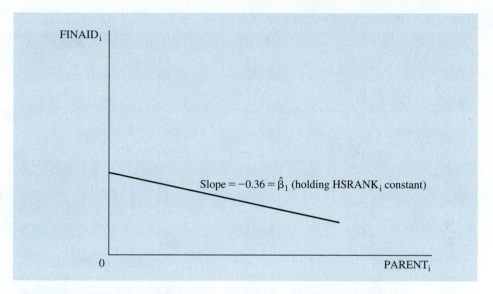

Figure 2.1 Financial Aid as a Function of Parents' Ability to Pay

In Equation 2.10, an increase of one dollar in the parents' ability to pay decreases the financial aid award by $0.36, holding constant high school rank.

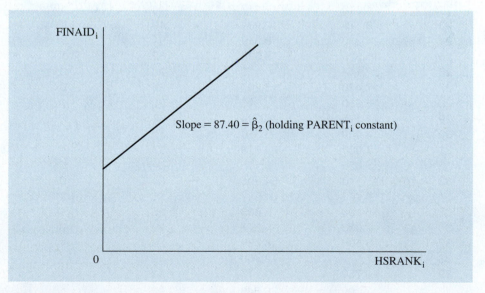

Figure 2.2 Financial Aid as a Function of High School Rank

In Equation 2.10, an increase of one percentage point in high school rank increases the financial aid award by $87.40, holding constant parents' ability to pay.

Table 2.2 Data for the Financial Aid Example

i	FINAID	PARENT	HSRANK	MALE
1	19,640	0	92	0
2	8,325	9,147	44	1
3	12,950	7,063	89	0
4	700	33,344	97	1
5	7,000	20,497	95	1
6	11,325	10,487	96	0
7	19,165	519	98	1
8	7,000	31,758	70	0
9	7,925	16,358	49	0
10	11,475	10,495	80	0
11	18,790	0	90	0
12	8,890	18,304	75	1
13	17,590	2,059	91	1
14	17,765	0	81	0
15	14,100	15,602	98	0
16	18,965	0	80	0
17	4,500	22,259	90	1
18	7,950	5,014	82	1
19	7,000	34,266	98	1
20	7,275	11,569	50	0
21	8,000	30,260	98	1
22	4,290	19,617	40	1
23	8,175	12,934	49	1
24	11,350	8,349	91	0
25	15,325	5,392	82	1
26	22,148	0	98	0
27	17,420	3,207	99	0
28	18,990	0	90	0
29	11,175	10,894	97	0
30	14,100	5,010	59	0
31	7,000	24,718	97	1
32	7,850	9,715	84	1
33	0	64,305	84	0
34	7,000	31,947	98	1
35	16,100	8,683	95	1
36	8,000	24,817	99	0
37	8,500	8,720	20	1
38	7,575	12,750	89	1
39	13,750	2,417	41	1
40	7,000	26,846	92	1
41	11,200	7,013	86	1
42	14,450	6,300	87	0

Table 2.2 (*continued*)

i	FINAID	PARENT	HSRANK	MALE
43	15,265	3,909	84	0
44	20,470	2,027	99	1
45	9,550	12,592	89	0
46	15,970	0	57	0
47	12,190	6,249	84	0
48	11,800	6,237	81	0
49	21,640	0	99	0
50	9,200	10,535	68	0

Datafile = FINAID2

on the dependent variable of a given independent variable, holding constant the other variables in the equation.

Total, Explained, and Residual Sums of Squares

Before going on, let's pause to develop some measures of how much of the variation of the dependent variable is explained by the estimated regression equation. Such comparison of the estimated values with the actual values can help a researcher judge the adequacy of an estimated regression.

Econometricians use the squared variations of Y around its mean as a measure of the amount of variation to be explained by the regression. This computed quantity is usually called the **total sum of squares**, or TSS, and is written as:

$$TSS = \sum_{i=1}^{N} (Y_i - \overline{Y})^2 \tag{2.12}$$

For Ordinary Least Squares, the total sum of squares has two components, variation that can be explained by the regression and variation that cannot:

$$\sum_i (Y_i - \overline{Y})^2 = \sum_i (\hat{Y}_i - \overline{Y})^2 + \sum_i e_i^2 \tag{2.13}$$

Total Sum	=	Explained	+	Residual
of		Sum of		Sum of
Squares		Squares		Squares
(TSS)		(ESS)		(RSS)

This is usually called the *decomposition of variance*.

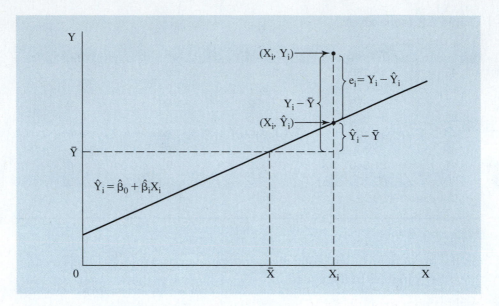

Figure 2.3 Decomposition of the Variance in Y

The variation of Y around its mean $(Y - \overline{Y})$ can be decomposed into two parts: (1) $(\hat{Y}_i - \overline{Y})$, the difference between the estimated value of $Y(\hat{Y})$ and the mean value of Y $(\overline{Y})$; and (2) $(Y_i - \hat{Y}_i)$, the difference between the actual value of Y and the estimated value of Y.

Figure 2.3 illustrates the decomposition of variance for a simple regression model. The estimated values of Y_i lie on the estimated regression line $\hat{Y}_i = \hat{\beta}_0 + \hat{\beta}_1 X_i$. The variation of Y around its mean $(Y_i - \overline{Y})$ can be decomposed into two parts: (1) $(\hat{Y}_i - \overline{Y})$, the difference between the estimated value of Y $(\hat{Y})$ and the mean value of Y $(\overline{Y})$; and (2) $(Y_i - \hat{Y}_i)$, the difference between the actual value of Y and the estimated value of Y.

The first component of Equation 2.13 measures the amount of the squared deviation of Y_i from its mean that is explained by the regression line. This component of the total sum of the squared deviations, called the **explained sum of squares**, or ESS, is attributable to the fitted regression line. The unexplained portion of TSS (that is, unexplained in an empirical sense by the estimated regression equation), is called the **residual sum of squares**, or RSS.[6]

---

6. Note that some authors reverse the definitions of RSS and ESS (defining ESS as $\sum e_i^2$), and other authors reverse the order of the letters, as in SSR.

We can see from Equation 2.13 that the smaller the RSS is relative to the TSS, the better the estimated regression line fits the data. OLS is the estimating technique that minimizes the RSS and therefore maximizes the ESS for a given TSS.

2.3 Evaluating the Quality of a Regression Equation

If the bread and butter of regression analysis is OLS estimation, then the heart and soul of econometrics is figuring out how good these OLS estimates are.

Many beginning econometricians have a tendency to accept regression estimates as they come out of a computer, or as they are published in an article, without thinking about the meaning or validity of those estimates. Such blind faith makes as much sense as buying an entire wardrobe of clothes without trying them on. Some of the clothes will fit just fine, but many others will turn out to be big (or small) mistakes.

Instead, the job of an econometrician is to carefully think about and evaluate every aspect of the equation, from the underlying theory to the quality of the data, before accepting a regression result as valid. In fact, most good econometricians spend quite a bit of time thinking about what to expect from an equation *before* they estimate that equation.

Once the computer estimates have been produced, however, it's time to evaluate the regression results. The list of questions that should be asked during such an evaluation is long. For example:

1. Is the equation supported by sound theory?
2. How well does the estimated regression fit the data?
3. Is the data set reasonably large and accurate?
4. Is OLS the best estimator to be used for this equation?
5. How well do the estimated coefficients correspond to the expectations developed by the researcher before the data were collected?
6. Are all the obviously important variables included in the equation?
7. Has the most theoretically logical functional form been used?
8. Does the regression appear to be free of major econometric problems?

The goal of this text is to help you develop the ability to ask and appropriately answer these kinds of questions. In fact, the number in front of each question above roughly corresponds to the chapter in which we'll address the issues raised by that question. Since this is Chapter 2, it'll come as no surprise to you to hear that the rest of the chapter will be devoted to the second of these topics—the overall fit of the estimated model.

2.4 Describing the Overall Fit of the Estimated Model

Let's face it: we expect that a good estimated regression equation will explain the variation of the dependent variable in the sample fairly accurately. If it does, we say that the estimated model fits the data well.

Looking at the overall fit of an estimated model is useful not only for evaluating the quality of the regression, but also for comparing models that have different data sets or combinations of independent variables. We can never be sure that one estimated model represents the truth any more than another, but evaluating the quality of the fit of the equation is one ingredient in a choice between different formulations of a regression model. Be careful, however! The quality of the fit is a minor ingredient in this choice, and many beginning researchers allow themselves to be overly influenced by it.

R²

The simplest commonly used measure of fit is R^2, or the coefficient of determination. **R^2** is the ratio of the explained sum of squares to the total sum of squares:

$$R^2 = \frac{ESS}{TSS} = 1 - \frac{RSS}{TSS} = 1 - \frac{\sum e_i^2}{\sum (Y_i - \overline{Y})^2} \qquad (2.14)$$

The higher R^2 is, the closer the estimated regression equation fits the sample data. Measures of this type are called "goodness of fit" measures. R^2 measures the percentage of the variation of Y around $\overline{Y}$ that is explained by the regression equation. Since OLS selects the coefficient estimates that minimize RSS, OLS provides the largest possible R^2, given a linear model. Since TSS, RSS, and ESS are all nonnegative (being squared deviations), and since ESS ≤ TSS, then R^2 must lie in the interval $0 \le R^2 \le 1$. A value of R^2 close to one shows an excellent overall fit, whereas a value near zero shows a failure of the estimated regression equation to explain the values of Y_i better than could be explained by the sample mean $\overline{Y}$.

Figures 2.4 through 2.6 demonstrate some extremes. Figure 2.4 shows an X and Y that are unrelated. The fitted regression line might as well be $\hat{Y} = \overline{Y}$, the same value it would have if X were omitted. As a result, the estimated

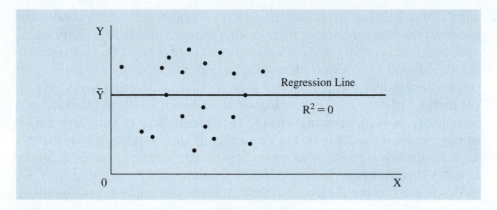

Figure 2.4

X and Y are not related; in such a case, R^2 would be 0.

linear regression is no better than the sample mean as an estimate of Y_i. The explained portion, ESS, = 0, and the unexplained portion, RSS, equals the total squared deviations TSS; thus, $R^2 = 0$.

Figure 2.5 shows a relationship between X and Y that can be "explained" quite well by a linear regression equation: the value of R^2 is .95. This kind of result is typical of a time-series regression with a good fit. Most of the variation has been explained, but there still remains a portion of the variation that is essentially random or unexplained by the model.

Goodness of fit is relative to the topic being studied. In time series data, we often get a very high R^2 because there can be significant time trends on both

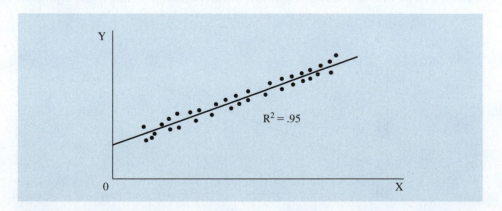

Figure 2.5

A set of data for X and Y that can be "explained" quite well with a regression line (R^2 = .95).

sides of the equation. In cross-sectional data, we often get low R^2s because the observations (say, countries) differ in ways that are not easily quantified. In such a situation, an R^2 of .50 might be considered a good fit, and researchers would tend to focus on identifying the variables that have a substantive impact on the dependent variable, not on R^2. In other words, there is no simple method of determining how high R^2 must be for the fit to be considered satisfactory. Instead, knowing when R^2 is relatively large or small is a matter of experience. It should be noted that a high R^2 does not imply that changes in X lead to changes in Y, as there may be an underlying variable whose changes lead to changes in both X and Y simultaneously.

Figure 2.6 shows a perfect fit of $R^2 = 1$. Such a fit implies that no estimation is required. The relationship is completely deterministic, and the slope and intercept can be calculated from the coordinates of any two points. In fact, reported equations with R^2s equal to (or very near) one should be viewed with suspicion; they very likely do not explain the movements of the dependent variable Y in terms of the causal proposition advanced, even though they explain them empirically. This caution applies to economic applications, but not necessarily to those in fields like physics or chemistry.

$\overline{R}^2$, The Adjusted R^2

A major problem with R^2 is that adding another independent variable to a particular equation can never decrease R^2. That is, if you compare two equations that are identical (same dependent variable and independent variables), except that one has an additional independent variable, the equation

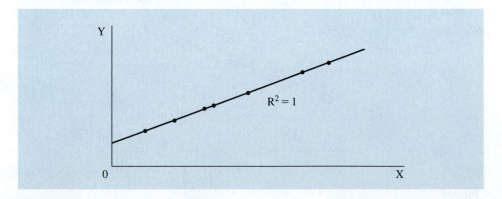

Figure 2.6

A perfect fit: all the data points are on the regression line, and the resulting R^2 is 1.

with the greater number of independent variables will always have a better (or equal) fit as measured by R^2.

To see this, recall the equation for R^2, Equation 2.14.

$$R^2 = \frac{ESS}{TSS} = 1 - \frac{RSS}{TSS} = 1 - \frac{\sum e_i^2}{\sum (Y_i - \bar{Y})^2} \qquad (2.14)$$

What will happen to R^2 if we add a variable to the equation? Adding a variable can't change TSS (can you figure out why?), but in most cases the added variable will reduce RSS, so R^2 will rise. You know that RSS will never increase because the OLS program could always set the coefficient of the added variable equal to zero, thus giving the same fit as the previous equation. The coefficient of the newly added variable being zero is the only circumstance in which R^2 will stay the same when a variable is added. Otherwise, R^2 will always increase when a variable is added to an equation.

Perhaps an example will make this clear. Let's return to our weight guessing regression, Equation 1.19:

Estimated weight $= 103.40 + 6.38$ Height (over five feet)

The R^2 for this equation is .74. If we now add a completely nonsensical variable to the equation (say, the campus post office box number of each individual in question), then it turns out that the results become:

Estimated weight $= 102.35 + 6.36$ (Height $>$ five feet) $+ 0.02$ (Box#)

but the R^2 for this equation is .75! Thus, an individual using R^2 alone as the measure of the quality of the fit of the regression would choose the second version as better fitting.

The inclusion of the campus post office box variable not only adds a nonsensical variable to the equation, but it also requires the estimation of another coefficient. This lessens the **degrees of freedom**, or the excess of the number of observations (N) over the number of coefficients (including the intercept) estimated $(K + 1)$. For instance, when the campus box number variable is added to the weight/height example, the number of observations stays constant at 20, but the number of estimated coefficients increases from 2 to 3, so the number of degrees of freedom falls from 18 to 17. This decrease has a cost, since the lower the degrees of freedom, the less reliable the estimates are likely to be. Thus, the increase in the quality of the fit caused by the addition of a variable needs to be compared to the decrease in the degrees of freedom before a decision can be made with respect to the statistical impact of the added variable.

To sum, R^2 is of little help if we're trying to decide whether adding a variable to an equation improves our ability to meaningfully explain the dependent variable. Because of this problem, econometricians have developed another measure of the quality of the fit of an equation. That measure is $\overline{R}^2$ (pronounced R-bar-squared), which is R^2 adjusted for degrees of freedom:

$$\overline{R}^2 = 1 - \frac{\sum e_i^2/(N-K-1)}{\sum (Y_i - \overline{Y})^2/(N-1)} \tag{2.15}$$

> $\overline{R}^2$ measures the percentage of the variation of Y around its mean that is explained by the regression equation, *adjusted for degrees of freedom.*

$\overline{R}^2$ will increase, decrease, or stay the same when a variable is added to an equation, depending on whether the improvement in fit caused by the addition of the new variable outweighs the loss of the degree of freedom. An increase in $\overline{R}^2$ indicates that the marginal benefit of adding a variable exceeds the cost, while a decrease in $\overline{R}^2$ indicates that the marginal cost exceeds the benefit. Indeed, the $\overline{R}^2$ for the weight-guessing equation *decreases* to .72 when the mail box variable is added. The mail box variable, since it has no theoretical relation to weight, should never have been included in the equation, and the $\overline{R}^2$ measure supports this conclusion.

The highest possible $\overline{R}^2$ is 1.00, the same as for R^2. The lowest possible $\overline{R}^2$, however, is not .00; if R^2 is extremely low, $\overline{R}^2$ can be slightly negative.

> $\overline{R}^2$ can be used to compare the fits of equations with the same dependent variable and different numbers of independent variables. Because of this property, most researchers automatically use $\overline{R}^2$ instead of R^2 when evaluating the fit of their estimated regression equations. Note, however, that $\overline{R}^2$ is not as useful when comparing the fits of two equations that have different dependent variables or dependent variables that are measured differently.

Finally, a warning is in order. Always remember that the quality of fit of an estimated equation is only one measure of the overall quality of that regression. As mentioned previously, the degree to which the estimated coefficients conform to economic theory and the researcher's previous expectations about those coefficients are just as important as the fit itself. For instance, an estimated equation with a good fit but with an implausible sign for an estimated coefficient might give implausible predictions and thus not be a very useful equation. Other factors, such as theoretical relevance and usefulness, also come into play. Let's look at an example of these factors.

2.5 An Example of the Misuse of $\overline{R}^2$

Section 2.4 implies that the higher the overall fit of a given equation, the better. Unfortunately, many beginning researchers assume that if a high $\overline{R}^2$ is good, then maximizing $\overline{R}^2$ is the best way to maximize the quality of an equation. Such an assumption is dangerous because a good overall fit is only one measure of the quality of an equation.

Perhaps the best way to visualize the dangers inherent in maximizing $\overline{R}^2$ without regard to the economic meaning or statistical significance of an equation is to look at an example of such misuse. This is important because it is one thing for a researcher to agree in theory that "$\overline{R}^2$ maximizing" is bad, and it is another thing entirely for that researcher to avoid subconsciously maximizing $\overline{R}^2$ on projects. It is easy to agree that the goal of regression is not to maximize $\overline{R}^2$, but many researchers find it hard to resist that temptation.

As an example, suppose you decide to combine your love of pizza with your love of economics, and think it might be a good idea to estimate a model of the determinants of mozzarella cheese consumption. You do some research and learn that mozzarella is a normal good, so you include income in your model. You collect a small sample, estimate the equation, and get the following results:

$$\widehat{MOZZARELLA}_t = -0.85 + 0.378INCOME_t \qquad (2.16)$$

$$N = 10 \quad \overline{R}^2 = .88$$

where: $MOZZARELLA_t$ = U.S. per capita consumption of mozzarella cheese (in pounds) in year t

$INCOME_t$ = U.S. real disposable per capita income (in thousands of dollars) in year t

You think, "What a great fit!" But like many budding econometricians, you wonder . . . could you do even better by adding another independent variable? You find some interesting data and, on a hunch, add a variable to the model and re-run the regression:[7]

$$\widehat{MOZZARELLA}_t = 3.33 + 0.248INCOME_t - 0.046DROWNINGS_t \quad (2.17)$$

$$N = 10 \qquad\qquad \overline{R}^2 = .97$$

where: $DROWNINGS_t$ = U.S. deaths due to drowning after falling out of a fishing boat in year t

---

7. This equation was created by Bruce Johnson of Centre College for the years 2000–2009. The data from MOZZARELLA and DROWNINGS come from tylervigen.com, while the data for INCOME are from the 2011 *Economic Report of the President*, Table B-31. For more examples of this type, see Tyler Vigen, *Spurious Correlation* (New York: Hachette Books, 2015).

The second equation has a much higher $\overline{R}^2$ than the first one, which you chose on the basis of theory. Does this mean your second model is better? Before you answer, reread the warning at the bottom of page 54 about the quality of fit ($\overline{R}^2$) being only one measure of the overall quality of a regression.

Did you read it? OK, then you probably know that the answer is . . . NO! Equation 2.17 has a better fit, but it's preposterous to think that the number of drownings belongs in an equation for per capita mozzarella cheese consumption. No reasonable economic theory could link drownings to cheese consumption! What happened here is that in this small sample, DROWNINGS is highly correlated with MOZZARELLA. For no particular reason other than coincidence, drowning deaths from falling out of fishing boats went steadily down from 2000 to 2009, while per capita consumption of mozzarella cheese went up, so adding DROWNINGS boosted $\overline{R}^2$. This increased fit, however, doesn't mean that the equation is better. Such a meaningless result is called a *spurious regression*[8] and it should be ignored. In all honesty, Equation 2.17 never should have been run in the first place. It's too fishy an idea to take seriously.

Thus, a researcher who uses $\overline{R}^2$ as the sole measure of the quality of an equation (at the expense of economic theory or statistical significance) increases the chances of having unrepresentative or misleading results. This practice should be avoided at all costs. No simple rule of econometric estimation is likely to work in all cases. Instead, a combination of technical competence, theoretical judgment, and common sense makes for a good econometrician.

To help avoid the natural urge to maximize $\overline{R}^2$ without regard to the rest of the equation, you might find it useful to imagine the following conversation:

You: Sometimes, it seems like the best way to choose between two models is to pick the one that gives the highest $\overline{R}^2$.

Your Conscience: But that would be wrong.

You: I know that the goal of regression analysis is to obtain the best possible estimates of the true population coefficients and not to get a high $\overline{R}^2$, but my results "look better" if my fit is good.

Your Conscience: Look better to whom? It's not at all unusual to get a high $\overline{R}^2$, but then find that some of the regression coefficients have signs or magnitudes that are contrary to theoretical expectations.

You: Well, I guess I should be more concerned with the logical relevance of the explanatory variables than with the fit, huh?

Your Conscience: Right! If in this process we obtain a high $\overline{R}^2$, well and good, but if $\overline{R}^2$ is high, it doesn't mean that the model is good.

---

8. For more on spurious regression and spurious correlation, see Section 12.5.

2.6 Summary

1. Ordinary Least Squares (OLS) is the most frequently used method of obtaining estimates of the regression coefficients from a set of data. OLS chooses those $\hat{\beta}$s that minimize the summed squared residuals ($\sum e_i^2$) for a particular sample.

2. R-bar-squared ($\overline{R}^2$) measures the percentage of the variation of Y around its mean that has been explained by a particular regression equation, adjusted for degrees of freedom. $\overline{R}^2$ increases when a variable is added to an equation only if the improvement in fit caused by the addition of the new variable more than offsets the loss of the degree of freedom that is used up in estimating the coefficient of the new variable. As a result, most researchers will automatically use $\overline{R}^2$ when evaluating the fit of their estimated regression equations.

3. Always remember that the fit of an estimated equation is only one of the measures of the overall quality of that regression. A number of other criteria, including the degree to which the estimated coefficients conform to economic theory and expectations (developed by the researcher before the data were collected) are more important than the size of $\overline{R}^2$.

EXERCISES

(The answers to the even-numbered exercises are in Appendix A.)

1. Write the meaning of each of the following terms without referring to the book (or your notes), and compare your definition with the version in the text for each:
   a. degrees of freedom (p. 53)
   b. estimate (p. 37)
   c. estimator (p. 37)
   d. multivariate regression coefficient (p. 41)
   e. Ordinary Least Squares (OLS) (p. 36)
   f. R^2 (p. 50)
   g. $\overline{R}^2$ (p. 54)
   h. total, explained, and residual sums of squares (pp. 47, 48)

2. Just as you are about to estimate a regression (due tomorrow), massive sunspots cause magnetic interference that ruins all electrically powered machines (e.g., computers). Instead of giving up and

flunking, you decide to calculate estimates from your data (on per capita income in thousands of U.S. dollars as a function of the percent of the labor force in agriculture in 10 developed countries) using methods like those used in Section 2.1 *without* a computer. Your data are:

Country	A	B	C	D	E	F	G	H	I	J
Per Capita Income	6	8	8	7	7	12	9	8	9	10
% in Agriculture	9	10	8	7	10	4	5	5	6	7

    a. Calculate $\hat{\beta}_0$ and $\hat{\beta}_1$.

    b. Calculate R^2 and $\overline{R}^2$.

    c. If the percent of the labor force in agriculture in another developed country was 8 percent, what level of per capita income (in thousands of U.S. dollars) would you guess that country had?

3. Consider the following two least-squares estimates of the relationship between interest rates and the federal budget deficit in the United States:

$$\text{Model A: } \hat{Y}_1 = 0.103 - 0.079X_1 \qquad R^2 = .00$$

where: Y_1 = the interest rate on Aaa corporate bonds
           X_1 = the federal budget deficit as a percentage of GNP
               (quarterly model: N = 56)

$$\text{Model T: } \hat{Y}_2 = 0.089 + 0.369X_2 + 0.887X_3 \qquad R^2 = .40$$

where: Y_2 = the interest rate on 3-month Treasury bills
           X_2 = the federal budget deficit in billions of dollars
           X_3 = the rate of inflation (in percent)
               (quarterly model: N = 38)

    a. What does "least-squares estimates" mean? What is being estimated? What is being squared? In what sense are the squares "least"?

    b. What does it mean to have an R^2 of .00? Is it possible for an R^2 to be negative?

    c. Based on economic theory, what signs would you have expected for the estimated slope coefficients of the two models?

    d. Compare the two equations. Which model has estimated signs that correspond to your prior expectations? Is Model T automatically better because it has a higher R^2? If not, which model do you prefer and why?

4. Let's return to the height-weight example on page 53 and recall what happened when we added a nonsensical variable that measured the student's campus post office box number (MAIL) to the equation. The estimated equation changed from:

$$\widehat{\text{WEIGHT}} = 103.40 + 6.38\text{HEIGHT}$$

to:

$$\widehat{\text{WEIGHT}} = 102.35 + 6.36\text{HEIGHT} + 0.02\text{MAIL}$$

   a. The estimated coefficient of HEIGHT changed when we added MAIL to the equation. Does that make sense? Why?
   b. In theory, someone's weight has nothing to do with their campus mail box number, yet R^2 went up from .74 to .75 when MAIL was added to the equation! How is it possible that adding a nonsensical variable to an equation can increase R^2?
   c. Adding the nonsensical variable to the equation decreased $\overline{R}^2$ from .73 to .72. Explain how it's possible that $\overline{R}^2$ can go down at the same time that R^2 goes up.
   d. If a person's campus mail box number truly is unrelated to their weight, shouldn't the estimated coefficient of that variable equal exactly 0.00? How is it possible for a nonsensical variable to get a nonzero estimated coefficient?

5. Suppose that you have been asked to estimate a regression model to explain the number of people jogging a mile or more on the school track to help decide whether to build a second track to handle all the joggers. You collect data by living in a press box for the spring semester, and you run two possible explanatory equations:

$$\text{A: } \hat{Y} = 125.0 - 15.0X_1 - 1.0X_2 + 1.5X_3 \qquad \overline{R}^2 = .75$$
$$\text{B: } \hat{Y} = 123.0 - 14.0X_1 + 5.5X_2 - 3.7X_4 \qquad \overline{R}^2 = .73$$

   where: Y = the number of joggers on a given day
   X_1 = inches of rain that day
   X_2 = hours of sunshine that day
   X_3 = the high temperature for that day (in degrees F)
   X_4 = the number of classes with term papers due the next day

   a. Which of the two (admittedly hypothetical) equations do you prefer? Why?

b. How is it possible to get different estimated signs for the coefficient of the same variable using the same data?

6. What's wrong with the following kind of thinking: "I understand that R^2 is not a perfect measure of the quality of a regression equation because it always increases when a variable is added to the equation. Once we adjust for degrees of freedom by using $\bar{R}^2$, though, it seems to me that the higher the $\bar{R}^2$, the better the equation."

7. Suppose that you work in the admissions office of a college that doesn't allow prospective students to apply by using the Common Application.[9] How might you go about estimating the number of extra applications that your college would receive if it allowed the use of the Common Application? An econometric approach to this question would be to build the best possible model of the number of college applications and then to examine the estimated coefficient of a dummy variable that equaled one if the college in question allowed the use of the "common app" (and zero otherwise).

For example, if we estimate an equation using the data in Table 2.3 for high-quality coed national liberal arts colleges, we get:

$$\widehat{\text{APPLICATION}}_i = 523.3 + 2.15\text{SIZE}_i - 32.1\text{RANK}_i$$
$$+ 1222\text{COMMONAPP}_i \qquad (2.18)$$

$$N = 49 \quad R^2 = .724 \quad \bar{R}^2 = .705$$

where: APPLICATION_i = the number of applications received by the ith college in 2007

SIZE_i = the total number of undergraduate students at the ith college in 2006

RANK_i = the *U.S. News*[10] rank of the ith college (1 = best) in 2006

COMMONAPP_i = a dummy variable equal to 1 if the ith college allowed the use of the Common Application in 2007 and 0 otherwise.

---

9. The Common Application is a computerized application form that allows high school students to apply to a number of different colleges and universities using the same basic data. For more information, go to www.commonap.org.

10. U.S. News and World Report Staff, *U.S. News Ultimate College Guide*. Naperville, Illinois: Sourcebooks, Inc., 2006–2008.

Table 2.3 Data for the College Application Example

COLLEGE	APPLICATION	COMMONAPP	RANK	SIZE
Amherst College	6680	1	2	1648
Bard College	4980	1	36	1641
Bates College	4434	1	23	1744
Bowdoin College	5961	1	7	1726
Bucknell University	8934	1	29	3529
Carleton College	4840	1	6	1966
Centre College	2159	1	44	1144
Claremont McKenna College	4140	1	12	1152
Colby College	4679	1	20	1865
Colgate University	8759	1	16	2754
College of the Holy Cross	7066	1	32	2790
Colorado College	4826	1	26	1939
Connecticut College	4742	1	39	1802
Davidson College	3992	1	10	1667
Denison University	5196	1	48	2234
DePauw University	3624	1	48	2294
Dickinson College	5844	1	41	2372
Franklin and Marshall College	5018	1	41	1984
Furman University	3879	1	41	2648
Gettysburg College	6126	1	45	2511
Grinnell College	3077	1	14	1556
Hamilton College	4962	1	17	1802
Harvey Mudd College	2493	1	14	729
Haverford College	3492	1	9	1168
Kenyon College	4626	1	32	1630
Lafayette College	6364	1	30	2322
Lawrence University	2599	1	53	1409
Macalester College	4967	1	24	1884
Middlebury College	7180	1	5	2363
Oberlin College	7014	1	22	2744
Occidental College	5275	1	36	1783
Pitzer College	3748	1	51	918
Pomona College	5907	1	7	1545
Reed College	3365	1	53	1365
Rhodes College	3709	1	45	1662
Sewanee-University of the South	2424	0	34	1498
Skidmore College	6768	1	48	2537
St. Lawrence University	4645	0	57	2148

(continued)

Table 2.3 (*continued*)

COLLEGE	APPLICATION	COMMONAPP	RANK	SIZE
St. Olaf College	4058	0	55	2984
Swarthmore College	5242	1	3	1477
Trinity College	5950	1	30	2183
Union College	4837	1	39	2178
University of Richmond	6649	1	34	2804
Vassar College	6393	1	12	2382
Washington and Lee University	3719	1	17	1749
Wesleyan University	7750	1	10	2798
Wheaton College	2160	1	55	1548
Whitman College	2892	1	36	1406
Williams College	6478	1	1	2820

Sources: U.S. News & World Report Staff, *U.S. News Ultimate College Guide*, Naperville, IL: Sourcebooks, Inc. 2006–2008.

Datafile = COLLEGE2 (Note that some colleges tied for the same rank.)

a. Take a look at the signs of each of the three estimated regression coefficients. Are they what you would have expected? Explain.

b. Carefully state the real-world meaning of the coefficients of SIZE and RANK. Does the fact that the coefficient of RANK is 15 times bigger (in absolute value) than the coefficient of SIZE mean that the ranking of a college is 15 times more important than the size of that college in terms of explaining the number of applications to that college? Why or why not?

c. Now carefully state the real-world meaning of the coefficient of COMMONAPP. Does this prove that 1,222 more students would apply if your college decided to allow the Common Application? Explain. (*Hint:* There are at least two good answers to this question. Can you get them both?)

d. To get some experience with your computer's regression software, use the data in Table 2.3 to estimate Equation 2.18. Do you get the same results?

e. Now use the same data and estimate Equation 2.18 again without the COMMONAPP variable. What is the new $\overline{R}^2$? Does $\overline{R}^2$ go up or down when you drop the variable? What, if anything, does this change tell you about whether COMMONAPP belongs in the equation?

2.7 Appendix: Econometric Lab #1

Throughout the text, you'll encounter "econometric labs" aimed at helping you get experience with the chapter topics.[11] We urge you to complete these labs, even if they aren't assigned as homework by your professor. Working through the labs on your own will make future econometric work much easier to understand and complete.

Our first lab is an exercise in simple regression analysis. You will collect a data set and then calculate regression coefficients and goodness of fit measures on your own (using Stata or another econometric software package to run the regression). Your goal is to estimate the relationship between the dependent variable WEIGHT and the independent variable HEIGHT, using your own sample, not the sample from the book.

Step 1: Gather the Data

Ask five students of your gender how tall they are, in inches, and how much they weigh, in pounds. Also report your own height and weight. Do not include names in the data. Record the variable HEIGHT in inches above five feet and the variable WEIGHT in pounds. Enter the data in an Excel spreadsheet (or directly into Stata) according to the following instructions. In the first row, type the first person's height in inches above five feet, the first person's weight in pounds, and the first person's gender—1 if male, 0 if female.

For the data, be sure to enter only numbers, not words such as pounds, inches, or male. Otherwise, Stata will get irritated and refuse to run the regression! In the height column, enter the height in inches above five feet. Enter the weight in pounds. If the observation is male, enter 1 in the MALE column. If female, enter 0.

After you enter all the data, your file might look like this:

HEIGHT	WEIGHT	MALE
4	127	0
9	152	0
6	130	0
2	130	0
6	112	0
3	119	0

---

11. These labs are simplified versions of labs designed by Bruce Johnson for use at Centre College. Instructors should consult the instructor's manual at http://www.pearson.com/studenmund for the answers to the labs and for suggestions on how best to use these labs in a classroom setting.

Now carry out the following tasks and answer the questions in order, using the data you collected.

Step 2: Calculate Summary Statistics

Use Stata to compute the summary statistics. What is the mean? Also look at the minimum, the maximum, and the sample size.

Step 3: Run the Regression

Run the regression in Stata. Can you find the estimated βs? Print the regression results if you are doing this lab as a class assignment.

Step 4: Interpret the Estimated Coefficients

State the precise meaning of the slope coefficient. Now compare your estimated coefficients with those in Equation 2.6. Are your results the same? If not, do you understand why they're different?

Step 5: Interpret $\overline{R}^2$

Can you find $\overline{R}^2$ in your results? What is it? State precisely the meaning of the $\overline{R}^2$ statistic.

Step 6: Estimate a Second Equation

Now add MALE to your equation as a second independent variable and estimate it again. Do you see a problem? Explain. Does this imply that gender has no relationship to weight?

Chapter 3

Learning to Use Regression Analysis

3.1 Steps in Applied Regression Analysis

3.2 Using Regression Analysis to Pick Restaurant Locations

3.3 Dummy Variables

3.4 Summary and Exercises

3.5 Appendix: Econometric Lab #2

From a quick reading of Chapter 2, it'd be easy to conclude that regression analysis is little more than the mechanical application of a set of equations to a sample of data. Such a notion would be similar to deciding that all that matters in golf is hitting the ball well. Golfers will tell you that it does little good to hit the ball well if you have used the wrong club or have hit the ball toward a trap, tree, or pond. Similarly, experienced econometricians spend much less time thinking about the OLS estimation of an equation than they do about a number of other factors. Our goal in this chapter is to introduce some of these "real-world" concerns.

The first section, an overview of the six steps typically taken in applied regression analysis, is the most important in the chapter. We believe that the ability to learn and understand a specific topic, like OLS estimation, is enhanced if the reader has a clear vision of the role that the specific topic plays in the overall framework of regression analysis. In addition, the six steps make it hard to miss the crucial function of theory in the development of sound econometric research.

This is followed by a complete example of how to use the six steps in applied regression: a location analysis for the "Woody's" restaurant chain that is based on actual company data and to which we will return in future chapters to apply new ideas and tests. The chapter concludes with a discussion of dummy variables and econometric lab #2.

3.1   Steps in Applied Regression Analysis

Although there are no hard and fast rules for conducting econometric research, most investigators commonly follow a standard method for applied regression analysis. The relative emphasis and effort expended on each step will vary, but normally all the steps are necessary for successful research. Note that we don't discuss the selection of the dependent variable; this choice is determined by the purpose of the research. We'll cover choosing a dependent variable in Chapter 11. Once a dependent variable is chosen, however, it's logical to follow these **six steps in applied regression analysis**.

1. Review the literature and develop the theoretical model.
2. Specify the model: Select the independent variables and the functional form.
3. Hypothesize the expected signs of the coefficients.
4. Collect the data. Inspect and clean the data.
5. Estimate and evaluate the equation.
6. Document the results.

The purpose of suggesting these steps is not to discourage the use of innovative or unusual approaches but rather to develop in the reader a sense of how regression ordinarily is done by professional economists and business analysts.

Step 1: Review the Literature and Develop the Theoretical Model

The first step in any applied research is to get a good theoretical grasp of the topic to be studied. That's right: the best data analysts don't start with data, but with theory! This is because many econometric decisions, ranging from which variables to include to which functional form to employ, are determined by the underlying theoretical model. It's virtually impossible to build a good econometric model without a solid understanding of the topic you're studying.

For most topics, this means that it's smart to review the scholarly literature before doing anything else. If a professor has investigated the theory behind your topic, you want to know about it. If other researchers have estimated equations for your dependent variable, you might want to apply one of their models to your data set. On the other hand, if you disagree with the approach of previous authors, you might want to head off in a new direction. In either case, you shouldn't have to "reinvent the wheel." You should start your investigation where earlier researchers left off. Any academic paper on an empirical topic should begin with a summary of the extent and quality of previous research.

The most convenient approaches to reviewing the literature are to obtain several recent issues of the *Journal of Economic Literature* or a business-oriented publication of abstracts, or to run an Internet search or an *EconLit* search[1] on your topic. Using these resources, find and read several recent articles on your topic. Pay attention to the bibliographies of these articles. If an older article is cited by a number of current authors, or if its title hits your topic on the head, trace back through the literature and find this article as well. We'll have more advice on reviewing the literature in Chapter 11.

In some cases, a topic will be so new or so obscure that you won't be able to find any articles on it. What then? We recommend two possible strategies. First, try to transfer theory from a similar topic to yours. For example, if you're trying to build a model of the demand for a new product, read articles that analyze the demand for similar, existing products. Second, if all else fails, contact someone who works in the field you're investigating. For example, if you're building a model of housing in an unfamiliar city, call a real estate agent who works there.

Step 2: Specify the Model: Select the Independent Variables and the Functional Form

The most important step in applied regression analysis is the specification of the theoretical regression model. After selecting the dependent variable, the **specification** of a model involves choosing the following components:

1. the independent variables and how they should be measured,
2. the functional (mathematical) form of the variables, and
3. the properties of the stochastic error term.

A regression equation is specified when each of these elements has been treated appropriately. We'll discuss the details of these specification decisions in Chapters 6, 7, and 4, respectively.

Each of the elements of specification is determined primarily on the basis of economic theory. A mistake in any of the three elements results in a

---

1. *EconLit* is an electronic bibliography of economics literature. *EconLit* contains abstracts, reviews, indexing, and links to full-text articles in economics journals. In addition, it abstracts books and indexes articles in books, working papers series, and dissertations. *EconLit* is available at libraries and on university websites throughout the world. For more, go to www.EconLit.org.

specification error. Of all the kinds of mistakes that can be made in applied regression analysis, specification error is usually the most disastrous to the validity of the estimated equation. Thus, the more attention paid to economic theory at the beginning of a project, the more satisfying the regression results are likely to be.

The emphasis in this text is on estimating behavioral equations, those that describe the behavior of economic entities. We focus on selecting independent variables based on the economic theory concerning that behavior. An explanatory variable is chosen because it is a theoretical determinant of the dependent variable; it is expected to explain at least part of the variation in the dependent variable. Recall that regression gives evidence but does not prove economic causality. Just as an example does not prove the rule, a regression result does not prove the theory.

There are dangers in specifying the wrong independent variables. Our goal should be to specify only relevant explanatory variables, those expected theoretically to assert a substantive influence on the dependent variable. Variables suspected of having little effect should be excluded unless their possible impact on the dependent variable is of some particular (e.g., policy) interest.

For example, an equation that explains the quantity demanded of a consumption good might use the price of the product and consumer income or wealth as likely variables. Theory also indicates that complementary and substitute goods are important. Therefore, you might decide to include the prices of complements and substitutes, but which complements and substitutes? Of course, selection of the closest complements and/or substitutes is appropriate, but how far should you go? The choice must be based on theoretical judgment, and such judgments are often quite subjective.

When researchers decide, for example, that the prices of only two other goods need to be included, they are said to impose their *priors* (i.e., previous theoretical belief) or their working hypotheses on the regression equation. Imposition of such priors is a common practice that determines the number and kind of hypotheses that the regression equation has to test. The danger is that a prior may be wrong and could diminish the usefulness of the estimated regression equation. Each of the priors therefore should be explained and justified in detail.

Step 3: Hypothesize the Expected Signs of the Coefficients

Once the variables have been selected, it's important to hypothesize the expected signs of the slope coefficients before you collect any data. In many cases, the basic theory is general knowledge, so you don't need to discuss the reasons for the expected sign. However, if any doubt surrounds the choice of an expected sign, then you should document the opposing theories and your reasons for hypothesizing a positive or a negative slope[2] coefficient.

For example, suppose that you're interested in the impact of class size on student learning at the elementary level in the United States. A reasonable dependent variable (Y) might be the student score on a test of grammar, math, and science. Likely independent variables would include the income level of the student's family (X_1) and the size (in students per teacher) of the student's class (X_2).

$$\overset{+}{} \quad \overset{-}{}$$
$$Y = \beta_0 + \beta_1 X_1 + \beta_2 X_2 + \epsilon \tag{3.1}$$

The signs above the coefficients in Equation 3.1 indicate the hypothesized sign of that particular coefficient. Take another look at the equation. Do you agree with the hypothesized signs? The expectation that higher income will improve test scores (holding constant class size) seems reasonable because of the extra learning opportunities that the money might allow, but the hypothesized sign for β_2 is a little trickier. Do you agree that it should be negative?

Step 4: Collect the Data. Inspect and Clean the Data

Obtaining an original data set and properly preparing it for regression is a surprisingly difficult task. This step entails more than a mechanical recording of data, because the type and size of the sample also must be chosen.

A general rule regarding sample size is "the more observations the better," as long as the observations are from the same general population. Ordinarily, researchers take all the roughly comparable observations that are readily available. In regression analysis, all the variables must have the same number of observations. They also should have the same frequency (monthly, quarterly, annual, etc.) and time period. Often, the frequency selected is determined by the availability of data.

The reason there should be as many observations as possible concerns the statistical concept of *degrees of freedom* first mentioned in Section 2.4. Consider fitting a straight line to two points on an X, Y coordinate system as in Figure 3.1. Such an exercise can be done mathematically without error. Both points lie on the line, so there is no estimation of the coefficients involved. The two points determine the two parameters, the intercept and the slope, precisely. Estimation takes place only when a straight line is fitted to

---

2. Note that while we hypothesize signs for the slope coefficients, we don't hypothesize an expected sign for the intercept. We'll explain why in Section 7.1.

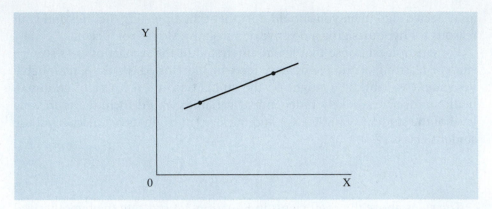

Figure 3.1 Mathematical Fit of a Line to Two Points

If there are only two points in a data set, as in Figure 3.1, a straight line can be fitted to those points mathematically without error, because two points completely determine a straight line.

three or more points that were generated by some process that is not exact. The excess of the number of observations (three) over the number of coefficients to be estimated (in this case two, the intercept and slope) is the degrees of freedom.[3] All that is necessary for estimation is a single degree of freedom, as in Figure 3.2, but the more degrees of freedom there are, the better. This is because when the number of degrees of freedom is large, every positive error is likely to be balanced by a negative error. When degrees of freedom are low, the random element is likely to fail to provide such offsetting observations. For example, the more a coin is flipped, the more likely it is that the observed proportion of heads will reflect the true probability of 0.5.

Another area of concern has to do with the *units of measurement of the variables.* Does it matter if a variable is measured in dollars or thousands of dollars? Does it matter if the measured variable differs consistently from the true variable by 10 units? Interestingly, such changes don't matter in terms of regression analysis except in interpreting the scale of the coefficients. All conclusions about signs, significance, and economic theory are independent of units of measurement. For example, it makes little difference whether an independent variable is measured in dollars or thousands of dollars. The

---

3. Throughout the text, we will calculate the number of degrees of freedom (d.f.) in a regression equation as d.f. $= (N - K - 1)$, where K is the number of independent variables in the equation. Equivalently, some authors will set $K' = K + 1$ and define d.f. $= (N - K')$. Since K' equals the number of independent variables plus 1 (for the constant), it equals the number of coefficients to be estimated in the regression.

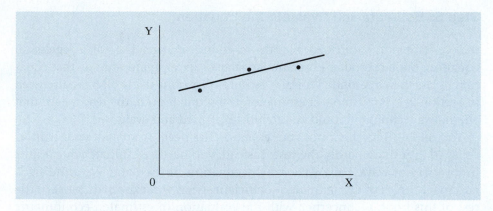

Figure 3.2 Statistical Fit of a Line to Three Points

If there are three (or more) points in a data set, as in Figure 3.2, then the line must almost always be fitted to the points statistically, using the estimation procedures of Section 2.1.

constant term and measures of overall fit remain unchanged. Such a multiplicative factor does change the slope coefficient, but only by the exact amount necessary to compensate for the change in the units of measurement of the independent variable. Similarly, a constant factor added to a variable alters only the intercept term without changing the slope coefficient itself.

The final step before estimating your equation is to inspect and clean the data. You should make it a point always to look over your data set to see if you can find any errors. The reason is obvious: why bother using sophisticated regression analysis if your data are incorrect?

To inspect the data, obtain a plot (graph) of the data and look for outliers. An *outlier* is an observation that lies outside the range of the rest of the observations, and looking for outliers is an easy way to find data entry errors. In addition, it's a good habit to look at the mean, maximum, and minimum of each variable and then think about possible inconsistencies in the data. Are any observations impossible or unrealistic? Did GDP double in one year? Does a student have a 7.0 GPA on a 4.0 scale? Is consumption negative?

Typically, the data can be cleaned of these errors by replacing an incorrect number with the correct one. In extremely rare circumstances, an observation can be dropped from the sample, but only if the correct number can't be found or if that particular observation clearly isn't from the same population as the rest of the sample. Be careful! The mere existence of an outlier is not a justification for dropping that observation from the sample. A regression needs to be able to explain all the observations in a sample, not just the well-behaved ones. For more on the details of data collection, see Sections 11.2 and 11.3. For more on generating your own data through an economic experiment, see Section 16.1.

Step 5: Estimate and Evaluate the Equation

Believe it or not, it can take months to complete steps 1–4 for a regression equation, but a computer program like Stata or EViews can estimate that equation in less than a second! Typically, estimation is done using OLS, as discussed in Section 2.1, but if another estimation technique is used, the reasons for that alternative technique should be carefully explained and evaluated.

You might think that once your equation has been estimated, your work is finished, but that's hardly the case. Instead, you need to evaluate your results in a variety of ways. How well did the equation fit the data? Were the signs and magnitudes of the estimated coefficients what you expected? Most of the rest of this book is concerned with the evaluation of estimated econometric equations, and beginning researchers should be prepared to spend a considerable amount of time doing this evaluation.

Once this evaluation is complete, don't automatically go to step 6. Regression results are rarely what one expects, and additional model development often is required. For example, an evaluation of your results might indicate that your equation is missing an important variable. In such a case, you'd go back to step 1 to review the literature and add the appropriate variable to your equation. You'd then go through each of the steps in order until you had estimated your new specification in step 5. You'd move on to step 6 only if you were satisfied with your estimated equation. Don't be too quick to make such adjustments, however, because we don't want to adjust the theory merely to fit the data. A researcher has to walk a fine line between making appropriate changes and avoiding inappropriate ones, and making these choices is one of the artistic elements of applied econometrics.

Finally, it's often worthwhile to estimate additional specifications of an equation in order to see how stable your observed results are. This approach, called *sensitivity analysis*, will be discussed in Section 6.4.

Step 6: Document the Results

A standard format usually is used to present estimated regression results:

$$\hat{Y}_i = 103.40 + 6.38X_i$$
$$(0.88) \tag{3.2}$$
$$t = 7.22$$
$$N = 20 \quad \overline{R}^2 = .73$$

The number in parentheses is the estimated standard error of the estimated coefficient, and the t-value is the one used to test the hypothesis that the true value of the coefficient is different from zero. These and other measures of the quality of the regression will be discussed in later chapters.[4] What is important to note is that the documentation of regression results using an easily understood format is considered part of the analysis itself. For time-series data sets, the documentation also includes the frequency (e.g., quarterly or annual) and the time period of the data.

One of the important parts of the documentation is the explanation of the model, the assumptions, and the procedures and data used. The written documentation must contain enough information so that the entire study could be replicated by others.[5] Unless the variables have been defined in a glossary or table, short definitions should be presented along with the equations. If there is a series of estimated regression equations, then tables should provide the relevant information for each equation. All data manipulations as well as data sources should be documented fully. When there is much to explain, this documentation usually is relegated to a data appendix. If the data are not available generally or are available only after computation, the data set itself might be included in this appendix.

3.2 Using Regression Analysis to Pick Restaurant Locations

To solidify your understanding of the six basic steps of applied regression analysis, let's work through a complete regression example. Suppose that you've been hired to determine the best location for the next Woody's restaurant, where Woody's is a moderately priced, 24-hour, family restaurant chain.[6] You decide to build a regression model to explain the gross sales volume at each of the restaurants in the chain as a function of various descriptors of the location of that branch. If you can come up with a sound equation to explain gross sales as a function of location, then you can use this equation to help Woody's decide where to build their newest eatery. Given data on

---

4. The standard error of the coefficient is discussed in more detail in Section 4.2; the *t*-value is developed in Section 5.2.

5. For example, the *Journal of Money, Credit, and Banking* and the *American Economic Review* have requested authors to submit their actual data sets so that regression results can be verified. See W. G. Dewald et al., "Replication in Empirical Economics," *American Economic Review*, Vol. 76, No. 4, pp. 587–603 and Daniel S. Hamermesh, "Replication in Economics," NBER Working Paper 13026, April 2007.

6. The data in this example are real (they're from a sample of 33 Denny's restaurants in Southern California), but the number of independent variables considered is much smaller than was used in the actual research. Datafile = WOODY3.

land costs, building costs, and local building and restaurant municipal codes, the owners of Woody's will be able to make an informed decision.

1. *Review the literature and develop the theoretical model.* You do some reading about the restaurant industry, but your review of the literature consists mainly of talking to various experts within the firm. They give you some good ideas about the attributes of a successful Woody's location. The experts tell you that all of the chain's restaurants are identical (indeed, this is sometimes a criticism of the chain) and that all the locations are in what might be called "suburban, retail, or residential" environments (as distinguished from central cities or rural areas, for example). Because of this, you realize that many of the reasons that might help explain differences in sales volume in other chains do not apply in this case because all the Woody's locations are similar. (If you were comparing Woody's to another chain, such variables might be appropriate.)

   In addition, discussions with the people in the Woody's strategic planning department convince you that price differentials and consumption differences between locations are not as important as the number of customers a particular location attracts. This causes you concern for a while because the variable you had planned to study originally, gross sales volume, would vary as prices changed between locations. Since your company controls these prices, you feel that you would rather have an estimate of the "potential" for such sales. As a result, you decide to specify your dependent variable as the number of customers served (measured by the number of checks or bills that the servers handed out) in a given location in the most recent year for which complete data are available.

2. *Specify the model: Select the independent variables and the functional form.* Your discussions lead to a number of suggested variables. After a while, you realize that there are three major determinants of sales (customers) on which virtually everyone agrees. These are the number of people who live near the location, the general income level of the location, and the number of direct competitors close to the location. In addition, there are two other good suggestions for potential explanatory variables. These are the number of cars passing the location per day and the number of months that the particular restaurant has been open. After some serious consideration of your alternatives, you decide not to include the last possibilities. All the locations have been open long enough to have achieved a stable clientele. In addition, it would be very expensive to collect data on the number of passing cars for all the locations. Should population prove to be a poor measure of the available customers in a location, you'll have to decide whether to ask your boss for the money to collect complete traffic data.

The exact definitions of the independent variables you decide to include are:

N = Competition: the number of direct market competitors within a two-mile radius of the Woody's location

P = Population: the number of people living within a three-mile radius of the Woody's location

I = Income: the average household income of the population measured in variable P

Since we have yet to develop any functional forms other than a linear functional form and a typical stochastic error term, that's what you decide to use.

3. *Hypothesize the expected signs of the coefficients.* After thinking about which variables to include, you expect hypothesizing signs will be easy. For two of the variables, you're right. Everyone expects that the more competition there is, the fewer customers (holding constant the population and income of an area) there will be, and also that the more people there are who live near a particular restaurant, the more customers (holding constant the competition and income) the restaurant will have. You expect that the greater the income is in a particular area, the more people will choose to eat in a family restaurant. However, people in especially high-income areas might want to eat in a restaurant that has more "atmosphere" than a family restaurant like Woody's. As a result, you worry that the income variable might be only weakly positive in its impact. To sum, you expect:

$$\overset{-}{} \overset{+}{} \overset{+?}{}$$
$$Y_i = \beta_0 + \beta_N N_i + \beta_P P_i + \beta_I I_i + \epsilon_i \tag{3.3}$$

where the signs above the coefficients indicate the expected impact of that particular independent variable on the dependent variable, holding constant the other two explanatory variables, and ϵ_i is a typical stochastic error term.

4. *Collect the data. Inspect and clean the data.* You want to include every local restaurant in the Woody's chain in your study, and, after some effort, you come up with data for your dependent variable and your independent variables for all 33 locations. You inspect the data, and you're confident that the quality of your data is excellent for three reasons: each manager measured each variable identically, you've included each restaurant in the sample, and all the information is from the same year. [The data set is included in this section, along with a sample computer output for the regression estimated by Stata (Tables 3.1 and 3.2).]

Table 3.1 Data for the Woody's Restaurant Example (Using the Stata Program)

	Y	N	P	I
1.	107919	3	65044	13240
2.	118866	5	101376	22554
3.	98579	7	124989	16916
4.	122015	2	55249	20967
5.	152827	3	73775	19576
6.	91259	5	48484	15039
7.	123550	8	138809	21857
8.	160931	2	50244	26435
9.	98496	6	104300	24024
10.	108052	2	37852	14987
11.	144788	3	66921	30902
12.	164571	4	166332	31573
13.	105564	3	61951	19001
14.	102568	5	100441	20058
15.	103342	2	39462	16194
16.	127030	5	139900	21384
17.	166755	6	171740	18800
18.	125343	6	149894	15289
19.	121886	3	57386	16702
20.	134594	6	185105	19093
21.	152937	3	114520	26502
22.	109622	3	52933	18760
23.	149884	5	203500	33242
24.	98388	4	39334	14988
25.	140791	3	95120	18505
26.	101260	3	49200	16839
27.	139517	4	113566	28915
28.	115236	9	194125	19033
29.	136749	7	233844	19200
30.	105067	7	83416	22833
31.	136872	6	183953	14409
32.	117146	3	60457	20307
33.	163538	2	65065	20111

(obs=33)

	Y	N	P	I
Y	1.0000			
N	−0.1442	1.0000		
P	0.3926	0.7263	1.0000	
I	0.5370	−0.0315	0.2452	1.0000

Table 3.2 Actual Computer Output (Using the Stata Program)

Source	SS	df	MS		
Model	9.9289e + 09	3	3.3096e + 09		
Residual	6.1333e + 09	29	211492485		
Total	1.6062e + 10	32	501943246		

Number of obs = 33
F(3, 29) = 15.65
Prob > F = 0.0000
R–squared = 0.6182
Adj R–squared = 0.5787
Root MSE = 14543

Y	Coef.	Std. Err.	t	P > |t|	[95% Conf.	Interval]
N	−9074.674	2052.674	−4.42	0.000	−13272.86	−4876.485
P	.3546684	.0726808	4.88	0.000	.2060195	.5033172
I	1.287923	.5432938	2.37	0.025	.1767628	2.399084
_cons	102192.4	12799.83	7.98	0.000	76013.84	128371

	Y	Yhat	residuals
1.	107919	115089.6	−7170.56
2.	118866	121821.7	−2955.74
3.	98579	104785.9	−6206.864
4.	122015	130642	−8627.041
5.	152827	126346.5	26480.55
6.	91259	93383.88	−2124.877
7.	123550	106976.3	16573.66
8.	160931	135909.3	25021.71
9.	98496	115677.4	−17181.36
10.	108052	116770.1	−8718.094
11.	144788	138502.6	6285.425
12.	164571	165550	−979.0342
13.	105564	121412.3	−15848.3
14.	102568	118275.5	−15707.47
15.	103342	118895.6	−15553.63
16.	127030	133978.1	−6948.114
17.	166755	132868.1	33886.91
18.	125343	120598.1	4744.898
19.	121886	116832.3	5053.7
20.	134594	137985.6	−3391.591
21.	152937	149717.6	3219.428
22.	109622	117903.5	−8281.508
23.	149884	171807.2	−21923.22
24.	98388	99147.65	−759.6514
25.	140791	132537.5	8253.518
26.	101260	114105.4	−12845.43
27.	139517	143412.3	−3895.303
28.	115236	113883.4	1352.599
29.	136749	146334.9	−9585.905
30.	105067	97661.88	7405.122
31.	136872	131544.4	5327.621
32.	117146	122564.5	−5418.45
33.	163538	133021	30517

5. *Estimate and evaluate the equation.* You take the data set and enter it into the computer. You then run an OLS regression on the data, but you do so only after thinking through your model once again to see if there are hints that you've made theoretical mistakes. You end up admitting that although you cannot be sure you are right, you've done the best you can, so you estimate the equation, obtaining:

$$\hat{Y}_i = 102,192 - 9075N_i + 0.355P_i + 1.288I_i \qquad (3.4)$$
$$\qquad\qquad (2053) \quad (0.073) \quad (0.543)$$
$$\qquad t = -4.42 \quad\;\; 4.88 \qquad 2.37$$
$$N = 33 \quad \overline{R}^2 = .579$$

This equation satisfies your needs in the short run. In particular, the estimated coefficients in the equation have the signs you expected. The overall fit, although not outstanding, seems reasonable for such a diverse group of locations. To predict Y, you obtain the values of N, P, and I for each potential new location and then plug them into Equation 3.4. Other things being equal, the higher the predicted Y, the better the location from Woody's point of view.

6. *Document the results.* The results summarized in Equation 3.4 meet our documentation requirements. (Note that we include the standard errors of the estimated coefficients and *t*-values[7] for completeness, even though we won't make use of them until Chapter 5.) However, it's not easy for a beginning researcher to wade through a computer's regression output to find all the numbers required for documentation. You'll probably have an easier time reading your own computer system's printout if you take the time to "walk through" the sample computer output for the Woody's model in Tables 3.1–3.2. This sample output was produced by the Stata computer program, but it's similar to those produced by EViews, SAS, SHAZAM, TSP, and others.

The first items listed are the actual data. These are followed by the simple correlation coefficients between all pairs of variables in the data set. Next comes a listing of the estimated coefficients, their estimated standard errors, and the associated *t*-values, and follows with R^2, $\overline{R}^2$, RSS, the *F*-ratio, and other items that we will explain in later chapters. Finally, we have a listing of the observed Ys, the predicted Ys, and

---

7. Throughout the text, the number in parentheses below a coefficient estimate typically will be the standard error of that estimated coefficient. Some authors put the *t*-value in parentheses, though, so be alert when reading journal articles or other books.

the residuals for each observation. Numbers followed by "$e + 06$" or "$e - 01$" are expressed in a scientific notation indicating that the printed decimal point should be moved six places to the right or one place to the left, respectively.

In future sections, we'll return to this example in order to apply various tests and ideas as we learn them.

3.3 Dummy Variables

Some concepts (for example, gender) might seem impossible to include in an equation because they're inherently qualitative in nature and can't be expressed as a number. Luckily, such concepts can be quantified by using dummy (or binary) variables. A **dummy variable** takes on the value of one or zero (and only those values) depending on whether a specified condition is met.

As an illustration of a dummy variable, suppose that Y_i represents the salary of the ith high school teacher and that salaries depend primarily on the experience of the teacher and the type of degree that the teacher has earned. All teachers have a B.A., but some also have a graduate degree like an M.A. An equation representing the relationship between earnings and these variables would be:

$$Y_i = \beta_0 + \overset{+}{\beta_1 X_i} + \overset{+}{\beta_2 D_i} + \epsilon_i \tag{3.5}$$

where:
Y_i = the income of the ith teacher in dollars
X_i = the number of years of teaching experience of the ith teacher
$D_i = \begin{cases} 1 \text{ if the } i\text{th teacher has a graduate degree} \\ 0 \text{ otherwise} \end{cases}$

The variable D_i takes on values of only zero or one, so D_i is called a dummy variable, or just a "dummy." Needless to say, the term has generated many a pun. In this case, the dummy variable represents the condition of having a graduate degree. The coefficient β_2 indicates the additional salary that can be attributed to having a graduate degree, holding teaching experience constant.

Since more experience and a graduate degree can be expected to increase the earnings of teachers, we expect positive coefficients for both variables, as indicated by the signs above the coefficients in Equation 3.5. Think for a second about what those expected signs would be if we had instead

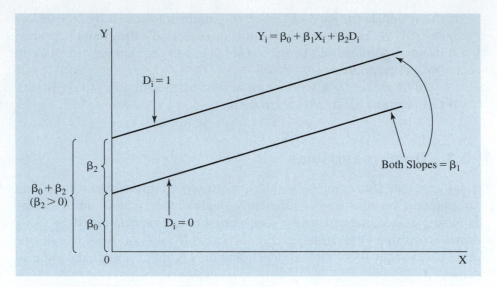

Figure 3.3 A Dummy Variable

If a dummy ($\beta_2 D_i$) is added to an equation, a graph of the equation will have different intercepts for the two qualitative conditions specified by the dummy variable. The difference between the two intercepts is β_2. The slopes are constant with respect to the qualitative condition.

defined D_i to be equal to one if the ith teacher has no graduate degree and equal to zero otherwise. This change shouldn't impact the expected sign of β_1, but do you see that the expected sign of β_2 now would be negative?[8]

As can be seen in Figure 3.3, the dummy changes the intercept depending on the value of D, but the slopes remain constant no matter what value D takes. This is true even if we define the dummy variable "reversed" and have $D = 0$ if the particular condition is met and $D = 1$ otherwise. The slopes still remain constant.

Note that in this example only one dummy variable is used even though there were two conditions. This is because one fewer dummy variable is constructed than conditions. The event not explicitly represented by a dummy variable, the **omitted condition**, forms the basis against which the included conditions are compared. Thus, for dual situations only one dummy variable is entered as an independent variable; the coefficient is interpreted as the effect of the included condition relative to the omitted condition. Be careful

8. The constant term will change as well.

never to use two dummy variables to describe the two conditions. If you were to make this mistake, sometimes called a *dummy variable trap*, you'd have perfect multicollinearity (to be described in Section 8.1).

For another example of the meaning of the coefficient of a dummy variable, let's look at a study of the relationship between fraternity/sorority membership and grade point average (GPA). Most noneconometricians would approach this research problem by calculating the mean grades of fraternity/sorority (so-called Greek) members and comparing them to the mean grades of nonmembers. However, such a technique would ignore the relationship that grades have to characteristics other than Greek membership.

Instead, we'd want to build a regression model that explains college GPA. Independent variables would include not only Greek membership but also other predictors of academic performance such as SAT scores and high school grades. Being a member of a social organization is a qualitative variable, however, so we'd have to create a dummy variable to represent fraternity or sorority membership quantitatively in a regression equation:

$$D_i = \begin{cases} 1 \text{ if the } i\text{th student is an active member} \\ \quad \text{ of a fraternity or sorority} \\ 0 \text{ otherwise} \end{cases}$$

If we collect data from all the students in our class and estimate the equation implied in this example, we obtain:

$$\widehat{CG_i} = 0.37 + 0.81HG_i + 0.00001S_i - 0.38D_i \qquad (3.6)$$
$$\overline{R}^2 = .45 \quad N = 25$$

where: CG_i = the cumulative college GPA (4-point scale) of the ith student

 HG_i = the cumulative high school GPA (4-point scale) of the ith student

 S_i = the sum of the highest verbal and mathematics SAT scores earned by the ith student

The meaning of the estimated coefficient of D_i in Equation 3.6 is very specific. Stop for a second and figure it out for yourself. What is it? The estimate that $\hat{\beta}_D = -0.38$ means that, for this sample, the GPA of fraternity/sorority members is 0.38 lower than for nonmembers, holding SATs and high school GPA constant. Thus, Greek members are doing about a third of a grade worse than otherwise might be expected. To understand this example better, try using Equation 3.6 to predict your own GPA; how close does it come?

Before you rush out and quit whatever social organization you're in, however, note that this sample is quite small and that we've surely omitted some important determinants of academic success from the equation. As a result, we shouldn't be too quick to conclude that Greeks are dummies.

Up to this point, we've used dummy variables to represent only those qualitative variables that have exactly two possibilities (such as gender). What about situations where a qualitative variable has three or more alternatives? For example, in our study of the salaries of high school teachers in Equation 3.5, what if we learn that some of the teachers have Ph.D.s? We now need to be able to distinguish teachers whose highest degree is a Ph.D. from teachers whose highest degree is an M.A. from teachers whose highest degree is a B.A. What can we do?

Well, the answer certainly isn't to define a variable such that Ph.D. = 2, M.A. = 1, and B.A. = 0, because we have no reason to think that the impact of having a Ph.D. is exactly twice that of having an M.A. If not that, then what?

The answer is to create one fewer dummy variable than there are possibilities (conditions) and to use each dummy to represent only one of the possible conditions. In the high school salary case, you'd create *two* dummy variables to represent the three conditions, for example:

$$PHD_i = \begin{cases} 1 \text{ if the } i\text{th teacher's highest degree is a Ph.D.} \\ 0 \text{ otherwise} \end{cases}$$

and

$$MA_i = \begin{cases} 1 \text{ if the } i\text{th teacher's highest degree is an M.A.} \\ 0 \text{ otherwise} \end{cases}$$

The omitted condition (when a B.A. is the highest degree) is represented by having both dummies equal to 0. This way you can measure the impact of each degree independently without having to link the impacts of having an M.A. and a Ph.D.

Thus Equation 3.5 now would look like this:

$$
\begin{array}{ccc}
+ & + & ? \\
\end{array}
$$
$$Y_i = \beta_0 + \beta_1 X_i + \beta_2 PHD_i + \beta_3 MA_i + \epsilon_i \qquad (3.7)$$

However, be careful! The interpretation of the coefficients when there are two or more related dummy variables is tricky. The coefficient tells you the increase in the dependent variable caused by the condition being met *compared to the omitted condition.* Thus β_3 measures the impact of having the highest degree be an M.A. (holding X and PHD constant) compared to the omitted condition, which is when the highest degree is a B.A. To make sure that you understand this, go back to Equation 3.7 and determine the expected sign of β_3. Did you decide it should be positive? That's right! We'd expect a high school teacher whose highest degree is an M.A. to have a higher salary than one whose highest degree is a B.A. (holding X and PHD constant).

A dummy variable that has only a single observation with a value of 1 while the rest of the observations are 0 (or vice versa) is to be avoided unless the variable is required by theory. Such a *one-time dummy* acts merely to eliminate that observation from the data set, improving the fit artificially by setting the dummy's coefficient equal to the residual for that observation. One would obtain exactly the same estimates of the other coefficients if that observation were deleted, but the deletion of an observation is rarely, if ever, appropriate.

While this is the end of the section, it's not the end of our coverage of dummy variables. In Section 7.4, we'll discuss slope dummy variables, and in Chapter 13 we'll analyze what happens when the *dependent* variable is a dummy.

3.4　Summary

1. Six steps typically taken in applied regression analysis for a given dependent variable are:
   a. Review the literature and develop the theoretical model.
   b. Specify the model: Select the independent variables and the functional form.
   c. Hypothesize the expected signs of the coefficients.
   d. Collect the data. Inspect and clean the data.
   e. Estimate and evaluate the equation.
   f. Document the results.

2. A dummy variable takes on only the values of 1 or 0, depending on whether some condition is met. An example of a dummy variable would be X equals 1 if a particular individual is female and 0 if the person is male.

EXERCISES

(The answers to the even-numberd exercises are in Appendix A.)

1. Write the meaning of each of the following terms without referring to the book (or your notes), and compare your definition with the version in the text for each:
    a. dummy variable (p. 79)
    b. omitted condition (p. 80)
    c. six steps in applied regression analysis (p. 66)
    d. specification (p. 67)
    e. specification error (p. 68)

2. Contrary to their name, dummy variables are not easy to understand without a little bit of practice:
    a. Specify a dummy variable that would allow you to distinguish between undergraduate students and graduate students in your econometrics class.
    b. Specify a regression equation to explain the grade (measured on a scale of 4.0) each student in your class received on his or her first econometrics test (Y) as a function of the student's grade in a previous course in statistics (G), the number of hours the student studied for the test (H), and the dummy variable you created above (D). Are there other variables you would want to add? Explain.
    c. What is the hypothesized sign of the coefficient of D? Does the sign depend on the exact way in which you defined D? (*Hint:* In particular, suppose that you had reversed the definitions of 1 and 0 in your answer to part a.) How?
    d. Suppose that you collected the data and ran the regression and found an estimated coefficient for D that had the expected sign and an absolute value of 0.5. What would this mean in real-world terms?
    e. Suppose three of the students in your class are high school seniors who are taking econometrics as part of an accelerated study program for especially talented youngsters. What's the best way to use dummy variables to distinguish between the three types of students in your class? Be specific as to the definition of the dummy variable(s) you'd use.

3. Do liberal arts colleges pay economists more than they pay other professors? To find out, we looked at a sample of 2,929 small-college faculty members and built a model of their salaries that included a number of variables, four of which were:

$$\hat{S}_i = 36{,}721 + 817M_i + 426A_i + 406R_i + 3539T_i + \cdots \qquad (3.8)$$
$$\quad\quad\;\; (259) \quad (456) \quad (24) \quad (458)$$
$$\overline{R}^2 = .77 \qquad N = 2929$$

where: S_i = the salary of the ith college professor
M_i = a dummy variable equal to 1 if the ith professor is a male and 0 otherwise
A_i = a dummy variable equal to 1 if the ith professor is African American and 0 otherwise
R_i = the years in rank of the ith professor
T_i = a dummy variable equal to 1 if the ith professor teaches economics and 0 otherwise

a. Carefully explain the meaning of the estimated coefficient of M.
b. The equation indicates that African Americans earn $426 more than members of other ethnic groups, holding constant the other variables in the equation. Does this coefficient have the sign you expected? Why or why not?
c. Is R a dummy variable? If not, what is it? Carefully explain the meaning of the coefficient of R. (*Hint:* A professor's salary typically increases each year based on rank.)
d. What's your conclusion? Do economists earn more than other professors at liberal arts colleges? Explain.
e. The fact that the equation ends with the notation "$+ \cdots$" indicates that there were more than four independent variables in the equation. If you could add a variable to the equation, what would it be? Explain.

4. Use Stata or your own computer regression software to estimate Equation 3.4 using the data in Table 3.1. Can you get the same results?

5. The Graduate Record Examination (GRE) subject test in economics was a multiple-choice measure of knowledge and analytical ability in economics that was used mainly as an entrance criterion for students applying to Ph.D. programs in the "dismal science." For years, critics claimed that the GRE, like the Scholastic Aptitude Test (SAT), was biased against women and some ethnic groups. To test the possibility that the GRE subject test in economics was biased against women,

Mary Hirschfeld, Robert Moore, and Eleanor Brown estimated the following equation (standard errors in parentheses):[9]

$$\widehat{GRE_i} = 172.4 + 39.7G_i + 78.9GPA_i + 0.203SATM_i + 0.110SATV_i$$
$$\quad\quad\quad (10.9)\quad (10.4)\quad\quad (0.071)\quad\quad\quad (0.058)$$
$$N = 149\quad \overline{R}^2 = .46 \quad\quad\quad\quad\quad (3.9)$$

where:
- GRE_i = the score of the ith student in the Graduate Record Examination subject test in economics
- G_i = a dummy variable equal to 1 if the ith student was a male, 0 otherwise
- GPA_i = the GPA in economics classes of the ith student (4 = A, 3 = B, etc.)
- $SATM_i$ = the score of the ith student on the mathematics portion of the Scholastic Aptitude Test
- $SATV_i$ = the score of the ith student on the verbal portion of the Scholastic Aptitude Test

a. Carefully explain the meaning of the coefficient of G in this equation. (*Hint:* Be sure to specify what 39.7 stands for.)
b. Does this result prove that the GRE is biased against women? Why or why not?
c. If you were going to add one variable to Equation 3.9, what would it be? Explain your reasoning.
d. Suppose that the authors had defined their gender variables as G_i = a dummy variable equal to 1 if the ith student was a female, 0 otherwise. What would the estimated Equation 3.9 have been in that case? (*Hint:* Only the intercept and the coefficient of the dummy variable change.)

6. Your boss is about to start production of her newest box-office smash-to-be, *Invasion of the Economists, Part II*, when she calls you in and asks you to build a model of the gross receipts of all the movies produced in the last five years. Your regression is (standard errors in parentheses):[10]

$$\hat{G}_i = 781 + 15.4T_i - 992F_i + 1770J_i + 3027S_i - 3160B_i + \cdots$$
$$\quad\quad (5.9)\quad (674)\quad\ (800)\quad (1006)\quad (2381)$$
$$\overline{R}^2 = .485\quad N = 254$$

---

9. Mary Hirschfeld, Robert L. Moore, and Eleanor Brown, "Exploring the Gender Gap on the GRE Subject Test in Economics," *Journal of Economic Education*, Vol. 26, No. 1, pp. 3–15.

10. This estimated equation (but not the question) comes from a final exam in managerial economics given at the Harvard Business School.

where: G_i = the final gross receipts of the ith motion picture (in thousands of dollars)

T_i = the number of screens (theaters) on which the ith film was shown in its first week

F_i = a dummy variable equal to 1 if the star of the ith film is a female and 0 otherwise

J_i = a dummy variable equal to 1 if the ith movie was released in June or July and 0 otherwise

S_i = a dummy variable equal to 1 if the star of the ith film is a superstar (like Tom Cruise or Milton) and 0 otherwise

B_i = a dummy variable equal to 1 if at least one member of the supporting cast of the ith film is a superstar and 0 otherwise

a. Hypothesize signs for each of the slope coefficients in the equation. Which, if any, of the signs of the estimated coefficients are different from your expectations?

b. Milton, the star of the original *Invasion of the Economists,* is demanding $4 million from your boss to appear in the sequel. If your estimates are trustworthy, should she say "yes" or hire Fred (a nobody) for $500,000?

c. Your boss wants to keep costs low, and it would cost $1.2 million to release the movie on an additional 200 screens. Assuming your estimates are trustworthy, should she spring for the extra screens?

d. The movie is scheduled for release in September, and it would cost $1 million to speed up production enough to allow a July release without hurting quality. Assuming your estimates are trustworthy, is it worth the rush?

e. You've been assuming that your estimates are trustworthy. Do you have any evidence that this is not the case? Explain your answer.

7. Let's get some more experience with the six steps in applied regression. Suppose that you're interested in buying an Apple iPod (either new or used) on eBay (the auction website) but you want to avoid overbidding. One way to get an insight into how much to bid would be to run a regression on the prices[11] for which iPods have sold in previous auctions.

---

11. This is an example of a hedonic model, in which the price of an item is the dependent variable and the independent variables are the attributes of that item rather than the quantity demanded/supplied of that item. For more on hedonic models, see Section 11.8.

The first step would be to review the literature, and luckily you find some good material—particularly a 2008 article by Leonardo Rezende[12] that analyzes eBay Internet auctions and even estimates a model of the price of iPods.

The second step would be to specify the independent variables and functional form for your equation, but you run into a problem. The problem is that you want to include a variable that measures the condition of the iPod in your equation, but some iPods are new, some are used and unblemished, and some are used and have a scratch or other defect.

a. Carefully specify a variable (or variables) that will allow you to quantify the three different conditions of the iPods. Please answer this question before moving on.

b. The third step is to hypothesize the signs of the coefficients of your equation. Assume that you choose the following specification. What signs do you expect for the coefficients of NEW, SCRATCH, and BIDRS? Explain.

$$\text{PRICE}_i = \beta_0 + \beta_1 \text{NEW}_i + \beta_2 \text{SCRATCH}_i + \beta_3 \text{BIDRS}_i + \epsilon_i$$

where: PRICE_i = the price at which the ith iPod sold on eBay

NEW_i = a dummy variable equal to 1 if the ith iPod was new, 0 otherwise

SCRATCH_i = a dummy variable equal to 1 if the ith iPod had a minor cosmetic defect, 0 otherwise

BIDRS_i = the number of bidders on the ith iPod

c. The fourth step is to collect your data. Luckily, Rezende has data for 215 silver-colored, 4 GB Apple iPod minis available on a website, so you download the data and are eager to run your first regression. Before you do, however, one of your friends points out that the iPod auctions were spread over a three-week period and worries that there's a chance that the observations are not comparable because they come from different time periods. Is this a valid concern? Why or why not?

---

12. Leonardo Rezende, "Econometrics of Auctions by Least Squares," *Journal of Applied Econometrics*, November/December 2008, pp. 925–948.

d. The fifth step is to estimate your specification using Rezende's data, producing:

$$\widehat{PRICE_i} = 109.24 + 54.99NEW_i - 20.44SCRATCH_i + 0.73BIDRS_i$$

$$ (5.34) \qquad (5.11) \qquad\qquad (0.59)$$

$$t = 10.28 \qquad -4.00 \qquad\qquad 1.23$$

$$N = 215$$

Do the estimated coefficients correspond to your expectations? Explain.

e. The sixth step is to document your results. Look over the regression results in part d. What, if anything, is missing that should be included in our normal documentation format?

f. (optional) Estimate the equation yourself (Datafile = IPOD3), and determine the value of the item that you reported missing in your answer to part e.

3.5   Appendix: Econometric Lab #2

This lab contains a section for each of the six steps in applied regression analysis. Your project is to estimate an aggregate consumption function for the U.S. economy for the period 1945–2014.

Step 1: Review the Literature and Develop the Theoretical Model

John Maynard Keynes, one of the most influential economists since Adam Smith, developed the notion of a consumption function, which explains total consumption as a function of disposable personal income. You probably learned about the Keynesian consumption function in your principles of macroeconomics class, your intermediate macroeconomics class, or both. Other variables, including interest rates, also affect aggregate consumption.

a.   One key analytical concept in the consumption function is the marginal propensity to consume. If you already know the definition of the marginal propensity to consume, write down that definition. If you don't know the definition, read through your macroeconomics textbook or find an appropriate website and write down the definition, being sure to specify your source with a full bibliographical reference.

b. Use the EconLit database or another source to find two articles from academic journals (not newspapers, blogs, or magazines) about the consumption function. You don't need to read the articles, but you must include the full bibliographic references for both articles.

Step 2: Specify the Model: Select the Independent Variables and the Functional Form

At this point, you would normally choose your independent variables and your functional form. Since we'd like everyone to estimate the same equation, we'll make those decisions for you. Please estimate a linear consumption function that includes disposable personal income and interest rates as your independent variables. The specific variables will be:

CON_t real personal consumption expenditures in year t, in billions of 2009 dollars

PYD_t real disposable personal income in year t, in billions of 2009 dollars

AAA_t the real interest rate in year t

Write out your equation for consumption as a function of disposable personal income and the interest rate, using the form of Equation 3.1 in the text but substituting the appropriate variable names for Y and X.

Step 3: Hypothesize the Expected Signs of the Coefficients

Hypothesize the expected signs of the slope coefficients of your model. Explain your reasoning—if you don't know, read about it. That's what literature reviews are for!

Step 4: Collect the Data. Inspect and Clean the Data

A handy source of macroeconomic data is the Federal Reserve Economic Data (FRED) website: https://research.stlouisfed.org/fred2/. It contains hundreds of thousands of downloadable time series from the U.S. and around the world. This lab assignment uses data from FRED and other sources. You can download this dataset from http://www.pearson.com/studenmund in Stata or other formats. The dataset name is LAB3.

Optional: Spot check the dataset yourself by using FRED to find real personal consumption expenditures in billions of 2009 dollars (annual, not seasonally adjusted) for 1946.

Finally, clean and inspect the data. To do this, print out the summary statistics (mean, standard deviation, minimum, maximum) for all three variables and look for unusual numbers. Do you see any maximum or minimum values that are impossible (like negative consumption) or unreasonably high (like interest rates over 100%)? If so, that's a clear indication that there is a mistake in the data.

Step 5: Estimate and Evaluate the Equation

Estimate your equation using Stata and print out the results. Then evaluate your results by answering the following questions:

a. Do the signs of the coefficients meet the expectations you developed in Step 3? If not, explain what differences there are.

b. What is $\overline{R}^2$? What is R^2? Why are they different?

c. According to your results, what is the value of the marginal propensity to consume (rounded to three decimal places)? By how much will consumption change if disposable personal income falls by $1 billion (holding constant the corporate bond Aaa interest rate)?

d. According to your results, by how much will consumption change if the corporate bond Aaa interest rate rises by three percentage points (holding constant disposable personal income)?

e. Based on your answers to parts a–d above, does your regression result seem reasonable, or do you think that you've made an error of some sort?

Step 6: Document the Results

Now reorganize your Stata regression results and put them into the standard format presented in Equation 3.4.

Chapter 4

The Classical Model

4.1 The Classical Assumptions

4.2 The Sampling Distribution of $\hat{\beta}$

4.3 The Gauss–Markov Theorem and the Properties
of OLS Estimators

4.4 Standard Econometric Notation

4.5 Summary and Exercises

The classical model of econometrics has nothing to do with ancient Greece or even the classical economic thinking of Adam Smith. Instead, the term *classical* refers to a set of fairly basic assumptions required to hold in order for OLS to be considered the "best" estimator available for regression models. When one or more of these assumptions do not hold, other estimation techniques (such as Generalized Least Squares, to be explained in Chapter 9) may be better than OLS.

As a result, one of the most important jobs in regression analysis is to decide whether the classical assumptions hold for a particular equation. If so, the OLS estimation technique is the best available. Otherwise, the pros and cons of alternative estimation techniques must be weighed. These alternatives usually are adjustments to OLS that take account of the particular assumption that has been violated. In a sense, most of the rest of this book deals in one way or another with the question of what to do when one of the classical assumptions is not met. Since econometricians spend so much time analyzing violations of them, it is crucial that they know and understand these assumptions.

4.1 The Classical Assumptions

The Classical Assumptions must be met in order for OLS estimators to be the best available. Because of their importance in regression analysis, the assumptions are presented here in tabular form as well as in words.

> ### The Classical Assumptions
>
>   I. The regression model is linear, is correctly specified, and has an additive error term.
>
> II. The error term has a zero population mean.
>
> III. All explanatory variables are uncorrelated with the error term.
>
> IV. Observations of the error term are uncorrelated with each other (no serial correlation).
>
>   V. The error term has a constant variance (no heteroskedasticity).
>
> VI. No explanatory variable is a perfect linear function of any other explanatory variable(s) (no perfect multicollinearity).
>
> VII. The error term is normally distributed (this assumption is optional but usually is invoked).

Subsequent chapters will investigate major violations of the assumptions and introduce estimation techniques that may provide better estimates in such cases.

An error term satisfying Assumptions I through V is called a **classical error term**, and if Assumption VII is added, the error term is called a *classical normal error term*.

I. *The regression model is linear, is correctly specified, and has an additive error term.* The regression model is assumed to be linear:

$$Y_i = \beta_0 + \beta_1 X_{1i} + \beta_2 X_{2i} + \cdots + \beta_K X_{Ki} + \epsilon_i \tag{4.1}$$

The assumption that the regression model is linear[1] does not require the underlying theory to be linear. For example, an exponential function:

$$Y_i = e^{\beta_0} X_i^{\beta_1} e^{\epsilon_i} \tag{4.2}$$

where e is the base of the natural log, can be transformed by taking the natural log of both sides of the equation:

$$\ln(Y_i) = \beta_0 + \beta_1 \ln(X_i) + \epsilon_i \tag{4.3}$$

---

1. The Classical Assumption that the regression model is "linear" technically requires the model to be "linear in the coefficients." You'll learn what it means for a model to be linear in the coefficients, particularly in contrast to being linear in the variables, in Section 7.2. We'll cover the application of regression analysis to equations that are nonlinear in the variables in that same section, but the application of regression analysis to equations that are nonlinear in the coefficients is beyond the scope of this textbook.

If the variables are relabeled as $Y_i^* = \ln(Y_i)$ and $X_i^* = \ln(X_i)$, then the form of the equation becomes linear:

$$Y_i^* = \beta_0 + \beta_1 X_i^* + \epsilon_i \qquad (4.4)$$

In Equation 4.4, the properties of the OLS estimator of the βs still hold because the equation is linear.

Two additional properties also must hold. First, we assume that the equation is correctly specified. If an equation has an omitted variable or an incorrect functional form, the odds are against that equation working well. Second, we assume that a stochastic error term has been added to the equation. This error term must be an additive one and cannot be multiplied by or divided into any of the variables in the equation.

II. *The error term has a zero population mean.* As was pointed out in Section 1.2, econometricians add a stochastic (random) error term to regression equations to account for variation in the dependent variable that is not explained by the model. The specific value of the error term for each observation is determined purely by chance. Probably the best way to picture this concept is to think of each observation of the error term as being drawn from a random variable distribution such as the one illustrated in Figure 4.1.

Classical Assumption II says that the mean of this distribution is zero. That is, when the entire population of possible values for the stochastic error

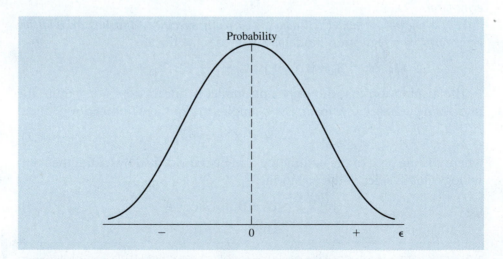

Figure 4.1 An Error Term Distribution with a Mean of Zero

Observations of stochastic error terms are assumed to be drawn from a random variable distribution with a mean of zero. If Classical Assumption II is met, the expected value (the mean) of the error term is zero.

term is considered, the average value of that population is zero. For a small sample, it is not likely that the mean is exactly zero, but as the size of the sample approaches infinity, the mean of the sample approaches zero.

What happens if the mean doesn't equal zero in a sample? As long as you have a constant term in the equation, the estimate of β_0 will absorb the non-zero mean. In essence, the constant term equals the *fixed* portion of Y that cannot be explained by the independent variables, and the error term equals the *stochastic* portion of the unexplained value of Y.

Although it's true that the error term never can be observed, it's instructive to pretend that we can do so to see how the constant term absorbs the non-zero mean of the error term in a sample. Consider a typical regression equation:

$$Y_i = \beta_0 + \beta_1 X_i + \epsilon_i \tag{4.5}$$

Suppose that the mean of ϵ_i is 3 instead of 0, then[2] $E(\epsilon_i - 3) = 0$. If we add 3 to the constant term and subtract it from the error term, we obtain:

$$Y_i = (\beta_0 + 3) + \beta_1 X_i + (\epsilon_i - 3) \tag{4.6}$$

Since Equations 4.5 and 4.6 are equivalent (do you see why?), and since $E(\epsilon_i - 3) = 0$, then Equation 4.6 can be written in a form that has a zero mean for the error term ϵ_i^*:

$$Y_i = \beta_0^* + \beta_1 X_i + \epsilon_i^* \tag{4.7}$$

where $\beta_0^* = \beta_0 + 3$ and $\epsilon_i^* = \epsilon_i - 3$. As can be seen, Equation 4.7 conforms to Assumption II. In essence, if Classical Assumption II is violated in an equation that includes a constant term, then the estimate of β_0 absorbs the non-zero mean of the error term, and the estimates of the other coefficients are unaffected.

III. *All explanatory variables are uncorrelated with the error term.* It is assumed that the observed values of the explanatory variables are independent of the values of the error term.

If an explanatory variable and the error term were instead correlated with each other, the OLS estimates would be likely to attribute to the X some of the variation in Y that actually came from the error term. If the error term and X were positively correlated, for example, then the estimated coefficient would probably be higher than it would otherwise have been (biased upward), because the OLS program would mistakenly attribute the variation

---

2. Here, as in Chapter 1, the "E" refers to the expected value (mean) of the item in parentheses after it. Thus $E(\epsilon_i - 3)$ equals the expected value of the stochastic error term epsilon minus 3. In this specific example, since we've defined $E(\epsilon_i) = 3$, we know that $E(\epsilon_i - 3) = 0$. One way to think about expected value is as our best guess of the long-run average value a specific random variable will have.

in Y caused by ϵ to X instead. As a result, it's important to ensure that the explanatory variables are uncorrelated with the error term.

Classical Assumption III is violated most frequently when a researcher omits an important independent variable from an equation.[3] As you learned in Chapter 1, one of the major components of the stochastic error term is omitted variables, so if a variable has been omitted, then the error term will change when the omitted variable changes. If this omitted variable is correlated with an included independent variable (as often happens in economics), then the error term is correlated with that independent variable as well. We have violated Assumption III! Because of this violation, OLS will attribute the impact of the omitted variable to the included variable, to the extent that the two variables are correlated.

IV. *Observations of the error term are uncorrelated with each other.* The observations of the error term are drawn independently from each other. If a systematic correlation exists between one observation of the error term and another, then OLS estimates will be less precise than estimates that account for the correlation. For example, if the fact that the ϵ from one observation is positive increases the probability that the ϵ from another observation also is positive, then the two observations of the error term are positively correlated. Such a correlation would violate Classical Assumption IV.

In economic applications, this assumption is most important in time-series models. In such a context, Assumption IV says that an increase in the error term in one time period (a random shock, for example) does not show up in or affect in any way the error term in another time period. In some cases, though, this assumption is unrealistic, since the effects of a random shock sometimes last for a number of time periods. For example, a natural disaster like the 2015 earthquake in Nepal will have a negative impact on a region long after the time period in which it was truly a random event. If, over all the observations of the sample, ϵ_{t+1} is correlated with ϵ_t, then the error term is said to be *serially correlated* (or *autocorrelated*), and Assumption IV is violated. Violations of this assumption are considered in more detail in Chapter 9.

V. *The error term has a constant variance.* The variance (or dispersion) of the distribution from which the observations of the error term are drawn is constant.[4] That is, the observations of the error term are assumed to be drawn continually from identical distributions (for example, the one pictured

---

3. Another important economic application that violates this assumption is any model that is simultaneous in nature. This will be considered in Chapter 14.

4. This is a simplification. The actual assumption (that error terms have positive finite second moments) is equivalent to this simplification in all but a few extremely rare cases.

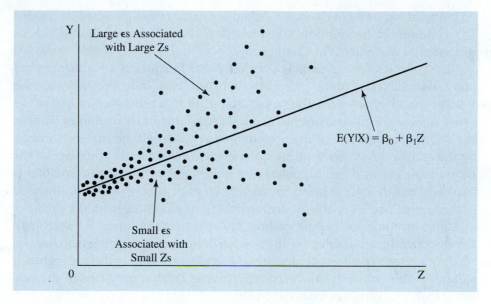

Figure 4.2 An Error Term Whose Variance Increases as Z Increases

One example of Classical Assumption V not being met is when the variance of the error term increases as Z increases. In such a situation (called heteroskedasticity), the observations are on average farther from the true regression line for large values of Z than they are for small values of Z.

in Figure 4.1). The alternative would be for the variance of the distribution of the error term to change for each observation or range of observations. In Figure 4.2, for example, the variance of the error term is shown to increase as the variable Z increases; such a pattern violates Classical Assumption V. The actual values of the error term are not directly observable, but the lack of a constant variance for the distribution of the error term causes OLS to generate inaccurate estimates of the standard error of the coefficients.[5]

For example, suppose that you're studying the amount of money that the 50 states spend on education. New York and California are more heavily populated than New Hampshire and Nevada, so it's probable that the variance of the error term for big states is larger than it is for small states. The amount of unexplained variation in educational expenditures seems likely to

---

5. Because some observations have errors with a large variance, those observations are not as reliable and so should be given less weight when minimizing the sum of squares. OLS, however, gives equal weight to each observation, so it will be less precise than estimators that weigh the observations more appropriately.

be larger in big states like New York than in small states like New Hampshire. The violation of Assumption V is referred to as *heteroskedasticity* and will be discussed in more detail in Chapter 10.

VI. *No explanatory variable is a perfect linear function of any other explanatory variable(s).* Perfect *collinearity* between two independent variables implies that they are really the same variable, or that one is a multiple of the other, and/or that a constant has been added to one of the variables. That is, the relative movements of one explanatory variable will be matched exactly by the relative movements of the other even though the absolute size of the movements might differ. Because every movement of one of the variables is matched exactly by a relative movement in the other, the OLS estimation procedure will be incapable of distinguishing one variable from the other.

Many instances of perfect collinearity (or *multicollinearity* if more than two independent variables are involved) are the result of the researcher not accounting for identities (definitional equivalences) among the independent variables. This problem can be corrected easily by dropping one of the perfectly collinear variables from the equation.

What's an example of perfect multicollinearity? Suppose that you decide to build a model of the profits of tire stores in your city and you include annual sales of tires (in dollars) at each store and the annual sales tax paid by each store as independent variables. Since the tire stores are all in the same city, they all pay the same percentage sales tax, so the sales tax paid will be a constant percentage of their total sales (in dollars). If the sales tax rate is 7%, then the total taxes paid will be 7% of sales for each and every tire store. Thus sales tax will be a perfect linear function of sales, and you'll have perfect multicollinearity!

Perfect multicollinearity also can occur when two independent variables always sum to a third or when one of the explanatory variables doesn't change within the sample. With perfect multicollinearity, OLS (or any other estimation technique) will be unable to estimate the coefficients of the collinear variables (unless there is a rounding error). While it's quite unusual for an experienced researcher to encounter perfect multicollinearity, even imperfect multicollinearity can cause problems for estimation, as you will see in Chapter 8.

VII. *The error term is normally distributed.* Although we have already assumed that observations of the error term are drawn independently (Assumption IV) from a distribution that has a zero mean (Assumption II) and that has a constant variance (Assumption V), we have said little about the shape of that distribution. Assumption VII states that the observations of the error term are drawn from a distribution that is normal (that is, bell-shaped, and generally following the symmetrical pattern portrayed in Figure 4.3).

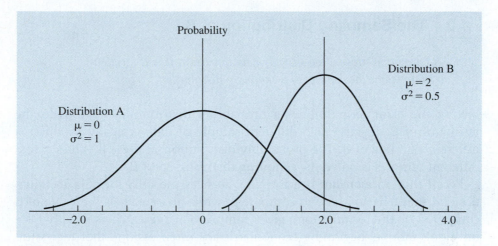

Figure 4.3 Normal Distributions

Although all normal distributions are symmetrical and bell-shaped, they do not necessarily have the same mean and variance. Distribution A has a mean of 0 and a variance
of 1, whereas distribution B has a mean of 2 and a variance of 0.5. As can be seen, the
whole distribution shifts when the mean changes, and the distribution gets fatter as the
variance increases.

This assumption of normality is not required for OLS estimation. Its major
application is in *hypothesis testing* and *confidence intervals*, which use the estimated regression coefficient to investigate hypotheses about economic behavior. Hypothesis testing is the subject of Chapter 5, and without the normality
assumption, most of the small sample tests of that chapter would be invalid.

Even though Assumption VII is optional, it's usually advisable to add the
assumption of normality to the other six assumptions for two reasons:

1. The error term ϵ_i can be thought of as the sum of a number of minor
    influences or errors. As the number of these minor influences gets
    larger, the distribution of the error term tends to approach the normal
    distribution.

2. The *t*-statistic and the *F*-statistic, which will be developed in Chapter 5,
    are not truly applicable unless the error term is normally distributed.

A quick look at Figure 4.3 shows how normal distributions differ when
the means and variances are different. In normal distribution A (a **Standard
Normal Distribution**), the mean is 0 and the variance is 1; in normal distribution B, the mean is 2, and the variance is 0.5. When the mean is different,
the entire distribution shifts. When the variance is different, the distribution
becomes fatter or skinnier.

4.2 The Sampling Distribution of $\hat{\beta}$

> *"It cannot be stressed too strongly how important it is for students to understand the concept of a sampling distribution."*[6]

Just as the error term follows a probability distribution, so too do the estimates of β. In fact, each different sample of data typically produces a different estimate of β. The probability distribution of these $\hat{\beta}$ values across different samples is called the **sampling distribution of $\hat{\beta}$**.

Recall that an *estimator* is a formula, such as the OLS formula in Equation 2.4 that tells you how to compute $\hat{\beta}$, while an *estimate* is the value of $\hat{\beta}$ computed by the formula for a given sample. Since researchers usually have only one sample, beginning econometricians often assume that regression analysis can produce only one estimate of β for a given population. In reality, however, each different sample from the same population will produce a different estimate of β. The collection of all the possible samples has a distribution, with a mean and a variance, and we need to discuss the properties of this sampling distribution of $\hat{\beta}$, even though in most real applications we will encounter only a single draw from it. Be sure to remember that a sampling distribution refers to the distribution of different values of $\hat{\beta}$ across different samples, not within one. These $\hat{\beta}$s usually are assumed to be normally distributed because the normality of the error term implies that the OLS estimates of β are normally distributed as well.

Let's look at an example of a sampling distribution of $\hat{\beta}$ by going back to the height and weight example of Chapter 1 (with weight measured in pounds and height measured in inches above five feet).

$$\text{WEIGHT}_i = \beta_0 + \beta_1 \text{HEIGHT}_i + \epsilon_i \tag{4.8}$$

Suppose you take a sample of six students and apply OLS to Equation 4.8 to get an estimate of β_1. So far, so good.

But what will happen if you select a second sample of six students and do the same thing? Will you get the exact same $\hat{\beta}_1$? Nope! Your second $\hat{\beta}_1$ will depend on the second sample, which almost surely will be different from your first sample. If your random sample includes a couple of football linemen, you're likely to get a really large coefficient. If you randomly choose some cross country runners, you'll get a low estimate. Even if there's nothing

6. Peter Kennedy, *A Guide to Econometrics* (Malden, MA: Blackwell, © 2008), p. 403.

unusual about your second sample, you'll almost certainly get a different $\hat{\beta}_1$. Why? Different data yield different estimates, so if you collect 100 samples, you're likely to get 100 different $\hat{\beta}_1$s.

All these $\hat{\beta}_1$ estimates come from a distribution with its own mean and variance, called a *sampling distribution*. To help you understand this, we took 100 different samples of six students and estimated Equation 4.8 100 times. Take a look at Figure 4.4. With the help of a histogram, we've graphed all 100 $\hat{\beta}_1$s so that we can get an idea of what the sampling distribution looks like.

While the histogram in Figure 4.4 isn't perfectly normally distributed (represented by the thin line), it's close. Notice how the estimates are clustered in the middle (near the mean of 7.75), with fewer and fewer estimates in the tails. With many more estimates of β_1, we'd expect the histogram to look even more like a normal curve.

For an estimation technique to be "good," the mean of the sampling distribution of the $\hat{\beta}$s it produces should equal the true population β. This property has a special name in econometrics: *unbiasedness*. There's much more to come on this idea.

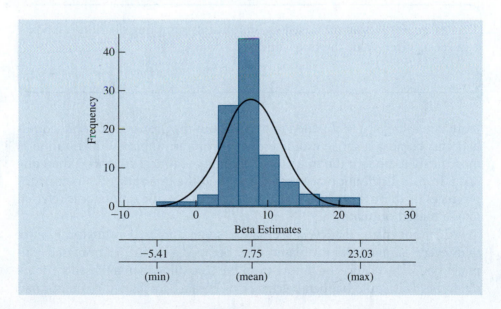

Figure 4.4 A Height and Weight Sampling Distribution of $\hat{\beta}$

We estimated Equation 4.8 (the height weight equation) with 100 samples of six students each and plotted the 100 $\hat{\beta}$s in Figure 4.4. The result is a sampling distribution of $\hat{\beta}$ with a mean of 7.75 and a pattern that is reasonably close to being normally distributed (the thin line).

Although we don't know the true β in this case, it's likely that if we took enough samples—thousands perhaps—the mean of the $\hat{\beta}_1$s would approach the true β. For example, when we took 1,000 samples of six, the mean of the $\hat{\beta}_1$s was 6.88. The chances are that 6.88 is closer to the true β than is 7.75, the mean of the 100 estimates shown in Figure 4.4.

The moral of the story is that while a single sample provides a single estimate of β_1, that estimate comes from a sampling distribution with a mean and a variance. Other estimates from that sampling distribution will most likely be different. When we discuss the properties of estimators in the next section, it will be important to remember that we are discussing the properties of a sampling distribution, not the properties of one sample.

Properties of the Mean

A desirable property of a distribution of estimates is that its mean equals the true mean of the variable being estimated. An estimator that yields such estimates is called an unbiased estimator.

> An estimator $\hat{\beta}$ is an **unbiased estimator** if its sampling distribution has as its expected value the true value of β.
>
> $$E(\hat{\beta}) = \beta \qquad (4.9)$$

Only one value of $\hat{\beta}$ is obtained in practice, but the property of unbiasedness is useful because a single estimate drawn from an unbiased distribution is more likely to be near the true value (assuming identical variances) than one taken from a distribution not centered around the true value. If an estimator produces $\hat{\beta}$s that are not centered around the true β, the estimator is referred to as a **biased estimator**.

We cannot ensure that every estimate from an unbiased estimator is better than every estimate from a biased one, because a particular unbiased estimate[7] could, by chance, be farther from the true value than a biased estimate might be. This could happen by chance or because the biased estimator had

---

7. Technically, since an estimate has just one value, an estimate cannot be unbiased (or biased). On the other hand, the phrase "estimate produced by an unbiased estimator" is cumbersome, especially if repeated 10 times on a page. As a result, many econometricians use "unbiased estimate" as shorthand for "a single estimate produced by an unbiased estimator."

a smaller variance. For example, a broken clock is a biased estimator of the time of day, but it has a zero variance and happens to be exactly right twice a day. Without any other information about the distribution of the estimates, however, we would always rather have an unbiased estimate than a biased one.

Properties of the Variance

Just as we would like the distribution of the β̂s to be centered around the true population β, we would also like that distribution to be as narrow (or precise) as possible. A distribution centered around the truth but with an extremely large variance might be of very little use because any given estimate would quite likely be far from the true β value. For a β̂ distribution with a small variance, the estimates are likely to be close to the mean of the sampling distribution. To see this more clearly, compare distributions A and B (both of which are unbiased) in Figure 4.5. Distribution A, which has a larger variance than distribution B, is less precise than distribution B.

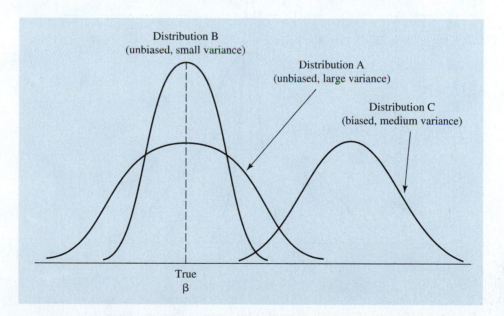

Figure 4.5 Distributions of β̂

Different distributions of β̂ can have different means and variances. Distributions A and B, for example, are both unbiased, but distribution A has a larger variance than does distribution B. Distribution C has a smaller variance than distribution A, but it is biased.

For comparison purposes, a biased distribution (distribution C) is also pictured; note that bias implies that the expected value of the distribution is to the right or left of the true β.

The variance of the distribution of the $\hat{\beta}$s can be decreased by increasing the size of the sample. This also increases the degrees of freedom, since the number of degrees of freedom equals the sample size minus the number of coefficients or parameters estimated. As the number of observations increases, other things held constant, the variance of the sampling distribution tends to decrease. Although it is not true that a sample of 60 will always produce estimates closer to the true β than a sample of 6, it is quite likely to do so; such larger samples should be sought. Figure 4.6 presents illustrative sampling distributions of $\hat{\beta}$s for 6, 60, and 600 observations for OLS estimators of β when the true β equals 1. The larger samples do indeed produce sampling distributions that are more closely centered around β.

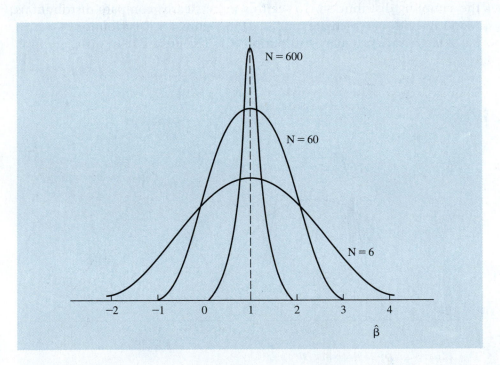

Figure 4.6 Sampling Distribution of $\hat{\beta}$ for Various Observations (N)

As the size of the sample increases, the variance of the distribution of $\hat{\beta}$s calculated from that sample tends to decrease. In the extreme case (not shown), a sample equal to the population would yield only an estimate equal to the mean of that distribution, which (for unbiased estimators) would equal the true β, and the variance of the estimates would be zero.

The powerful lesson illustrated by Figure 4.6 is that if you want to maximize your chances of getting an estimate close to the true value, apply OLS to a large sample. There's no guarantee that you'll get a more accurate estimate from a large sample, but your chances are better. Larger samples, all else equal, tend to result in more precise estimates. And if the estimator is unbiased, more precise estimates are more accurate estimates.

Think of it this way. Having a couple of cross country runners might lead to a pretty wacky estimate from a sample of 6, but their influence on $\hat{\beta}_1$ is going to be much smaller in a sample of 60. You could imagine getting 2 cross country runners in a random sample of 6 students, but it would be virtually impossible to get 20 cross country runners in a sample of 60. So try to get larger samples.

In econometrics, we must rely on general tendencies. The element of chance, a random occurrence, is always present in estimating regression coefficients, and some estimates may be far from the true value no matter how good the estimating technique. However, if the distribution is centered on the true value and has as small a variance as possible, the element of chance is less likely to induce a poor estimate. If the sampling distribution is centered around a value other than the true β (that is, if $\hat{\beta}$ is *biased*) then a lower variance implies that most of the sampling distribution of $\hat{\beta}$ is concentrated on the wrong value. However, if this value is not very different from the true value, which is usually not known in practice, then the greater precision will still be valuable.

One method of deciding whether this decreased variance in the distribution of the $\hat{\beta}$s is valuable enough to offset the bias is to compare different estimation techniques by using a measure called the Mean Square Error (MSE). The *Mean Square Error* is equal to the variance plus the square of the bias. The lower the MSE, the better.

A final item of importance is that as the variance of the error term increases, so too does the variance of the distribution of $\hat{\beta}$. The reason for the increased variance of $\hat{\beta}$ is that with the larger variance of ϵ_i, the more extreme values of ϵ_i are observed with more frequency, and the error term becomes more important in determining the values of Y_i.

The Standard Error of $\hat{\beta}$

Since the standard error of the estimated coefficient, **SE($\hat{\beta}$)**, is the square root of the estimated variance of the $\hat{\beta}$s, it is similarly affected by the size of the sample and the other factors we've mentioned. For example, an increase in sample size will cause SE($\hat{\beta}$) to fall; the larger the sample, the more precise our coefficient estimates will be.

4.3 The Gauss–Markov Theorem and the Properties of OLS Estimators

The Gauss–Markov Theorem proves two important properties of OLS estimators. This theorem is proven in all advanced econometrics textbooks, but for a regression user, it's more important to know what the theorem implies than to be able to prove it. The **Gauss–Markov Theorem** states that:

> Given Classical Assumptions I through VI (Assumption VII, normality, is not needed for this theorem), the Ordinary Least Squares estimator of β_k is the minimum variance estimator from among the set of all linear unbiased estimators of β_k, for $k = 0, 1, 2, \ldots, K$.

The Gauss–Markov Theorem is perhaps most easily remembered by stating that "OLS is BLUE" where **BLUE** stands for "*B*est (meaning minimum variance) *L*inear *U*nbiased *E*stimator." Students who might forget that "best" stands for minimum variance might be better served by remembering "OLS is MvLUE," but such a phrase is hardly catchy or easy to remember.

If an equation's coefficient estimation is unbiased (that is, if each of the estimated coefficients is produced by an unbiased estimator of the true population coefficient), then:

$$E(\hat{\beta}_k) = \beta_k \qquad (k = 0, 1, 2, \ldots, K)$$

Best means that each $\hat{\beta}_k$ has the smallest variance possible (in this case, out of all the linear unbiased estimators of β_k). An unbiased estimator with the smallest variance is called *efficient*, and that estimator is said to have the property of **efficiency**. Since the variance typically falls as the sample size increases, larger samples almost always produce more accurate coefficient estimates than do smaller ones.

The Gauss–Markov Theorem requires that just the first six of the seven classical assumptions be met. What happens if we add in the seventh assumption, that the error term is normally distributed? In this case, the result of the Gauss–Markov Theorem is strengthened because the OLS estimator can be shown to be the best (minimum variance) unbiased estimator out of *all* the possible estimators, not just out of the linear estimators. In other words, if all seven assumptions are met, OLS is "BUE."

Given all seven classical assumptions, the OLS coefficient estimators can be shown to have the following properties:

1. *They are unbiased.* That is, $E(\hat{\beta})$ is β. This means that the OLS estimates of the coefficients are centered around the true population values of the parameters being estimated.

2. *They are minimum variance.* The distribution of the coefficient estimates around the true parameter values is as tightly or narrowly distributed as is possible for an unbiased distribution. No other unbiased estimator has a lower variance for each estimated coefficient than OLS.

3. *They are consistent.* As the sample size approaches infinity, the estimates converge to the true population parameters. Put differently, as the sample size gets larger, the variance gets smaller, and each estimate approaches the true value of the coefficient being estimated.[8]

4. *They are normally distributed.* The $\hat{\beta}$s are $N(\beta, \text{VAR}[\hat{\beta}])$. Thus various statistical tests based on the normal distribution may indeed be applied to these estimates, as will be done in Chapter 5.

4.4 Standard Econometric Notation

This section presents the standard notation used throughout the econometrics literature. Table 4.1 presents various alternative notational devices used to represent the different population (true) parameters and their corresponding estimates (based on samples).

The measure of the central tendency of the sampling distribution of $\hat{\beta}$, which can be thought of as the mean of the $\hat{\beta}$s, is denoted as $E(\hat{\beta})$, read as "the expected value of beta-hat." The variance of $\hat{\beta}$ is the typical measure of dispersion of the sampling distribution of $\hat{\beta}$. The variance (or, alternatively, the square root of the variance, called the *standard deviation*) has several alternative notational representations, including $\text{VAR}(\hat{\beta})$ and $\sigma^2(\hat{\beta})$, read as the "variance of beta-hat."

The variance of the estimates is a population parameter that is never actually observed in practice; instead, it is estimated with $\hat{\sigma}^2(\hat{\beta}_k)$, also written as $s^2(\hat{\beta}_k)$. Note, by the way, that the variance of the true β, $\sigma^2(\beta)$, is zero, since there is only one true β_k with no distribution around it. Thus, the estimated

---

8. Technically, OLS estimates are consistent only if the independent variables continue to fluctuate as the sample size increases. See Halbert White, *Asymptotic Theory for Econometricians* (Orlando: Academic Press, 1984), p. 20.

Table 4.1 Notation Conventions

| Population Parameter (True Values, but Unobserved) | | Estimate (Observed from Sample) | |
Name	Symbol(s)	Name	Symbol(s)
Regression coefficient	β_k	Estimated regression coefficient	$\hat{\beta}_k$
Expected value of the estimated coefficient	$E(\hat{\beta}_k)$		
Variance of the error term	σ^2 or $VAR(\epsilon_i)$	Estimated variance of the error term	s^2 or $\hat{\sigma}^2$
Standard deviation of the error term	σ	An estimate of the standard deviation of the error term	s or SE
Variance of the estimated coefficient	$\sigma^2(\hat{\beta}_k)$ or $VAR(\hat{\beta}_k)$	Estimated variance of the estimated coefficient	$s^2(\hat{\beta}_k)$ or $\widehat{VAR}(\hat{\beta}_k)$
Standard deviation of the estimated coefficient	$\sigma_{\hat{\beta}k}$ or $\sigma(\hat{\beta}_k)$	Standard error of the estimated coefficient	$\hat{\sigma}(\hat{\beta}_k)$ or $SE(\hat{\beta}_k)$
Error or disturbance term	ϵ_i	Residual (estimate of error in a loose sense)	e_i

variance of the estimated coefficient is defined and observed, the true variance of the estimated coefficient is unobservable, and the true variance of the true coefficient is zero. The square root of the estimated variance of the coefficient estimate is the standard error of $\hat{\beta}$, $SE(\hat{\beta}_k)$, which we will use extensively in hypothesis testing.

4.5 Summary

1. The seven Classical Assumptions state that the regression model is linear with an additive error term that has a mean of zero, is uncorrelated with the explanatory variables and other observations of the error term, has a constant variance, and is normally distributed (optional). In addition, explanatory variables must not be perfect linear functions of each other.

2. The two most important properties of an estimator are unbiasedness and minimum variance. An estimator is unbiased when the expected value of the estimated coefficient is equal to the true value. Minimum variance holds when the estimating distribution has the smallest variance of all the estimators in a given class of estimators (for example, unbiased estimators).

3. Given the Classical Assumptions, OLS can be shown to be the minimum variance, linear, unbiased estimator (or BLUE, for best linear unbiased estimator) of the regression coefficients. This is the Gauss–Markov Theorem. When one or more of the classical properties do not hold (excluding normality), OLS is no longer BLUE, although it still may provide better estimates in some cases than the alternative estimation techniques discussed in subsequent chapters.

4. Because the sampling distribution of the OLS estimator of $\hat{\beta}_k$ is BLUE, it has desirable properties. Moreover, the variance, or the measure of dispersion of the sampling distribution of $\hat{\beta}_k$, decreases as the number of observations increases.

5. There is a standard notation used in the econometric literature. Table 4.1 presents this fairly complex set of notational conventions for use in regression analysis. This table should be reviewed periodically as a refresher.

EXERCISES

(The answers to the even-numbered exercises are in Appendix A.)

1. Write the meaning of each of the following terms without referring to the book (or to your notes), and compare your definition with the version in the text for each:
   a. biased estimator (p. 102)
   b. BLUE (p. 106)
   c. classical error term (p. 93)
   d. efficiency (p. 106)
   e. Gauss–Markov Theorem (p. 106)
   f. sampling distribution of $\hat{\beta}$ (p. 100)
   g. SE($\hat{\beta}$) (p. 105)
   h. standard normal distribution (p. 99)
   i. the Classical Assumptions (p. 92)
   j. unbiased estimator (p. 102)

2. Consider the following estimated regression equation (standard errors in parentheses):

$$\hat{Y}_t = -120 + 0.10F_t + 5.33R_t \qquad \bar{R}^2 = .50$$
$$\qquad\qquad\quad (0.05)\quad (1.00)$$

where: Y_t = the corn yield (bushels/acre) in year t
F_t = fertilizer intensity (pounds/acre) in year t
R_t = rainfall (inches) in year t

a. Carefully state the meaning of the coefficients 0.10 and 5.33 in this equation in terms of the impact of F and R on Y.
b. Does the constant term of -120 really mean that *negative* amounts of corn are possible? If not, what is the meaning of that estimate?
c. Suppose you were told that the true value of β_F is *known* to be 0.20. Does this show that the estimate is biased? Why or why not?
d. Suppose you were told that the equation does not meet all the classical assumptions and therefore is not BLUE. Does this mean that the true β_R is definitely *not* equal to 5.33? Why or why not?

3. Which of the following pairs of independent variables would violate Assumption VI? (That is, which pairs of variables are perfect linear functions of each other?)
a. right shoe size and left shoe size (of students in your class)
b. consumption and disposable income (in the United States over the last 30 years)
c. X_i and $2X_i$
d. X_i and $(X_i)^2$

4. Edward Saunders published an article that tested the possibility that the stock market is affected by the weather on Wall Street. Using daily data from 28 years, he estimated an equation with the following variables (standard errors in parentheses):[9]

$$\widehat{DJ}_t = \hat{\beta}_0 + 0.10R_{t-1} + 0.0010J_t - 0.017M_t + 0.0005C_t$$
$$\qquad\quad (0.01)\qquad (0.0006)\quad (0.004)\quad (0.0002)$$
$$N = 6{,}911 \text{ (daily)} \quad \bar{R}^2 = .02$$

9. Edward M. Saunders, Jr., "Stock Prices and Wall Street Weather," *American Economic Review,* Vol. 76, No. 1, pp. 1337–1346. (Published by the American Economic Association, © 1993.) Saunders also estimated equations for the New York and American Stock Exchange indices, both of which had much higher R²s than did this equation. R_{t-1} was included in the equation "to account for nonsynchronous trading effects" (p. 1341).

where: DJ_t = the percentage change in the Dow Jones industrial average on day t

R_t = the daily index capital gain or loss for day t

J_t = a dummy variable equal to 1 if the *i*th day was in January, 0 otherwise

M_t = a dummy variable equal to 1 if the *i*th day was a Monday, 0 otherwise

C_t = a variable equal to 1 if the cloud cover was 20 percent or less, equal to -1 if the cloud cover was 100 percent, 0 otherwise

a. Saunders did not include an estimate of the constant term in his published regression results. Which of the Classical Assumptions supports the conclusion that you shouldn't spend much time analyzing estimates of the constant term? Explain.

b. Which of the Classical Assumptions would be violated if you decided to add a dummy variable to the equation that was equal to 1 if the *i*th day was a Tuesday, Wednesday, Thursday, or Friday, and equal to 0 otherwise? (*Hint:* The stock market is not open on weekends.)

c. Carefully state the meaning of the coefficients of R and M, being sure to take into account the fact that R is lagged (one time period behind) in this equation for valid theoretical reasons.

d. The variable C is a measure of the percentage of cloud cover from sunrise to sunset on the *i*th day and reflects the fact that approximately 85 percent of all New York's rain falls on days with 100 percent cloud cover. Is C a dummy variable? What assumptions (or conclusions) did the author have to make to use this variable? What constraints does it place on the equation?

e. Saunders concludes that these findings cast doubt on the hypothesis that security markets are entirely rational. Based just on the small portion of the author's work that we include in this question, would you agree or disagree? Why?

5. In Hollywood, most nightclubs hire "promoters," or people who walk around near the nightclub and try to convince passersby to enter the club. One of the nightclub owners asked a marketing consultant to estimate the effectiveness of such promoters in terms of their ability to attract patrons to the club. The consultant did some research and found that the main entertainment at the nightclubs was attractive dancers and that the most popular nightclubs were on Hollywood

Boulevard or attached to hotels, so he hypothesized the following model of nightclub attendance:

$$\text{PEOPLE}_i = \beta_0 + \overset{+}{\beta_1\text{HOLLY}_i} + \overset{+}{\beta_2\text{PROMO}_i} + \overset{+}{\beta_3\text{HOTEL}_i} + \overset{+}{\beta_4\text{GOGO}_i} + \epsilon_i$$

where: PEOPLE_i = attendance at the ith nightclub at midnight on Saturday 11/24/07

HOLLY_i = equal to 1 if the ith nightclub is on Hollywood Boulevard, 0 otherwise

PROMO_i = number of promoters working at the ith nightclub that night

HOTEL_i = equal to 1 if the ith nightclub is part of a hotel, 0 otherwise

GOGO_i = number of dancers working at the ith nightclub that night

He then collected data from 25 similarly sized nightclubs on or near Hollywood Boulevard and came up with the following estimates (standard errors in parentheses):

$$\widehat{\text{PEOPLE}}_i = 162.8 + 47.4\text{HOLLY}_i + 22.3\text{PROMO}_i + 214.5\text{HOTEL}_i + 26.9\text{GOGO}_i$$
$$(21.7) \qquad (11.8) \qquad (46.0) \qquad (7.2)$$
$$N = 25 \quad \overline{R}^2 = .57$$

Let's work through the classical assumptions to see which assumptions might or might not be met by this model. As we analyze each assumption, make sure that you can state the assumption from memory and that you understand how the following questions help us understand whether the assumption has been met.

a. Assumption I: Is the equation linear with an additive error term? Is there a chance that there's an omitted variable or an incorrect functional form?

b. Assumption II: Is there a constant term in the equation?

c. Assumption III: Is there a chance that there's an omitted variable or that this equation is part of a simultaneous system?

d. Assumption IV: Is the model estimated with time-series data with the chance that a random event in one time period could affect the regression in subsequent time periods?

e. Assumption V: Is the model estimated with cross-sectional data with dramatic variations in the size of the dependent variable?

f. Assumption VI: Is any independent variable a perfect linear function of any other independent variable?

g. Assume that dancers earn about as much per hour as promoters. If the equation is accurate, should the nightclub owner hire one more promoter or one more dancer if they want to increase attendance? Explain your answer.

6. In 2001, Donald Kenkel and Joseph Terza published an article in which they investigated the impact on an individual's alcohol consumption of a physician's advice to reduce drinking.[10] In that article, Kenkel and Terza used econometric techniques well beyond the scope of this text to conclude that such physician advice can play a significant role in reducing alcohol consumption.

We took a fifth (no pun intended) of the authors' dataset[11] and estimated the following equation (standard errors in parentheses):

$$\widehat{DRINKS_i} = 13.00 + 11.36 ADVICE_i - 0.20 EDUC_i + 2.85 DIVSEP_i + 14.20 UNEMP_i$$
$$(2.12) \qquad (0.31) \qquad (2.55) \qquad (5.16)$$
$$t = 5.37 \qquad -0.65 \qquad 1.11 \qquad 2.75$$
$$N = 500 \quad \overline{R}^2 = .07$$

where: $DRINKS_i$ = drinks consumed by the ith individual in the last two weeks

$ADVICE_i$ = 1 if a physician had advised the ith individual to cut back on drinking alcohol, 0 otherwise

$EDUC_i$ = years of schooling of the ith individual

$DIVSEP_i$ = 1 if the ith individual was divorced or separated, 0 otherwise

$UNEMP_i$ = 1 if the ith individual was unemployed, 0 otherwise

a. Carefully state the meaning of the estimated coefficients of DIVSEP and UNEMP. Do the signs of the coefficients make sense to you? Do the relative sizes of the coefficients make sense to you? Explain.

---

10. Donald S. Kenkel and Joseph V. Terza, "The Effect of Physician Advice on Alcohol Consumption: Count Regression with an Endogenous Treatment Effect," *Journal of Applied Econometrics*, 2001, pp. 165–184.

11. The dataset, which is available on the *JAE* website, consists of more than 20 variables for 2467 males who participated in the 1990 National Health Interview Survey and who were current drinkers with high blood pressure. Because roughly 30 percent of the sample had zero drinks, many econometricians wouldn't use OLS to estimate this equation. Instead, they'd use techniques that, while similar to those covered in Chapter 13, are beyond the scope of this text.

b. Carefully state the meaning of the estimated coefficient of ADVICE. Does the sign of the coefficient make sense to you? If so, explain. If not, this unexpected sign might be related to a violation of one of the Classical Assumptions. What Classical Assumption (other than Assumption I) is this equation almost surely violating? (*Hint:* Think about what might cause a physician to advise a patient to cut back on alcohol drinking and then review the Classical Assumptions one more time.)

c. We broke up our sample of 500 observations into five different samples of 100 observations each and calculated $\hat{\beta}$s for four of the five samples. The results (for $\hat{\beta}_{ADVICE}$) were:

1st sample: $\hat{\beta}_{ADVICE} = 10.43$

2nd sample: $\hat{\beta}_{ADVICE} = 13.52$

3rd sample: $\hat{\beta}_{ADVICE} = 14.39$

4th sample: $\hat{\beta}_{ADVICE} = 8.01$

The $\hat{\beta}$s are different! Explain in your own words how it's possible to get different $\hat{\beta}$s when you're estimating identical specifications on data that are drawn from the same source. What term would you use to describe this group of $\hat{\beta}$s?

d. The data for the fifth sample of 100 observations are in dataset DRINKS4 on the text's website. Use these data to estimate DRINKS = f(ADVICE, EDUC, DIVSEP, and UNEMP) with Stata, EViews, or another regression program. What value do you get for $\hat{\beta}_{ADVICE}$? How do your estimated coefficients compare to those of the entire sample of 500?

Chapter 5

Hypothesis Testing and Statistical Inference

In this chapter, we return to the essence of econometrics—an effort to quantify economic relationships by analyzing sample data—and ask what conclusions we can draw from this quantification. Hypothesis testing goes beyond calculating estimates of the true population parameters to a much more complex set of questions. Hypothesis testing and statistical inference allow us to answer important questions about the real world from a sample. Is it likely that our result could have been obtained by chance? Would the results generated from our sample lead us to reject our original theories? How confident can we be that our estimate is close to the true value of the parameter? This chapter starts with a brief introduction to the topic of hypothesis testing. We then examine the *t*-test, typically used for hypothesis tests of individual regression coefficients. We next look at the confidence interval, a tool for evaluating the precision of our estimates, and we end the chapter by learning how to use the *F*-test to determine whether whole groups of coefficients affect the dependent variable.

Hypothesis testing and the *t*-test should be familiar topics to readers with strong backgrounds in statistics, who are encouraged to skim this chapter and focus on only those applications that seem somewhat new. The development of hypothesis testing procedures is explained here in terms of the regression model, however, so parts of the chapter may be instructive even to those already skilled in statistics.

Our approach will be classical in nature, since we assume that the sample data are our best and only information about the population. An alternative, *Bayesian statistics*, uses a completely different definition of probability and does not use the sampling distribution concept.[1]

5.1 What Is Hypothesis Testing?

Hypothesis testing is used in a variety of settings. The Food and Drug Administration (FDA), for example, tests new products before allowing their sale. If the sample of people exposed to the new product shows some side effect significantly more frequently than would be expected to occur by chance, the FDA is likely to withhold approval of marketing that product. Similarly, economists have been statistically testing various relationships between consumption and income for almost a century; theories developed by John Maynard Keynes and Milton Friedman, among others, have been tested on macroeconomic and microeconomic data sets.

Although researchers are always interested in learning whether the theory in question is supported by estimates generated from a sample of real-world observations, it's almost impossible to *prove* that a given hypothesis is correct. All that can be done is to state that a particular sample conforms to a particular hypothesis. Even though we cannot prove that a given theory is "correct" using hypothesis testing, we often can *reject* a given hypothesis with a certain level of confidence. In such a case, the researcher concludes that it is very unlikely that the sample result would have been observed if the hypothesized theory were correct.

Classical Null and Alternative Hypotheses

The first step in hypothesis testing is to state the hypotheses to be tested. This should be done *before* the equation is estimated because hypotheses

---

1. Bayesians, by being forced to state explicitly their prior expectations, tend to do most of their thinking before estimation, which is a good habit for a number of important reasons. For more on this approach, see Peter Kennedy, *A Guide to Econometrics* (Malden, MA: Blackwell, 2008), pp. 213–231. For more advanced coverage, see Tony Lancaster, *An Introduction to Bayesian Econometrics* (Oxford: Blackwell Publishing, 2004).

developed after estimation run the risk of being justifications of particular results rather than tests of the validity of those results.

The **null hypothesis** typically is a statement of the values that the researcher does not expect. The notation used to specify the null hypothesis is "H_0:" followed by a statement of the range of values you do not expect. For example, if you expect a positive coefficient, then you don't expect a zero or negative coefficient, and the null hypothesis is:

Null hypothesis $H_0: \beta \leq 0$ (the values you do not expect)

The **alternative hypothesis** typically is a statement of the values that the researcher expects. The notation used to specify the alternative hypothesis is "H_A:" followed by a statement of the range of values you expect. To continue our previous example, if you expect a positive coefficient, then the alternative hypothesis is:

Alternative hypothesis $H_A: \beta > 0$ (the values you expect)

To test yourself, take a moment and think about what the null and alternative hypotheses will be if you expect a negative coefficient. That's right, they're:

$$H_0: \beta \geq 0$$
$$H_A: \beta < 0$$

The above hypotheses are for a **one-sided test** because the alternative hypotheses have values on only one side of the null hypothesis. Another approach is to use a **two-sided test** (or a *two-tailed test*) in which the alternative hypothesis has values on both sides of the null hypothesis. For a two-sided test around zero, the null and alternative hypotheses are:

$$H_0: \beta = 0$$
$$H_A: \beta \neq 0$$

We should note that there are a few rare cases in which we must violate our rule that the value you expect goes in the alternative hypothesis. Classical hypothesis testing requires that the null hypothesis contain the equal sign in some form (whether it be $=$, $\leq$, or $\geq$). This requirement means that researchers are forced to put the value they expect in the null hypothesis if their expectation includes an equal sign. This typically happens when the researcher specifies a particular value rather than a range. Luckily, such exceptions are unusual in elementary applications.

With the exception of the unusual cases previously mentioned, economists always put what they expect in the alternative hypothesis. This allows us to make rather strong statements when we reject a null hypothesis. However, we can never say that we *accept* the null hypothesis; we must always say that we *cannot reject* the null hypothesis. As put by Jan Kmenta:

> Just as a court pronounces a verdict as *not guilty* rather than *innocent*, so the conclusion of a statistical test is *do not reject* rather than *accept*.[2]

Type I and Type II Errors

The typical testing technique in econometrics is to hypothesize an expected sign (or value) for each regression coefficient (except the constant term) and then to determine whether to reject the null hypothesis. Since the regression coefficients are only estimates of the true population parameters, it would be unrealistic to think that conclusions drawn from regression analysis will always be right.

There are two kinds of errors we can make in such hypothesis testing:

> Type I: We reject a true null hypothesis.
> Type II: We do not reject a false null hypothesis.

We will refer to these errors as **Type I** and **Type II Errors**, respectively.

Suppose we have the following null and alternative hypotheses:

$$H_0: \beta \leq 0$$
$$H_A: \beta > 0$$

Even if the true parameter β is not positive, the particular estimate obtained by a researcher may be sufficiently positive to lead to the rejection of the null hypothesis that $\beta \leq 0$. This is a Type I Error; we have rejected the truth!

Alternatively, it's possible to obtain an estimate of β that is close enough to zero (or negative) to be considered "not significantly positive." Such a result may lead the researcher to "accept"[3] the hypothesis that $\beta \leq 0$ when in truth $\beta > 0$. This is a Type II Error; we have failed to reject a false null hypothesis!

As an example of Type I and Type II Errors, let's suppose that you're on a jury in a murder case.[4] In such a situation, the presumption of "innocent until proven guilty" implies that:

> H_0: *The defendant is innocent.*
> H_A: *The defendant is guilty.*

---

2. Jan Kmenta, *Elements of Econometrics* (Ann Arbor: University of Michigan Press, © 1986), p. 112. (Emphasis added.)

3. We will consistently put the word accept in quotes whenever we use it. In essence, "accept" means *do not reject*.

4. This example comes from and is discussed in much more detail in Ed Leamer, *Specification Searches* (New York: John Wiley and Sons, 1978), pp. 93–98.

What would a Type I Error be? Rejecting the null hypothesis would mean sending the defendant to jail, so a Type I Error, rejecting a true null hypothesis, would mean:

Type I Error = Sending an innocent defendant to jail.

Similarly,

Type II Error = Freeing a guilty defendant.

Most reasonable jury members would want both levels of error to be quite small, but such certainty is almost impossible. After all, couldn't there be a mistaken identification or a lying witness? In the real world, decreasing the probability of a Type I Error (sending an innocent defendant to jail) means increasing the probability of a Type II Error (freeing a guilty defendant). If we never sent an innocent defendant to jail, we'd be freeing quite a few murderers!

Decision Rules of Hypothesis Testing

A **decision rule** is a method of deciding whether to reject a null hypothesis. Typically, a decision rule involves comparing a sample statistic with a pre-selected *critical value* found in tables such as those in the end of this text.

A decision rule should be formulated before regression estimates are obtained. The range of possible values of $\hat{\beta}$ is divided into two regions, an *"acceptance" region* and a *rejection region*, where the terms are expressed relative to the null hypothesis. To define these regions, we must determine a *critical value* (or, for a two-tailed test, two critical values) of $\hat{\beta}$. Thus, a **critical value** is a value that divides the "acceptance" region from the rejection region when testing a null hypothesis. Graphs of these "acceptance" and rejection regions are presented in Figures 5.1 and 5.2.

To use a decision rule, we need to select a critical value. Let's suppose that the critical value is 1.8. If the observed $\hat{\beta}$ is greater than 1.8, we can reject the null hypothesis that β is zero or negative. To see this, take a look at Figure 5.1. Any $\hat{\beta}$ above 1.8 can be seen to fall into the rejection region, whereas any $\hat{\beta}$ below 1.8 can be seen to fall into the "acceptance" region.

The rejection region measures the probability of a Type I Error if the null hypothesis is true. Some students react to this news by suggesting that we make the rejection region as small as possible. Unfortunately, decreasing the chance of a Type I Error means increasing the chance of a Type II Error (not rejecting a false null hypothesis). If you make the rejection region so small that you almost never reject a true null hypothesis, then you're going to be unable to reject almost every null hypothesis, whether they're true or not! As a result, the probability of a Type II Error will rise.

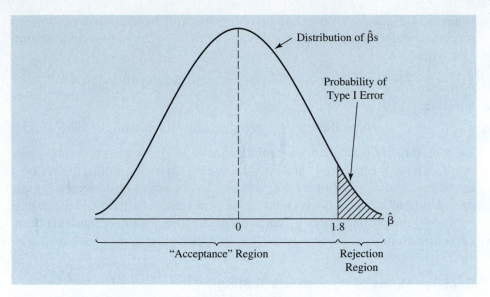

Figure 5.1 "Acceptance" and Rejection Regions for a One-Sided Test of β

For a one-sided test of H_0: $\beta \leq 0$ vs. H_A: $\beta > 0$, the critical value divides the distribution of $\hat{\beta}$ (centered around zero on the assumption that H_0 is true) into "acceptance" and rejection regions.

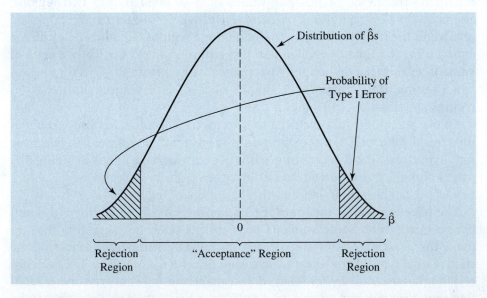

Figure 5.2 "Acceptance" and Rejection Regions for a Two-Sided Test of β

For a two-sided test of H_0: $\beta = 0$ vs. H_A: $\beta \neq 0$, we divided the distribution of $\hat{\beta}$ into an "acceptance" region and *two* rejection regions.

Given that, how do you choose between Type I and Type II Errors? The answer is easiest if you know that the cost (to society or the decision maker) of making one kind of error is dramatically larger than the cost of making the other. If you worked for the FDA, for example, you'd want to be very sure that you hadn't released a product that had horrible side effects. We'll discuss this dilemma for the *t*-test on page 126.

5.2 The *t*-Test

Econometricians generally use the *t*-test to test hypotheses about individual regression slope coefficients. Tests of more than one coefficient at a time (joint hypotheses) are typically done with the *F*-test, presented in Section 5.6.

The *t*-test is easy to use because it accounts for differences in the units of measurement of the variables and in the standard deviations of the estimated coefficients. More important, the *t*-statistic is the appropriate test to use when the stochastic error term is normally distributed and when the variance of that distribution must be estimated. Since these usually are the case, the use of the *t*-test for hypothesis testing has become standard practice in econometrics.

The *t*-Statistic

For a typical multiple regression equation:

$$Y_i = \beta_0 + \beta_1 X_{1i} + \beta_2 X_{2i} + \epsilon_i \tag{5.1}$$

we can calculate *t*-values for each of the estimated coefficients in the equation. For reasons that will be explained in Section 7.1, *t*-tests are usually done only on the slope coefficients; for these, the relevant form of the **t-statistic** for the *k*th coefficient is

$$t_k = \frac{(\hat{\beta}_k - \beta_{H_0})}{SE(\hat{\beta}_k)} \qquad (k = 1, 2, \ldots, K) \tag{5.2}$$

where: $\hat{\beta}_k$ = the estimated regression coefficient of the *k*th variable

β_{H_0} = the border value (usually zero) implied by the null hypothesis for β_k

$SE(\hat{\beta}_k)$ = the estimated standard error of $\hat{\beta}_k$ (that is, the square root of the estimated variance of the distribution of the $\hat{\beta}_k$; note that there is no "hat" attached to SE because SE is already defined as an estimate)

How do you decide what *border* is implied by the null hypothesis? Some null hypotheses specify a particular value. For these, β_{H_0} is simply that value; if $H_0: \beta = S$, then $\beta_{H_0} = S$. Other null hypotheses involve ranges, but we are concerned only with the value in the null hypothesis that is closest to the border between the "acceptance" region and the rejection region. This border value then becomes the β_{H_0}. For example, if $H_0: \beta \geq 0$ and $H_A: \beta < 0$, then the value in the null hypothesis closest to the border is zero, and $\beta_{H_0} = 0$.

Since most regression hypotheses test whether a particular regression coefficient is significantly different from zero, β_{H_0} is typically zero. Zero is particularly meaningful because if the true β equals zero, then the variable doesn't belong in the equation. Before we drop the variable from the equation and effectively force the coefficient to be zero, however, we need to be careful and test the null hypothesis that $\beta = 0$. Thus, the most-used form of the t-statistic becomes

$$t_k = \frac{(\hat{\beta}_k - 0)}{SE(\hat{\beta}_k)} \qquad (k = 1, 2, \ldots, K)$$

which simplifies to

$$t_k = \frac{\hat{\beta}_k}{SE(\hat{\beta}_k)} \qquad (k = 1, 2, \ldots, K) \tag{5.3}$$

or the estimated coefficient divided by the estimate of its standard error. This is the t-statistic formula used by most computer programs.

For an example of this calculation, let's consider the equation for the check volume at Woody's restaurants from Section 3.2:

$$\hat{Y}_i = 102,192 - 9075N_i + 0.3547P_i + 1.288I_i \tag{5.4}$$
$$(2053) \quad (0.0727) \quad (0.543)$$
$$t = -4.42 \quad 4.88 \quad 2.37$$
$$N = 33 \quad \bar{R}^2 = .579$$

In Equation 5.4, the numbers in parentheses underneath the estimated regression coefficients are the estimated standard errors of the estimated $\hat{\beta}$s, and the numbers below them are t-values calculated according to Equation 5.3. The format used to document Equation 5.4 is the one we'll use whenever possible throughout this text. Note that the sign of the t-value is always the same as that of the estimated regression coefficient, and the standard error is always positive.

Using the regression results in Equation 5.4, let's calculate the t-value for the estimated coefficient of P, the population variable. Given the values in

Equation 5.4 of 0.3547 for $\hat{\beta}_P$ and 0.0727 for $SE(\hat{\beta}_P)$, and given H_0: $\beta_P \leq 0$, the relevant *t*-value is indeed 4.88, as specified in Equation 5.4:

$$t_P = \frac{\hat{\beta}_P}{SE(\hat{\beta}_P)} = \frac{0.3547}{0.0727} = 4.88$$

The larger in absolute value this *t*-value is, the greater the likelihood that the estimated regression coefficient is different from zero.

The Critical *t*-Value and the *t*-Test Decision Rule

To decide whether to reject or not to reject a null hypothesis based on a calculated *t*-value, we use a critical *t*-value. A *critical t-value* is the value that distinguishes the "acceptance" region from the rejection region. The critical *t*-value, t_c, is selected from a *t*-table (see Statistical Table B-1 in the back of the book) depending on whether the test is one-sided or two-sided, on the level of Type I Error you specify, and on the degrees of freedom, which we have defined as the number of observations minus the number of coefficients estimated (including the constant) or $N - K - 1$. The level of Type I Error in a hypothesis test is also called the *level of significance* of that test and will be discussed in more detail later in this section. The *t*-table was created to save time during research; it consists of critical *t*-values given specific areas underneath curves such as those in Figure 5.1 for Type I Errors. A critical *t*-value is thus a function of the probability of Type I Error that the researcher wants to specify.

Once you have obtained a calculated *t*-value t_k and a critical *t*-value t_c, you reject the null hypothesis if the calculated *t*-value is greater in absolute value than the critical *t*-value and if the calculated *t*-value has the sign implied by H_A.

Thus, the rule to apply when testing a single regression coefficient is that you should:

> Reject H_0 if $|t_k| > t_c$ and if t_k also has the sign implied by H_A. Do not reject H_0 otherwise.

This decision rule works for calculated *t*-values and critical *t*-values for one-sided hypotheses around zero:

$$H_0: \beta_k \leq 0$$
$$H_A: \beta_k > 0$$

$$H_0: \beta_k \geq 0$$
$$H_A: \beta_k < 0$$

for two-sided hypotheses around zero:

$$H_0: \beta_k = 0$$
$$H_A: \beta_k \neq 0$$

for one-sided hypotheses based on hypothesized values other than zero:

$$H_0: \beta_k \leq S$$
$$H_A: \beta_k > S$$

$$H_0: \beta_k \geq S$$
$$H_A: \beta_k < S$$

and for two-sided hypotheses based on hypothesized values other than zero:

$$H_0: \beta_k = S$$
$$H_A: \beta_k \neq S$$

The decision rule is the same: Reject the null hypothesis if the appropriately calculated t-value, t_k, is greater in absolute value than the critical t-value, t_c, as long as the sign of t_k is the same as the sign of the coefficient implied in H_A. Otherwise, do not reject H_0. Always use Equation 5.2 whenever the hypothesized value is not zero.

Statistical Table B-1 contains the critical values t_c for varying degrees of freedom and levels of significance. The columns indicate the levels of significance according to whether the test is one-sided or two-sided, and the rows indicate the degrees of freedom. For an example of the use of this table and the decision rule, let's return to the Woody's restaurant example and, in particular, to the t-value for $\hat{\beta}_P$ calculated in the previous section. Recall that we hypothesized that population's coefficient would be positive, so this is a one-sided test:

$$H_0: \beta_p \leq 0$$
$$H_A: \beta_p > 0$$

There are 29 degrees of freedom (equal to $N - K - 1$, or $33 - 3 - 1$) in this regression, so the appropriate t-value with which to test the calculated t-value is a one-tailed critical t-value with 29 degrees of freedom. To find this value, pick a level of significance, say 5 percent, and turn to Statistical Table B-1. Take a look for yourself. Do you agree that the number there is 1.699?

Given that, should you reject the null hypothesis? The decision rule is to reject H_0 if $|t_k| > t_c$ and if t_k has the sign implied by H_A. Since the 5-percent, one-sided, 29 degrees of freedom critical t-value is 1.699, and since the sign implied by H_A is positive, the decision rule (for this specific case) becomes:

Reject H_0 if $|t_P| > 1.699$ and if t_P is positive

or, combining the two conditions:

$$\text{Reject } H_0 \text{ if } t_P > 1.699$$

What is t_P? In the previous section, we found that t_P was $+4.88$, so we would reject the null hypothesis and conclude that population does indeed tend to have a positive relationship with Woody's check volume (holding the other variables in the equation constant).

Note from Statistical Table B-1 that the critical *t*-value for a one-tailed test at a given level of significance is exactly equal to the critical *t*-value for a two-tailed test at twice the level of significance as the one-tailed test. This relationship between one-sided and two-sided tests is illustrated in Figure 5.3. The critical value $t_c = 1.699$ is for a one-sided, 5-percent level of significance, but it also represents a two-sided, 10-percent level of significance because if one tail represents 5 percent, then both tails added together represent 10 percent.

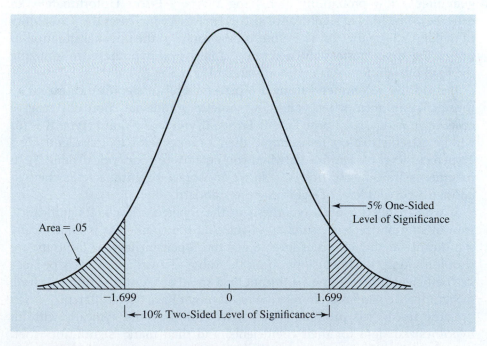

Figure 5.3 One-Sided and Two-Sided *t*-Tests

The t_c for a one-sided test at a given level of significance is equal exactly to the t_c for a two-sided test with twice the level of significance of the one-sided test. For example, $t_c = 1.699$ for a 10-percent two-sided test *and* for a 5-percent one-sided test (for 29 degrees of freedom).

Choosing a Level of Significance

To complete the previous example, it was necessary to pick a level of significance before a critical t-value could be found in Statistical Table B-1. The words "significantly positive" usually carry the statistical interpretation that H_0 ($\beta \leq 0$) was rejected in favor of H_A ($\beta > 0$) according to the preestablished decision rule, which was set up with a given level of significance. The **level of significance** indicates the probability of observing an estimated t-value greater than the critical t-value if the null hypothesis were correct. It measures the amount of Type I Error implied by a particular critical t-value. If the level of significance is 10 percent and we reject the null hypothesis at that level, then this result would have occurred only 10 percent of the time that the null hypothesis was indeed correct.

How should you choose a level of significance? Most beginning econometricians (and many published ones, too) assume that the lower the level of significance, the better. After all, they say, doesn't a low level of significance guarantee a low probability of making a Type I Error? Unfortunately, an extremely low level of significance also dramatically increases the probability of making a Type II Error. Therefore, unless you're in the unusual situation of not caring about mistakenly "accepting" a false null hypothesis, minimizing the level of significance is *not* good standard practice.

Instead, we recommend using a 5-percent level of significance except in those circumstances when you know something unusual about the relative costs of making Type I and Type II Errors. If you know that a Type II Error will be extremely costly, for example, then it makes sense to consider using a 10-percent level of significance when you determine your critical value. Such judgments are difficult, however, so we encourage beginning researchers to adopt a 5-percent level of significance as standard.

If we can reject a null hypothesis at the 5-percent level of significance, we can summarize our results by saying that the coefficient is "statistically significant" at the 5-percent level. Since the 5-percent level is arbitrary, we shouldn't jump to conclusions about the value of a variable simply because its coefficient misses being significant by a small amount; if a different level of significance had been chosen, the result might have been different.

Some researchers produce tables of regression results, typically without hypothesized signs for their coefficients, and then mark "significant" coefficients with asterisks. The asterisks indicate when the t-score is larger in absolute value than the two-sided 10-percent critical value (which merits one asterisk), the two-sided 5-percent critical value (**), or the two-sided 1-percent critical value (***). Such a use of the t-value should be regarded as a descriptive rather than a hypothesis-testing use of statistics.

Now and then researchers will use the phrase "degree of confidence" or "level of confidence" when they test hypotheses. What do they mean? The *level of confidence* is nothing more than 100 percent minus the level of significance. Thus a *t*-test for which we use a 5-percent level of significance can also be said to have a 95-percent level of confidence. Since the two terms have identical meanings, we will use level of significance throughout this text. Another reason we prefer the term level of significance to level of confidence is to avoid any possible confusion with the related concept of confidence intervals, which will be covered in Section 5.5.

Some researchers avoid choosing a level of significance by simply stating the lowest level of significance possible for each estimated regression coefficient. The resulting significance levels are called *p-values*.

p-Values

There's an alternative to the *t*-test based on a measure called the *p*-value, or *marginal significance level*. A **p-value** for a *t*-score is the probability of observing a *t*-score that size or larger (in absolute value) if the null hypothesis were true. Graphically, it's two times the area under the curve of the *t*-distribution between the absolute value of the actual *t*-score and infinity.

A *p*-value is a probability, so it runs from 0 to 1. It tells us the lowest level of significance at which we could reject the null hypothesis (assuming that the estimate is in the expected direction). A small *p*-value casts doubt on the null hypothesis, so to reject a null hypothesis, we need a low *p*-value.

How do we calculate a *p*-value? One option would be to comb through pages and pages of statistical tables, looking for the level of significance that exactly matches the regression result. That could take days! Luckily, standard regression software packages calculate *p*-values automatically and print them out for every estimated coefficient.[5] You're thus able to read *p*-values off your regression output just as you would your $\hat{\beta}$s. Be careful, however, because virtually every regression package prints out *p*-values for two-sided alternative hypotheses. Such two-sided *p*-values include the area in both "tails," so two-sided *p*-values are twice the size of one-sided ones. If your test is one-sided, you need to divide the *p*-value in your regression output by 2 before doing any tests.

How would you use a *p*-value to run a *t*-test? If your chosen level of significance is 5 percent and the *p*-value is less than .05, then you can reject

---

5. Different software packages use different names for *p*-values. Stata uses $P > |t|$. To see this, turn to page 77 and look in the center of the top of the page. Note that such *p*-values are for $H_0: \beta = 0$.

your null hypothesis as long as the sign is in the expected direction. Thus the p-value decision rule is:

> Reject H_0 if p-value$_K$ < the level of significance and if $\hat{\beta}_K$ has the sign implied by H_A. Do not reject H_0 otherwise.

Let's look at an example of the use of a p-value to run a t-test. If we return to the Woody's example of Equation 5.4 and run a one-sided test on the coefficient of I, the income variable, we have the following null and alternative hypotheses:

$$H_0: \beta_I \leq 0$$
$$H_A: \beta_I > 0$$

As you can see from the regression output for the Woody's equation on page 77, the p-value for $\hat{\beta}_I$ is .025. This is a two-sided p-value and we're running a one-sided test, so we need to divide .025 by 2, getting .0125. Since .0125 is lower than our chosen level of significance of .05, and since the sign of $\hat{\beta}_I$ is positive and agrees with that in H_A, we can reject H_0. Not surprisingly, this is the same result we'd get if we ran a conventional t-test.

p-values have a number of advantages. They're easy to use, and they allow readers of research to choose their own levels of significance instead of being forced to use the level chosen by the original researcher. In addition, p-values convey information to the reader about the relative strength with which we can reject a null hypothesis. Because of these benefits, many researchers use p-values on a consistent basis.

Despite these advantages, we will not use p-values in this text. We think that beginning researchers benefit from learning the standard t-test procedure, particularly since it's more likely to force them to remember to hypothesize the sign of the coefficient and to use a one-sided test when a particular sign can be hypothesized. In addition, if you know how to use the standard t-test approach, it's easy to switch to the p-value approach, but the reverse isn't necessarily true.

However, we acknowledge that practicing econometricians today spend far more energy estimating models and coefficients than they spend testing hypotheses. This is because most researchers are more confident in their theories (say, that demand curves slope downward) than they are in the quality of their data or their regression methods. In such situations, where the statistical tools are being used more for descriptive purposes than for hypothesis testing purposes, it's clear that the use of p-values saves time and conveys more information than does the standard t-test procedure.

5.3   Examples of *t*-Tests

Examples of One-Sided *t*-Tests

The most common use of the one-sided *t*-test is to determine whether a regression coefficient is significantly different from zero in the direction predicted by theory. Let's face it: if you expect a positive sign for a coefficient and you get a negative $\hat{\beta}$, it's hard to reject the possibility that the true β might be negative (or zero). On the other hand, if you expect a positive sign and get a positive $\hat{\beta}$, things get a bit tricky. If $\hat{\beta}$ is positive but fairly close to zero, then a one-sided *t*-test should be used to determine whether the $\hat{\beta}$ is different enough from zero to allow the rejection of the null hypothesis. Recall that in order to be able to control the amount of Type I Error we make, such a theory implies an alternative hypothesis of $H_A: \beta > 0$ (the expected sign) and a null hypothesis of $H_0: \beta \leq 0$. Let's look at some complete examples of these kinds of one-sided *t*-tests.

Consider a simple model of the aggregate annual retail sales of new cars that specifies that sales of new cars (CARS) are a function of real disposable income (YD) and the average retail price of a car adjusted by the consumer price index (PRICE). Suppose you spend some time reviewing the literature on the automobile industry and are inspired to test a new theory. You decide to add a third independent variable, the number of sports utility vehicles sold (SUV) to take account of the fact that some potential new car buyers purchase SUVs instead. You therefore hypothesize the following model:

$$\overset{+}{} \qquad \overset{-}{} \qquad \overset{-}{}$$
$$\text{CARS} = \beta_0 + \beta_1 \text{YD} + \beta_2 \text{PRICE} + \beta_3 \text{SUV} + \epsilon \qquad (5.5)$$

As you can see from the hypothesized signs above the coefficients in Equation 5.5, you expect β_1 to be positive and β_2 and β_3 to be negative. This makes sense, since you'd expect higher incomes, lower prices, or lower sales of SUVs to increase new car sales, holding the other variables in the equation constant.

The four steps to use when working with the *t*-test are:

1. Set up the null and alternative hypotheses.

2. Choose a level of significance and therefore a critical *t*-value.

3. Run the regression and obtain an estimated *t*-value (or *t*-score).

4. Apply the decision rule by comparing the calculated *t*-value with the critical *t*-value in order to reject or not reject the null hypothesis.

Let's look at each step in more detail.

1. *Set up the null and alternative hypotheses.*[6] From Equation 5.5, the one-sided hypotheses are set up as:

$$\text{1. } H_0: \beta_1 \leq 0$$
$$H_A: \beta_1 > 0$$

$$\text{2. } H_0: \beta_2 \geq 0$$
$$H_A: \beta_2 < 0$$

$$\text{3. } H_0: \beta_3 \geq 0$$
$$H_A: \beta_3 < 0$$

Remember that a *t*-test typically is not run on the estimate of the constant term β_0.

2. *Choose a level of significance and therefore a critical t-value.* Assume that you have considered the various costs involved in making Type I and Type II Errors and have chosen 5 percent as the level of significance with which you want to test. There are 10 observations in the data set that is going to be used to test these hypotheses, and so there are $10 - 3 - 1 = 6$ degrees of freedom. At a 5-percent level of significance, the critical *t*-value, t_c, can be found in Statistical Table B-1 to be 1.943. Note that the level of significance does not have to be the same for all the coefficients in the same regression equation. It could well be that the costs involved in an incorrectly rejected null hypothesis for one coefficient are much higher than for another, so lower levels of significance would be used. In this equation, though, for all three variables:

$$t_c = 1.943$$

3. *Run the regression and obtain an estimated t-value.* You now use the data (annual from 2000 to 2009) to run the regression on your OLS computer package, getting:

$$\text{CARS}_t = 1.30 + 4.91\text{YD}_t + 0.00123\text{PRICE}_t - 7.14\text{SUV}_t \quad (5.6)$$
$$(2.38) \quad (0.00044) \quad (71.38)$$
$$t = 2.1 \quad \quad 2.8 \quad \quad \quad -0.1$$

---

6. The null hypothesis can be stated either as $H_0: \beta \leq 0$ or $H_0: \beta = 0$ because the value used to test $H_0: \beta \leq 0$ is the value in the null hypothesis closest to the border between the acceptance and the rejection regions. When the amount of Type I Error is calculated, this border value of β is the one that is used, because over the whole range of $\beta \leq 0$, the value $\beta = 0$ gives the maximum amount of Type I Error. The classical approach limits this maximum amount to a preassigned level—the chosen level of significance.

where:　CARS$_t$　= new car sales (in hundreds of thousands of units) in year t

YD$_t$　= real U.S. disposable income (in hundreds of billions of dollars)

PRICE$_t$　= the average real price of a new car in year t (in dollars)

SUV$_t$　= the number of sports utility vehicles sold in year t (in millions)

Once again, we use our standard documentation notation, so the figures in parentheses are the estimated standard errors of the $\hat{\beta}$s. The *t*-values to be used in these hypothesis tests are printed out by standard OLS programs:

$$t_k = \frac{\hat{\beta}_k}{SE(\hat{\beta}_k)} \qquad (k = 1, 2, \ldots, K) \qquad (5.3)$$

For example, the estimated coefficient of SUV divided by its estimated standard error is $-7.14/71.38 = -0.1$. Note that since standard errors are always positive, a negative estimated coefficient implies a negative *t*-value.

4. *Apply the decision rule by comparing the calculated t-value with the critical t-value in order to reject or not reject the null hypothesis.* As stated in Section 5.2, the decision rule for the *t*-test is to

Reject H$_0$ if $|t_k| > t_c$ and if t_k also has the sign implied by H$_A$.
Do not reject H$_0$ otherwise.

What would these decision rules be for the three hypotheses, given the relevant critical *t*-value (1.943) and the calculated *t*-values?

For β_1: Reject H$_0$ if $|2.1| > 1.943$ and if 2.1 is positive.

In the case of disposable income, you reject the null hypothesis that $\beta_1 \leq 0$ since 2.1 is indeed greater than 1.943. The result (that is, H$_A$: $\beta_1 > 0$) is as you expected on the basis of theory, since the more income in the country, the more new car sales you'd expect.

For β_2: Reject H$_0$ if $|2.8| > 1.943$ and if 2.8 is negative.

For prices, the *t*-statistic is large in absolute value (being greater than 1.943) but has a sign that is contrary to our expectations, since the alternative hypothesis implies a negative sign. Since both conditions in the decision rule must be met before we can reject H$_0$, you cannot reject the null hypothesis that prices have a zero or positive effect on new car sales!

Despite your surprise,[7] you stick with your contention that prices belong in the equation and that their expected impact should be negative.

Notice that the coefficient of PRICE is quite small, 0.00123, but that this size has no effect on the t-calculation other than its relationship to the standard error of the estimated coefficient.

For β_3: Reject H_0 if $|-0.1| > 1.943$ and if -0.1 is negative.

For sales of sports utility vehicles, the coefficient $\hat{\beta}_3$ is not statistically different from zero, since $|-0.1| < 1.943$, and you cannot reject the null hypothesis that $\beta \geq 0$ even though the estimated coefficient has the sign implied by the alternative hypothesis. After thinking this model over again, you come to the conclusion that you were hasty in adding the variable to the equation.

Figure 5.4 illustrates all three of these outcomes by plotting the critical t-value and the calculated t-values for all three null hypotheses on a t-distribution that is centered around zero (the value in the null hypothesis closest to the border between the acceptance and rejection regions). Students are urged to analyze the results of tests on the estimated coefficients of Equation 5.6 assuming different numbers of observations and different levels of significance. Exercise 2 has a number of such specific combinations, with answers in Appendix A.

The purpose of this example is to provide practice in testing hypotheses, and the results of such a poorly thought-out equation for such a small number of observations should not be taken too seriously. Given all that, however, it's still instructive to note that you did not react the same way to your inability to reject the null hypotheses for the price and sports utility vehicle variables. That is, the failure of the sports utility vehicle variable's coefficient to be significantly negative caused you to realize that perhaps the addition of this variable was ill-advised. The failure of the price variable's coefficient to be significantly negative did not cause you to consider the possibility that price has no effect on new car sales. Put differently, estimation results should never be allowed to cause you to want to adjust theoretically sound variables or hypotheses, but if they make you realize you

---

7. Actually, it shouldn't be a surprise to occasionally get a positive estimated coefficient for price in a demand equation, particularly in such a small sample. Supply and demand are determined simultaneously, but we didn't specify a supply equation in our model. Thus our "demand" equation might be picking up the positive impact of price on quantity from the omitted supply equation. We'll deal with the simultaneity issue in Chapter 14.

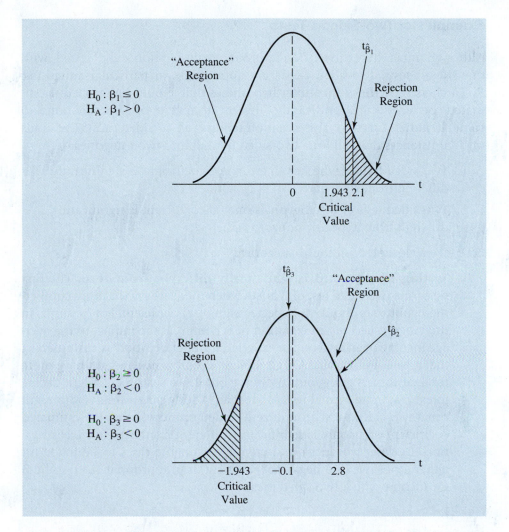

Figure 5.4 One-Sided *t*-Tests of the Coefficients of the New Car Sales Model

Given the estimates in Equation 5.6 and the critical *t*-value of 1.943 for a 5-percent level of significance, one-sided, 6 degrees of freedom *t*-test, we can reject the null hypothesis for $\hat{\beta}_1$, but not for $\hat{\beta}_2$ or $\hat{\beta}_3$.

have made a serious mistake, then it would be foolhardy to ignore that mistake. What to do about the positive coefficient of price, on the other hand, is what the "art" of econometrics is all about. Surely a positive coefficient is unsatisfactory, but throwing the price variable out of the equation seems even more so. Possible answers to such issues are addressed more than once in the chapters that follow.

Examples of Two-Sided *t*-Tests

Although most hypotheses in regression analysis should be tested with one-sided *t*-tests, two-sided *t*-tests are appropriate in particular situations. Researchers sometimes encounter hypotheses that should be rejected if estimated coefficients are significantly different from zero, or a specific nonzero value, in either direction. This situation requires a two-sided *t*-test. The kinds of circumstances that call for a two-sided test fall into two categories:

1. Two-sided tests of whether an estimated coefficient is significantly different from zero, and

2. Two-sided tests of whether an estimated coefficient is significantly different from a specific nonzero value.

Let's take a closer look at these categories:

1. **Testing whether a $\hat{\beta}$ is statistically different from zero.** The first case for a two-sided test of $\hat{\beta}$ arises when there are two or more conflicting hypotheses about the expected sign of a coefficient. For example, in the Woody's restaurant equation of Section 3.2, the impact of the average income of an area on the expected number of Woody's customers in that area is ambiguous. A high-income neighborhood might have more total customers going out to dinner, but those customers might decide to eat at a more formal restaurant than Woody's. As a result, you might run a two-sided *t*-test around zero to determine whether the estimated coefficient of income is significantly different from zero in *either* direction. In other words, since there are reasonable cases to be made for either a positive or a negative coefficient, it is appropriate to test the $\hat{\beta}$ for income with a two-sided *t*-test:

$$H_0: \beta_I = 0$$
$$H_A: \beta_I \neq 0$$

As Figure 5.5 illustrates, a two-sided test implies two different rejection regions (one positive and one negative) surrounding the acceptance region. A critical *t*-value, t_c, must be increased in order to achieve the same level of significance with a two-sided test as can be achieved with a one-sided test.[8] As a result, there is an advantage to testing hypotheses with a one-sided test if the underlying theory allows because, for the same *t*-values, the possibility of Type I Error is half as much for a one-sided

---

8. See Figure 5.3. In that figure, the same critical *t*-value has double the level of significance for a two-sided test as for a one-sided test.

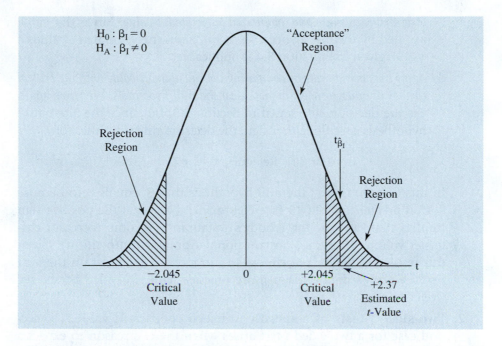

Figure 5.5 Two-Sided *t*-Test of the Coefficient of Income in the Woody's Model

Given the estimates of Equation 5.4 and the critical *t*-values of ± 2.045 for a 5-percent level of significance, two-sided, 29 degrees of freedom *t*-test, we can reject the null hypothesis that $\beta_1 = 0$.

test as for a two-sided test. In cases where there are powerful theoretical arguments on both sides, however, the researcher has no alternative to using a two-sided *t*-test around zero. To see how this works, let's follow through the Woody's income variable example in more detail.

a. *Set up the null and alternative hypotheses.*

$$H_0: \beta_1 = 0$$
$$H_A: \beta_1 \neq 0$$

b. *Choose a level of significance and therefore a critical t-value.* You decide to keep the level of significance at 5 percent, but now this amount must be distributed between two rejection regions for 29 degrees of freedom. Hence, the correct critical *t*-value is 2.045 (found in Statistical Table B-1 for 29 degrees of freedom and a 5-percent, two-sided test). Note that, technically, there now are two critical *t*-values, $+2.045$ and -2.045.

c. *Run the regression and obtain an estimated t-value.* Since the value implied by the null hypothesis is still zero, the estimated *t*-value of +2.37 given in Equation 5.4 is applicable.

d. *Apply the decision rule by comparing the calculated t-value with the critical t-value in order to reject or not reject the null hypothesis.* We once again use the decision rule stated in Section 5.2, but since the alternative hypothesis specifies either sign, the decision rule simplifies to:

$$\text{For } \beta_I: \quad \text{Reject } H_0 \text{ if } |2.37| > 2.045$$

In this case, you reject the null hypothesis that β_I equals zero because 2.37 is greater than 2.045 (see Figure 5.5). Note that the positive sign implies that, at least for Woody's restaurants, income increases customer volume (holding constant population and competition). Given this result, we might well choose to run a one-sided *t*-test on the next year's Woody's data set. For more practice with two-sided *t*-tests, see Exercise 5.

2. **Two-sided *t*-tests of a specific nonzero coefficient value.** The second case for a two-sided *t*-test arises when there is reason to expect a specific nonzero value for an estimated coefficient. For example, if a previous researcher has stated that the true value of some coefficient almost surely equals a particular number, β_{H_0}, then that number would be the one to test by creating a two-sided *t*-test around the hypothesized value, β_{H_0}.

In such a case, the null and alternative hypotheses become:

$$H_0: \beta_k = \beta_{H_0}$$
$$H_A: \beta_k \neq \beta_{H_0}$$

where β_{H_0} is the specific nonzero value hypothesized.

Since the hypothesized β value is no longer zero, the formula with which to calculate the estimated *t*-value is Equation 5.2, repeated here:

$$t_k = \frac{(\hat{\beta}_k - \beta_{H_0})}{SE(\hat{\beta}_k)} \qquad (k = 1, 2, \ldots, K) \qquad (5.2)$$

This *t*-statistic is still distributed around zero if the null hypothesis is correct, because we have subtracted β_{H_0} from the estimated regression coefficient whose expected value is supposed to be β_{H_0} when H_0 is true. Since the *t*-statistic is still centered around zero, the decision rule developed earlier still is applicable.

5.4 Limitations of the *t*-Test

One problem with the *t*-test is that it is easy to misuse. *t*-scores are printed out by computer regression packages and the *t*-test seems easy to work with, so beginning researchers sometimes attempt to use the *t*-test to "prove" things that it was never intended to even test. For that reason, it's probably just as important to know the limitations of the *t*-test[9] as it is to know the applications of that test. Perhaps the most important of these limitations, that the usefulness of the *t*-test diminishes rapidly as more and more specifications are estimated and tested, is the subject of Section 6.4. The purpose of the present section is to give additional examples of how the *t*-test should *not* be used.

The *t*-Test Does Not Test Theoretical Validity

Recall that the purpose of the *t*-test is to help the researcher make inferences about a particular population coefficient based on an estimate obtained from a sample of that population. Some beginning researchers conclude that any *statistically* significant result is also a *theoretically* correct one. This is dangerous because such a conclusion confuses statistical significance with theoretical validity.

Consider for instance, the following estimated regression that explains the consumer price index in the United Kingdom:[10]

$$\hat{P} = 10.9 - 3.2C + 0.39C^2 \tag{5.7}$$
$$(0.23)\ (0.02)$$
$$t = -13.9 \quad 19.5$$
$$\overline{R}^2 = .982 \quad N = 21$$

Apply the *t*-test to these estimates. Do you agree that the two slope coefficients are statistically significant?

The catch is that P is the consumer price index and C is the cumulative amount of rainfall in the United Kingdom! We have just shown that rain is statistically significant in explaining consumer prices, but does that also show that the underlying theory is valid? Of course not. Why is the statistical result so significant? The answer is that by chance there is a common trend on both sides of the equation. This common trend does *not* have any meaning. The

---

9. These limitations also apply to the use of *p*-values. For example, many beginning students conclude that the variable with the lowest *p*-value is the most important variable in an equation, but this is just as false for *p*-values as it is for the *t*-test.

10. These results, and others similar to them, can be found in David F. Hendry, "Econometrics— Alchemy or Science?" *Economica*, Vol. 47, pp. 383–406. This is another example of spurious regression, first mentioned in Section 2.5 and covered in more detail in Section 12.4.

moral should be clear: Never conclude that statistical significance, as shown by the *t*-test, is the same as theoretical validity.

Occasionally, estimated coefficients will be significant in the direction opposite from that hypothesized, and some beginning researchers may be tempted to change their hypotheses. For example, a student might run a regression in which the hypothesized sign is positive, get a "statistically significant" negative sign, and be tempted to change the theoretical expectations to "expect" a negative sign after "rethinking" the issue. Although it is admirable to be willing to reexamine incorrect theories on the basis of new evidence, that evidence should be, for the most part, theoretical in nature. If the evidence causes a researcher to go back to the theoretical underpinnings of a model and find a mistake, then the null hypothesis should be changed, but then this new hypothesis should be tested using a completely different data set. After all, we already know what the result will be if the hypothesis is tested on the old one.

The *t*-Test Does Not Test "Importance"

One possible use of a regression equation is to help determine which independent variable has the largest relative effect (importance) on the dependent variable. Some beginning researchers draw the unwarranted conclusion that the most statistically significant variable in their estimated regression is also the most important in terms of explaining the largest portion of the movement of the dependent variable. Statistical significance says little—if anything—about which variables determine the major portion of the variation in the dependent variable. To determine importance, a measure such as the size of the coefficient multiplied by the average size of the independent variable or the standard error of the independent variable would make more sense.

Consider the following hypothetical equation:

$$\hat{Y} = 300.0 + 10.0X_1 + 200.0X_2 \tag{5.8}$$
$$(1.0) \qquad (25.0)$$
$$t = 10.0 \qquad 8.0$$
$$\overline{R}^2 = .90 \qquad N = 30$$

where: Y = mail-order sales of *O'Henry's Oyster Recipes*
X_1 = hundreds of dollars of advertising expenditures in *Gourmets' Magazine*
X_2 = hundreds of dollars of advertising expenditures on the *Julia Adult TV Cooking Show*

Assume that all other factors, including prices, quality, and competition, remain constant during the estimation period. Where should O'Henry be spending his advertising money? That is, which independent variable has the biggest impact per dollar on Y? Given that X_2's coefficient is 20 times X_1's coefficient, you'd have to agree that X_2 is more important as defined, and yet which coefficient is more statistically significantly different from zero? With a t-score of 10.0, X_1 is more statistically significant than X_2 and its t-score of 8.0, but all that means is that we have more evidence that the coefficient is positive, not that the variable itself is necessarily more important in determining Y.

The *t*-Test Is Not Intended for Tests of the Entire Population

The t-test helps make inferences about the true value of a parameter from an estimate calculated from a sample of the *population* (the group from which the sample is being drawn). If a coefficient is calculated from the entire population, then an unbiased estimate already measures the population value and a significant t-test adds nothing to this knowledge. One might forget this property and attach too much importance to t-scores that have been obtained from samples that approximate the population in size.

This point can perhaps best be seen by remembering that the t-score is the estimated regression coefficient divided by the standard error of the estimated regression coefficient. If the sample size is large enough to approach the population, then the standard error will approach zero and the t-score will eventually become:

$$t = \frac{\hat{\beta}}{0} = \infty$$

Thus, the mere existence of a large t-score for a huge sample has no real substantive significance.

5.5 Confidence Intervals

Now that you've learned how to do hypothesis tests using the t-statistic and the p-value, you're probably thinking it would be fun to learn a third way. OK, maybe not! But there is indeed a third way. It's based on the concept of a confidence interval.

A **confidence interval** is a range of values that will contain the true value of β a certain percentage of the time, say 90 or 95 percent. The formula for a confidence interval is

$$\text{Confidence interval} = \hat{\beta} \pm t_c \cdot \text{SE}(\hat{\beta}) \tag{5.9}$$

where t_c is the two-sided critical value of the t-statistic for whatever significance level we choose. If you want a 90-percent confidence interval, you'd choose the critical value for the 10-percent significance level. For a 95-percent confidence interval, you'd use a 5-percent critical value.

To see how confidence intervals can be used for hypothesis tests, let's return to Equation 5.4 and test the significance of the income coefficient:

$$\hat{Y}_i = 102{,}192 - 9075N_i + 0.3547P_i + 1.288I_i \qquad (5.4)$$
$$\phantom{\hat{Y}_i = 102{,}192} (2053) \quad (0.0727) \quad (0.543)$$
$$\phantom{\hat{Y}_i = 102{,}192} t = -4.42 \qquad 4.88 \qquad 2.37$$
$$\phantom{\hat{Y}_i = 10} N = 33 \qquad \overline{R}^2 = .579$$

We'd typically expect sales at a restaurant to rise as income rises (a normal good), but Woody's is a fairly low-priced restaurant chain, so there's a chance that sales will tail off if income gets too high (an inferior good). As a result, many econometricians would choose $\beta_I = 0$ as their null hypothesis and therefore run a two-sided test of β_I. In a situation where a two-sided test is appropriate, a confidence interval makes a lot of sense.

What would a 90-percent confidence interval for β_I look like? Well, $\hat{\beta}_I = 1.288$ and $SE(\hat{\beta}_I) = 0.543$, so all we need is a 10-percent two-sided critical t-value for 29 degrees of freedom. Using Statistical Table B-1, we see $t_c = 1.699$. Substituting these values into Equation 5.9, we get:

$$\text{90-percent confidence interval around } \hat{\beta}_I = 1.288 \pm 1.699 \cdot 0.543$$
$$= 1.288 \pm 0.923$$
$$\text{and therefore } 0.365 \le \beta_I \le 2.211$$

What exactly does this mean? If the Classical Assumptions hold true, the confidence interval formula produces ranges that contain the true value of β 90 percent of the time. In this case, there's a 90 percent chance the true value of β_I is between 0.365 and 2.211. If it's not in that range, it's due to an unlucky sample.

How can we use a confidence interval for a two-tailed hypothesis test? If the null hypothesis is $\beta_I = 0$, we can reject it at the 10-percent level because 0 is not in the confidence interval. If the null hypothesis is that $\beta_I = 1.0$, we cannot reject it because 1.0 is in the interval. In general, if your null hypothesis border value is in the confidence interval, you cannot reject the null hypothesis.

Thus, confidence intervals can be used for two-sided tests, but they are more complicated. So why bother with them? It turns out that confidence intervals are very useful in telling us how precise a coefficient estimate is. And for many people using econometrics in the real world, this may be more important than hypothesis testing. An example will make it easier to understand.

Meet Grace, a building contractor who specializes in starter homes for young families. It's a really competitive business, so to make a profit she needs to build appealing but inexpensive houses. As a result, Grace wants to know which features she can add to her houses that will increase the selling price more than they increase her costs. Since she took econometrics in college, she decides to estimate a model of starter home prices in her city using 13 independent variables (such as square footage, number of bathrooms, etc.). She hopes to use the results to decide which features might turn a profit for her on the houses that she's planning on building.

Let's focus on how much an additional bathroom might increase the sales price. Grace knows that her marginal cost of adding a bathroom is about $8,000. She collects 100 observations on recently sold starter homes in her city and estimates her model.

The results appear in the first row of Table 5.1. The estimate of the coefficient of bathrooms is about $21,770, well above the $8,000 marginal cost. Sounds like a no-brainer to add a bathroom, right? Not so fast. Look at the 90-percent confidence interval in the first row of Table 5.1. It is huge, ranging from about $187 to $43,356. If the true value is in that interval, there's a pretty big chance it could be below $8,000, meaning Grace would lose money by adding a bathroom. Or, she could come out way ahead. What should she do?

Remember one of the lessons of Section 4.2 on sampling distributions: Bigger samples decrease the variance of $\hat{\beta}$. In plain English, as the sample size grows, $\hat{\beta}$ tends to get closer and closer to the true value of β. As a result, the confidence interval for β shrinks. Let's see what happens if Grace increases her sample to 1,000 observations.

The results for $\hat{\beta}_{bath}$ when $N = 1,000$ appear in Table 5.1, right below those for $N = 100$. Notice that $\hat{\beta}_{bath}$ has fallen from almost $22,000 to less than $13,000. Does this mean Grace should not add a bathroom? Not at all! Look at the 90-percent confidence interval. The lower end has risen to $8,346.29, a bit more than the $8,000 marginal cost. While Grace could still lose money on the deal, it looks like a much safer bet than the small sample results suggest.

Why does a confidence interval become so much narrower with a bigger sample? Well, take a look at Equation 5.9. As you can see, the width of a

Table 5.1 Selected Results from Two Regressions on Selling Prices of Starter Homes as a Function of House Characteristics

obs	variable	Coef.	Std. Err.	t	p-value	[90% Conf. Interval]
100	bath	21771.65	12981.1	1.68	0.097	187.1275 to 43356.18
1000	bath	12935.06	2787.154	4.64	0.000	8346.288 to 17523.83

These results were generated with data from Nashville, TN house sales in 2012. Because the model included 13 independent variables, the first regression has 86 degrees of freedom, and the second has 986 degrees of freedom.

confidence interval depends entirely on the product of t_c and $SE(\hat{\beta})$. What happens to t_c and $SE(\hat{\beta})$ as the sample size rises? If you take a look at Table B-1, you'll see that as the sample size rises, t_c falls. Simultaneously, as the sample size rises, the variance of the sampling distribution falls, so the $SE(\hat{\beta})$ (the square root of the estimated variance) must fall as well. If both t_c and $SE(\hat{\beta})$ fall, then their multiple must fall, and a bigger sample will indeed lead to a narrower confidence interval.

This example illustrates how confidence intervals provide information on how precise an estimated coefficient is. In addition, confidence intervals also are extremely useful in forecasting, and we'll cover that topic in Chapter 15.

5.6 The *F*-Test

Although the *t*-test is invaluable for hypotheses about individual regression coefficients, it can't be used to test multiple hypotheses simultaneously. Such a limitation is unfortunate because many interesting ideas involve a number of hypotheses or involve one hypothesis about multiple coefficients. For example, suppose that you want to test the null hypothesis that there is no seasonal variation in a quarterly regression equation that has dummy variables for the seasons. To test such a hypothesis, most researchers would use the *F*-test.

What Is the *F*-Test?

The **F-test** is a formal hypothesis test that is designed to deal with a null hypothesis that contains multiple hypotheses or a single hypothesis about a group of coefficients.[11] Such "joint" or "compound" null hypotheses are appropriate whenever the underlying economic theory specifies values for multiple coefficients simultaneously.

The way in which the *F*-test works is fairly ingenious. The first step is to translate the particular null hypothesis in question into constraints that will be placed on the equation. The resulting constrained equation can be thought of as what the equation would look like if the null hypothesis were correct; you substitute the hypothesized values into the regression equation in order to see what would happen if the equation were constrained to agree with the null hypothesis. As a result, in the *F*-test the null hypothesis always leads to a constrained equation, even if this violates our standard practice that the alternative hypothesis contains what we expect is true.

---

11. As you will see, the *F*-test works by placing constraints or restrictions on the equation to be tested. Because of this, it's equivalent to say that the *F*-test is for tests that involve multiple linear restrictions.

The second step in an *F*-test is to estimate this constrained equation with OLS and compare the fit of this constrained equation with the fit of the unconstrained equation. If the fits of the constrained equation and the unconstrained equation are not substantially different, the null hypothesis should not be rejected. If the fit of the unconstrained equation is substantially better than that of the constrained equation, then we reject the null hypothesis. The fit of the constrained equation is never superior to the fit of the unconstrained equation, as we'll explain next.

The fits of the equations are compared with the general *F*-statistic:

$$F = \frac{(RSS_M - RSS)/M}{RSS/(N - K - 1)} \tag{5.10}$$

where: RSS   = residual sum of squares from the unconstrained equation

RSS_M = residual sum of squares from the constrained equation

M   = number of constraints placed on the equation (usually equal to the number of βs eliminated from the unconstrained equation)

$(N - K - 1)$ = degrees of freedom in the unconstrained equation

RSS_M is always greater than or equal to RSS. Imposing constraints on the coefficients instead of allowing OLS to select their values can never decrease the summed squared residuals. (Recall that OLS selects that combination of values of the coefficients that minimizes RSS.) At the extreme, if the unconstrained regression yields exactly the same estimated coefficients as does the constrained regression, then the RSS are equal and the *F*-statistic is zero. In this case, H_0 is not rejected because the data indicate that the constraints appear to be correct. As the difference between the constrained coefficients and the unconstrained coefficients increases, the data indicate that the null hypothesis is less likely to be true. Thus, when F gets larger than the critical *F*-value, the hypothesized restrictions specified in the null hypothesis are rejected by the test.

The decision rule to use in the *F*-test is to reject the null hypothesis if the calculated *F*-value (F) from Equation 5.10 is greater than the appropriate critical *F*-value (F_c):

> Reject H_0 if $F > F_c$
> Do not reject H_0 if $F \leq F_c$

The critical F-value, F_c, is determined from Statistical Table B-2 or B-3, depending on the level of significance chosen by the researcher and on the degrees of freedom. The F-statistic has two types of degrees of freedom: the degrees of freedom for the numerator of Equation 5.10 (M, the number of constraints implied by the null hypothesis) and the degrees of freedom for the denominator of Equation 5.10 ($N - K - 1$, the degrees of freedom in the unconstrained regression equation). The underlying principle here is that if the calculated F-value (or F-ratio) is greater than the critical value, then the estimated equation's fit is substantially better than the constrained equation's fit, and we can reject the null hypothesis of no effect.

The *F*-Test of Overall Significance

Although R^2 and $\overline{R}^2$ measure the overall degree of fit of an equation, they don't provide a formal hypothesis test of that overall fit. Such a test is provided by the F-test. The null hypothesis in an F-test of overall significance is that all the slope coefficients in the equation equal zero simultaneously. For an equation with K independent variables, this means that the null and alternative hypotheses would be[12]:

$$H_0: \beta_1 = \beta_2 = \cdots = \beta_K = 0$$
$$H_A: H_0 \text{ is not true}$$

To show that the overall fit of the estimated equation is statistically significant, we must be able to reject this null hypothesis using the F-test.

For the F-test of overall significance, Equation 5.10 simplifies to:

$$F = \frac{\text{ESS}/K}{\text{RSS}/(N - K - 1)} = \frac{\sum(\hat{Y}_i - \overline{Y})^2/K}{\sum e_i^2/(N - K - 1)} \qquad (5.11)$$

This is the ratio of the explained sum of squares (ESS) to the residual sum of squares (RSS), adjusted for the number of independent variables (K) and the number of observations in the sample (N). In this case, the "constrained equation" to which we're comparing the overall fit is:

$$Y_i = \beta_0 + \epsilon_i \qquad (5.12)$$

which is nothing more than saying $\hat{Y}_i = \overline{Y}$. Thus the F-test of overall significance is really testing the null hypothesis that the fit of the equation is no better than that provided by using the mean alone.

---

12. Note that we don't hypothesize that $\beta_0 = 0$. This would imply that $E(\overline{Y}) = 0$. Note also that for the test of overall significance, $M = K$.

To see how this works, let's test the overall significance of the Woody's restaurant model of Equation 3.4. Since there are three independent variables, the null and alternative hypotheses are:

$$H_0: \beta_N = \beta_P = \beta_I = 0$$
$$H_A: H_0 \text{ is not true}$$

To decide whether to reject or not reject this null hypothesis, we need to calculate Equation 5.11 for the Woody's example. There are three constraints in the null hypothesis, so $K = 3$. If we check the Stata output for the Woody's equation on pages 76 and 77, we can see that $N = 33$, RSS $= 6,133,300,000$, and ESS $= 9,928,900,000$.[13] Thus the appropriate F-ratio is:

$$F = \frac{\text{ESS}/K}{\text{RSS}/(N - K - 1)} = \frac{9,928,900,000/3}{6,133,300,000/29} = 15.65 \qquad (5.13)$$

In practice, this calculation is never necessary, since virtually every computer regression package routinely provides the computed F-ratio for a test of overall significance as a matter of course. On the Woody's computer output, the value of the F-statistic can be found near the top of the right-hand column.

Our decision rule tells us to reject the null hypothesis if the calculated F-value is greater than the critical F-value. To determine that critical F-value, we need to know the level of significance and the degrees of freedom. If we assume a 5-percent level of significance, the appropriate table to use is Statistical Table B-2. The numerator degrees of freedom equal 3 (K), and the denominator degrees of freedom equal 29 ($N - K - 1$), so we need to look in Statistical Table B-2 for the critical F-value for 3 and 29 degrees of freedom. As the reader can verify,[14] $F_c = 2.93$ is well below the calculated F-value of 15.65, so we can reject the null hypothesis and conclude that the Woody's equation does indeed have a significant overall fit.

Just as p-values provide an alternative approach to the t-test, so too can p-values provide an alternative approach to the F-test of overall significance.

---

13. Stata calls the RSS the "Residual SS" and calls the ESS the "Model SS." The e + 09 indicates that you should move the decimal point nine places to the right.

14. Note that this critical F-value must be interpolated. The critical value for 30 denominator degrees of freedom is 2.92, and the critical value for 25 denominator degrees of freedom is 2.99. Since both numbers are well below the calculated F-value of 15.65, however, the interpolation isn't necessary to reject the null hypothesis. As a result, many researchers don't bother with such interpolations unless the calculated F-value is inside the range of the interpolation.

Most standard regression estimation programs report not only the *F*-value for the test of overall significance but also the *p*-value associated with that test. To see this for the Woody's output, look for "Prob > F" in the right-hand column on the top of page 77. If the *p*-value is less than your chosen level of significance, you can reject the null hypothesis.

Other Uses of the *F*-Test

There are many other uses of the *F*-test besides the test of overall significance. For example, let's take a look at the problem of testing the significance of seasonal dummies. **Seasonal dummies** are dummy variables that are used to account for seasonal variation in the data in time-series models. In a quarterly model, if:

$$X_{1t} = \begin{cases} 1 \text{ in quarter 1} \\ 0 \text{ otherwise} \end{cases}$$

$$X_{2t} = \begin{cases} 1 \text{ in quarter 2} \\ 0 \text{ otherwise} \end{cases}$$

$$X_{3t} = \begin{cases} 1 \text{ in quarter 3} \\ 0 \text{ otherwise} \end{cases}$$

then:

$$Y_t = \beta_0 + \beta_1 X_{1t} + \beta_2 X_{2t} + \beta_3 X_{3t} + \beta_4 X_{4t} + \epsilon_t \qquad (5.14)$$

where X_4 is a nondummy independent variable and t is quarterly. Notice that only three dummy variables are required to represent four seasons. In this formulation β_1 shows the extent to which the expected value of Y in the first quarter differs from its expected value in the fourth quarter, the omitted condition. β_2 and β_3 can be interpreted similarly.

Inclusion of a set of seasonal dummies "deseasonalizes" Y. This procedure may be used as long as Y and X_4 are not "seasonally adjusted" prior to estimation. Many researchers avoid the type of seasonal adjustment done prior to estimation because they think it distorts the data in unknown and arbitrary ways, but seasonal dummies have their own limitations such as remaining constant for the entire time period. As a result, there is no unambiguously best approach to deseasonalizing data.

To test the hypothesis of significant seasonality in the data, one must test the hypothesis that all the dummies equal zero simultaneously rather than test the dummies one at a time. In other words, the appropriate test of seasonality in a regression model using seasonal dummies involves the use of the *F*-test instead of the *t*-test.

In this case, the null hypothesis is that there is *no* seasonality:

$$H_0: \beta_1 = \beta_2 = \beta_3 = 0$$
$$H_A: H_0 \text{ is not true}$$

The constrained equation would then be $Y = \beta_0 + \beta_4 X_4 + \epsilon$. To determine whether the whole set of seasonal dummies should be included, the fit of the estimated constrained equation would be compared to the fit of the estimated unconstrained equation by using the *F*-test in Equation 5.10. Note that this example uses the *F*-test to test null hypotheses that include only a subset of the slope coefficients. Also note that in this case M = 3, because three coefficients (β_1, β_2, and β_3) have been eliminated from the equation.

The exclusion of some seasonal dummies because their estimated coefficients have low *t*-scores is not recommended. Seasonal dummy coefficients should be tested with the *F*-test instead of with the *t*-test because seasonality is usually a single compound hypothesis rather than 3 individual hypotheses (or 11 with monthly data) having to do with each quarter (or month). To the extent that a hypothesis is a joint one, it should be tested with the *F*-test. If the hypothesis of seasonal variation can be summarized into a single dummy variable, then the use of the *t*-test will cause no problems. Often, where seasonal dummies are unambiguously called for, no hypothesis testing at all is undertaken.

5.7 Summary

1. Hypothesis testing makes inferences about the validity of specific economic (or other) theories from a sample of the population for which the theories are supposed to be true. The four basic steps of hypothesis testing (using a *t*-test as an example) are:
   a. Set up the null and alternative hypotheses.
   b. Choose a level of significance and, therefore, a critical *t*-value.
   c. Run the regression and obtain an estimated *t*-value.
   d. Apply the decision rule by comparing the calculated *t*-value with the critical *t*-value in order to reject or not reject the null hypothesis.

2. The null hypothesis states the range of values that the regression coefficient is expected to take on if the researcher's theory is not correct. The alternative hypothesis is a statement of the range of values that the regression coefficient is expected to take if the researcher's theory is correct.

3. The two kinds of errors we can make in such hypothesis testing are:

   Type I: We reject a null hypothesis that is true.
   Type II: We do not reject a null hypothesis that is false.

4. The *t*-test tests hypotheses about individual coefficients from regression equations. The form for the *t*-statistic is

$$t_k = \frac{(\hat{\beta}_k - \beta_{H_0})}{SE(\hat{\beta}_k)} \qquad (k = 1, 2, \ldots, K)$$

In many regression applications, β_{H_0} is zero. Once you have calculated a *t*-value and chosen a critical *t*-value, you reject the null hypothesis if the *t*-value is greater in absolute value than the critical *t*-value and if the *t*-value has the sign implied by the alternative hypothesis.

5. The *t*-test is easy to use for a number of reasons, but care should be taken when using the *t*-test to avoid confusing statistical significance with theoretical validity or empirical evidence.

6. The *F*-test is a formal hypothesis test designed to deal with a null hypothesis that contains multiple hypotheses or a single hypothesis about a group of coefficients. The most common use of the *F*-test is to test the overall significance of an estimated equation.

EXERCISES

(The answers to the even-numbered exercises are in Appendix A.)

1. Write the meaning of each of the following terms without referring to the book (or your notes), and compare your definition with the version in the text for each.
    a. alternative hypothesis (p. 117)
    b. confidence interval (p. 139)
    c. critical value (p. 119)
    d. decision rule (p. 119)
    e. *F*-Test (p. 142)
    f. level of significance (p. 126)
    g. null hypothesis (p. 117)
    h. one-sided test (p. 117)
    i. *p*-value (p. 127)
    j. seasonal dummies (p. 146)
    k. *t*-statistic (p. 121)
    l. two-sided test (p. 117)
    m. Type I Error (p. 118)
    n. Type II Error (p. 118)

2. Return to Section 5.3 and test the hypotheses implied by Equation 5.5 with the results in Equation 5.6 for all three coefficients under the following circumstances:
   a. 10 percent significance and 15 observations
   b. 10 percent significance and 28 observations
   c. 1 percent significance and 10 observations

3. Create null and alternative hypotheses for the following coefficients:
   a. the impact of height on weight (Section 1.4)
   b. all the coefficients in Equation A in Exercise 5, Chapter 2
   c. all the coefficients in $Y = \beta_0 + \beta_1 X_1 + \beta_2 X_2 + \beta_3 X_3 + \epsilon$, where Y is total gasoline used on a particular trip, X_1 is miles traveled, X_2 is the weight of the car, and X_3 is the average speed traveled
   d. the impact of the decibel level of the grunt of a shot-putter on the length of the throw involved (shot-putters are known to make loud noises when they throw, but there is little theory about the impact of this yelling on the length of the put). Assume all relevant "nongrunt" variables are included in the equation.

4. Return to Section 5.2 and test the appropriate hypotheses with the results in Equation 5.4 for all three coefficients under the following circumstances:
   a. 5 percent significance and 6 degrees of freedom
   b. 10 percent significance and 29 degrees of freedom
   c. 1 percent significance and 2 degrees of freedom

5. Using the techniques of Section 5.3, test the following two-sided hypotheses:
   a. For Equation 5.8, test the hypothesis that:

$$H_0: \beta_2 = 160.0$$
$$H_A: \beta_2 \neq 160.0$$

   at the 5-percent level of significance.
   b. For Equation 5.4, test the hypothesis that:

$$H_0: \beta_3 = 0$$
$$H_A: \beta_3 \neq 0$$

   at the 1-percent level of significance.
   c. For Equation 5.6, test the hypothesis that:

$$H_0: \beta_2 = 0$$
$$H_A: \beta_2 \neq 0$$

   at the 5-percent level of significance.

6. Suppose that you estimate a model of house prices to determine the impact of having beach frontage on the value of a house.[15] You do some research, and you decide to use the size of the lot instead of the size of the house for a number of theoretical and data availability reasons. Your results (standard errors in parentheses) are:

$$\widehat{PRICE_i} = 40 + 35.0\,LOT_i - 2.0\,AGE_i + 10.0\,BED_i - 4.0\,FIRE_i + 100\,BEACH_i$$
$$\quad\quad\quad (5.0)\quad\quad (1.0)\quad\quad (10.0)\quad\quad (4.0)\quad\quad (10)$$
$$N = 30 \quad\quad\quad\quad \overline{R}^2 = .63$$

where: $PRICE_i$ = the price of the ith house (in thousands of dollars)

LOT_i = the size of the lot of the ith house (in thousands of square feet)

AGE_i = the age of the ith house in years

BED_i = the number of bedrooms in the ith house

$FIRE_i$ = a dummy variable for a fireplace (1 = yes for the ith house)

$BEACH_i$ = a dummy for having beach frontage (1 = yes for the ith house)

a. You expect the variables LOT, BED, and BEACH to have positive coefficients. Create and test the appropriate hypotheses to evaluate these expectations at the 5-percent level.

b. You expect AGE to have a negative coefficient. Create and test the appropriate hypotheses to evaluate these expectations at the 10-percent level.

c. At first you expect FIRE to have a positive coefficient, but one of your friends says that fireplaces are messy and are a pain to keep clean, so you're not sure. Run a two-sided t-test around zero to test these expectations at the 5-percent level.

d. What problems appear to exist in your equation? (*Hint:* Do you have any unexpected signs? Do you have any coefficients that are not significantly different from zero?)

e. Which of the problems that you outlined in part d is the most worrisome? Explain your answer.

f. What explanation or solution can you think of for this problem?

---

15. This hypothetical result draws on Rachelle Rush and Thomas H. Bruggink, "The Value of Ocean Proximity on Barrier Island Houses," *The Appraisal Journal*, April 2000, pp. 142–150.

7. Suppose that you've been asked by the San Diego Padres baseball team to evaluate the economic impact of their new stadium by analyzing the team's attendance per game in the last year at their old stadium. After some research on the topic, you build the following model (standard errors in parentheses):

$$\widehat{ATT_i} = 25000 + 15000\,WIN_i + 4000\,FREE_i - 3000\,DAY_i - 12000\,WEEK_i$$
$$(15000)(2000)(3000)(3000)$$
$$N = 35\overline{R}^2 = .41$$

where: ATT_i = the attendance at the ith game
WIN_i = the winning percentage of the opponent in the ith game
$FREE_i$ = a dummy variable equal to 1 if the ith game was a "promotion" game at which something was given free to each fan, 0 otherwise
DAY_i = a dummy variable equal to 1 if the ith game was a day game and equal to 0 if the game was a night or twilight game
$WEEK_i$ = a dummy variable equal to 1 if the ith game was during the week and equal to 0 if it was on the weekend

a. You expect the variables WIN and FREE to have positive coefficients. Create and test the appropriate hypotheses to evaluate these expectations at the 5-percent level.

b. You expect WEEK to have a negative coefficient. Create and test the appropriate hypotheses to evaluate these expectations at the 1-percent level.

c. You've included the day game variable because your boss thinks it's important, but you're not sure about the impact of day games on attendance. Run a two-sided t-test around zero to test these expectations at the 5-percent level.

d. What problems appear to exist in your equation? (*Hint:* Do you have any unexpected signs? Do you have any coefficients that are not significantly different from zero?)

e. Which of the problems that you outlined in part d is the most worrisome? Explain your answer.

f. What explanation or solution can you think of for this problem? (*Hint:* You don't need to be a sports fan to answer this question. If you like music, think about attendance at outdoor concerts.)

8. Let's return to the model of iPod prices on eBay that was developed in Exercise 7 in Chapter 3. That equation was:

$$\widehat{PRICE}_i = 109.24 + 54.99NEW_i - 20.44SCRATCH_i + 0.73BIDRS_i$$
$$(5.34) \qquad (5.11) \qquad\qquad (0.59)$$
$$t = 10.28 \qquad -4.00 \qquad\qquad 1.23$$
$$N = 215 \qquad F = 55.09$$

where: $PRICE_i$ = the price at which the *i*th iPod sold on eBay

   NEW_i = a dummy variable equal to 1 if the *i*th iPod was new, 0 otherwise

   $SCRATCH_i$ = a dummy variable equal to 1 if the *i*th iPod had a minor cosmetic defect, 0 otherwise

   $BIDRS_i$ = the number of bidders on the *i*th iPod

a. Create and test hypotheses for the coefficients of NEW and SCRATCH at the 5-percent level. (*Hint:* Use the critical value for 120 degrees of freedom.)

b. In theory, the more bidders there are on a given iPod, the higher the price should be. Create and test hypotheses at the 1-percent level to see if this theory can be supported by the results.

c. Based on the hypothesis tests you conducted in parts a and b, are there any variables that you think should be dropped from the equation? Explain.

d. If you could add one variable to this equation, what would it be? Explain. (*Hint:* All the iPods in the sample are silver-colored, 4 GB Apple iPod minis.)

e. Test the overall significance of this equation with the *F*-test at the 5-percent level. Be sure to state the correct null and alternative hypotheses and to be specific with respect to your critical value.

9. Frederick Schut and Peter VanBergeijk[16] published an article in which they attempted to see if the pharmaceutical industry practiced international price discrimination by estimating a model of the prices of pharmaceuticals in a cross section of 32 countries. The authors felt that if price discrimination existed, then the coefficient of per capita income in a properly specified price equation would be strongly positive. The reason they felt that the coefficient of per capita income

---

16. Frederick T. Schut and Peter A. G. VanBergeijk, "International Price Discrimination: The Pharmaceutical Industry," *World Development*, Vol. 14, No. 9, pp. 1141–1150. The estimated coefficients we list are those produced by EViews using the original data and differ slightly from those in the original article.

would measure price discrimination went as follows: the higher the ability to pay, the lower (in absolute value) the price elasticity of demand for pharmaceuticals and the higher the price a price discriminator could charge. In addition, the authors expected that prices would be higher if pharmaceutical patents were allowed and that prices would be lower if price controls existed, if competition was encouraged, or if the pharmaceutical market in a country was relatively large. Their estimates were (standard errors in parentheses):

$$\hat{P}_i = 38.22 + 1.43GDPN_i - 0.6CVN_i + 7.31PP_i \qquad (5.15)$$
$$\phantom{\hat{P}_i = 38.22 + } (0.21) \qquad\quad (0.22) \qquad (6.12)$$
$$t = \qquad 6.69 \qquad\quad -2.66 \qquad 1.19$$

$$\phantom{\hat{P}_i = } - 15.63DPC_i - 11.38PC_i$$
$$\phantom{\hat{P}_i = xxxx} (6.93) \qquad\quad (7.16)$$
$$t = -2.25 \qquad\quad -1.59$$

$$N = 32 \qquad \overline{R}^2 = .775$$

where: P_i = the pharmaceutical price level in the *i*th country divided by that of the United States

$GDPN_i$ = per capita domestic product in the *i*th country divided by that of the United States

CVN_i = per capita volume of consumption of pharmaceuticals in the *i*th country divided by that of the United States

PP_i = a dummy variable equal to 1 if patents for pharmaceutical products are recognized in the *i*th country, 0 otherwise

DPC_i = a dummy variable equal to 1 if the *i*th country applied strict price controls, 0 otherwise

PC_i = a dummy variable equal to 1 if the *i*th country encouraged price competition, 0 otherwise

a. Develop and test appropriate hypotheses concerning the regression coefficients using the *t*-test at the 5-percent level.
b. Set up 90-percent confidence intervals for each of the estimated slope coefficients.
c. Do you think Schut and VanBergeijk concluded that international price discrimination exists? Why or why not?
d. How would the estimated results have differed if the authors had not divided each country's prices, per capita income, and per capita pharmaceutical consumption by that of the United States? Explain your answer.

e. Reproduce their regression results by using the Stata computer program (datafile DRUGS5) or your own computer program and the data from Table 5.2.

Table 5.2 Data for the Pharmaceutical Price Discrimination Exercise

Country	P	GDPN	CV	N	CVN	PP	PC	DPC
Malawi	60.83	4.9	0.014	2.36	0.6	1	0	0
Kenya	50.63	6.56	0.07	6.27	1.1	1	0	0
India	31.71	6.56	18.66	282.76	6.6	0	0	1
Pakistan	38.76	8.23	3.42	32.9	10.4	0	1	1
Sri Lanka	15.22	9.3	0.42	6.32	6.7	1	1	1
Zambia	96.58	10.3	0.05	2.33	2.2	1	0	0
Thailand	48.01	13.0	2.21	19.60	11.3	0	0	0
Philippines	51.14	13.2	0.77	19.70	3.9	1	0	0
South Korea	35.10	20.7	2.20	16.52	13.3	0	0	0
Malaysia	70.74	21.5	0.50	5.58	8.9	1	0	0
Colombia	48.07	22.4	1.56	11.09	14.1	0	1	0
Jamaica	46.13	24.0	0.21	0.96	22.0	1	0	0
Brazil	63.83	25.2	10.48	50.17	21.6	0	1	0
Mexico	69.68	34.7	7.77	28.16	27.6	0	0	0
Yugoslavia	48.24	36.1	3.83	9.42	40.6	0	1	1
Iran	70.42	37.7	3.27	15.33	21.3	0	0	0
Uruguay	65.95	39.6	0.44	1.30	33.8	0	0	0
Ireland	73.58	42.5	0.57	1.49	38.0	1	0	0
Hungary	57.25	49.6	2.36	4.94	47.8	0	1	1
Poland	53.98	50.1	8.08	15.93	50.7	0	1	1
Italy	69.01	53.8	12.02	26.14	45.9	0	0	1
Spain	69.68	55.9	9.01	16.63	54.2	0	0	0
United Kingdom	71.19	63.9	9.96	26.21	38.0	1	1	1
Japan	81.88	68.4	28.58	52.24	54.7	0	0	1
Austria	139.53	69.6	1.24	3.52	35.2	0	0	0
Netherlands	137.29	75.2	1.54	6.40	24.1	1	0	0
Belgium	101.73	77.7	3.49	4.59	76.0	1	0	1
France	91.56	81.9	25.14	24.70	101.8	1	0	1
Luxembourg	100.27	82.0	0.10	0.17	60.5	1	0	1
Denmark	157.56	82.4	0.70	2.35	29.5	1	0	0
Germany, West	152.52	83.0	24.29	28.95	83.9	1	0	0
United States	100.00	100.0	100.00	100.00	100.0	1	1	0

Source: Frederick T. Schut and Peter A. G. VanBergeijk, "International Price Discrimination: The Pharmaceutical Industry," *World Development*, Vol. 14, No. 9, p. 1144.

Datafile = DRUGS5

5.8 Appendix: Econometric Lab #3

This lab focuses on hypothesis testing. You will estimate models of life expectancy at birth across the 50 states and the District of Columbia using economic and demographic variables. The data are in the dataset LIFE5 on the textbook's website and include the following variables:

Table 5.3 Variable Listing

Variable	Description
lifeexpect$_i$	Life expectancy at birth, in years, in state i, 2010
medinc$_i$	The median household income in state i (thousands of dollars), 2010
uninsured$_i$	The percentage of the population (aged 0–64) in state i that was without health insurance coverage, 2008–2010
smoke$_i$	The percentage of adults in state i who smoked, 2006–2012
obesity$_i$	The percentage of adults in state i who were obese (Body Mass Index greater than or equal to 30), 2006–2012
teenbirth$_i$	The number of births to teenaged mothers in state i per 1,000 females aged 15 to 19 years, 2010
gunlaw$_i$	A dummy variable = 1 if state i had a firearm law protecting children, 0 otherwise, 2010
metro$_i$	The percentage of the population in state i that lived in a metropolitan statistical area, 2010

Step 1: Specify the Model

Specify (i.e., write out) a linear regression equation for **lifeexpect** with all seven independent variables included, using the format of Equation 5.1 in the text. Use proper subscripts and Greek letters where appropriate.

Step 2: Hypothesize the Signs of the Coefficients

For all seven independent variables, hypothesize the sign of each regression coefficient.

Step 3: Summary Statistics

Check the means, maximums, and minimums for each of the variables. Do you spot any obvious anomalies? If so, what are they? If you see no anomalies, go on to Step 4.

Step 4: Estimation

Run the regression using all seven independent variables and print out your regression results.

Step 5: Hypothesis Testing (*t*-statistics)

Test the slope coefficients of **smoke**, **teenbirth**, **medinc**, and **uninsured** at the 5-percent level of significance using the *t*-table in the textbook. Show your null and alternative hypotheses and list the critical *t*-statistic used for each hypothesis test. For which coefficients can you reject the null hypothesis?

Step 6: Hypothesis Testing (*p*-values)

Test the slope coefficients of **gunlaw**, **metro**, and **obesity** at the 5-percent level of significance using *p*-values. List the *p*-value used for each test. For which coefficients can you reject the null hypothesis?

Step 7: Overall *F*-test

Use the overall *F*-statistic to test whether the regression is significant at the 5-percent level. Show your null and alternative hypotheses and your decision rule, and use the *F*-table.

Step 8: Drawing Conclusions

The absolute value of the coefficient of **gunlaw** is much larger than the absolute value of the coefficient of **smoke**. Does this mean that passing a gun law to protect children will have a bigger impact on life expectancy than reducing smoking by three percentage points? Explain.

Chapter 6

Specification: Choosing the Independent Variables

6.1 Omitted Variables

6.2 Irrelevant Variables

6.3 An Illustration of the Misuse of Specification Criteria

6.4 Specification Searches

6.5 An Example of Choosing Independent Variables

6.6 Summary and Exercises

6.7 Appendix: Additional Specification Criteria

Before any equation can be estimated, it must be specified. *Specifying* an econometric equation consists of three parts: choosing the correct independent variables, the correct functional form, and the correct form of the stochastic error term.

A **specification error** results when any one of these choices is made incorrectly. This chapter is concerned with only the first of these, choosing the variables; the second and third choices will be taken up in later chapters.

The fact that researchers can decide which independent variables to include in regression equations is a source of both strength and weakness in econometrics. The strength is that the equations can be formulated to fit individual needs, but the weakness is that researchers can estimate many different specifications until they find the one that "proves" their point, even if many other results disprove it. A major goal of this chapter is to help you understand how to choose variables for your regressions without falling prey to the various errors that result from misusing the ability to choose.

The primary consideration in deciding whether an independent variable belongs in an equation is whether the variable is essential to the regression on the basis of theory. If the answer is an unambiguous yes, then the variable definitely should be included in the equation, even if it seems to be

---

157

lacking in statistical significance. If theory is ambivalent or less emphatic, a dilemma arises. Leaving a relevant variable out of an equation is likely to bias the remaining estimates, but including an irrelevant variable leads to higher variances of the estimated coefficients. Although we'll develop statistical tools to help us deal with this decision, it's difficult in practice to be sure that a variable is relevant, and so the problem often remains unresolved.

We devote the fourth section of the chapter to specification searches and the pros and cons of various approaches to such searches. For example, poorly done specification searches often cause bias or make the usual tests of significance inapplicable. Instead, we suggest trying to minimize the number of regressions estimated and relying as much as possible on theory rather than statistical fit when choosing variables. There are no pat answers, however, and so the final decisions must be left to each individual researcher.

6.1 Omitted Variables

Suppose that you forget to include one of the relevant independent variables when you first specify an equation (after all, no one's perfect!). Or suppose that you can't get data for one of the variables that you *do* think of. The result in both these situations is an **omitted variable**, defined as an important explanatory variable that has been left out of a regression equation.

Whenever you have an omitted (or *left-out*) variable, the interpretation and use of your estimated equation become suspect. Leaving out a relevant variable, like price from a demand equation, not only prevents you from getting an estimate of the coefficient of price but also usually causes bias in the estimated coefficients of the variables that are in the equation.

The bias caused by leaving a variable out of an equation is called **omitted variable bias**. In an equation with more than one independent variable, the coefficient β_k represents the change in the dependent variable Y caused by a one-unit increase in the independent variable X_k, holding constant the other independent variables in the equation. If a variable is omitted, then it is not included as an independent variable, and it is not held constant for the calculation and interpretation of $\hat{\beta}_k$. This omission can cause bias: It can force the expected value of the estimated coefficient away from the true value of the population coefficient.

Thus, omitting a relevant variable is usually evidence that the entire estimated equation is suspect, because of the likely bias in the coefficients of the variables that remain in the equation. Let's look at this issue in more detail.

The Consequences of an Omitted Variable

What happens if you omit an important variable from your equation (perhaps because you can't get the data for the variable or didn't even think of the variable in the first place)? The major consequence of omitting a relevant independent variable from an equation is to cause bias in the regression coefficients that remain in the equation. Suppose that the true regression model is:

$$Y_i = \beta_0 + \beta_1 X_{1i} + \beta_2 X_{2i} + \epsilon_i \tag{6.1}$$

where ϵ_i is a classical error term. If you omit X_2 from the equation, then the equation becomes:

$$Y_i = \beta_0^* + \beta_1^* X_{1i} + \epsilon_i^* \tag{6.2}$$

where ϵ_i^* equals:

$$\epsilon_i^* = \epsilon_i + \beta_2 X_{2i} \tag{6.3}$$

because the stochastic error term includes the effects of any omitted variables, as mentioned in Section 1.2. Why does Equation 6.2 include β_0^* and β_1^* instead of β_0 and β_1? The answer lies in the meaning of a regression coefficient. β_1 is the impact of a one-unit increase in X_1 on Y, *holding X_2 constant*, but X_2 isn't in Equation 6.2, so OLS can't hold it constant. As a result, β_1^* is the impact of a one-unit increase in X_1 on Y, *not holding X_2 constant*.

From Equations 6.2 and 6.3, it might seem as though we could get unbiased estimates even if we left X_2 out of the equation. Unfortunately, this is not the case,[1] because the included coefficients almost surely pick up some of the effect of the omitted variable and therefore will change, causing bias. To see why, take another look at Equations 6.2 and 6.3. Most pairs of variables are correlated to some degree, so X_1 and X_2 almost surely are correlated. When X_2 is omitted from the equation, the impact of X_2 goes into ϵ^*, so ϵ^* and X_2 are correlated. Thus if X_2 is omitted from the equation and X_1 and X_2 are correlated, both X_1 and ϵ^* will change when X_2 changes, and the error term will no longer be independent of the explanatory variable. That violates Classical Assumption III!

In other words, if we leave an important variable out of an equation, we violate Classical Assumption III (that the explanatory variables are independent of the error term), unless the omitted variable is uncorrelated with all the included independent variables (which is extremely unlikely). In general,

---

1. To avoid bias, X_1 and X_2 must be perfectly uncorrelated in the sample—an extremely unlikely result.

when there is a violation of one of the Classical Assumptions, the Gauss–Markov Theorem does not hold, and the OLS estimates are not BLUE. Given linear estimators, this means that the estimated coefficients are no longer unbiased or are no longer minimum variance (for all linear unbiased estimators), or both. In such a circumstance, econometricians first determine the exact property (unbiasedness or minimum variance) that no longer holds and then suggest an alternative estimation technique that might be better than OLS.

An omitted variable causes Classical Assumption III to be violated in a way that causes bias. Estimating Equation 6.2 when Equation 6.1 is the truth will cause bias. This means that:

$$E(\hat{\beta}_1^*) \neq \beta_1 \tag{6.4}$$

Instead of having an expected value equal to the true β_1, the estimate will compensate for the fact that X_2 is missing from the equation. If X_1 and X_2 are correlated and X_2 is omitted from the equation, then the OLS estimation procedure will attribute to X_1 variations in Y that are actually caused by X_2, and a biased estimate of β_1 will result.

To see how an omitted variable can cause bias, let's look at an extremely early application of regression analysis.[2] During World War II, the Allies were interested in improving the accuracy of their bombers, so they estimated an equation where the dependent variable was bomber accuracy and the independent variables included such things as the speed and altitude of the bombing group and the amount of enemy fighter opposition. As expected, the estimated coefficients supported the hypotheses that higher speeds and higher altitudes led to larger aiming errors, but the researchers were shocked to discover that more enemy fighter opposition appeared to improve the accuracy of the pilot and bombardier! What was going on?

The answer is omitted variable bias. It turns out that the equation didn't include a variable for cloud cover over the target, and cloud cover typically prevented enemy fighters from flying. When it was cloudy, the bombers couldn't see the ground and made large errors, but OLS attributed these errors to the lack of enemy fighter opposition because there was no variable for cloud cover in the equation and because few fighters could fly when it was cloudy. Put differently, the coefficient of enemy fighters picked up the impact of the omitted variable of cloud cover because the two variables were highly correlated. This is omitted variable bias!

---

2. Adapted from Frederick Mosteller and John Tukey, *Data Analysis and Regression: A Second Course in Statistics* (Reading, MA: Addison-Wesley, 1977), p. 318.

To generalize for a model with two independent variables, the expected value of the coefficient of an included variable (X_1) when a relevant variable (X_2) is omitted from the equation equals:

$$E(\hat{\beta}_1^*) = \beta_1 + \beta_2 \cdot \hat{\alpha}_1 \qquad (6.5)$$

where $\hat{\alpha}_1$ is an estimate of the slope coefficient of the secondary regression that relates X_2 to X_1:

$$\hat{X}_{2i} = \hat{\alpha}_0 + \hat{\alpha}_1 X_{1i} \qquad (6.6)$$

If X_1 and X_2 are positively correlated, $\hat{\alpha}_1$ will be positive. If X_1 and X_2 are negatively correlated, $\hat{\alpha}_1$ will be negative. If X_1 and X_2 are uncorrelated, $\hat{\alpha}_1$ will be zero.

Let's take a look at Equation 6.5. It states that the expected value of the included variable's coefficient is equal to its true value plus the omitted variable's true coefficient times a function of the correlation between the included and omitted variables.[3] Since the expected value of an unbiased estimate equals the true value, the right-hand term in Equation 6.5 measures the omitted variable bias in the equation:

$$\text{Bias} = \beta_2 \hat{\alpha}_1 \qquad (6.7)$$

In general terms, the bias thus equals the coefficient of the omitted variable times a function of the correlation between the included and omitted variables.

This bias exists unless:

1. the true coefficient equals zero, or

2. the included and omitted variables are uncorrelated in the sample.

The term $\beta_2 \hat{\alpha}_1$ is the amount of **expected bias** introduced into the estimate of the coefficient of the included variable by leaving out the omitted variable. Although it's true that there is no bias if the included and excluded variables are uncorrelated, there almost always is some correlation between any two variables in the real world, and so bias is almost always caused by the omission of a relevant variable.

---

3. Equations 6.5 and 6.7 hold when there are exactly two independent variables, but the more general equations are quite similar.

An Example of Omitted Variable Bias

For an example of omitted variable bias, let's go back to Equation 5.4, the Woody's restaurants model that we first studied in Section 3.2:

$$\hat{Y}_i = 102,192 - 9075N_i + 0.3547P_i + 1.288I_i \qquad (5.4)$$
$$(2053) \quad (0.0727) \quad (0.543)$$
$$t = -4.42 \qquad 4.88 \qquad 2.37$$
$$N = 33 \qquad \overline{R}^2 = .579$$

where Y = customers (check volume), N = the number of competitive restaurants nearby, P = the population nearby, and I = the average household income nearby.

Let's take a look at what happens if we drop population (P) from the equation:

$$Y_i = 84,439 - 1487N_i + 2.322I_i \qquad (6.8)$$
$$(1778) \quad (0.664)$$
$$t = \qquad -0.84 \qquad +3.50$$
$$N = 33 \qquad \overline{R}^2 = .258$$

Stop for a minute and compare Equations 5.4 and 6.8. The most noticeable difference is that $\overline{R}^2$ has fallen from .579 to .258 because we've omitted population. However, check out the estimated coefficient and t-score for competition (N). The coefficient has changed from -9075 to -1487, and the t-score has changed from -4.42 to -0.84. What a disaster! The coefficient of N now is insignificantly different from zero! How could this have happened?

The answer is omitted variable bias. Population and competition are understandably quite correlated; the more people there are in an area, the more restaurants you'd expect to find. As a result, when population is dropped from the equation, OLS attributes the impact of the omitted variable to the included variables to the extent that they're correlated with the omitted variable. Was this positive or negative bias? Well, $\hat{\beta}_N$ increased from a large negative number to a smaller negative number, so the bias is positive. The positive impact of population almost completely offset the negative impact of competition, resulting in a coefficient not far from zero.

Note that we could have predicted that the bias was going to be positive by using our expected bias equation,[4] Equation 6.7. Because the expected sign of

---

4. It is important to note the distinction between expected bias and any actual observed differences between coefficient estimates. Because of the random nature of the error term (and hence the $\hat{\beta}$s), the change in an estimated coefficient brought about by dropping a relevant variable from the equation will not necessarily be in the expected direction. Biasedness refers to the central tendency of the sampling distribution of the $\hat{\beta}$s, not to every single drawing from that distribution. However, we usually (and justifiably) rely on these general tendencies.

β_P is positive and because we'd expect $\hat{\alpha}_1$ (related to the correlation between population and competition) to be positive, the expected bias in $\hat{\beta}_N$ is positive:

$$\text{Expected bias in } \hat{\beta}_N = \beta_P \cdot \hat{\alpha}_1 = (+)(+) = + \qquad (6.9)$$

Just as we would have predicted, omitting N caused positive bias. Leaving population out of the equation caused the coefficient of competition to pick up the impact of population to the extent that the two variables were correlated.

To sum, if a relevant variable is left out of a regression equation,

1. there is no longer an estimate of the coefficient of that variable in the equation, and

2. the coefficients of the remaining variables are likely to be biased.

Although the amount of the bias might not be very large in some cases (when, for instance, there is little correlation between the included and excluded variables), it is extremely likely that at least a small amount of omitted variable bias will be present in all such situations.

Correcting for an Omitted Variable

In theory, the solution to a problem of omitted variable bias seems easy: Add the omitted variable to the equation! Unfortunately, that's easier said than done, for a couple of reasons.

First, omitted variable bias is hard to detect. The amount of bias introduced can be small and not immediately detectable. This is especially true when there is no reason to believe that you have misspecified the model. Some indications of specification bias are obvious (such as an estimated coefficient that is significant in the direction opposite from that expected), but others are not so clear. The best indicators of an omitted relevant variable are the theoretical underpinnings of the model itself. What variables *must* be included? What signs do you expect? Do you have any notions about the range into which the coefficient values should fall? The best way to avoid omitting an important variable is to invest the time in thinking carefully through the equation before the data are entered into the computer.

A second source of complexity is the problem of choosing which variable to add to an equation once you decide that it is suffering from omitted variable bias. Some beginning researchers, when faced with this dilemma, will add all the possible relevant variables to the equation at once, but this process leads to less precise estimates, as will be discussed in the next section. Other beginning researchers will test a number of different variables and keep the one in the equation that does the best statistical job of appearing to reduce the bias (by giving plausible signs and satisfactory *t*-values). This technique, adding a "left-out" variable to "fix" a strange-looking regression result, is invalid because the variable that best corrects a case of specification bias might do so only by chance rather than by being the true solution to the problem. In such an instance, the "fixed" equation may give superb statistical results for the sample at hand but then do terribly when applied to other samples because it does not describe the characteristics of the true population.

Dropping a variable will not help cure omitted variable bias. If the sign of an estimated coefficient is different from expected, it cannot be changed to the expected direction by dropping a variable that has a *t*-score lower (in absolute value) than the *t*-score of the coefficient estimate that has the unexpected sign. Furthermore, the sign in general will not likely change even if the variable to be deleted has a large *t*-score.[5]

If an unexpected result leads you to believe that you have an omitted variable, one way to decide which variable to add to the equation is to use expected bias analysis. If the sign of the expected bias (using Equation 6.7) is the same as the sign of your unexpected result, then the variable might be the source of the apparent bias. If the sign of the expected bias is *not* the same as the sign of your unexpected result, however, then the variable is extremely unlikely to have caused your unexpected result. Expected bias analysis should be used only when you're choosing between theoretically sound potential variables.

Although you can never actually observe bias (since you don't know the true β), the use of this technique to screen potential causes of specification bias should reduce the number of regressions run and increase the validity of the results.

A brief warning: It may be tempting to conduct what might be called "residual analysis" by examining a plot of the residuals in an attempt to find patterns that suggest variables that have been accidentally omitted. A major problem with this approach is that the coefficients of the estimated equation will possibly have some of the effects of the left-out variable already altering their estimated values. Thus, residuals may show a pattern that only vaguely resembles the pattern of the actual omitted variable. The chances are high that the pattern shown in the residuals may lead to the selection of an incorrect variable. In addition, care should be taken to use residual analysis only to choose between theoretically sound candidate variables rather than to generate those candidates.

---

5. Ignazio Visco, "On Obtaining the Right Sign of a Coefficient Estimate by Omitting a Variable from the Regression," *Journal of Econometrics*, Vol. 7, No. 1, pp. 115–117.

6.2   Irrelevant Variables

What happens if you include a variable in an equation that doesn't belong there? This case, **irrelevant variables**, is the converse of omitted variables and can be analyzed using the model we developed in Section 6.1. The addition of a variable to an equation where it doesn't belong does not cause bias, but it does increase the variances of the estimated coefficients of the included variables.

Impact of Irrelevant Variables

If the true regression specification is:

$$Y_i = \beta_0 + \beta_1 X_{1i} + \epsilon_i \tag{6.10}$$

but the researcher for some reason includes an extra variable,

$$Y_i = \beta_0 + \beta_1 X_{1i} + \beta_2 X_{2i} + \epsilon_i^{**} \tag{6.11}$$

the misspecified equation's error term can be seen to be:

$$\epsilon_i^{**} = \epsilon_i - \beta_2 X_{2i} \tag{6.12}$$

Such a mistake won't cause bias if the true coefficient of the irrelevant variable is zero. That is, an estimate of β_1 in Equation 6.11 is unbiased when $\beta_2 = 0$.

However, the inclusion of an irrelevant variable will increase the variance of the estimated coefficients, and this increased variance will tend to decrease the absolute magnitude of their t-scores. Also, an irrelevant variable usually will decrease the $\overline{R}^2$ (but not the R^2).

Thus, although the irrelevant variable causes no bias, it causes problems for the regression because it reduces the t-scores and $\overline{R}^2$.

An Example of an Irrelevant Variable

Let's return to the Woody's equation and see what happens when we add an irrelevant variable to the model. The original equation was:

$$\hat{Y}_i = 102{,}192 - 9075 N_i + 0.3547 P_i + 1.288 I_i \tag{5.4}$$
$$(2053) \quad (0.0727) \quad (0.543)$$
$$t = -4.42 \qquad 4.88 \qquad 2.37$$
$$N = 33 \qquad \overline{R}^2 = .579$$

where Y = customers (check volume), N = the number of competitive restaurants nearby, P = the population nearby, and I = the average household income nearby.

What's the most irrelevant variable that you can think of? How about A_i = the last three digits of the street address of the ith Woody's restaurant? That's pretty random! If we add A_i to Equation 5.4, we get:

$$\hat{Y}_i = 98,125 - 8975N_i + 0.360P_i + 1.301I_i + 58.07A_i \qquad (6.13)$$
$$\phantom{\hat{Y}_i = 98,125} (2082) \quad (0.074) \quad (0.550) \quad (95.21)$$
$$t = \quad -4.31 \quad +4.86 \quad +2.37 \quad +0.61$$
$$N = 33 \qquad \overline{R}^2 = .569$$

A comparison of Equations 5.4 and 6.13 will make the theory in Section 6.2 come to life. First of all, $\overline{R}^2$ has fallen slightly, indicating the reduction in fit adjusted for degrees of freedom. Second, none of the regression coefficients from the original equation changed very much; compare these results with the larger differences between Equations 5.4 and 6.9. Further, the standard errors of the estimated coefficients increased. Finally, the t-score for the potential variable (A) is small, indicating that it is not significantly different from zero. Given the theoretical shakiness of the new variable, these results indicate that it is irrelevant and never should have been included in the regression.

Four Important Specification Criteria

We have now discussed at least four valid criteria to help decide whether a given variable belongs in the equation. We think these criteria are so important that we urge beginning researchers to work through them every time a variable is added or subtracted.

1. *Theory:* Is the variable's place in the equation unambiguous and theoretically sound?
2. *t-Test:* Is the variable's estimated coefficient significant in the expected direction?
3. $\overline{R}^2$: Does the overall fit of the equation (adjusted for degrees of freedom) improve when the variable is added to the equation?
4. *Bias:* Do other variables' coefficients change significantly when the variable is added to the equation?

If all these conditions hold, the variable belongs in the equation; if none of them do, the variable is irrelevant and can be safely excluded from the equation. When a typical omitted relevant variable is included in the equation, its inclusion probably will increase $\overline{R}^2$ and change at least one other coefficient.

If an irrelevant variable, on the other hand, is included, it will reduce $\overline{R}^2$, have an insignificant t-score, and have little impact on the other variables' coefficients.

In many cases, all four criteria do not agree. It is possible for a variable to have an insignificant t-score that is greater than one, for example. In such a case, it can be shown that $\overline{R}^2$ will go up when the variable is added to the equation and yet the t-score still will be insignificant.

Whenever our four specification criteria disagree, the econometrician must use careful judgment and should not rely on a single criterion like $\overline{R}^2$ to determine the specification. Researchers should not misuse this freedom by testing various combinations of variables until they find the results that appear to statistically support the point they want to make. All such decisions are a bit easier when you realize that the single most important determinant of a variable's relevance is its theoretical justification. No amount of statistical evidence should make a theoretical necessity into an "irrelevant" variable. Once in a while, a researcher is forced to leave a theoretically important variable out of an equation for lack of data; in such cases, the usefulness of the equation is limited.

6.3 An Illustration of the Misuse of Specification Criteria

At times, the four specification criteria outlined in the previous section will lead the researcher to an incorrect conclusion if those criteria are applied to a problem without proper concern for economic principles or common sense. In particular, a t-score can often be insignificant for reasons other than the presence of an irrelevant variable. Since economic theory is the most important test for including a variable, an example of why a variable should not be dropped from an equation simply because it has an insignificant t-score is in order.

Suppose you believe that the demand for Brazilian coffee in the United States is a negative function of the real price of Brazilian coffee (P_{bc}) and a positive function of both the real price of tea (P_t) and real disposable income in the United States (Y_d).[6] Suppose further that you obtain the data, run the implied regression, and observe the following results:

$$\widehat{COFFEE} = 9.1 + 7.8P_{bc} + 2.4P_t + 0.0035Y_d \qquad (6.14)$$
$$(15.6) \quad (1.2) \quad (0.0010)$$
$$t = 0.5 \quad 2.0 \quad 3.5$$
$$\overline{R}^2 = .60 \quad N = 25$$

---

6. This example was inspired by a similar one concerning Ceylonese tea published in Potluri Rao and Roger LeRoy Miller, *Applied Econometrics* (Belmont, CA: Wadsworth, 1971), pp. 38–40. This wonderful book is now out of print.

The coefficients of the second and third variables, P_t and Y_d, appear to be fairly significant in the direction you hypothesized, but the first variable, P_{bc}, appears to have an insignificant coefficient with an unexpected sign. If you think there is a possibility that the demand for Brazilian coffee is price-inelastic (that is, its coefficient is zero), you might decide to run the same equation without the price variable, obtaining:

$$\widehat{COFFEE} = 9.3 + 2.6P_t + 0.0036Y_d \qquad (6.15)$$
$$(1.0) \quad (0.0009)$$
$$t = 2.6 \qquad 4.0$$
$$\overline{R}^2 = .61 \quad N = 25$$

By comparing Equations 6.14 and 6.15, we can apply our four specification criteria for the inclusion of a variable in an equation that were outlined in the previous section:

1. *Theory:* If it's possible that the demand for coffee could be price-inelastic, the theory behind dropping the variable seems plausible.
2. *t-Test:* The *t*-score of the possibly irrelevant variable is 0.5, insignificant at any level.
3. $\overline{R}^2$: $\overline{R}^2$ increases when the variable is dropped, indicating that the variable is irrelevant.
4. *Bias:* The remaining coefficients change only a small amount when P_{bc} is dropped, suggesting that there is little—if any—bias caused by excluding the variable.

Based upon this analysis, you might conclude that the demand for Brazilian coffee is indeed price-inelastic and that the variable is therefore irrelevant and should be dropped from the model. As it turns out, this conclusion would be unwarranted. Although the elasticity of demand for coffee in general might be fairly low (actually, the evidence suggests that it is inelastic only over a particular range of prices), it is hard to believe that Brazilian coffee is immune to price competition from other kinds of coffee. Indeed, one would expect quite a bit of sensitivity in the demand for Brazilian coffee with respect to the price of, for example, Colombian coffee. To test this hypothesis, the price of Colombian coffee (P_{cc}) should be added to the original Equation 6.14:

$$\widehat{COFFEE} = 10.0 + 8.0P_{cc} - 5.6P_{bc} + 2.6P_t + 0.0030Y_d \qquad (6.16)$$
$$(4.0) \quad (2.0) \quad (1.3) \quad (0.0010)$$
$$t = 2.0 \quad -2.8 \quad 2.0 \quad 3.0$$
$$\overline{R}^2 = .65 \quad N = 25$$

By comparing Equations 6.14 and 6.16, we can once again apply our four specification criteria:

1. *Theory:* Both prices should always have been included in the model; their logical justification is quite strong.

2. *t-Test:* The *t*-score of the new variable, the price of Colombian coffee, is 2.0, significant at most levels.

3. $\overline{R}^2$: $\overline{R}^2$ increases with the addition of the variable, indicating that the variable was an omitted variable.

4. *Bias:* Although two of the coefficients remain virtually unchanged, indicating that the correlations between these variables and the price of Colombian coffee variable are low, the coefficient for the price of Brazilian coffee does change significantly, indicating bias in the original result.

The moral to be drawn is that theoretical considerations never should be discarded, even in the face of statistical insignificance. If a variable known to be extremely important from a theoretical point of view turns out to be statistically insignificant in a particular sample, that variable should be left in the equation despite the fact that it makes the results look bad.

Don't conclude that the particular path outlined in this example is the correct way to specify an equation. Trying a long string of possible variables until you get the particular one that makes the coefficient of P_{bc} turn negative and significant is not the way to obtain a result that will stand up well to other samples or alternative hypotheses. The original equation should never have been run without the Colombian coffee price variable. Instead, the problem should have been analyzed enough so that such errors of omission were unlikely before any regressions were attempted at all. The more thinking that's done before the first regression is run, and the fewer alternative specifications that are estimated, the better the regression results are likely to be.

6.4 Specification Searches

One of the weaknesses of econometrics is that a researcher potentially can manipulate a data set to produce almost *any* result by specifying different regressions until estimates with the desired properties are obtained. Because the integrity of all empirical work is thus open to question, the subject of how to search for the best specification is quite controversial among econometricians. Our goal in this section isn't to summarize or settle this controversy; instead, we hope to provide some guidance and insight for beginning researchers.

Best Practices in Specification Searches

The issue of how best to choose a specification from among alternative possibilities is a difficult one, but our experience leads us to make the following recommendations:

1. Rely on theory rather than statistical fit as much as possible when choosing variables, functional forms, and the like.
2. Minimize the number of equations estimated (except for sensitivity analysis, to be discussed later in this section).
3. Reveal, in a footnote or appendix, all alternative specifications estimated.

If theory, not $\overline{R}^2$ or t-scores, is the most important criterion for the inclusion of a variable in a regression equation, then it follows that most of the work of specifying a model should be done before you attempt to estimate the equation. Since it's unreasonable to expect researchers to be perfect, there will be times when additional specifications must be estimated. However, these new estimates should be few in number and should be thoroughly grounded in theory. In addition, they should be explicitly taken into account when testing for significance and/or summarizing results. In this way, the danger of misleading the reader about the statistical properties of the final equation will be reduced.

Sequential Specification Searches

Most econometricians tend to specify equations by estimating an initial equation and then sequentially dropping or adding variables (or changing functional forms) until a plausible equation is found with "good statistics." Faced with knowing that a few variables are relevant (on the basis of theory) but not knowing whether other additional variables also are relevant, the generally accepted practice appears to be inspecting $\overline{R}^2$ and t-tests for all variables for each specification. Indeed, casual reading of the previous section might make it seem as if such a sequential specification search is the best way to go about finding the "truth." Instead, as we shall see, there is a vast difference between a sequential specification search and our recommended approach.

The **sequential specification search** technique allows a researcher to estimate an undisclosed number of regressions and then present a final choice (which is based upon an unspecified set of expectations about the signs and significance of the coefficients) as if it were the only specification estimated. Such a method misstates the statistical validity of the regression results for two reasons:

1. The statistical significance of the results is overestimated because the estimations of the previous regressions are ignored.

2. The expectations used by the researcher to choose between various regression results rarely, if ever, are disclosed. Thus the reader has no way of knowing whether all the other regression results had opposite signs or insignificant coefficients for the important variables.

Unfortunately, there is no universally accepted way of conducting sequential searches, primarily because the appropriate test at one stage in the procedure depends on which tests previously were conducted, and also because the tests have been very difficult to invent.

Instead we recommend trying to keep the number of regressions estimated as low as possible; to focus on theoretical considerations when choosing variables or functional forms; and to document all the various specifications investigated. That is, we recommend combining parsimony (using theory and analysis to limit the number of specifications estimated) with disclosure (reporting all the equations estimated).

Not everyone agrees with our advice. Some researchers feel that the true model will show through if given the chance and that the best statistical results (including signs of coefficients, etc.) are most likely to have come from the true specification. In addition, reasonable people often disagree as to what the "true" model should look like. As a result, different researchers can look at the same data set and come up with very different "best" equations. Because this can happen, the distinction between good and bad econometrics is not always as clear-cut as is implied by the previous paragraphs. As long as researchers have a healthy respect for the dangers inherent in specification searches, they are very likely to proceed in a reasonable way.

Bias Caused by Relying on the *t*-Test or $\overline{R}^2$ to Choose Variables

In the previous section, we stated that sequential specification searches are likely to mislead researchers about the statistical properties of their results. In particular, the practice of dropping a potential independent variable simply because its coefficient has a low *t*-score or because it lowers $\overline{R}^2$ will cause systematic bias in the estimated coefficients (and their *t*-scores) of the remaining variables.

Let's say the hypothesized model is:

$$Y_i = \beta_0 + \beta_1 X_{1i} + \beta_2 X_{2i} + \epsilon_i \tag{6.17}$$

Assume further that, on the basis of theory, we are certain that X_1 belongs in the equation but that we are not as certain that X_2 belongs. Many inexperienced researchers use only the t-test on $\hat{\beta}_2$ to determine whether X_2 should be included. If this preliminary t-test indicates that $\hat{\beta}_2$ is significantly different from zero, then these researchers leave X_2 in the equation. If, however, the t-test does *not* indicate that $\hat{\beta}_2$ is significantly different from zero, then such researchers drop X_2 from the equation and consider Y to be a function of X_1.

Two kinds of mistakes can be made using such a system. First, X_2 sometimes can be left in the equation when it does not belong there, but such a mistake does not change the expected value of $\hat{\beta}_1$.

Second, X_2 sometimes can be dropped from the equation when it belongs. In this second case, the estimated coefficient of X_1 will be biased. In other words, $\hat{\beta}_1$ will be biased every time X_2 belongs in the equation and is left out, and X_2 will be left out every time that its estimated coefficient is not significantly different from zero. We will have systematic bias in our equation!

To summarize, the t-test is biased by sequential specification searches. Since most researchers consider a number of different variables before settling on the final model, someone who relies on the t-test or $\overline{R}^2$ is likely to encounter this problem systematically.

Data Mining

Data mining involves estimating a wide variety of alternative specifications *before* a "best" equation is chosen. Readers of this text will not be surprised to hear that we urge extreme caution when data mining. Improperly done data mining is worse than doing nothing at all.

Done properly, data mining involves exploring a data set not for the purpose of testing hypotheses or finding a specification, but for the purpose of uncovering empirical regularities that can inform economic theory.[7] After all, we can't expect economic theorists to think of everything!

Be careful, however! If you develop a hypothesis using data mining techniques, you must test that hypothesis on a *different* data set (or in a different context) than the one you used to develop the hypothesis. A new data set

---

7. For an excellent presentation of this approach, see Lawrence H. Summers, "The Scientific Illusion in Empirical Macroeconomics," *Scandinavian Journal of Economics*, Vol. 93, No. 2, pp. 129–148.

must be used because our typical statistical tests have little meaning if the new hypothesis is tested on the data set that was used to generate it. After all, the researcher already knows ahead of time what the results will be! The use of dual data sets is easiest when there is a plethora of data. This sometimes is the case in cross-sectional research projects but rarely is the case for time series research.

Data mining without using dual data sets is almost surely the worst way to choose a specification. In such a situation, a researcher could estimate virtually every possible combination of the various alternative independent variables, could choose the results that "look" the best, and then could report the "best" equation as if no data mining had been done. This improper use of data mining ignores the fact that a number of specifications have been examined before the final one is reported.

In addition, data mining will cause you to choose specifications that reflect the peculiarities of your particular data set. How does this happen? Suppose you have 100 true null hypotheses and you run 100 tests of these hypotheses. At the 5-percent level of significance, you'd expect to reject about five true null hypotheses and thus make about five Type I Errors. By looking for high t-values, a data mining search procedure will find these Type I Errors and incorporate them into your specification. As a result, the reported t-scores will overstate the statistical significance of the estimated coefficients.

In essence, improper data mining to obtain desired statistics for the final regression equation is a potentially unethical empirical research method. Whether the improper data mining is accomplished by estimating one equation at a time or by estimating batches of equations or by techniques like stepwise regression procedures,[8] the conclusion is the same. Hypotheses developed by data mining should always be tested on a data set different from the one that was used to develop the hypothesis. Otherwise, the researcher hasn't found any scientific evidence to support the hypothesis; rather, a specification has been chosen in a way that is essentially misleading. As put by one econometrician, "if you torture the data long enough, they will confess."[9]

---

8. A stepwise regression involves the use of an automated computer program to choose the independent variables in an equation. The researcher specifies a "shopping list" of possible independent variables, and then the computer estimates a number of equations until it finds the one that maximizes $\overline{R}^2$. Such stepwise techniques are deficient in the face of multicollinearity (to be discussed in Chapter 8) and they run the risk that the chosen specification will have little theoretical justification and/or will have coefficients with unexpected signs. Because of these pitfalls, econometricians avoid stepwise procedures.

9. Thomas Mayer, "Economics as a Hard Science: Realistic Goal or Wishful Thinking?" *Economic Inquiry*, Vol. 18, No. 2, p. 175. (This quote also has been attributed to Ronald Coase.)

Sensitivity Analysis

Throughout this text, we've encouraged you to estimate as few specifications as possible and to avoid depending on fit alone to choose between those specifications. If you read the current economics literature, however, it won't take you long to find well-known researchers who have estimated five or more specifications and then have listed all their results in an academic journal article. What's going on?

In almost every case, these authors have employed a technique called sensitivity analysis. **Sensitivity analysis** consists of purposely running a number of alternative specifications to determine whether particular results are *robust* (not statistical flukes). In essence, we're trying to determine how sensitive a potential "best" equation is to a change in specification because the true specification isn't known. Researchers who use sensitivity analysis run (and report on) a number of different reasonable specifications and tend to discount a result that appears significant in some specifications and insignificant in others. Indeed, the whole purpose of sensitivity analysis is to gain confidence that a particular result is significant in a variety of alternative specifications, functional forms, variable definitions, and/or subsets of the data.

6.5   An Example of Choosing Independent Variables

It's time to get some experience choosing independent variables. After all, every equation so far in the text has come with the specification already determined, but once you've finished this course you'll have to make all such specification decisions on your own. In future chapters, we'll use a technique called "interactive regression learning exercises" to allow you to make your own actual specification choices and get feedback on your choices. To start, though, let's work through a specification together.

To keep things as simple as possible, we'll begin with a topic near and dear to your heart—your GPA! Suppose a friend who attends a small liberal arts college surveys all 25 members of her econometrics class, obtains data on the variables listed here, and asks for your help in choosing a specification:

GPA_i = the cumulative college grade point average of the *i*th student on a four-point scale

$HGPA_i$ = the cumulative high school grade point average of the *i*th student on a four-point scale

$MSAT_i$ = the highest score earned by the *i*th student on the math section of the SAT test (800 maximum)

$VSAT_i$ = the highest score earned by the ith student on the verbal section of the SAT test (800 maximum)

SAT_i = $MSAT_i + VSAT_i$

$GREK_i$ = a dummy variable equal to 1 if the ith student is a member of a fraternity or sorority, 0 otherwise

HRS_i = the ith student's estimate of the average number of hours spent studying per course per week in college

$PRIV_i$ = a dummy variable equal to 1 if the ith student graduated from a private high school, 0 otherwise

$JOCK_i$ = a dummy variable equal to 1 if the ith student is or was a member of a varsity intercollegiate athletic team for at least one season, 0 otherwise

$lnEX_i$ = the natural log of the number of full courses that the ith student has completed in college

Assuming that GPA_i is the dependent variable, which independent variables would you choose? Before you answer, think through the possibilities carefully. What does the literature tell us on this subject? (Is there literature?) What are the expected signs of each of the coefficients? How strong is the theory behind each variable? Which variables seem obviously important? Which variables seem potentially irrelevant or redundant? Are there any other variables that you wish your friend had collected?

To get the most out of this example, you should take the time to *write down* the exact specification that you would run:

$$GPA_i = f(?, ?, ?, ?, ?) + \epsilon$$

It's hard for most beginning econometricians to avoid the temptation of including *all* of these variables in a GPA equation and then dropping any variables that have insignificant t-scores. Even though we mentioned in the previous section that such a specification search procedure will result in biased coefficient estimates, most beginners don't trust their own judgment and tend to include too many variables. With this warning in mind, do you want to make any changes in your proposed specification?

No? OK, let's compare notes. We believe that grades are a function of a student's ability, how hard the student works, and the student's experience taking college courses. Consequently, our specification would be:

$$\overset{+}{} \qquad \overset{+}{} \qquad \overset{+}{}$$
$$GPA_i = \beta_0 + \beta_1 HGPA_i + \beta_2 HRS_i + \beta_3 lnEX_i + \epsilon_i$$

We can already hear you complaining! What about SATs, you say? Everyone knows they're important. How about jocks and Greeks? Don't they have lower

GPAs? Don't prep schools grade harder and prepare students better than public high schools?

Before we answer, it's important to note that we think of specification choice as choosing which variables to *include*, not which variables to *exclude*. That is, we don't assume automatically that a given variable should be included in an equation simply because we can't think of a good reason for dropping it.

Given that, however, why did we choose the variables we did? First, we think that the best predictor of a student's college GPA is his or her high school GPA. We have a hunch that once you know HGPA, SATs are redundant, at least at a liberal arts college[10] where there are few multiple choice tests. In addition, we're concerned that possible racial and gender bias in the SAT test makes it a questionable measure of academic potential, but we recognize that we could be wrong on this issue.

As for the other variables, we're more confident. For example, we feel that once we know how many hours a week a student spends studying, we couldn't care less what that student does with the rest of his or her time, so JOCK and GREK are superfluous once HRS is included. In addition, the higher lnEX is, the better student study habits are and the more likely students are to be taking courses in their major. Finally, while we recognize that some private schools are superb and that some public schools are not, we'd guess that PRIV is irrelevant; it probably has only a minor effect.

If we estimate this specification on the 25 students, we obtain:

$$\widehat{GPA}_i = -0.26 + 0.49 HGPA_i + 0.06 HRS_i + 0.42 lnEX_i \qquad (6.18)$$
$$\phantom{\widehat{GPA}_i = -0.26 + } (0.21) \qquad\quad (0.02) \qquad\;\; (0.14)$$
$$\phantom{\widehat{GPA}_i =} t = 2.33 \qquad\qquad 3.00 \qquad\quad 3.00$$
$$\phantom{\widehat{GPA}_i} N = 25 \quad \overline{R}^2 = .585$$

Since we prefer this specification on theoretical grounds, since the overall fit seems reasonable, and since each coefficient meets our expectations in terms of sign, size, and significance, we consider this an acceptable equation. The only circumstance under which we'd consider estimating a second specification would be if we had theoretical reasons to believe that we had omitted a

10. In contrast, SATs tend to have a statistically significant effect on GPAs at large research universities. For example, see Andrew Barkley and Jerry Forst, "The Determinants of First-Year Academic Performance in the College of Agriculture at Kansas State University, 1990–1999," *Journal of Agricultural and Applied Economics*, Vol. 36, No 2, pp. 437–448.

relevant variable. The only variable that might meet this description is SAT_i (which we prefer to the individual MSAT and VSAT):

$$\widehat{GPA}_i = -0.92 + 0.47HGPA_i + 0.05HRS_i \qquad (6.19)$$
$$\phantom{\widehat{GPA}_i = -0.92 +}(0.22) \qquad\quad (0.02)$$
$$\phantom{\widehat{GPA}_i = -0.92 +}t = 2.12 \qquad\qquad 2.50$$
$$\phantom{\widehat{GPA}_i =}+ 0.44lnEX_i \;\; + 0.00060SAT_i$$
$$\phantom{\widehat{GPA}_i = +0.44}(0.14) \qquad\quad (0.00064)$$
$$\phantom{\widehat{GPA}_i = +0.44}t = 3.12 \qquad\qquad 0.93$$
$$N = 25 \quad \overline{R}^2 = .583$$

Let's use our four specification criteria to compare Equations 6.18 and 6.19:

1. *Theory:* As discussed previously, the theoretical validity of SAT tests is a matter of some academic controversy, but they still are one of the most-cited measures of academic potential in this country.

2. *t-Test:* The coefficient of SAT is positive, as we'd expect, but it's not significantly different from zero.

3. $\overline{R}^2$: As you'd expect (since SAT's t-score is under 1), $\overline{R}^2$ falls slightly when SAT is added.

4. *Bias:* None of the estimated slope coefficients changes substantially when SAT is added, though some of the t-scores do change because of the increase in the $SE(\hat{\beta})$s caused by the addition of SAT.

Thus, the statistical criteria do not convincingly contradict our theoretical contention that SAT is irrelevant.

Finally, it's important to recognize that different researchers could come up with different final equations on this topic. A researcher whose prior expectation was that SAT unambiguously belonged in the equation would have estimated Equation 6.19 and accepted that equation without bothering to estimate Equation 6.18. Other researchers, in the spirit of sensitivity analysis, would report both equations.

6.6 Summary

1. The omission of a variable from an equation will cause bias in the estimates of the remaining coefficients to the extent that the omitted variable is correlated with included variables.

2. The bias to be expected from leaving a variable out of an equation equals the coefficient of the excluded variable times a function of the simple correlation coefficient between the excluded variable and the included variable in question.

3. Including a variable in an equation in which it is actually irrelevant does not cause bias, but it will usually increase the variances of the included variables' estimated coefficients, thus lowering their t-values, widening their confidence intervals, and lowering $\overline{R}^2$.

4. Four useful criteria for the inclusion of a variable in an equation are:
   a. theory
   b. t-test
   c. $\overline{R}^2$
   d. bias

5. Theory, not statistical fit, should be the most important criterion for the inclusion of a variable in a regression equation. To do otherwise runs the risk of producing incorrect and/or disbelieved results.

EXERCISES

(The answers to the even-numbered exercises are in Appendix A.)

1. Write the meaning of each of the following terms without referring to the book (or your notes), and compare your definition with the version in the text for each:
   a. expected bias (p. 161)
   b. irrelevant variable (p. 165)
   c. omitted variable (p. 158)
   d. omitted variable bias (p. 158)
   e. sensitivity analysis (p. 174)
   f. sequential specification search (p. 170)
   g. specification error (p. 157)
   h. the four specification criteria (p. 166)

2. You've been hired by "Indo," the new Indonesian automobile manufacturer, to build a model of U.S. car prices in order to help the company undercut U.S. prices. Allowing Friedmaniac zeal to overwhelm any patriotic urges, you build the following model of the price of 35 different American-made 2016 U.S. sedans (standard errors in parentheses):

$$\text{Model A: } \hat{P}_i = 9.0 + 0.28W_i + 1.2T_i + 5.8C_i + 0.19L_i$$
$$(0.07) \quad (0.4) \quad (2.9) \quad (0.20)$$
$$\overline{R}^2 = .92$$

where: P_i = the list price of the ith car (thousands of dollars)
           W_i = the weight of the ith car (hundreds of pounds)
           T_i = a dummy equal to 1 if the ith car has an automatic trans-
                 mission, 0 otherwise
           C_i = a dummy equal to 1 if the ith car has cruise control, 0
                 otherwise
           L_i = the size of the engine of the ith car (in liters)

a. Your firm's pricing expert hypothesizes positive signs for all the slope coefficients in Model A. Test her expectations at the 5-percent level.

b. What econometric problems appear to exist in Model A? In particular, does the size of the coefficient of C cause any concern? Why? What could be the problem?

c. You decide to test the possibility that L is an irrelevant variable by dropping it and rerunning the equation, obtaining the following Model T equation. Which model do you prefer? Why? (*Hint:* Be sure to use our four specification criteria.)

$$\text{Model T: } \hat{P} = 24 + 0.29W_i + 1.2T_i + 5.9C_i$$
$$(0.07) \quad (0.30) \ (2.9)$$
$$\overline{R}^2 = .93$$

3. Consider the following annual model of the death rate (per million population) due to coronary heart disease in the United States (Y_t):

$$\hat{Y}_t = 140 + 10.0C_t + 4.0E_t - 1.0M_t$$
$$(2.5) \quad (1.0) \quad (0.5)$$
$$t = 4.0 \qquad 4.0 \quad -2.0$$
$$N = 31 \ (1975-2005) \quad \overline{R}^2 = .678$$

where: C_t = per capita cigarette consumption (pounds of tobacco) in year t
           E_t = per capita consumption of edible saturated fats (pounds of butter, margarine, and lard) in year t
           M_t = per capita consumption of meat (pounds) in year t

a. Create and test appropriate hypotheses at the 10-percent level. What, if anything, seems to be wrong with the estimated coefficient of M?

b. The most likely cause of a coefficient that is significant in the unexpected direction is omitted variable bias. Which of the following variables could possibly be an omitted variable that is causing $\hat{\beta}_M$'s unexpected sign? Explain. (*Hint:* Be sure to analyze expected bias in your explanation.)

B_t = per capita consumption of hard liquor (gallons) in year t

F_t = the average fat content (percentage) of the meat that was consumed in year t

W_t = per capita consumption of wine and beer (gallons) in year t

R_t = per capita number of miles run in year t

H_t = per capita open-heart surgeries in year t

O_t = per capita amount of oat bran eaten in year t

c. If you had to choose a variable not listed in part b to add to the equation, what would it be? Explain your answer.

4. For each of the following situations, determine the *sign* (and, if possible, comment on the likely size) of the expected bias introduced by omitting a variable:

a. In an equation for the demand for peanut butter, the impact on the coefficient of disposable income of omitting the price of peanut butter variable. (*Hint:* Start by hypothesizing signs.)

b. In an earnings equation for workers, the impact on the coefficient of experience of omitting the variable for age.

c. In a production function for airplanes, the impact on the coefficient of labor of omitting the capital variable.

d. In an equation for daily attendance at outdoor concerts, the impact on the coefficient of the weekend dummy variable (1 = weekend) of omitting a variable that measures the probability of precipitation at concert time.

5. Let's return to the model of financial aid awards at a liberal arts college that was first introduced in Section 2.2. In that section, we estimated the following equation (standard errors in parentheses):

$$\widehat{\text{FINAID}}_i = 8927 - 0.36 \, \text{PARENT}_i + 87.4 \, \text{HSRANK}_i \qquad (6.20)$$
$$(0.03) \qquad\qquad (20.7)$$
$$t = \qquad -11.26 \qquad\qquad 4.22$$
$$\overline{R}^2 = .73 \qquad N = 50$$

where: FINAID_i = the financial aid (measured in dollars of grant) awarded to the *i*th applicant

PARENT_i = the amount (in dollars) that the parents of the *i*th student are judged able to contribute to college expenses

HSRANK_i = the *i*th student's GPA rank in high school, measured as a percentage (ranging from a low of 0 to a high of 100)

a. Create and test hypotheses for the coefficients of the independent variables.

b. What econometric problems do you see in the equation? Are there any signs of an omitted variable? Of an irrelevant variable? Explain your answer.

c. Suppose that you now hear a charge that financial aid awards at the school are unfairly tilted toward males, so you decide to attempt to test this charge by adding a dummy variable for gender ($MALE_i = 1$ if the ith student is a male, 0 if female) to your equation, getting the following results:

$$\widehat{FINAID_i} = 9813 - 0.34\ PARENT_i + 83.3\ HSRANK_i - 1570\ MALE_i \quad (6.21)$$
$$\phantom{\widehat{FINAID_i} = 9813}\ (0.03)(20.1)(784)$$
$$t = -10.884.13-2.00$$
$$\overline{R}^2 = .75N = 50$$

d. Carefully explain the real-world meaning of the estimated coefficient of MALE. What would Equation 6.21 look like if you used FEMALE ($= 1$ if the ith student is a female and 0 otherwise) instead of MALE in the equation? (Hint: Be specific.)

e. Which equation is better, Equation 6.20 or Equation 6.21? Carefully use our four specification criteria to make your decision, being sure to state which criteria support which equation and why.

6. Suppose that you run a regression to determine whether gender or race has any significant impact on scores on a test of the economic understanding of children.[11] You model the score of the ith student on the test of elementary economics (S_i) as a function of the composite score on the Iowa Tests of Basic Skills of the ith student, a dummy variable equal to 1 if the ith student is female (0 otherwise), the average number of years of education of the parents of the ith student, and a dummy variable equal to 1 if the ith student is nonwhite (0 otherwise). Unfortunately, a rainstorm floods the computer center and makes it impossible to read the part of the computer output that identifies which variable is which. All you know is that the regression results are (standard errors in parentheses):

$$\hat{S}_i = 5.7 - 0.63X_{1i} - 0.22X_{2i} + 0.16X_{3i} + 1.20X_{4i}$$
$$\phantom{\hat{S}_i = 5.7}\ (0.63)(0.88)(0.08)(0.10)$$
$$N = 24\overline{R}^2 = .54$$

---

11. These results have been jiggled to meet the needs of this question, but this research actually was done. See Stephen Buckles and Vera Freeman, "Male-Female Differences in the Stock and Flow of Economic Knowledge," *Review of Economics and Statistics*, Vol. 65, No. 2, pp. 355–357.

a. Attempt to identify which result corresponds to which variable. Be specific.

b. Explain the reasoning behind your answer to part a.

c. Assuming that your answer is correct, create and test appropriate hypotheses (at the 5-percent level) and come to conclusions about the effects of gender and race on the test scores of this particular sample.

d. Did you use a one-tailed or two-tailed test in part c? Why?

7. Let's return to the model of Exercises 3-7 and 5-8 of the auction price of iPods on eBay. In that model, we used datafile IPOD3 to estimate the following equation:

$$\widehat{PRICE}_i = 109.24 + 54.99NEW_i - 20.44SCRATCH_i + 0.73BIDRS_i \qquad (6.22)$$
$$\begin{array}{cccc} & (5.34) & (5.11) & (0.59) \\ t = & 10.28 & -4.00 & 1.23 \\ & N = 215 \end{array}$$

where: $PRICE_i$ = the price at which the ith iPod sold on eBay
            NEW_i = a dummy variable equal to 1 if the ith iPod was new, 0 otherwise
            $SCRATCH_i$ = a dummy variable equal to 1 if the ith iPod had a minor cosmetic defect, 0 otherwise
            $BIDRS_i$ = the number of bidders on the ith iPod

The dataset also includes a variable $(PERCENT_i)$ that measures the percentage of customers of the seller of the ith iPod who gave that seller a positive rating for quality and reliability in previous transactions.[12] In theory, the higher the rating of a seller, the more a potential bidder would trust that seller, and the more that potential bidder would be willing to bid. If you add PERCENT to the equation, you obtain

$$\widehat{PRICE}_i = 82.67 + 55.42NEW_i - 20.95SCRATCH_i + 0.63BIDRS_i + 0.28PERCENT_i$$
$$\begin{array}{ccccc} & (5.34) & (5.12) & (0.59) & (0.20) \\ t = & 10.38 & -4.10 & 1.07 & 1.40 \\ & N = 215 & & & (6.23) \end{array}$$

a. Use our four specification criteria to decide whether you think PERCENT belongs in the equation. Be specific. (*Hint:* $\overline{R}^2$ isn't given, but you're capable of determining which equation had the higher $\overline{R}^2$.)

---

12. For more on this dataset and this variable, see Leonardo Rezende, "Econometrics of Auctions by Least Squares," *Journal of Applied Econometrics*, November/December 2008, pp. 925–948.

    b. Do you think that PERCENT is an accurate measure of the quality and reliability of the seller? Why or why not? (*Hint:* Among other things, consider the case of a seller with very few previous transactions.)

    c. (optional) With datafile IPOD3, use Stata, EViews, or your own regression program to estimate the equation with and without PERCENT. What are the $\overline{R}^2$ figures for the two specifications? Were you correct in your determination (in part a) as to which equation had the higher $\overline{R}^2$?

8. Look back at Exercise 9 in Chapter 5, the equation on international price discrimination in pharmaceuticals. In that cross-sectional study, Schut and VanBergeijk estimated two equations in addition to the one cited in the exercise.[13] These two equations tested the possibility that CV_i, total volume of consumption of pharmaceuticals in the ith country, and N_i, the population of the ith country, belonged in the original equation, Equation 5.15, repeated here:

$$\hat{P}_i = 38.22 + 1.43GDPN_i - 0.6CVN_i + 7.31PP_i \qquad (5.15)$$
$$\phantom{\hat{P}_i = 38.22 + } (0.21) \qquad (0.22) \qquad (6.12)$$
$$t = 6.69 \qquad\quad -2.66 \qquad 1.19$$

$$ -15.63DPC_i - 11.38PC_i$$
$$ (6.93) \qquad\quad (7.16)$$
$$t = -2.25 \qquad\quad -1.59$$
$$N = 32 \quad \overline{R}^2 = .775$$

where:

P_i	=	the pharmaceutical price level in the ith country divided by that of the United States
$GDPN_i$	=	per capita domestic product in the ith country divided by that of the United States
CVN_i	=	per capita volume of consumption of pharmaceuticals in the ith country divided by that of the United States
PP_i	=	a dummy variable equal to 1 if patents for pharmaceutical products are recognized in the ith country, 0 otherwise
DPC_i	=	a dummy variable equal to 1 if the ith country applied strict price controls, 0 otherwise
PC_i	=	a dummy variable equal to 1 if the ith country encouraged price competition, 0 otherwise

---

13. Frederick T. Schut and Peter A. G. VanBergeijk, "International Price Discrimination: The Pharmaceutical Industry," *World Development*, Vol. 14, No. 9, pp. 1141–1150.

    a. Using Stata, or your own computer program, and datafile DRUG5 (or Table 5.2), estimate:
      i. Equation 5.15 with CV_i added, and
      ii. Equation 5.15 with N_i added
    b. Use our four specification criteria to determine whether CV and N are irrelevant or omitted variables. (*Hint:* The authors expected that prices would be lower if market size were larger because of possible economies of scale and/or enhanced competition.)
    c. Why didn't the authors run Equation 5.15 with *both* CV and N included? (*Hint:* While you can estimate this equation yourself, you don't have to do so to answer the question.)
    d. Why do you think that the authors reported all three estimated specifications in their results when they thought that Equation 5.15 was the best?

6.7 Appendix: Additional Specification Criteria

So far in this chapter, we've suggested four criteria for choosing the independent variables (economic theory, $\overline{R}^2$, the *t*-test, and possible bias in the coefficients). Sometimes, however, these criteria don't provide enough information for a researcher to feel confident that a given specification is best. For instance, there can be two different specifications that both have excellent theoretical underpinnings. In such a situation, many econometricians use additional, often more formal, specification criteria to provide comparisons of the properties of the alternative estimated equations.

The use of formal specification criteria is not without problems, however. First, no test, no matter how sophisticated, can "prove" that a particular specification is the true one. The use of specification criteria, therefore, must be tempered with a healthy dose of economic theory and common sense. A second problem is that more than 20 such criteria have been proposed. How do we decide which one(s) to use? Because many of these criteria overlap with one another or have varying levels of complexity, a choice between the alternatives is a matter of personal preference.

In this section, we'll describe the use of three of the most popular specification criteria, J. B. Ramsey's RESET test, Akaike's Information Criterion, and the Bayesian Information Criterion. Our inclusion of just these techniques does not imply that other tests and criteria are not appropriate or useful. Indeed, the reader will find that most other formal specification criteria have quite a bit in common with at least one of the techniques that we include. We think that you'll be better able to use and understand other formal specification criteria[14] once you've mastered these three.

Ramsey's Regression Specification Error Test (RESET)

One of the most-used formal specification criteria other than $\overline{R}^2$ is the Ramsey Regression Specification Error Test (RESET).[15] The **Ramsey RESET test** is a general test that determines the likelihood of specification error by measuring whether the fit of a given equation can be significantly improved by the addition of $\hat{Y}^2$, $\hat{Y}^3$, and $\hat{Y}^4$ terms.

What's the intuition behind RESET? The additional terms act as proxies for any possible (unknown) omitted variables or incorrect functional forms. If the proxies can be shown by the F-test to have improved the overall fit of the original equation, then we have evidence that there is some sort of specification error in our equation. The $\hat{Y}^2$, $\hat{Y}^3$, and $\hat{Y}^4$ terms form a *polynomial* functional form. Such a polynomial is a powerful curve-fitting device that has a good chance of acting as a proxy for a specification error if one exists. If there is no specification error, then we'd expect the coefficients of the added terms to be insignificantly different from zero because there is nothing for them to act as a proxy for.

The Ramsey RESET test involves three steps:

1. Estimate the equation to be tested using OLS:

$$\hat{Y}_i = \hat{\beta}_0 + \hat{\beta}_1 X_{1i} + \hat{\beta}_2 X_{2i} \tag{6.24}$$

2. Take the $\hat{Y}_i$ values from Equation 6.24 and create $\hat{Y}_i^2$, $\hat{Y}_i^3$, and $\hat{Y}_i^4$ terms. Then add these terms to the original equation as additional explanatory variables and estimate the new equation with OLS:

$$Y_i = \beta_0 + \beta_1 X_{1i} + \beta_2 X_{2i} + \beta_3 \hat{Y}_i^2 + \beta_4 \hat{Y}_i^3 + \beta_5 \hat{Y}_i^4 + \epsilon_i \tag{6.25}$$

3. Compare the fits of Equations 6.24 and 6.25, using the F-test. Specifically, test the hypothesis that the coefficients of all three of the added terms are equal to zero:

$$H_0: \quad \beta_3 = \beta_4 = \beta_5 = 0$$
$$H_A: \quad \text{otherwise}$$

---

14. For example, the likelihood ratio test can be used as a specification test. For an introductory level summary of six other specification criteria, see Ramu Ramanathan, *Introductory Econometrics* (Fort Worth: Harcourt Brace Jovanovich, 1998, pp. 164–166).

15. J. B. Ramsey, "Tests for Specification Errors in Classical Linear Squares Regression Analysis," *Journal of the Royal Statistical Society*, Vol. 31, No. 2, pp. 350–371.

If the two equations are significantly different in overall fit, we can conclude that it's likely that Equation 6.24 is misspecified.

The appropriate *F*-statistic to use is Equation 5.10 from Section 5.6:

$$F = \frac{(RSS_M - RSS)/M}{RSS/(N - K - 1)} \tag{5.10}$$

where RSS_M is the residual sum of squares from the constrained equation (Equation 6.24), RSS is the residual sum of squares from the unconstrained equation[16] (Equation 6.25), M is the number of constraints (3 in this case), and $(N - K - 1)$ is the number of degrees of freedom in the unconstrained equation. If F is greater than the critical *F*-value with M and $(N - K - 1)$ degrees of freedom, then we can reject the null hypothesis and conclude that there is a specification error in Equation 6.24. Many econometric software programs, including Stata,[17] have a command that will automatically run Equation 6.25 and calculate the *F*-statistic using Equation 5.10.

While the Ramsey RESET test is fairly easy to use, it does little more than signal *when* a major specification error might exist. If you encounter a significant Ramsey RESET test, then you face the daunting task of figuring out exactly *what* the error is! Thus, the test often ends up being more useful in "supporting" (technically, not refuting) a researcher's contention that a given specification has no major specification errors than it is in helping find an otherwise undiscovered flaw.[18]

---

16. Because of the obvious correlation between the three $\hat{Y}$ values, Equation 6.25 (with most RESET equations) suffers from extreme multicollinearity. Since the purpose of the RESET equation is to see whether the overall fit can be improved by adding in proxies for an omitted variable (or other specification error), this extreme multicollinearity is not a concern.

17. To carry out the Ramsey RESET test in Stata, estimate Equation 6.24 and then run the "ovtest" command. For details, see the *Using Stata* guide on the textbook's website at http://www.pearsonhighered.com/studenmund.

18. The particular version of the Ramsey RESET test we describe in this section is only one of a number of possible formulations of the test. For example, some researchers delete the $\hat{Y}^4$ term from Equation 6.25. At present, there is a mild split among econometricians about RESET. Jeff Wooldridge, "Score Diagnostics for Linear Models Estimated by Two Stage Least Squares," in G.S. Maddala, P.C.B. Phillips, and T.N. Srinivasan (eds.), *Advances in Econometrics and Quantitative Economics* (Oxford: Blackwell, 1995), pp. 66–87, argues that RESET is primarily a functional form test. However, many applied econometricians continue to rely on RESET for a variety of specification tests, some even going so far as to use RESET in an to attempt to distinguish between pure and impure serial correlation and heteroskedasticity (to be discussed in Chapters 9 and 10).

Akaike's Information Criterion and the Bayesian Information Criterion

A second category of formal specification criteria involves adjusting the summed squared residuals (RSS) by one factor or another to create an index of the fit of an equation. The most popular criterion of this type is $\overline{R}^2$, but a number of interesting alternatives have been proposed.

Akaike's Information Criterion (AIC) and the **Bayesian Information Criterion (BIC)** are methods of comparing alternative specifications by adjusting RSS for the sample size (N) and the number of independent variables (K).[19] These criteria can be used to augment our four basic specification criteria when we try to decide if the improved fit caused by an additional variable is worth the decreased degrees of freedom and increased complexity caused by the addition. Their equations are:

$$AIC = Log(RSS/N) + 2(K + 1)/N \tag{6.26}$$

$$BIC = Log(RSS/N) + Log(N)(K + 1)/N \tag{6.27}$$

In practice, these calculations may not be necessary because AIC and BIC are automatically calculated by some regression software packages, including Stata.

To use AIC and BIC, estimate two alternative specifications and calculate AIC and BIC for each equation. The lower AIC or BIC are, the better the specification. Note that even though the two criteria were developed independently to maximize different object functions, their equations are quite similar. Both criteria tend to penalize the addition of another explanatory variable more than $\overline{R}^2$ does. As a result, AIC and BIC will quite often[20] be

---

19. Hirotogu Akaike, "Likelihood of a Model and Information Criteria," *Journal of Econometrics*, Vol. 16, No. 1, pp. 3–14 and G. Schwarz, "Estimating the Dimension of a Model," *The Annals of Statistics*, Vol. 6, pp. 461–464. (The BIC is sometimes called the *Schwarz Criterion*.) The definitions of AIC and BIC we use produce slightly different numbers than the versions used by Stata, but the versions map on a one-to-one basis and therefore produce identical conclusions.

20. Using a Monte Carlo study, Judge et al. showed that (given specific simplifying assumptions) a specification chosen by maximizing $\overline{R}^2$ is more than 50 percent more likely to include an irrelevant variable than is one chosen by minimizing AIC or BIC. See George C. Judge, R. Carter Hill, W. E. Griffiths, Helmut Lutkepohl, and Tsoung-Chao Lee, *Introduction to the Theory and Practice of Econometrics* (New York: Wiley, 1988), pp. 849–850. At the same time, minimizing AIC or BIC will omit a relevant variable more frequently than will maximizing $\overline{R}^2$

minimized by an equation with fewer independent variables than the ones that maximize $\overline{R}^2$.

AIC and BIC require the researcher to come up with a particular alternative specification, whereas Ramsey's RESET does not. Such a distinction makes RESET easier to use, but it makes AIC and BIC more informative if a specification error is found. Thus our additional specification criteria serve different purposes. RESET is useful as a general test of the existence of a specification error, whereas AIC and BIC are useful as means of comparing two or more alternative specifications.

Chapter 7

Specification: Choosing a Functional Form

Even after you've chosen your independent variables, the job of specifying the equation is not over. The next step is to choose the functional form of the relationship between each independent variable and the dependent variable. Should the equation go through the origin? Do you expect a curve instead of a straight line? Does the effect of a variable peak at some point and then start to decline? An affirmative answer to any of these questions suggests that an equation other than the standard linear model of the previous chapters might be appropriate. Such alternative specifications are important for two reasons: a correct explanatory variable may well appear to be insignificant or to have an unexpected sign if an inappropriate functional form is used, and the consequences of an incorrect functional form for interpretation and forecasting can be severe.

Theoretical considerations usually dictate the form of a regression model. The basic technique involved in deciding on a functional form is to choose the shape that best exemplifies the expected underlying economic or business principles and then to use the mathematical form that produces that shape. To help with that choice, this chapter contains plots of the most commonly used functional forms along with the mathematical equations that correspond to each.

The chapter begins with a brief discussion of the constant term. In particular, we suggest that the constant term should be retained in equations and that estimates of the constant term should not be relied on for inference or analysis. The chapter concludes with a discussion of slope dummy variables.

7.1   The Use and Interpretation of the Constant Term

In the linear regression model, β_0 is the intercept or constant term. It is the expected value of Y when all the explanatory variables (and the error term) equal zero. An estimate of β_0 has at least three components:

1. the true β_0,
2. the constant impact of any specification errors (an omitted variable, for example), and
3. the mean of ϵ for the correctly specified equation (if not equal to zero).

Unfortunately, these components can't be distinguished from one another because we can observe only $\hat{\beta}_0$, the sum of the three components. The result is that we have to analyze $\hat{\beta}_0$ differently from the way we analyze the other coefficients in the equation.[1]

At times, β_0 is of theoretical importance. Consider, for example, the following cost equation:

$$C_i = \beta_0 + \beta_1 Q_i + \epsilon_i$$

where C_i is the total cost of producing output Q_i. The term $\beta_1 Q_i$ represents the total variable cost associated with output level Q_i, and β_0 represents the total fixed cost, defined as the cost when output $Q_i = 0$. Thus, a regression equation might seem useful to a researcher who wanted to determine the relative magnitudes of fixed and variable costs. This would be an example of relying on the constant term for inference.

On the other hand, the product involved might be one for which it is known that there are few—if any—fixed costs. In such a case, a researcher might want to eliminate the constant term; to do so would conform to the notion of zero fixed costs and would conserve a degree of freedom (which would presumably make the estimate of β_1 more precise). This would be an example of suppressing the constant term.

---

1. If the second and third components of β_0 are small compared to the first component, then this difference diminishes. See R. C. Allen and J. H. Stone, "Textbook Neglect of the Constant Coefficient," *The Journal of Economic Education*, Fall 2005, pp. 379–384.

Neither suppressing the constant term nor relying on it for inference is advisable, however, and the reasons for these conclusions are explained in the following sections.

Do Not Suppress the Constant Term

In most cases, suppressing the constant term leads to a violation of the Classical Assumptions, because it's very rare that economic theory implies that the true intercept, β_0, equals zero. If you omit the constant term, then the impact of the constant is forced into the estimates of the other coefficients, causing potential bias. This is demonstrated in Figure 7.1. Given the pattern of the X and Y observations, estimating a regression equation with a constant term would likely produce an estimated regression line very similar to the true regression line, which has a constant term (β_0) quite different from zero. The slope of this estimated line is very low, and the *t*-score of the estimated slope coefficient may be very close to zero.

However, if the researcher were to suppress the constant term, which implies that the estimated regression line must pass through the origin, then the estimated regression line shown in Figure 7.1 would result. The slope

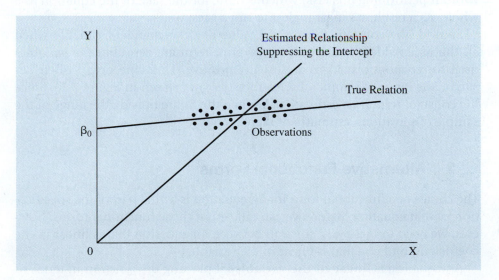

Figure 7.1 The Harmful Effect of Suppressing the Constant Term

If the constant (or intercept) term is suppressed, the estimated regression will go through the origin. Such an effect potentially biases the $\hat{\beta}$s and inflates their *t*-scores. In this particular example, the true slope is close to zero in the range of the sample, but forcing the regression through the origin makes the slope appear to be significantly positive.

coefficient is biased upward compared with the true slope coefficient. The *t*-score is biased upward as well, and it may very well be large enough to indicate that the estimated slope coefficient is statistically significantly positive. Such a conclusion would be incorrect.

Thus, even though some regression packages allow the constant term to be suppressed (set to zero), the general rule is: *Don't!*

Do Not Rely on Estimates of the Constant Term

It would seem logical that if it's a bad idea to suppress the constant term, then the constant term must be an important analytical tool to use in evaluating the results of the regression. Unfortunately, there are at least two reasons that suggest that the intercept should *not* be relied on for purposes of analysis or inference.

First, the error term is generated, in part, by the omission of a number of marginal independent variables, the mean effect of which is placed in the constant term. The constant term acts as a garbage collector, with an unknown amount of this mean effect being dumped into it. The constant term's estimated coefficient may be different from what it would have been without performing this task, which is done for the sake of the equation as a whole. As a result, it's meaningless to run a *t*-test on $\hat{\beta}_0$.

Second, the constant term is the value of the dependent variable when all the independent variables and the error term are zero, but the variables used for economic analysis are usually positive. Thus, the origin often lies *outside* the range of sample observations (as can be seen in Figure 7.1). Since the constant term is an estimate of Y when the Xs are outside the range of the sample observations, estimates of it are tenuous.

7.2 Alternative Functional Forms

The choice of a functional form for an equation is a vital part of the specification of that equation. Before we can talk about those functional forms, however, we need to make a distinction between an equation that is linear in the coefficients and one that is linear in the variables.

An equation is **linear in the variables** if plotting the function in terms of X and Y generates a straight line. For example, Equation 7.1:

$$Y = \beta_0 + \beta_1 X + \epsilon \tag{7.1}$$

is linear in the variables, but Equation 7.2:

$$Y = \beta_0 + \beta_1 X^2 + \epsilon \tag{7.2}$$

is not linear in the variables, because if you were to plot Equation 7.2 it would be a quadratic, not a straight line.

An equation is **linear in the coefficients** only if the coefficients (the βs) appear in their simplest form—they are not raised to any powers (other than one), are not multiplied or divided by other coefficients, and do not themselves include some sort of function (like logs or exponents). For example, Equation 7.1 is linear in the coefficients, but Equation 7.3:

$$Y = \beta_0 + X^{\beta_1} \tag{7.3}$$

is not linear in the coefficients β_0 and β_1. Equation 7.3 is not linear because there is no rearrangement of the equation that will make it linear in the βs of original interest, β_0 and β_1. In fact, of all possible equations for a single explanatory variable, *only* functions of the general form:

$$f(Y) = \beta_0 + \beta_1 f(X) \tag{7.4}$$

are linear in the coefficients β_0 and β_1. Linear regression analysis can be applied to an equation that is nonlinear in the variables as long as the equation is linear in the coefficients. Indeed, when econometricians use the phrase "linear regression" (for example, in the Classical Assumptions), they usually mean "regression that is linear in the coefficients."

The use of OLS requires that the equation be linear in the coefficients, but there is a wide variety of functional forms that are linear in the coefficients while being nonlinear in the variables. Indeed, in previous chapters we've already used several equations that are linear in the coefficients and nonlinear in the variables, but we've said little about when to use such nonlinear equations. The purpose of the current section is to present the details of the most frequently used functional forms to help the reader develop the ability to choose the correct one when specifying an equation.

The choice of a functional form almost always should be based on the underlying theory and only rarely on which form provides the best fit. The logical form of the relationship between the dependent variable and the independent variable in question should be compared with the properties of various functional forms, and the one that comes closest to that underlying theory should be chosen. To allow such a comparison, the paragraphs that follow characterize the most frequently used forms in terms of graphs, equations, and examples. In some cases, more than one functional form will be applicable, but usually a choice between alternative functional forms can be made on the basis of the information we'll present.

Linear Form

The linear regression model, used almost exclusively in this text thus far, is based on the assumption that the slope of the relationship between the independent variable and the dependent variable is constant:[2]

$$\frac{\Delta Y}{\Delta X_k} = \beta_k \qquad k = 1, 2, \ldots, K$$

If the hypothesized relationship between Y and X is such that the slope of the relationship can be expected to be constant, then the linear functional form should be used.

Since the slope is constant, the **elasticity** of Y with respect to X (the percentage change in the dependent variable caused by a 1-percent increase in the independent variable, holding the other variables in the equation constant) can be calculated fairly easily:

$$\text{Elasticity}_{Y, X_k} = \frac{\Delta Y/Y}{\Delta X_k/X_k} = \frac{\Delta Y}{\Delta X_k} \cdot \frac{X_k}{Y} = \beta_k \frac{X_k}{Y}$$

Unless theory, common sense, or experience justifies using some other functional form, you should use the linear model. Because, in effect, it's being used by default, the linear model is sometimes referred to as the *default* functional form.

Double-Log Form

The double-log form is the most common functional form that is nonlinear in the variables while still being linear in the coefficients. Indeed, the double-log form is so popular that some researchers use it as their default functional form instead of the linear form. In a **double-log functional form**, the natural log of Y is the dependent variable and the natural log of X is the independent variable:

$$\ln Y = \beta_0 + \beta_1 \ln X_1 + \beta_2 \ln X_2 + \epsilon \tag{7.5}$$

where lnY refers to the natural log of Y, and so on. For a brief review of the meaning of a natural log, see the boxed feature on pages 196 and 197.

---

2. Throughout this section, the "delta" notation (Δ) will be used instead of the calculus notation to make for easier reading. The specific definition of Δ is "change," and it implies a small change in the variable it is attached to. For example, the term ΔX should be read as "change in X." Since a regression coefficient represents the change in the expected value of Y brought about by a one-unit increase in X_k (holding constant all other variables in the equation), then $\beta_k = \Delta Y/\Delta X_k$. Those comfortable with calculus should substitute partial derivative signs for Δs.

The double-log form, sometimes called the log-log form, often is used because a researcher has specified that the elasticities of the model are constant and the slopes are not. This is in contrast to the linear model, in which the slopes are constant but the elasticities are not.

In a double-log equation, an individual regression coefficient can be interpreted as an elasticity because:

$$\beta_k = \frac{\Delta(\ln Y)}{\Delta(\ln X_k)} = \frac{\Delta Y/Y}{\Delta X_k/X_k} = \text{Elasticity}_{Y,X_k} \qquad (7.6)$$

Since regression coefficients are constant, the condition that the model have a constant elasticity is met by the double-log equation.

The way to interpret β_k in a double-log equation is that if X_k increases by 1 percent while the other Xs are held constant, then Y will change by β_k percent. Since elasticities are constant, the slopes are now no longer constant.

Figure 7.2 is a graph of the double-log function (ignoring the error term). The panel on the left shows the economic concept of an isoquant or an indifference curve. Isoquants from production functions show the different combinations of factors X_1 and X_2, probably capital and labor, that can be used to produce a given level of output Y. The panel on the right of Figure 7.2 shows

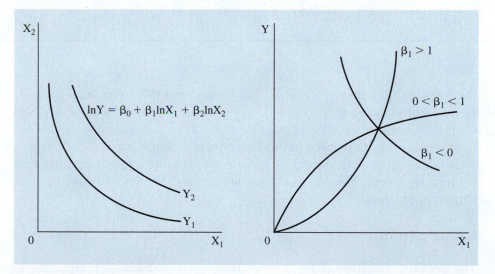

Figure 7.2 Double-Log Functions

Depending on the values of the regression coefficients, the double-log functional form can take on a number of shapes. The left panel shows the use of a double-log function to depict a shape useful in describing the economic concept of an isoquant or an indifference curve. The right panel shows various shapes that can be achieved with a double-log function if X_2 is held constant or is not included in the equation.

What Is a Log?

What the heck is a log? If e (a constant equal to 2.71828) to the "*b*th power" produces x, then b is the log of x:

$$b \text{ is the log of x to the base e if:}\quad e^b = x$$

Thus, a **log** (or logarithm) is the exponent to which a given base must be taken in order to produce a specific number. While logs come in more than one variety, we'll use only **natural logs** (logs to the base e) in this text. The symbol for a natural log is "ln," so $\ln(x) = b$ means that $(2.71828)^b = x$ or, more simply,

$$\ln(x) = b \qquad \text{means that} \qquad e^b = x$$

For example, since $e^2 = (2.71828)^2 = 7.389$, we can state that:

$$\ln(7.389) = 2$$

Thus, the natural log of 7.389 is 2! Two is the power of e that produces 7.389. Let's look at some other natural log calculations:

$$\ln(100) \quad = \quad 4.605$$
$$\ln(1000) \quad = \quad 6.908$$

the relationship between Y and X_1 that would exist if X_2 were held constant or were not included in the model. Note that the shape of the curve depends on the sign and magnitude of coefficient β_1. If β_1 is negative, a double-log functional form can be used to model a typical demand curve.

Double-log models should be run only when the logged variables take on positive values. Dummy variables, which can take on the value of zero, should not be logged.

Semilog Form

The **semilog functional form** is a variant of the double-log equation in which some but not all of the variables (dependent and independent) are expressed in terms of their natural logs. For example, you might choose to use the logarithm of one of the original independent variables, as in:

$$Y_i = \beta_0 + \beta_1 \ln X_{1i} + \beta_2 X_{2i} + \epsilon_i \tag{7.7}$$

In this case, the economic meanings of the two slope coefficients are different, since X_2 is linearly related to Y while X_1 is nonlinearly related to Y.

$$\ln(10000) \quad = \quad 9.210$$
$$\ln(100000) \quad = \quad 11.513$$
$$\ln(1000000) = 13.816$$

Note that as a number goes from 100 to 1,000,000, its natural log goes from 4.605 to only 13.816! Since logs are exponents, even a small change in a log can mean a big change in impact. As a result, logs can be used in econometrics if a researcher wants to reduce the absolute size of the numbers associated with the same actual meaning.

One useful property of natural logs in econometrics is that they make it easier to figure out impacts in percentage terms. If you run a double-log regression, the meaning of a slope coefficient is the percentage change in the dependent variable caused by a one percentage point increase in the independent variable, holding the other independent variables in the equation constant.[3] It's because of this percentage change property that the slope coefficients in a double-log equation are elasticities.

---

3. This is because the derivative of a natural log of X equals dX/X (or ΔX/X), which is the same as percentage change.

The right-hand side of Figure 7.3 shows the relationship between Y and X_1 in this kind of semilog equation when X_2 is held constant. Note that if β_1 is greater than zero, the impact of changes in X_1 on Y decreases as X_1 gets bigger. Thus, the semilog functional form should be used when the relationship between X_1 and Y is hypothesized to have this "increasing at a decreasing rate" form.[4]

Applications of the semilog form are quite frequent. For example, most consumption functions tend to increase at a decreasing rate past

---

4. Another functional form that can be used when you anticipate that the relationship between X and Y has an "increasing at a decreasing rate" shape is the inverse functional form. This form expresses Y as a function of the reciprocal (or inverse) of one or more of the independent variables (in this case X_1):

$$Y_i = \beta_0 + \beta_1(1/X_{1i}) + \beta_2 X_{2i} + \epsilon_i$$

The inverse functional form should be used when the impact of a particular independent variable is expected to approach zero as that independent variable approaches infinity. To see this, note that as X_1 gets larger, its impact on Y decreases.

Be careful, however, because X_1 cannot equal zero, since if X_1 equaled zero, dividing it into anything would result in infinite or undefined values.

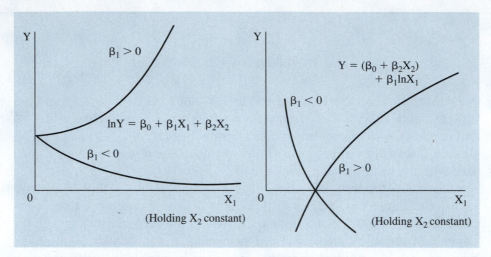

Figure 7.3 Semilog Functions

The semilog functional form on the right (lnX) can be used to depict a situation in which the impact of X_1 on Y is expected to increase at a decreasing rate as X_1 gets bigger as long as β_1 is greater than zero (holding X_2 constant). The semilog functional form on the left (lnY) can be used to depict a situation in which an increase in X_1 causes Y to increase at an increasing rate.

some level of income. These *Engel curves* tend to flatten out because as incomes get higher, a smaller percentage of income goes to consumption and a greater percentage goes to saving. Consumption thus increases at a decreasing rate. If Y is the consumption of an item and X_1 is disposable income (with X_2 standing for all the other independent variables), then the use of the semilog functional form is justified whenever the item's consumption can be expected to increase at a decreasing rate as income increases.

For example, recall the beef demand equation, Equation 2.7, from Chapter 2:

$$\widehat{CB}_t = 37.54 - 0.88P_t + 11.9Yd_t \qquad (2.7)$$
$$\phantom{\widehat{CB}_t = 37.54 - }(0.16) \quad (1.76)$$
$$t = \qquad -5.36 \quad 6.75$$
$$\overline{R}^2 = 0.631 \quad N = 28 \text{ (annual)}$$

where: CB = per capita consumption of beef

P   = the price of beef in cents per pound

Yd = U.S. disposable income in thousands of dollars

If we substitute the log of disposable income ($\ln Yd_t$) for disposable income in Equation 2.7, we get:

$$\widehat{CB}_t = -71.75 - 0.87P_t + 98.87\ln Yd_t \qquad (7.8)$$
$$\phantom{\widehat{CB}_t = -71.75 -} (0.13) \quad (11.11)$$
$$t = -6.93 \qquad 8.90$$
$$\overline{R}^2 = .750 \quad N = 28 \text{ (annual)}$$

In Equation 7.8, the independent variables include the price of beef and the *log* of disposable income. Equation 7.8 would be appropriate if we hypothesize that as income rises, consumption will increase at a decreasing rate. For other products, perhaps like yachts or summer homes, no such decreasing rate could be hypothesized, and the semilog function would not be appropriate.

Not all semilog functions have the log on the right-hand side of the equation, as in Equation 7.7. The alternative semilog form is to have the log on the left-hand side of the equation. This would mean that the natural log of Y would be a function of unlogged values of the Xs, as in:

$$\ln Y = \beta_0 + \beta_1 X_1 + \beta_2 X_2 + \epsilon \qquad (7.9)$$

This model has neither a constant slope nor a constant elasticity, but the coefficients do have a very useful interpretation. If X_1 increases by one *unit*, then Y will change in *percentage* terms. Specifically, Y will change by $\beta_1 \cdot 100$ percent for every unit that X_1 increases, holding X_2 constant. The left-hand side of Figure 7.3 shows such a semilog function.

This fact means that the lnY semilog function of Equation 7.9 is perfect for any model in which the dependent variable adjusts in percentage terms to a unit change in an independent variable. The most common economic and business application of Equation 7.9 is in a model of the earnings of individuals, where firms often give annual raises in percentage terms. In such a model, Y would be the salary or wage of the *i*th employee, and X_1 would be the experience of the *i*th worker. Each year X_1 would increase by one, and β_1 would measure the percentage raises given by the firm.

Note that we now have two different kinds of semilog functional forms, creating possible confusion. As a result, many econometricians use phrases like "right-side semilog" or "lin-log functional form" to refer to Equation 7.7 while using "left-side semilog" or "log-lin functional form" to refer to Equation 7.9.

Polynomial Form

In most average cost functions, the slope of the cost curve changes sign as output changes. If the slopes of a relationship are expected to depend on the level of the variable itself, then a polynomial model should be considered. **Polynomial**

functional forms express Y as a function of independent variables, some of which are raised to powers other than 1. For example, in a second-degree polynomial (also called a quadratic) equation, at least one independent variable is squared:

$$Y_i = \beta_0 + \beta_1 X_{1i} + \beta_2 (X_{1i})^2 + \beta_3 X_{2i} + \epsilon_i \qquad (7.10)$$

Such a model can indeed produce slopes that change sign as the independent variables change. The slope of Y with respect to X_1 in Equation 7.10 is:

$$\frac{\Delta Y}{\Delta X_1} = \beta_1 + 2\beta_2 X_1 \qquad (7.11)$$

Note that the slope depends on the level of X_1. For small values of X_1, β_1 might dominate, but for large values of X_1, β_2 will always dominate. If this were a cost function, with Y being the average cost of production and X_1 being the level of output of the firm, then we would expect β_1 to be negative and β_2 to be positive if the firm has the typical U-shaped cost curve depicted in the left half of Figure 7.4.

For another example, consider a model of annual employee earnings as a function of the age of each employee and a number of other measures of productivity such as education. What is the expected impact of age on earnings? As a young worker gets older, his or her earnings will typically increase.

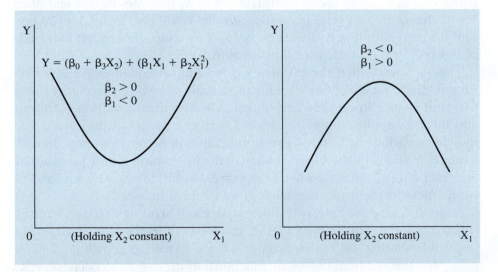

Figure 7.4 Polynomial Functions

Quadratic functional forms (polynomials with squared terms) take on U or inverted U shapes, depending on the values of the coefficients (holding X_2 constant). The left panel shows the shape of a quadratic function that could be used to show a typical cost curve; the right panel allows the description of an impact that rises and then falls (like the impact of age on earnings).

Beyond some point, however, an increase in age will not increase earnings by very much at all, and around retirement we'd expect earnings to start to fall abruptly with age. As a result, a logical relationship between earnings and age might look something like the right half of Figure 7.4; earnings would rise, level off, and then fall as age increased. Such a theoretical relationship could be modeled with a quadratic equation:

$$\text{Earnings}_i = \beta_0 + \beta_1 \text{Age}_i + \beta_2 \text{Age}_i^2 + \cdots + \epsilon_i \qquad (7.12)$$

What would the expected signs of $\hat{\beta}_1$ and $\hat{\beta}_2$ be? Since you expect the impact of age to rise and fall, you'd thus expect $\hat{\beta}_1$ to be positive and $\hat{\beta}_2$ to be negative (all else being equal). In fact, this is exactly what many researchers in labor economics have observed.

With polynomial regressions, the interpretation of the individual regression coefficients becomes difficult, and the equation may produce unwanted results for particular ranges of X. Great care must be taken when using a polynomial regression equation to ensure that the functional form will achieve what is intended by the researcher and no more.

Choosing a Functional Form

The best way to choose a functional form for a regression model is to select the specification that best matches the underlying theory of the equation. In a majority of cases, the linear form will be adequate, and for most of the rest, common sense will point out a fairly easy choice from the alternatives outlined above. Table 7.1 contains a summary of the properties of the various alternative functional forms.

Table 7.1 Summary of Alternative Functional Forms

Functional Form	Equation (one X only)	The Change in Y when X Changes
Linear	$Y_i = \beta_0 + \beta_1 X_i + \epsilon_i$	If X increases by one unit, Y will change by β_1 units.
Double-log	$\ln Y_i = \beta_0 + \beta_1 \ln X_i + \epsilon_i$	If X increases by one percent, Y will change by β_1 percent. (Thus β_1 is the elasticity of Y with respect to X.)
Semilog (lnX)	$Y_i = \beta_0 + \beta_1 \ln X_i + \epsilon_i$	If X increases by one percent, Y will change by $\beta_1/100$ units.
Semilog (lnY)	$\ln Y_i = \beta_0 + \beta_1 X_i + \epsilon_i$	If X increases by one unit, Y will change by roughly $100\beta_1$ percent.
Polynomial	$Y_i = \beta_0 + \beta_1 X_i + \beta_2 X_i^2 + \epsilon_i$	If X increases by one unit, Y will change by $(\beta_1 + 2\beta_2 X)$ units.

7.3 Lagged Independent Variables

Virtually all the regressions we've studied so far have been "instantaneous" in nature. In other words, they have included independent and dependent variables from the same time period, as in:

$$Y_t = \beta_0 + \beta_1 X_{1t} + \beta_2 X_{2t} + \epsilon_t \tag{7.13}$$

where the subscript t is used to refer to a particular point in time. If all variables have the same subscript, then the equation is instantaneous.

However, not all economic or business situations imply such instantaneous relationships between the dependent and independent variables. In many cases time elapses between a change in the independent variable and the resulting change in the dependent variable. The period of time between the cause (the change in X) and the effect (the change in Y) is called a **lag**. Time periods can be measured in days, months, years, etc. Many econometric equations include one or more lagged independent variables like X_{1t-1}, where the subscript $t-1$ indicates that the observation of X_1 is from the time period previous to time period t, as in the following equation:

$$Y_t = \beta_0 + \beta_1 X_{1t-1} + \beta_2 X_{2t} + \epsilon_t \tag{7.14}$$

In this equation, X_1 has been lagged by one time period, but the relationship between Y and X_2 is still instantaneous. While this one-time-period lag is the most frequent lag in economics, lags of two or more time periods can be used when justified by the underlying theory.

For an example of a lagged independent variable, think about the process by which the supply of an agricultural product is determined. Since agricultural goods take time to grow, decisions on how many acres to plant or how many eggs to let hatch into egg-producing hens (instead of selling them immediately) must be made months, if not years, before the product is actually supplied to the consumer. Any change in an agricultural market, such as an increase in the price that the farmer can earn for providing cotton, has a lagged effect on the supply of that product:

$$\overset{+}{\phantom{C_t = \beta_0 + \beta_1 PC_{t-1}}} \quad \overset{-}{}$$
$$C_t = \beta_0 + \beta_1 PC_{t-1} + \beta_2 PF_t + \epsilon_t \tag{7.15}$$

where: C_t = the quantity of cotton supplied in year t
PC_{t-1} = the price of cotton in year $t-1$
PF_t = the price of farm labor in year t

Note that this equation hypothesizes a lag between the price of cotton and the production of cotton, but not between the price of farm labor and the production of cotton. It's reasonable to think that if cotton prices change, farmers won't be able to react immediately because it takes a while for cotton to be planted and to grow.

The meaning of the regression coefficient of a lagged variable is not the same as the meaning of the coefficient of an unlagged variable. The estimated coefficient of a lagged X measures the change in *this year's* Y attributed to a one-unit increase in *last year's* X (holding constant the other Xs in the equation). Thus β_1 in Equation 7.15 measures the extra number of units of cotton that would be produced this year as a result of a one-unit increase in last year's price of cotton, holding this year's price of farm labor constant.

If the lag structure is hypothesized to take place over more than one time period, or if a lagged dependent variable is included on the right-hand side of an equation, the question becomes significantly more complex. Such cases, called *distributed lags*, will be dealt with in Chapter 12.

7.4 Slope Dummy Variables

In Section 3.3 we introduced the concept of a dummy variable, which we defined as one that takes on the values of 0 or 1, depending on a qualitative attribute such as gender. In that section our sole focus was on the use of a dummy variable as an **intercept dummy**, which changes the constant or intercept term, depending on whether the qualitative condition is met. These take the general form:

$$Y_i = \beta_0 + \beta_1 X_i + \beta_2 D_i + \epsilon_i \tag{7.16}$$

$$\text{where } D_i = \begin{cases} 1 \text{ if the } i\text{th observation meets a particular condition} \\ 0 \text{ otherwise} \end{cases}$$

Until now, every independent variable in this text has been multiplied by exactly one other item: the slope coefficient. To see this, take another look at Equation 7.16. As you can see, X is multiplied only by β_1, and D is multiplied only by β_2, and there are no other factors involved.

This restriction does not apply to a new kind of variable called an interaction term. An **interaction term** is an independent variable in a regression equation that is the *multiple* of two or more other independent variables. Each interaction term has its own regression coefficient, so the end result is that the interaction term has three or more components, as in $\beta_3 X_i D_i$. Such interaction terms are used when the change in Y with respect to one independent variable (in this case X) depends on the level of another independent variable (in this case D). For an example of the use of interaction terms, see Exercise 8.

Interaction terms can involve two quantitative variables ($\beta_3 X_1 X_2$) or two dummy variables ($\beta_3 D_1 D_2$), but the most frequent application of interaction terms involves one quantitative variable and one dummy variable ($\beta_3 X_1 D_1$), a combination that is typically called a *slope dummy*. **Slope dummy** *variables* allow the slope of the relationship between the dependent variable and an independent variable to be different depending on whether the condition specified by a dummy variable is met. This is in contrast to an intercept dummy variable, which changes the intercept, but does not change the slope, when a particular condition is met.

In general, a slope dummy is introduced by adding to the equation a variable that is the multiple of the independent variable that has a slope you want to change and the dummy variable that you want to cause the changed slope. The general form of a slope dummy equation is:

$$Y_i = \beta_0 + \beta_1 X_i + \beta_2 D_i + \beta_3 X_i D_i + \epsilon_i \qquad (7.17)$$

Note that Equation 7.17 is the same as Equation 7.16, except that we have added an interaction term in which the dummy variable is multiplied by an independent variable ($\beta_3 X_i D_i$). Let's check to make sure that the slope of Y with respect to X does indeed change if D changes:

$$\text{When } D = 0, \quad \Delta Y / \Delta X = \beta_1$$
$$\text{When } D = 1, \quad \Delta Y / \Delta X = (\beta_1 + \beta_3)$$

In essence, the coefficient of X *changes* when the condition specified by D is met. To see this, substitute $D = 0$ and $D = 1$, respectively, into Equation 7.17 and factor out X.

Note that Equation 7.17 includes both a slope dummy and an intercept dummy. It turns out that whenever a slope dummy is used, it's vital to also have $\beta_1 X_i$ and $\beta_2 D$ in the equation to avoid bias in the estimate of the coefficient of the slope dummy term. If there are other Xs in an equation, they should not be multiplied by D unless you hypothesize that their slopes change with respect to D as well.

Take a look at Figure 7.5, which has both a slope dummy and an intercept dummy. In Figure 7.5 the intercept will be β_0 when $D = 0$ and $\beta_0 + \beta_2$ when $D = 1$. In addition, the slope of Y with respect to X will be β_1 when $D = 0$ and $\beta_1 + \beta_3$ when $D = 1$. As a result, there really are two equations:

$$Y_i = \beta_0 \qquad\qquad + \beta_1 X_i + \epsilon_i \qquad [\text{when } D = 0]$$
$$Y_i = (\beta_0 + \beta_2) + (\beta_1 + \beta_3) X_i + \epsilon_i \qquad [\text{when } D = 1]$$

In practice, slope dummies have many realistic uses. For example, consider the question of earnings differentials between men and women. Although there is little argument that these differentials exist, there is quite a bit of

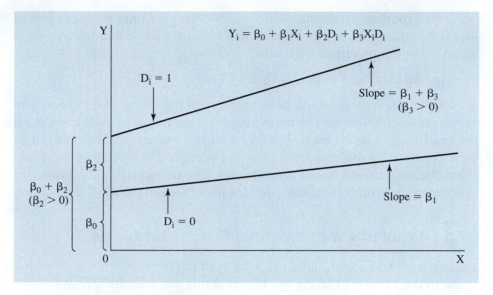

Figure 7.5 Slope and Intercept Dummies

If slope dummy ($\beta_3 X_i D_i$) and intercept dummy ($\beta_2 D_i$) terms are added to an equation, a graph of the equation will have different intercepts *and* different slopes depending on the value of the qualitative condition specified by the dummy variable. The difference between the two intercepts is β_2, whereas the difference between the two slopes is β_3.

controversy over the extent to which these differentials are caused by sexual discrimination (as opposed to other factors). Suppose you decide to build a model of earnings to get a better view of this controversy. If you hypothesized that men earn more than women on average, then you would want to use an intercept dummy variable for gender in an earnings equation that included measures of experience, special skills, education, and so on, as independent variables:

$$\ln(\text{Earnings}_i) = \beta_0 + \beta_1 D_i + \beta_2 \text{EXP}_i + \cdots + \epsilon_i \qquad (7.18)$$

where: D_i = 1 if the *i*th worker is male and 0 otherwise
$\quad\quad\quad$ EXP_i = the years experience of the *i*th worker
$\quad\quad\quad$ ϵ_i = a classical error term

In Equation 7.18, $\hat{\beta}_1$ would be an estimate of the average difference in earnings between males and females, holding constant their experience and the other factors in the equation. Equation 7.18 also forces the impact of increases in experience (and the other factors in the equation) to have the same effect for females as for males because the slopes are the same for both genders.

If you hypothesized that men also increase their earnings more per year of experience than women, then you would include a slope dummy as well as an intercept dummy in such a model:

$$\ln(\text{Earnings}_i) = \beta_0 + \beta_1 D_i + \beta_2 EXP_i + \beta_3 D_i EXP_i + \cdots + \epsilon_i \quad (7.19)$$

In Equation 7.19, $\hat{\beta}_3$ would be an estimate of the differential impact of an extra year of experience on earnings between men and women. We could test the possibility of a positive true β_3 by running a one-tailed t-test on $\hat{\beta}_3$. If $\hat{\beta}_3$ were significantly different from zero in a positive direction, then we could reject the null hypothesis of no difference due to gender in the impact of experience on earnings, holding constant the other variables in the equation.

7.5 Problems with Incorrect Functional Forms

Once in a while a circumstance will arise in which the model is logically nonlinear in the variables, but the exact form of this nonlinearity is hard to specify. In such a case, the linear form is not correct, and yet a choice between the various nonlinear forms cannot be made on the basis of economic theory. Even in these cases, however, it still pays (in terms of understanding the true relationships) to avoid choosing a functional form on the basis of fit alone.

If functional forms are similar, and if theory does not specify exactly which form to use, why should we try to avoid using goodness of fit over the sample to determine which equation to use? This section will highlight two answers to this question:

1. $\overline{R}^2$s are difficult to compare if the dependent variable is transformed.

2. An incorrect functional form may provide a reasonable fit within the sample but have the potential to make large forecast errors when used outside the range of the sample.

$\overline{R}^2$s Are Difficult to Compare When Y Is Transformed

When the dependent variable is transformed from its linear version, the overall measure of fit, the $\overline{R}^2$, cannot be used for comparing the fit of the nonlinear equation with the original linear one.[5] This problem is not especially important in most cases because the emphasis in applied regression analysis

---

5. This warning also applies to other measures of overall fit, for example Akaike's Information Criterion (AIC) and the Bayesian Information Criterion (BIC) of Section 6.7, the appendix on additional specification criteria.

is usually on the coefficient estimates. However, if $\overline{R}^2$s are ever used to compare the fit of two different functional forms, then it becomes crucial that this lack of comparability be remembered. For example, suppose you were trying to compare a linear equation:

$$Y = \beta_0 + \beta_1 X_1 + \beta_2 X_2 + \epsilon \tag{7.20}$$

with a semilog version of the same equation (using the version of a semilog function that takes the log of the dependent variable):

$$\ln Y = \beta_0 + \beta_1 X_1 + \beta_2 X_2 + \epsilon \tag{7.21}$$

Notice that the only difference between Equations 7.20 and 7.21 is the functional form of the dependent variable. The reason that the $\overline{R}^2$s of the respective equations cannot be used to compare overall fits of the two equations is that the total sum of squares (TSS) of the dependent variable around its mean is different in the two formulations. That is, the $\overline{R}^2$s are not comparable because the dependent variables are different. There is no reason to expect that different dependent variables will have the identical (or easily comparable) degrees of dispersion around their means.

Incorrect Functional Forms Outside the Range of the Sample

If an incorrect functional form is used, then the probability of mistaken inferences about the true population parameters will increase. Using an incorrect functional form is a kind of specification error that is similar to the omitted variable bias discussed in Section 6.1. Even if an incorrect functional form provides good statistics within a sample, large residuals almost surely will arise when the misspecified equation is used on data that were not part of the sample used to estimate the coefficients.

In general, the extrapolation of a regression equation to data that are outside the range over which the equation was estimated runs increased risks of large forecasting errors and incorrect conclusions about population values. This risk is heightened if the regression uses a functional form that is inappropriate for the particular variables being studied.

Two functional forms that behave similarly over the range of the sample may behave quite differently outside that range. If the functional form is chosen on the basis of theory, then the researcher can take into account how the equation would act over any range of values, even if some of those values are outside the range of the sample. If functional forms are chosen on the basis of fit, then extrapolating outside the sample becomes tenuous.

Figure 7.6 contains a number of hypothetical examples. As can be seen, some functional forms have the potential to fit quite poorly outside the

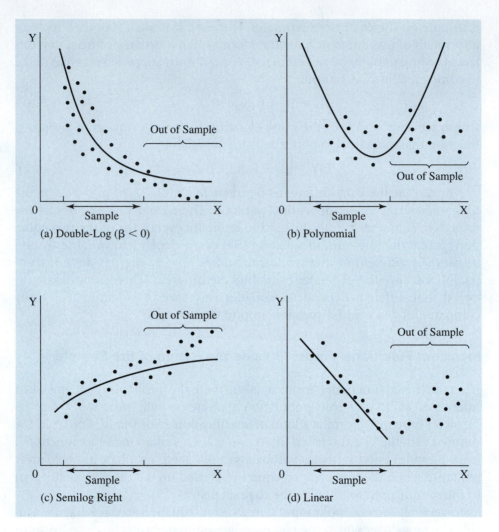

Figure 7.6 Incorrect Functional Forms Outside the Sample Range

If an incorrect form is applied to data outside the range of the sample on which it was estimated, the probability of large mistakes increases. In particular, note how the polynomial functional form can change slope rapidly outside the sample range (panel b) and that even a linear form can cause mistakes if the true functional form is nonlinear (panel d).

sample range. Such graphs are meant as examples of what could happen, not as statements of what necessarily will happen, when incorrect functional forms are pushed outside the range of the sample over which they were estimated. Do not conclude from these diagrams that nonlinear functions should be avoided. If the true relationship is nonlinear, then the *linear* functional form will make large forecasting errors outside the sample. Instead, the researcher must take the time to think through how the equation will act for values both inside and outside the sample before choosing a functional form to use to estimate the equation. If the theoretically appropriate nonlinear equation appears to work well over the relevant range of possible values, then it should be used without concern over this issue.

7.6 Summary

1. Do not suppress the constant term. On the other hand, don't rely on estimates of the constant term for inference even if it appears to be statistically significant.

2. The choice of a functional form should be based on the underlying economic theory to the extent that theory suggests a shape similar to that provided by a particular functional form. A form that is linear in the variables should be used unless a specific hypothesis suggests otherwise.

3. Functional forms that are nonlinear in the variables include the double-log form, the semilog form, and the polynomial form. The double-log form is especially useful if the elasticities involved are expected to be constant. The semilog form has the advantage of allowing the effect of an independent variable to tail off as that variable increases. The polynomial form is useful if the slopes are expected to change sign, depending on the level of an independent variable.

4. A slope dummy is a dummy variable that is multiplied by an independent variable to allow the slope of the relationship between the dependent variable and the particular independent variable to change, depending on whether a particular condition is met.

5. The use of nonlinear functional forms has a number of potential problems. In particular, the $\overline{R}^2$s are difficult to compare if Y has been transformed, and the residuals are potentially large if an incorrect functional form is used for forecasting outside the range of the sample.

EXERCISES

(The answers to the even-numbered exercises are in Appendix A.)

1. Write the meaning of each of the following terms without referring to the book (or your notes), and compare your definition with the version in the text for each.
   a. double-log functional form (p. 194)
   b. elasticity (p. 194)
   c. interaction term (p. 203)
   d. intercept dummy (p. 203)
   e. lag (p. 202)
   f. linear in the coefficients (p. 193)
   g. linear in the variables (p. 192)
   h. log (p. 196)
   i. natural log (p. 196)
   j. polynomial functional form (p. 199)
   k. semilog functional form (p. 196)
   l. slope dummy (p. 204)

2. For each of the following pairs of dependent (Y) and independent (X) variables, pick the functional form that you think is likely to be appropriate, and then explain your reasoning (assume that all other relevant independent variables are included in the equation):
   a. Y = sales of shoes
      X = disposable income
   b. Y = the attendance at the Hollywood Bowl outdoor symphony concerts on a given night
      X = whether the orchestra's most famous conductor was scheduled to conduct that night
   c. Y = aggregate consumption of goods and services in the United States
      X = aggregate disposable income in the United States
   d. Y = the money supply in the United States
      X = the interest rate on Treasury Bills (in a demand function)
   e. Y = the average production cost of a box of pasta
      X = the number of boxes of pasta produced

3. Look over the following equations and decide whether they are linear in the variables, linear in the coefficients, both, or neither:

a. $Y_i = \beta_0 + \beta_1 X_i^3 + \epsilon_i$

b. $Y_i = \beta_0 + \beta_1 \ln X_i + \epsilon_i$

c. $\ln Y_i = \beta_0 + \beta_1 \ln X_i + \epsilon_i$

d. $Y_i = \beta_0 + \beta_1 X_i^{\beta_2} + \epsilon_i$

e. $Y_i^{\beta_0} = \beta_1 + \beta_2 X_i^2 + \epsilon_i$

4. In 2003, Ray Fair[6] analyzed the relationship between stock prices and risk aversion by looking at the 1996–2000 performance of the 65 companies that had been a part of Standard and Poor's famous index (the S&P 500) since its inception in 1957. Fair focused on the P/E ratio (the ratio of a company's stock price to its earnings per share) and its relationship to the beta coefficient (a measure of a company's riskiness—a high beta implies high risk). Hypothesizing that the stock price would be a positive function of earnings growth and dividend growth, he estimated the following equation:

$$\widehat{LNPE_i} = 2.74 - 0.22 BETA_i + 0.83 EARN_i + 2.81 DIV_i$$
$$(0.11) \qquad (0.57) \qquad (0.84)$$
$$t = \qquad -1.99 \qquad 1.44 \qquad 3.33$$
$$N = 65 \quad R^2 = .232 \quad \overline{R}^2 = .194$$

where: $LNPE_i$ = the log of the median P/E ratio of the *i*th company from 1996 to 2000

$BETA_i$ = the mean beta coefficient of the *i*th company from 1958 to 1994

$EARN_i$ = the median percentage earnings growth rate for the *i*th company from 1996 to 2000

DIV_i = the median percentage dividend growth rate for the *i*th company from 1996 to 2000

a. Create and test appropriate hypotheses about the slope coefficients of this equation at the 5-percent level.

b. One of these variables is lagged and yet this is a cross-sectional equation. Explain which variable is lagged and why you think Fair lagged it.

c. Is one of Fair's variables potentially irrelevant? Which one? Use Stata, EViews, or your own regression program on the data in Table 7.2 to estimate Fair's equation without your potentially

---

6. Ray C. Fair, "Risk Aversion and Stock Prices," Cowles Foundation Discussion Papers 1382, Cowles Foundation: Yale University, revised February 2003 © 2003. Most of the article is well beyond the scope of this text, but Fair generously included the data (including proprietary data that he generated) necessary to replicate his regression results. Note that the beta coefficient is not the same as the β regression coefficient used in econometrics.

Table 7.2 Data for the Stock Price Example

	COMPANY	PE	BETA	EARN	DIV
1	Alcan	12.64	0.466	0.169	−0.013
2	TXU Corp.	10.80	0.545	0.016	0.014
3	Procter & Gamble	19.90	0.597	0.066	0.050
4	PG&E	11.30	0.651	0.021	0.014
5	Phillips Petroleum	13.27	0.678	0.071	0.006
6	AT&T	13.71	0.697	−0.004	−0.008
7	Minnesota Mining & Mfg.	17.61	0.781	0.054	0.051
8	Alcoa	15.97	0.795	0.120	−0.015
9	American Electric Power	10.68	0.836	−0.001	−0.021
10	Public Service Entrp	9.63	0.845	−0.018	−0.011
11	Hercules	16.07	0.851	0.077	−0.008
12	Air Products & Chemicals	16.20	0.865	0.051	0.074
13	Bristol Myers Squibb	17.01	0.866	0.068	0.110
14	Kimberly-Clark	13.42	0.869	0.063	0.018
15	Aetna	8.98	0.894	−0.137	0.007
16	Wrigley	14.49	0.898	0.062	0.044
17	Halliburton	17.84	0.906	0.120	−0.011
18	Deere & Co.	12.15	0.916	−0.010	0.004
19	Kroger	11.82	0.931	0.010	0.000
20	Intl Business Machines	16.08	0.944	0.081	0.045
21	Caterpillar	16.95	0.952	−0.043	−0.005
22	Goodrich	12.06	0.958	0.028	−0.015
23	General Mills	17.16	0.965	0.060	0.048
24	Winn-Dixie Stores	16.10	0.973	0.045	0.047
25	Heinz (H J)	13.49	0.979	0.079	0.079
26	Eastman Kodak	28.28	0.983	0.023	0.009
27	Campbell Soup	16.33	0.986	0.028	0.025
28	Philip Morris	12.25	0.993	0.129	0.130
29	Southern Co.	11.26	0.995	0.034	0.000
30	Du Pont	14.16	0.996	0.099	0.001
31	Phelps Dodge	11.47	1.008	0.186	−0.011
32	Pfizer Inc.	17.63	1.019	0.052	0.062
33	Hershey Foods	14.66	1.022	0.025	0.058
34	Ingersoll-Rand	14.24	1.024	0.045	−0.018

(continued)

Table 7.2 (*continued*)

	COMPANY	PE	BETA	EARN	DIV
35	FPL Group	11.86	1.048	0.038	0.019
36	Pitney Bowes	16.11	1.064	0.049	0.086
37	Archer-Daniels-Midland	14.43	1.073	0.073	−0.011
38	Rockwell	9.42	1.075	0.062	0.020
39	Dow Chemical	15.25	1.081	0.042	0.026
40	General Electric	15.16	1.091	0.051	0.015
41	Abbott Laboratories	17.58	1.097	0.114	0.098
42	Merck & Co.	23.29	1.122	0.066	0.072
43	J C Penney	13.14	1.133	0.094	−0.003
44	Union Pacific Corp.	12.99	1.136	0.010	0.021
45	Schering-Plough	18.18	1.137	0.112	0.060
46	Pepsico	18.94	1.147	0.082	0.046
47	McGraw-Hill	16.93	1.150	0.051	0.052
48	Household International	8.36	1.184	0.019	0.008
49	Emerson Electric	17.52	1.196	0.047	0.044
50	General Motors	11.21	1.206	0.052	−0.023
51	Colgate-Palmolive	16.60	1.213	0.067	0.025
52	Eaton Corp.	10.64	1.216	0.137	0.001
53	Dana Corp.	10.26	1.222	0.069	−0.011
54	Sears Roebuck	12.41	1.256	0.030	−0.014
55	Corning Inc.	19.33	1.258	0.052	−0.013
56	General Dynamics	9.06	1.285	0.056	−0.023
57	Coca-Cola	21.68	1.290	0.085	0.055
58	Boeing	11.93	1.306	0.169	0.017
59	Ford	8.62	1.308	0.016	0.026
60	Peoples Energy	9.58	1.454	0.000	0.005
61	Goodyear	12.02	1.464	0.022	0.012
62	May Co.	11.32	1.525	0.050	0.006
63	ITT Industries	9.92	1.630	0.038	0.018
64	Raytheon	11.75	1.821	0.112	0.050
65	Cooper Industries	12.41	1.857	0.108	0.037

Source: Ray C. Fair, "Risk Aversion and Stock Prices," Cowles Foundation Discussion Papers 1382, Cowles Foundation: Yale University, revised February 2003 © 2003.

Datafile = STOCK7

irrelevant variable and then use our four specification criteria to determine whether the variable is indeed irrelevant.

d. What functional form does Fair use? Does this form seem appropriate on the basis of theory? (*Hint:* A review of the literature would certainly help you answer this question, but before you start that review, think through the meaning of the slope coefficients in this functional form.)

e. (optional) Suppose that your review of the literature makes you concerned that Fair should have used a double-log functional form for his equation. Use the data in Table 7.2 to estimate that functional form on Fair's data. What is your estimated result? Does it support your concern? Explain.

5. In an effort to explain regional wage differentials, you collect wage data from 7,338 unskilled workers, divide the country into four regions (Northeast, South, Midwest, and West), and estimate the following equation (standard errors in parentheses):

$$\hat{Y}_i = 4.78 - 0.038E_i - 0.041S_i - 0.048W_i$$
$$\phantom{\hat{Y}_i = 4.78 -} (0.019)\quad (0.010)\quad (0.012)$$
$$\bar{R}^2 = .49 \qquad N = 7,338$$

where: Y_i = the hourly wage (in dollars) of the *i*th unskilled worker

E_i = a dummy variable equal to 1 if the *i*th worker lives in the Northeast, 0 otherwise

S_i = a dummy variable equal to 1 if the *i*th worker lives in the South, 0 otherwise

W_i = a dummy variable equal to 1 if the *i*th worker lives in the West, 0 otherwise

a. What is the omitted condition in this equation?

b. If you add a dummy variable for the omitted condition to the equation without dropping E_i, S_i, or W_i, what will happen?

c. If you add a dummy variable for the omitted condition to the equation and drop E_i, what will the sign of the new variable's estimated coefficient be?

d. Which of the following three statements is most correct? Least correct? Explain your answers.

   i.   The equation explains 49 percent of the variation of Y around its mean with regional variables alone, so there must be quite a bit of wage variation by region.

    ii.   The coefficients of the regional variables are virtually identical, so there must not be much wage variation by region.

    iii.   The coefficients of the regional variables are quite small compared with the average wage, so there must not be much wage variation by region.

6. Suggest the appropriate functional forms for the relationships between the following variables. Be sure to explain your reasoning:

    a. The age of the ith house in a cross-sectional equation for the sales price of houses in Cooperstown, New York. (*Hint:* Cooperstown is known as a lovely town with a number of elegant historic homes.)

    b. The price of natural gas in year t in a demand-side time-series equation for the consumption of natural gas in the United States.

    c. The income of the ith individual in a cross-sectional equation for the number of suits owned by individuals.

    d. A dummy variable for being a student ($1 =$ yes) in the equation specified in part c.

7. V. N. Murti and V. K. Sastri[7] investigated the production characteristics of various Indian industries, including cotton and sugar. They specified Cobb–Douglas production functions for output (Q) as a double-log function of labor (L) and capital (K):

$$\ln Q_i = \beta_0 + \beta_1 \ln L_i + \beta_2 \ln K_i + \epsilon_i$$

and obtained the following estimates (standard errors in parentheses):

Industry	$\hat{\beta}_0$	$\hat{\beta}_1$	$\hat{\beta}_2$	R^2
Cotton	0.97	0.92 (0.03)	0.12 (0.04)	.98
Sugar	2.70	0.59 (0.14)	0.33 (0.17)	.80

    a. What are the elasticities of output with respect to labor and capital for each industry?

    b. What economic significance does the sum ($\hat{\beta}_1 + \hat{\beta}_2$) have?

    c. Murti and Sastri expected positive slope coefficients. Test their hypotheses at the 5-percent level of significance. (*Hint:* This is much harder than it looks!)

7. V. N. Murti and V. K. Sastri, "Production Functions for Indian Industry," *Econometrica*, Vol. 25, No. 2, pp. 205–221.

8. Richard Fowles and Peter Loeb studied the interactive effect of drinking and altitude on traffic deaths.[8] The authors hypothesized that drunk driving fatalities are more likely at high altitude than at low altitude because higher elevations diminish the oxygen intake of the brain, increasing the impact of a given amount of alcohol. To test this hypothesis, they used an interaction variable between altitude and beer consumption. They estimated the following cross-sectional model (by state for the continental United States) of the motor vehicle fatality rate (Note: t-scores in parentheses):

$$\hat{F}_i = -3.36 - 0.002B_i + 0.17S_i - 0.31D_i + 0.011B_iA_i \qquad (7.22)$$
$$(-0.08) \quad (1.85)(-1.29) \quad (4.05)$$
$$N = 48 \qquad \overline{R}^2 = .499$$

where: F_i = traffic fatalities per motor vehicle mile driven in the *i*th state

B_i = per capita consumption of beer (malt beverages) in state *i*

S_i = average highway driving speed in state *i*

D_i = a dummy variable equal to 1 if the *i*th state had a vehicle safety inspection program, 0 otherwise

A_i = the average altitude of metropolitan areas in state *i* (in thousands)

a. Carefully state and test appropriate hypotheses about the coefficients of B, S, and D at the 5-percent level. Do these results give any indication of econometric problems in the equation? Explain.

b. Think through the interaction variable. What is it measuring? Carefully state the meaning of the coefficient of B*A.

c. Create and test appropriate hypotheses about the coefficient of the interaction variable at the 5-percent level.

d. Note that A_i is included in the equation in the interaction variable but not as an independent variable on its own. If an equation includes an interaction variable, should both components of the

8. Richard Fowles and Peter D. Loeb, "The Interactive Effect of Alcohol and Altitude on Traffic Fatalities," *Southern Economic Journal*, Vol. 59, pp. 108–111. To focus the analysis, we have omitted the coefficients of three other variables (the minimum legal drinking age, the percent of the population between 18 and 24, and the variability of highway driving speeds) that were insignificant in Equations 7.22 and 7.23.

interaction be independent variables in the equation as a matter of course? Why or why not? (*Hint:* Recall that with slope dummies, we emphasized that both the intercept dummy term and the slope dummy variable term should be in the equation.)

e. When the authors included A_i in their model, the results were as in Equation 7.23 (with *t*-scores once again in parenthesis). Which equation do you prefer? Explain.

$$\hat{F}_i = -2.33 - 0.024B_i + 0.14S_i - 0.24D_i - 0.35A_i + 0.023B_i\,A_i \qquad (7.23)$$
$$\phantom{\hat{F}_i = }(-0.80) \quad (1.53)(-0.96)\,(-1.07) \quad (1.97)$$

$$N = 48 \quad \overline{R}^2 = .501$$

7.7) Appendix: Econometric Lab #4

This lab is an exercise in specification: choosing the variables and the functional form. It also will give you experience in transforming variables and conducting joint hypothesis tests in Stata or your computer's econometric software program. The dependent variable that we're going to study is the price of a used farm tractor that was sold at auction in the United States.

Step 1: Review the Literature

Since you're probably not an expert on the prices of used tractors, let's start with a quick review of the literature. This is a model of the price of a used tractor as a function of the attributes of that tractor and the time of the sale, so this is another example of a *hedonic* model. For more on hedonic models, see page 358.

Believe it or not, there have been a number of econometric studies of tractor prices. Most significantly, in 2008 Diekmann et al.[9] studied used tractor prices utilizing a semilog left functional form and found that key independent variables included make, horsepower, age, hours of use, sale date, drive (four-wheel drive or two-wheel drive), automatic transmission, and fuel (diesel or gas). This provides a useful starting point.

9. Florian Diekmann, Brian E. Roe, and Marvin T. Batte, "Tractors on eBay: Differences between Internet and In-Person Auctions." *American Journal of Agricultural Economics*, Vol. 90, No. 2, pp. 306–320. Also see Gregory Perry, Ahmet Bayaner, and Clair J. Nixon, "The Effect of Usage and Size on Tractor Depreciation," *American Journal of Agricultural Economics*, Vol. 72, No. 2, pp. 317–325.

Table 7.3 Variable Definitions for the Used Tractor Price Model

Variable	Description	Hypoth. Sign of Coef.
Y_i = saleprice$_i$	The price paid for tractor i in dollars	n/a
Tractor Specifications:		
horsepower$_i$	The horsepower of tractor i	+
age$_i$	The number of years since tractor i was manufactured	−
enghours$_i$	The number of hours of use recorded on tractor i	−
diesel$_i$	A dummy variable = 1 if tractor i runs on diesel fuel, 0 otherwise	+
fwd$_i$	A dummy variable = 1 if tractor i has four-wheel drive, 0 otherwise	+
manual$_i$	A dummy variable = 1 if tractor i transmission is manual, 0 otherwise	−
johndeere$_i$	A dummy variable = 1 if tractor i is manufactured by John Deere, 0 otherwise	+
cab$_i$	A dummy variable = 1 if tractor i has an enclosed cab, 0 otherwise	+
Time of year:		
spring$_i$	A dummy variable = 1 if tractor i was sold in April or May, 0 otherwise	?
summer$_i$	A dummy variable = 1 if tractor i was sold June–September, 0 otherwise	?
winter$_i$	A dummy variable = 1 if tractor i was sold December–March, 0 otherwise	?

Step 2: Estimate the Basic Model

As our basic model, let's estimate a variation of Diekmann's model using a more current dataset. Table 7.3 contains the definitions of the variables we'll need to attempt to replicate Diekmann's regression. The dependent variable is the price of a used farm tractor that was sold at auction in the United States between June 1, 2011 and May 31, 2012. The data[10] are available on this text's website as dataset TRACTOR7. Table 7.3 also has the hypothesized expected sign of the coefficient of each variable, given the underlying theory. Now:

---

10. The data were collected by Preston Cahill of Centre College.

a. Estimate an equation with the natural log of the sale price (saleprice$_i$) as the dependent variable and all the other variables in Table 7.3 as the independent variables. (*Hints:* Don't forget to generate lnsaleprice before you run your regression, and make sure not to include any variables that are not listed in Table 7.3.)

b. Take a look at your regression results. What is $\overline{R}^2$? Does this seem reasonable? Explain your thinking.

c. Do any of your estimated coefficients have unexpected signs? If so, which ones?

d. Run one-sided 5-percent *t*-tests on the coefficients of all your independent variables except for the seasonal dummies. For which coefficients can you reject the null hypothesis?

e. Carefully interpret the coefficient of johndeere. What does it mean in real-world terms?

f. What econometric problems (if any) appear to exist in the basic model?

Step 3: Consider a Polynomial Functional Form for Horsepower

Suppose you show the results of your basic model to a used tractor dealer who happened to take econometrics in college. He says that your results are promising, but he's found it very difficult to sell overpowered used tractors because these tractors waste fuel and provide no extra benefit to the buyer. He thinks that new tractor buyers often overestimate how much power they'll need and that used tractor buyers don't make this mistake as often. He therefore suggests that it could be that as horsepower increases, the price increases, at least up to a point, but beyond that point, further increases in horsepower start to have a negative effect on price. You decide to take his advice and consider changing the functional form of horsepower to a polynomial.

a. Generate the new variable and run the new regression. (*Hint:* Did you remember to hypothesize the signs of the coefficients of horsepower and its square before you ran the regression?)

b. Run 5-percent one-sided *t*-tests on your hypotheses for the coefficients of horsepower and its square.

c. At what horsepower (to the nearest round number) does the value of a tractor reach an extreme (other things being equal)? Is the extreme a minimum or a maximum?

d. Which equation do you prefer between the basic equation and the polynomial equation? Why? (Be sure to cite evidence to support your choice.)

Step 4: Add a Potential Omitted Variable to Your Step 3 Model

As you're leaving the used tractor lot, you happen to notice that quite a few of the tractors have enclosed cabs. Since such a cab would come in handy in bad weather, you have a sudden sinking feeling that you might have an omitted variable! To test this, you find the data for cab (luckily also in TRACTOR7). Now:

a. Add cab to the model you preferred in Step 3, part d, and re-estimate the equation.
b. Use our four specification criteria to decide whether cab belongs in the equation. (*Hint:* Write out specific answers for all four criteria and then justify your conclusion.)

Step 5: Joint Hypothesis Testing

Go back to the basic model of Step 2, and test at the 5-percent level the joint hypothesis that the time of year of the sale has no effect on the price of tractors:

a. What is the omitted condition in this seasonal model? What's unusual about this?
b. Carefully write out your null and alternative hypotheses.
c. Estimate your constrained equation.
d. Run the appropriate *F*-test at the 5-percent level. Calculate F and look up the appropriate critical *F*-value.
e. What's your conclusion? Do used tractor prices have a seasonal pattern?

(Optional) Step 6: Consider a Slope Dummy That Interacts Diesel with Use

It is well known that diesel engines tend to be more durable than gasoline engines. That fact raises the question of whether an additional hour of use affects the value of a diesel tractor differently than for a gasoline tractor. Generate the variable you need to test this hypothesis, add this variable to the basic model of Step 2, estimate the revised slope dummy model, and test the appropriate slope dummy hypothesis at the 5-percent level. What is your *t*-value? Can you reject the null hypothesis?

Chapter 8

Multicollinearity

8.1 Perfect versus Imperfect Multicollinearity

8.2 The Consequences of Multicollinearity

8.3 The Detection of Multicollinearity

8.4 Remedies for Multicollinearity

8.5 An Example of Why Multicollinearity Often Is Best Left Unadjusted

8.6 Summary and Exercises

8.7 Appendix: The SAT Interactive Regression Learning Exercise

The next three chapters deal with violations of the Classical Assumptions and remedies for those violations. This chapter addresses multicollinearity, and the next two chapters address serial correlation and heteroskedasticity. For each of these three problems, we will attempt to answer the following questions:

1. What is the nature of the problem?
2. What are the consequences of the problem?
3. How is the problem diagnosed?
4. What remedies for the problem are available?

Strictly speaking, *perfect multicollinearity* is the violation of Classical Assumption VI—that no independent variable is a perfect linear function of one or more other independent variables. Perfect multicollinearity is rare, but severe imperfect multicollinearity, although not violating Classical Assumption VI, still causes substantial problems.

Recall that the coefficient β_k can be thought of as the impact on the dependent variable of a one-unit increase in the independent variable X_k, holding constant the other independent variables in the equation. If two explanatory variables are significantly related, then the OLS computer program will find

---

221

it difficult to distinguish the effects of one variable from the effects of the other.

In essence, the more highly correlated two (or more) independent variables are, the more difficult it becomes to accurately estimate the coefficients of the true model. If two variables move identically, then there is no hope of distinguishing between their impacts, but if the variables are only roughly correlated, then we still might be able to estimate the two effects accurately enough for most purposes.

8.1 Perfect versus Imperfect Multicollinearity

Perfect Multicollinearity

Perfect multicollinearity[1] violates Classical Assumption VI, which specifies that no explanatory variable is a perfect linear function of any other explanatory variable. The word *perfect* in this context implies that the variation in one explanatory variable can be *completely* explained by movements in another explanatory variable. Such a perfect linear function between two independent variables would be:

$$X_{1i} = \alpha_0 + \alpha_1 X_{2i} \tag{8.1}$$

where the αs are constants and the Xs are independent variables in:

$$Y_i = \beta_0 + \beta_1 X_{1i} + \beta_2 X_{2i} + \epsilon_i \tag{8.2}$$

Notice that there is no error term in Equation 8.1. This implies that X_1 can be exactly calculated given X_2 and the equation. Typical equations for such perfect linear relationships would be:

$$X_{1i} = 3X_{2i} \tag{8.3}$$

$$X_{1i} = 2 + 4X_{2i} \tag{8.4}$$

What are some real-world examples of perfect multicollinearity? The simplest examples involve the same variable measured in different units. Think about the distance between two cities measured in miles with X_1 and in kilometers with X_2. The data for the variables look quite different, but they're

---

1. The word *collinearity* describes a linear correlation between two independent variables, and *multicollinearity* indicates that more than two independent variables are involved. In common usage, multicollinearity is used to apply to both cases, and so we'll typically use that term in this text even though many of the examples and techniques discussed relate, strictly speaking, to collinearity.

perfectly correlated! A more subtle example is when the two variables always add up to the same amount, for instance P_1, the percent of voters who voted in favor of a proposition, and P_2, the percent who voted against it (assuming no abstentions), would always add up to 100% and therefore would be perfectly (negatively) correlated.

Figure 8.1 shows a graph of explanatory variables that are perfectly correlated. As can be seen in Figure 8.1, a perfect linear function has all data points on the same straight line. There is none of the variation that accompanies the data from a typical regression.

What happens to the estimation of an econometric equation where there is perfect multicollinearity? OLS is incapable of generating estimates of the regression coefficients, and most OLS computer programs will print out an error message in such a situation. Using Equation 8.2 as an example, we theoretically would obtain the following estimated coefficients and standard errors:

$$\hat{\beta}_1 = \text{indeterminate} \qquad SE(\hat{\beta}_1) = \infty \qquad (8.5)$$
$$\hat{\beta}_2 = \text{indeterminate} \qquad SE(\hat{\beta}_2) = \infty \qquad (8.6)$$

Perfect multicollinearity ruins our ability to estimate the coefficients because the two variables cannot be distinguished. You cannot "hold all the other independent variables in the equation constant" if every time one variable changes, another changes in an identical manner.

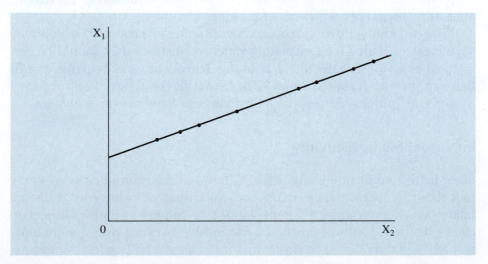

Figure 8.1 Perfect Multicollinearity

With perfect multicollinearity, an independent variable can be completely explained by the movements of one or more other independent variables. Perfect multicollinearity can usually be avoided by careful screening of the independent variables before a regression is run.

Fortunately, instances in which one explanatory variable is a perfect linear function of another are rare. More important, perfect multicollinearity should be fairly easy to discover before a regression is run. You can detect perfect multicollinearity by asking whether one variable equals a multiple of another or if one variable can be derived by adding a constant to another or if a variable equals the sum of two other variables. If so, then one of the variables should be dropped because there is no essential difference between the two.

A special case related to perfect multicollinearity occurs when a variable that is definitionally related to the dependent variable is included as an independent variable in a regression equation. Such a **dominant variable** is by definition so highly correlated with the dependent variable that it completely masks the effects of all other independent variables in the equation. In a sense, this is a case of perfect collinearity between the dependent variable and an independent variable.

For example, if you include a variable measuring the amount of raw materials used by the shoe industry in a production function for that industry, the raw materials variable would have an extremely high t-score, but otherwise important variables like labor and capital would have quite insignificant t-scores. Why? In essence, if you knew how much leather was used by a shoe factory, you could predict the number of pairs of shoes produced without knowing *anything* about labor or capital. The relationship is definitional, and the dominant variable should be dropped from the equation to get reasonable estimates of the coefficients of the other variables.

Be careful, though! Dominant variables shouldn't be confused with highly significant or important explanatory variables. Instead, they should be recognized as being virtually identical to the dependent variable. While the fit between the two is superb, knowledge of that fit could have been obtained from the definitions of the variables without any econometric estimation.

Imperfect Multicollinearity

Since perfect multicollinearity is fairly easy to avoid, econometricians rarely talk about it. Instead, when we use the word multicollinearity, we really are talking about severe imperfect multicollinearity. **Imperfect multicollinearity** can be defined as a linear functional relationship between two or more independent variables that is so strong that it can significantly affect the estimation of the coefficients of the variables.

In other words, imperfect multicollinearity occurs when two (or more) explanatory variables are imperfectly linearly related, as in:

$$X_{1i} = \alpha_0 + \alpha_1 X_{2i} + u_i \tag{8.7}$$

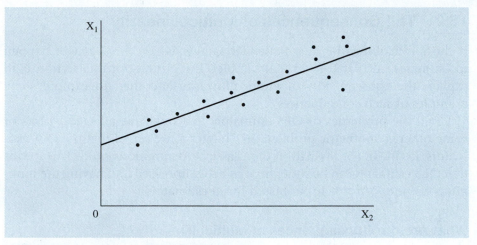

Figure 8.2 Imperfect Multicollinearity

With imperfect multicollinearity, an independent variable is a strong but not perfect linear function of one or more other independent variables. Imperfect multicollinearity varies in degree from sample to sample.

Compare Equation 8.7 to Equation 8.1; notice that Equation 8.7 includes u_i, a stochastic error term. This implies that although the relationship between X_1 and X_2 might be fairly strong, it is not strong enough to allow X_1 to be completely explained by X_2; some unexplained variation still remains. Figure 8.2 shows the graph of two explanatory variables that might be considered imperfectly multicollinear. Notice that although all the observations in the sample are fairly close to the straight line, there is still some variation in X_1 that cannot be explained by X_2.

Imperfect multicollinearity is a strong linear relationship between the explanatory variables. The stronger the relationship is between the two (or more) explanatory variables, the more likely it is that they'll be considered significantly multicollinear. Two variables that might be only slightly related in one sample might be so strongly related in another that they could be considered to be imperfectly multicollinear. In this sense, it is fair to say that multicollinearity is a sample phenomenon as well as a theoretical one. This contrasts with perfect multicollinearity because two variables that are perfectly related probably can be detected on a logical basis. The detection of multicollinearity will be discussed in more detail in Section 8.3.

8.2 The Consequences of Multicollinearity

If the multicollinearity in a particular sample is severe, what will happen to estimates calculated from that sample? The purpose of this section is to explain the consequences of multicollinearity and then to explore some examples of such consequences.

Recall the properties of OLS estimators that might be affected by this or some other econometric problem. In Chapter 4, we stated that the OLS estimators are BLUE (or MvLUE) if the Classical Assumptions hold. This means that OLS estimates can be thought of as being unbiased and having the minimum variance possible for unbiased linear estimators.

What Are the Consequences of Multicollinearity?

The major consequences of multicollinearity are:

1. *Estimates will remain unbiased.* Even if an equation has significant multicollinearity, the estimates of the βs still will be centered around the true population βs if the first six Classical Assumptions are met for a correctly specified equation.

2. *The variances and standard errors of the estimates will increase.* This is the principal consequence of multicollinearity. Since two or more of the explanatory variables are significantly related, it becomes difficult to precisely identify the separate effects of the multicollinear variables. When it becomes hard to distinguish the effect of one variable from the effect of another, we're much more likely to make large errors in estimating the βs than we were before we encountered multicollinearity. As a result, the estimated coefficients, although still unbiased, now come from distributions with much larger variances and, therefore, larger standard errors.

   Even though the variances and standard errors are larger with multicollinearity than they are without it, OLS is still BLUE when multicollinearity exists. That is, no other linear unbiased estimation technique can get lower variances than OLS even in the presence of multicollinearity. Thus, although the effect of multicollinearity is to increase the variance of the estimated coefficients, OLS still has the property of minimum variance. These "minimum variances" are just fairly large.

   Figure 8.3 compares a distribution of β̂s from a sample with severe multicollinearity to one with virtually no correlation between any of the independent variables. Notice that the two distributions have the same mean, indicating that multicollinearity does not cause bias. Also

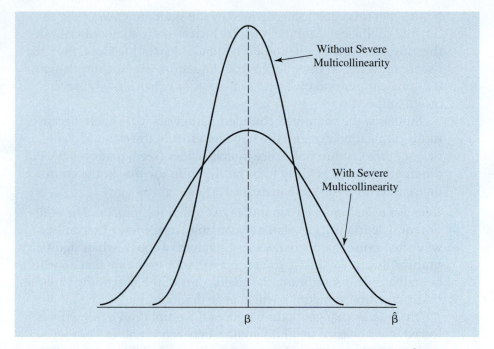

Figure 8.3 Severe Multicollinearity Increases the Variances of the $\hat{\beta}$s

Severe multicollinearity produces a distribution of the $\hat{\beta}$s that is centered around the true β but that has a much wider variance. Thus, the distribution of $\hat{\beta}$s with multicollinearity is much wider than otherwise.

note how much wider the distribution of $\hat{\beta}$ becomes when multicollinearity is severe; this is the result of the increase in the standard error of $\hat{\beta}$ that is caused by multicollinearity.

Because of this larger variance, multicollinearity increases the likelihood of obtaining an unexpected sign[2] for a coefficient even though, as mentioned earlier, multicollinearity causes no bias.

3. *The computed t-scores will fall.* Multicollinearity tends to decrease the *t*-scores of the estimated coefficients mainly because of the formula for the *t*-statistic:

$$t_k = \frac{(\hat{\beta}_k - \beta_{H_0})}{SE(\hat{\beta}_k)} \tag{8.8}$$

2. These unexpected signs generally occur because the distribution of the $\hat{\beta}$s with multicollinearity is wider than it would be without it, increasing the chance that a particular observed $\hat{\beta}$ will be on the other side of zero from the true β (have an unexpected sign).

Notice that this equation is divided by the standard error of the estimated coefficient. Multicollinearity increases the standard error of the estimated coefficient, and if the standard error increases, then the t-score must fall, as can be seen from Equation 8.8. Not surprisingly, it's quite common to observe low t-scores in equations with severe multicollinearity.

Similarly, the computed confidence intervals will widen. Because multicollinearity increases the standard error of the estimated coefficient, it makes the confidence interval wider (see Equation 5.9). Put differently, since $\hat{\beta}$ is likely to be farther from the true β, the confidence interval is forced to increase.

4. *Estimates will become very sensitive to changes in specification.* The addition or deletion of an explanatory variable or of a few observations will often cause major changes in the values of the $\hat{\beta}$s when significant multicollinearity exists. If you drop a variable, even one that appears to be statistically insignificant, the coefficients of the remaining variables in the equation sometimes will change dramatically.

These large changes occur because OLS estimation is sometimes forced to emphasize small differences between variables in order to distinguish the effect of one multicollinear variable from that of another. If two variables are virtually identical throughout most of the sample, the estimation procedure relies on the observations in which the variables move differently in order to distinguish between them. As a result, a specification change that drops a variable that has an unusual value for one of these crucial observations can cause the estimated coefficients of the multicollinear variables to change dramatically.

5. *The overall fit of the equation and the estimation of the coefficients of nonmulticollinear variables will be largely unaffected.* Even though the individual t-scores are often quite low in a multicollinear equation, the overall fit of the equation, as measured by $\overline{R}^2$, will not fall much, if at all, in the face of significant multicollinearity. Given this, one of the first indications of severe multicollinearity is the combination of a high $\overline{R}^2$ with no statistically significant individual regression coefficients. Similarly, if an explanatory variable in an equation is not multicollinear with the other variables, then the estimation of its coefficient and standard error usually will not be affected.

Because the overall fit is largely unchanged, it's possible for the F-test of overall significance to reject the null hypothesis even though none of the t-tests on individual coefficients can do so. Such a result is a clear indication of severe imperfect multicollinearity.

Finally, since multicollinearity has little effect on the overall fit of the equation, it also will have little effect on the use of that equation for prediction or forecasting, as long as the independent variables maintain the same pattern of multicollinearity in the forecast period that they demonstrated in the sample.

Two Examples of the Consequences of Multicollinearity

To see what severe multicollinearity does to an estimated equation, let's look at a hypothetical example. Suppose you decide to estimate a "student consumption function." After the appropriate preliminary work, you come up with the following hypothesized equation:

$$\overset{+}{CO_i} = \beta_0 + \beta_1 Yd_i \overset{-}{+ \beta_2 LA_i} + \epsilon_i \tag{8.9}$$

where: CO_i = the annual consumption expenditures of the ith student on items other than tuition and room and board

Yd_i = the annual disposable income (including gifts) of that student

LA_i = the liquid assets (savings, etc.) of the ith student

ϵ_i = a stochastic error term

You then collect a small amount of data from people who are sitting near you in class:

Student	CO_i	Yd_i	LA_i
Mary	$2000	$2500	$25000
Robby	2300	3000	31000
Bevin	2800	3500	33000
Lesley	3800	4000	39000
Brandon	3500	4500	48000
Bruce	5000	5000	54000
Harwood	4500	5500	55000

Datafile = CONS8

If you run an OLS regression on your data set for Equation 8.9, you obtain:

$$\widehat{CO_i} = -367.83 + 0.5113 Yd_i + 0.0427 LA_i \tag{8.10}$$
$$(1.0307) \quad (0.0942)$$
$$t = 0.496 \qquad 0.453$$
$$\overline{R}^2 = .835$$

On the other hand, if you had consumption as a function of disposable income alone, then you would have obtained:

$$\widehat{CO}_i = -471.43 + 0.9714Yd_i \tag{8.11}$$
$$(0.157)$$
$$t = 6.187$$
$$\overline{R}^2 = .861$$

Notice from Equations 8.10 and 8.11 that the *t*-score for disposable income increases more than tenfold when the liquid assets variable is dropped from the equation. Why does this happen? First of all, the correlation between Yd and LA is quite high. This high degree of correlation causes the standard errors of the estimated coefficients to be very high when both variables are included. In the case of $\hat{\beta}_{Yd}$, the standard error goes from 0.157 to 1.03 with the inclusion of LA! In addition, the coefficient estimate itself changes somewhat. Further, note that the $\overline{R}^2$s of the two equations are quite similar despite the large differences in the significance of the explanatory variables in the two equations. It's quite common for $\overline{R}^2$ to stay virtually unchanged when multicollinear variables are dropped. All of these results are typical of equations with multicollinearity.

Which equation is better? If the liquid assets variable theoretically belongs in the equation, then to drop it will run the risk of omitted variable bias, but to include the variable will mean certain multicollinearity. There is no automatic answer when dealing with multicollinearity. We'll discuss this issue in more detail in Sections 8.4 and 8.5.

A second example of the consequences of multicollinearity is based on actual rather than hypothetical data. Suppose you've decided to build a cross-sectional model of the demand for gasoline by state:

$$PCON_i = \beta_0 + \overset{+}{\beta_1 UHM_i} + \overset{-}{\beta_2 TAX_i} + \overset{+}{\beta_3 REG_i} + \epsilon_i \tag{8.12}$$

where: $PCON_i$ = petroleum consumption in the *i*th state (trillions of BTUs)

UHM_i = urban highway miles within the *i*th state

TAX_i = the gasoline tax rate in the *i*th state (cents per gallon)

REG_i = motor vehicle registrations in the *i*th state (thousands)

Given the definitions, let's move on to the estimation of Equation 8.12 using a linear functional form (assuming a classical error term):

$$\widehat{PCON}_i = 389.6 + 60.8UHM_i - 36.5TAX_i - 0.061REG_i \tag{8.13}$$
$$(10.3) \qquad (13.2) \qquad (0.043)$$
$$t = 5.92 \qquad -2.77 \qquad -1.43$$
$$N = 50 \qquad \overline{R}^2 = .919$$

What's wrong with this equation? The motor vehicle registrations variable has an insignificant coefficient with an unexpected sign, but it's hard to believe that the variable is irrelevant. Is an omitted variable causing bias? It's possible, but adding a variable is unlikely to fix things. Does it help to know that the correlation between REG and UHM is extremely high? Given that, it seems fair to say that one of the two variables is redundant; both variables are really measuring the *size* of the state, so we have multicollinearity.

Notice the impact of the multicollinearity on the equation. The coefficient of a variable such as motor vehicle registrations, which has a very strong theoretical relationship to petroleum consumption, is insignificant and has a sign contrary to our expectations. This is mainly because the multicollinearity has increased the variance of the distribution of the estimated $\hat{\beta}$s.

What would happen if we were to drop one of the multicollinear variables?

$$\widehat{PCON}_i = 551.7 - 53.6TAX_i + 0.186REG_i \qquad (8.14)$$
$$(16.9) \qquad (0.012)$$
$$t = -3.18 \qquad 15.88$$
$$N = 50 \qquad \overline{R}^2 = .861$$

Dropping UHM has made REG extremely significant. Why did this occur? The answer is that the standard error of the coefficient of REG has fallen substantially (from 0.043 to 0.012) now that the multicollinearity has been removed from the equation. Also note that the sign of the estimated coefficient has now become positive as hypothesized. The reason is that REG and UHM are virtually indistinguishable from an empirical point of view, and so the OLS program latched on to minor differences between the variables to explain the movements of PCON. Once the multicollinearity was removed, the direct positive relationship between REG and PCON was obvious.

Either UHM or REG could have been dropped with similar results because the two variables are, in a quantitative sense, virtually identical. In fact, our guess is that a majority of experienced econometricians, when faced with the results in Equation 8.13 and the high correlation between REG and UHM, would have dropped REG and kept UHM. Why did we do the opposite? Our opinion is that because UHM is an urban variable and REG is a statewide variable, REG is preferable from a theoretical standpoint if we're trying to understand statewide petroleum consumption. Since the two are identical quantitatively and REG is preferable theoretically, we'd keep REG, but we recognize that others could look at the same results and come to a different conclusion. Even though $\overline{R}^2$ fell when UHM was dropped, Equation 8.14 should be considered superior to Equation 8.13. This is an example of the point, first made in Chapter 2, that the fit of the equation is not the most important criterion to be used in determining its overall quality.

8.3 The Detection of Multicollinearity

How do we decide whether an equation has a severe multicollinearity problem? A first step is to recognize that some multicollinearity exists in every equation. It's virtually impossible in a real-world example to find a set of explanatory variables that are totally uncorrelated with each other (except for designed experiments). Our main purpose in this section will be to learn to determine *how much* multicollinearity exists in an equation, not *whether* any multicollinearity exists.

A second key point is that the severity of multicollinearity in a given equation can change from sample to sample depending on the characteristics of the sample. As a result, the theoretical underpinnings of the equation are not quite as important in the detection of multicollinearity as they are in the detection of an omitted variable or an incorrect functional form. Instead, we tend to rely more on data-oriented techniques to determine the severity of the multicollinearity in a given sample. Of course, we can never ignore the theory behind an equation. The trick is to find variables that are theoretically relevant (for meaningful interpretation) and that are also statistically non-multicollinear (for meaningful inference).

Because multicollinearity is a sample phenomenon and the level of damage of its impact is a matter of degree, many of the methods used to detect it are informal tests without critical values or levels of significance. Indeed, there are no generally accepted, true statistical tests for multicollinearity. Most researchers develop a general feeling for the severity of multicollinearity in an estimated equation by looking at a number of the characteristics of that equation. Let's examine two of the most frequently used characteristics.

High Simple Correlation Coefficients

One way to detect severe multicollinearity is to examine the simple correlation coefficients between the explanatory variables. The **simple correlation coefficient**, r, is a measure of the strength and direction of the linear relationship between two variables.[3] The range of r is from $+1$ to -1, and the sign of r indicates the direction of the correlation between the two variables. The

---

3. The equation for r_{12}, the simple correlation coefficient between X_1 and X_2, is:

$$r_{12} = \frac{\sum[(X_{1i} - \overline{X}_1)(X_{2i} - \overline{X}_2)]}{\sqrt{\sum(X_{1i} - \overline{X}_1)^2 \sum(X_{2i} - \overline{X}_2)^2}}$$

Interestingly, it turns out that r and R^2 are related if the estimated equation has exactly one independent variable. The square of r equals R^2 for a regression where one of the two variables is the dependent variable and the other is the only independent variable.

closer the absolute value of r is to 1, the stronger is the correlation between the two variables. Thus:

> If two variables are perfectly positively correlated, then $r = +1$
>
> If two variables are perfectly negatively correlated, then $r = -1$
>
> If two variables are totally uncorrelated, then $r = 0$

If an r is high in absolute value, then we know that these two particular Xs are quite correlated and that multicollinearity is a potential problem. For example, in Equation 8.10, the simple correlation coefficient between disposable income and liquid assets is 0.986. A simple correlation coefficient this high, especially in an equation with only two independent variables, is a certain indication of severe multicollinearity.

How high is high? Some researchers pick an arbitrary number, such as 0.80, and become concerned about multicollinearity any time the absolute value of a simple correlation coefficient exceeds 0.80. A better answer might be that r is high if it causes unacceptably large variances in the coefficient estimates in which we're interested.

Be careful: The use of simple correlation coefficients as an indication of the extent of multicollinearity involves a major limitation if there are more than two explanatory variables. It is quite possible for groups of independent variables, acting together, to cause multicollinearity without any single simple correlation coefficient being high enough to indicate that multicollinearity is in fact severe. As a result, simple correlation coefficients must be considered to be sufficient but not necessary tests for multicollinearity. Although a high r does indeed indicate the probability of severe multicollinearity, a low r by no means proves otherwise.[4]

High Variance Inflation Factors (VIFs)

The use of tests to give an indication of the severity of multicollinearity in a particular sample is controversial. Some econometricians reject even the simple correlation coefficient, mainly because of the limitations cited. Others tend to use a variety of more formal tests.[5]

---

4. Most authors criticize the use of simple correlation coefficients to detect multicollinearity in equations with large numbers of explanatory variables, but many researchers continue to do so because a scan of the simple correlation coefficients is a "quick and dirty" way to get a feel for the degree of multicollinearity in an equation.

5. Perhaps the best of these is the Condition number. For more on the Condition number, which is a single index of the degree of multicollinearity in the overall equation, see D. A. Belsley, *Conditioning Diagnostics* (New York: Wiley, 1991).

One measure of the severity of multicollinearity that is easy to use and that is gaining in popularity is the variance inflation factor. The **variance inflation factor (VIF)** is a method of detecting the severity of multicollinearity by looking at the extent to which a given explanatory variable can be explained by all the other explanatory variables in the equation. There is a VIF for each explanatory variable in an equation. The VIF is an index of how much multicollinearity has increased the variance of an estimated coefficient. A high VIF indicates that multicollinearity has increased the estimated variance of the estimated coefficient by quite a bit, yielding a decreased t-score.

Suppose you want to use the VIF to attempt to detect multicollinearity in an original equation with K independent variables:

$$Y = \beta_0 + \beta_1 X_1 + \beta_2 X_2 + \cdots + \beta_K X_K + \epsilon$$

Doing so requires calculating K different VIFs, one for each X_i. Calculating the VIF for a given X_i involves two steps:

1. *Run an OLS regression that has X_i as a function of all the other explanatory variables in the equation.* For $i = 1$, this equation would be:

$$X_1 = \alpha_1 + \alpha_2 X_2 + \alpha_3 X_3 + \cdots + \alpha_K X_K + v \tag{8.15}$$

   where v is a classical stochastic error term. Note that X_1 is not included on the right-hand side of Equation 8.15, which is referred to as an auxiliary or secondary regression. Thus there are K auxiliary regressions, one for each independent variable in the original equation.

2. *Calculate the variance inflation factor for $\hat{\beta}_i$:*

$$\mathrm{VIF}(\hat{\beta}_i) = \frac{1}{(1 - R_i^2)} \tag{8.16}$$

   where R_i^2 is the coefficient of determination (the unadjusted R^2) of the auxiliary regression in step one. Since there is a separate auxiliary regression for each independent variable in the original equation, there also is an R_i^2 and a $\mathrm{VIF}(\hat{\beta}_i)$ for each X_i. The higher the VIF, the more severe the effects of multicollinearity.

How high is high? An R_i^2 of 1, indicating perfect multicollinearity, produces a VIF of infinity, whereas an R_i^2 of 0, indicating no multicollinearity at all, produces a VIF of 1. While there is no table of formal critical VIF values, a common rule of thumb is that if $\mathrm{VIF}(\beta_i) > 5$, the multicollinearity is severe. As the number of independent variables increases, it makes sense to increase this number slightly.

For example, let's return to Equation 8.10 and calculate the VIFs for both independent variables. Both VIFs equal 36, confirming the quite severe multicollinearity we already know exists. It's no coincidence that the VIFs for the two variables are equal. In an equation with exactly two independent variables, the two auxiliary equations will have identical R_i^2s, leading to equal VIFs.[6]

Some authors and statistical software programs replace the VIF with its reciprocal, $(1 - R_i^2)$, called *tolerance*, or TOL. Whether we calculate VIF or TOL is a matter of personal preference, but either way, the general approach is the most comprehensive multicollinearity detection technique we've discussed in this text.

Unfortunately, there are a couple of problems with using VIFs. First, as mentioned, there is no hard-and-fast VIF decision rule. Second, it's possible to have multicollinear effects in an equation that has no large VIFs. For instance, if the simple correlation coefficient between X_1 and X_2 is 0.88, multicollinear effects are quite likely, and yet the VIF for the equation (assuming no other Xs) is only 4.4.

In essence, then, the VIF is a sufficient but not necessary test for multicollinearity, just like the other test described in this section. Indeed, as is probably obvious to the reader by now, there is no test that allows a researcher to reject the possibility of multicollinearity with any real certainty.

8.4 Remedies for Multicollinearity

What can be done to minimize the consequences of severe multicollinearity? There is no automatic answer to this question because multicollinearity is a phenomenon that could change from sample to sample even for the same specification of a regression equation. The purpose of this section is to outline a number of alternative remedies for multicollinearity that might be appropriate under certain circumstances.

Do Nothing

The first step to take once severe multicollinearity has been diagnosed is to decide whether anything should be done at all. As we'll see, it turns out that every remedy for multicollinearity has a drawback of some sort, and so it often happens that doing nothing is the correct course of action.

One reason for doing nothing is that multicollinearity in an equation will not always reduce the *t*-scores enough to make them insignificant or change

---

6. Another use for the R^2s of these auxiliary equations is to compare them with the overall equation's R^2. If an auxiliary equation's R^2 is higher, it's yet another sign of multicollinearity.

the $\hat{\beta}$s enough to make them differ from expectations. In other words, the mere existence of multicollinearity does not necessarily mean anything. A remedy for multicollinearity should be considered only if the consequences cause insignificant t-scores or unreliable estimated coefficients. For example, it's possible to observe a simple correlation coefficient of .97 between two explanatory variables and yet have each individual t-score be significant. It makes no sense to consider remedial action in such a case, as long as both variables belong in the equation on theoretical grounds, because any remedy for multicollinearity would probably cause other problems for the equation. In a sense, multicollinearity is similar to a non-life-threatening human disease that requires general anesthesia to operate on the patient: The risk of the operation should be undertaken only if the disease is causing a significant problem.

A second reason for doing nothing is that the deletion of a multicollinear variable that belongs in an equation will cause specification bias. If we drop a theoretically important variable, then we are *purposely* creating bias. Given all the effort typically spent avoiding omitted variables, it seems foolhardy to consider running that risk on purpose. As a result, experienced econometricians often will leave multicollinear variables in equations despite low t-scores.

The final reason for considering doing nothing to offset multicollinearity is that every time a regression is rerun, we risk encountering a specification that fits because it accidentally works for the particular data set involved, not because it is the truth. The larger the number of experiments, the greater the chances of finding the accidental result. To make things worse, when there is significant multicollinearity in the sample, the odds of strange results increase rapidly because of the sensitivity of the coefficient estimates to slight specification changes.

To sum, it is often best to leave an equation unadjusted in the face of all but extreme multicollinearity. Such advice might be difficult for beginning researchers to take, however, if they think that it's embarrassing to report that their final regression is one with insignificant t-scores. Compared to the alternatives of possible omitted variable bias or accidentally significant regression results, the low t-scores seem like a minor problem. For an example of "doing nothing" in the face of severe multicollinearity, see Section 8.5.

Drop a Redundant Variable

On occasion, the simple solution of dropping one of the multicollinear variables is a good one. For example, some inexperienced researchers include too many variables in their regressions, not wanting to face omitted variable bias.

As a result, they often have two or more variables in their equations that are measuring essentially the same thing. In such a case the multicollinear variables are not irrelevant, since any one of them is quite probably theoretically and statistically sound. Instead, the variables might be called **redundant**; only one of them is needed to represent the effect on the dependent variable that all of them currently represent. For example, in an aggregate demand function, it would not make sense to include disposable income and GDP because both are measuring the same thing: income. A bit more subtle is the inference that population and disposable income should not both be included in the same aggregate demand function because, once again, they really are measuring the same thing: the size of the aggregate market. As population rises, so too will income. Dropping these kinds of redundant multicollinear variables is doing nothing more than making up for a specification error; the variables should never have been included in the first place.

To see how this solution would work, let's return to the student consumption function example of Equation 8.10:

$$\widehat{CO}_i = -367.83 + 0.5113Yd_i + 0.0427LA_i \tag{8.10}$$
$$(1.0307) \quad (0.0942)$$
$$t = 0.496 \quad 0.453 \quad \overline{R}^2 = .835$$

where CO = consumption, Yd = disposable income, and LA = liquid assets. When we first discussed this example, we compared this result to the same equation without the liquid assets variable:

$$\widehat{CO}_i = -471.43 + 0.9714Yd_i \tag{8.11}$$
$$(0.157)$$
$$t = 6.187 \quad \overline{R}^2 = .861$$

If we had instead dropped the disposable income variable, we would have obtained:

$$\widehat{CO}_i = -199.44 + 0.08876LA_i \tag{8.17}$$
$$(0.01443)$$
$$t = 6.153 \quad \overline{R}^2 = .860$$

Note that dropping one of the multicollinear variables has eliminated both the multicollinearity between the two explanatory variables and the low t-score of the coefficient of the remaining variable. By dropping Yd, we were able to increase t_{LA} from 0.453 to 6.153. Since dropping a variable changes the meaning of the remaining coefficient (because the dropped variable is no longer being held constant), such dramatic changes are not unusual. The coefficient of the remaining included variable also now measures almost all of the joint impact on the dependent variable of the multicollinear explanatory variables.

Assuming you want to drop a variable, how do you decide which variable to drop? In cases of severe multicollinearity, it makes no statistical difference which variable is dropped. As a result, it doesn't make sense to pick the variable to be dropped on the basis of which one gives superior fit or which one is more significant (or has the expected sign) in the original equation. Instead, the theoretical underpinnings of the model should be the basis for such a decision. In the example of the student consumption function, there is more theoretical support for the hypothesis that disposable income determines consumption than there is for the liquid assets hypothesis. Therefore, Equation 8.11 should be preferred to Equation 8.17.

Increase the Size of the Sample

Another way to deal with multicollinearity is to attempt to increase the size of the sample to reduce the degree of multicollinearity. Although such an increase may be impossible, it's a useful alternative to be considered when feasible.

The idea behind increasing the size of the sample is that a larger data set (often requiring new data collection) will allow more accurate estimates than a small one, since the larger sample normally will reduce the variance of the estimated coefficients, diminishing the impact of the multicollinearity.

For most time series data sets, however, this solution isn't feasible. After all, samples typically are drawn by getting all the available data that seem similar. As a result, new data are generally impossible or quite expensive to find. Going out and generating new data is much easier with a cross-sectional or experimental data set than it is when the observations must be generated by the passage of time.

8.5   An Example of Why Multicollinearity Often Is Best Left Unadjusted

Let's look at an example of the idea that multicollinearity often should be left unadjusted. Suppose you work in the marketing department of a hypothetical soft drink company and you build a model of the impact on sales of your firm's advertising:

$$\hat{S}_t = 3080 - 75{,}000P_t + 4.23A_t - 1.04B_t \qquad (8.18)$$
$$\qquad\quad (25{,}000) \quad (1.06) \quad (0.51)$$
$$t = -3.00 \quad\;\; 3.99 \quad -2.04$$
$$\bar{R}^2 = .825 \qquad N = 28$$

where: S_t = sales of the soft drink in year t
P_t = average relative price of the drink in year t
A_t = advertising expenditures for the company in year t
B_t = advertising expenditures for the company's main competitor in year t

Assume that there are no omitted variables. All variables are measured in real dollars; that is, the nominal values are divided, or deflated, by a price index.

On the face of it, this is a reasonable-looking result. Estimated coefficients are significant in the directions implied by the underlying theory, and both the overall fit and the size of the coefficients seem acceptable. Suppose you now were told that advertising in the soft drink industry is cut-throat in nature and that firms tend to match their main competitor's advertising expenditures. This would lead you to suspect that significant multicollinearity was possible. Further suppose that the simple correlation coefficient between the two advertising variables is .974 and that their respective VIFs are well over 5.

Such a correlation coefficient is evidence that there is severe multicollinearity in the equation, but there is no reason even to consider doing anything about it, because the coefficients are so powerful that their t-scores remain significant, even in the face of severe multicollinearity. Unless multicollinearity causes problems in the equation, it should be left unadjusted. To change the specification might give us better-looking results, but the adjustment would decrease our chances of obtaining the best possible estimates of the true coefficients. Although it's certainly lucky that there were no major problems due to multicollinearity in this example, that luck is no reason to try to fix something that isn't broken.

When a variable is dropped from an equation, its effect will be absorbed by the other explanatory variables to the extent that they are correlated with the newly omitted variable. It's likely that the remaining multicollinear variable(s) will absorb virtually all the bias, since the variables are highly correlated. This bias may destroy whatever usefulness the estimates had before the variable was dropped.

For example, if a variable, say B, is dropped from the equation to fix the multicollinearity, then the following might occur:

$$\hat{S}_t = 2586 - 78{,}000P_t + 0.52A_t \qquad (8.19)$$
$$(24{,}000) \quad (4.32)$$
$$t = -3.25 \qquad 0.12$$
$$\overline{R}^2 = .531 \qquad N = 28$$

What's going on here? The company's advertising coefficient becomes less significant instead of more significant when one of the multicollinear variables is dropped. To see why, first note that the expected bias on $\hat{\beta}_A$ is negative because the product of the expected sign of the coefficient of B and of the correlation between A and B is negative:

$$\text{Bias} = \beta_B \cdot \hat{\alpha}_1 = (-)(+) = - \tag{8.20}$$

Second, this negative bias is strong enough to decrease the estimated coefficient of A until it is insignificant. Although this problem could have been avoided by using a relative advertising variable (A divided by B, for instance), that formulation would have forced identical absolute coefficients on A and 1/B. Such identical coefficients will sometimes be theoretically expected or empirically reasonable but, in most cases, these kinds of constraints will force bias onto an equation that previously had none.

This example is simplistic, but its results are typical in cases in which equations are adjusted for multicollinearity by dropping a variable without regard to the effect that the deletion is going to have. The point here is that it's quite often theoretically or operationally unwise to drop a variable from an equation and that multicollinearity in such cases is best left unadjusted.

8.6 Summary

1. Perfect multicollinearity is the violation of the assumption that no explanatory variable is a perfect linear function of other explanatory variable(s). Perfect multicollinearity results in indeterminate estimates of the regression coefficients and infinite standard errors of those estimates, making OLS estimation impossible.

2. Imperfect multicollinearity, which is what is typically meant when the word "multicollinearity" is used, is a linear relationship between two or more independent variables that is strong enough to significantly affect the estimation of the equation. Multicollinearity is a sample phenomenon as well as a theoretical one. Different samples can exhibit different degrees of multicollinearity.

3. The major consequence of severe multicollinearity is to increase the variances of the estimated regression coefficients and therefore decrease the calculated t-scores of those coefficients and expand the confidence intervals. Multicollinearity causes no bias in the estimated coefficients, and it has little effect on the overall significance of the regression or on the estimates of the coefficients of any nonmulticollinear explanatory variables.

4. Since multicollinearity exists, to one degree or another, in virtually every data set, the question to be asked in detection is how severe the multicollinearity in a particular sample is.

5. Two useful methods for the detection of severe multicollinearity are:
   a. Are the simple correlation coefficients between the explanatory variables high?
   b. Are the variance inflation factors high?

   If either of these answers is yes, then multicollinearity certainly exists, but multicollinearity can also exist even if the answers are no.

6. The three most common remedies for multicollinearity are:
   a. Do nothing (and thus avoid specification bias).
   b. Drop a redundant variable.
   c. Increase the size of the sample.

7. Quite often, doing nothing is the best remedy for multicollinearity. If the multicollinearity has not decreased t-scores to the point of insignificance, then no remedy should even be considered as long as the variables are theoretically strong. Even if the t-scores are insignificant, remedies should be undertaken cautiously, because all impose costs on the estimation that may be greater than the potential benefit of ridding the equation of multicollinearity.

EXERCISES

(The answers to the even-numbered exercises are in Appendix A.)

1. Write the meaning of each of the following terms without referring to the book (or your notes), and compare your definition with the version in the text for each.
   a. dominant variable (p. 224)
   b. imperfect multicollinearity (p. 224)
   c. perfect multicollinearity (p. 222)
   d. redundant variable (p. 237)
   e. simple correlation coefficient (p. 232)
   f. variance inflation factor (p. 234)

2. A recent study of the salaries of elementary school teachers in a small school district in Northern California came up with the following estimated equation (*Note: t*-scores in parentheses!):

$$\widehat{\ln SAL_i} = 10.5 - 0.006EMP_i + 0.002UNITS_i + 0.079LANG_i + 0.020EXP_i$$
$$(-0.98) \qquad (2.39) \qquad (2.08) \qquad (4.97)$$
$$\overline{R}^2 = .866 \quad N = 25 \tag{8.21}$$

where: SAL_i = the salary of the ith teacher (in dollars)
EMP_i = the years that the ith teacher has worked in this school district
$UNITS_i$ = the units of graduate work completed by the ith teacher
$LANG_i$ = a dummy variable equal to 1 if the ith teacher speaks two languages
EXP_i = the total years of teaching experience of the ith teacher

a. Make up and test appropriate hypotheses for the coefficients of this equation at the 5-percent level.
b. What is the functional form of this equation? Does it seem appropriate? Explain.
c. What econometric problems (out of irrelevant variables, omitted variables, and multicollinearity) does this equation appear to have? Explain.
d. Suppose that you now are told that the simple correlation coefficient between EMP and EXP is .89 and that the VIFs for EMP and EXP are both just barely over 5. Does this change your answer to part c above? How?
e. What remedy for the problem you identify in part d do you recommend? Explain.
f. If you drop EMP from the equation, the estimated equation becomes Equation 8.22. Use our four specification criteria to decide whether you prefer Equation 8.21 or Equation 8.22. Which do you like better? Why?

$$\widehat{lnSAL_i} = 10.5 + 0.002UNITS_i + 0.081LANG_i + 0.015EXP_i \quad (8.22)$$
$$(2.47) \qquad (2.09) \qquad (8.65)$$
$$\overline{R}^2 = .871 \quad N = 25$$

3. A researcher once attempted to estimate an asset demand equation that included the following three explanatory variables: current wealth W_t, wealth in the previous quarter W_{t-1}, and the change in wealth $\Delta W_t = W_t - W_{t-1}$. What problem did this researcher encounter? What should have been done to solve this problem?

4. In each of the following situations, determine whether the variable involved is a dominant variable:
a. games lost in year t in an equation for the number of games won in year t by a baseball team that plays the same number of games each year

b. number of Woody's restaurants in a model of the total sales of the entire Woody's chain of restaurants
c. disposable income in an equation for aggregate consumption expenditures
d. number of tires purchased in an annual model of the number of automobiles produced by an automaker that does not make its own tires
e. number of acres planted in an agricultural supply function

5. In 1998, Mark McGwire hit 70 homers to break Roger Maris's old record of 61, and yet McGwire wasn't voted the Most Valuable Player (MVP) in his league. To try to understand how this happened, you collect the following data on MVP votes, batting average (BA), home runs (HR), and runs batted in (RBI) from the 1998 National League:

Name	Votes	BA	HR	RBI
Sosa	438	.308	66	158
McGwire	272	.299	70	147
Alou	215	.312	38	124
Vaughn	185	.272	50	119
Biggio	163	.325	20	88
Galarraga	147	.305	44	121
Bonds	66	.303	37	122
Jones	56	.313	34	107

Datafile = MVP8

Just as you are about to run the regression, your friend warns you that you probably have multicollinearity.

a. What should you do about your friend's warning before running the regression?
b. Run the regression implied in this example (votes as a function of BA, HR, and RBI), with positive expected signs for all three slope coefficients. What signs of multicollinearity are there?
c. What suggestions would you make for another run of this equation? In particular, what would you do about multicollinearity?

6. Consider the following regression result paraphrased from a study conducted by the admissions office at the Stanford Business School (standard errors in parentheses):

$$\hat{G}_i = 1.00 + 0.005M_i + 0.20B_i - 0.10A_i + 0.25S_i$$
$$\phantom{\hat{G}_i = 1.00 + } (0.001) \quad (0.20) \quad (0.10) \quad (0.10)$$
$$\overline{R}^2 = .20 \qquad N = 1000$$

where: G_i = the Stanford Business School GPA of the ith student (4 = high)

M_i = the score on the graduate management admission test of the ith student (800 = high)

B_i = the number of years of business experience of the ith student

A_i = the age of the ith student

S_i = dummy equal to 1 if the ith student was an economics major, 0 otherwise

a. Theorize the expected signs of all the coefficients (try not to look at the results) and test these expectations with appropriate hypotheses (including choosing a significance level).

b. Do any problems appear to exist in this equation? Explain your answer.

c. How would you react if someone suggested a polynomial functional form for A? Why?

d. What suggestions (if any) would you have for another run of this equation?

7. Calculating VIFs typically involves running sets of auxiliary regressions, one regression for each independent variable in an equation. To get practice with this procedure, calculate the following:

a. the VIFs for N, P, and I from the Woody's data in Table 3.1

b. the VIFs for BETA, EARN, and DIV from the stock price example data in Table 7.2

c. the VIF for X_1 in an equation where X_1 and X_2 are the only independent variables, given that the VIF for X_2 is 3.8 and N = 28

d. the VIF for X_1 in an equation where X_1 and X_2 are the only independent variables, given that the simple correlation coefficient between X_1 and X_2 is 0.80 and N = 15

8.7 Appendix: The SAT Interactive Regression Learning Exercise

Econometrics is difficult to learn by reading examples, no matter how good they are. Most econometricians, the author included, had trouble understanding how to use econometrics, particularly in the area of specification choice, until they ran their own regression projects. This is because there's an element of econometric understanding that is better learned by *doing* than by reading about what someone else is doing.

Unfortunately, mastering the art of econometrics by running your own regression projects without any feedback is also difficult because it takes quite a while to learn to avoid some fairly simple mistakes. Probably the best way to learn is to work on your own regression project, analyzing your own problems and making your own decisions, but with a more experienced econometrician nearby to give you one-on-one feedback on exactly which of your decisions were inspired and which were flawed (and why).

This section is an attempt to give you an opportunity to make independent specification decisions and to then get feedback on the advantages or disadvantages of those decisions. Using the interactive learning exercise of this section requires neither a computer nor a tutor, although either would certainly be useful. Instead, we have designed an exercise that can be used on its own to help to bridge the gap between the typical econometrics examples (which require no decision making) and the typical econometrics projects (which give little feedback). An additional interactive learning exercise is presented in Chapter 11.

STOP!

To get the most out of the exercise, it's important to follow the instructions carefully. Reading the pages in order as with any other example will waste your time, because once you have seen even a few of the results, the benefits to you of making specification decisions will diminish. In addition, you shouldn't look at any of the regression results until you have specified your first equation.

Building a Model of Scholastic Aptitude Test Scores

The dependent variable for this interactive learning exercise is the combined "two-test" SAT score, math plus verbal, earned by students in the senior class at Arcadia High School. Arcadia is an upper-middle-class suburban community located near Los Angeles, California. Out of a graduating class of about 640, a total of 65 students who had taken the SATs were randomly selected for inclusion in the data set. In cases in which a student had taken the test more than once, the highest score was recorded.

A review of the literature on the SAT shows many more psychological studies and popular press articles than econometric regressions. Many articles have been authored by critics of the SAT, who maintain (among other things) that it is biased against women and minorities. In support of this argument, these critics have pointed to national average scores for women and some minorities, which in recent years have been significantly lower than the national averages for white males. Any reader interested in reviewing a portion of the applicable literature should do so now before continuing on with the section.[7]

If you were going to build a single-equation linear model of SAT scores, what factors would you consider? First, you'd want to include some measures of a student's academic ability. Three such variables are cumulative high school grade point average (GPA) and participation in advanced placement math and English courses (APMATH and APENG). Advanced placement (AP) classes are academically rigorous courses that may help a student do well on the SAT. More important, students are invited to be in AP classes on the basis of academic potential, and students who choose to take AP classes are revealing their interest in academic subjects, both of which bode well for SAT scores. GPAs at Arcadia High School are weighted GPAs; each semester that a student takes an AP class adds one extra point to his or her total grade points. (For example, a semester grade of "A" in an AP math class counts for five grade points as opposed to the conventional four points.)

A second set of important considerations includes qualitative factors that may affect performance on the SAT. Available dummy variables in this category include measures of a student's gender (GEND), ethnicity (RACE), and native language (ESL). All of the students in the sample are either Asian or Caucasian, and RACE is assigned a value of 1 if a student is Asian. Asian students are a substantial proportion of the student body at Arcadia High. The ESL dummy is given a value of 1 if English is a student's second language. In addition, studying for the test may be relevant, so a dummy variable indicating whether or not a student has attended an SAT preparation class (PREP) is also included in the data.

To sum, the explanatory variables available for you to choose for your model are:

GPA_i = the weighted GPA of the ith student

$APMATH_i$ = a dummy variable equal to 1 if the ith student has taken AP math, 0 otherwise

$APENG_i$ = a dummy variable equal to 1 if the ith student has taken AP English, 0 otherwise

AP_i = a dummy variable equal to 1 if the ith student has taken AP math and/or AP English, 0 if the ith student has taken neither

---

7. See, for example, James Fallows, "The Tests and the 'Brightest': How Fair Are the College Boards?" *The Atlantic,* Vol. 245, No. 2, pp. 37–48. We are grateful to former Occidental student Bob Sego for his help in preparing this interactive exercise.

ESL_i = a dummy variable equal to 1 if English is not the ith student's first language, 0 otherwise

$RACE_i$ = a dummy variable equal to 1 if the ith student is Asian, 0 if the student is Caucasian

$GEND_i$ = a dummy variable equal to 1 if the ith student is male, 0 if the student is female

$PREP_i$ = a dummy variable equal to 1 if the ith student has attended an SAT preparation course, 0 otherwise

The data for these variables are presented in Table 8.1.

Now:

1. Hypothesize expected signs for the coefficients of each of these variables in an equation for the SAT score of the ith student. Examine each variable carefully; what is the theoretical content of your hypothesis?

2. Choose carefully the best set of explanatory variables. Start off by including GPA, APMATH, and APENG; what other variables do you think should be specified? Don't simply include all the variables, intending to drop the insignificant ones. Instead, think through the problem carefully and find the best possible equation.

Once you've specified your equation, you're ready to move on. Keep following the instructions in the exercise until you have specified your equation completely. You may take some time to think over the questions or take a break, but when you return to the interactive exercise, make sure to go back to the exact point from which you left rather than starting all over again. To the extent you can do it, try to avoid looking at the hints until after you've completed the entire project. The hints are there to help you if you get stuck, not to allow you to check every decision you make.

One final bit of advice: Each regression result is accompanied by a series of questions. Take the time to answer all these questions, in writing if possible. Rushing through this interactive exercise will lessen its effectiveness.

The SAT Score Interactive Regression Exercise

To start, choose the specification you'd like to estimate, find the regression run number[8] of that specification in the list on pages 250 and 251, and then turn to that regression. Note that the simple correlation coefficient matrix for this data set is in Table 8.2 just before the results begin.

---

8. All the regression results appear exactly as they are produced by the Stata regression package.

Table 8.1 Data for the SAT Interactive Learning Exercise

SAT	GPA	APMATH	APENG	AP	ESL	GEND	PREP	RACE
1060	3.74	0	1	1	0	0	0	0
740	2.71	0	0	0	0	0	1	0
1070	3.92	0	1	1	0	0	1	0
1070	3.43	0	1	1	0	0	1	0
1330	4.35	1	1	1	0	0	1	0
1220	3.02	0	1	1	0	1	1	0
1130	3.98	1	1	1	1	0	1	0
770	2.94	0	0	0	0	0	1	0
1050	3.49	0	1	1	0	0	1	0
1250	3.87	1	1	1	0	1	1	0
1000	3.49	0	0	0	0	0	1	0
1010	3.24	0	1	1	0	0	1	0
1320	4.22	1	1	1	1	1	0	1
1230	3.61	1	1	1	1	1	1	1
840	2.48	1	0	1	1	1	0	1
940	2.26	1	0	1	1	0	0	1
910	2.32	0	0	0	1	1	1	1
1240	3.89	1	1	1	0	1	1	0
1020	3.67	0	0	0	0	1	0	0
630	2.54	0	0	0	0	0	1	0
850	3.16	0	0	0	0	0	1	0
1300	4.16	1	1	1	1	1	1	0
950	2.94	0	0	0	0	1	1	0
1350	3.79	1	1	1	0	1	1	0
1070	2.56	0	0	0	0	1	0	0
1000	3.00	0	0	0	0	1	1	0
770	2.79	0	0	0	0	0	1	0
1280	3.70	1	0	1	1	0	1	1
590	3.23	0	0	0	1	0	1	1
1060	3.98	1	1	1	1	1	0	1
1050	2.64	1	0	1	0	0	0	0
1220	4.15	1	1	1	1	1	1	1

(continued)

Table 8.1 (*continued*)

SAT	GPA	APMATH	APENG	AP	ESL	GEND	PREP	RACE
930	2.73	0	0	0	0	1	1	0
940	3.10	1	1	1	1	0	0	1
980	2.70	0	0	0	1	1	1	1
1280	3.73	1	1	1	0	1	1	0
700	1.64	0	0	0	1	0	1	1
1040	4.03	1	1	1	1	0	1	1
1070	3.24	0	1	1	0	1	1	0
900	3.42	0	0	0	0	1	1	0
1430	4.29	1	1	1	0	1	0	0
1290	3.33	0	0	0	0	1	0	0
1070	3.61	1	0	1	1	0	1	1
1100	3.58	1	1	1	0	0	1	0
1030	3.52	0	1	1	0	0	1	0
1070	2.94	0	0	0	0	1	1	0
1170	3.98	1	1	1	1	1	1	0
1300	3.89	1	1	1	0	1	0	0
1410	4.34	1	1	1	1	0	1	1
1160	3.43	1	1	1	0	1	1	0
1170	3.56	1	1	1	0	0	0	0
1280	4.11	1	1	1	0	0	1	0
1060	3.58	1	1	1	1	0	1	0
1250	3.47	1	1	1	0	1	1	0
1020	2.92	1	0	1	1	1	1	1
1000	4.05	0	1	1	1	0	0	1
1090	3.24	1	1	1	1	1	1	1
1430	4.38	1	1	1	1	0	0	1
860	2.62	1	0	1	1	0	0	1
1050	2.37	0	0	0	0	1	0	0
920	2.77	0	0	0	0	0	1	0
1100	2.54	0	0	0	0	1	1	0
1160	3.55	1	0	1	1	1	1	1
1360	2.98	0	1	1	1	0	1	0
970	3.64	1	1	1	0	0	1	0

Datafile = SAT8

Table 8.2 Means, Standard Deviations, and Simple Correlation Coefficients for the SAT Interactive Regression Learning Exercise

Means and Standard Deviations:

Variable	Obs	Mean	Std. Dev.	Min	Max
OBS	65	33	18.90767	1	65
AP	65	.6769231	.4712912	0	1
APENG	65	.5538462	.5009606	0	1
APMATH	65	.5230769	.5033541	0	1
ESL	65	.4	.4937104	0	1
GEND	65	.4923077	.5038315	0	1
GPA	65	3.362308	.6127392	1.64	4.38
PREP	65	.7384615	.4428926	0	1
RACE	65	.3230769	.4712912	0	1
SAT	65	1075.538	191.3605	590	1430

Simple Correlation Coefficients:
(obs=65)

	OBS	AP	APENG	APMATH	ESL	GEND	GPA
OBS	1.0000						
AP	0.0859	1.0000					
APENG	0.0049	0.7697	1.0000				
APMATH	0.2298	0.7235	0.4442	1.0000			
ESL	0.1891	0.2955	0.0379	0.4024	1.0000		
GEND	0.0754	-0.1093	-0.0448	0.0777	-0.0503	1.0000	
GPA	-0.0148	0.5854	0.7094	0.4971	0.0718	-0.0083	1.0000
PREP	-0.0709	-0.1117	0.0293	-0.1477	-0.0857	-0.0442	0.0011
RACE	0.1490	0.1959	-0.1079	0.3303	0.8461	-0.0223	-0.0259
SAT	0.1738	0.5798	0.6081	0.5129	0.0241	0.2938	0.6787

	PREP	RACE	SAT
PREP	1.0000		
RACE	-0.1877	1.0000	
SAT	-0.1006	-0.0860	1.0000

All the equations include SAT as the dependent variable and GPA, APMATH, and APENG as explanatory variables. Find the combination of explanatory variables (from ESL, GEND, PREP, and RACE) that you wish to include and go to the indicated regression:

None of them, go to regression run 8.1

ESL only, go to regression run 8.2

GEND only, go to regression run 8.3

PREP only, go to regression run 8.4

RACE only, go to regression run 8.5

ESL and GEND, go to regression run 8.6

ESL and PREP, go to regression run 8.7

ESL and RACE, go to regression run 8.8

GEND and PREP, go to regression run 8.9

GEND and RACE, go to regression run 8.10

PREP and RACE, go to regression run 8.11

ESL, GEND, and PREP, go to regression run 8.12

ESL, GEND, and RACE, go to regression run 8.13

ESL, PREP, and RACE, go to regression run 8.14

GEND, PREP, and RACE, go to regression run 8.15

All four, go to regression run 8.16

Regression Run 8.1:

```
  Source |      SS           df       MS              Number of obs =      65
---------+------------------------------              F(  3,     61) =   22.41
   Model | 1228849.32         3   409616.439          Prob > F       =  0.0000
Residual | 1114756.84        61   18274.7022          R-squared      =  0.5243
---------+------------------------------              Adj R-squared  =  0.5009
   Total | 2343606.15        64   36618.8462          Root MSE       =  135.18


------------------------------------------------------------------------------
     SAT |     Coef.    Std. Err.       t     P>|t|     [95% Conf. Interval]
---------+--------------------------------------------------------------------
     GPA | 131.8512     40.86212     3.23    0.002     50.14236     213.5601
  APMATH |  78.60445    39.13018     2.01    0.049      .3588106    156.8501
   APENG |  82.77424    48.40687     1.71    0.092    -14.02128     179.5698
   _cons | 545.2537    117.8141      4.63    0.000    309.6699      780.8376
------------------------------------------------------------------------------
```

Answer each of the following questions for this regression run.

a. Evaluate this result with respect to its economic meaning, overall fit, and the signs and significance of the individual coefficients.

b. What econometric problems (out of omitted variables, irrelevant variables, or multicollinearity) does this regression have? Why? If you need feedback on your answer, see hint 2 in the material on this chapter in Appendix A.

c. Which of the following statements comes closest to your recommendation for further action to be taken in the estimation of this equation?

i. No further specification changes are advisable (go to page 272).
ii. I would like to add ESL to the equation (go to run 8.2).
iii. I would like to add GEND to the equation (go to run 8.3).
iv. I would like to add PREP to the equation (go to run 8.4).
v. I would like to add RACE to the equation (go to run 8.5).

If you need feedback on your answer, see hint 6 in the material on this chapter in Appendix A.

Regression Run 8.2:

Source	SS	df	MS
Model	1256418.66	4	314104.665
Residual	1087187.5	60	18119.7916
Total	2343606.15	64	36618.8462

Number of obs = 65
$F(4, 60) = 17.33$
Prob > F = 0.0000
R-squared = 0.5361
Adj R-squared = 0.5052
Root MSE = 134.61

SAT	Coef.	Std. Err.	t	P>|t|	[95% Conf. Interval]	
GPA	128.3402	40.788	3.15	0.003	46.75208	209.9284
APMATH	101.5886	43.19023	2.35	0.022	15.19531	187.9819
APENG	77.30713	48.40462	1.60	0.115	-19.51652	174.1308
ESL	-46.72721	37.88203	-1.23	0.222	-122.5025	29.04813
_cons	566.7551	118.6016	4.78	0.000	329.5165	803.9937

Answer each of the following questions for this regression run.

a. Evaluate this result with respect to its economic meaning, overall fit, and the signs and significance of the individual coefficients.

b. What econometric problems (out of omitted variables, irrelevant variables, or multicollinearity) does this regression have? Why? If you need feedback on your answer, see hint 3 in the material on this chapter in Appendix A.

c. Which of the following statements comes closest to your recommendation for further action to be taken in the estimation of this equation?

i. No further specification changes are advisable (go to page 272).
ii. I would like to drop ESL from the equation (go to run 8.1).
iii. I would like to add GEND to the equation (go to run 8.6).
iv. I would like to add RACE to the equation (go to run 8.8).
v. I would like to add PREP to the equation (go to run 8.7).

If you need feedback on your answer, see hint 6 in the material on this chapter in Appendix A.

Regression Run 8.3:

Source	SS	df	MS
Model	1429979.75	4	357494.937
Residual	913626.408	60	15227.1068
Total	2343606.15	64	36618.8462

```
Number of obs =      65
F( 4,    60) =   23.48
Prob > F      =  0.0000
R-squared     =  0.6102
Adj R-squared =  0.5842
Root MSE      =   123.4
```

SAT	Coef.	Std. Err.	t	P>|t|	[95% Conf. Interval]	
GPA	131.5798	37.2997	3.53	0.001	56.96932	206.1903
APMATH	65.04046	35.91313	1.81	0.075	-6.796506	136.8774
APENG	94.10841	44.29652	2.12	0.038	5.502183	182.7146
GEND	112.0465	30.82961	3.63	0.001	50.37809	173.7149
_cons	491.8225	108.5429	4.53	0.000	274.7044	708.9407

Answer each of the following questions for this regression run.

a. Evaluate this result with respect to its economic meaning, overall fit, and the signs and significance of the individual coefficients.

b. What econometric problems (out of omitted variables, irrelevant variables, or multicollinearity) does this regression have? Why? If you need feedback on your answer, see hint 5 in the material on this chapter in Appendix A.

c. Which of the following statements comes closest to your recommendation for further action to be taken in the estimation of this equation?

 i. No further specification changes are advisable (go to page 272).
 ii. I would like to add ESL to the equation (go to run 8.6).
 iii. I would like to add PREP to the equation (go to run 8.9).
 iv. I would like to add RACE to the equation (go to run 8.10).

If you need feedback on your answer, see hint 19 in the material on this chapter in Appendix A.

Regression Run 8.4:

```
 Source |      SS          df        MS              Number of obs =      65
--------+-------------------------------            F( 4,    60) =    16.95
  Model | 1243189.44        4     310797.36          Prob > F      =   0.0000
Residual | 1100416.71       60    18340.2786         R-squared     =   0.5305
--------+-------------------------------            Adj R-squared =   0.4992
  Total | 2343606.15        64    36618.8462         Root MSE      =   135.43
```

```
   SAT |     Coef.    Std. Err.      t     P>|t|      [95% Conf. Interval]
-------+----------------------------------------------------------------------
   GPA |   132.7666   40.94846     3.24    0.002      50.85753     214.6757
APMATH |   72.29444   39.84456     1.81    0.075      -7.406535    151.9954
 APENG |   85.68562   48.60529     1.76    0.083      -11.53944    182.9107
  PREP |  -34.38129   38.88201    -0.88    0.380      -112.1569    43.39431
 _cons |   569.2532   121.1058     4.70    0.000      327.0056     811.5009
```

Answer each of the following questions for this regression run.

a. Evaluate this result with respect to its economic meaning, overall fit, and the signs and significance of the individual coefficients.

b. What econometric problems (out of omitted variables, irrelevant variables, or multicollinearity) does this regression have? Why? If you need feedback on your answer, see hint 8 in the material on this chapter in Appendix A.

c. Which of the following statements comes closest to your recommendation for further action to be taken in the estimation of this equation?

   i. No further specification changes are advisable (go to page 272).

   ii. I would like to drop PREP from the equation (go to run 8.1).

   iii. I would like to add ESL to the equation (go to run 8.7).

   iv. I would like to add GEND to the equation (go to run 8.9).

   v. I would like to replace APMATH and APENG with AP, a linear combination of the two variables (go to run 8.17).

If you need feedback on your answer, see hint 12 in the material on this chapter in Appendix A.

Regression Run 8.5:

Source	SS	df	MS		
Model	1270629.16	4	317657.29		
Residual	1072976.99	60	17882.9499		
Total	2343606.15	64	36618.8462		

Number of obs =					65
F(4, 60) =					17.76
Prob > F =					0.0000
R-squared =					0.5422
Adj R-squared =					0.5116
Root MSE =					133.73

SAT	Coef.	Std. Err.	t	P>|t|	[95% Conf. Interval]	
GPA	128.2798	40.48924	3.17	0.002	47.28924	209.2703
APMATH	106.2137	42.71559	2.49	0.016	20.76982	191.6576
APENG	67.42362	48.92704	1.38	0.173	-30.44503	165.2923
RACE	-60.33471	39.4733	-1.53	0.132	-139.2931	18.62364
_cons	570.8148	117.7382	4.85	0.000	335.3035	806.3262

Answer each of the following questions for this regression run.

a. Evaluate this result with respect to its economic meaning, overall fit, and the signs and significance of the individual coefficients.

b. What econometric problems (out of omitted variables, irrelevant variables, or multicollinearity) does this regression have? Why? If you need feedback on your answer, see hint 3 in the material on this chapter in Appendix A.

c. Which of the following statements comes closest to your recommendation for further action to be taken in the estimation of this equation?

   i. No further specification changes are advisable (go to page 272).
   ii. I would like to drop RACE from the equation (go to run 8.1).
   iii. I would like to add ESL to the equation (go to run 8.8).
   iv. I would like to add GEND to the equation (go to run 8.10).
   v. I would like to add PREP to the equation (go to run 8.11).

If you need feedback on your answer, see hint 14 in the material on this chapter in Appendix A.

Regression Run 8.6:

Source	SS	df	MS
Model	1444109.93	5	288821.987
Residual	899496.22	59	15245.6986
Total	2343606.15	64	36618.8462

```
Number of obs =      65
F(  5,    59) =   18.94
Prob > F      =  0.0000
R-squared     =  0.6162
Adj R-squared =  0.5837
Root MSE      =  123.47
```

SAT	Coef.	Std. Err.	t	P>|t|	[95% Conf. Interval]	
GPA	129.0595	37.41416	3.45	0.001	54.19399	203.9251
APMATH	81.97538	40.0095	2.05	0.045	1.916549	162.0342
APENG	89.8496	44.54376	2.02	0.048	.7177482	178.9815
ESL	-33.64469	34.94751	-0.96	0.340	-103.5745	36.28511
GEND	108.8598	31.02552	3.51	0.001	46.77785	170.9417
_cons	508.8237	110.0355	4.62	0.000	288.6432	729.0041

Answer each of the following questions for this regression run.

a. Evaluate this result with respect to its economic meaning, overall fit, and the signs and significance of the individual coefficients.

b. What econometric problems (out of omitted variables, irrelevant variables, or multicollinearity) does this regression have? Why? If you need feedback on your answer, see hint 7 in the material on this chapter in Appendix A.

c. Which of the following statements comes closest to your recommendation for further action to be taken in the estimation of this equation?

   i. No further specification changes are advisable (go to page 272).
   ii. I would like to drop ESL from the equation (go to run 8.3).
   iii. I would like to add PREP to the equation (go to run 8.12).
   iv. I would like to add RACE to the equation (go to run 8.13).

If you need feedback on your answer, see hint 4 in the material on this chapter in Appendix A.

Regression Run 8.7:

```
    Source |       SS         df        MS              Number of obs =       65
-----------+------------------------------              F(  5,    59) =    13.99
     Model |  1271126.11       5   254225.223           Prob > F      =   0.0000
  Residual |  1072480.04      59   18177.6278           R-squared     =   0.5424
-----------+------------------------------              Adj R-squared =   0.5036
     Total |  2343606.15      64   36618.8462           Root MSE      =   134.82


-------------------------------------------------------------------------------
       SAT |    Coef.    Std. Err.      t      P>|t|     [95% Conf. Interval]
-----------+-------------------------------------------------------------------
       GPA |  129.2439    40.86539     3.16    0.002     47.47242     211.0153
    APMATH |  95.35163    43.81128     2.18    0.034     7.685451     183.0178
     APENG |  80.21916    48.58978     1.65    0.104    -17.00876     177.4471
       ESL | -47.03944    37.94402    -1.24    0.220    -122.9653     28.88638
      PREP | -34.82031    38.71083    -0.90    0.372    -112.2805     42.63988
     _cons |  591.2047    121.8609     4.85    0.000     347.3616     835.0478
-------------------------------------------------------------------------------
```

Answer each of the following questions for this regression run.

a. Evaluate this result with respect to its economic meaning, overall fit, and the signs and significance of the individual coefficients.

b. What econometric problems (out of omitted variables, irrelevant variables, or multicollinearity) does this regression have? Why? If you need feedback on your answer, see hint 8 in the material on this chapter in Appendix A.

c. Which of the following statements comes closest to your recommendation for further action to be taken in the estimation of this equation?

  i. No further specification changes are advisable (go to page 272).
  ii. I would like to drop ESL from the equation (go to run 8.4).
  iii. I would like to drop PREP from the equation (go to run 8.2).
  iv. I would like to add GEND to the equation (go to run 8.12).
  v. I would like to add RACE to the equation (go to run 8.14).

If you need feedback on your answer, see hint 18 in the material on this chapter in Appendix A.

Regression Run 8.8:

```
       Source |       SS          df       MS              Number of obs =        65
--------------+------------------------------              F(  5,     59) =     13.97
        Model |  1270643.65        5    254128.731         Prob > F        =   0.0000
     Residual |  1072962.5        59    18185.8051         R-squared       =   0.5422
--------------+------------------------------              Adj R-squared   =   0.5034
        Total |  2343606.15       64    36618.8462         Root MSE        =   134.85


-----------------------------------------------------------------------------------
          SAT |     Coef.    Std. Err.       t     P>|t|      [95% Conf. Interval]
--------------+--------------------------------------------------------------------
          GPA |   128.3251    40.86223      3.14    0.003      46.55999    210.0903
        APMATH |   106.031    43.5594       2.43    0.018      18.86883    193.1932
        APENG |   67.23015    49.81328      1.35    0.182     -32.446      166.9063
          ESL |   1.885689    66.79448      0.03    0.978    -131.7698     135.5411
         RACE |  -61.96231    70.05962     -0.88    0.380    -202.1513      78.22667
         _cons |   570.6367   118.8985      4.80    0.000      332.7213     808.5521
-----------------------------------------------------------------------------------
```

Answer each of the following questions for this regression run.

a. Evaluate this result with respect to its economic meaning, overall fit, and the signs and significance of the individual coefficients.

b. What econometric problems (out of omitted variables, irrelevant variables, or multicollinearity) does this regression have? Why? If you need feedback on your answer, see hint 9 in the material on this chapter in Appendix A.

c. Which of the following statements comes closest to your recommendation for further action to be taken in the estimation of this equation?

   i. No further specification changes are advisable (go to page 272).
   ii. I would like to drop ESL from the equation (go to run 8.5).
   iii. I would like to drop RACE from the equation (go to run 8.2).
   iv. I would like to add GEND to the equation (go to run 8.13).
   v. I would like to add PREP to the equation (go to run 8.14).

If you need feedback on your answer, see hint 15 in the material on this chapter in Appendix A.

Regression Run 8.9:

```
   Source |       SS          df       MS              Number of obs =      65
----------+-----------------------------------         F(  5,     59) =   18.87
    Model |  1441871.27        5   288374.253          Prob > F        =  0.0000
 Residual |  901734.887       59   15283.6422          R-squared       =  0.6152
----------+-----------------------------------         Adj R-squared   =  0.5826
    Total |  2343606.15       64   36618.8462          Root MSE        =  123.63


-----------------------------------------------------------------------------------
      SAT |     Coef.    Std. Err.       t      P>|t|       [95% Conf. Interval]
----------+------------------------------------------------------------------------
      GPA |   132.4152    37.38088     3.54     0.001      57.61629     207.2142
    APMATH |   59.37168    36.54919     1.62     0.110     -13.76309     132.5064
    APENG |   96.69438     44.4754     2.17     0.034      7.699308     185.6895
     GEND |   111.3943    30.89564     3.61     0.001      49.57224     173.2163
     PREP |  -31.31762    35.50451    -0.88     0.381     -102.362      39.72674
    _cons |   513.9945    111.6115     4.61     0.000      290.6604     737.3286
-----------------------------------------------------------------------------------
```

Answer each of the following questions for this regression run.

a. Evaluate this result with respect to its economic meaning, overall fit, and the signs and significance of the individual coefficients.

b. What econometric problems (out of omitted variables, irrelevant variables, or multicollinearity) does this regression have? Why? If you need feedback on your answer, see hint 8 in the material on this chapter in Appendix A.

c. Which of the following statements comes closest to your recommendation for further action to be taken in the estimation of this equation?

   i. No further specification changes are advisable (go to page 272).
   ii. I would like to drop PREP from the equation (go to run 8.3).
   iii. I would like to add ESL to the equation (go to run 8.12).
   iv. I would like to add RACE to the equation (go to run 8.15).

If you need feedback on your answer, see hint 17 in the material on this chapter in Appendix A.

Regression Run 8.10:

```
    Source |       SS         df       MS              Number of obs =      65
-----------+----------------------------------        F(  5,    59) =   19.44
     Model | 1458295.57        5   291659.113          Prob > F      = 0.0000
  Residual | 885310.588       59   15005.2642          R-squared     = 0.6222
-----------+----------------------------------        Adj R-squared = 0.5902
     Total | 2343606.15       64   36618.8462          Root MSE      =  122.5


-------------------------------------------------------------------------------
       SAT |     Coef.    Std. Err.      t     P>|t|     [95% Conf. Interval]
-----------+-------------------------------------------------------------------
       GPA |  128.6381    37.08886     3.47    0.001     54.42347    202.8528
     APMATH |  88.26401    39.45591     2.24    0.029     9.312909    167.2151
     APENG |  81.07941    44.98391     1.80    0.077    -8.93318     171.092
      GEND |  108.5953    30.70716     3.54    0.001     47.15043    170.0402
      RACE | -49.83756    36.27973    -1.37    0.175    -122.4331    22.75801
      _cons |  514.5822   109.0157     4.72    0.000     296.4423    732.7221
-------------------------------------------------------------------------------
```

Answer each of the following questions for this regression run.

a. Evaluate this result with respect to its economic meaning, overall fit, and the signs and significance of the individual coefficients.

b. What econometric problems (out of omitted variables, irrelevant variables, or multicollinearity) does this regression have? Why? If you need feedback on your answer, see hint 10 in the material on this chapter in Appendix A.

c. Which of the following statements comes closest to your recommendation for further action to be taken in the estimation of this equation?

i. No further specification changes are advisable (go to page 272).
ii. I would like to drop RACE from the equation (go to run 8.3).
iii. I would like to add ESL to the equation (go to run 8.13).
iv. I would like to add PREP to the equation (go to run 8.15).

If you need feedback on your answer, see hint 4 in the material on this chapter in Appendix A.

Regression Run 8.11:

```
  Source |       SS         df       MS                   Number of obs =       65
---------+------------------------------                  F(  5,    59) =     14.49
   Model |   1291862.27      5    258372.454              Prob > F      =    0.0000
Residual |   1051743.88     59    17826.1675              R-squared     =    0.5512
---------+------------------------------                  Adj R-squared =    0.5132
   Total |   2343606.15     64    36618.8462              Root MSE      =    133.51


-----------------------------------------------------------------------------------
     SAT |     Coef.    Std. Err.        t     P>|t|      [95% Conf. Interval]
---------+-------------------------------------------------------------------------
     GPA |   129.0898   40.43172       3.19    0.002       48.1861      209.9935
  APMATH |   100.8919   42.92558       2.35    0.022       14.998       186.7858
   APENG |    69.6507   48.8919        1.42    0.160      -28.18177     167.4832
    PREP |   -42.14969  38.62038      -1.09    0.280      -119.4289      35.12952
    RACE |   -65.60984  39.70586      -1.65    0.104      -145.0611      13.84141
   _cons |   602.4718  121.0769        4.98    0.000       360.1975     844.7462
-----------------------------------------------------------------------------------
```

Answer each of the following questions for this regression run.

a. Evaluate this result with respect to its economic meaning, overall fit, and the signs and significance of the individual coefficients.

b. What econometric problems (out of omitted variables, irrelevant variables, or multicollinearity) does this regression have? Why? If you need feedback on your answer, see hint 8 in the material on this chapter in Appendix A.

c. Which of the following statements comes closest to your recommendation for further action to be taken in the estimation of this equation?

  i. No further specification changes are advisable (go to page 272).
  ii. I would like to drop PREP from the equation (go to run 8.5).
  iii. I would like to drop RACE from the equation (go to run 8.4).
  iv. I would like to add GEND to the equation (go to run 8.15).
  v. I would like to replace APMATH and APENG with AP, a linear combination of the two variables (go to run 8.18).

If you need feedback on your answer, see hint 18 in the material on this chapter in Appendix A.

Regression Run 8.12:

```
  Source |      SS         df       MS              Number of obs =      65
---------+------------------------------            F(  6,    58) =   15.87
   Model |   1456310.3      6   242718.383          Prob > F      =  0.0000
Residual |   887295.854    58   15298.2044          R-squared     =  0.6214
---------+------------------------------            Adj R-squared =  0.5822
   Total |   2343606.15    64   36618.8462          Root MSE      =  123.69


     SAT |     Coef.    Std. Err.      t      P>|t|     [95% Conf. Interval]
---------+-------------------------------------------------------------------
     GPA |   129.8782   37.48974     3.46    0.001     54.83437    204.9221
   APMATH |   76.41832   40.55854    1.88    0.065     -4.768418   157.6051
   APENG |   92.42253   44.71331     2.07    0.043     2.919109    181.926
     ESL |  -34.01275   35.01006    -0.97    0.335     -104.093    36.06751
    GEND |   108.1642   31.08865     3.48    0.001     45.93352    170.3949
    PREP |  -31.72391   35.52388    -0.89    0.376     -102.8327   39.38488
    _cons |   531.4692  113.1041     4.70    0.000     305.0668    757.8717
```

Answer each of the following questions for this regression run.

a. Evaluate this result with respect to its economic meaning, overall fit, and the signs and significance of the individual coefficients.

b. What econometric problems (out of omitted variables, irrelevant variables, or multicollinearity) does this regression have? Why? If you need feedback on your answer, see hint 8 in the material on this chapter in Appendix A.

c. Which of the following statements comes closest to your recommendation for further action to be taken in the estimation of this equation?

   i. No further specification changes are advisable (go to page 272).
   ii. I would like to drop ESL from the equation (go to run 8.9).
   iii. I would like to drop PREP from the equation (go to run 8.6).
   iv. I would like to add RACE to the equation (go to run 8.16).

If you need feedback on your answer, see hint 17 in the material on this chapter in Appendix A.

Regression Run 8.13:

Source	SS	df	MS
Model	1459451.8	6	243241.967
Residual	884154.352	58	15244.0406
Total	2343606.15	64	36618.8462

Number of obs =		65
F(6, 58) =		15.96
Prob > F	=	0.0000
R-squared	=	0.6227
Adj R-squared =		0.5837
Root MSE	=	123.47

SAT	Coef.	Std. Err.	t	P>|t|	[95% Conf. Interval]	
GPA	129.046	37.41213	3.45	0.001	54.15754	203.9345
APMATH	86.52973	40.26408	2.15	0.036	5.93242	167.127
APENG	79.42187	45.73811	1.74	0.088	-12.1329	170.9766
ESL	16.88299	61.30223	0.28	0.784	-105.8267	139.5927
GEND	109.1893	31.02557	3.52	0.001	47.08487	171.2937
RACE	-64.35243	64.14694	-1.00	0.320	-192.7565	64.05161
_cons	512.6796	110.0966	4.66	0.000	292.2973	733.0619

Answer each of the following questions for this regression run.

a. Evaluate this result with respect to its economic meaning, overall fit, and the signs and significance of the individual coefficients.

b. What econometric problems (out of omitted variables, irrelevant variables, or multicollinearity) does this regression have? Why? If you need feedback on your answer, see hint 9 in the material on this chapter in Appendix A.

c. Which of the following statements comes closest to your recommendation for further action to be taken in the estimation of this equation?

  i. No further specification changes are advisable (go to page 272).
  ii. I would like to drop ESL from the equation (go to run 8.10).
  iii. I would like to drop RACE from the equation (go to run 8.6).
  iv. I would like to add PREP to the equation (go to run 8.16).

If you need feedback on your answer, see hint 15 in the material on this chapter in Appendix A.

Regression Run 8.14:

```
      Source |       SS          df       MS              Number of obs =      65
-------------+------------------------------              F( 6,     58) =   11.89
       Model | 1292628.98          6   215438.164         Prob > F       =  0.0000
    Residual | 1050977.17         58   18120.296          R-squared      =  0.5516
-------------+------------------------------              Adj R-squared  =  0.5052
       Total | 2343606.15         64   36618.8462         Root MSE       =  134.61


         SAT |     Coef.    Std. Err.       t    . P>|t|     [95% Conf. Interval]
-------------+----------------------------------------------------------------------
         GPA |  129.4491    40.80133      3.17    0.002      47.77639     211.1219
      APMATH |  99.37976    43.89816      2.26    0.027      11.50805     187.2515
       APENG |  68.29405    49.73286      1.37    0.175     -31.25709     167.8452
         ESL |  13.89708    67.55991      0.21    0.838    -121.3388     149.1329
        PREP | -43.45964    39.45502     -1.10    0.275    -122.4375     35.51817
        RACE | -77.76882    71.39042     -1.09    0.281    -220.6723     65.13464
       _cons |  602.1427    122.0822      4.93    0.000      357.7687     846.5168
```

Answer each of the following questions for this regression run.

a. Evaluate this result with respect to its economic meaning, overall fit, and the signs and significance of the individual coefficients.

b. What econometric problems (out of omitted variables, irrelevant variables, or multicollinearity) does this regression have? Why? If you need feedback on your answer, see hint 9 in the material on this chapter in Appendix A.

c. Which of the following statements comes closest to your recommendation for further action to be taken in the estimation of this equation?

   i. No further specification changes are advisable (go to page 272).
   ii. I would like to drop ESL from the equation (go to run 8.11).
   iii. I would like to drop PREP from the equation (go to run 8.8).
   iv. I would like to add GEND to the equation (go to run 8.16).
   v. I would like to replace APMATH and APENG with AP, a linear combination of the two variables (go to run 8.19).

If you need feedback on your answer, see hint 15 in the material on this chapter in Appendix A.

Regression Run 8.15:

```
  Source |       SS         df      MS              Number of obs =        65
---------+------------------------------            F(  6,     58) =     16.43
   Model | 1475443.65        6  245907.275          Prob > F        =    0.0000
Residual | 868162.501       58   14968.319          R-squared       =    0.6296
---------+------------------------------            Adj R-squared   =    0.5912
   Total | 2343606.15       64   36618.8462         Root MSE        =    122.35


     SAT |    Coef.   Std. Err.       t     P>|t|      [95% Conf. Interval]
---------+------------------------------------------------------------------
     GPA |  129.3628   37.04936     3.49    0.001      55.2004     203.5251
  APMATH |   83.66463  39.64091     2.11    0.039       4.314729   163.0145
   APENG |   82.94048  44.96213     1.84    0.070      -7.060989   172.942
    GEND |  107.47     30.68735     3.50    0.001      46.04258    168.8974
    PREP |  -37.90098  35.41026    -1.07    0.289     -108.7823     32.98036
    RACE |  -54.68974  36.51752    -1.50    0.140     -127.7875     18.40802
   _cons |  543.6309  112.2128      4.84    0.000      319.0125    768.2493
```

Answer each of the following questions for this regression run.

a. Evaluate this result with respect to its economic meaning, overall fit, and the signs and significance of the individual coefficients.

b. What econometric problems (out of omitted variables, irrelevant variables, or multicollinearity) does this regression have? Why? If you need feedback on your answer, see hint 8 in the material on this chapter in Appendix A.

c. Which of the following statements comes closest to your recommendation for further action to be taken in the estimation of this equation?

  i. No further specification changes are advisable (go to page 272).
  ii. I would like to drop PREP from the equation (go to run 8.10).
  iii. I would like to drop RACE from the equation (go to run 8.9).
  iv. I would like to add ESL to the equation (go to run 8.16).

If you need feedback on your answer, see hint 17 in the material on this chapter in Appendix A.

Regression Run 8.16:

```
    Source |       SS          df       MS              Number of obs =      65
-----------+------------------------------              F(  7,    57) =    13.92
     Model |  1478535.29        7   211219.327          Prob > F      =   0.0000
  Residual |  865070.867       57   15176.6819          R-squared     =   0.6309
-----------+------------------------------              Adj R-squared =   0.5855
     Total |  2343606.15       64   36618.8462          Root MSE      =   123.19
```

```
-----------------------------------------------------------------------------
      SAT |     Coef.    Std. Err.      t     P>|t|    [95% Conf. Interval]
----------+------------------------------------------------------------------
      GPA |   130.0882    37.34094     3.48   0.001     55.31421     204.8621
    APMATH |   80.47642    40.53608     1.99   0.052    -.6956791     161.6485
    APENG |   80.32262    45.64401     1.76   0.084    -11.07795     171.7232
      ESL |    27.9651    61.95989     0.45   0.653    -96.10744     152.0376
     GEND |   108.3766    30.96543     3.50   0.001     46.36945     170.3838
     PREP |  -40.50116    36.11828    -1.12   0.267    -112.8268     31.82444
     RACE |  -79.06514    65.33603    -1.21   0.231    -209.8983     51.76799
    _cons |   542.4723    113.0203     4.80   0.000      316.153     768.7915
-----------------------------------------------------------------------------
```

Answer each of the following questions for this regression run.

a. Evaluate this result with respect to its economic meaning, overall fit, and the signs and significance of the individual coefficients.

b. What econometric problems (out of omitted variables, irrelevant variables, or multicollinearity) does this regression have? Why? If you need feedback on your answer, see hint 9 in the material on this chapter in Appendix A.

c. Which of the following statements comes closest to your recommendation for further action to be taken in the estimation of this equation?

i. No further specification changes are advisable (go to page 272).
ii. I would like to drop ESL from the equation (go to run 8.15).
iii. I would like to drop PREP from the equation (go to run 8.13).
iv. I would like to drop RACE from the equation (go to run 8.12).

If you need feedback on your answer, see hint 15 in the material on this chapter in Appendix A.

Regression Run 8.17:

```
    Source |       SS          df       MS              Number of obs =      65
-----------+------------------------------              F(  3,    61) =    21.70
     Model |   1210002.3        3    403334.101         Prob > F      =   0.0000
  Residual |   1133603.85      61   18583.6697          R-squared     =   0.5163
-----------+------------------------------              Adj R-squared =   0.4925
     Total |   2343606.15      64   36618.8462          Root MSE      =   136.32


------------------------------------------------------------------------------
       SAT |      Coef.   Std. Err.       t     P>|t|     [95% Conf. Interval]
-----------+------------------------------------------------------------------
       GPA |    163.4716   34.41783      4.75   0.000     94.64887    232.2943
        AP |     107.746   45.02942      2.39   0.020     17.70408    197.7879
      PREP |   -30.92277   38.84976     -0.80   0.429    -108.6077    46.76214
      _cons |    475.7963   104.7275      4.54   0.000     266.3807    685.2118
------------------------------------------------------------------------------
```

Answer each of the following questions for this regression run.

a. Evaluate this result with respect to its economic meaning, overall fit, and the signs and significance of the individual coefficients.

b. What econometric problems (out of omitted variables, irrelevant variables, or multicollinearity) does this regression have? Why? If you need feedback on your answer, see hint 11 in the material on this chapter in Appendix A.

c. Which of the following statements comes closest to your recommendation for further action to be taken in the estimation of this equation?

   i.   No further specification changes are advisable (go to page 272).
   ii. I would like to drop PREP from the equation (go to run 8.20).
   iii. I would like to add RACE to the equation (go to run 8.18).
   iv. I would like to replace the AP combination variable with APMATH and APENG (go to run 8.4).

If you need feedback on your answer, see hint 16 in the material on this chapter in Appendix A.

Regression Run 8.18:

Source	SS	df	MS			
Model	1259042.71	4	314760.679			
Residual	1084563.44	60	18076.0573			
Total	2343606.15	64	36618.8462			

Number of obs = 65
F(4, 60) = 17.41
Prob > F = 0.0000
R-squared = 0.5372
Adj R-squared = 0.5064
Root MSE = 134.45

SAT	Coef.	Std. Err.	t	P>|t|	[95% Conf. Interval]	
GPA	154.0768	34.42039	4.48	0.000	85.22576	222.9278
AP	125.9048	45.75812	2.75	0.008	34.37493	217.4347
PREP	-41.06153	38.80679	-1.06	0.294	-118.6867	36.56361
RACE	-61.63421	37.41938	-1.65	0.105	-136.4841	13.2157
_cons	522.492	107.1073	4.88	0.000	308.2455	736.7385

Answer each of the following questions for this regression run.

a. Evaluate this result with respect to its economic meaning, overall fit, and the signs and significance of the individual coefficients.

b. What econometric problems (out of omitted variables, irrelevant variables, or multicollinearity) does this regression have? Why? If you need feedback on your answer, see hint 11 in the material on this chapter in Appendix A.

c. Which of the following statements comes closest to your recommendation for further action to be taken in the estimation of this equation?

   i. No further specification changes are advisable (go to page 272).
   ii. I would like to drop RACE from the equation (go to run 8.17).
   iii. I would like to add ESL to the equation (go to run 8.19).
   iv. I would like to replace the AP combination variable with APMATH and APENG (go to run 8.11).

If you need feedback on your answer, see hint 16 in the material on this chapter in Appendix A.

Regression Run 8.19:

```
  Source |       SS         df        MS            Number of obs =      65
---------+----------------------------------        F(  5,    59) =    13.76
   Model |  1261778.06      5   252355.613          Prob > F       =   0.0000
Residual |  1081828.09     59   18336.0693          R-squared      =   0.5384
---------+----------------------------------        Adj R-squared  =   0.4993
   Total |  2343606.15     64   36618.8462          Root MSE       =   135.41


     SAT |     Coef.    Std. Err.      t     P>|t|     [95% Conf. Interval]
---------+-------------------------------------------------------------------
     GPA |   153.7341    34.67841     4.43    0.000     84.34277    223.1255
      AP |   122.3201    47.0113      2.60    0.012     28.25071    216.3895
     ESL |   26.00898    67.33954     0.39    0.701    -108.7371    160.7551
    PREP |  -43.55594    39.61488    -1.10    0.276    -122.8251    35.71325
    RACE |  -84.43699    70.04203    -1.21    0.233    -224.5908    55.71678
   _cons |   524.8762    108.0514     4.86    0.000     308.6659    741.0865
```

Answer each of the following questions for this regression run.

a. Evaluate this result with respect to its economic meaning, overall fit, and the signs and significance of the individual coefficients.

b. What econometric problems (out of omitted variables, irrelevant variables, or multicollinearity) does this regression have? Why? If you need feedback on your answer, see hint 11 in the material on this chapter in Appendix A.

c. Which of the following statements comes closest to your recommendation for further action to be taken in the estimation of this equation?

    i. No further specification changes are advisable (go to page 272).

    ii. I would like to drop ESL from the equation (go to run 8.18).

    iii. I would like to replace the AP combination variable with APMATH and APENG (go to run 8.14).

If you need feedback on your answer, see hint 16 in the material on this chapter in Appendix A.

Regression Run 8.20:

```
    Source |       SS          df       MS              Number of obs =        65
-----------+------------------------------             F(  2,    62) =     32.43
     Model |  1198228.64        2    599114.322         Prob > F      =    0.0000
  Residual |  1145377.51       62    18473.8308         R-squared     =    0.5113
-----------+------------------------------             Adj R-squared =    0.4955
     Total |  2343606.15       64    36618.8462         Root MSE      =    135.92


------------------------------------------------------------------------------
       SAT |     Coef.    Std. Err.       t      P>|t|     [95% Conf. Interval]
-----------+------------------------------------------------------------------
       GPA |   161.2106    34.19889      4.71    0.000     92.84795     229.5732
        AP |   112.7129    44.46296      2.53    0.014     23.83273     201.5931
     _cons |    457.201   101.7863      4.49    0.000      253.733      660.6689
------------------------------------------------------------------------------
```

Answer each of the following questions for this regression run.

a. Evaluate this result with respect to its economic meaning, overall fit, and the signs and significance of the individual coefficients.

b. What econometric problems (out of omitted variables, irrelevant variables, or multicollinearity) does this regression have? Why? If you need feedback on your answer, see hint 13 in the material on this chapter in Appendix A.

c. Which of the following statements comes closest to your recommendation for further action to be taken in the estimation of this equation?

   i. No further specification changes are advisable (go to page 272).
   ii. I would like to add PREP to the equation (go to run 8.17).
   iii. I would like to replace the AP combination variable with APMATH and APENG (go to run 8.1).

If you need feedback on your answer, see hint 13 in the material on this chapter in Appendix A.

Evaluating the Results from Your Interactive Exercise

Congratulations! If you've reached this section, you must have found a specification that met your theoretical and econometric goals. Which one did you pick? Our experience is that most beginning econometricians end up with either regression run 8.3, 8.6, or 8.10, but only after looking at three or more regression results (or a hint or two) before settling on that choice.

In contrast, we've found that most experienced econometricians gravitate to regression run 8.6, usually after inspecting, at most, one other specification. What lessons can we learn from this difference?

1. *Learn that a variable isn't irrelevant simply because its t-score is low.* In our opinion, ESL belongs in the equation for strong theoretical reasons, and a slightly insignificant *t*-score in the expected direction isn't enough evidence to get us to rethink the underlying theory.

2. *Learn to spot redundant (multicollinear) variables.* ESL and RACE wouldn't normally be redundant, but in this high school, with its particular ethnic diversity, they are. Once one is included in the equation, the other shouldn't even be considered.

3. *Learn to spot false variables.* At first glance, PREP is a tempting variable to include because prep courses almost surely improve the SAT scores of the students who choose to take them. The problem is that a student's decision to take a prep course isn't independent of his or her previous SAT scores (or expected scores). We trust the judgment of students who feel a need for a prep course, and we think that all the course will do is bring them up to the level of their peers who didn't feel they needed a course. As a result, we wouldn't expect a significant effect in either direction.

If you enjoyed and learned from this interactive regression learning exercise, you'll be interested to know that there is another in Chapter 11. Good luck!

Chapter 9

Serial Correlation

In the next two chapters we'll investigate the final component of the specification of a regression equation—choosing the correct form of the stochastic error term. Our first topic, serial correlation, is the violation of Classical Assumption IV that different observations of the error term are uncorrelated with each other. Serial correlation, also called autocorrelation, can exist in any research study in which the order of the observations has some meaning and occurs most frequently in time-series data sets. In essence, serial correlation implies that the value of the error term from one time period depends in some systematic way on the value of the error term in other time periods. Since time-series data are used in many applications of econometrics, it's important to understand serial correlation and its consequences for OLS estimators.

The approach of this chapter to the problem of serial correlation will be similar to that used in the previous chapter. We'll attempt to answer the same four questions:

1. What is the nature of the problem?
2. What are the consequences of the problem?
3. How is the problem diagnosed?
4. What remedies for the problem are available?

9.1 Time Series

Virtually every equation in the text so far has been cross-sectional in nature, but that's going to change dramatically in this chapter. As a result, it's probably worthwhile to talk about some of the characteristics of time-series equations.

Time-series data involve a single entity (like a person, corporation, or state) over multiple points in time. Such a time-series approach allows researchers to investigate analytical issues that can't be examined very easily with a cross-sectional regression. For example, macroeconomic models and supply-and-demand models are best studied using time-series, not cross-sectional, data.

The notation for a time-series study is different from that for a cross-sectional one. Our familiar cross-sectional notation (for one time period and N different entities) is:

$$Y_i = \beta_0 + \beta_1 X_{1i} + \beta_2 X_{2i} + \beta_3 X_{3i} + \epsilon_i$$

where i goes from 1 to N.

A time-series regression has one entity and T different time periods, however, so we'll switch to this notation:

$$Y_t = \beta_0 + \beta_1 X_{1t} + \beta_2 X_{2t} + \beta_3 X_{3t} + \epsilon_t$$

where t goes from 1 to T.

Thus:

$Y_1 = \beta_0 + \beta_1 X_{11} + \beta_2 X_{21} + \beta_3 X_{31} + \epsilon_1$ refers to observations from the first time period

$Y_2 = \beta_0 + \beta_1 X_{12} + \beta_2 X_{22} + \beta_3 X_{32} + \epsilon_2$ refers to observations from the second time period

. . .

$Y_T = \beta_0 + \beta_1 X_{1T} + \beta_2 X_{2T} + \beta_3 X_{3T} + \epsilon_T$ refers to observations from the Tth time period

What's so tough about that, you say? All we've done is change from i to t and change from N to T. Well, it turns out that time-series studies have some characteristics that make them more difficult to deal with than cross-sections:

1. *The order of observations in a time series is fixed.* With a cross-sectional data set, you can enter the observations in any order you want, but with time-series data, you must keep the observations in chronological order.

2. *Time-series samples tend to be much smaller than cross-sectional ones.* Most time-series populations have many fewer potential observations than do cross-sectional ones, and these smaller data sets make statistical inference more difficult. In addition, it's much harder to generate a

time-series observation than a cross-sectional one. After all, it takes a year to get one more observation in an annual time series!

3. *The theory underlying time-series analysis can be quite complex.* In part because of the problems mentioned above, time-series econometrics includes a number of complex topics that require advanced estimation techniques. We'll tackle these topics in Chapters 12, 14, and 15.

4. *The stochastic error term in a time-series equation is often affected by events that took place in a previous time period.* This is serial correlation, the topic of our chapter, so let's get started!

9.2 Pure versus Impure Serial Correlation

Pure Serial Correlation

Pure serial correlation occurs when Classical Assumption IV, which assumes uncorrelated observations of the error term, is violated in a correctly specified equation. If there is correlation between observations of the error term, then the error term is said to be serially correlated. When econometricians use the term serial correlation without any modifier, they are referring to pure serial correlation.

The most commonly assumed kind of serial correlation is **first-order serial correlation**, in which the current value of the error term is a function of the previous value of the error term:

$$\epsilon_t = \rho\epsilon_{t-1} + u_t \tag{9.1}$$

where: ϵ = the error term of the equation in question
ρ = the first-order autocorrelation coefficient
u = a classical (not serially correlated) error term

The functional form in Equation 9.1 is called a first-order Markov scheme. The new symbol, ρ (rho, pronounced "row"), called the **first-order autocorrelation coefficient**, measures the functional relationship between the value of an observation of the error term and the value of the previous observation of the error term.

The magnitude of ρ indicates the strength of the serial correlation in an equation. If ρ is zero, then there is no serial correlation (because ϵ would equal u, a classical error term). As ρ approaches 1 in absolute value, the value of the previous observation of the error term becomes more important in determining the current value of ϵ_t, and a high degree of serial correlation exists. For ρ to be greater than 1 in absolute value is unreasonable because it implies that the error term has a tendency to continually increase in absolute value over time ("explode"). As a result of this, we can state that:

$$-1 < \rho < +1 \qquad (9.2)$$

The sign of ρ indicates the nature of the serial correlation in an equation. A positive value for ρ implies that the error term tends to have the same sign from one time period to the next; this is called **positive serial correlation**. Such a tendency means that if ϵ_t happens by chance to take on a large value in one time period, subsequent observations would tend to retain a portion of this original large value and would have the same sign as the original. For example, in time-series models, the effects of a large external shock to an economy (like an earthquake) in one period may linger for several time periods. The error term will tend to be positive for a number of observations, then negative for several more, and then back positive again.

Figure 9.1 shows two different examples of positive serial correlation. The error term observations plotted in Figure 9.1 are arranged in chronological order, with the first observation being the first period for which data are available, the second being the second, and so on. To see the difference between error terms with and without positive serial correlation, compare the patterns in Figure 9.1 with the depiction of no serial correlation ($\rho = 0$) in Figure 9.2.

A negative value of ρ implies that the error term has a tendency to switch signs from negative to positive and back again in consecutive observations; this is called **negative serial correlation**. It implies that there is some sort of cycle (like a pendulum) behind the drawing of stochastic disturbances. Figure 9.3 shows two different examples of negative serial correlation. For instance, negative serial correlation might exist in the error term of an equation that is in first differences because *changes* in a variable often follow a cyclical pattern. In most time-series applications, however, negative pure serial correlation is much less likely than positive pure serial correlation. As a result, most econometricians analyzing pure serial correlation concern themselves primarily with positive serial correlation.

Serial correlation can take on many forms other than first-order serial correlation. For example, in a quarterly model, the current quarter's error term observation may be functionally related to the observation of the error term from the same quarter in the previous year. This is called *seasonally based serial correlation*:

$$\epsilon_t = \rho \epsilon_{t-4} + u_t$$

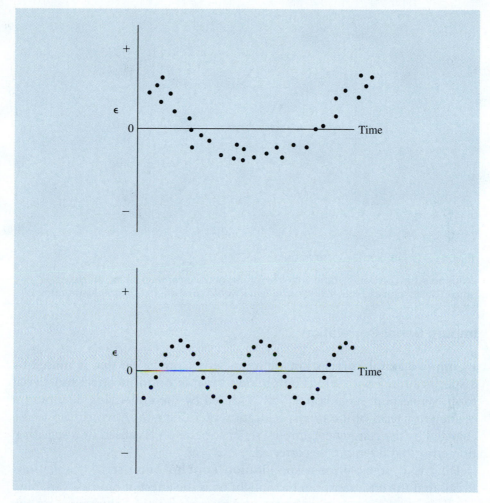

Figure 9.1 Positive Serial Correlation

With positive first-order serial correlation, the current observation of the error term tends to have the same sign as the previous observation of the error term. An example of positive serial correlation would be external shocks to an economy that take more than one time period to completely work through the system.

Similarly, it is possible that the error term in an equation might be a function of more than one previous observation of the error term:

$$\epsilon_t = \rho_1 \epsilon_{t-1} + \rho_2 \epsilon_{t-2} + u_t$$

Such a formulation is called *second-order* serial correlation.

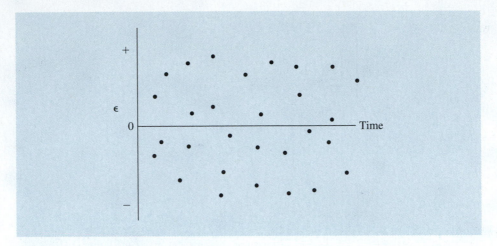

Figure 9.2 No Serial Correlation

With no serial correlation, different observations of the error term are completely uncorrelated with each other. Such error terms would conform to Classical Assumption IV.

Impure Serial Correlation

By **impure serial correlation** we mean serial correlation that is caused by a specification error such as an omitted variable or an incorrect functional form. While pure serial correlation is caused by the underlying distribution of the error term of the true specification of an equation (which cannot be changed by the researcher), impure serial correlation is caused by a specification error that often can be corrected.

How is it possible for a specification error to cause serial correlation? Recall that the error term can be thought of as the effect of omitted variables, nonlinearities, measurement errors, and pure stochastic disturbances on the dependent variable. This means, for example, that if we omit a relevant variable or use the wrong functional form, then the portion of that omitted effect that cannot be represented by the included explanatory variables must be absorbed by the error term. The error term for an incorrectly specified equation thus includes a portion of the effect of any omitted variables and/or a portion of the effect of the difference between the proper functional form and the one chosen by the researcher. This new error term might be serially correlated even if the true one is not. If this is the case, the serial correlation has been caused by the researcher's choice of a specification and not by the pure error term associated with the correct specification.

As you'll see in Section 9.5, the proper remedy for serial correlation depends on whether the serial correlation is likely to be pure or impure. Not

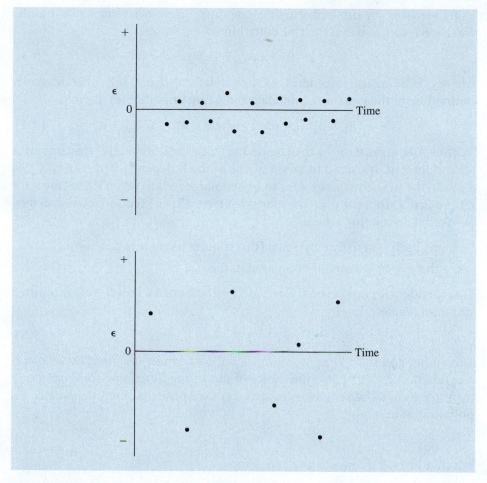

Figure 9.3 Negative Serial Correlation

With negative first-order serial correlation, the current observation of the error term tends to have the opposite sign from the previous observation of the error term. In most time-series applications, negative serial correlation is much less likely than positive serial correlation.

surprisingly, the best remedy for impure serial correlation is to attempt to find the omitted variable (or at least a good proxy) or the correct functional form for the equation. Both the bias and the impure serial correlation will disappear if the specification error is corrected. As a result, most econometricians try to make sure they have the best specification possible before they spend too much time worrying about pure serial correlation.

To see how an omitted variable can cause the error term to be serially correlated, suppose that the true equation is:

$$Y_t = \beta_0 + \beta_1 X_{1t} + \beta_2 X_{2t} + \epsilon_t \tag{9.3}$$

where ϵ_t is a classical error term. As shown in Section 6.1, if X_2 is accidentally omitted from the equation (or if data for X_2 are unavailable), then:

$$Y_t = \beta_0 + \beta_1 X_{1t} + \epsilon_t^* \quad \text{where} \quad \epsilon_t^* = \beta_2 X_{2t} + \epsilon_t \tag{9.4}$$

Thus, the error term in the omitted variable case is not the classical error term ϵ. Instead, it's also a function of one of the independent variables, X_2. As a result, the new error term, ϵ^*, can be serially correlated even if the true error term ϵ is not. In particular, the new error term ϵ^* will tend to exhibit detectable serial correlation when:

1. X_2 itself is serially correlated (this is quite likely in a time series) *and*
2. the size of ϵ is small[1] compared to the size of $\beta_2 \overline{X}_2$.

These tendencies hold even if there are a number of included and/or omitted variables. Therefore:

$$\epsilon_t^* = \rho \epsilon_{t-1}^* + u_t \tag{9.5}$$

Another common kind of impure serial correlation is caused by an incorrect functional form. Here, the choice of the wrong functional form can cause the error term to be serially correlated. Let's suppose that the true equation is polynomial in nature:

$$Y_t = \beta_0 + \beta_1 X_{1t} + \beta_2 X_{1t}^2 + \epsilon_t \tag{9.6}$$

but that instead a linear regression is run:

$$Y_t = \alpha_0 + \alpha_1 X_{1t} + \epsilon_t^* \tag{9.7}$$

The new error term ϵ^* is now a function of the true error term ϵ and of the differences between the linear and the polynomial functional forms. As can be seen in Figure 9.4, these differences often follow fairly autoregressive patterns. That is, positive differences tend to be followed by positive differences, and negative differences tend to be followed by negative differences. As a

---

1. If typical values of ϵ are significantly larger in absolute size than $\beta_2 \overline{X}_2$, then even a serially correlated omitted variable (X_2) will not change ϵ^* very much. In addition, recall that the omitted variable, X_2, will cause bias in the estimate of β_1, depending on the correlation between the two Xs. If $\hat{\beta}_1$ is biased because of the omission of X_2, then a portion of the $\beta_2 \overline{X}_2$ effect must have been absorbed by $\hat{\beta}_1$ and will not end up in the residuals. As a result, tests for serial correlation based on those residuals may give incorrect readings. Such residuals may leave misleading clues as to possible specification errors.

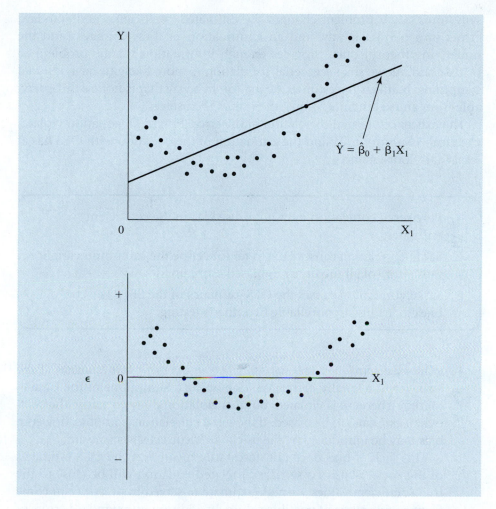

Figure 9.4 Incorrect Functional Form as a Source of Impure Serial Correlation

The use of an incorrect functional form tends to group positive and negative residuals together, causing positive impure serial correlation.

result, using a linear functional form when a nonlinear one is appropriate will usually result in positive impure serial correlation.

9.3 The Consequences of Serial Correlation

The consequences of serial correlation are quite different in nature from the consequences of the problems discussed so far in this text. Omitted variables, irrelevant variables, and multicollinearity all have fairly recognizable external symptoms. Each problem changes the estimated coefficients and standard errors in a particular way, and an examination of these changes (and the underlying theory) often provides enough information for the problem to be detected. As we shall see, serial correlation is more likely to have internal symptoms; it affects the estimated equation in a way that is not easily observable from an examination of just the results themselves.

The existence of serial correlation in the error term of an equation violates Classical Assumption IV, and the estimation of the equation with OLS has at least three consequences:[2]

---

1. Pure serial correlation does not cause bias in the coefficient estimates.

2. Serial correlation causes OLS to no longer be the minimum variance estimator (of all the linear unbiased estimators).

3. Serial correlation causes the OLS estimates of the $SE(\hat{\beta})$s to be biased, leading to unreliable hypothesis testing.

---

1. *Pure serial correlation does not cause bias in the coefficient estimates.* If the error term is serially correlated, one of the assumptions of the Gauss–Markov Theorem is violated, but this violation does not cause the coefficient estimates to be biased. If the serial correlation is impure, however, bias may be introduced by the use of an incorrect specification.

    This lack of bias does not necessarily mean that the OLS estimates of the coefficients of a serially correlated equation will be close to the true coefficient values. A single estimate observed in practice can come from a wide range of possible values. In addition, the standard errors of these estimates will typically be increased by the serial correlation. This increase will raise the probability that a $\hat{\beta}$ will differ significantly from the true β value. What unbiased means in this case is that the distribution of the $\hat{\beta}$s is still centered around the true β.

2. *Serial correlation causes OLS to no longer be the minimum variance estimator (of all the linear unbiased estimators).* Although the violation of Classical Assumption IV causes no bias, it does affect the other main conclusion of the Gauss–Markov Theorem, that of minimum variance. In particular,

---

2. If the regression includes a lagged dependent variable as an independent variable, then the problems worsen significantly. For more on this topic (called a dynamic model), see Chapter 12.

we cannot prove that the distribution of the OLS $\hat{\beta}$s is minimum variance (among the linear unbiased estimators) when Assumption IV is violated.

The serially correlated error term causes the dependent variable to fluctuate in a way that the OLS estimation procedure sometimes attributes to the independent variables. Thus, OLS is more likely to misestimate the true β in the face of serial correlation. On balance, the $\hat{\beta}$s are still unbiased because overestimates are just as likely as underestimates, but these errors increase the variance of the distribution of the estimates, increasing the amount that any given estimate is likely to differ from the true β.

3. *Serial correlation causes the OLS estimates of the SE($\hat{\beta}$)s to be biased, leading to unreliable hypothesis testing.* With serial correlation, the OLS formula for the standard error produces biased estimates of the SE($\hat{\beta}$)s. Because the SE($\hat{\beta}$) is a prime component in the *t*-statistic, these biased SE($\hat{\beta}$)s cause biased *t*-scores and unreliable hypothesis testing in general. In essence, serial correlation causes OLS to produce *incorrect* SE($\hat{\beta}$)s and *t*-scores! Not surprisingly, most econometricians therefore are very hesitant to put much faith in hypothesis tests that were conducted in the face of pure serial correlation.[3]

What sort of bias does serial correlation tend to cause? Typically, the bias in the estimate of SE($\hat{\beta}$) is negative, meaning that OLS underestimates the size of the standard errors of the coefficients. This comes about because serial correlation usually results in a pattern of observations that allows a better fit than the actual (not serially correlated) observations would otherwise justify. This tendency of OLS to underestimate the SE($\hat{\beta}$) means that OLS typically overestimates the *t*-scores of the estimated coefficients, since:

$$t = \frac{(\hat{\beta} - \beta_{H_0})}{SE(\hat{\beta})} \tag{9.8}$$

Thus the *t*-scores printed out by a typical software regression package in the face of serial correlation are likely to be too high. Similarly, confidence intervals for the coefficients will tend to be too narrow.

What will happen to hypothesis testing if OLS underestimates the SE($\hat{\beta}$)s and therefore overestimates the *t*-scores? Well, the "too low" SE($\hat{\beta}$) will cause

---

3. While our discussion here involves the *t*-test, the same conclusion of unreliability in the face of serial correlation applies to all other test statistics.

a "too high" t-score for a particular coefficient, and this will make it more likely that we will reject a null hypothesis (for example $H_0: \beta \le 0$) when it is in fact true. This increased chance of rejecting H_0 means that we're more likely to reject a true null hypothesis, so we're more likely to make the mistake of keeping an irrelevant variable in an equation because its coefficient's t-score has been overestimated. In other words, hypothesis testing becomes unreliable when we have pure serial correlation.

9.4 The Detection of Serial Correlation

How can we detect serial correlation? While the first indication of serial correlation often occurs when we observe a pattern in the residuals similar to Figure 9.1, most econometricians rely on more formal tests like the Durbin–Watson test and the Lagrange Multiplier test.

The Durbin–Watson Test

The **Durbin–Watson test** is used to determine if there is first-order serial correlation in the error term of an equation by examining the *residuals* of a particular estimation of that equation.[4] It's important to use the Durbin–Watson test only when the assumptions that underlie its derivation are met:

1. The regression model includes an intercept term.

2. The serial correlation is first-order in nature:

$$\epsilon_t = \rho\epsilon_{t-1} + u_t \tag{9.9}$$

where ρ is the autocorrelation coefficient and u is a classical (normally distributed) error term.

3. The regression model does not include a lagged dependent variable (discussed in Chapter 12) as an independent variable.[5]

The equation for the *Durbin–Watson statistic* for T observations is:

$$d = \sum_{2}^{T} (e_t - e_{t-1})^2 \Big/ \sum_{1}^{T} e_t^2 \tag{9.10}$$

---

4. J. Durbin and G. S. Watson, "Testing for Serial Correlation in Least-Squared Regression," *Biometrika*, 1951, pp. 159–177.

5. In such a circumstance, the Durbin–Watson test is biased toward 2.

where the e_ts are the OLS residuals. Note that the numerator has one fewer observation than the denominator because an observation must be used to calculate e_{t-1}. The Durbin–Watson statistic equals 0 if there is extreme positive serial correlation, 2 if there is no serial correlation, and 4 if there is extreme negative serial correlation. To see this, let's put appropriate residual values into Equation 9.10 for these three cases:

1. Extreme Positive Serial Correlation: d = 0
   In this case, $e_t = e_{t-1}$, so $(e_t - e_{t-1}) = 0$ and d = 0.

2. Extreme Negative Serial Correlation: d ≈ 4
   In this case, $e_t = -e_{t-1}$, and $(e_t - e_{t-1}) = (2e_t)$. Substituting into Equation 9.10, we obtain $d = \sum(2e_t)^2 / \sum(e_t)^2$ and d ≈ 4.

3. No Serial Correlation: d ≈ 2
   When there is no serial correlation, the mean of the distribution of d is equal to 2.[6] That is, if there is no serial correlation, d ≈ 2.

Using the Durbin–Watson Test

The Durbin–Watson test is unusual in two respects. First, econometricians almost never test the one-sided null hypothesis that there is negative serial correlation in the residuals because negative serial correlation, as mentioned previously, is quite difficult to explain theoretically in economic or business analysis. Its existence usually means that impure serial correlation has been caused by some specification error.

Second, the Durbin–Watson test is sometimes inconclusive. Whereas previously explained decision rules always have had only "acceptance" regions and rejection regions, the Durbin–Watson test has a third possibility, called the inconclusive region. For reasons outlined in Section 9.5, we do not recommend the application of a remedy for serial correlation if the Durbin–Watson test is inconclusive.[7]

---

6. To see this, multiply out the numerator of Equation 9.10, obtaining

$$d = \left[\sum_{2}^{T} e_t^2 - 2\sum_{2}^{T}(e_t e_{t-1}) + \sum_{2}^{T} e_{t-1}^2 \right] \Big/ \sum_{1}^{T} e_t^2 \approx \left[\sum_{2}^{T} e_t^2 + \sum_{2}^{T} e_{t-1}^2 \right] \Big/ \sum_{1}^{T} e_t^2 \approx 2 \quad (9.11)$$

If there is no serial correlation, then e_t and e_{t-1} are not related, and, on average, $\sum(e_t e_{t-1}) = 0$.

7. This inconclusive region is troubling, but the development of exact Durbin–Watson tests may eliminate this problem in the future. Some computer programs allow the user the option of calculating an exact Durbin–Watson probability (of first-order serial correlation). Alternatively, it's worth noting that there is a growing trend toward the use of d_U as a sole critical value. This trend runs counter to our view that if the Durbin–Watson test is inconclusive, then no remedial action should be taken except to search for a possible cause of impure serial correlation.

With these exceptions, the use of the Durbin–Watson test is quite similar to the use of the t-test. To test for positive serial correlation, the following steps are required:

1. Obtain the OLS residuals from the equation to be tested and calculate the d statistic by using Equation 9.10.

2. Determine the sample size and the number of explanatory variables and then consult Statistical Table B-4 in Appendix B to find the upper critical d value, d_U, and the lower critical d value, d_L, respectively. Instructions for the use of this table are also in that appendix.

3. Given the null hypothesis of no positive serial correlation and a one-sided alternative hypothesis:

$$H_0: \rho \leq 0 \quad \text{(no positive serial correlation)} \quad (9.12)$$
$$H_A: \rho > 0 \quad \text{(positive serial correlation)}$$

the appropriate decision rule is:

$$
\begin{aligned}
&\text{If } d < d_L && \text{Reject } H_0 \\
&\text{If } d > d_U && \text{Do not reject } H_0 \\
&\text{If } d_L \leq d \leq d_U && \text{Inconclusive}
\end{aligned}
$$

In rare circumstances, perhaps first differenced equations, a two-sided Durbin–Watson test might be appropriate. In such a case, steps 1 and 2 are still used, but step 3 is now:

Given the null hypothesis of no serial correlation and a two-sided alternative hypothesis:

$$H_0: \rho = 0 \quad \text{(no serial correlation)} \quad (9.13)$$
$$H_A: \rho \neq 0 \quad \text{(serial correlation)}$$

the appropriate decision rule is:

$$
\begin{aligned}
&\text{if } d < d_L && \text{Reject } H_0 \\
&\text{if } d > 4 - d_L && \text{Reject } H_0 \\
&\text{if } 4 - d_U > d > d_U && \text{Do not reject } H_0 \\
&\text{otherwise} && \text{Inconclusive}
\end{aligned}
$$

Examples of the Use of the Durbin–Watson Statistic

Let's work through some applications of the Durbin–Watson test. First, turn to Statistical Table B-4. Note that the upper and lower critical d values (d_U and d_L) depend on the number of explanatory variables (do not count the constant term), the sample size, and the level of significance of the test.

Now let's set up a one-sided 5-percent test for a regression with three explanatory variables and 25 observations. As can be seen from 5-percent table B-4, the critical values are $d_L = 1.12$ and $d_U = 1.66$. As a result, if the hypotheses are:

$$H_0: \rho \leq 0 \quad \text{(no positive serial correlation)}$$
$$H_A: \rho > 0 \quad \text{(positive serial correlation)}$$

the appropriate decision rule is:

$$\text{if } d < 1.12 \quad \text{Reject } H_0$$
$$\text{if } d > 1.66 \quad \text{Do not reject } H_0$$
$$\text{if } 1.12 \leq d \leq 1.66 \quad \text{Inconclusive}$$

A computed Durbin–Watson statistic of 1.78, for example, would indicate that there is no evidence of positive serial correlation, a value of 1.28 would be inconclusive, and a value of 0.60 would imply positive serial correlation. Figure 9.5 provides a graph of the "acceptance," rejection, and inconclusive regions for this example.

For a real-world example, let's look at a simple time-series model of the annual consumption of chicken in the United States. There are a variety of

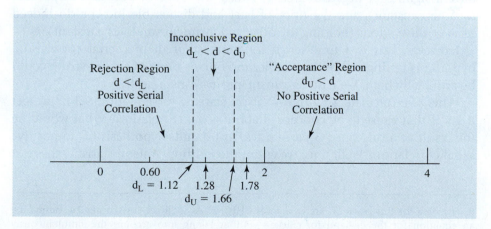

Figure 9.5 An Example of a One-Sided Durbin–Watson Test

In a one-sided Durbin–Watson test for positive serial correlation, only values of d significantly below 2 cause the null hypothesis of no positive serial correlation to be rejected. In this example, a d of 1.78 would indicate no positive serial correlation, a d of 0.60 would indicate positive serial correlation, and a d of 1.28 would be inconclusive.

variables that might make sense in such an equation, and at least three variables seem obvious. We'd expect the demand for chicken to be a negative function of the price of chicken and a positive function of income and the price of a substitute (in this case, beef):

$$Y_t = \beta_0 \overset{-}{+} \beta_1 PC_t \overset{+}{+} \beta_2 PB_t \overset{+}{+} \beta_3 YD_t + \epsilon_t$$

where: Y_t = per capita chicken consumption (in pounds) in year t
PC_t = the price of chicken (in cents per pound) in year t
PB_t = the price of beef (in cents per pound) in year t
YD_t = U.S. per capita disposable income (in hundreds of dollars) in year t

If we collect data for these variables for the years 1974 through 2002, we can estimate[8] the following equation:

$$\hat{Y}_t = 27.7 - 0.11PC_t + 0.03PB_t + 0.23YD_t \qquad (9.14)$$
$$\phantom{\hat{Y}_t = 27.7} (0.03) \quad (0.02) \quad (0.01)$$
$$t = \qquad -3.38 \quad +1.86 \quad +15.7$$
$$\bar{R}^2 = .9904 \quad N = 29 \text{ (annual 1974–2002)}$$

How does our estimated equation look? The overall fit of Equation 9.14 is excellent, and each of the individual regression coefficients is significantly different from zero in the expected direction. The price of chicken does indeed have a significant negative effect (holding the price of beef and disposable income constant), and the price of beef and disposable income do indeed have positive effects (holding the other independent variables constant).

However, this is a time-series equation, so if there's serial correlation, hypothesis testing will be unreliable, and one or more of these t-scores could be artificially high. We'd better run a Durbin–Watson test!

When we calculate a Durbin–Watson statistic for Equation 9.14,[9] we get 0.99. Is that cause to be concerned about serial correlation? What would be the result of a one-sided 5-percent test of the null hypothesis of no positive serial correlation? Well, once we've got the Durbin–Watson statistic, the next

---

8. The data for this equation are in dataset CHICK9. As we'll see in Chapter 14, estimating an equation for the demand for chicken without taking into account the simultaneously determined supply of chicken runs the risk of bias, particularly in the coefficient of the price of chicken.

9. Luckily, you don't actually need to calculate the Durbin–Watson statistic yourself. Some econometric software programs, including EViews, calculate the Durbin–Watson statistic automatically, while others, including Stata, allow you to do so quite simply. In Stata, for example, the command is *estat dwatson*.

step is to consult Statistical Table B-4. In that table, with K (the number of explanatory variables[10]) equal to 3 and N (the number of observations) equal to 29, we find that the critical d values are $d_L = 1.20$ and $d_U = 1.65$. (It's probably a good idea to check these d values yourself to make sure that you know how to look them up.)

The decision rule would thus be:

$$\begin{array}{ll} \text{if } d < 1.20 & \text{Reject } H_0 \\ \text{if } d > 1.65 & \text{Do not reject } H_0 \\ \text{if } 1.20 \leq d \leq 1.65 & \text{Inconclusive} \end{array}$$

Since 0.99 is less than the critical lower limit of the *d* statistic, we would reject the null hypothesis of no positive serial correlation, and we would have to decide how to cope with that serial correlation.

The Lagrange Multiplier (LM) test

Unfortunately, the Durbin–Watson test has a number of limitations. As mentioned, it can be used only when the serial correlation is first-order, when a constant is included in the equation, and when the equation doesn't include a lagged dependent variable. The Durbin–Watson test's inconclusive region also is a drawback, particularly since the size of the inconclusive region increases as the number of independent variables increases.

A popular alternative to the Durbin–Watson test is the **Lagrange Multiplier (LM) test**, which checks for serial correlation by analyzing how well the lagged residuals explain the residual of the original equation in an equation that also includes all the explanatory variables of the original model. If the lagged residuals are significant in explaining this time's residuals (as shown by the chi-square test), then we can reject the null hypothesis of no serial correlation.[11] The LM serial correlation test is just one application of a

---

10. Be careful! While we define K as the number of explanatory variables, some other sources, including Stata and the Stanford University Durbin–Watson tables, define K as the number of coefficients (which is equivalent to K + 1 in our notation). As long as you're aware of this difference, it won't cause you any problems. Incidentally, the Stanford tables, which are online at http://web.stanford.edu/~clint/bench/dwcrit.htm, have many more observations than can be printed in a textbook, so they're quite useful if you have a large sample.

11. The Lagrange Multiplier test for serial correlation is sometimes referred to as the Breusch–Godfrey test, which is why the Stata command for this test is *estat bgodfrey, lag (1)*. Note that if we're testing for first-order serial correlation, we need to specify that the lag equals 1. If we are concerned with second-order serial correlation, then the lag would equal 2, etc.

general Lagrange Multiplier testing approach that can be applied to a variety of econometric problems.[12]

Using the Lagrange Multiplier (LM) test to investigate the possibility of serial correlation involves three steps:

1. Obtain the residuals from the estimated equation. For an equation with two independent variables, this would equal:

$$e_t = Y_t - \hat{Y}_t = Y_t - \hat{\beta}_0 - \hat{\beta}_1 X_{1t} - \hat{\beta}_2 X_{2t} \tag{9.15}$$

2. Use these residuals as the dependent variable in an auxiliary equation that includes as independent variables all those on the right-hand side of the original equation as well as the lagged residuals:

$$e_t = \alpha_0 + \alpha_1 X_{1t} + \alpha_2 X_{2t} + \alpha_3 e_{t-1} + u_t \tag{9.16}$$

3. Estimate Equation 9.16 using OLS and then test the null hypothesis that $\alpha_3 = 0$ with the following test statistic:

$$LM = NR^2$$

where N is the sample size and R^2 is the unadjusted coefficient of determination, both of the auxiliary equation, Equation 9.16.

For large samples, LM has a chi-square distribution with degrees of freedom equal to one (the number of restrictions in the null hypothesis). If LM is greater than the critical chi-square value from Statistical Table B-6, then we reject the null hypothesis that $\alpha_3 = 0$ and conclude that there is serial correlation in the original equation. Note that even though α_3 tends to be positive in economic examples, this is a two-sided test.

An Example of the Lagrange Multiplier Test

As an example of the Lagrange Multiplier test, let's run a 5-percent test for serial correlation on our chicken demand model, Equation 9.14. The appropriate LM equation to run is:

$$e_t = \alpha_0 + \alpha_1 PC_t + \alpha_2 PB_t + \alpha_3 YD_t + \alpha_4 e_{t-1} + u_t \tag{9.17}$$

where e_t is the residual from Equation 9.14, the equation that we're testing for serial correlation.

---

12. For example, the White test for heteroskedasticity (to be explained in Section 10.3) also is an application of the Lagrange Multiplier approach. For a survey of the various uses to which Lagrange Multiplier tests can be put, see Rob Engle, "Wald, Likelihood Ratio, and Lagrange Multiplier Tests in Econometrics," in Z. Griliches and M. D. Intrilligator (eds.), *Handbook of Econometrics*, Vol. II (Amsterdam, Elsevier Science Publishers, 1984).

Since there are three independent variables, the null hypothesis becomes $H_0: \alpha_4 = 0$. If we estimate Equation 9.17, we get an R^2 of .291. Since the sample size is 29, this means that:

$$LM = NR^2 = 8.439$$

The decision rule is to reject the null hypothesis if NR^2 is greater than the critical chi-square value with 1 degree of freedom, so the next step is to consult Table B-6 and look up the critical value. As you can see if you take a look at Table B-6, the 5-percent chi-square critical value with 1 degree of freedom is 3.84. Since $8.439 > 3.84$, we can reject the null hypothesis and conclude that we have serial correlation in the chicken demand model. This is a two-sided test, but it confirms the result of our one-sided Durbin–Watson test. It seems clear that the chicken demand equation has serial correlation!

9.5 Remedies for Serial Correlation

Suppose that the Durbin–Watson or LM test detects serial correlation in the residuals of your equation. Is there a remedy? Some students suggest reordering the observations of Y and the Xs to avoid serial correlation. They think that if this time's error term appears to be affected by last time's error term, why not reorder the data randomly to get rid of the problem? The answer is that the reordering of the data does not get rid of the serial correlation; it just makes the problem harder to detect. If $\epsilon_2 = f(\epsilon_1)$ and we reorder the data, then the error term observations are still related to each other, but they now no longer follow each other, and it becomes almost impossible to discover the serial correlation. Interestingly, reordering the data changes the Durbin–Watson statistic but does not change the estimates of the coefficients or their standard errors at all.[13]

> The place to start in correcting a serial correlation problem is to look carefully at the specification of the equation for possible errors that might be causing impure serial correlation. Is the functional form correct? Are you sure that there are no omitted variables? Only after the specification of the equation has been reviewed carefully should the possibility of an adjustment for pure serial correlation be considered.

---

13. This can be proven mathematically, but it is usually more instructive to estimate a regression yourself, change the order of the observations, and then reestimate the regression. See Exercise 3 at the end of the chapter.

It's worth noting that if an omitted variable increases or decreases over time, as is often the case, or if the data set is logically reordered (say, according to the magnitude of one of the variables), then the Durbin–Watson or LM test can help detect impure serial correlation. A significant Durbin–Watson or LM test result can easily be caused by an omitted variable or an incorrect functional form. In such circumstances, the Durbin–Watson or LM tests do not distinguish between pure and impure serial correlation, but the detection of negative serial correlation is often a strong hint that the serial correlation is impure.

If you conclude that you have pure serial correlation, then the appropriate response is to consider the application of Generalized Least Squares or Newey–West standard errors, as described in the following sections.

Generalized Least Squares

Generalized least squares (GLS) is a method of ridding an equation of pure first-order serial correlation and in the process restoring the minimum variance property to its estimation. GLS starts with an equation that does not meet the Classical Assumptions (due in this case to the pure serial correlation in the error term) and transforms it into one (Equation 9.22) that does meet those assumptions.

At this point, you could skip directly to Equation 9.22, but it's easier to understand the GLS estimator if you examine the transformation from which it comes. Start with an equation that has first-order serial correlation:

$$Y_t = \beta_0 + \beta_1 X_{1t} + \epsilon_t \tag{9.18}$$

which, if $\epsilon_t = \rho\epsilon_{t-1} + u_t$ (due to pure serial correlation), also equals:

$$Y_t = \beta_0 + \beta_1 X_{1t} + \rho\epsilon_{t-1} + u_t \tag{9.19}$$

where ϵ is the serially correlated error term, ρ is the autocorrelation coefficient, and u is a classical (not serially correlated) error term.

If we could get the $\rho\epsilon_{t-1}$ term out of Equation 9.19, the serial correlation would be gone, because the remaining portion of the error term (u_t) has no serial correlation in it. To rid $\rho\epsilon_{t-1}$ from Equation 9.19, multiply Equation 9.18 by ρ and then lag the new equation by one time period, obtaining

$$\rho Y_{t-1} = \rho\beta_0 + \rho\beta_1 X_{1t-1} + \rho\epsilon_{t-1} \tag{9.20}$$

Notice that we now have an equation with a $\rho\epsilon_{t-1}$ term in it. If we now subtract Equation 9.20 from Equation 9.19, the equivalent equation that remains no longer contains the serially correlated component of the error term:

$$Y_t - \rho Y_{t-1} = \beta_0(1 - \rho) + \beta_1(X_{1t} - \rho X_{1t-1}) + u_t \tag{9.21}$$

Equation 9.21 can be rewritten as:

$$Y_t^* = \beta_0^* + \beta_1 X_{1t}^* + u_t \tag{9.22}$$

where:
$$Y_t^* = Y_t - \rho Y_{t-1} \tag{9.23}$$
$$X_{1t}^* = X_{1t} - \rho X_{1t-1}$$
$$\beta_0^* = \beta_0 - \rho \beta_0$$

Equation 9.22 is called a Generalized Least Squares (or "quasi-differenced") version of Equation 9.19. Notice that:

1. The error term is not serially correlated. As a result, OLS estimation of Equation 9.22 will be minimum variance. (This is true if we know ρ or if we accurately estimate ρ.)

2. The slope coefficient β_1 is the same as the slope coefficient of the original serially correlated equation, Equation 9.19. Thus coefficients estimated with GLS have the same meaning as those estimated with OLS.

3. The dependent variable has changed compared to that in Equation 9.19. This means that the GLS $\overline{R}^2$ is not necessarily comparable to the OLS $\overline{R}^2$.

Unfortunately we can't use OLS to estimate a Generalized Least Squares model because GLS equations are inherently nonlinear in the coefficients. To see why, take a look at Equation 9.21. We need to estimate values not only for β_0 and β_1 but also for ρ, and ρ is multiplied by β_0 and β_1 (which you can see if you multiply out the right-hand side of the equation). Since OLS requires that the equation be linear in the coefficients, we need a different estimation procedure.

Luckily, there are a number of techniques that can be used to estimate GLS equations. While the best-known of these is the *Cochrane–Orcutt method*,[14] our recommendation is to use a slightly different approach, the Prais–Winsten method. The **Prais–Winsten method**[15] is a two–step iterative technique that rids an equation of serial correlation by first producing

---

14. D. Cochrane and G. H. Orcutt, "Application of Least Squares Regression to Relationships Containing Autocorrelated Error Terms," *Journal of the American Statistical Association*, 1949, pp. 32–61.

15. S. J. Prais and C. B. Winsten, "Trend Estimators and Serial Correlation," *Cowles Commission Discussion Paper No. 383* (1954) Chicago. The Prais–Winsten method (sometimes called Yule–Walker) is very similar to Cochrane–Orcutt, but the Prais–Winsten estimate of ρ is more accurate because it uses the first observation in Step 1 while Cochrane–Orcutt does not. For more, see Masahito Kobayashi, "Comparison of Efficiencies of Several Estimators for Linear Regressions with Autocorrelated Errors," *Journal of the American Statistical Association*, 1985, pp. 951–953.

an estimate of ρ and then estimating the GLS equation using that $\hat{\rho}$. The two steps are:

1. Estimate ρ by running a regression based on the residuals of the equation suspected of having serial correlation:

$$e_t = \rho e_{t-1} + u_t \tag{9.24}$$

where the e_ts are the OLS residuals from the equation suspected of having pure serial correlation and u_t is a classical (non-serially-correlated) error term.

2. Use this $\hat{\rho}$ to estimate the GLS equation by substituting $\hat{\rho}$ into Equation 9.21 and using OLS to estimate Equation 9.21 with the adjusted data.

These two steps are repeated (iterated) until further improvement results in little change in $\hat{\rho}$. Once $\hat{\rho}$ has converged (usually in just a few iterations), the last estimate of step 2 is used as the final estimate of Equation 9.21.

Unfortunately, all methods of estimating GLS equations use iterative non-linear regression techniques that are well beyond the scope of this text. As a result, most researchers rely on their econometric software packages to estimate their GLS equations for them. In Stata, for example, the Prais–Winsten method can be run using the command *prais* followed by a listing of the dependent and independent variables.[16]

Let's apply Generalized Least Squares, using the Prais–Winsten method, to the chicken demand example that was found to have serial correlation in the previous section. Recall that we estimated the per capita demand for chicken as a function of the price of chicken, the price of beef, and disposable income:

$$\hat{Y}_t = 27.7 - 0.11PC_t + 0.03PB_t + 0.23YD_t \tag{9.14}$$
$$(0.03) \quad (0.02) \quad (0.01)$$
$$t = -3.38 \quad +1.86 \quad +15.7$$

$$\overline{R}^2 = .9904 \quad N = 29 \quad DW = 0.99$$

Note that we have added the Durbin–Watson statistic to the documentation with the notation DW. All future time-series results will include the DW statistic, but cross-sectional documentation of the DW is not required unless the observations are ordered in some meaningful manner (like smallest to largest or youngest to oldest).

---

16. In Stata, the command to apply GLS (using Prais–Winsten) to Equation 9.14 thus would be *prais Y PC PB YD*. In EViews, the easiest way to estimate a GLS equation is to add AR(1) to the equation as an independent variable, as in: LS Y C PC PB YD AR(1). The result is a GLS estimate where $\hat{\rho}$ will appear as the estimated coefficient of the variable AR(1).

If we reestimate Equation 9.14 with the Prais–Winsten approach to GLS, we obtain:

$$Y_t = 28.5 - 0.08PC_t + 0.016PB_t + 0.24YD_t$$
$$(0.04) \quad (0.021) \quad (0.02)$$
$$t = -2.13 \quad +0.74 \quad +13.12$$

$$\overline{R}^2 = .963 \quad N = 29 \quad \hat{\rho} = 0.56$$

(9.25)

Let's compare Equations 9.14 and 9.25. Note that the $\hat{\rho}$ used in Equation 9.25 is 0.56. This means that Y was actually run as $Y^* = Y_t - 0.56Y_{t-1}$, PC as $PC^* = PC_t - 0.56PC_{t-1}$, etc. Second, $\hat{\rho}$ replaces DW in the documentation of GLS estimates in part because the DW of Equation 9.25 isn't strictly comparable to non-GLS DWs (it is biased toward 2).

Generalized Least Squares estimates, no matter how they are produced, have at least two problems. First, even though serial correlation causes no bias in the estimates of the $\hat{\beta}$s, the GLS estimates usually are different from the OLS ones. For example, note that all three slope coefficients change as we move from OLS in Equation 9.14 to GLS in Equation 9.25. This isn't surprising, since different estimates can have different values even though their expected values are the same. The second problem is more important, however. It turns out that GLS works well if $\hat{\rho}$ is close to the actual ρ, but the GLS $\hat{\rho}$ is biased in small samples. If $\hat{\rho}$ is biased, then the biased $\hat{\rho}$ introduces bias into the GLS estimates of the $\hat{\beta}$s. Luckily, there is a remedy for serial correlation that helps avoid both of these problems: Newey–West standard errors.

Newey–West Standard Errors

Not all corrections for pure serial correlation involve Generalized Least Squares. **Newey–West standard errors** are SE($\hat{\beta}$)s that take account of serial correlation without changing the $\hat{\beta}$s themselves in any way.[17] The logic behind Newey–West standard errors is powerful. If serial correlation does not cause bias in the $\hat{\beta}$s but does impact the standard errors, then it makes sense to adjust the estimated equation in a way that changes the SE($\hat{\beta}$)s but not the $\hat{\beta}$s.

---

17. W. K. Newey and K. D. West, "A Simple, Positive Semi-Definite Heteroskedasticity and Autocorrelation Consistent Covariance Matrix," *Econometrica*, 1987, pp. 703–708. Newey–West standard errors are similar to HC standard errors (or White standard errors), to be discussed in Section 10.4.

Thus Newey–West standard errors have been calculated specifically to avoid the consequences of pure first-order serial correlation. The Newey–West procedure yields an estimator of the standard errors that, while they are biased, is generally more accurate than uncorrected standard errors for large samples (greater than 100) in the face of serial correlation. As a result, Newey–West standard errors can be used for t-tests and other hypothesis tests in most samples without the errors of inference potentially caused by serial correlation. Typically, Newey–West $SE(\hat{\beta})$s are larger than OLS $SE(\hat{\beta})$s, thus producing lower t-scores and decreasing the probability that a given estimated coefficient will be significantly different from zero.

To see how Newey–West standard errors work, let's apply them to the same serially correlated chicken demand equation to which we applied GLS in Equation 9.14. If we use Newey–West standard errors in the estimation of Equation 9.14, we get:

$$\hat{Y}_t = 27.7 - 0.11PC_t + 0.03PB_t + 0.23YD_t \qquad (9.26)$$
$$(0.03) \quad (0.02) \quad (0.01)$$
$$t = -3.30 \quad + 2.12 \quad +19.2$$

$$\bar{R}^2 = .9904 \qquad N = 29$$

Let's compare Equations 9.14 and 9.26. First of all, the $\hat{\beta}$s are identical in Equations 9.14 and 9.26. This is because Newey–West standard errors do not change the OLS $\hat{\beta}$s. Second, while we can't observe the change because of rounding, the Newey–West standard errors must be different from the OLS standard errors because the t-scores have changed even though the estimated coefficients are identical. However, two of the Newey–West $SE(\hat{\beta})$s are slightly lower than the OLS $SE(\hat{\beta})$s, which is a surprise even in a small sample like this one. Such a result indicates that there may well be an omitted variable or nonstationarity (to be discussed in Chapter 12) in this equation.

9.6 Summary

1. Serial correlation, or autocorrelation, is the violation of Classical Assumption IV that the observations of the error term are uncorrelated with each other. Usually, econometricians focus on first-order serial correlation, in which the current observation of the error term is assumed to be a function of the previous observation of the error term and a not-serially-correlated error term (u):

$$\epsilon_t = \rho \epsilon_{t-1} + u_t \qquad -1 < \rho < 1$$

where ρ is "rho," the autocorrelation coefficient.

2. Pure serial correlation is serial correlation that is a function of the error term of the correctly specified regression equation. Impure serial correlation is caused by specification errors such as an omitted variable or an incorrect functional form. While impure serial correlation can be positive $(0 < \rho < +1)$ or negative $(-1 < \rho < 0)$ pure serial correlation in economics or business situations is almost always positive (unless first differences are involved).

3. The major consequence of serial correlation is bias in the OLS SE $(\hat{\beta})$s, causing unreliable hypothesis testing. Pure serial correlation does not cause bias in the estimates of the βs.

4. A commonly used method of detecting first-order serial correlation is the Durbin–Watson test, which uses the residuals of an estimated regression to test the possibility of serial correlation in the error term. An often-preferred alternative is the Lagrange Multiplier (LM) test, which is far more general than the Durbin–Watson test.

5. The first step in ridding an equation of serial correlation is to check for possible specification errors. Only once the possibility of impure serial correlation has been reduced to a minimum should remedies for pure serial correlation be considered.

6. Generalized Least Squares (GLS) is a method of transforming an equation to rid it of pure first-order serial correlation. The use of GLS requires the estimation of ρ.

7. Newey–West standard errors are an alternative remedy for serial correlation that adjusts the OLS estimates of the SE $(\hat{\beta})$s to take account of the serial correlation without changing the $\hat{\beta}$s.

EXERCISES

(The answers to the even-numbered exercises are in Appendix A.)

1. Write the meaning of each of the following terms without referring to the book (or your notes), and compare your definition with the version in the text for each.
   a. Durbin–Watson test (p. 284)
   b. first-order auto correlation coefficient (p. 275)
   c. first-order serial correlation (p. 275)
   d. Generalized Least Squares (GLS) (p. 292)
   e. impure serial correlation (p. 278)

f. Lagrange Multiplier (LM) test (p. 289)
g. negative serial correlation (p. 276)
h. Newey–West standard errors (p. 295)
i. positive serial correlation (p. 276)
j. Prais–Winsten method (p. 293)
k. pure serial correlation (p. 275)

2. Consider the following equation for U.S. per capita consumption of beef:

$$\widehat{CB}_t = -330.3 + 49.1\ln Y_t - 0.34PB_t + 0.33PRP_t - 15.4D_t \quad (9.27)$$
$$(7.4) \quad (0.13) \quad (0.12) \quad (4.1)$$
$$t = 6.6 \quad -2.6 \quad 2.7 \quad -3.7$$
$$\overline{R}^2 = .700 \quad N = 28 \quad DW = 0.94$$

where: CB_t = the annual per capita pounds of beef consumed in the United States in year t

$\ln Y_t$ = the log of per capita disposable real income in the U.S. in year t

PB_t = average annualized real wholesale price of beef in year t (in cents per pound)

PRP_t = average annualized real wholesale price of pork in year t (in cents per pound)

D_t = a dummy variable equal to 1 for years in which there was a "health scare" about the dangers of red meat, 0 otherwise

a. Develop and test your own hypotheses with respect to the individual estimated slope coefficients.
b. Test for serial correlation in Equation 9.27 using the Durbin–Watson test at the 5-percent level.
c. What econometric problem(s) (if any) does Equation 9.27 appear to have? What remedy would you suggest?
d. You take your own advice and apply GLS to Equation 9.27, obtaining:

$$\widehat{CB}_t = -193.3 + 35.2\ln Y_t - 0.38PB_t + 0.10PRP_t - 5.7D_t \quad (9.28)$$
$$(14.1) \quad (0.10) \quad (0.09) \quad (3.9)$$
$$t = 2.5 \quad -3.7 \quad 1.1 \quad -1.5$$
$$\overline{R}^2 = .857 \quad N = 28 \quad \hat{\rho} = 0.82$$

Compare Equations 9.27 and 9.28. Which do you prefer? Why?

3. Recall from Section 9.5 that switching the order of a data set will not change its coefficient estimates. A revised order will change the Durbin–Watson statistic, however. To see both these points, run

regressions $(HS = \beta_0 + \beta_1 P + \epsilon)$ and compare the coefficient estimates and DW statistics for this data set:

Year	Housing Starts	Population
1	9090	2200
2	8942	2222
3	9755	2244
4	10327	2289
5	10513	2290

in the following three orders (in terms of year):
a. 1, 2, 3, 4, 5
b. 5, 4, 3, 2, 1
c. 2, 4, 3, 5, 1

4. Suppose that the data in a time-series study were entered in reverse chronological order. Would this change in any way the testing or adjusting for serial correlation? How? In particular:
   a. What happens to the Durbin–Watson statistic's ability to detect serial correlation if the order is reversed?
   b. What happens to the GLS method's ability to adjust for serial correlation if the order is reversed?
   c. What is the intuitive economic explanation of reverse serial correlation?

5. Your friend is just finishing a study of attendance at Los Angeles Laker regular-season home basketball games when she hears that you've read a chapter on serial correlation and asks your advice. Before running the equation on last season's data, she "reviewed the literature" by interviewing a number of basketball fans. She found out that fans like to watch winning teams. In addition, she learned that while some fans like to watch games throughout the season, others are most interested in games played late in the season. Her estimated equation (standard errors in parentheses) was:

$$\hat{A}_t = 14123 + 20L_t + 2600P_t + 900W_t$$
$$\phantom{\hat{A}_t = 14123 + } (500) \quad (1000) \quad (300)$$

$$DW = 0.85 \qquad N = 40 \qquad \overline{R}^2 = .46$$

where: A_t = the attendance at game t
  L_t = the winning percentage (games won divided by games played) of the Lakers before game t

P_t = the winning percentage before game t of the Lakers' opponent in that game

W_t = a dummy variable equal to 1 if game t was on Friday, Saturday, or Sunday, 0 otherwise

a. Test for serial correlation using the Durbin–Watson test at the 5-percent level.

b. Make and test appropriate hypotheses about the slope coefficients at the 1-percent level.

c. Compare the size and significance of the estimated coefficient of L with that for P. Is this difference surprising? Is L an irrelevant variable? Explain your answer.

d. If serial correlation exists, would you expect it to be pure or impure serial correlation? Why?

e. Your friend omitted the first game of the year from the sample because the first game is always a sellout and because neither team had a winning percentage yet. Was this a good decision?

6. In a 1988 article, Josef Brada and Ronald Graves built an interesting model of defense spending in the Soviet Union just before the breakup of that nation.[18] The authors felt sure that Soviet defense spending was a function of U.S. defense spending and Soviet GNP but were less sure about whether defense spending also was a function of the ratio of Soviet nuclear warheads to U.S. nuclear warheads. Using a double-log functional form, the authors estimated a number of alternative specifications, including (standard errors in parentheses):

$$\widehat{\ln SDH_t} = -1.99 + 0.056\ln USD_t + 0.969\ln SY_t + 0.057\ln SP_t \quad (9.29)$$
$$(0.074)(0.065)(0.032)$$
$$t = 0.7614.981.80$$

$$N = 25 \text{ (annual 1960–1984)} \quad \overline{R}^2 = .979 \quad DW = 0.49$$

$$\widehat{\ln SDH_t} = -2.88 + 0.105\ln USD_t + 1.066\ln SY_t \quad (9.30)$$
$$(0.073)(0.038)$$
$$t = 1.4428.09$$
$$N = 25 \text{ (annual 1960–1984)} \quad \overline{R}^2 = .977 \quad DW = 0.43$$

---

18. Josef C. Brada and Ronald L. Graves, "The Slowdown in Soviet Defense Expenditures," *Southern Economic Journal*, Vol. 54, No. 4, pp. 969–984. In addition to the variables used in this exercise, Brada and Graves also provide data for SFP_t, the rate of Soviet factor productivity in year t, which we include in Table 9.1.

Table 9.1 Data on Soviet Defense Spending

Year	SDH	SDL	USD	SY	SFP	NR	NU
1960	31	23	200.54	232.3	7.03	415	1734
1961	34	26	204.12	245.3	6.07	445	1846
1962	38	29	207.72	254.5	3.90	485	1942
1963	39	31	206.98	251.7	2.97	531	2070
1964	42	34	207.41	279.4	1.40	580	2910
1965	43	35	185.42	296.8	1.87	598	4110
1966	44	36	203.19	311.9	4.10	674	4198
1967	47	39	241.27	326.3	4.90	1058	4338
1968	50	42	260.91	346.0	4.07	1270	4134
1969	52	43	254.62	355.9	2.87	1662	4026
1970	53	44	228.19	383.3	4.43	2047	5074
1971	54	45	203.80	398.2	3.77	3199	6282
1972	56	46	189.41	405.7	2.87	2298	7100
1973	58	48	169.27	435.2	3.87	2430	8164
1974	62	51	156.81	452.2	4.30	2534	8522
1975	65	53	155.59	459.8	6.33	2614	9170
1976	69	56	169.91	481.8	0.63	3219	9518
1977	70	56	170.94	497.4	2.23	4345	9806
1978	72	57	154.12	514.2	1.03	5097	9950
1979	75	59	156.80	516.1	0.17	6336	9945
1980	79	62	160.67	524.7	0.27	7451	9668
1981	83	63	169.55	536.1	0.47	7793	9628
1982	84	64	185.31	547.0	0.07	8031	10124
1983	88	66	201.83	567.5	1.50	8730	10201
1984	90	67	211.35	578.9	1.63	9146	10630

Source: Josef C. Brada and Ronald L. Graves, "The Slowdown in Soviet Defense Expenditures," *Southern Economic Journal,* Vol. 54, No. 4, p. 974.

Datafile = DEFEND9

where: SDH_t = the CIA's "high" estimate of Soviet defense expenditures in year t (billions of 1970 rubles)

USD_t = U.S. defense expenditures in year t (billions of 1980 dollars)

SY_t = Soviet GNP in year t (billions of 1970 rubles)

SP_t = the ratio of the number of USSR nuclear warheads (NR_t) to the number of U.S. nuclear warheads (NU_t) in year t

a. The authors expected positive signs for all the slope coefficients of both equations. Test these hypotheses at the 5-percent level.
b. Use our four specification criteria to determine whether SP is an irrelevant variable. Explain your reasoning.
c. Test both equations for positive first-order serial correlation. Does the high probability of serial correlation cause you to reconsider your answer to part b? Explain.
d. Someone might argue that because the DW statistic improved when lnSP was added, the serial correlation was impure and that GLS was not called for. Do you agree with this conclusion? Why or why not?
e. If we run a GLS version of Equation 9.29, we get Equation 9.31. Does this result cause you to reconsider your answer to part b? Explain

$$\widehat{lnSDH}_t = -2.65 + 0.104 lnUSD_t + 1.034\, lnSY_t - 0.032\, lnSP_t \qquad (9.31)$$
$$ (0.087) \qquad\quad (0.078) \qquad\quad (0.034)$$
$$ t = 1.20 \qquad\qquad 13.30 \qquad\qquad 0.93$$
$$N = 24\ (\text{annual } 1960\text{–}1984) \quad \overline{R}^2 = .986 \quad \hat{\rho} = 0.75$$

7. As an example of impure serial correlation caused by an incorrect functional form, let's return to the equation for the percentage of putts made (P_i) as a function of the length of the putt in feet (L_i) that we discussed originally in Exercise 3 in Chapter 1. The complete documentation of that equation is

$$\hat{P}_i = 83.6 - 4.1L_i \qquad\qquad (9.32)$$
$$\phantom{\hat{P}_i = 83.6 -} (0.4)$$
$$\phantom{\hat{P}_i = 83.} t = -10.6$$
$$N = 19 \qquad \overline{R}^2 = .861 \qquad DW = 0.48$$

a. Test Equation 9.32 for serial correlation using the Durbin–Watson test at the 5-percent level.
b. Why might the linear functional form be inappropriate for this study? Explain your answer.
c. If we now reestimate Equation 9.32 using a double-log functional form, we obtain:

$$\widehat{lnP}_i = 5.50 - 0.92\, lnL_i \qquad\qquad (9.33)$$
$$\phantom{\widehat{lnP}_i = 5.50 -} (0.07)$$
$$\phantom{\widehat{lnP}_i = 5.} t = -13.0$$
$$N = 19 \qquad \overline{R}^2 = .903 \qquad DW = 1.22$$

Test Equation 9.33 for serial correlation using the Durbin–Watson test at the 5-percent level.

d. Compare Equations 9.32 and 9.33. Which equation do you prefer? Why?

9.7 Appendix: Econometric Lab #5

In this lab, you'll expand on Econometric Lab #2 by estimating an aggregate consumption function for the U.S. economy for the period 1945–2006, testing your equation for serial correlation, and, if appropriate, taking corrective action.[19]

Step 1: State the Variables and the Expected Signs of the Coefficients

As in Econometric Lab #2, our goal is to model U.S. aggregate consumption as a function of disposable personal income and the real interest rate. Once again, the data are from the St. Louis Federal Reserve FRED database and the *Economic Report of the President.* Descriptions of the variables are in Table 9.2, along with the hypothesized signs for the coefficients, and the dataset itself is on the text's website as CONS9.

Table 9.2 Variable Definitions

Variable	Description	Expected sign
con_t	Real personal consumption expenditures in year t, in billions of 2009 dollars	NA
dpi_t	Real disposable personal income in year t, in billions of 2009 dollars	+
aaa_t	The real interest rate on Aaa corporate bonds in year t	−
$year_t$	Year t	NA

---

19. Econometric Lab #2 used a sample for the period 1945–2014, but we end Lab #5's sample in 2006 to avoid the (admittedly interesting) complications introduced by the Great Recession.

Step 2: Estimate the Aggregate Consumption Function

Now estimate the consumption function, using disposable personal income and the real interest rate as the independent variables.[20]

Step 3: Examine the Residuals

Generate the residuals from the regression in Step 2 (naming them "e") and plot them as a line graph against $year_t$ (with $year_t$ on the x-axis). Does the plot look entirely random? Explain.

Step 4: Run the Durbin–Watson Test

Conduct a Durbin–Watson test for positive serial correlation.

a. Carefully write down the null and alternative hypotheses.
b. Run a Durbin–Watson test for positive serial correlation at the 5-percent level. What are the upper and lower critical values in this case? What can you conclude? Explain.

Step 5: Run the Lagrange Multiplier Serial Correlation Test

Let's see if our Durbin–Watson results can be confirmed with the Lagrange Multiplier test.

a. Are the null and alternative hypotheses for the Lagrange Multiplier test the same as for the Durbin–Watson test? Why or why not?
b. Conduct a Lagrange Multiplier test for serial correlation at the 5-percent level. What can you conclude? Explain.

Step 6: Estimate the Model with Generalized Least Squares

a. If you encountered serial correlation in either of the previous steps, re-estimate our aggregate consumption model using Generalized Least Squares.

---

20. If you're using Stata, be sure to tell Stata that this is a time series and that $year_t$ is the time variable.

b. Are the GLS coefficients and *t*-statistics the same as the OLS coefficients and *t*-statistics? Explain.

c. After the GLS transformation, does serial correlation still appear to exist? Support your answer.

Step 7: Calculate Newey-West Standard Errors

a. If you ran a GLS model in Step 6, now estimate the aggregate consumption model using the Newey–West method with a lag of 1.

b. After the Newey–West calculation, are the coefficients the same as the OLS coefficients? Explain.

c. Why are the Newey–West *t*-statistics different from the OLS *t*-statistics? Which do you prefer? Why?

Chapter 10

Heteroskedasticity

Heteroskedasticity is the violation of Classical Assumption V, which states that the observations of the error term are drawn from a distribution that has a constant variance.[1] The assumption of constant variances for different observations of the error term (homoskedasticity) is not always realistic. For example, in a model explaining heights, it's likely that error term observations associated with the height of a basketball player would come from distributions with larger variances than those associated with the height of a mouse. Heteroskedasticity is important because OLS, when applied to heteroskedastic models, is no longer the minimum variance estimator (it still is unbiased, however).

In general, heteroskedasticity is more likely to take place in cross-sectional models than in time-series models. This focus on cross-sectional models is not to say that heteroskedasticity in time-series models is impossible, though. In fact, heteroskedasticity has turned out to be an important factor in time-series studies of financial markets.

---

1. Various authors spell this "heteroscedasticity," but Huston McCulloch appears to settle this controversy in favor of "heteroskedasticity" because of the word's Greek origin. See J. Huston McCulloch, "On Heteros*edasticity," *Econometrica*, Vol. 53, No. 2, p. 483. Although heteroskedasticity is a difficult word to spell, at least it's an impressive comeback when parents ask, "What'd you learn for all that money?"

The structure of this chapter will be quite familiar. We'll attempt to answer the same four questions for heteroskedasticity that we answered for multicollinearity and serial correlation in the previous two chapters:

1. What is the nature of the problem?
2. What are the consequences of the problem?
3. How is the problem diagnosed?
4. What remedies for the problem are available?

10.1 Pure versus Impure Heteroskedasticity

Heteroskedasticity, like serial correlation, can be divided into pure and impure versions. Pure heteroskedasticity is caused by the error term of the correctly specified equation; impure heteroskedasticity is caused by a specification error such as an omitted variable.

Pure Heteroskedasticity

Pure heteroskedasticity refers to heteroskedasticity that is a function of the error term of a correctly specified regression equation. As with serial correlation, use of the word "heteroskedasticity" without any modifier (like pure or impure) implies *pure* heteroskedasticity.

Such **pure heteroskedasticity** occurs when Classical Assumption V, which assumes that the variance of the error term is constant, is violated in a correctly specified equation. Assumption V assumes that:

$$VAR(\epsilon_i) = \sigma^2 = \text{a constant} \qquad (i = 1, 2, \ldots, N) \qquad (10.1)$$

If this assumption is met, all the observations of the error term can be thought of as being drawn from the same distribution: a distribution with a mean of zero and a variance of σ^2. The property of having σ^2 not change for different observations of the error term is called **homoskedasticity**. A homoskedastic error term distribution is pictured in the top half of Figure 10.1; note that the variance of the distribution is constant (even though individual observations drawn from that sample will vary quite a bit).

With heteroskedasticity, this error term variance is not constant; instead, the variance of the distribution of the error term depends on exactly which observation is being discussed:

$$VAR(\epsilon_i) = \sigma_i^2 \qquad (i = 1, 2, \ldots, N) \qquad (10.2)$$

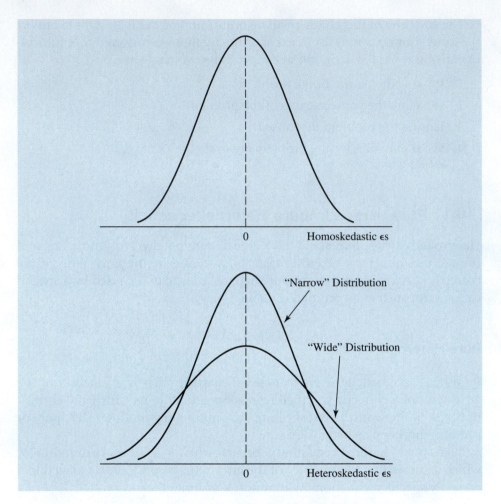

Figure 10.1 Homoskedasticity versus Discrete Heteroskedasticity

In homoskedasticity, the distribution of the error term has a constant variance, so the observations are continually drawn from the same distribution (shown in the top panel). In the simplest heteroskedastic case, discrete heteroskedasticity, there would be two different error term variances and, therefore, two different distributions (one wider than the other, as in the bottom panel) from which the observations of the error term could be drawn.

Note that the only difference between Equations 10.1 and 10.2 is the subscript "i" attached to σ^2, which implies that instead of being constant over all the observations, a heteroskedastic error term's variance can change depending on the observation (hence the subscript).

Heteroskedasticity often occurs in data sets in which there is a wide disparity between the largest and smallest observed value of the dependent variable.

The larger the disparity between the size of observations of the dependent variable in a sample is, the larger the likelihood is that the error term observations associated with them will have different variances and therefore be heteroskedastic. That is, we'd expect that the error term distribution for very large observations might have a large variance, and that the error term distribution for small observations might have a small variance.

In cross-sectional data sets, it's easy to get such a large range between the highest and lowest values of the variables. The difference between California and Rhode Island in terms of the dollar value of the consumption of goods and services, for instance, is quite large (comparable in percentage terms to the difference between the heights of a basketball player and a mouse). Since cross-sectional models often include observations of widely different sizes in the same sample (cross-state studies of the United States usually include California and Rhode Island as individual observations, for example), heteroskedasticity is hard to avoid if economic topics are going to be studied cross sectionally.

The simplest way to visualize pure heteroskedasticity is to picture a world in which the observations of the error term could be grouped into just two different distributions, "wide" and "narrow." We'll call this simple version of the problem *discrete heteroskedasticity*. Here, both distributions would be centered around zero, but one would have a larger variance than the other, as indicated in the bottom half of Figure 10.1. Note the difference between the two halves of the figure. With homoskedasticity, all the error term observations come from the same distribution; with heteroskedasticity, they come from different distributions.

For an example of discrete heteroskedasticity, we need go no further than our discussion of the heights of basketball players and mice. We'd certainly expect the variance of ϵ to be larger for basketball players as a group than for mice, so the distribution of ϵ for the heights of basketball players might look like the "wide" distribution in Figure 10.1, and the distribution of ϵ for mice would be much narrower than the "narrow" distribution in Figure 10.1.

Heteroskedasticity takes on many more complex forms. In fact, the number of different models of heteroskedasticity is virtually limitless, and an analysis of even a small percentage of these alternatives would be a huge task. Instead, we'd like to address the general principles of heteroskedasticity by focusing on the most frequently specified model of pure heteroskedasticity, just as we focused on pure, positive, first-order serial correlation in the previous chapter. However, don't let this focus mislead you into concluding that econometricians are concerned only with one kind of heteroskedasticity.

In this model of heteroskedasticity, the variance of the error term is related to an exogenous variable Z_i. For a typical regression equation:

$$Y_i = \beta_0 + \beta_1 X_{1i} + \beta_2 X_{2i} + \epsilon_i \qquad (10.3)$$

the variance of the otherwise classical error term ϵ might be equal to:

$$\mathrm{VAR}(\epsilon_i) = \sigma^2 Z_i \tag{10.4}$$

where Z may or may not be one of the Xs in the equation. The variable Z is called a **proportionality factor** because the variance of the error term changes proportionally to Z_i. The higher the value of Z_i, the higher the variance of the distribution of the ith observation of the error term. There would be N different distributions, one for each observation, from which the observations of the error term could be drawn depending on the number of different values that Z takes. To see what homoskedastic and heteroskedastic distributions of the error term look like with respect to Z, compare Figures 10.2 and 10.3. Note that the heteroskedastic distribution gets wider as Z increases but that the homoskedastic distribution maintains the same width no matter what value Z takes.

What is an example of a proportionality factor Z? How is it possible for an exogenous variable such as Z to change the whole distribution of an error term? Think about a function that relates the consumption expenditures in a state to its income. The expenditures of a small state like Rhode Island are not likely to be as variable in absolute value as the expenditures of a large state like California because a 10-percent change in spending for a large state involves a lot more money than a 10-percent change for a small one. In such a case, the dependent variable would be consumption expenditures and a likely proportionality factor, Z, would be population. As population rose, so too would the variance of the error term of an equation built to explain

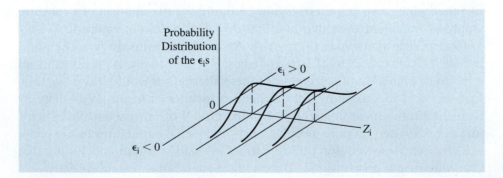

Figure 10.2 A Homoskedastic Error Term with Respect to Z_i

If an error term is homoskedastic with respect to Z_i, the variance of the distribution of the error term is the same (constant) no matter what the value of Z_i is: $\mathrm{VAR}(\epsilon_i) = \sigma^2$.

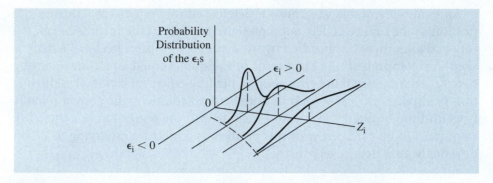

Figure 10.3 A Heteroskedastic Error Term with Respect to Z_i

If an error term is heteroskedastic with respect to Z_i, the variance of the distribution of the error term changes systematically as a function of Z_i. In this example, the variance is an increasing function of Z_i, as in $VAR(\epsilon_i) = \sigma^2 Z_i$.

expenditures. The error term distributions would look something like those in Figure 10.3, where the Z in Figure 10.3 is population.

This example helps emphasize that heteroskedasticity is likely to occur in cross-sectional models because of the large variation in the size of the dependent variable involved. An exogenous disturbance that might seem huge to a small state could seem miniscule to a large one, for instance.

Heteroskedasticity can occur in a time-series model with a significant amount of change in the dependent variable. If you were modeling sales of DVD players from 1994 to 2015, it's quite possible that you would have a heteroskedastic error term. As the phenomenal growth of the industry took place, the variance of the error term probably increased as well. Such a possibility is unlikely in time series that have low rates of change, however.

Heteroskedasticity also can occur in any model, time series or cross sectional, where the quality of data collection changes dramatically within the sample. As data collection techniques get better, the variance of the error term should fall because measurement errors are included in the error term. As measurement errors decrease in size, so should the variance of the error term. For more on this topic (called "errors in the variables"), see Section 14.6.

Impure Heteroskedasticity

Heteroskedasticity that is caused by an error in specification, such as an omitted variable, is referred to as **impure heteroskedasticity**. Impure heteroskedasticity thus is similar to impure serial correlation.

An omitted variable can cause a heteroskedastic error term because the portion of the omitted effect not represented by one of the included explanatory variables must be absorbed by the error term. If this effect has a heteroskedastic component, the error term of the misspecified equation might be heteroskedastic even if the error term of the true equation is not. This distinction is important because with impure heteroskedasticity the correct remedy is to find the omitted variable and include it in the regression. It's therefore important to be sure that your specification is correct before trying to detect or remedy pure heteroskedasticity.

10.2 The Consequences of Heteroskedasticity

If the error term of your equation is known to be heteroskedastic, what does that mean for the estimation of your coefficients? If the error term of an equation is heteroskedastic, there are three major consequences:[2]

1. *Pure heteroskedasticity does not cause bias in the coefficient estimates.* Even if the error term of an equation is known to be purely heteroskedastic, that heteroskedasticity will not cause bias in the OLS estimates of the coefficients. This is true because even though large positive errors are more likely, so too are large negative errors. The two tend to average each other out, leaving the OLS estimator still unbiased.

   As a result, we can say that an otherwise correctly specified equation that has pure heteroskedasticity still has the property that:

$$E(\hat{\beta}) = \beta \qquad \text{for all } \beta s$$

   Lack of bias does not guarantee "accurate" coefficient estimates, especially since heteroskedasticity increases the variance of the estimates, but the distribution of the estimates is still centered around the true β. Equations with impure heteroskedasticity caused by an omitted variable, of course, will have possible specification bias.

2. *Heteroskedasticity typically causes OLS to no longer be the minimum-variance estimator (of all the linear unbiased estimators).* Pure heteroskedasticity causes no bias in the estimates of the OLS coefficients,

---

2. It turns out that the consequences of heteroskedasticity are almost identical in general framework to those of serial correlation, though the two problems are quite different.

but it does affect the minimum-variance property. If the error term of an equation is heteroskedastic with respect to a proportionality factor Z:

$$VAR(\epsilon_i) = \sigma^2 Z_i \qquad (10.5)$$

then the minimum-variance portion of the Gauss–Markov Theorem cannot be proven because there are other linear unbiased estimators that have smaller variances. This is because the heteroskedastic error term causes the dependent variable to fluctuate, and the OLS estimation procedure attributes this fluctuation to the independent variables. Thus, OLS is more likely to misestimate the true β in the face of heteroskedasticity. The $\hat{\beta}$s still are unbiased because overestimates are just as likely as underestimates.

3. *Heteroskedasticity causes the OLS estimates of the SE($\hat{\beta}$)s to be biased, leading to unreliable hypothesis testing and confidence intervals.* With heteroskedasticity, the OLS formula for the standard error produces biased estimates of the SE($\hat{\beta}$)s. Because the SE($\hat{\beta}$) is a prime component in the *t*-statistic, these biased SE($\hat{\beta}$)s cause biased *t*-scores and unreliable hypothesis testing in general. In essence, heteroskedasticity causes OLS to produce incorrect SE($\hat{\beta}$)s and *t*-scores! Not surprisingly, most econometricians therefore are very hesitant to put much faith in hypothesis tests that were conducted in the face of pure heteroskedasticity.[3]

What sort of bias in the standard errors does heteroskedasticity tend to cause? Typically, heteroskedasticity causes OLS estimates of the standard errors to be biased downward, making them too small. Sometimes, however, they're biased upward; it's hard to predict in any given case. But either way, it's a big problem for hypothesis testing and confidence intervals.

What'll happen if OLS underestimates a standard error? Well, the "too low" SE($\hat{\beta}$) will cause a "too high" *t*-score for a particular coefficient, and this will make it more likely that we will reject a null hypothesis (for example, $H_0: \beta \leq 0$) when it is in fact true. This increased chance of rejecting H_0 means that we're more likely to make a Type I error and we're more likely to make the mistake of keeping an irrelevant variable in an equation. Also, because the confidence interval depends directly on SE($\hat{\beta}$) (see Equation 5.9),

---

3. While our discussion here involves the *t*-test, the same conclusion of unreliability in the face of heteroskedasticity applies to all other test statistics, including confidence intervals.

the underestimation of $SE(\hat{\beta})$ will fool us into thinking that our estimate is more precise than it really is.[4]

In other words, pure heteroskedasticity can make quite a mess of our results. Hypothesis testing will become unreliable, and confidence intervals will be misleading.

10.3 Testing for Heteroskedasticity

As we've seen, heteroskedasticity is a potentially nasty problem. The good news is that there are many tests for heteroskedasticity. The bad news is heteroskedasticity can take many different forms and no single test can find them all.

In this section, we'll describe two of the most popular and powerful tests for heteroskedasticity, the *Breusch–Pagan test* and the *White test*.[5] While neither test can "prove" that heteroskedasticity exists, these tests often can give us a pretty good idea of whether or not it's a problem.

Before using any test for heteroskedasticity, it's a good idea to start with the following preliminary questions:

1. Are there any obvious specification errors? Are there any likely omitted variables? Have you specified a linear model when a double-log model is more appropriate? Don't test for heteroskedasticity until the specification is as good as possible. After all, if you find heteroskedasticity in an incorrectly specified model, there's a chance it will be impure.

2. Are there any early warning signs of heteroskedasticity? Just as certain kinds of clouds can warn of potential storms, certain kinds of data can signal possible heteroskedasticity. In particular, if the dependent variable's maximum value is many, many times larger than its minimum, beware of heteroskedasticity.

3. Does a graph of the residuals show any evidence of heteroskedasticity? It sometimes saves time to plot the residuals against a potential Z proportionality factor or against the dependent variable. If you see a pattern in the residuals, you've got a problem. See Figure 10.4 for a few examples of heteroskedastic patterns in the residuals.

---

4. If OLS overestimates the standard error, then we'll have the same problems but in reverse. The "too high" $SE(\hat{\beta})$ will lead to a "too low" *t*-score. If the *t*-score is lowered enough, we might be fooled into failing to reject a false null hypothesis, thus increasing the risk that we'll drop a relevant variable from the model. In addition, the confidence intervals will be too wide, leading to similar potential mistakes.

5. Both tests belong to a general group of tests based on the Lagrange Multiplier (LM), which you first met in Chapter 9.

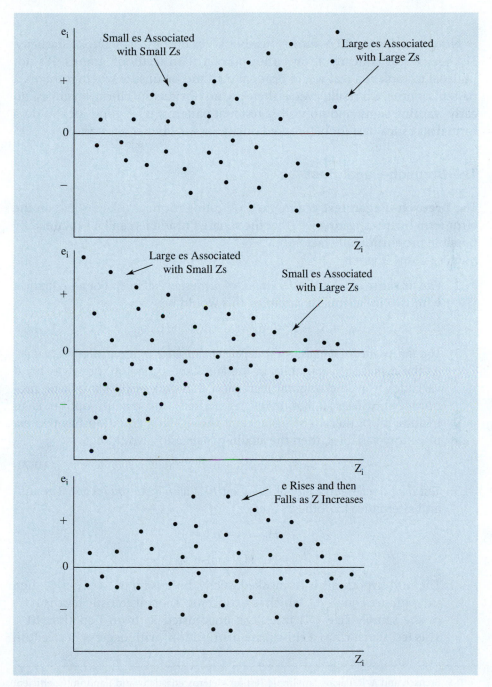

Figure 10.4 Eyeballing Residuals for Possible Heteroskedasticity

If you plot the residuals of an equation with respect to a potential Z proportionality factor, a pattern in the residuals is an indication of possible heteroskedasticity.

Note that Figure 10.4 shows "textbook" examples of heteroskedasticity. The real world is nearly always a lot messier than textbook graphs. It's not unusual to look at a real-world residual plot and be unsure whether there's a pattern or not. As a result, even if there are no obvious specification errors, no early warning signs, and no visible residual patterns, it's a good idea to do a formal statistical test for heteroskedasticity, so we'd better get started.

The Breusch–Pagan Test

The **Breusch–Pagan test** is a method of testing for heteroskedasticity in the error term by investigating whether the squared residuals can be explained by possible proportionality factors.[6]

Here's how it works.

1. *Obtain the residuals from the estimated regression equation.* For an equation with two independent variables, this would be:

$$e_i = Y_i - \hat{Y}_i = Y_i - \hat{\beta}_0 - \hat{\beta}_1 X_{1i} - \hat{\beta}_2 X_{2i} \qquad (10.6)$$

2. *Use the squared residuals as the dependent variable in an auxiliary equation.* As the explanatory variables in the auxiliary regression, use right-hand variables from the original regression that you suspect might be pro-portionality factors. For many researchers, the default option is to include all of them. For instance, if the original equation has two ex-planatory variables, then the auxiliary regression would be:

$$e_i^2 = \alpha_0 + \alpha_1 X_{1i} + \alpha_2 X_{2i} + u_i \qquad (10.7)$$

3. *Test the overall significance of Equation 10.7 with a chi-square test.* The null and alternative hypotheses are:

$$H_0: \alpha_1 = \alpha_2 = 0$$

$$H_A: H_0 \text{ is false}$$

The null hypothesis is homoskedasticity, because if $\alpha_1 = \alpha_2 = 0$, then the variance equals α_0, which is a constant. The test statistic here is NR^2, or the sample size (N) times the unadjusted R^2 from Equation 10.7. This test statistic has a chi-square distribution[7] with degrees of freedom

---

6. T. S. Breusch and A. R. Pagan, "A Simple Test for Heteroscedasticity and Random Coefficient Variation," *Econometrica*, Vol. 47, pp. 1287–1294.

7. You might wonder why the test statistic is not the overall *F*-statistic of the auxiliary regres-sion. It turns out that the *F*-statistic is valid only if the errors are normally distributed, and in this case, with squared residuals as the dependent variable, it's not safe to assume the errors are normally distributed. With non-normal errors, the proper test is a chi-square test.

equal to the number of slope coefficients in the auxiliary regression (Equation 10.7). If NR^2 is greater than or equal to the critical chi-square value, then we reject the null hypothesis of homoskedasticity.

If you strongly suspect that only certain variables are plausible Z factors, then you should run the Breusch–Pagan test using only an intercept and the suspect variables. The degrees of freedom for the chi-square statistic of course would change in such a situation, because they're equal to the number of right-hand-side variables in the auxiliary equation. If you're certain you know the one and only proportionality factor Z and that there are no other forms of heteroskedasticity present, you don't even need to fool with the chi-square statistic. You can just do a two-sided t-test[8] on the $\hat{\alpha}$ for Z.

The strengths of the Breusch–Pagan test are that it's easy to use and it's powerful if heteroskedasticity is related to one or more linear proportionality factors. Its weakness is that if it fails to find heteroskedasticity, it only means there is no evidence of heteroskedasticity related to the Zs you've chosen. If you're pretty certain that the Xs in the auxiliary regression are the only plausible proportionality factors, you can rest easy. But if you're not certain, you might want to use the White test, which we'll discuss shortly.

As an example of the use of the Breusch–Pagan test, let's return to the Woody's restaurants example of Section 3.2 and use the residuals of Equation 3.4 to test for heteroskedasticity. Recall that the regression explained the number of customers, as measured by the check volume (Y) for a cross section of 33 different Woody's restaurants as a function of the number of nearby competitors (N), the nearby population (P), and the average household income of the local area (I):

$$\hat{Y}_i = 102{,}192 - 9075N_i + 0.355P_i + 1.288I_i \qquad (3.4)$$
$$(2053)\ \ (0.073)\ \ (0.543)$$
$$t = -4.42\quad 4.88\quad\ \ 2.37$$
$$N = 33\qquad \bar{R}^2 = .579$$

The first step in the Breusch–Pagan test is to obtain the residuals from Equation 3.4. You can find these residuals in Table 3.2 on page 77. The

8. A Breusch–Pagan test with a single Z is a linear version of the *Park test*, which uses a double-log equation to test whether the squared residuals can be explained by a single potential Z proportionality factor. See R. E. Park, "Estimation with Heteroskedastic Error Terms," *Econometrica*, Vol. 54, p. 888. A major disadvantage of the Park test, of course, is that the researcher must choose a single Z proportionality factor.

second step is to square the residuals and use them as the dependent variable in an auxiliary regression. If we include all the independent variables in Equation 3.4 in our auxiliary equation, we get:

$$e_i^2 = \alpha_0 + \alpha_1 N_i + \alpha_2 P_i + \alpha_3 I_i + u_i \qquad (10.8)$$

If we estimate Equation 10.8, we find that the unadjusted $R^2 = .0441$. We know that $N = 33$, so we can calculate that the chi-square statistic $= NR^2 = 33(.0441) = 1.455$. Since the 5-percent critical value of chi-square with 3 degrees of freedom is 7.81, we can't reject the null hypothesis that $\alpha_1 = \alpha_2 = \alpha_3 = 0$. As a result, the Breusch–Pagan test doesn't provide any evidence that Equation 3.4 suffers from heteroskedasticity. This makes sense. Even though the Woody's sample is cross-sectional, the largest value of the dependent variable isn't even twice the size of the smallest one, so we have no reason to suspect pure heteroskedasticity.

The White Test

Probably the most popular of all the heteroskedasticity tests is the White test[9] because it can find more types of heteroskedasticity than any other test. That's a distinct advantage in a world where just about any variable or combination of variables, linear or nonlinear, could trip us up with a heteroskedastic stumbling block. Let's see how it works.

The **White test** investigates the possibility of heteroskedasticity in an equation by seeing if the squared residuals can be explained by the equation's independent variables, their squares, and their cross–products. To run the White test:

1. *Obtain the residuals of the estimated regression equation.*

2. *Estimate an auxiliary regression, using the squared residuals as the dependent variable, with each X from the original equation, the square of each X, and the product of each X times every other X as the explanatory variables. For example, if the original equation's independent variables are X_1 and X_2, the White test equation is:*

$$e_i^2 = \alpha_0 + \alpha_1 X_{1i} + \alpha_2 X_{2i} + \alpha_3 X_{1i}^2 + \alpha_4 X_{2i}^2 + \alpha_5 X_{1i} X_{2i} + u_i \qquad (10.9)$$

---

9. Halbert White, "A Heteroskedasticity-Consistent Covariance Matrix Estimator and a Direct Test for Heteroskedasticity, *Econometrica*, Vol. 48, pp. 817–838.

3. *Test the overall significance of Equation 10.9 with a chi-square test.* Once again, the test statistic is NR^2, the sample size (N) times the unadjusted R^2 of Equation 10.9. This test statistic has a chi-square distribution with degrees of freedom equal to the number of slope coefficients in the auxiliary regression. The null hypothesis is that all the slope coefficients in Equation 10.9 equal zero, and if NR^2 is greater than the chi-square critical value, then we can reject the null hypothesis and conclude that there's evidence of heteroskedasticity.

Check out the explanatory variables in Equation 10.9. They include every variable in the original model, their squares, and their cross products. Including all the variables from the original model allows the White test to check to see if any or all of them are Z proportionality factors. Including all the squared terms and cross products allows us to test for more exotic and complex types of heteroskedasticity. This is the White test's greatest strength.

However, the White test contains more right-hand-side variables than the original regression, sometimes a *lot* more. This can be its greatest weakness. To see why, note that as the number of explanatory variables in an original regression rises, the number of right-hand variables in the White test auxiliary regression goes up much faster. For example, there are five right-hand variables in Equation 10.9 even though the original model had only two, X_1 and X_2. With three variables in the original model, the White regression could have nine. With 12 explanatory variables in the original model, there could[10] be 90 in the White regression with all the squares and interactive terms included!

And this is where the weakness becomes a real problem. If the number of right-hand variables in the auxiliary regression exceeds the number of observations, you can't run the White test regression because you would have negative degrees of freedom in the auxiliary equation! Even if the degrees of freedom in the auxiliary equation are positive but small, the White test might do a poor job of detecting heteroskedasticity because the fewer the degrees of

---

10. There could be fewer explanatory variables if one or more of the original independent variables is a dummy, since the square of a dummy is the same as a dummy and the cross product of a variable times a dummy equals the original variable itself or zero. Because of the large number of variables and this possible duplication, it's tedious to create and check all the variables for the White test. Luckily, Stata and most other econometric software packages have simple commands to do the work for you.

freedom there are, the less powerful the statistical test is. In such a situation, you'd be limited to the Breusch–Pagan test or an alternative.[11]

As an example of the White test, let's again return to the Woody's restaurants model of Section 3.2. As with the Breusch–Pagan test, the first step is to obtain the residuals of the original Woody's equation. The second step in the White test is to square the residuals and use them as the dependent variable in an auxiliary regression that includes N, P, I, their squares, and their cross products as independent variables:

$$e_i^2 = \alpha_0 + \alpha_1 N_i + \alpha_2 P_i + \alpha_3 I_i + \alpha_4 N_i^2 + \alpha_5 P_i^2 + \alpha_6 I_i^2$$
$$+ \alpha_7 N_i P_i + \alpha_8 N_i I_i + \alpha_9 P_i I_i + u_i$$

If we estimate this equation with the Woody's data, we find that the unadjusted $R^2 = .1218$. Since $N = 33$, the chi-square $NR^2 = 33(.1218) = 4.02$. That's less than 16.92, the 5-percent critical chi-square value with nine degrees of freedom (do you see why it's nine?), so we once again can't reject the null hypothesis of homoskedasticity.

10.4   Remedies for Heteroskedasticity

The first thing to do if the Breusch–Pagan test or the White test indicates the possibility of heteroskedasticity is to examine the equation carefully for specification errors. Although you should never include an explanatory variable simply because a test indicates the possibility of heteroskedasticity, you ought to rigorously think through the specification of the equation. If this rethinking allows you to discover a variable that should have been in the regression from the beginning, then that variable should be added to the equation. Similarly, if you had the wrong functional form to begin with, the discovery of heteroskedasticity might be the hint you need to rethink the specification and switch to the functional form that best represents the underlying theory. However, if there are no obvious specification errors, the heteroskedasticity is probably pure in nature, and one of the remedies described in this section should be considered.

---

11. For instance, there is an alternative form of the White test that has many fewer degrees of freedom in the auxiliary equation. You perform this alternative White test by replacing all the right-hand variables in Equation 10.9 with the fitted Y values and the squares of the fitted Y values from the original model. That is, run: $e_i^2 = \alpha_0 + \alpha_1 \hat{Y}_i + \alpha_2 \hat{Y}_i^2 + u_i$ with the null hypothesis being $\alpha_1 = \alpha_2 = 0$ and the rest of the test being the same. This isn't as good as the full White test, but if the full White test is impossible to run, this may be an excellent alternative. For more, see Christopher F. Baum, *An Introduction to Modern Econometrics Using Stata* (College Station, TX: Stata Press, 2006), p. 146.

Heteroskedasticity-Corrected Standard Errors

The most popular remedy for heteroskedasticity is heteroskedasticity-corrected standard errors, which adjust the estimation of the $SE(\hat{\beta})$s for heteroskedasticity while still using the OLS estimates of the slope coefficients. The logic behind this approach is powerful. Since heteroskedasticity causes problems with the $SE(\hat{\beta})$s but not with the $\hat{\beta}$s, it makes sense to improve the estimation of the $SE(\hat{\beta})$s in a way that doesn't alter the estimates of the slope coefficients. This approach is virtually identical to the use of Newey–West standard errors as a remedy for serial correlation.

Thus, **heteroskedasticity-corrected (HC) standard errors** are $SE(\hat{\beta})$s that have been calculated specifically to avoid the consequences of heteroskedasticity. The HC procedure yields an estimator of the standard errors that, while they are biased, are generally more accurate than uncorrected standard errors for large samples in the face of heteroskedasticity. As a result, the HC $SE(\hat{\beta})$s can be used in t-tests and other hypothesis tests in most samples without the errors of inference potentially caused by heteroskedasticity. Typically, the HC $SE(\hat{\beta})$s are larger than the OLS $SE(\hat{\beta})$s, thus producing lower t-scores and decreasing the probability that a given estimated coefficient will be significantly different from zero. The technique was suggested by Halbert White in the same article in which he proposed the White test for heteroskedasticity.[12]

There are a few problems with using heteroskedasticity-corrected standard errors. First, the technique works best in large samples, so it's best to avoid HC $SE(\hat{\beta})$s in small samples. Second, details of the calculation of the HC $SE(\hat{\beta})$s are beyond the scope of this text and imply a model that is substantially more general than the basic theoretical construct, $VAR(\epsilon_i) = \sigma^2 Z_i$, of this chapter. In addition, not all computer regression software packages calculate heteroskedasticity-corrected standard errors.

Redefining the Variables

Another approach to ridding an equation of heteroskedasticity is to go back to the basic underlying theory of the equation and redefine the variables in a way that avoids heteroskedasticity. A redefinition of the variables often is useful in allowing the estimated equation to focus more on the behavioral

---

12. Note that Newey–West standard errors, introduced in Section 9.4, also can be used as HC standard errors. Indeed, some econometric software packages provide a choice between the White and Newey–West procedures. Unless otherwise noted, however, HC standard errors should be assumed to be of the White variety. Most authors refer to this method as HCCM, for heteroskedasticity-consistent covariance matrix.

aspects of the relationship. Such a rethinking is a difficult and discouraging process because it appears to dismiss all the work already done. However, once the theoretical work has been reviewed, the alternative approaches that are discovered are often exciting in that they offer possible ways to avoid problems that had previously seemed insurmountable. Be careful, however. Redefining your variables is a functional form specification change that can dramatically change your equation.

In some cases, the only redefinition that's needed to rid an equation of heteroskedasticity is to switch from a linear functional form to a double-log functional form. The double-log form has inherently less variation than the linear form, so it's less likely to encounter heteroskedasticity. In addition, there are many research topics for which the double-log form is just as theoretically logical as the linear form. This is especially true if the linear form was chosen by default, as is often the case.

In other situations, it might be necessary to completely rethink the research project in terms of its underlying theory. For example, consider a cross-sectional model of the total expenditures by the governments of different cities. Logical explanatory variables to consider in such an analysis are the aggregate income, the population, and the average wage in each city. The larger the total income of a city's residents and businesses, for example, the larger the city government's expenditures (see Figure 10.5). In this case, it's not very enlightening to know that the larger cities have larger incomes and larger expenditures (in absolute magnitude) than the smaller ones.

Fitting a regression line to such data (see the line in Figure 10.5) also gives undue weight to the larger cities because they would otherwise give rise to large squared residuals. That is, since OLS minimizes the summed squared residuals, and since the residuals from the large cities are likely to be large due simply to the size of the city, the regression estimation will be especially sensitive to the residuals from the larger cities. This is often called "spurious correlation" due to size.

In addition, the residuals may indicate heteroskedasticity. It makes sense to consider reformulating the model in a way that will discount the scale factor (the size of the cities) and emphasize the underlying behavior. In this case, per capita expenditures would be a logical dependent variable. Such a transformation is shown in Figure 10.6. This form of the equation places New York and Los Angeles on the same scale as, say, Pasadena or New Brunswick, and thus gives them the same weight in estimation. If an explanatory variable happened not to be a function of the size of the city, however, it would not need to be adjusted to per capita terms. If the equation included the average wage of city workers, for example, that wage would not be divided through by population in the transformed equation.

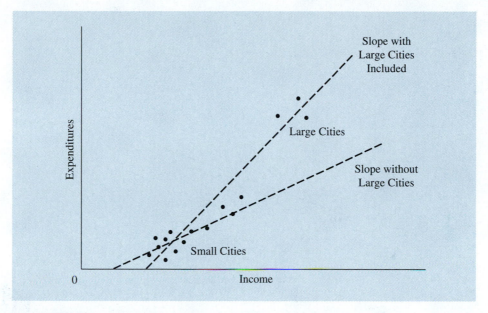

Figure 10.5 An Aggregate City Expenditures Function

If city expenditures are explained in an aggregate model, the larger cities play a major role in the determination of the coefficient values. Note how the slope would be somewhat lower without the heavy influence of the larger cities. In addition, heteroskedasticity is a potential problem in an aggregate model because the wide range of sizes of the dependent variable makes different error term variances more likely.

Suppose your original equation is:

$$EXP_i = \beta_0 + \beta_1 POP_i + \beta_2 INC_i + \beta_3 WAGE_i + \epsilon_i \qquad (10.10)$$

where EXP_i refers to expenditures, INC_i refers to income, $WAGE_i$ refers to the average wage, and POP_i refers to the population of the ith city.

The transformed equation would be[13]

$$EXP_i/POP_i = \alpha_0 + \alpha_1 INC_i/POP_i + \alpha_2 WAGE_i + u_i \qquad (10.12)$$

---

13. This transformed equation is very similar to the equation for Weighted Least Squares (WLS). *Weighted Least Squares* is a remedy for heteroskedasticity that consists of dividing the entire equation (including the constant and the heteroskedastic error term) by the proportionality factor Z and then re-estimating the equation with OLS. For the example in this section, the WLS equation would be:

$$EXP_i/POP_i = \beta_0/POP_i + \beta_1 + \beta_2 INC_i/POP_i + \beta_3 WAGE_i/POP_i + u_i \qquad (10.11)$$

where the variables and βs in Equation 10.11 are identical to those in Equation 10.10. Dividing through by Z means that u is a homoskedastic error term as long as Z is the correct proportionality factor. This is not a trivial problem, however, and other transformations and HCSEs are much easier to use than WLS is, so we no longer recommend the use of WLS.

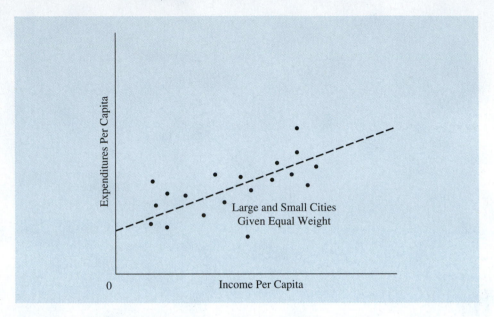

Figure 10.6 A Per Capita City Expenditures Function

If city expenditures are explained in a per capita model, then large and small cities have equal weights. In addition, heteroskedasticity is less likely, because the dependent variable does not vary over a wide range of sizes.

where u_i is a classical homoskedastic error term. While the directly transformed Equation 10.12 probably avoids heteroskedasticity, such a solution should be considered incidental to the benefits of rethinking the equation in a way that focuses on the basic behavior being examined.

Note that it's possible that the *reformulated* Equation 10.12 could have heteroskedasticity; the error variances might be larger for the observations having the larger per capita values for expenditures than they are for smaller per capita values. Thus, it is legitimate to suspect and test for heteroskedasticity even in this transformed model. Such heteroskedasticity in the transformed equation is unlikely, however, because there will be little of the variation in size normally associated with heteroskedasticity.

10.5 A More Complete Example

Let's work through a more complete example involving heteroskedasticity, a cross-sectional model of petroleum consumption by state.

Possible explanatory variables include functions of the size of the state (such as the number of miles of roadway, the number of motor vehicle registrations, or the population) and variables that are *not* functions of the size of the state (such as the price of gasoline or the speed limit). Since there is little to be gained by including more than one variable that measures the size of the state (because such an addition would be theoretically redundant and likely to cause needless multicollinearity), and since the speed limit was the same for all states (it would be a useful variable in a time-series model, however) a reasonable model to consider might be:

$$\overset{+}{} \qquad \overset{-}{}$$
$$PCON_i = \beta_0 + \beta_1 REG_i + \beta_2 PRICE_i + \epsilon_i \qquad (10.13)$$

where: $PCON_i$ = petroleum consumption in the ith state (trillions of BTUs)
 REG_i = motor vehicle registrations in the ith state (thousands)
 $PRICE_i$ = the price of gasoline in the ith state (cents per gallon)
 ϵ_i = a classical error term

The more cars there are registered in a state, we would think, the more petroleum would be consumed, while a high gasoline price would decrease aggregate gasoline purchases in that state.[14] If we now collect data from 2005 for this example (see Table 10.1) we can estimate:

$$\widehat{PCON_i} = 4101 + 0.16 REG_i - 1885 PRICE_i \qquad (10.14)$$
$$\phantom{\widehat{PCON_i} = 4101 +} (0.01) \qquad (750)$$
$$t = 12.4 \qquad -2.51$$
$$N = 50 \qquad \overline{R}^2 = .76$$

This equation seems to have no problems; the coefficients are significant in the hypothesized directions, and the overall equation is statistically significant. No Durbin–Watson statistic is shown because there is no "natural" order of the observations to test for serial correlation (if you're curious, the DW for the order in Table 10.1 is 2.15).

Given the discussion in the previous sections, let's investigate the possibility of heteroskedasticity caused by variation in the size of the states. To test this possibility, we obtain the residuals from Equation 10.14, and run Breusch–Pagan and White tests on them.

---

14. An alternative to using PRICE as an independent variable in this equation is to use PRICE*REG or PRICE*POP (where POP_i is the population of the ith state). These are more sophisticated examples of the interaction terms we introduced in Section 7.4 in our discussion of slope dummy variables.

Table 10.1 Data for the Petroleum Consumption Example

PCON	PRICE	REG	POP	STATE
580	2.11	4545	4548	Alabama
284	2.13	673	663	Alaska
537	2.23	3972	5953	Arizona
377	2.10	1940	2776	Arkansas
3837	2.47	32487	36154	California
463	2.19	1808	4663	Colorado
463	2.17	3059	3501	Connecticut
148	2.07	737	842	Delaware
1940	2.21	15691	17768	Florida
1058	2.09	8063	9133	Georgia
270	2.47	948	1273	Hawaii
139	2.14	1374	1429	Idaho
1313	2.22	9458	12765	Illinois
901	2.19	4955	6266	Indiana
393	2.13	3398	2966	Iowa
434	2.17	2368	2748	Kansas
664	2.14	3428	4173	Kentucky
1610	2.10	3819	4507	Louisiana
262	2.16	1075	1318	Maine
561	2.15	4322	5590	Maryland
734	2.08	5420	6433	Massachusetts
1010	2.24	8247	10101	Michigan
694	2.11	4647	5127	Minnesota
484	2.11	1978	2908	Mississippi
737	2.09	4589	5798	Missouri
161	2.17	1009	935	Montana
231	2.21	1703	1758	Nebraska
242	2.38	1349	2412	Nevada
198	2.08	1174	1307	New Hampshire
1233	1.99	6262	8703	New Jersey
250	2.19	1548	1926	New Mexico
1776	2.23	11863	19316	New York
947	2.14	6148	8672	North Carolina
121	2.19	695	635	North Dakota
1340	2.19	10634	11471	Ohio
545	2.08	3725	3543	Oklahoma
370	2.28	2897	3639	Oregon
1466	2.14	9864	12405	Pennsylvania
102	2.12	812	1074	Rhode Island
517	2.06	3339	4247	South Carolina

PCON	PRICE	REG	POP	STATE
113	2.20	854	775	South Dakota
782	2.11	4980	5956	Tennessee
5628	2.07	17470	22929	Texas
276	2.12	2210	2490	Utah
86	2.13	508	622	Vermont
965	2.10	6591	7564	Virginia
793	2.28	5598	6292	Washington
255	2.20	1352	1814	West Virginia
597	2.26	4725	5528	Wisconsin
162	2.08	646	509	Wyoming

Source: *2008 Statistical Abstract* (U.S. Department of Commerce).

Datafile = GAS10

Before we can run a Breusch–Pagan test, we must decide which variables to include on the right-hand side of the auxiliary equation. REG (motor vehicle registrations) is a measure of market size, so it's an obvious proportionality factor. On the other hand, PRICE (gasoline prices) seems unlikely to vary significantly with the size of the state, so it's less likely to be a Z. However, many researchers automatically include all the independent variables from the original equation in the Breusch–Pagan auxiliary equation, so let's use that approach and estimate the auxiliary equation (Equation 10.7) with both REG and PRICE:

$$e_i^2 = 5164290 + 83.33REG_i - 2475027PRICE_i \qquad (10.15)$$
$$(25.1) \qquad (1476765)$$
$$t = \qquad 3.32 \qquad -1.68$$
$$N = 50 \qquad R^2 = .197$$

The Breusch–Pagan test specifies that we should reject the null hypothesis of homoskedasticity ($\alpha_1 = \alpha_2 = 0$) if $NR^2 >$ the appropriate critical chi-square value. Since $N = 50$ and $R^2 = .197$, $NR^2 = 50(.197) = 9.85$. If you take a look at Table B-6, you'll see that the 5-percent critical chi-square value equals 5.99, so since $9.85 > 5.99$, we can reject the null hypothesis of homoskedasticity.[15] We have heteroskedasticity!

---

15. If we run the Breusch–Pagan test with REG as the only proportionality factor, we also can reject the null hypothesis of homoskedasticity at the 5-percent level because the *t*-score of 2.90 is greater than 2.01, the 5-percent two-sided critical *t*-score with 48 degrees of freedom. (Table B-1 doesn't include a value for 48 degrees of freedom, but we can interpolate to get a critical value of 2.01.)

To see whether the White test also will detect this heteroskedasticity, we'll need to modify Equation 10.9 to fit our example. The dependent variable will be the square of the residuals in Equation 10.14, and the independent variables will be REG, PRICE, their squares, and their cross-product:

$$e_i^2 = \alpha_0 + \alpha_1 REG_i + \alpha_2 PRICE_i + \alpha_3 REG_i^2 \qquad (10.16)$$
$$+ \alpha_4 PRICE_i^2 + \alpha_5 REG_i * PRICE_i + u_i$$

If we estimate Equation 10.16 with the residuals from Equation 10.14 and the data from Table 10.1, we obtain an R^2 of .85.

Since $N = 50$, $NR^2 = 50*.85 = 42.5$. As you can confirm by looking at Table B-6, the critical chi-square value at the 5-percent level for 5 degrees of freedom is 11.07. This means that our decision rule is:

> Do not reject the null hypothesis of homoskedasticity if $NR^2 < 11.07$
> Reject the null hypothesis of homoskedasticity if $NR^2 \geq 11.07$

$NR^2 = 42.5 > 11.07$, so we can reject the null hypothesis of homoskedasticity.

Since there appears to be heteroskedasticity in the residuals of Equation 10.14, what should we do? First, we should think through the specification of the equation in search of an omitted variable. While there are a number of possible omitted variables, it turns out that the heteroskedasticity in the equation is pure heteroskedasticity for the most part.

Let's apply the most popular of our remedies, heteroskedasticity-corrected standard errors, to this example. If we start with Equation 10.14 and use White's suggested method for estimating $SE(\hat{\beta})$s that are minimum variance (for large samples) in the face of heteroskedasticity, we obtain:

$$\widehat{PCON_i} = 4101 + 0.16 REG_i - 1885 PRICE_i \qquad (10.17)$$
$$(0.03) \qquad (1360)$$
$$t = \quad 4.85 \qquad -1.39$$

Compare Equation 10.14 with Equation 10.17. Note that the slope coefficients are identical, as you'd expect, since the HC approach uses OLS to estimate the coefficients. Also note that the HC $SE(\hat{\beta})$s are higher than the OLS $SE(\hat{\beta})$s, as is usually but not necessarily the case. While the resulting t-scores are lower, they are still reasonably large in the direction we expected, making Equation 10.17 very appealing indeed.

A second possible remedy for heteroskedasticity is to change to a double-log functional form. If we use the data in Table 10.1 to estimate a double-log equation, we get:

$$\widehat{\ln PCON_i} = -0.32 + 0.90\ln REG_i - 0.89\ln PRICE_i \qquad (10.18)$$
$$(0.04) \qquad (1.03)$$
$$t = \qquad 20.3 \qquad\quad -0.87$$
$$N = 50 \qquad \overline{R}^2 = .89$$

As can be seen, switching to logs improves $\overline{R}^2$ and the significance of the coefficient of lnREG, but the t-score for the coefficient of lnPRICE is below 1. We'd normally be concerned about such a low t-score, but the estimated coefficient is in the expected direction, and PRICE unambiguously belongs in the equation for theoretical reasons, so there's no reason to consider the possibility that PRICE might be irrelevant. As we'd hope, the White test indicates that the residuals of Equation 10.18 are indeed homoskedastic.

Finally, an alternative is to rethink the purpose of the regression and reformulate the variables of the equation to try to avoid heteroskedasticity resulting from spurious correlation due to size. If we were to rethink Equation 10.14, we might decide to attempt to explain per capita petroleum consumption, coming up with:

$$PCON_i/POP_i = \beta_0 + \beta_1 REG_i/POP_i + \beta_2 PRICE_i + \epsilon_i \qquad (10.19)$$

where POP_i is the population of the ith state in thousands of people.

If we estimate Equation 10.19, we obtain:

$$\widehat{PCON_i/POP_i} = 0.23 + 0.15 REG_i/POP_i - 0.10 PRICE_i \qquad (10.20)$$
$$(0.06) \qquad\qquad (0.10)$$
$$t = \qquad 2.52 \qquad\qquad -1.00$$
$$N = 50 \qquad \overline{R}^2 = .12$$

If we compare Equation 10.20 with Equations 10.17 and 10.18, we see that this approach is quite different and not necessarily better. The statistical properties of Equation 10.20, though not directly comparable to the other equations, do not appear as strong as they might[16] be, but this is not necessarily the deciding factor. One positive note is that the residuals of Equation 10.20 do indeed appear to be homoskedastic.

---

16. Petroleum-producing states like Texas, Louisiana, and Alaska consume petroleum products for many reasons other than their use in motor vehicles, so it might be tempting to add a variable measuring petroleum production to the equation. A better approach, however, would be to limit the dependent variable to the consumption of petroleum for use in motor vehicles. In addition, there is evidence that the *Statistical Abstract of the United States* data for REG may well have been incorrect for Colorado. Adjusting for this possible error improves the fit of the per-capita model dramatically. We are grateful to Ron Michener for both of these insights.

Which remedy is best: HC standard errors, the double-log functional form, or reformulating the equation? Most econometricians would prefer HC standard errors, though the sample size of 50 makes it unlikely that the large sample properties of HC estimators hold in this case. However, this answer could change depending on the underlying theory of your equation. If theory strongly supports either the double-log or the reformulated functional form, then that model clearly is best. In such a situation, however, it's worth asking why the theoretically superior functional form wasn't chosen in the first place. Finally, in the fairly unusual case that t-scores aren't used to test hypotheses or retain variables, then it's not at all clear that any sort of remedy for heteroskedasticity is required at all.

10.6 Summary

1. Heteroskedasticity is the violation of Classical Assumption V that the observations of the error term are drawn from a distribution with a constant variance. Homoskedastic error term observations are drawn from a distribution that has a constant variance for all observations, and heteroskedastic error term observations are drawn from distributions whose variances differ from observation to observation. Heteroskedasticity occurs most frequently in cross-sectional data sets.

2. The variance of a heteroskedastic error term is not equal to σ^2, a constant. Instead, it equals σ_i^2, where the subscript i indicates that the variance can change from observation to observation. Many different kinds of heteroskedasticity are possible, but a common model is one in which the variance changes systematically as a function of some other variable, a proportionality factor Z:

$$\text{VAR}(\epsilon_i) = \sigma^2 Z_i$$

The proportionality factor Z is usually a variable related in some way to the size or accuracy of the dependent variable.

3. Pure heteroskedasticity is a function of the error term of the correctly specified regression equation. Impure heteroskedasticity is caused by a specification error such as an omitted variable.

4. The major consequence of heteroskedasticity is bias in the OLS $\text{SE}(\hat{\beta})$s, causing unreliable hypothesis testing. Pure heteroskedasticity does not cause bias in the estimates of the βs themselves.

5. Two popular tests for heteroskedasticity are the Breusch–Pagan test and the White test. Both test for heteroskedasticity by analyzing the extent to which the squared residuals of the original equation can be explained by an auxiliary equation.

6. The first step in correcting heteroskedasticity is to check for a specification error that might be causing impure heteroskedasticity. If the specification is as good as possible, then solutions such as HC standard errors or redefining the variables should be considered.

EXERCISES

(The answers to the even-numbered exercises are in Appendix A.)

1. Write the meaning of each of the follow terms without referring to the book (or your notes), and compare your definition with the version in the text for each.
   a. the Breusch–Pagan test (p. 316)
   b. heteroskedasticity (p. 307)
   c. heteroskedasticity-corrected standard errors (p. 321)
   d. impure heteroskedasticity (p. 311)
   e. proportionality factor (p. 310)
   f. pure heteroskedasticity (p. 307)
   g. the White test (p. 318)

2. Let's return to the analysis of the international pharmaceutical industry that we started in Exercise 9 of Chapter 5. That study was cross sectional and included countries as large as the United States and as small as Luxembourg, so you'd certainly expect heteroskedasticity to be a potential problem. Luckily, the dependent variable in the original research was P_i, the pharmaceutical price level in the ith country divided by that of the United States, so the researchers didn't encounter the wide variations in size typically associated with heteroskedasticity. (Do you see why?)

   Suppose, however, that we use the same data set to build a model of pharmaceutical consumption:

$$\widehat{CV}_i = -15.9 + 0.18N_i + 0.22P_i + 14.3PC_i \qquad (10.21)$$
$$(0.05) \quad (0.09) \quad (6.4)$$
$$t = \quad 3.32 \quad 2.53 \quad 2.24$$
$$N = 32 \quad \overline{R}^2 = .31$$

where: CV_i = the volume of consumption of pharmaceuticals in the ith country divided by that of the United States

N_i = the population of the ith country divided by that of the United States

PC_i = a dummy variable equal to 1 if the ith country encouraged price competition, 0 otherwise

a. Does heteroskedasticity seem more likely when CV is the dependent variable than when P is the dependent variable? Explain your reasoning.

b. Use the data in Table 5.2 (datafile = DRUGS5) to test for heteroskedasticity in Equation 10.21 with both the Breusch–Pagan and the White test at the 5-percent level.

c. If your answer to part b is heteroskedasticity, estimate HC standard errors for Equation 10.21.

d. Similarly, if you encountered heteroskedasticity, re-estimate Equation 10.21 using a double-log functional form.

e. Similarly, if you encountered heteroskedasticity, reformulate the variables in Equation 10.21 to avoid heteroskedasticity and estimate your reformulated equation.

f. Which of our three remedies for heteroskedasticity do you think is best in this case? Why?

g. In Chapter 5, we estimated an equation with P as a function of CVN (CV per capita), and now we've estimated an equation with CV as a function of PC. Which Classical Assumption are you worried that we might have violated? Explain.

3. Of all the econometric problems we've encountered, heteroskedasticity is the one that seems the most difficult to understand. Close your book and attempt to write an explanation of heteroskedasticity in your own words. Be sure to include a diagram in your description.

4. A. Ando and F. Modigliani collected the following data on the income and consumption of non-self-employed homeowners:[17]

---

17. Albert Ando and Franco Modigliani, "The 'Permanent Income' and 'Life Cycle' Hypotheses of Saving Behavior: Comparisons and Tests," in I. Friend and R. Jones, eds. *Consumption and Saving*, Vol. II, 1960, p. 154.

Income Bracket ($)	Average Income ($)	Average Consumption ($)
0–999	556	2760
1000–1999	1622	1930
2000–2999	2664	2740
3000–3999	3587	3515
4000–4999	4535	4350
5000–5999	5538	5320
6000–7499	6585	6250
7500–9999	8582	7460
10000–above	14033	11500

a. Run a regression to explain average consumption as a function of average income.

b. Use the Breusch–Pagan test to test the residuals from the equation you ran in part a for heteroskedasticity at the 5-percent level.

c. Run a 5-percent White test on the same residuals.

d. If the tests run in parts b or c show evidence of heteroskedasticity, then what, if anything, should be done about it?

5. James Stock and Mark Watson suggest a quite different approach to heteroskedasticity. They state that "economic theory rarely gives any reason to believe that the errors are homoskedastic. It therefore is prudent to assume that the errors might be heteroskedastic unless you have compelling reasons to believe otherwise."[18] As a result, Stock and Watson automatically use HC standard errors without testing for heteroskedasticity. In fact, since they adjust every equation for heteroskedasticity, they don't even list homoskedasticity as a Classical Assumption.

a. What do you think? Do you agree with Stock and Watson? Explain your reasoning.

b. If Stock and Watson are right, does this mean that we don't need to learn about heteroskedasticity in the first place? Did you waste your time reading this chapter?

---

18. James Stock and Mark Watson, *Introduction to Econometrics* (Boston: Pearson, 2015), p. 163.

6. R. Bucklin, R. Caves, and A. Lo estimated the following double-log model to explain the yearly circulation of metropolitan newspapers (standard errors in parentheses):[19]

$$\hat{C}_i = -8.2 - 0.56P_i + 0.90I_i + 0.76Q_i + 0.27A_i + 0.08S_i - 0.77T_i$$
$$\phantom{\hat{C}_i = -8.2 } (0.58) \quad (0.14) \quad (0.21) \quad (0.14) \quad (0.05) \quad (0.27)$$

$$N = 50$$

where: C_i = yearly circulation of the ith newspaper

P_i = the weighted average single copy price of the ith newspaper

I_i = the total disposable income of the metropolitan area of the ith newspaper

Q_i = the number of personnel in editorial positions at the ith newspaper

A_i = the volume of retail advertising in the ith newspaper

S_i = amount of competition from suburban dailies in the ith newspaper's region

T_i = the number of television stations in the ith newspaper's region

(All variables are in logarithmic form.)

a. Hypothesize signs and run t-tests on each of the individual slope coefficients.

b. Does heteroskedasticity seem theoretically likely? Explain.

c. Given your responses to parts a and b, what econometric problems (out of omitted variables, irrelevant variables, incorrect functional form, multicollinearity, serial correlation, and heteroskedasticity) appear to exist in this equation?

d. If you could suggest just one change in the specification of this equation, what would that change be? Carefully explain your answer.

7. Let's investigate the possibility of heteroskedasticity in time-series data by looking at a model of the black market for U.S. dollars in Brazil that was studied by R. Dornbusch and C. Pechman.[20] In

19. R. E. Bucklin, R. E. Caves, and A. W. Lo, "Games of Survival in the U.S. Newspaper Industry," *Applied Economics*, Vol. 21, pp. 631–650.

20. Rudiger Dornbusch and Clarice Pechman, "The Bid-Ask Spread in the Black Market for Dollars in Brazil," *Journal of Money, Credit and Banking*, Vol. 17, pp. 517–520. The data for this study were not published with the original article but are on the data diskette that accompanies William F. Lott and Subhash C. Ray, *Applied Econometrics: Problems with Data Sets* (Fort Worth: Dryden/Harcourt Brace, 1992). The analytical approach of this question also comes from Lott and Ray, pp. 169–173.

particular, the authors wanted to know if the Demsetz-Bagehot bid-ask theory, previously tested on cross-sectional data from the United States, could be extended to time-series data outside the United States.[21] They estimated the following model on monthly data from Brazil for March 1979 through December 1983:

$$S_t = \beta_0 + \overset{+}{\beta_1 I_t} + \overset{+}{\beta_2 \ln(1 + V_t)} + \epsilon_t \tag{10.22}$$

where: S_t = the average daily spread between the bid and asking prices for the U.S. dollar on the Brazilian black market in month t

I_t = the average interest rate in month t

V_t = the variance of the daily premium between the black market rate and the official exchange rate for the dollar in month t

a. Use the authors' data in Table 10.2 (datafile = BID10) to estimate Equation 10.22 and test the residuals for positive first-order serial correlation.

b. If serial correlation appears to exist, reestimate Equation 10.22 using GLS. Do the coefficient estimates change? Which equation do you prefer? Why?

c. The authors noted that S nearly doubled in size during their sample period. Does this make you concerned about the possibility of heteroskedasticity? Why or why not?

d. Test the residuals of Equation 10.22 for heteroskedasticity using the Breusch–Pagan test. (*Hint:* A possible proportionality factor is a time-trend variable that equals 1 for March 1979 and that increases by 1 for each following month.)

e. Test the residuals of your GLS version of Equation 10.22 for heteroskedasticity. Did running GLS change the possibility of heteroskedasticity?

f. What remedy would you suggest for any heteroskedasticity that might exist in such a time-series model? Be specific.

---

21. For a review of this literature at the time of Dornbusch and Pechman's research, see Kalman Cohen et al., "Market Makers and the Market Spread: A Review of Recent Literature," *Journal of Financial and Quantitative Studies*, Vol. 14, No. 4, pp. 813–835.

Table 10.2   Data on the Brazilian Black Market for Dollars

Month	S	I	V
1979:03	2.248	4.15	20.580
1979:04	2.849	4.04	12.450
1979:05	2.938	2.68	21.230
1979:06	2.418	2.81	26.300
1979:07	2.921	1.92	22.600
1979:08	2.587	2.37	18.750
1979:09	2.312	3.59	20.040
1979:10	2.658	2.03	31.110
1979:11	2.262	2.41	29.040
1979:12	4.056	4.09	20.590
1980:01	3.131	3.28	11.770
1980:02	3.404	2.89	7.900
1980:03	2.835	3.44	6.150
1980:04	3.309	2.43	6.780
1980:05	3.042	2.13	8.550
1980:06	3.417	2.94	13.380
1980:07	2.929	3.19	11.870
1980:08	3.821	3.26	15.560
1980:09	2.753	3.98	24.560
1980:10	2.633	3.69	21.110
1980:11	2.608	4.43	15.000
1980:12	2.168	5.86	7.480
1981:01	2.273	4.36	2.820
1981:02	1.892	5.66	1.540
1981:03	2.283	4.60	1.520
1981:04	2.597	4.42	4.930
1981:05	2.522	5.41	10.790
1981:06	2.865	4.63	17.160
1981:07	4.206	5.46	30.590
1981:08	2.708	5.88	23.900
1981:09	2.324	5.52	20.620
1981:10	2.736	6.07	18.900
1981:11	3.277	5.48	26.790
1981:12	3.194	6.79	29.640
1982:01	3.473	5.46	32.870
1982:02	2.798	6.20	30.660
1982:03	3.703	6.19	40.740
1982:04	3.574	6.06	48.040
1982:05	3.484	6.26	33.510
1982:06	2.726	6.27	23.650

Month	S	I	V
1982:07	4.430	6.89	37.080
1982:08	4.158	7.55	51.260
1982:09	5.633	6.93	60.450
1982:10	5.103	8.14	83.980
1982:11	3.691	7.80	69.490
1982:12	3.952	9.61	68.030
1983:01	3.583	7.01	85.630
1983:02	4.459	7.94	77.060
1983:03	6.893	10.06	71.490
1983:04	5.129	11.82	51.520
1983:05	4.171	11.18	43.660
1983:06	5.047	10.92	59.500
1983:07	8.434	11.72	61.070
1983:08	5.143	9.54	75.380
1983:09	3.980	9.78	72.205
1983:10	4.340	9.91	59.258
1983:11	4.330	9.61	38.860
1983:12	4.350	10.09	33.380

Source: William F. Lott and Subhash C. Ray, *Applied Econometrics: Problems with Data Sets* (Fort Worth: Dryden/Harcourt Brace, 1992). (data diskette)

Datafile = BID10

10.7 Appendix: Econometric Lab #6

This laboratory assignment is an exercise in the detection and correction of heteroskedasticity.

Several years ago, an airplane pilot took econometrics, and for his project he estimated a hedonic model of the determinants of used, single-engine airplane prices in the year 2000. This lab uses data from his project as the basis for an exercise in the detection and correction of heteroskedasticity. The dataset, PLANES10, consists of the variables in Table 10.3.

Step 1: Use the Data to Estimate the Model with OLS

Use lnprice$_i$ as the dependent variable and use all the other variables in Table 10.3 as independent variables in your regression. Which variables have coefficients that are significant in the expected direction at the 5-percent level?

Table 10.3   Variable Listing

Variable	Description	Hypoth. Sign of Coef.
lnprice$_i$	Natural log of the price in dollars for used, basic single-engine aircraft i	n/a
lnceiling$_i$	Natural log of the service ceiling, or the highest possible altitude plane i can fly, in feet	+
lncruise$_i$	Natural log of the cruising speed in miles per hour of airplane i	+
lnhorse$_i$	Natural log of horsepower of the engine of airplane i	+
fixgear$_i$	Equal to 1 if aircraft i's landing gear is fixed (not retractable), 0 otherwise	−
lnfuel$_i$	Natural log of the volume of the fuel tank of aircraft i, in gallons	+
pass$_i$	The number of passengers aircraft i can accommodate during flight	+
tdrag$_i$	Equal to 1 if aircraft i is a tail dragger, 0 otherwise (*A tail dragger is an aircraft that has a wheel connected to its tail—hence, a tail dragger.*)	−
wtop$_i$	Equal to 1 if aircraft i has wings above the fuselage, 0 otherwise	−
lnage$_i$	Natural log of the age in years of aircraft i	−

Step 2: Multicollinearity Concerns

Could severe imperfect multicollinearity account for any of the coefficients being insignificant at the 5-percent level? If so, which ones? Use simple correlation coefficients and VIFs to support your answer.

Step 3: Heteroskedasticity Concerns

Plot the residuals from your OLS regression against the passenger capacity. Do the residuals look heteroskedastic? Explain.

Step 4: Conduct a Breusch–Pagan Test for Heteroskedasticity

Use all the right-hand variables in the original model to run the Breusch–Pagan auxiliary regression.

Write the null and alternative hypotheses, compute the test statistic, and conduct the test at the 5-percent level. Does heteroskedasticity appear to be present?

Step 5: Conduct a White Test for Heteroskedasticity

Test the regression in Step 1 at the 5-percent level for heteroskedasticity using the White test. Use the White test command in your regression package to run the auxiliary regression and to calculate the test statistic. How many variables are on the right-hand side of the auxiliary regression? What is the chi-square critical value? According to the White test, does there appear to be heteroskedasticity in the model?

Step 6: Estimate the Equation with Heteroskedasticity-Corrected Standard Errors

Re-estimate the model in Step 1 with heteroskedasticity-corrected standard errors, also known as White standard errors. Are the coefficients and $\overline{R}^2$ the same?

Step 7: Compare the Results

Compare the OLS results from Step 1 with the heteroskedasticity-corrected results in Step 6. For how many of the coefficients are the heteroskedasticity-corrected standard errors larger than the OLS standard errors? Doesn't this make the equation worse? If so, why bother to estimate the heteroskedasticity-corrected errors?

Chapter 11

Running Your Own Regression Project

We believe that econometrics is best learned by doing, not by reading books, listening to lectures, or taking tests. To us, learning the art of econometrics has more in common with learning to fly a plane or learning to play golf than it does with learning about history or literature. In fact, we developed the interactive exercises of this chapter and Chapter 8 precisely because of our confidence in learning by doing.

Although interactive exercises are a good bridge between textbook examples and running your own regressions, they don't go far enough. You still need to "get your hands dirty." We think that you should run your own regression project before you finish reading this book even if you're not required to do so. We're not alone. Some professors substitute a research project for the final exam as their class's comprehensive learning experience.

Running your own regression project has three major components:

1. Choosing a topic
2. Applying the six steps in regression analysis to that topic
3. Writing your research report

The first and third of these components are the topics of Sections 11.1 and 11.5, respectively. The rest of the chapter focuses on helping you carry out the six steps in regression analysis.

11.1 Choosing Your Topic

The purpose of an econometric research project is to use regression analysis to build the best explanatory equation for a particular dependent variable for a particular sample. Often, though, the hardest part is getting started. How can you choose a good topic?

There are at least three keys to choosing a topic. First, try to pick a field that you find interesting and that you know something about. If you enjoy working on your project, the hours involved will seem to fly by. In addition, if you know something about your subject, you'll be more likely to make correct specification choices and to notice subtle indications of data errors or theoretical problems. A second key is to make sure that data are readily available with a reasonable sample (we suggest at least 25 observations). Nothing is more frustrating than searching through data source after data source in search of numbers for your dependent variable or one of your independent variables, so before you lock yourself into a topic, see if the data are there. The final key is to make sure that there is some substance to your topic. Try to avoid topics that are purely descriptive or virtually tautological in nature. Instead, look for topics that address an inherently interesting economic or behavioral question or choice.

Perhaps the best place to look for ideas for topics is to review your textbooks and notes from previous economics classes or to look over the examples and exercises of the first 10 chapters of this book. Often, you can take an idea from a previous study and update the data to see if the idea can be applied in a different context. Other times, reading an example will spark an idea about a similar or related study that you'd be interested in doing. Don't feel that your topic has to contain an original hypothesis or equation. On your first or second project, it's more important to get used to the econometrics than it is to create a publishable masterpiece.

Another way to find a topic is to read through issues of economics journals, looking for article topics that you find interesting and that might be possible to model. For example, Table 11.1 contains a list of the journals cited so far in this textbook (in order of the frequency of citation). These journals would be a great place to start if you want to try to replicate or update a previous research study. Although this is an excellent way to get ideas, it's also frustrating, because most current articles use econometric techniques that go beyond those that we've covered so far in this text. As a result, it's often difficult to compare your results to those in the article.

Table 11.1 Sources of Potential Topic Ideas

Econometrica
American Economic Review
Journal of Applied Econometrics
American Journal of Agricultural Economics
Journal of Economic Education
Journal of the American Statistical Association
World Development
Applied Economics
Assessment and Evaluation in Higher Education
Economic Inquiry
Economica
Journal of Agricultural and Applied Economics
Journal of Econometrics
Journal of Economic Literature
Journal of Money, Credit and Banking
Journal of the Royal Statistical Society
National Tax Review
NBER working papers
Review of Economics and Statistics
Scandinavian Journal of Economics
Southern Economic Journal
The Appraisal Journal

If you get stuck for a topic, go directly to the data sources themselves. That is, instead of thinking of a topic and then seeing if the data are available, look over what data are available and see if they help you generate ideas for topics. Quite often, a reference will have data not only for a dependent variable but also for most of the relevant independent variables all in one place, minimizing time spent collecting data.

Once you pick a topic, don't rush out and run your first regression. Remember, the more time you spend reviewing the literature and analyzing your expectations on a topic, the better the econometric analysis and, ultimately, your research report will be.

11.2 Collecting Your Data

Before any quantitative analysis can be done, the data must be collected, organized, and entered into a computer. Usually, this is a time-consuming and frustrating task because of the difficulty of finding data, the existence of definitional differences between theoretical variables and their empirical counterparts, and the high probability of data entry errors or data transmission errors. In general, though, time spent thinking about and collecting the data is well spent, since a researcher who knows the data sources and definitions is much less likely to make mistakes using or interpreting regressions run on those data.

What Data to Look For

Before you settle on a research topic, make sure that data for your dependent variable and all relevant independent variables are available. However, checking for data availability means deciding what specific variables you want to study. Half of the time that beginning researchers spend collecting data is wasted by looking for the wrong variables in the wrong places. A few minutes thinking about what data to look for will prevent hours of frustration later.

For example, if the dependent variable is the quantity of television sets demanded per year, then most independent variables should be measured annually as well. It would be inappropriate and possibly misleading to define the price of TVs as the price from a particular month. An average of prices over the year (usually weighted by the number of TVs sold per month) would be more meaningful. If the dependent variable includes all TV sets sold regardless of brand, then the price would appropriately be an aggregate based on prices of all brands. Calculating such aggregate variables, however, is not straightforward. Researchers typically make their best efforts to compute the respective aggregate variables and then acknowledge that problems still remain. For example, if the price data for all the various brands are not available, a researcher may be forced to compromise and use the price of one or a few of the major brands as a substitute for the proper aggregate price.

Another issue is suggested by the TV example. Over the years of the sample, it's likely that the market shares of particular kinds of TV sets have changed. For example, flat-screen HD TV sets might have made up a majority of the market in one decade, but black-and-white sets might have been the favorite 40 years before. In cases where the composition of the market share, the size, or the quality of the various brands have changed over time, it would make little sense to measure the dependent variable as the number of TV sets because a "TV set" from one year has little in common with a "TV set" from another. The approach usually taken to deal with this problem is to measure the variable in dollar terms, under the assumption that value encompasses size and quality. Thus, we would work with the dollar sales of TVs rather than the number of sets sold.

A third issue, whether to use nominal or real variables, usually depends on the underlying theory of the research topic. Nominal (or money) variables are measured in current dollars and thus include increases caused by inflation. If theory implies that inflation should be filtered out, then it's best to state the variables in real (constant-dollar) terms by selecting an appropriate price deflator, such as the Consumer Price Index, and adjusting the money (or nominal) value by it.

As an example, the appropriate price index for Gross Domestic Product is called the GDP deflator. Real GDP is calculated by multiplying nominal GDP by the ratio of the GDP deflator from the base year to the GDP deflator from the current year:

Real GDP = nominal GDP × (base GDP deflator/current GDP deflator)

In 2007, U.S. nominal GDP was $13,807.5 billion and the GDP deflator was 119.82 (for a base year of 2000 = 100), so real GDP was:[1]

Real GDP = $13,807.5 (100/119.82) = $11,523.9 billion

That is, the goods and services produced in 2007 were worth $13,807.5 billion if 2007 dollars were used but were worth only $11,523.9 billion if 2000 dollars were used.

Fourth, recall that all economic data are either time series or cross sectional in nature. Since time-series data are for the same economic entity from different time periods, whereas cross-sectional data are from the same time period but for different economic entities, the appropriate definitions of the variables depend on whether the sample is a time series or a cross section.

To understand this, consider the TV set example once again. A time-series model might study the sales of TV sets in the United States from 1967 to 2015, and a cross-sectional model might study the sales of TV sets by state for 2015. The time-series data set would have 49 observations, each of which would refer to a particular year. In contrast, the cross-sectional model data set would have 50 observations, each of which would refer to a particular state. A variable that might be appropriate for the time-series model might be completely inappropriate for the cross-sectional model, and vice versa; at the very least, it would have to be measured differently. National advertising in a particular year would be appropriate for the time-series model, for example, while advertising in or near each particular state would make more sense for the cross-sectional one.

Finally, learn to be a critical reader of the descriptions of variables in econometric research. Are variables measured in nominal or real terms?

---

1. *2009 Economic Report of the President*, pp. 282–285.

Where did the data originate? A careful reader would want to know the answers to these questions before analyzing any results.

Where to Look for Economic Data

Although some researchers generate their own data through surveys or other techniques (and we'll address this possibility in Section 11.3), the vast majority of regressions are run on publicly available data. The best sources for such data are government publications and machine-readable data files. In fact, the U.S. government has been called the most thorough statistics-collecting agency in history.

Excellent government publications include the annual *Economic Report of the President*, the *Handbook of U.S. Labor Statistics*, and *Historical Statistics of the U.S.* (published in 1975). One of the best places to start with U.S. data[2] is the annual *Census Catalog and Guide*, which provides overviews and abstracts of data sources and various statistical products as well as details on how to obtain each item. Consistent international data are harder to come by, but the United Nations publishes a number of compilations of figures. The best of these are the *U.N. Statistical Yearbook* and the *U.N. Yearbook of National Account Statistics*.

However, most researchers use online computer databases to find data instead of plowing through stacks of printed volumes. These online databases, available through most college and university libraries, contain complete series on literally thousands of possible variables. Perhaps the best source of economic data on the Internet is FRED, the Federal Reserve Economic Database, which contains more than 268,000 U.S. and international time series, all downloadable in Excel spreadsheets. It is hosted and maintained by the Federal Reserve Bank of St. Louis at https://research.stlouisfed.org/fred2/. The best guides to Internet data are "Resources for Economists on the Internet" and "Economagic." Other good Internet resources are EconLit, which is an online summary of the *Journal of Economic Literature*, and "ProQuest, Dialog," which provides online access to a large number of data sets.[3]

---

2. For older data, the *Statistical Abstract of the United States* is a great source. Sadly, this is no longer published by the government, but it is commercially available both in print and online as the *ProQuest Statistical Abstract of the United States* (Lanham, MD: Bernan, 2015).

3. The website addresses of these resources are:
Resources for Economists: https://www.aeaweb.org/RFE/showCat.php?cat_id=2
Economagic: http://www.economagic.com/
EconLit: https://www.aeaweb.org/econlit/
Proquest Dialog: http://www.proquest.com/products-services/ProQuest-Dialog.html

Missing Data

Suppose the data aren't there? What happens if you choose the perfect variable and look in all the right sources and can't find the data?

The answer to this question depends on how much is missing. If a few observations have incomplete data in a cross-sectional study, you usually can afford to drop these observations from the sample. If the incomplete data are from a time series, you can sometimes estimate the missing value by interpolating (taking the mean of adjacent values). Similarly, if one variable is available only annually in an otherwise quarterly model, you may want to consider quarterly interpolations of that variable. In either case, interpolation can be justified only if the variable moves in a slow and smooth manner. Extreme caution should always be exercised when "creating" data in such a way (and full documentation is required).

If no data at all exist for a theoretically relevant variable, then the problem worsens significantly. Omitting a relevant variable runs the risk of biased coefficient estimates, as you learned in Chapter 6. After all, how can you hold a variable constant if it's not included in the equation? In such cases, most researchers resort to the use of proxy variables.

Proxy variables can sometimes substitute for theoretically desired variables for which data are missing. For example, the value of net investment is a variable that is not measured directly in a number of countries. As a result, a researcher might use the value of gross investment as a proxy, the assumption being that the value of gross investment is directly proportional to the value of net investment. This proportionality (which is similar to a change in units) is required because the regression analyzes the relationship between changes among variables, rather than the absolute levels of the variables.

In general, a proxy variable is a "good" proxy when its movements correspond relatively well to movements in the theoretically correct variable. Since the latter is unobservable whenever a proxy must be used, there is usually no easy way to examine a proxy's "goodness" directly. Instead, the researcher must document as well as possible why the proxy is likely to be a good or bad one. Poor proxies and variables with large measurement errors constitute "bad" data, but the degree to which the data are bad is a matter of judgment by the individual researcher.

11.3 Advanced Data Sources

So far, all the data sets in this text have been cross sectional or time series in nature, and we have collected our data by observing the world around us, instead of by creating the data ourselves. It turns out, however, that time-series and cross-sectional data can be pooled to form *panel data*, and that data can be generated through *surveys*. The purpose of this short section is to introduce you to these more advanced data sources and to explain why it probably doesn't make sense to use these data sources on your first regression project.

Surveys

Surveys are everywhere in our society. Marketing firms use surveys to learn more about products and competition, political candidates use surveys to fine-tune their campaign advertising or strategies, and governments use surveys for all sorts of purposes, including keeping track of their citizens with instruments like the U.S. Census. As a result, many beginning researchers (particularly those who are having trouble obtaining data for their project) are tempted to run their own surveys in the hope that it'll be an easy way to generate the data they need.

However, running a survey is not as easy as it might seem. For example, the topics to be covered in the survey need to be thought through carefully, because once a survey has been run, it's virtually impossible to go back to the respondents and add another question. In addition, the questions themselves need to be worded precisely (and pretested) to avoid confusing the respondent or "leading" the respondent to a particular answer. Perhaps most importantly, it's crucial for the sample to be random in order to avoid selection, survivor, and nonresponse biases. In fact, running a survey properly is so difficult that entire books and courses are devoted to the topic. To top it all off, most colleges and universities require a lengthy institutional review before allowing an on-campus survey.

As a result, we don't encourage beginning researchers to run their own surveys, and we're cautious when we analyze the results of surveys run by others. As put by the American Statistical Association, "The quality of a survey is best judged not by its size, scope, or prominence, but by how much attention is given to preventing, measuring, and dealing with the many important problems that can arise."[4]

Panel Data

As mentioned previously, **panel data** are formed when cross-sectional and time-series data sets are pooled to create a single data set. Why would you want to use panel data? In some cases, researchers use panel data to increase

---

4. As quoted in "Best Practices for Research," on the website of the American Association for Public Opinion Research: www.aapor.org. The best practices outlined on this website are a good place to start if you decide to create your own survey.

their sample size, but the main reason for using panel data is to provide an insight into an analytical question that can't be obtained by using time-series or cross-sectional data alone.

What's an example of panel data? Suppose that we're interested in the relationship between budget deficits and interest rates but we have only 10 years' worth of comparable annual data to study. Ten observations is too small a sample for a reasonable regression, so it might seem as if we're out of luck. However, if we can find time-series data on the same economic variables—interest rates and budget deficits—for the same ten years for six different countries, we'll end up with a sample of 10*6 = 60 observations, which is more than enough to use. The result is a pooled cross-section time-series data set—a panel data set!

Unfortunately, panel data can't be analyzed fully with the econometric techniques you've learned to date in this text, so we don't encourage beginning researchers to attempt to run regressions on panel data. Instead, we've devoted the majority of a chapter (Chapter 16) to panel data, and we urge you to read that chapter if you're interested. Chapter 16 also covers experimental methods in economics, since such experiments often generate panel data.

11.4   Practical Advice for Your Project

The purpose of this section is to give you some practical advice about actually doing applied econometric work. Such advice often is missing from econometrics textbooks and courses, but the advice is crucial because many of the skills of an applied econometrician are judgmental and subjective in nature. No single text or course can teach these skills, and that's not our goal. Instead, we want to alert you to some technical suggestions that a majority of experienced applied econometricians would be likely to support.

What to Check If You Get an Unexpected Sign

An all-too-familiar problem for a beginning econometrician is to run a regression and find that the sign of one or more of the estimated coefficients is the opposite of what was expected. While an unexpected sign certainly is frustrating, it's not entirely bad news. Rather than considering this a disaster, a researcher should consider it a blessing—this result is a friendly message that some detective work needs to be done—there is undoubtedly some shortcoming in the theory, data, specification, or estimation procedure. If the "correct" signs had been obtained, odds are that the analysis would not be double-checked. What should be checked?

1. *Recheck the expected sign.* Every once in a while, a variable that is defined "upside down" will cause a researcher to expect the wrong sign. For example, in an equation for student SATs, the variable "high school rank in class" (where a rank of 1 means that the student was first in his or her class) can sometimes lure a beginning researcher into expecting a positive coefficient for rank.

2. *Check your data for input errors and/or outliers.* If you have data errors or oddball observations, the chances of getting an unexpected sign—even a significant unexpected sign—increase dramatically.

3. *Check for an omitted variable.* The most frequent source of a significant unexpected sign for the coefficient of a relevant independent variable is an omitted variable. Think hard about what might have been omitted, and remember to use our equation for expected bias.

4. *Check for an irrelevant variable.* A frequent source of insignificant unexpected signs is that the variable doesn't actually belong in the equation in the first place. If the true coefficient for an irrelevant variable is zero, then you're likely to get an unexpected sign half the time.

5. *Check for multicollinearity.* Multicollinearity increases the variances and standard errors of the estimated coefficients, increasing the chance that a coefficient could have an unexpected sign. The sampling distributions will be widely spread and may straddle zero, implying that it is quite possible that a draw from this distribution will produce an unexpected sign. Indeed, one of the casual indicators of multicollinearity is the presence of unexpected signs.

6. *Check for sample selection bias.* An unexpected sign sometimes can be due to the fact that the observations included in the data were not obtained randomly.

7. *Check your sample size.* Multicollinearity isn't the only source of high variances; they also could result from a small sample size or minimal variation in the explanatory variables. In some cases, all it takes to fix an unexpected sign is to increase the sample.

8. *Check your theory.* If you've exhausted every logical econometric explanation for your unexpected sign, there are only two likely remaining explanations. Either your theory is wrong, or you've got a bad data set. If your theory is wrong, then you of course have to change your expected sign, but remember to test this new expectation on a different data set. However, be careful! It's amazing how economists

can conjure up rationales for unexpected signs after the regression has been run! One theoretical source of bias, and therefore unexpected signs, is if the underlying model is simultaneous in nature (we'll cover simultaneous equations in Chapter 14).

A Dozen Practical Tips Worth Reiterating

Here are a number of practical tips for applied econometrics[5] that we've made in previous chapters that are worth emphasizing. They work!

1. Don't attempt to maximize $\overline{R}^2$. (Chapter 2)

2. Always review the literature and hypothesize the signs of your coefficients before estimating a model. (Chapter 3)

3. Remember to inspect and clean your data before estimating a model. Know that outliers should not be automatically omitted; instead, they should be investigated to make sure that they belong in the sample. (Chapter 3)

4. Know the Classical Assumptions *cold*! (Chapter 4)

5. In general, use a one-sided *t*-test unless the expected sign of the coefficient actually is in doubt. (Chapter 5)

6. Don't automatically discard a variable with an insignificant *t*-score. In general, be willing to live with a variable with a *t*-score lower than the critical value in order to decrease the chance of omitting a relevant variable. (Chapter 6)

7. Know how to analyze the size and direction of the bias caused by an omitted variable. (Chapter 6)

8. Understand all the different functional form options and their common uses, and remember to choose your functional form primarily on the basis of theory, not fit. (Chapter 7)

9. Remember that multicollinearity doesn't create bias; the estimated variances are large, but the estimated coefficients themselves are unbiased. As a result, the most-used remedy for multicollinearity is to do nothing. (Chapter 8)

10. If you get a significant Durbin–Watson, Breusch–Pagan, or White test, remember to consider the possibility that a specification error might be

---

5. For more practical tips of a similar nature, see Peter Kennedy, "Sinning in the Basement: What are the Rules? The Ten Commandments of Applied Econometrics," *Journal of Economic Surveys*, Vol. 16, No. 4, pp. 569–589.

causing impure serial correlation or heteroskedasticity. Don't change your estimation technique from OLS to GLS or use adjusted standard errors until you have the best possible specification. (Chapters 9 and 10)

11. Remember that adjusted standard errors like Newey–West standard errors or HC standard errors use the OLS coefficient estimates. It's the standard errors of the estimated coefficients that change, not the estimated coefficients themselves. (Chapters 9 and 10)

12. Finally, and perhaps most importantly, if in doubt, rely on common sense and economic theory, not on statistical tests.

The Ethical Econometrician

One conclusion that a casual reader of this book might draw from the large number of specifications we include is that we encourage the estimation of numerous regression results as a way of ensuring the discovery of these best possible estimates.

Nothing could be further from the truth!

As every reader of this book should know by now, our opinion is that the best models are those on which much care has been spent to develop the theoretical underpinnings and only a short time is spent pursuing alternative estimations of that equation. Many econometricians, ourselves included, would hope to be able to estimate only *one* specification of an equation for each data set. Econometricians are fallible and our data are sometimes imperfect, however, so it is unusual for a first attempt at estimation to be totally problem free. As a result, two or even more regressions are often necessary to rid an estimation of fairly simple difficulties that perhaps could have been avoided in a world of perfect foresight.

Unfortunately, a beginning researcher usually has little motivation to stop running regressions until he or she likes the way the result looks. If running another regression provides a result with a better fit, why shouldn't one more specification be tested?

The reason is a compelling one. Every time an extra regression is run and a specification choice is made on the basis of fit or statistical significance, the chances of making a mistake of inference increase dramatically. This can happen in at least two ways:

1. If you consistently drop a variable when its coefficient is insignificant but keep it when it is significant, it can be shown, as discussed in Section 6.4, that you bias your estimates of the coefficients of the equation and of the *t*-scores.

2. If you choose to use a lag structure, or a functional form or an estimation procedure other than OLS, on the basis of fit rather than on the basis of previously theorized hypotheses, you run the risk that your equation will work poorly when it's applied to data outside your sample. If you restructure your equation to work well on one data set, you might decrease the chance of it working well on another.

What might be thought of as ethical econometrics is also in reality *good* econometrics. That is, the real reason to avoid running too many different specifications is that the fewer regressions you run, the more reliable and more consistently trustworthy are your results. The instance in which professional ethics come into play is when a number of changes are made (different variables, lag structures, functional forms, estimation procedures, data sets, dropped outliers, and so on), but the regression results are presented to colleagues, clients, editors, or journals as if the final and best equation had been the first and only one estimated. Our recommendation is that all estimated equations be reported even if footnotes or an appendix have to be added to the documentation.

We think that there are two reasonable goals for econometricians when estimating models:

1. Run as few different specifications as possible while still attempting to avoid the major econometric problems. The only exception to our recommendation to run as few specifications as possible is sensitivity analysis, described in Section 6.4.

2. Report honestly the number and type of different specifications estimated so that readers of the research can evaluate how much weight to give to your results.

Therefore, the art of econometrics boils down to attempting to find the best possible equation in the fewest possible number of regression runs. Only careful thinking and reading before estimating the first regression can bring this about. An ethical econometrician is honest and complete in reporting the different specifications and/or data sets used.

11.5 Writing Your Research Report

Once you've finished your research, it's important to write a report on your results so that others can benefit from what you found out (or didn't find out) or so that you can get feedback on your econometric techniques from someone else. Most good research reports have a number of elements in common:

- A brief introduction that defines the dependent variable and states the goals of the research.

- A short review of relevant previous literature and research.

- An explanation of the specification of the equation (model). This should include explaining why particular independent variables and functional forms were chosen as well as stating the expected signs of (or other hypotheses about) the slope coefficients.

- A description of the data (including generated variables), data sources, and any irregularities with the data.

- A presentation of each estimated specification, using our standard documentation format. If you estimate more than one specification, be sure to explain which one is best (and why).

- A careful analysis of the regression results that includes a discussion of any econometric problems encountered and complete documentation of all equations estimated and all tests run. (Beginning researchers are well advised to test for every possible econometric problem; with experience, you'll learn to focus on the most likely difficulties.)

- A short summary/conclusion that includes any policy recommendations or suggestions for further research.

- A bibliography.

- An appendix that includes all data, all regression runs, and all relevant computer output. Do this carefully; readers appreciate a well-organized and labeled appendix.

We think that the easiest way to write such a research report is to keep a research journal as you go along. In this journal, you can keep track of *a priori* hypotheses, regression results, statistical tests, different specifications you considered, and theoretical analyses of what you thought was going on in your equation. You'll find that when it comes time to write your research report, this journal will almost write your paper for you! The alternative to keeping a journal is to wait until you've finished all your econometric work before starting to write your research report, but by doing this, you run the risk of forgetting the thought process that led you to make a particular decision (or some other important item).

11.6 A Regression User's Checklist and Guide

Table 11.2 contains a list of the items that a researcher checks when reviewing the output from a computer regression package. Not every item in the checklist will be produced by your computer package, and not every item in your computer output will be in the checklist, but the checklist can be a very useful reference. In most cases, a quick glance at the checklist will remind you of the

Table 11.2 Regression User's Checklist

Symbol	Checkpoint	Reference	Decision
X, Y	Data observations	Check for errors. Check means, maximums, and minimums.	Correct any errors.
df	Degrees of freedom	$N - K - 1 > 0$ N = number of observations K = number of explanatory variables	If $N - K - 1 \leq 0$, equation cannot be estimated, and if the degrees of freedom are low, precision is low. In such a case, try to include more observations.
$\hat{\beta}$	Estimated coefficient	Compare signs and magnitudes to expected values.	If they are unexpected, respecify model if appropriate.
t	t-statistic $t_k = \dfrac{\hat{\beta}_k - \beta_{H_0}}{SE(\hat{\beta}_k)}$ or $t_k = \dfrac{\hat{\beta}_k}{SE(\hat{\beta}_k)}$ for computer-supplied t-scores or whenever $\beta_{H_0} = 0$	Two-sided test: $H_0: \beta_k = \beta_{H_0}$ $H_A: \beta_k \neq \beta_{H_0}$ One-sided test: $H_0: \beta_k \leq \beta_{H_0}$ $H_A: \beta_k > \beta_{H_0}$ β_{H_0}, the hypothesized β, is supplied by the researcher, and is often zero.	Reject H_0 if $|t_k| > t_c$ and if the estimate is of the expected sign. t_c is the critical value of α level of significance and $N - K - 1$ degrees of freedom.
R^2	Coefficient of determination	The percentage of the variation of Y around its mean explained by the regression equation.	Measures the degree of overall fit of the model to the data.
$\overline{R}^2$	R^2 adjusted for degrees of freedom	The percentage of the variation of Y around its mean explained by the regression equation, adjusted for degrees of freedom.	One indication that an explanatory variable is irrelevant is if the $\overline{R}^2$ falls when it is included.
F	F-statistic $F = \dfrac{(RSS_M - RSS)/M}{RSS/(N - K - 1)}$		Can be used to test joint hypotheses about two or more coefficients. A special case is the F-test of overall significance.

Symbol	Checkpoint	Reference	Decision
DW	Durbin–Watson statistic	Tests: $H_0: \rho \leq 0$ $H_A: \rho > 0$ For positive serial correlation.	Reject H_0 if $DW < d_L$. Inconclusive if $d_L \leq DW \leq d_U$. (d_L and d_U are critical DW values.)
e_i	Residual	Check for heteroske-dasticity by examining the pattern of the residuals.	May take appropriate corrective action, but test first.
SE	Standard error of the regression	An estimate of the standard error of the error term.	A guide to the overall fit.
TSS	Total sum of squares	$TSS = \sum_i (Y_i - \bar{Y})^2$	Used to compute F, R^2, and $\bar{R}^2$.
RSS	Residual sum of squares	$RSS = \sum_i (Y_i - \hat{Y}_i)^2$	Same as above.
$SE(\hat{\beta}_k)$	Standard error of $\hat{\beta}_k$	Used in t-statistics and confidence intervals.	A measure of the imprecision of the estimated coefficient.
$\hat{\rho}$	Estimated first-order autocorrelation coefficient	Usually provided by an autoregressive routine.	If negative, implies a specification error or that the data were differenced.
r_{12}	Simple correlation coefficient between X_1 and X_2	Used to detect multicollinearity.	Suspect severe multicol-linearity if $r_{12} > .8$.
VIF	Variance inflation factor	Used to detect multicollinearity.	Suspect severe multicol-linearity if $VIF > 5$.

text sections that deal with the item, but if this is not the case, the fairly mini-mal explanation in the checklist should *not* be relied on to cover everything needed for complete analysis and judgment. Instead, you should look up the item in the index. In addition, note that the actions in the right-hand column are merely suggestions. The circumstances of each individual research project are much more reliable guides than any dogmatic list of actions.

There are two ways to use the checklist. First, you can refer to it as a "glossary of packaged computer output terms" when you encounter something in your regression result that you don't understand. Second, you can work your way through the checklist in order, finding the items in your computer output and marking them. As with the Regression User's Guide (Table 11.3),

Table 11.3 Regression User's Guide

What Can Go Wrong?	What Are the Consequences?	How Can It Be Detected?	How Can It Be Corrected?
Omitted Variable The omission of a relevant independent variable	Bias in the coefficient estimates (the $\hat{\beta}$s) of the included Xs.	Theory, significant unexpected signs, or surprisingly poor fits.	Include the omitted variable or a proxy.
Irrelevant Variable The inclusion of a variable that does not belong in the equation	Decreased precision in the form of higher standard errors, lower t-scores and wider confidence intervals.	1. Theory 2. t-test on $\hat{\beta}$ 3. $\bar{R}^2$ 4. Impact on other coefficients if X is dropped.	Delete the variable if its inclusion is not required by the underlying theory.
Incorrect Functional Form The functional form is inappropriate	Biased estimates, poor fit, and difficult interpretation.	Examine the theory carefully; think about the relationship between X and Y.	Transform the variable or the equation to a different functional form.
Multicollinearity Some of the independent variables are (imperfectly) correlated	No biased $\hat{\beta}$s, but estimates of the separate effects of the Xs are not reliable, i.e., high $SE(\hat{\beta})$s and low t-scores.	No universally accepted rule or test is available. Use high r_{12}s or the VIF test.	Drop redundant variables, but to drop others might introduce bias. Often doing nothing is best.
Serial Correlation Observations of the error term are correlated, as in: $\epsilon_t = \rho\epsilon_{t-1} + u_t$	No biased $\hat{\beta}$s, but OLS no longer is minimum variance, and hypothesis testing and confidence intervals are unreliable.	Use Durbin–Watson test; if significantly less than 2, positive serial correlation exists.	If impure, fix the specification. Otherwise, consider Generalized Least Squares or Newey–West standard errors.
Heteroskedasticity The variance of the error term is not constant for all observations, as in: $VAR(\epsilon_i) = \sigma^2 Z_i$	Same as for serial correlation.	Use residual plots and the Breusch–Pagan or White tests.	If impure, fix the specification. Otherwise, use HC standard errors or reformulate the variables.

the use of the Regression User's Checklist will be most helpful for beginning researchers, but we also find ourselves referring back to it once in a while even after years of experience.

Be careful. All simplified tables, like the two in this chapter, must trade completeness for ease of use. As a result, strict adherence to a set of rules is not recommended even if the rules come from one of our tables. Someone who understands the purpose of the research, the exact definitions of the variables, and the problems in the data is much more likely to make a correct judgment than is someone equipped with a set of rules created to apply to a wide variety of possible applications.

Table 11.3, the Regression User's Guide, contains a brief summary of the major econometric maladies discussed so far in this text. For each econometric problem, we list:

1. Its nature.

2. Its consequences for OLS estimation.

3. How to detect it.

4. How to attempt to get rid of it.

How might you use the guide? If an estimated equation has a particular problem, such as an insignificant coefficient estimate, a quick glance at the guide can give some idea of the econometric problems that might be causing the symptom. Both multicollinearity and irrelevant variables can cause regression coefficients to have insignificant t-scores, for example, and someone who remembered only one of these potential causes might take the wrong corrective action. After some practice, the use of this guide will decrease until it eventually will seem fairly limiting and simplistic. Until then, however, our experience is that those about to undertake their first econometric research can benefit by referring to this guide.

(11.7) Summary

1. Running your own regression project involves choosing your dependent variable, applying the six steps in applied regression (of Chapter 3) to that dependent variable, and then writing a research report that summarizes your work.

2. A great research topic is one that you know something about, one that addresses an inherently interesting economic or behavioral question or choice, and one for which data are available not only for the dependent variable but also for the obvious independent variables.

3.   Don't underestimate the difficulty and importance of collecting a complete and accurate data set. It's a lot of work, but it's worth it!

4.   The art of econometrics boils down to finding the best possible equation in the fewest possible number of regression runs. The only way to do this is to spend quite a bit of time thinking through the underlying principles of your research project before you run your first regression.

5.   Before you complete your research project, be sure to review the practical hints and regression user's guide and checklist in Sections 11.4 and 11.6.

11.8 Appendix: The Housing Price Interactive Exercise

This interactive regression learning exercise is somewhat different from the previous one in Section 8.7. Our goal is still to bridge the gap between textbook and computer, but we feel that if you completed the previous interactive exercise, you should be ready to do the computer work on your own. As a result, this interactive exercise will provide you with a short literature review and the data, but you'll be asked to calculate your own estimates. Feedback on your specification choices will once again be found in the hints in Appendix A.

Since the only difference between this interactive exercise and the first one is that this one requires you to estimate your chosen specification(s) with the computer, our guidelines for interactive exercises still apply:

1.   Take the time to look over a portion of the reading list before choosing a specification.

2.   Try to estimate as few regression runs as possible.

3.   Avoid looking at the hints until after you've reached what you think is your best specification.

We believe that the benefits you get from an interactive exercise are directly proportional to the effort you put into it. If you have to delay this exercise until you have the time and energy to do your best, that's probably a good idea.

Building a Hedonic Model of Housing Prices

In the next section, we're going to ask you to specify the independent variables and functional form for an equation whose dependent variable is the price of a house in Southern California. Before making these choices, it's vital to review the housing price literature and to think through the theory behind such models. Such a review is especially important in this case because the model we'll be building will be *hedonic* in nature.

What is a hedonic model? Recall that in Section 1.5 we estimated an equation for the price of a house as a function of the size of that house. Such a model is called **hedonic** because it uses measures of the quality of a product as independent variables instead of measures of the market for that product (like quantity demanded, income, etc.). Hedonic models are most useful when the product being analyzed is heterogeneous in nature because we need to analyze what causes products to be different and therefore to have different prices. With a homogeneous product, hedonic models are virtually useless.

Perhaps the most-cited early hedonic housing price study is that of G. Grether and P. Mieszkowski,[6] who collected a seven-year data set and built a number of linear models of housing price using different combinations of variables. They included square feet of space, the number of bathrooms, and the number of rooms, although the number of rooms turned out to be insignificant. They also included lot size and the age of the house as variables, specifying a quadratic function for the age variable. Most innovatively, they used several slope dummies in order to capture the interaction effects of various combinations of variables (like a hardwood-floors dummy times the size of the house).

Peter Linneman[7] estimated a housing price model on data from Los Angeles, Chicago, and the entire United States. His goal was to create a model that worked for the two individual cities and then to apply it to the nation to test the hypothesis of a national housing market. Linneman did not include any lot characteristics, nor did he use any interaction variables. His only measures of the size of the living space were the number of bathrooms and the number of nonbathrooms. Except for an age variable, the rest of the independent variables were dummies describing quality characteristics of the house and neighborhood. Although many of the dummy variables were quite fickle, the coefficients of age, number of bathrooms, and the number of nonbathrooms were relatively stable and significant. Central air conditioning had a negative, insignificant coefficient for the Los Angeles regression.

---

6. G. M. Grether and Peter Mieszkowski, "Determinants of Real Estate Values," *Journal of Urban Economics*, Vol. 1, pp. 127–146. Another classic article of the same era is J. Kain and J. Quigley, "Measuring the Value of Housing Quality," *Journal of the American Statistical Association*, Vol. 45, pp. 532–548.

7. Peter Linneman, "Some Empirical Results on the Nature of the Hedonic Price Functions for the Urban Housing Market," *Journal of Urban Economics*, Vol. 8, No. 1, pp. 47–68.

K. Ihlanfeldt and J. Martinez-Vasquez[8] investigated sample bias in various methods of obtaining house price data and concluded that a house's sales price is the least biased of all measures. Unfortunately, they went on to estimate an equation by starting with a large number of variables and then dropping all those that had *t*-scores below 1, almost surely introducing bias into their equation.

Finally, Allen Goodman[9] added some innovative variables to an estimate on a national data set. He included measures of specific problems like rats, cracks in the plaster, holes in the floors, plumbing breakdowns, and the level of property taxes. Although the property tax variable showed the capitalization of low property taxes, as would be expected, the rats coefficient was insignificant, and the cracks variable's coefficient asserted that cracks significantly increase the value of a house.

The Housing Price Interactive Exercise

Now that we've reviewed at least a portion of the literature, it's time to build your own model. Recall that in Section 1.5, we built a simple model of the price of a house as a function of the size of that house, Equation 1.21:

$$\hat{P}_i = 40.0 + 0.138S_i \tag{1.21}$$

where: P_i = the price (in thousands of dollars) of the *i*th house
S_i = the size (in square feet) of the *i*th house

Equation 1.21 was estimated on a sample of 43 houses that were purchased in the same Southern California town (Monrovia) within a few weeks of each other. It turns out that we have a number of additional independent variables for the data set we used to estimate Equation 1.21. Also available are:

N_i = the quality of the neighborhood of the *i*th house (1 = best, 4 = worst) as rated by two local real estate agents
A_i = the age of the *i*th house in years
BE_i = the number of bedrooms in the *i*th house
BA_i = the number of bathrooms in the *i*th house

8. Keith Ihlanfeldt and Jorge Martinez-Vasquez, "Alternate Value Estimates of Owner-Occupied Housing: Evidence on Sample Selection Bias and Systematic Errors," *Journal of Urban Economics*, Vol. 20, No. 3, pp. 356–369. Also see Eric Cassel and Robert Mendelsohn, "The Choice of Functional Forms for Hedonic Price Equations: Comment," *Journal of Urban Economics*, Vol. 18, No. 2, pp. 135–142.

9. Allen C. Goodman, "An Econometric Model of Housing Price, Permanent Income, Tenure Choice, and Housing Demand," *Journal of Urban Economics*, Vol. 23, pp. 327–353.

CA_i = a dummy variable equal to 1 if the *i*th house has central air conditioning, 0 otherwise

SP_i = a dummy variable equal to 1 if the *i*th house has a pool, 0 otherwise

Y_i = the size of the yard around the *i*th house (in square feet)

Read through the list of variables again, developing your own analyses of the theory behind each variable. What are the expected signs of the coefficients? Which variables seem potentially redundant? Which variables *must* you include?

In addition, there are a number of functional form modifications that can be made. For example, you might consider a quadratic polynomial for age, as Grether and Mieszkowski did, or you might consider creating slope dummies such as SP · S or CA · S. Finally, you might consider interactive variables that involve the neighborhood proxy variable such as N · S or N · BA. What hypotheses would each of these imply?

Develop your specification carefully. Think through each variable and/or functional form decision, and take the time to write out your expectations for the sign and size of each coefficient. Don't take the attitude that you should include *every* possible variable and functional form modification and then drop the insignificant ones. Instead, try to design the best possible hedonic model of housing prices you can the first time around.

Once you've chosen a specification, estimate your equation, using the data in Table 11.4 and analyze the result.

Table 11.4 Data for the Housing Price Interactive Exercise

P	S	N	A	BE	BA	CA	SP	Y
107	736	4	39	2	1	0	0	3364
133	720	3	63	2	1	0	0	1780
141	768	2	66	2	1	0	0	6532
165	929	3	41	3	1	0	0	2747
170	1080	2	44	3	1	0	0	5520
173	942	2	65	2	1	0	0	6808
182	1000	2	40	3	1	0	0	6100
200	1472	1	66	3	2	0	0	5328
220	1200	1.5	69	3	1	0	0	5850
226	1302	2	49	3	2	0	0	5298
260	2109	2	37	3	2	1	0	3691
275	1528	1	41	2	2	0	0	5860

(continued)

Table 11.4 (*continued*)

P	S	N	A	BE	BA	CA	SP	Y
280	1421	1	41	3	2	0	1	6679
289	1753	1	1	3	2	1	0	2304
295	1528	1	32	3	2	0	0	6292
300	1643	1	29	3	2	0	1	7127
310	1675	1	63	3	2	0	0	9025
315	1714	1	38	3	2	1	0	6466
350	2150	2	75	4	2	0	0	14825
365	2206	1	28	4	2.5	1	0	8147
503	3269	1	5	4	2.5	1	0	10045
135	936	4	75	2	1	0	0	5054
147	728	3	40	2	1	0	0	1922
165	1014	3	26	2	1	0	0	6416
175	1661	3	27	3	2	1	0	4939
190	1248	2	42	3	1	0	0	7952
191	1834	3.5	40	3	2	0	1	6710
195	989	2	41	3	1	0	0	5911
205	1232	1	43	2	2	0	0	4618
210	1017	1	38	2	1	0	0	5083
215	1216	2	77	2	1	0	0	6834
228	1447	2	44	2	2	0	0	4143
242	1974	1.5	65	4	2	0	1	5499
250	1600	1.5	63	3	2	1	0	4050
250	1168	1.5	63	3	1	0	1	5182
255	1478	1	50	3	2	0	0	4122
255	1756	2	36	3	2	0	1	6420
265	1542	2	38	3	2	0	0	6833
265	1633	1	32	4	2	0	1	7117
275	1500	1	42	2	2	1	0	7406
285	1734	1	62	3	2	0	1	8583
365	1900	1	42	3	2	1	0	19580
397	2468	1	10	4	2.5	1	0	6086

Datafile = HOUSE11

1. Test your hypotheses for each coefficient with the *t*-test. Pay special attention to any functional form modifications.

2. Decide what econometric problems exist in the equation, testing, if appropriate, for multicollinearity, serial correlation, or heteroskedasticity.

3. Decide whether to accept your first specification as the best one or to make a modification in your equation and estimate again. Make sure you avoid the temptation to estimate an additional specification "just to see what it looks like."

Once you've decided to make no further changes, you're finished—congratulations! Now turn to the hints in Appendix A for feedback on your choices.

Chapter 12

Time-Series Models

12.1 **Distributed Lag Models**

12.2 **Dynamic Models**

12.3 **Serial Correlation and Dynamic Models**

12.4 **Granger Causality**

12.5 **Spurious Correlation and Nonstationarity**

12.6 **Summary and Exercises**

The purpose of this chapter is to provide an introduction to a number of interesting models that have been designed to cope with and take advantage of the special properties of time-series data. Working with time-series data often causes complications that simply can't happen with cross-sectional data. Most of these complications involve the order of the observations because order matters quite a bit in time-series data but doesn't matter much (if at all) in cross-sectional data.

The most important of the topics concerns a class of dynamic models in which a lagged value of the dependent variable appears on the right-hand side of the equation. As you will see, the presence of a lagged dependent variable on the right-hand side of the equation implies that the impact of the independent variables can be spread out over a number of time periods.

Why would you want to distribute the impact of an independent variable over a number of time periods? To see why, consider the impact of advertising on sales. Most analysts believe that people remember advertising for more than one time period, so advertising affects sales in the future as well as in the current time period. As a result, models of sales should include current *and lagged* values of advertising, thus distributing the impact of advertising over a number of different lags.

While this chapter focuses on such dynamic models, you'll also learn about models in which different numbers of lags appear and we'll investigate how the presence of these lags affects our estimators. The chapter concludes with a brief introduction to a topic called nonstationarity. If variables have significant changes in basic properties (like their mean or variance) over time, they are said to be nonstationary, and it turns out that nonstationary variables have the potential to inflate t-scores and measures of overall fit in an equation.

12.1 Distributed Lag Models

As described in Section 7.3, lagged independent variables can be used whenever you expect X to affect Y after a period of time. For example, if the underlying theory suggests that X_1 affects Y with a one-time-period lag (but X_2 has an instantaneous impact on Y), we use equations like:

$$Y_t = \beta_0 + \beta_1 X_{1t-1} + \beta_2 X_{2t} + \epsilon_t \qquad (7.14)$$

Such lags are called simple lags, and the estimation of β_1 with OLS is no more difficult than the estimation of the coefficients of nonlagged equations, except for possible impure serial correlation if the lag is misspecified. Remember, however, that the coefficients of such equations should be interpreted carefully. For example, β_2 in Equation 7.14 measures the effect of a one-unit increase in this time's X_2 on this time's Y holding *last time's* X_1 constant.

A case that's more complicated than this one-period lag occurs when the impact of an independent variable is expected to be spread out over a number of time periods. Suppose, for example, that we're interested in studying the impact of a change in the money supply on GDP. Theoretical and empirical studies have provided evidence that, because of rigidities in the marketplace, it takes time for the economy to react completely to a change in the money supply. If it takes two years, some of the effect will take place immediately, some will take place with a lag of one year, and the rest will occur with a lag of two years. In such a case, the appropriate econometric model would be:

$$Y_t = \beta_0 + \beta_1 X_t + \beta_2 X_{t-1} + \beta_3 X_{t-2} + \epsilon_t \qquad (12.1)$$

where Y would be GDP and X would be the money supply. The right-hand side of Equation 12.1 is unusual, because X appears three times, each with a different lag, distributing the impact of X over a number of time periods. This is a **distributed lag model**; it explains the current value of Y as a function of current and past values of X.

Can you think of another example of a dependent variable that might be appropriately explained with a distributed lag? For instance, is your grade on an econometrics exam a function only of how much you studied the night before the test, or is it impacted by your work during the previous days and weeks? Most people would agree that with a few notable exceptions, a distributed lag model would indeed be a good way to measure the impact of studying on an exam grade.

The estimation of Equation 12.1 with OLS typically is straightforward. There will be some unavoidable multicollinearity between the Xs, but otherwise a distributed lag model like Equation 12.1 will be quite useful in a variety of applications.

However, the impact of X on Y often can be expected to continue over a large number of time periods, so in many cases we'll need more lagged values of X than are shown in Equation 12.1. If we were building a *quarterly* model of the impact of a change in the money supply on GDP, for example, then we'd need quite a few lagged independent variables, and a more general distributed lag equation would be appropriate:

$$Y_t = \alpha_0 + \beta_0 X_t + \beta_1 X_{t-1} + \beta_2 X_{t-2} + \cdots + \beta_p X_{t-p} + \epsilon_t \qquad (12.2)$$

where p is the maximum number of periods by which X is lagged. In our quarterly GDP model, p might be as high as 10 or 11. (Note that in order to have the subscript of β equal the lag in X, we've defined the constant term as α_0 and β_0 now is a slope coefficient.)

Take a careful look at Equation 12.2. The slope coefficients β_0 through β_p measure the effects of the various lagged values of X on the current value of Y (holding constant the other independent variables in the equation). In most economic applications, including our GDP example, we'd expect the impact of X on Y to decrease as the length of the lag (indicated by the subscript of the β) increases. As a result, we'd always expect β_0 and β_1 to be larger in absolute value than β_9 or β_{10}.

Unfortunately, the estimation of Equation 12.2 with OLS causes a number of problems:

1. The various lagged values of X are likely to be severely multicollinear, making coefficient estimates imprecise.

2. In large part because of this multicollinearity, there is no guarantee that the estimated βs will follow the smoothly declining pattern that economic theory would suggest. Instead, it's quite typical for the estimated coefficients of Equation 12.2 to follow a fairly irregular pattern, for example:

$$\hat{\beta}_0 = 0.26 \quad \hat{\beta}_1 = 0.07 \quad \hat{\beta}_2 = 0.17 \quad \hat{\beta}_3 = -0.03 \quad \hat{\beta}_4 = 0.08$$

3. The degrees of freedom tend to decrease, sometimes substantially, for two reasons. First, we have to estimate a coefficient for each lagged X, thus increasing K and lowering the degrees of freedom ($N - K - 1$).

Second, unless data for lagged Xs outside the sample are available, we have to decrease the sample size by 1 for each lagged X we calculate, thus lowering the number of observations, N, and therefore the degrees of freedom.

As a result of these problems with OLS estimation of distributed lag equations like Equation 12.2, it's standard practice to consider a simplifying assumption in such situations. The most commonly used simplification is to replace all the lagged independent variables with a lagged value of the dependent variable, and we'll call that kind of equation a *dynamic model*.

12.2 Dynamic Models

The simplest dynamic model is:

$$Y_t = \alpha_0 + \beta_0 X_t + \lambda Y_{t-1} + u_t \tag{12.3}$$

Note that Y is on both sides of the equation! Luckily, the subscripts are different in that the Y on the left-hand side is Y_t, and the Y on the right-hand side is Y_{t-1}. It's this difference in time period that makes the equation dynamic. Thus, the simplest **dynamic model** is an equation in which the current value of the dependent variable Y is a function of the current value of X and a lagged value of Y itself. Such a model with a lagged dependent variable is often called an *autoregressive* equation.

Let's look at Equation 12.3 to try to see why it can be used to represent a distributed lag model or any model in which the impact of X on Y is distributed over a number of lags. Suppose that we lag Equation 12.3 one time period:

$$Y_{t-1} = \alpha_0 + \beta_0 X_{t-1} + \lambda Y_{t-2} + u_{t-1} \tag{12.4}$$

If we now substitute Equation 12.4 for Y_{t-1} in Equation 12.3, we get:

$$Y_t = \alpha_0 + \beta_0 X_t + \lambda(\alpha_0 + \beta_0 X_{t-1} + \lambda Y_{t-2} + u_{t-1}) + u_t \tag{12.5}$$

or

$$Y_t = (\alpha_0 + \lambda\alpha_0) + \beta_0 X_t + \lambda\beta_0 X_{t-1} + \lambda^2 Y_{t-2} + (\lambda u_{t-1} + u_t) \tag{12.6}$$

If we do this one more time (that is, if we lag Equation 12.3 two time periods, substitute it into Equation 12.5, and rearrange), we get:

$$Y_t = \alpha_0^* + \beta_0 X_t + \lambda\beta_0 X_{t-1} + \lambda^2\beta_0 X_{t-2} + \lambda^3 Y_{t-3} + u_t^* \tag{12.7}$$

where α_0^* is the new (combined) intercept and u_t^* is the new (combined) error term. We've shown that a dynamic model can indeed be used to represent a distributed lag model!

In addition, note that the coefficients of the lagged Xs follow a clear pattern. To see this, let's go back to Equation 12.2:

$$Y_t = \alpha_0 + \beta_0 X_t + \beta_1 X_{t-1} + \beta_2 X_{t-2} + \cdots + \beta_p X_{t-p} + \epsilon_t \qquad (12.2)$$

and compare the coefficients in Equation 12.2 to those in Equation 12.7. We get:

$$\beta_1 = \lambda\beta_0 \qquad\qquad (12.8)$$
$$\beta_2 = \lambda^2\beta_0$$
$$\beta_3 = \lambda^3\beta_0$$
$$\cdot$$
$$\cdot$$
$$\cdot$$
$$\beta_p = \lambda^p\beta_0$$

As long as λ is between 0 and 1, these coefficients will indeed smoothly decline,[1] as shown in Figure 12.1.

Dynamic models like Equation 12.3 avoid the three major problems with distributed lag equations that we outlined in the previous section. The degrees of freedom have increased dramatically, and the multicollinearity problem has disappeared. If u_t is well behaved, OLS estimation of Equation 12.3 can be shown to have desirable properties for large samples. How large is "large enough"? Our recommendation, based more on experience than proof, is to aim for a sample of at least 50 observations. The smaller the sample, the more likely you are to encounter bias. In particular, estimates of λ will be biased downward, and the bias will be especially severe for larger values of λ and in the presence of additional independent variables, even irrelevant ones. As a result, samples below 30 should be avoided, in part because of this bias and in part because hypothesis testing can become unreliable.[2]

In addition to this sample size issue, dynamic models face another serious problem. It turns out that serial correlation almost surely will cause bias in the OLS estimates of dynamic models. This problem will be discussed in Section 12.3.

---

1. This model is sometimes referred to as a Koyck distributed lag model because it was originally developed by L. M. Koyck in *Distributed Lags and Investment Analysis* (Amsterdam: North-Holland Publishing, 1954).

2. David Grubb and James Symons, "Bias in Regressions with a Lagged Dependent Variable," *Econometric Theory*, Vol. 3, No. 3, pp. 371–386.

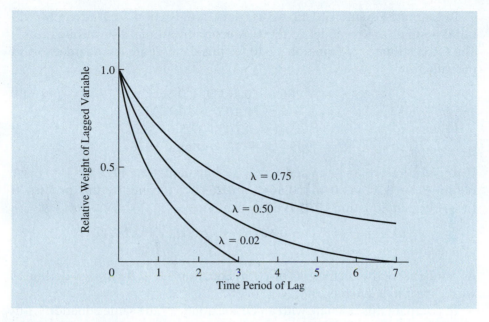

Figure 12.1 Geometric Weighting Schemes for Various Dynamic Models

As long as λ is between 0 and 1, a dynamic model has the impact of the independent variable declining as the length of the lag increases.

An Example of a Dynamic Model

As an example of a dynamic model, let's look at an aggregate consumption function from a macroeconomic equilibrium GDP model. Many economists argue that in such a model, consumption (CO_t) is not just an instantaneous function of disposable income (YD_t). Instead, they believe that current consumption is also influenced by past levels of disposable income (YD_{t-1}, YD_{t-2}, etc.):

$$CO_t = \alpha_0 + \beta_0 YD_t + \beta_1 YD_{t-1} + \beta_2 YD_{t-2} + \cdots + \beta_p YD_{t-p} + \epsilon_t \quad (12.9)$$

Such an equation fits well with simple models of consumption, but it makes sense only if the coefficients of past levels of income decrease as the length of the lag increases. That is, the impact of lagged income on current consumption should decrease as the lag gets bigger. Thus we'd expect the coefficient of YD_{t-2} to be less than the coefficient of YD_{t-1}, and so on.

As a result, most econometricians would model Equation 12.9 with a dynamic model:

$$CO_t = \alpha_0 + \beta_0 YD_t + \lambda CO_{t-1} + u_t \quad (12.10)$$

To estimate Equation 12.10, we use data from Section 14.3, where we will build a small macromodel of the U.S. economy from 1976 through 2007. The OLS estimates of Equation 12.10 for this data set are (standard errors in parentheses):

$$\widehat{CO}_t = -266.6 + 0.46YD_t + 0.56CO_{t-1} \qquad (12.11)$$
$$\phantom{\widehat{CO}_t = -266.6 +} (0.10) \qquad (0.10)$$
$$\phantom{\widehat{CO}_t = -266.6 +} t = 4.70 \qquad 5.66$$
$$\bar{R}^2 = .999 \quad N = 32 \quad \text{(annual 1976–2007)}$$

If we substitute $\hat{\beta}_0 = 0.46$ and $\hat{\lambda} = 0.56$ into Equation 12.3 for $i = 1$, we obtain $\hat{\beta}_1 = \hat{\beta}_0\hat{\lambda}^1 = (0.46)(0.56)^1 = 0.26$. If we continue this process, it turns out that Equation 12.11 is equivalent to:

$$\widehat{CO}_t = -605.91 + 0.46YD_t + 0.26YD_{t-1} + 0.14YD_{t-2} \qquad (12.12)$$
$$+ 0.08YD_{t-3} + \cdots$$

As can be seen, the coefficients of YD in Equation 12.12 do indeed decline as we'd expect in a dynamic model.

To compare this estimate with an OLS estimate of the same equation without the dynamic model format, we'd need to estimate a distributed lag equation with at least three lagged variables.

$$CO_t = \alpha_0 + \beta_0 YD_t + \beta_1 YD_{t-1} + \beta_2 YD_{t-2} + \beta_3 YD_{t-3} + \epsilon_t \qquad (12.13)$$

If we estimate Equation 12.13 using the same data set, we get:

$$\widehat{CO}_t = -695.89 + 0.73YD_t + 0.39YD_{t-1} + 0.006YD_{t-2} - 0.08YD_{t-3}$$
$$(12.14)$$

How do the coefficients of Equation 12.14 look? As the lag increases, the coefficients of YD decrease sharply, actually going negative for t–3. Neither economic theory nor common sense leads us to expect this pattern. Such a poor result is due to the severe multicollinearity between the lagged Xs. Most econometricians therefore estimate consumption functions with a lagged dependent variable simplification scheme like the dynamic model in Equation 12.10.

An interesting interpretation of the results in Equation 12.11 concerns the long-run multiplier implied by the model. The long-run multiplier measures the total impact of a change in income on consumption after all the lagged effects have been felt. One way to get this estimate would be to add up all the $\hat{\beta}$s, but an easier alternative is to calculate $\hat{\beta}_0[1/(1 - \hat{\lambda})]$, which in this case equals $0.46[1/(1 - 0.56)]$ or 1.05. A sample of this size is likely to encounter small sample bias, however, so we shouldn't overanalyze the results. For more on this data set and the other equations in the model, see Section 14.3. For more on testing and adjusting dynamic equations like Equation 12.11 for serial correlation, let's move on to the next section.

12.3 Serial Correlation and Dynamic Models

The consequences of serial correlation depend crucially on the type of model we're talking about. For a distributed lag model such as Equation 12.2, serial correlation has the effects outlined in Section 9.3: Serial correlation causes: (1) OLS to no longer be the minimum variance unbiased estimator, (2) the $SE(\hat{\beta})$s to be biased, and (3) no bias in the OLS $\hat{\beta}$s themselves.

For dynamic models such as Equation 12.3, however, all this changes, and serial correlation does indeed cause bias in the $\hat{\beta}$s produced by OLS. Compounding this is the fact that the detection of and remedies for serial correlation that we discussed in Chapter 9 need to be modified in the presence of a lagged dependent variable.

Serial Correlation Causes Bias in Dynamic Models

If an equation with a lagged dependent variable as an independent variable has a serially correlated error term, then OLS estimates of the coefficients will be biased, even in large samples.

To see where this bias comes from, let's start with a dynamic model:

$$Y_t = \alpha_0 + \beta_0 X_t + \lambda Y_{t-1} + u_t \tag{12.3}$$

and lag it one time period:

$$\overset{\uparrow}{Y_{t-1}} = \alpha_0 + \beta_0 X_{t-1} + \lambda Y_{t-2} + \overset{\uparrow}{u_{t-1}} \tag{12.15}$$

As you can see from the upward-pointing arrows above Equation 12.15, if u_{t-1} is positive, then Y_{t-1} will be higher than it would have been otherwise.

In addition, if u_t is serially correlated, then we know that:

$$\overset{\uparrow}{u_t} = \overset{\uparrow}{\rho u_{t-1}} + \epsilon_t \tag{12.16}$$

where ϵ_t is a classical error term with an expected value of zero. As you can see from the arrows above Equation 12.16, if u_{t-1} is positive, then u_t will be higher than it would have been otherwise as long as ρ is positive, as it typically is in economic applications.

If we add the arrows from Equations 12.15 and 12.16 to Equation 12.3, we get:

$$Y_t = \alpha_0 + \beta_0 X_t + \overset{\uparrow}{\lambda Y_{t-1}} + \overset{\uparrow}{u_t} \tag{12.3}$$

Take a look at the arrows in Equation 12.3. Y_{t-1} and u_t are correlated! Such a correlation violates Classical Assumption III, which assumes that the error term is not correlated with any of the explanatory variables. (If u_{t-1} is negative, then both u_t and Y_{t-1} will be lower than they would have been otherwise, which again violates Classical Assumption III.)

The consequences of this correlation include biased estimates, in particular of the coefficient λ, because OLS attributes to Y_{t-1} some of the change in Y_t actually caused by u_t. In essence, the uncorrected serial correlation acts like an omitted variable (u_{t-1}). Since an omitted variable causes bias whenever it is correlated with one of the included independent variables, and since u_{t-1} is correlated with Y_{t-1}, the combination of a lagged dependent variable and serial correlation causes bias in the coefficient estimates. This bias is in addition to the bias mentioned on page 368.

Testing for Serial Correlation in Dynamic Models

If serial correlation causes bias in a dynamic model, then tests for serial correlation are obviously important. Unfortunately, however, the Durbin–Watson test is potentially invalid for an equation that contains a lagged dependent variable as an independent variable because the Durbin–Watson statistic is biased toward 2 in a dynamic equation. This bias toward 2 means that serial correlation in a dynamic model is more likely to evade detection by the Durbin–Watson test.[3]

Luckily, the *Lagrange Multiplier (LM)* serial correlation test of Section 9.4 still is valid even in the face of a lagged dependent variable. Using the Lagrange Multiplier to test for serial correlation in a typical dynamic model involves three steps that should seem familiar:

1. Obtain the residuals from the estimated equation:

$$e_t = Y_t - \hat{Y}_t = Y_t - \hat{\alpha}_0 - \hat{\beta}_0 X_{1t} - \hat{\lambda} Y_{t-1} \tag{12.17}$$

2. Use these residuals as the dependent variable in an auxiliary equation that includes as independent variables all those on the right-hand side of the original equation as well as the lagged residuals:

$$e_t = a_0 + a_1 X_t + a_2 Y_{t-1} + a_3 e_{t-1} + u_t \tag{12.18}$$

---

3. The opposite is not a problem. A Durbin–Watson test that indicates serial correlation in the presence of a lagged dependent variable, despite the bias toward 2, is an even stronger affirmation of serial correlation.

3. Estimate Equation 12.18 using OLS and then test the null hypothesis that $a_3 = 0$ with the following test statistic:

$$LM = NR^2 \qquad (12.19)$$

where N is the sample size and R^2 is the unadjusted coefficient of determination, both of the auxiliary equation, Equation 12.18. For large samples, NR^2 has a chi-square distribution with degrees of freedom equal to the number of restrictions in the null hypothesis (in this case, one). If NR^2 is greater than the critical chi-square value from Statistical Table B-6, then we reject the null hypothesis that $a_3 = 0$ and conclude that there is indeed serial correlation in the original equation.

As an example of testing for serial correlation in a dynamic model, let's run a Lagrange Multiplier (LM) serial correlation test on Equation 12.11, the consumption function we estimated in the previous section. If we estimate the auxiliary equation for that model, we get an R^2 of .4025 which, when multiplied by the sample size of 31 (do you see why it's 31 and not 32?), produces an NR^2 of 12.48. 12.48 is greater than 3.84, the 5-percent critical chi-square value with one degree of freedom, so we have strong evidence of serial correlation in Equation 12.11. What should we do?

Correcting for Serial Correlation in Dynamic Models

If the Lagrange Multiplier test indicates serial correlation in a dynamic model, the first step is to consider the possibility that the serial correlation is impure, perhaps caused by omission of a relevant variable and/or by failure to capture the actual distributed lag pattern accurately.

If the serial correlation appears to be pure, then the theoretically preferred solution is to transform the equation so as to eliminate the serial correlation and re-estimate the model. The required transformation is quite similar to the Generalized Least Squares approach to serial correlation described in Section 9.5. Unfortunately, the iterative nonlinear estimation of the transformed equation is well beyond the scope of this text, so it's not a realistic alternative for most readers.[4] Instead, our suggestion is to use one of two alternatives, depending on the underlying theory of the model and the size of the sample.

If theory indicates that only a few lagged values of X are meaningful in explaining Y, then a potential way to avoid the bias due to serial correlation

---

4. Readers interested in this approach should see Sean Becketti, "Introduction to Time Series Using Stata" (College Station: Stata Press, 2013), pp. 192–195.

is to estimate a distributed lag model (Equation 12.2 with p = 1 or 2) instead of a dynamic model. The distributed lag model will have potential multicollinearity but will not likely face the other problems typically associated with distributed lag models because p is so low. Most econometricians would prefer to deal with the consequences of multicollinearity than to face bias, so this is an improvement. There's a second advantage to distributed lags. The X_{t-p} terms, in essence, are acting as proxies for Y_{t-1}. As we'll learn in Chapter 14, such proxies are similar to *instrumental variables*, and they are especially useful because they will eliminate bias if they're uncorrelated with the error term.

In a small sample, the best approach may well be to continue to use OLS even in the face of serial correlation in a dynamic model. For a nontrivial subset of real-world examples, OLS actually outperforms more sophisticated techniques. One reason is that in a small sample, the estimation bias in λ mentioned in Section 12.2 and the bias introduced by serial correlation often are of opposite signs, so they offset each other. As a result, OLS can do better than a technique that eliminates only the bias caused by serial correlation.[5] The second reason is that there's evidence from Monte Carlo studies that the size of the bias introduced by serial correlation in small samples often is fairly low.[6]

To sum, unless you're comfortable with iterative nonlinear least squares, our suggestion for dealing with serial correlation in dynamic models depends on theory and the sample size. If theory calls for very few lagged Xs, we suggest the distributed lag approach. If the sample is small, we think continuing to use OLS, even in the face of serial correlation, presents the best alternative. If both the sample and the meaningful number of lagged Xs are large, we'd recommend using distributed lags because of the benefits of the instrumental variable approach.

12.4 Granger Causality

One application of distributed lag models is to provide evidence about the direction of causality in economic relationships. Such a test is useful when we know that two variables are related but we don't know which variable causes the other to move. For example, most economists believe that increases in the

5. Asatoshi Maeshiro, "Teaching Regressions with a Lagged Dependent Variable and Autocorrelated Disturbances," *Journal of Economic Education*, Vol. 27, No. 1, pp. 72–84.

6. Luke Keele and Nathan Kelly, "Dynamic Models for Dynamic Theories: The Ins and Outs of Lagged Dependent Variables," *Political Analysis*, Vol. 14, No. 2, pp. 186–205.

money supply stimulate GDP, but others feel that increases in GDP eventually lead the monetary authorities to increase the money supply. Who's right?

One approach to such a question of indeterminate causality is to theorize that the two variables are determined simultaneously. We'll address the estimation of simultaneous equation models in Chapter 14. A second approach to the problem is to test for what is called "Granger causality."

How can we claim to be able to test for causality? After all, didn't we say in Chapter 1 that even though most economic relationships are causal in nature, regression analysis can't prove such causality? The answer is that we don't actually test for theoretical causality; instead, we test for Granger causality.

Granger causality, or precedence, is a circumstance in which one time-series variable consistently and predictably changes before another variable.[7] Granger causality is important because it allows us to analyze which variable precedes or "leads" the other, and, as we shall see, such leading variables are extremely useful for forecasting purposes.

Despite the value of Granger causality, however, we shouldn't let ourselves be lured into thinking that it allows us to prove economic causality in any rigorous way. If one variable precedes ("Granger causes") another, we can't be sure that the first variable "causes" the other to change.[8] As a result, even if we're able to show that event A always happens before event B, we have not shown that event A "causes" event B.

There are a number of different tests for Granger causality, and all the various methods involve lagged dependent variables in one way or another.[9] Our preference is to use an expanded version of a test originally developed by Granger. Granger suggested that to see if A Granger-caused Y, we should run:

$$Y_t = \beta_0 + \beta_1 Y_{t-1} + \cdots + \beta_p Y_{t-p} + \alpha_1 A_{t-1} + \cdots + \alpha_p A_{t-p} + \epsilon_t \qquad (12.20)$$

7. See C. W. J. Granger, "Investigating Causal Relations by Econometric Models and Cross-Spectral Methods," *Econometrica*, Vol. 37, No. 3, pp. 424–438.

8. In a previous edition, we ended this paragraph by saying, "For example, Christmas cards typically arrive before Christmas, but it's clear that Christmas wasn't caused by the arrival of the cards." However, this isn't a true example of Granger causality, because the date of Christmas is fixed and therefore isn't a "time-series variable." See Erdal Atukeren, "Christmas cards, Easter bunnies, and Granger-causality," *Quality & Quantity*, Vol. 42, No. 6, Dec. 2008, pp. 835–844. For an in-depth discussion of causality, see Kevin Hoover, *Causality in Macroeconomics* (Cambridge: Cambridge University Press, 2001).

9. See John Geweke, R. Meese, and W. Dent, "Comparing Alternative Tests of Causality in Temporal Systems," *Journal of Econometrics*, Vol. 21, pp. 161–194, and Rodney Jacobs, Edward Leamer, and Michael Ward, "Difficulties with Testing for Causation," *Economic Inquiry*, Vol. 17, No. 3, pp. 401–413.

and test the null hypothesis that the coefficients of the lagged As (the αs) jointly equal zero.[10] If we can reject this null hypothesis using the F-test, then we have evidence that A Granger-causes Y. Note that if p = 0, Equation 12.20 is similar to the dynamic model, Equation 12.3.

Applications of this test involve running two Granger tests, one in each direction. That is, run Equation 12.20 and also run:

$$A_t = \beta_0 + \beta_1 A_{t-1} + \cdots + \beta_p A_{t-p} + \alpha_1 Y_{t-1} + \cdots + \alpha_p Y_{t-p} + \epsilon_t \qquad (12.21)$$

testing for Granger causality in both directions by testing the null hypothesis that the coefficients of the lagged Ys (again, the αs) jointly equal zero. If the F-test is significant for Equation 12.20 but not for Equation 12.21, then we can conclude that A Granger-causes Y.

12.5   Spurious Correlation and Nonstationarity

One problem with time-series data is that independent variables can appear to be more significant than they actually are if they have the same underlying trend as the dependent variable. In a country with rampant inflation, for example, almost any nominal variable will appear to be highly correlated with all other nominal variables. Why? Nominal variables are unadjusted for inflation, so every nominal variable will have a powerful inflationary component. This inflationary component will usually outweigh any real causal relationship, making nominal variables appear to be correlated even if they aren't.

Such a problem is an example of **spurious correlation**, a strong relationship between two or more variables that is not caused by a real underlying causal relationship. If you run a regression in which the dependent variable and one or more independent variables are spuriously correlated, the result is a *spurious regression*, and the t-scores and overall fit of such spurious regressions are likely to be overstated and untrustworthy.

There are many causes of spurious correlation. In a cross-sectional data set, for example, spurious correlation can be caused by dividing both the dependent variable and at least one independent variable by a third variable that varies considerably more than do the others. The focus of this section, however, will be on time-series data and in particular on spurious correlation caused by *nonstationary time series*.

---

10. Such a joint test requires the use of the F-test of Section 5.6.

Stationary and Nonstationary Time Series

A stationary series is one whose basic properties, for example, its mean and its variance, do not change over time. In contrast, a nonstationary series has one or more basic properties that *do* change over time. For instance, the real per capita output of an economy typically increases over time, so it's nonstationary. By contrast, the growth *rate* of real per capita output often does not increase over time, so this variable is stationary even though the variable it's based on, real per capita output, is nonstationary. A time series can be nonstationary even with a constant mean if another property, such as the variance, changes over time.

More formally, a time-series variable, X_t, is **stationary** if:

1. the mean of X_t is constant over time,
2. the variance of X_t is constant over time, and
3. the simple correlation coefficient between X_t and X_{t-k} depends on the length of the lag (k) but on no other variable (for all k).[11]

If one or more of these properties is not met, then X_t is **nonstationary**. And if a series is nonstationary, that problem is referred to as *nonstationarity*.

Although our definition of a stationary series focuses on stationary and nonstationary *variables*, it's important to note that *error terms* (and, therefore, residuals) also can be nonstationary. In fact, we've already had experience with a nonstationary error term. Many cases of heteroskedasticity in time-series data involve an error term with a variance that tends to increase with time. That kind of heteroskedastic error term is also nonstationary!

The major consequence of nonstationarity for regression analysis is spurious correlation that inflates R^2 and the *t*-scores of the nonstationary independent variables, which in turn leads to incorrect model specification. This occurs because the regression estimation procedure attributes to the nonstationary X_t changes in Y_t that were actually caused by some factor (trend, for example) that also affects X_t. Thus, the variables move together because of the nonstationarity, increasing R^2 and the relevant *t*-scores. This is especially

---

11. There are two different definitions of stationarity. The particular definition we use here is a simplification of the most frequently cited definition, referred to by various authors as weak, wide-sense, or covariance stationarity. In addition, there are many models of nonstationarity, for example ARCH and GARCH, that are significantly more sophisticated than the model of nonstationarity introduced in this section.

important in macroeconometrics, and the macroeconomic literature includes many articles that examine various series for signs of nonstationarity.[12]

Some variables are nonstationary mainly because they increase rapidly over time. Spurious regression results involving these kinds of variables often can be avoided by the addition of a simple time trend ($t = 1, 2, 3, \ldots, T$) to the equation as an independent variable.

Unfortunately, many economic time-series variables are nonstationary even after the removal of a time trend. This nonstationarity often takes the form of the variable behaving as though it were a "random walk." A **random walk** is a time-series variable in which the next period's value equals this period's value plus a stochastic error term. A random-walk variable is nonstationary because it can wander up and down without an inherent equilibrium and without approaching a long-term mean of any sort.

To get a better understanding of how a random walk gives rise to nonstationarity, let's suppose that Y_t is generated by an equation that includes only past values of itself (an *autoregressive* equation):

$$Y_t = \gamma Y_{t-1} + v_t \tag{12.22}$$

where v_t is a classical error term.

Take a look at Equation 12.22. Can you see that if $|\gamma| < 1$, then the expected value of Y_t will eventually approach 0 (and therefore be stationary) as the sample size gets bigger and bigger? (Remember, since v_t is a classical error term, its expected value $= 0$.) Similarly, can you see that if $|\gamma| > 1$, then the expected absolute value of Y_t will continuously increase, making Y_t nonstationary? This is nonstationarity due to a trend, but it still can cause spurious regression results.

Most importantly, what about if $|\gamma| = 1$? In this case,

$$Y_t = Y_{t-1} + v_t \tag{12.23}$$

It's a random walk! The expected value of Y_t does not converge on any value, meaning that it is nonstationary. This circumstance, where $\gamma = 1$ in Equation 12.23 (or similar equations), is called a **unit root**. If a variable has a unit root, then Equation 12.23 holds, and the variable follows a random walk and is nonstationary. The relationship between unit roots and nonstationarity is so strong that some econometricians use the words interchangeably, even though they recognize that many factors other than unit roots can cause nonstationarity.

---

12. See, for example, C. R. Nelson and C. I. Plosser, "Trends and Random Walks in Macroeconomics Time Series: Some Evidence and Implication," *Journal of Monetary Economics*, Vol. 10, pp. 169–182, and J. Campbell and N. G. Mankiw, "Permanent and Transitory Components in Macroeconomic Fluctuations," *American Economic Review*, Vol. 77, No. 2, pp. 111–117.

Spurious Regression

As noted at the beginning of this section, if the dependent variable and at least one independent variable in an equation are trending, as they will if they contain unit roots, it's possible for the results of an OLS regression to be spurious.[13]

Consider the linear regression model

$$Y_t = \alpha_0 + \beta_0 X_t + u_t \tag{12.24}$$

If both X and Y are nonstationary, then they can be highly correlated for non-causal reasons, and our standard regression inference measures will be very misleading in that they'll overstate $\overline{R}^2$ and the t-score for $\hat{\beta}_0$.

For example, take a look at the following estimated equation:

$$\widehat{PRICE}_t = -27.8 + 0.070 TUITION_t \tag{12.25}$$
$$(0.006)$$
$$t = 11.4$$
$$\overline{R}^2 = .94 \qquad T = 10(\text{annual})$$

The $\overline{R}^2$ of this equation and the t-score for the coefficient of TUITION are clearly significant, but what are the definitions of the variables? Well, PRICE is the price of a gallon of gasoline in Portland, Oregon, and TUITION is the tuition for a semester of study at Occidental College (Oxy) in Los Angeles (both measured in nominal dollars). Is it possible that an increase in the tuition at Oxy caused gas prices in Portland to go up? Not unless every Oxy student was the child of a Portland gas station owner! What's going on? Well, this regression is from the 1970s, a decade of inflation, so any nominally measured variables are likely to result in an equation that fits as well as Equation 12.25. Both variables are nonstationary, and this particular regression result clearly is spurious.

To avoid spurious regression results, it's crucial to be sure that time-series variables are stationary before running regressions.

The Dickey–Fuller Test

To ensure that the equations we estimate are not spurious, it's important to test for nonstationarity. If we can be reasonably sure that all the variables are stationary, then we need not worry about spurious regressions. How can you tell if a time series is nonstationary? The first step is to visually examine the

---

13. See C. W. J. Granger and P. Newbold, "Spurious Regression in Econometrics," *Journal of Econometrics*, Volume 2, pp. 111–120.

data. For many time series, a quick glance at the data (or a diagram of the data) will tell you that the mean of a variable is increasing dramatically over time and that the series is nonstationary.

After this trend has been removed, the standard method of testing for non-stationarity is the **Dickey–Fuller test**,[14] which examines the hypothesis that the variable in question has a unit root[15] and, as a result, is likely to benefit from being expressed in first-difference form.

To best understand how the Dickey–Fuller test works, let's return to the discussion of the role that unit roots play in the distinction between stationarity and nonstationarity. Recall that we looked at the value of γ in Equation 12.22 to help us determine if Y was stationary or nonstationary:

$$Y_t = \gamma Y_{t-1} + v_t \tag{12.22}$$

We decided that if $|\gamma| < 1$, then Y is stationary, and that if $|\gamma| > 1$, then Y_t is nonstationary. However, if $|\gamma| = 1$, then Y_t is nonstationary due to a unit root. Thus we concluded that the autoregressive model is stationary if $|\gamma| < 1$ and nonstationary otherwise.

From this discussion of stationarity and unit roots, it makes sense to esti-mate Equation 12.22 and determine if $|\gamma| < 1$ to see if Y is stationary, and that's almost exactly how the Dickey–Fuller test works. First, we subtract Y_{t-1} from both sides of Equation 12.22, yielding:

$$(Y_t - Y_{t-1}) = (\gamma - 1)Y_{t-1} + v_t \tag{12.26}$$

If we define $\Delta Y_t = Y_t - Y_{t-1}$ then we have the simplest form of the Dickey–Fuller test:

$$\Delta Y_t = \beta_1 Y_{t-1} + v_t \tag{12.27}$$

where $\beta_1 = \gamma - 1$. The null hypothesis is that Y_t contains a unit root and is therefore nonstationary, and the alternative hypothesis is that Y_t is stationary. If Y_t contains a unit root, $\gamma = 1$ and $\beta_1 = 0$. If Y_t is stationary, $|\gamma| < 1$ and $\beta_1 < 0$. Hence we construct a one-sided t-test on the hypothesis that $\beta_1 = 0$:

$$H_0: \beta_1 = 0$$
$$H_A: \beta_1 < 0$$

---

14. D. A. Dickey and W. A. Fuller, "Distribution of the Estimators for Autoregressive Time-Series with a Unit Root," *Journal of the American Statistical Association*, Vol. 74, pp. 427–431.

15. For more on unit roots, see John Y. Campbell and Pierre Peron, "Pitfalls and Opportuni-ties: What Macroeconomists Should Know About Unit Roots," *NBER Macroeconomics Annual* (Cambridge, MA: MIT Press, 1991), pp. 141–219.

The Dickey–Fuller test actually comes in three versions:

1. Equation 12.27,
2. Equation 12.27 with a constant term added (Equation 12.28), and
3. Equation 12.27 with a constant term and a trend term added (Equation 12.29).

The form of the Dickey–Fuller test in Equation 12.27 is correct if Y_t follows Equation 12.22, but most econometricians add a constant term to the equation, for reasons similar to those mentioned in Section 7.1, so the basic Dickey–Fuller test equation becomes:

$$\Delta Y_t = \beta_0 + \beta_1 Y_{t-1} + v_t \qquad (12.28)$$

Alternatively, if we believe Y_t contains a trend "t" ($t = 1, 2, 3, \ldots, T$), then we'd add "t" to the equation as a *variable* with a coefficient, and the appropriate Dickey–Fuller test equation is:

$$\Delta Y_t = \beta_0 + \beta_1 Y_{t-1} + \beta_2 t + v_t \qquad (12.29)$$

How do we decide whether to use Equation 12.28 or Equation 12.29? If you compare the two equations, you can see that the only difference between them is a trend term ($\beta_2 t$) that's in Equation 12.29 but not in Equation 12.28. Thus Equation 12.29 is appropriate if Y is growing and Equation 12.28 is appropriate if Y is not growing. Perhaps the best way to make this decision is to plot Y over time and then judge whether or not it appears to be growing.[16] GDP and consumption are good examples of variables that usually are growing over time, while most rates (like interest rates and unemployment rates) are good examples of variables that are not growing.

No matter which form of the Dickey–Fuller test we use, the decision rule is the same. If $\hat{\beta}_1$ is significantly less than 0 as measured by a *t*-test, then we can reject the null hypothesis of a unit root; this implies that the variable is stationary. If $\hat{\beta}_1$ is not significantly less than 0, then we cannot reject the null hypothesis of a unit root; this implies that the variable is nonstationary. (Recall from Chapter 5 that if we're not able to reject the null hypothesis, we still have not "proven" that Y is nonstationary.)

---

16. John Elder and Peter Kennedy, "Testing for Unit Roots: What Should Students Be Taught?" *Journal of Economic Education*, Vol. 32, No. 2, pp. 137–146. Elder and Kennedy also investigate what to do in the unlikely case that the growth status of Y is unknown.

Be careful, however. The standard *t*-table does not apply to Dickey–Fuller tests. Instead the critical values are somewhat higher than those in Statistical Table B-1, and they also depend on the version of the Dickey–Fuller test you use. In Table 12.1,[17] we list critical values for the two versions of the Dickey–Fuller test we have discussed the most, Equations 12.28 and 12.29. For example, a 5-percent one-sided test of β_1 in Equation 12.28 with a sample size of 25 has a critical *t*-value of 3.00 compared to 1.717 for a standard *t*-test (with 22 degrees of freedom since K = 2).

The Dickey–Fuller specifications in Equations 12.28 and 12.29 and the critical values for those specifications are derived under the assumption that the error term is serially uncorrelated. If the error term is serially correlated, then the test must be modified to take this serial correlation into account. This adjustment, called the Augmented Dickey–Fuller test (ADF), adds a series of lagged values of ΔY to the Dickey–Fuller test. While the ADF is the most-used version of the Dickey–Fuller test, it is beyond the scope of this textbook, at least in part because choosing how many lagged ΔY values to include can be quite complicated.

Cointegration

If the Dickey–Fuller test reveals nonstationarity, what should we do?

The traditional approach is to take the first differences ($\Delta Y = Y_t - Y_{t-1}$ and $\Delta X = X_t - X_{t-1}$) and use them in place of Y_t and X_t in the equation.

Table 12.1 5-Percent One-Sided Critical Values for the Dickey–Fuller test

Sample Size (T)	For Equation 12.28 (Y not growing)	For Equation 12.29 (Y growing)
25	3.00	3.60
50	2.93	3.50
100	2.89	3.45
∞	2.86	3.41

17. Most sources list negative critical values for the Dickey–Fuller test, because the unit root test is one-sided with a negative expected value. However, the *t*-test decision rule of this text is based on the absolute value of the *t*-score, so negative critical values would cause every null hypothesis to be rejected. As a result, the critical values in Table 12.1 are positive. For adjusted critical *t*-values for the Dickey–Fuller test, including those in Table 12.1, see J. G. MacKinnon, "Critical Values of Cointegration Tests," in Rob Engle and C. W. J. Granger, eds., *Long-Run Economic Relationships: Readings in Cointegration* (New York: Oxford University Press, 1991), Chapter 13. Most software packages provide these critical values with the output from a Dickey–Fuller test.

With economic data, taking a first difference usually is enough to convert a nonstationary series into a stationary one. Unfortunately, using first differences to correct for nonstationarity throws away information that economic theory can provide in the form of equilibrium relationships between the variables when they are expressed in their original units (X_t and Y_t). As a result, first differences should not be used without carefully weighing the costs and benefits of that shift, and in particular first differences should not be used until the residuals have been tested for *cointegration*.

Cointegration consists of matching the degree of nonstationarity of the variables in an equation in a way that makes the error term (and residuals) of the equation stationary and rids the equation of any spurious regression results. Even though individual variables might be nonstationary, it's possible for linear combinations of nonstationary variables to be stationary, or *cointegrated*. If a long-run equilbrium relationship exists between a set of variables, those variables are said to be cointegrated. If the variables are cointegrated, then you can avoid spurious regressions even though the dependent variable and at least one independent variable are nonstationary.

To see how this works, let's return to Equation 12.24:

$$Y_t = \alpha_0 + \beta_0 X_t + u_t \tag{12.24}$$

As we saw in the previous section, if X_t and Y_t are nonstationary, it's likely that we'll get spurious regression results. To understand how it's possible to get sensible results from Equation 12.24 if the nonstationary variables are cointegrated, let's focus on the case in which both X_t and Y_t contain one unit root. The key to cointegration is the behavior of u_t.

If we solve Equation 12.24 for u_t, we get:

$$u_t = Y_t - \alpha_0 - \beta_0 X_t \tag{12.30}$$

In Equation 12.30, u_t is a function of two nonstationary variables, so you'd certainly expect u_t also to be nonstationary, but that's not necessarily the case. In particular, suppose that X_t and Y_t are related? More specifically, if economic theory supports Equation 12.24 as an equilibrium, then departures from that equilibrium should not be arbitrarily large.

Hence, if Y_t and X_t are related, then the error term u_t may well be stationary even though X_t and Y_t are nonstationary. If u_t is stationary, then the unit roots in Y_t and X_t have "cancelled out" and Y_t and X_t are said to be cointegrated.[18]

---

18. For more on cointegration, see Peter Kennedy, *A Guide to Econometrics* (Malden, MA: Blackwell, 2008), pp. 309–313 and 327–330, and B. Bhaskara Rau, ed., *Cointegration for the Applied Economist* (New York: St. Martin's Press, 1994).

We thus see that if X_t and Y_t are cointegrated, then OLS estimation of the coefficients in Equation 12.24 can avoid spurious results. To determine if X_t and Y_t are cointegrated, we begin with OLS estimation of Equation 12.24 and calculate the OLS residuals:

$$e_t = Y_t - \hat{\alpha}_0 - \hat{\beta}_0 X_t \tag{12.31}$$

We then perform a Dickey–Fuller test on the residuals. Once again, the standard critical t-values do not apply to this application, so adjusted critical t-values should be used.[19] If we are able to reject the null hypothesis of a unit root in the residuals, we can conclude that Y_t and X_t are cointegrated and our OLS estimates are not spurious.

To sum, if the Dickey–Fuller test reveals that our variables have unit roots, the first step is to test for cointegration in the residuals. If the nonstationary variables are not cointegrated, then the equation should be estimated using first differences (ΔY and ΔX). However, if the nonstationary variables are cointegrated, then the equation can be estimated in its original units.[20]

A Standard Sequence of Steps for Dealing with Nonstationary Time Series

This material is fairly complex, at least compared to previous chapters, so let's pause for a moment to summarize the various steps suggested in Section 12.5. To deal with the possibility that nonstationary time series might be

---

19. See J. G. MacKinnon, "Critical Values of Cointegration Tests," in Rob Engle and C. W. J. Granger, eds., *Long-Run Economic Relationships: Readings in Cointegration* (New York: Oxford University Press, 1991), Chapter 13, and Rob Engle and C. W. J. Granger, "Co-integration and Error Correction: Representation, Estimation and Testing," *Econometrica*, Vol. 55, No. 2.

20. In this case, it's common practice to use a version of the original equation called the Error Correction Model (ECM). While the equation for the ECM is fairly complex, the model itself is a logical extension of the cointegration concept. If two variables are cointegrated, then there is an equilibrium relationship connecting them. A regression on these variables therefore is an estimate of this equilibrium relationship along with a residual, which is a measure of the extent to which these variables are out of equilibrium. When formulating a dynamic relationship between the variables, economic theory suggests that the current change in the dependent variable should be affected not only by the current change in the independent variable but also by the extent to which these variables were out of equilibrium in the preceding period (the residual from the cointegrating process). The resulting equation is the ECM. For more on the ECM, see Peter Kennedy, *A Guide to Econometrics* (Malden, MA: Blackwell, 2008), pp. 299–301 and 322–323.

causing regression results to be spurious, most empirical work in time series follows a standard sequence of steps:

1. Specify the model. This model might be a time-series equation with no lagged variables, a distributed lag model or a dynamic model.

2. Test all variables for unit roots using the appropriate version of the Dickey–Fuller test.

3. If the variables don't have unit roots, estimate the equation in its original units (Y and X).

4. If the variables have unit roots, test the residuals of the equation for cointegration using the Dickey–Fuller test.

5. If the variables have unit roots but are not cointegrated, then change the functional form of the model to first differences (ΔY and ΔX) and estimate the equation.

6. If the variables have unit roots and also are cointegrated, then estimate the equation in its original units.

12.6 Summary

1. A distributed lag explains the current value of Y as a function of current and past values of X, thus "distributing" the impact of X over a number of lagged time periods. OLS estimation of distributed lag equations without any constraints encounters problems with multicollinearity, degrees of freedom, and a noncontinuous pattern of estimated coefficients over time.

2. A dynamic model avoids these problems by assuming that the coefficients of the lagged independent variables decrease in a geometric fashion the longer the lag. Given this, the dynamic model is:

$$Y_t = \alpha_0 + \beta_0 X_t + \lambda Y_{t-1} + u_t$$

where Y_{t-1} is a lagged dependent variable and $0 < \lambda < 1$.

3. In small samples, OLS estimates of a dynamic model are biased and have unreliable hypothesis testing properties. Even in large samples, OLS will produce biased estimates of the coefficients of a dynamic model if the error term is serially correlated.

4. In a dynamic model, the Durbin–Watson test is biased toward 2, so it should not be used. The most-used alternative is the Lagrange Multiplier test.

5. Granger causality, or precedence, is a circumstance in which one time-series variable consistently and predictably changes before another variable does. If one variable precedes (Granger-causes) another, we still can't be sure that the first variable "causes" the other to change.

6. A nonstationary series is one that exhibits significant changes (for example, in its mean and variance) over time. If the dependent variable and at least one independent variable are nonstationary or trending, a regression may encounter spurious correlation that inflates $\overline{R}^2$ and t-scores.

7. Nonstationarity can be detected using the Dickey–Fuller test. If the variables have unit roots and therefore are nonstationary, then the residuals of the equation should be tested for cointegration using the Dickey–Fuller test. If the variables are nonstationary but are not cointegrated, then the equation should be estimated with first differences. If the variables are nonstationary and also are cointegrated, then the equation can be estimated in its original units.

EXERCISES

(Answers to the even-numbered exercises are in Appendix A.)

1. Write the meaning of each of the following terms without referring to the book (or your notes), and then compare your definition with the version in the text for each:
   a. cointegration (p. 383)
   b. Dickey–Fuller test (p. 380)
   c. distributed lag model (p. 365)
   d. dynamic model (p. 367)
   e. Granger causality (p. 375)
   f. nonstationary (p. 377)
   g. random walk (p. 378)
   h. spurious correlation (p. 376)
   i. stationary (p. 377)
   j. unit root (p. 378)

2. Consider the following equation aimed at estimating the demand for real cash balances in Mexico (standard errors in parentheses):

$$\widehat{\ln M_t} = 2.00 - 0.10 \ln R_t + 0.70 \ln Y_t + 0.60 \ln M_{t-1}$$
$$(0.10) \qquad (0.35) \qquad (0.10)$$
$$\overline{R}^2 = .90 \qquad DW = 1.80 \qquad N = 26$$

where: M_t = the money stock in year t (millions of pesos)
R_t = the long-term interest rate in year t (percent)
Y_t = the real GNP in year t (millions of pesos)

a. What economic relationship between Y and M is implied by the equation?
b. How are Y and R similar in terms of their relationship to M?
c. Does this equation seem likely to have serial correlation? Explain.

3. You've been hired to determine the impact of advertising on gross sales revenue for "Four Musketeers" candy bars. Four Musketeers has the same price and more or less the same ingredients as competing candy bars, so it seems likely that only advertising affects sales. You decide to build a model of sales as a function of advertising, but you're not sure whether a distributed lag or a dynamic model is appropriate.

Using data on Four Musketeers candy bars from Table 12.2, estimate both of the following equations from 1985–2009 and compare the lag structures implied by the estimated coefficients. (*Hint:* Be careful to use the correct sample.)
a. distributed lag model (4 lags)
b. a dynamic model

4. Test for serial correlation in the estimated dynamic model you got as your answer to Exercise 3b.

5. Some farmers were interested in predicting inches of growth of corn as a function of rainfall on a monthly basis, so they collected data from the growing season and estimated an equation of the following form:

$$G_t = \beta_0 + \beta_1 R_t + \beta_2 G_{t-1} + \epsilon_t$$

where: G_t = inches of growth of corn in month t
R_t = inches of rain in month t
ϵ_t = a normally distributed classical error term

The farmers expected a negative sign for β_2 (they felt that since corn can only grow so much, if it grows a lot in one month, it won't grow much in the next month), but they got a positive estimate instead. What suggestions would you have for this problem?

Table 12.2 Data for the Four Musketeers Exercise

Year	Sales	Advertising
1981	*	30
1982	*	35
1983	*	36
1984	320	39
1985	360	40
1986	390	45
1987	400	50
1988	410	50
1989	400	50
1990	450	53
1991	470	55
1992	500	60
1993	500	60
1994	490	60
1995	580	65
1996	600	70
1997	700	70
1998	790	60
1999	730	60
2000	720	60
2001	800	70
2002	820	80
2003	830	80
2004	890	80
2005	900	80
2006	850	75
2007	840	75
2008	850	75
2009	850	75
Datafile = MOUSE12		

6. Run 5-percent Dickey–Fuller tests for the following variables from the chicken demand equation, using dataset CHICK9 on the text's website, and determine which variables, if any, you think are nonstationary.
   a. Y_t
   b. PC_t
   c. PB_t
   d. YD_t

7. In 2001, Heo and Tan published an article[21] in which they used the Granger causality model to test the relationship between economic growth and democracy. For years, political scientists have noted a strong positive relationship between economic growth and democracy, but the authors of previous studies (which included Granger causality studies) disagreed about the causality involved. Heo and Tan studied 32 developing countries and found that economic growth "Granger-caused" democracy in 11 countries, while democracy "Granger-caused" economic growth in 10 others.

   a. How is it possible to get significant Granger causality results in two different directions in the same study? Is this evidence that the study was done incorrectly? Is this evidence that Granger causality tests cannot be applied to this topic?

   b. Based on the evidence presented, what's your conclusion about the relationship between economic growth and democracy? Explain.

   c. If this were your research project, what would your next step be? (*Hint:* In particular, is there anything to be gained by learning more about the countries in the two different Granger causality groups?[22])

---

21. Uk Heo and Alexander Tan, "Democracy and Economic Growth: a Causal Analysis," *Comparative Politics*, Vol. 33, No. 4 (July 2001), pp. 463–473.

22. For the record, the 11 countries in which growth Granger-caused democracy were Costa Rica, Egypt, Guatemala, India, Israel, South Korea, Mexico, Nicaragua, Thailand, Uruguay, and Venezuela, and the 10 countries in which democracy Granger-caused growth were Bolivia, Burma, Colombia, Ecuador, El Salvador, Indonesia, Iran, Paraguay, the Philippines, and South Africa.

Chapter 13

Dummy Dependent Variable Techniques

13.1 The Linear Probability Model

13.2 The Binomial Logit Model

13.3 Other Dummy Dependent Variable Techniques

13.4 Summary and Exercises

Until now, our discussion of dummy variables has been restricted to dummy independent variables. However, there are many important research topics for which the *dependent* variable is appropriately treated as a dummy, equal only to 0 or 1.

In particular, researchers analyzing consumer choice often must cope with dummy dependent variables (also called qualitative dependent variables). For example, how do high school students decide whether to go to college? What distinguishes Pepsi drinkers from Coke drinkers? How can we convince people to use public transportation instead of driving? For an econometric study of these topics, or of any topic that involves a *discrete* choice of some sort, the dependent variable is typically a dummy variable.

In the first two sections of this chapter, we'll present two frequently used ways to estimate equations that have dummy dependent variables: the linear probability model and the binomial logit model. In the last section, we'll briefly discuss the binomial probit model and multinomial models.

13.1 The Linear Probability Model

What Is a Linear Probability Model?

The most obvious way to estimate a model with a dummy dependent variable is to run OLS on a typical linear econometric equation. A **linear probability**

model is just that, a linear-in-the-coefficients equation used to explain a dummy dependent variable:

$$D_i = \beta_0 + \beta_1 X_{1i} + \beta_2 X_{2i} + \epsilon_i \tag{13.1}$$

where D_i is a dummy variable and the Xs, βs, and ε are typical independent variables, regression coefficients, and an error term, respectively.

For instance, suppose you're interested in understanding why some states have female governors and others don't. In such a model, the appropriate dependent variable would be a dummy, for example D_i equal to 1 if the *i*th state has a female governor and equal to 0 otherwise. If we hypothesize that states with a high percentage of females and a low percentage of social conservatives would be likely to have a female governor, then a linear probability model would be:

$$
\begin{array}{cc} + & - \end{array}
$$
$$D_i = \beta_0 + \beta_1 F_i + \beta_2 R_i + \epsilon_i \tag{13.2}$$

where: D_i = 1 if the *i*th state has a female governor, 0 otherwise
F_i = females as a percent of the *i*th state's population
R_i = conservatives as a percent of the *i*th state's registered voters

The term *linear probability model* comes from the fact that the right side of the equation is linear while the expected value of the left side measures the probability that $D_i = 1$. To understand this second statement, let's assume that we estimate Equation 13.2 and get a $\hat{D}_i$ of 0.10 for a particular state. What does that mean? Well, since D = 1 if the governor is female and D = 0 if the governor is male, a state with a $\hat{D}_i$ of 0.10 can perhaps best be thought of as a state in which there is a 10 percent chance that the governor will be female, based on the state's values for the independent variables. Thus $\hat{D}_i$ is an estimate of the probability that $D_i = 1$ for the *i*th observation, and:

$$\hat{D}_i = \overbrace{\Pr(D_i = 1)} = \hat{\beta}_0 + \hat{\beta}_1 F_i + \hat{\beta}_2 R_i \tag{13.3}$$

where $\Pr(D_i = 1)$ indicates the probability that $D_i = 1$ for the *i*th observation.

How should we interpret the coefficients of Equation 13.3? Since $\hat{D}_i$ measures the probability that $D_i = 1$, then a coefficient in a linear probability model is an estimate of the change in the probability that $D_i = 1$ caused by a one-unit increase in the independent variable in question, holding constant the other independent variables in the equation.

Let's define P_i to be the true probability that $D_i = 1$. We can never observe P_i, just as we can never observe true βs, because it reflects the underlying situation before a discrete choice is made. After the choice is made, we can observe only the outcome of that choice, and so the dependent variable D_i can take on the values of only 0 or 1. Thus, even though P_i can be any value between 0 and 1, we can observe only the two extremes (0 and 1) in D_i.

Problems with the Linear Probability Model

Unfortunately, using OLS to estimate the coefficients of an equation with a dummy dependent variable faces at least three problems:

1. *$\overline{R}^2$ is not an accurate measure of overall fit.* For models with a dummy dependent variable, $\overline{R}^2$ tells us very little about how well the model explains the choices of the decision makers. To see why, take a look at Figure 13.1. D_i can equal only 1 or 0, but $\hat{D}_i$ must move in a continuous fashion from one extreme to the other. This means that $\hat{D}_i$ is likely to be quite different from D_i for some range of X_i. Thus, $\overline{R}^2$ is likely to be much lower than 1 even if the model actually does an exceptional job of explaining the choices involved. As a result, $\overline{R}^2$ (or R^2) should not be relied on as a measure of the overall fit of a model with a dummy dependent variable.

2. *$\hat{D}_i$ is not bounded by 0 and 1.* Since D_i is a dummy variable, we'd expect $\hat{D}_i$ to be limited to a range of from 0 to 1. After all, the prediction that a probability equals 2.6 (or -2.6, for that matter) is almost meaningless. However, take another look at Equation 13.3. Depending on the values of the independent variables and the $\hat{β}$s, the right-hand side might well be outside the meaningful range. For instance, if F, R, and all the $\hat{β}$s in Equation 13.3 equal 1.0, then $\hat{D}_i$ equals 3.0, which is substantially greater than 1.0.

3. *The error term is neither homoskedastic nor normally distributed.* In addition, the error term in a linear probability model is heteroskedastic and is not distributed normally, mainly because D_i takes on only two values (0 and 1). In practice, however, the impact of these problems on OLS estimation is minor, so many researchers ignore potential heteroskedasticity and nonnormality and apply OLS directly to the linear probability model.[1]

---

1. See R. G. McGilvray, "Estimating the Linear Probability Function," *Econometrica*, Vol. 38, pp. 775–776.

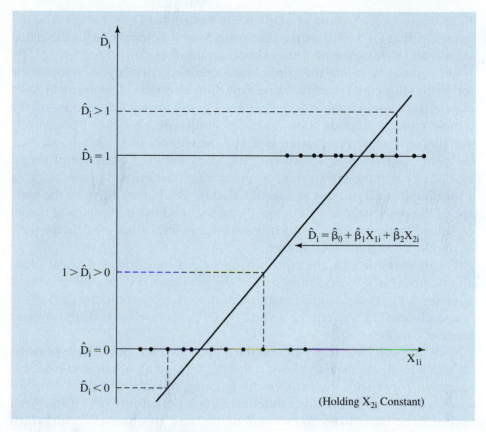

Figure 13.1 A Linear Probability Model

In a linear probability model, all the observed D_is equal either 0 or 1, but $\hat{D}_i$ moves linearly from one extreme to the other. As a result, $\overline{R}^2$ is often quite low even if the model does an excellent job of explaining the decision maker's choice. In addition, exceptionally large or small values of X_{1i} (holding X_{2i} constant) can produce values of $\hat{D}_i$ outside the meaningful range of 0 to 1.

The first of these problems isn't impossible to deal with, because there are a variety of alternatives to $\overline{R}^2$ for equations with dummy dependent variables.[2] Our preference is to create a measure based on the percentage of the observations in the sample that a particular estimated equation explains correctly.

2. See M. R. Veal and K. F. Zimmerman, "Pseudo-R^2 Measures for Some Common Limited Dependent Variables Models," *Journal of Economic Surveys*, Vol. 10, No. 3, pp. 241–259 and C. S. McIntosh and J. J. Dorfman, "Qualitative Forecast Evaluation: A Comparison of Two Performance Measures," *American Journal of Agricultural Economics*, Vol. 74, pp. 209–214.

To use this approach, consider a $\hat{D}_i > 0.5$ to predict that $D_i = 1$ and a $\hat{D}_i < 0.5$ to predict that $D_i = 0$. If we then compare these predictions[3] with the actual D_i, we can calculate the percentage of observations explained correctly.

Unfortunately, using the percentage explained correctly as a substitute for $\overline{R}^2$ for the entire sample has a flaw. Suppose that 85 percent of your observations are 1s and 15 percent are 0s. Explaining 85 percent of the sample correctly sounds good, but your results are no better than naively guessing that every observation is a 1! A better way might be to calculate the percentage of 1s explained correctly, calculate the percentage of zeroes explained correctly, and then report the average of these two percentages. As a shorthand, we'll call this average $\overline{R}_p^2$. That is, we'll define $\overline{R}_p^2$ to be the average of the percentage of 1s explained correctly and the percentage of zeroes explained correctly. Since $\overline{R}_p^2$ is a new statistic, we'll calculate and discuss both $\overline{R}_p^2$ and $\overline{R}^2$ throughout this chapter.

For most researchers, therefore, the major difficulty with the linear probability model is the unboundedness of the predicted D_is. Take another look at Figure 13.1 for a graphical interpretation of the situation. Because of the linear relationship between the X_is and $\hat{D}_i$, $\hat{D}_i$ can fall well outside the relevant range of 0 to 1.

One simplistic way to get around the unboundedness problem is to assign $\hat{D}_i = 1.0$ to all values of $\hat{D}_i$ above 1 and $\hat{D}_i = 0.0$ to all negative values. This approach copes with the problem by ignoring it, since an observation for which the linear probability model predicts a probability of 2.0 has been judged to be more likely to be equal to 1.0 than an observation for which the model predicts a 1.0, and yet they are lumped together. Even $\hat{D}_i = 1$ isn't very useful, because it implies that events will happen with certainty, which is surely a foolish prediction to make. What is needed is a systematic method of forcing the $\hat{D}_i$s to range from 0 to 1 in a smooth and meaningful fashion. We'll present such a method, the binomial logit, in Section 13.2.

Using the linear probability model, despite this unboundedness problem, may not cause insurmountable difficulties. In particular, the signs and general significance levels of the estimated coefficients of the linear probability model are often similar to those of the alternatives we will discuss later in this chapter.

---

3. Although it's standard to use $\hat{D}_i = 0.5$ as the value that distinguishes a prediction of $D_i = 1$ from a prediction of $D_i = 0$, there's no rule that requires that 0.5 be used. This is because it's possible to imagine circumstances in which 0.5 is too high or too low. For example, if the pay-off when you're right if you classify $D_i = 1$ is much lower than the payoff when you're right if you classify $D_i = 0$, then a value other than 0.5 might make sense.

An Example of a Linear Probability Model

Let's take a look at an example of a linear probability model: a disaggregate study of the labor force participation of women.

A person is defined as being in the labor force if she either has a job or is actively looking for a job. Thus, a disaggregate (cross-sectional by person) study of women's labor force participation is appropriately modeled with a dummy dependent variable:

$$D_i = 1 \text{ if the } i\text{th woman has or is looking for a job,}$$
$$0 \text{ otherwise (not in the labor force)}$$

A review of the literature reveals that there are many potentially relevant independent variables. Two of the most important are the marital status and the number of years of schooling of the woman. The expected signs for the coefficients of these variables are fairly straightforward, since a woman who is unmarried and well educated is much more likely to be in the labor force than her opposite. If we choose a linear functional form, we've got a linear probability model:

$$
\overset{\displaystyle -\qquad\ +}{D_i = \beta_0 + \beta_1 M_i + \beta_2 S_i + \epsilon_i} \tag{13.4}
$$

where: $M_i = 1$ if the ith woman is married and 0 otherwise
S_i = the number of years of schooling of the ith woman

The data are presented in Table 13.1. The sample size is limited to 30 in order to make it easier for readers to enter the dataset on their own. Unfortunately, such a small sample will make hypothesis testing fairly unreliable. Table 13.1 also includes the age of the ith woman, A_i. Another typically used variable, O_i = other income available to the ith woman, is not available for this sample, introducing possible omitted variable bias.

If we now estimate Equation 13.4 with the data on the labor force participation of women from Table 13.1, we obtain (standard errors in parentheses):

$$\hat{D}_i = -0.28 - 0.38M_i + 0.09S_i \tag{13.5}$$
$$(0.15)\quad (0.03)$$
$$N = 30 \qquad \overline{R}^2 = .32 \qquad \overline{R}_p^2 = .81$$

How do these results look? Despite the small sample and the possible bias due to omitting O_i, both independent variables have estimated coefficients that are significant in the expected direction. In addition, the $\overline{R}^2$ of .32 is fairly high for a linear probability model. (Since D_i equals only 0 or 1, it's

Table 13.1 Data on the Labor Force Participation of Women

Observation #	D_i	M_i	A_i	S_i	$\hat{D}_i$
1	1.0	0.0	31.0	16.0	1.20
2	1.0	1.0	34.0	14.0	0.63
3	1.0	1.0	41.0	16.0	0.82
4	0.0	0.0	67.0	9.0	0.55
5	1.0	0.0	25.0	12.0	0.83
6	0.0	1.0	58.0	12.0	0.45
7	1.0	0.0	45.0	14.0	1.01
8	1.0	0.0	55.0	10.0	0.64
9	0.0	0.0	43.0	12.0	0.83
10	1.0	0.0	55.0	8.0	0.45
11	1.0	0.0	25.0	11.0	0.73
12	1.0	0.0	41.0	14.0	1.01
13	0.0	1.0	62.0	12.0	0.45
14	1.0	1.0	51.0	13.0	0.54
15	0.0	1.0	39.0	9.0	0.17
16	1.0	0.0	35.0	10.0	0.64
17	1.0	1.0	40.0	14.0	0.63
18	0.0	1.0	43.0	10.0	0.26
19	0.0	1.0	37.0	12.0	0.45
20	1.0	0.0	27.0	13.0	0.92
21	1.0	0.0	28.0	14.0	1.01
22	1.0	1.0	48.0	12.0	0.45
23	0.0	1.0	66.0	7.0	−0.01
24	0.0	1.0	44.0	11.0	0.35
25	0.0	1.0	21.0	12.0	0.45
26	1.0	1.0	40.0	10.0	0.26
27	1.0	0.0	41.0	15.0	1.11
28	0.0	1.0	23.0	10.0	0.26
29	0.0	1.0	31.0	11.0	0.35
30	1.0	1.0	44.0	12.0	0.45

Datafile = WOMEN13

almost impossible to get an $\overline{R}^2$ much higher than .70.) Further evidence of good fit is the fairly high $\overline{R}_p^2$ of .81, meaning that an average of 81 percent of the choices were explained "correctly" by Equation 13.5.

We need to be careful when we interpret the estimated coefficients in Equation 13.5, however. Remember that the slope coefficient in a linear probability model represents the change in the probability that D_i equals 1 caused by a one-unit increase in the independent variable (holding the other independent variables constant). Viewed in this context, do the estimated coefficients make economic sense? The answer is yes: The probability of a woman participating in the labor force falls by 38 percentage points if she is married (holding constant schooling). Each year of schooling increases the probability of labor force participation by 9 percentage points (holding constant marital status).

The values for $\hat{D}_i$ have been included in Table 13.1. Note that $\hat{D}_i$ is indeed often outside the meaningful range of 0 and 1, causing most of the problems cited earlier. To attack this problem of the unboundedness of $\hat{D}_i$, however, we need a new estimation technique, so let's take a look at one.

13.2 The Binomial Logit Model

What Is the Binomial Logit?

The **binomial logit** is an estimation technique for equations with dummy dependent variables that avoids the unboundedness problem of the linear probability model by using a variant of the cumulative logistic function:

$$P_i = \frac{1}{1 + e^{-[\beta_0 + \beta_1 X_{1i} + \beta_2 X_{2i}]}} \tag{13.6}$$

where P_i is the true probability that $D_i = 1$. We can't observe P_i, so we need to use observed D_is to estimate a logit equation like Equation 13.6. That estimation will produce $\hat{D}_i$s that we can compare to the $\hat{D}_i$s produced by an estimated linear probability model like Equation 13.3.

Are the $\hat{D}_i$s produced by a logit now limited by 0 and 1? The answer is yes, but to see why we need to take a close look at Equation 13.6. What is the largest that $\hat{D}_i$ can be? Well, if $\hat{\beta}_0 + \hat{\beta}_1 X_{1i} + \hat{\beta}_2 X_{2i}$ equals infinity, then:

$$\hat{D}_i = \frac{1}{1 + e^{-\infty}} = \frac{1}{1} = 1 \tag{13.7}$$

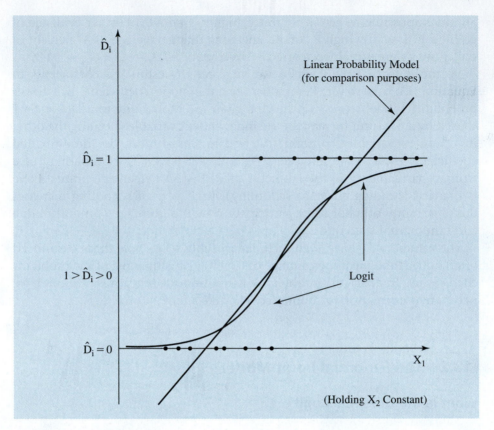

Figure 13.2 $\hat{D}_i$ Is Bounded by 0 and 1 in a Binomial Logit Model

In a binomial logit model, $\hat{D}_i$ is nonlinearly related to X_1, so even exceptionally large or small values of X_{1i}, holding X_{2i} constant, will not produce values of $\hat{D}_i$ outside the meaningful range of 0 to 1.

because e to the minus infinity equals 0. What's the smallest that $\hat{D}_i$ can be? If $\hat{\beta}_0 + \hat{\beta}_1 X_{1i} + \hat{\beta}_2 X_{2i}$ equals minus infinity, then:

$$\hat{D}_i = \frac{1}{1 + e^{\infty}} = \frac{1}{\infty} = 0 \qquad (13.8)$$

Thus, $\hat{D}_i$ is bounded by 1 and 0. As can be seen in Figure 13.2, $\hat{D}_i$ approaches 1 and 0 very slowly (asymptotically). The binomial logit model therefore avoids the major problem that the linear probability model encounters in dealing with dummy dependent variables. In addition, the logit is quite satisfying to most researchers because it turns out that real-world data often are described well by S-shape patterns like that in Figure 13.2.

Logits cannot be estimated using OLS. Instead, we use **maximum likelihood** (ML), an iterative estimation technique that is especially useful for equations that are nonlinear in the coefficients. ML estimation is inherently different from least squares in that it chooses coefficient estimates that *maximize the likelihood* of the sample data set being observed.[4] Interestingly, OLS and ML estimates are not necessarily different; for a linear equation that meets the Classical Assumptions (including the normality assumption), ML estimates are identical to the OLS ones.

One of the reasons that maximum likelihood is used is that ML has a number of desirable large sample properties; ML is consistent (homes in on true parameter values) and asymptotically efficient (minimum variance for large samples). With very large samples, ML often has the added advantage of converging to a normal distribution, allowing the use of typical hypothesis testing techniques. As a result, sample sizes for logits should be substantially larger than they are for linear regressions. Some researchers aim for samples of 500 or more.

It's also important to make sure that a logit sample contains a reasonable representation of both alternative choices. For instance, if 98 percent of a sample chooses alternative A and 2 percent chooses B, a random sample of 500 might have only 10 observations that choose B. In such a situation, our estimated coefficients would be overly reliant on the characteristics of those 10 observations. A better technique would be to disproportionately sample from those who choose B. It turns out that using different sampling rates for subgroups within the sample does not cause bias in the slope coefficients of a logit model,[5] even though it might do so in a linear regression.

When we estimate a logit, we apply the ML technique to Equation 13.6, but that equation's functional form is complex, so let's try to simplify it a bit. First, a few mathematical steps can allow us to rewrite Equation 13.6 so that the right side of the equation looks like the linear probability model:

$$\ln\left(\frac{P_i}{[1 - P_i]}\right) = \beta_0 + \beta_1 X_{1i} + \beta_2 X_{2i} \tag{13.9}$$

where P_i is the true probability that $D_i = 1$.

4. Actually, the ML program chooses coefficient estimates that maximize the probability (or likelihood) of observing the particular set of values of the dependent variable in the sample $(Y_1, Y_2, \ldots, Y_N)$ for a given set of Xs. For more on maximum likelihood, see Robert S. Pindyck and Daniel L. Rubinfeld, *Economic Models and Economic Forecasts* (New York: McGraw-Hill, 1998), pp. 51–53 and 329–330.

5. The constant term, however, needs to be adjusted. Multiply $\hat{\beta}_0$ by $[\ln(p_1) - \ln(p_2)]$, where p_1 is the proportion of the observations chosen if $D_i = 1$ and p_2 is the proportion of the observations chosen if $D_i = 0$. See G. S. Maddala, *Limited-Dependent and Qualitative Variables in Econometrics* (Cambridge: Cambridge University Press, 1983), pp. 90–91.

Even Equation 13.9 is a bit cumbersome, however, since the left side of the equation contains the log of the ratio of P_i to $(1 - P_i)$, sometimes called the "log of the odds." To make things simpler still, let's adopt a shorthand for the logit functional form on the left side of Equation 13.9. Let's define:

$$L{:}Pr(D_i = 1) = \ln\left(\frac{P_i}{[1 - P_i]}\right) \tag{13.10}$$

The L indicates that the equation is a logit of the functional form in Equation 13.9 (derived from Equation 13.6), and the "$Pr(D_i = 1)$" is a reminder that the dependent variable is a dummy and that a $\hat{D}_i$ produced by an estimated logit equation is an estimate of the probability that $D_i = 1$. If we now substitute Equation 13.10 into Equation 13.9, we get:

$$L{:}Pr(D_i = 1) = \beta_0 + \beta_1 X_{1i} + \beta_2 X_{2i} \tag{13.11}$$

Equation 13.11 will be our standard documentation format for estimated logit equations.

Interpreting Estimated Logit Coefficients

Once you've estimated a binomial logit, then hypothesis testing and the analysis of potential econometric problems can be undertaken using techniques similar to those discussed in previous chapters. The signs of the coefficients have the same meaning as they do in a linear probability model, and tests of hypotheses about logit coefficients can be run.[6]

When it comes to the economic interpretation of the estimated logit coefficients, however, all this changes. In particular, the absolute sizes of estimated logit coefficients tend to be quite different from the absolute sizes of estimated linear probability model coefficients for the same specification and the same data. What's going on?

There are two powerful reasons for these differences. First, as you can see by comparing Equations 13.1 and 13.9, the dependent variable in a logit equation isn't the same as the dependent variable in a linear probability

---

6. Different econometric software programs provide a variety of information in support of this hypothesis testing, at least in part because the t-test isn't appropriate for hypothesis testing for logits with small samples. Stata produces z-statistics, which require the Normal Distribution table in Appendix B-5. SAS, on the other hand, produces chi-square statistics, which use Table B-6. Our suggestion is to use p-values because they're produced by virtually all the econometric packages and because their use doesn't require the researcher to decide whether the t-distribution, normal distribution, or chi-square distribution is appropriate in any given case.

model. Since the dependent variable is different, it makes complete sense that the coefficients are different. The second reason that logit coefficients are different is even more dynamic. Take a look at Figure 13.2. The slope of the graph of the logit changes as $\hat{D}_i$ moves from 0 to 1! Thus the change in the probability that $\hat{D}_i = 1$ caused by a one-unit increase in an independent variable (holding the other independent variables constant) will vary as we move from $\hat{D}_i = 0$ to $\hat{D}_i = 1$.

Given all this, how can we interpret estimated logit coefficients? How can we use them to measure the impact of an independent variable on the probability that $D_i = 1$? It turns out that there are three reasonable ways of answering this question:

1. *Change an average observation.* Create an "average" observation by plugging the means of all the independent variables into the estimated logit equation and then calculating an "average" $\hat{D}_i$. Then increase the independent variable of interest by one unit and recalculate the $\hat{D}_i$. The difference between the two $\hat{D}_i$s tells you the impact of a one-unit increase in that independent variable on the probability that $\hat{D}_i = 1$ (holding constant the other independent variables) for an average observation. This approach has the weakness of not being very meaningful when one or more of the independent variables is a dummy variable (after all, what is an average gender?), but it's possible to work around this weakness if you estimate the impact for an "average female" and an "average male" by setting the dummy independent variable equal first to 0 and then to 1.

2. *Use a partial derivative.* It turns out that if you take a derivative of the logit, you'll find that the change in the expected value of $\hat{D}_i$ caused by a one-unit increase in X_{1i}, holding constant the other independent variables in the equation, equals $\beta_1 P_i(1 - P_i)$. To use this formula, plug in your estimates of β_1 and P_i ($\hat{\beta}_1$ and $\hat{D}_i$). As you can see, the marginal impact of X does indeed depend on the value of $\hat{D}_i$.

3. *Use a rough estimate of 0.25.* The previous two methods are reasonably accurate, but they're hardly very handy. However, if you plug $\hat{D}_i = 0.5$ into $\beta_1 P_i(1 - P_i)$, you get the much more useful result that if you multiply a logit coefficient by 0.25, you'll get an equivalent linear probability model coefficient.[7]

---

7. See, for example, Jeff Wooldridge, *Introductory Econometrics* (Mason, OH: Southwestern, 2009), p. 584. Wooldridge also suggests a multiple of 0.40 for converting a probit coefficient into a linear probability coefficient. We'll briefly cover probits in Section 13.3.

On balance, what do we recommend? For all situations except those requiring precise accuracy, we find ourselves gravitating toward the third approach. To get a rough approximation of the economic meaning of a logit coefficient, multiply by 0.25 (or, equivalently, divide by 4). Remember, however, that the dependent variable in question still is the probability that $D_i = 1$.

Measuring the overall fit also is not straightforward. Recall from Section 7.5 that since the functional form of the dependent variable has been changed, $\overline{R}^2$ should not be used to compare the fit of a logit with an otherwise comparable linear probability model. In addition, don't forget the general faults inherent in using $\overline{R}^2$ with equations with dummy dependent variables. Our suggestion is to use the mean percentage of correct predictions, $\overline{R}_p^2$, from Section 13.1.

To get some practice interpreting logit estimates, let's estimate a logit on the same women's labor force participation data that we used in the previous section. The OLS linear probability model estimate of that model, Equation 13.5, was:

$$\hat{D}_i = -0.28 - 0.38M_i + 0.09S_i \tag{13.5}$$
$$(0.15) \quad (0.03)$$
$$N = 30 \quad \overline{R}^2 = .32 \quad \overline{R}_p^2 = .81$$

where: $D_i = 1$ if the ith woman is in the labor force, 0 otherwise
          $M_i = 1$ if the ith woman is married, 0 otherwise
          S_i = the number of years of schooling of the ith woman

If we estimate a logit on the same data (from Table 13.1) and the same independent variables, we obtain:

$$\overset{\frown}{L{:}Pr(D_i = 1)} = -5.90 - 2.59M_i + 0.69S_i \tag{13.12}$$
$$(1.18) \quad (0.32)$$
$$N = 30 \quad \overline{R}_p^2 = .81 \quad \text{iterations} = 5$$

Let's compare Equations 13.5 and 13.12. As expected, the signs and general significance of the slope coefficients are the same. Even if we divide the logit coefficients by 4, as suggested earlier, they still are larger than the linear probability model coefficients. Despite these differences, the overall fits are comparable, especially after taking account of the different dependent variables and estimation techniques. In this example, then, the two estimation procedures differ mainly in that the logit does not produce $\hat{D}_i$s outside the range of 0 and 1.

However, if the size of the sample in this example is too small for a linear probability model, it certainly is too small for a logit, making any in-depth analysis of Equation 13.12 problematic. Instead, we're better off finding an example with a much larger sample.

A More Complete Example of the Use of the Binomial Logit

For a more complete example of the binomial logit, let's look at a model of the probability of passing the California State Department of Motor Vehicles drivers' license test. To obtain a license, each driver must pass a written and a behind-the-wheel test. Even though the tests are scored from 0 to 100, all that matters is that you pass and get your license.

Since the written test requires some boning up on traffic and safety laws, driving students have to decide how much time to spend studying. If they don't study enough, they waste time because they have to retake the test. If they study too much, however, they also waste time, because there's no bonus for scoring above the minimum, especially since there is no evidence that doing well on the written test has much to do with driving well after the test (this, of course, might be worth its own econometric study).

Recently, two students decided to collect data on test takers in order to build an equation explaining whether someone passed the Department of Motor Vehicles written test. They hoped that the model, and in particular the estimated coefficient of study time, would help them decide how much time to spend studying for the test. (Of course, it took more time to collect the data and run the model than it would have taken to memorize the entire traffic code, but that's another story.)

After reviewing the literature, choosing variables, and hypothesizing signs, the students realized that the appropriate functional form was a binomial logit because their dependent variable was a dummy variable:

$$D_i = \begin{cases} 1 \text{ if the } i\text{th test taker passed the test on the first try} \\ 0 \text{ if the } i\text{th test taker failed the test on the first try} \end{cases}$$

They chose four independent variables (all with positive expected coefficients):

A_i = the age of the ith test taker

H_i = the number of hours the ith test taker studied (usually less than one hour!)

E_i = a dummy variable equal to 1 if the ith test taker's primary language was English, 0 otherwise

C_i = a dummy variable equal to 1 if the ith test taker had any college education, 0 otherwise

After collecting data from 480 test takers, the students estimated the following equation:

$$\widehat{L:Pr(D_i = 1)} = -1.18 + 0.011A_i + 2.70H_i + 1.62E_i + 3.97C_i \quad (13.13)$$
$$(0.009) \quad (0.54) \quad (0.34) \quad (0.99)$$

$$N = 480 \qquad \overline{R}_p^2 = .74 \qquad \text{iterations} = 5$$

Note how similar these results look to a typical linear regression result. All the estimated coefficients have the expected signs, and all but one appear to be significantly different from 0. Remember that the logit coefficients need to be divided by 4 to get meaningful estimates of the impact of the independent variables on the probability of passing the test. Note that $\overline{R}_p^2$ is .74, indicating that the equation correctly explained almost three quarters of the sample based on nothing but the four variables in Equation 13.13.

And what about the two students? Did the equation help them? How much did they end up deciding to study? They found that given their ages, their college education, and their English-speaking backgrounds, the expected value of $\hat{D}_i$ for each of them was quite high, even if H_i was set equal to 0. So what did they actually do? They studied for a half hour "just to be on the safe side" and passed with flying colors, having devoted more time to passing the test than anyone else in the history of the state.

13.3 Other Dummy Dependent Variable Techniques

Although the binomial logit is the most frequently used estimation technique for equations with dummy dependent variables, it's by no means the only one. In this section, we'll mention two alternatives, but our main goal is to briefly describe these estimation techniques, not to cover them in any detail.[8]

The Binomial Probit Model

The **binomial probit model** is an estimation technique for equations with dummy dependent variables that avoids the unboundedness problem of

---

8. For more, see G. S. Maddala, *Limited Dependent Variables and Qualitative Variables in Econometrics* (Cambridge: Cambridge University Press, 1983) and T. Amemiya, "Qualitative Response Models: A Survey," *Journal of Economic Literature*, Vol. 19, pp. 1483–1536. These surveys also cover additional techniques, like the Tobit model, that are useful with bounded dependent variables or other special situations.

the linear probability model by using a variant of the cumulative normal distribution.

$$P_i = \frac{1}{\sqrt{2\pi}} \int_{-\infty}^{Z_i} e^{-s^2/2}\, ds \qquad (13.14)$$

where: P_i = the probability that the dummy variable $D_i = 1$
$Z_i = \beta_0 + \beta_1 X_{1i} + \beta_2 X_{2i}$
s = a standardized normal variable

As different as this probit looks from the logit that we examined in the previous section, it can be rewritten to look quite familiar:

$$Z_i = \Phi^{-1}(P_i) = \beta_0 + \beta_1 X_{1i} + \beta_2 X_{2i} \qquad (13.15)$$

where Φ^{-1} is the inverse of the normal cumulative distribution function. Probit models typically are estimated by applying maximum likelihood techniques to the model in the form of Equation 13.14, but the results often are presented in the format of Equation 13.15.

The fact that both the logit and the probit are cumulative distribution functions means that the two have similar properties. For example, a graph of the probit looks almost exactly like the logit in Figure 13.2. In addition, the probit has the same requirement of a fairly large sample before hypothesis testing becomes meaningful. Finally, $\overline{R}^2$ continues to be of questionable value as a measure of overall fit.

For an example of a probit, let's estimate one using the same women's labor force participation data employed in the previous logit and linear probability examples (standard errors in parentheses):

$$\hat{Z}_i = \widehat{\Phi^{-1}(P_i)} = -3.44 - 1.44 M_i + 0.40 S_i \qquad (13.16)$$
$$(0.62) \quad (0.17)$$
$$N = 30 \quad \overline{R}_p^2 = 0.81 \quad \text{iterations} = 4$$

Compare this result with Equation 13.12 from the previous section. Note that except for a slight difference in the scale of the coefficients, the logit and probit models provide virtually identical results in this example.

Multinomial Models

In many cases, there are more than two qualitative choices available. In some cities, for instance, a commuter has a choice of car, bus, or subway for the trip to work. How could we build and estimate a model of choosing from more than two alternatives?

One answer is to hypothesize that choices are made sequentially and to model a multichoice decision as a series of binary decisions. For example, we might hypothesize that the commuter would first decide whether to drive to work, and we could build a binary model of car versus public transportation. For those commuters who choose public transportation, the next step would be to choose whether to take the bus or the subway, and we could build a second binary model of that choice. This method, called a **sequential binary logit**, is cumbersome and at times unrealistic, but it does allow a researcher to use a binary technique to model an inherently multichoice decision.

If a decision among more than two alternatives truly is made simultaneously, then the sequential binary logit can't be used. There are a number of alternative estimation procedures that are appropriate in this situation, but unfortunately they are beyond the scope of this text.[9]

13.4 Summary

1. A linear probability model is a linear-in-the-coefficients equation used to explain a dummy dependent variable (D_i). $\hat{D}_i$ is an estimate of the probability that D_i equals 1.

2. The estimation of a linear probability model with OLS faces at least three major problems:
   a. $\overline{R}^2$ is not an accurate measure of overall fit.
   b. The expected value of $\hat{D}_i$ is not limited by 0 and 1.
   c. The error term is neither homoskedastic nor normally distributed.

3. When measuring the overall fit of equations with dummy dependent variables, an alternative to $\overline{R}^2$ is $\overline{R}_p^2$, the average percentage of the observations in the sample that a particular estimated equation would have explained correctly.

4. The binomial logit is an estimation technique for equations with dummy dependent variables that avoids the unboundedness problem of the linear probability model by using a variant of the cumulative logistic function:

$$L: \Pr(D_i = 1) = \ln\left(\frac{P_i}{[1 - P_i]}\right) = \beta_0 + \beta_1 X_{1i} + \beta_2 X_{2i}$$

---

9. These alternative procedures include the multinomial logit and the ordered logit. See William H. Greene, *Econometric Analysis* (Boston: Pearson Education, 2012), pp. 803–806 and pp. 824–827.

5. The binomial logit is best estimated using the maximum likelihood (ML) technique and a large sample. A slope coefficient from a logit measures the impact of a one-unit increase of the independent variable in question (holding the other explanatory variables constant) on the log of the odds of a given choice.

6. The binomial probit model is an estimation technique for equations with dummy dependent variables that uses the cumulative normal distribution function. The binomial probit has properties quite similar to those of the binomial logit.

EXERCISES

(The answers to the even-numbered exercises are in Appendix A.)

1. Write the meaning of each of the following terms without referring to the book (or your notes), and compare your definition with the version in the text for each:
   a. binomial logit (p. 397)
   b. binomial probit (p. 404)
   c. interpreting estimated logit coefficients (p. 400)
   d. linear probability model (p. 390)
   e. maximum likelihood (p. 399)
   f. $\overline{R}_p^2$ (p. 394)
   g. sequential binary logit (p. 406)

2. R. Amatya[10] estimated the following logit model of birth control for 1,145 continuously married women aged 35 to 44 in Nepal:

$$\widehat{L:Pr(D_i = 1)} = -4.47 + 2.03WN_i + 1.45ME_i$$
$$(0.36) \qquad (0.14)$$

where: D_i = 1 if the ith woman has ever used a recognized form of birth control, 0 otherwise

WN_i = 1 if the ith woman wants no more children, 0 otherwise

ME_i = number of methods of birth control known to the ith woman

---

10. Ramesh Amatya, "Supply-Demand Analysis of Differences in Contraceptive Use in Seven Asian Nations" (paper presented at the Annual Meetings of the Western Economic Association, 1988, Los Angeles).

a. Explain the theoretical meaning of the coefficients for WN and ME. How would your answer differ if this were a linear probability model?

b. Do the signs, sizes, and significance of the estimated slope coefficients meet your expectations? Why or why not?

c. What is the theoretical significance of the constant term in this equation?

d. If you could make one change in the specification of this equation, what would it be? Explain your reasoning.

3. Because their college had just upgraded its residence halls, two seniors decided to build a model of the decision to live on campus. They collected data from 533 upper-class students (first-year students were required to live on campus) and estimated the following equation:

$$L{:}Pr\left(D_i = 1\right) = 3.26 + 0.03UNIT_i - 0.13ALCO_i - 0.99YEAR_i - 0.39GREK_i$$
$$\quad\quad\quad (0.04)\quad\quad (0.08)\quad\quad (0.12)\quad\quad (0.21)$$
$$N = 533 \quad \overline{R}_p^2 = .668 \quad \text{iterations} = 4$$

where: D_i = 1 if the ith student lived on campus, 0 otherwise

$UNIT_i$ = the number of academic units the ith student was taking

$ALCO_i$ = the nights per week that the ith student consumed alcohol

$YEAR_i$ = 2 if the ith student was a sophomore, 3 if a junior, and 4 if a senior

$GREK_i$ = 1 if the ith student was a member of a fraternity/sorority, 0 otherwise

a. The two seniors expected UNIT to have a positive coefficient and the other variables to have negative coefficients. Do the results support these hypotheses?

b. What problem do you see with the definition of the YEAR variable? What constraint does this definition place on the estimated coefficients?

c. Carefully state the meaning of the coefficient of ALCO and analyze the size of the coefficient. (*Hint:* Be sure to discuss how the size of the coefficient compares with your expectations.)

d. If you could add one variable to this equation, what would it be? Explain.

4. Return to our data on women's labor force participation and consider the possibility of adding A_i, the age of the ith woman, to the equation. Be careful when you develop your expected sign and functional form because the expected impact of age on labor force participation is difficult to pin down. For instance, some women drop out of the labor force when they get married, but others continue working even while they're raising their children. Still others work until they get married, stay at home with young children, and then return to the workforce once the children reach school age. Malcolm Cohen et al., for example, found the age of a woman to be relatively unimportant in determining labor force participation, except for women who were 65 and older and were likely to have retired.[11] The net result for our model is that age appears to be a theoretically irrelevant variable. A possible exception, however, is a dummy variable equal to 1 if the ith woman is 65 or over, 0 otherwise.

   a. Look over the data set in Table 13.1. What problems do you see with adding an independent variable equal to 1 if the ith woman is 65 or older and 0 otherwise?

   b. To get practice in actually estimating your own linear probability and logit equations, test the possibility that age (A_i) is actually a relevant variable in our women's labor force participation model. That is, take the data from Table 13.1 and estimate linear probability and logit versions. Then use our specification criteria to compare your equation with the parallel version in the text (without A_i). Explain why you do or do not think that age is a relevant variable. (*Hint:* Be sure to calculate $\overline{R}_p^2$.)

5. In 2008, Goldman and Romley[12] studied hospital demand by analyzing how 8,721 Medicare-covered pneumonia patients chose from among 117 hospitals in the greater Los Angeles area. The authors concluded that clinical quality (as measured by a low pneumonia mortality rate) played a smaller role in hospital choice than did a variety of other factors.

   Let's focus on a subset of the Goldman–Romley sample: the 499 patients who chose either the UCLA Medical Center or the nearby Cedars Sinai Medical Center. Typically, economists would expect price to have a major influence on such a choice, but Medicare patients pay

11. Malcolm Cohen, Samuel A. Rea, Jr., and Robert I. Lerman, *A Micro Model of Labor Supply* (Washington, D.C.: U.S. Bureau of Labor Statistics, 1970), p. 212.

12. Dana Goldman and John Romley, "Hospitals as Hotels: The Role of Patient Amenities in Hospital Demand," *NBER Working Paper* 14619, December 2008. We appreciate the permission of the authors to use a portion of their data set.

roughly the same price no matter what hospital they choose. Instead, factors like the distance the patient lives from the hospital and the age and income of the patient become potentially important factors:

$$\overset{\frown}{L}:Pr(D_i = 1) = 4.41 - 0.38DISTANCE_i - 0.072INCOME_i - 0.29OLD_i \qquad (13.17)$$
$$\qquad\qquad (0.05) \qquad\qquad (0.036) \qquad\qquad (0.31)$$
$$N = 499 \qquad\qquad \overline{R}_p^2 = .66 \qquad\qquad \text{iterations} = 8$$

where: D_i = 1 if the ith patient chose Cedars Sinai, 0 if they chose UCLA

$DISTANCE_i$ = the distance from the ith patient's home (according to zip code) to Cedars Sinai *minus* the distance from that point to the UCLA Medical Center (in miles)

$INCOME_i$ = the income of the ith patient (as measured by the average income of their zip code in thousands of dollars)

OLD_i = 1 if the ith patient was older than 75, 0 otherwise

a. Create and test appropriate hypotheses about the coefficient of DISTANCE.

b. Carefully state the meaning of the estimated coefficient of DISTANCE in terms of the "per mile" impact on the probability of choosing Cedars Sinai Medical Center.

c. Think about the definition of DISTANCE. Why do you think we defined DISTANCE as the difference between the distances as opposed to entering the distance to Cedars and the distance to UCLA as two different independent variables?

d. This data set is available on our Web site (www.pearsonhighered. com/studenmund) as datafile = HOSPITAL13. Load the data into your computer and use Stata or your computer's regression program to estimate the linear probability model version of this equation. What is the coefficient of DISTANCE in your estimate? Which do you prefer, the logit or the linear probability model? Explain.

e. (optional) Now create a slope dummy by adding OLD∗DISTANCE to Equation 13.17 and estimating a new logit equation. Why do you think we're suggesting this particular slope dummy? Create and test the appropriate hypotheses about the slope dummy. Which equation do you prefer, Equation 13.17 or the new slope dummy logit? Explain.

Chapter 14

Simultaneous Equations

The most important models in economics and business are simultaneous in nature. Supply and demand, for example, is obviously simultaneous. To study the demand for chicken without also looking at the supply of chicken is to take a chance on missing important linkages and thus making significant mistakes. Virtually all the major approaches to macroeconomics, from Keynesian aggregate demand models to rational expectations schemes, are inherently simultaneous. Even models that appear to be inherently single-equation in nature often turn out to be much more simultaneous than you might think. The price of housing, for instance, is dramatically affected by the level of economic activity, the prevailing rate of interest in alternative assets, and a number of other simultaneously determined variables.

All this wouldn't mean much to econometricians if it weren't for the fact that the estimation of simultaneous equations systems with OLS causes a number of difficulties that aren't encountered with single equations. Most important, Classical Assumption III, which states that all explanatory variables should be uncorrelated with the error term, is violated in simultaneous models. Mainly because of this, OLS coefficient estimates are biased in simultaneous models. As a result, an alternative estimation procedure called Two-Stage Least Squares usually is employed in such models instead of OLS.

You're probably wondering why we've waited until now to discuss simultaneous equations if they're so important in economics and if OLS encounters bias when estimating them. The answer is that the simultaneous estimation of an equation changes every time the specification of any equation in the entire system is changed, so a researcher must be well equipped to deal with specification problems like those of previous chapters. As a result, it does not make sense to learn how to estimate a simultaneous system until you are fairly adept at estimating a single equation.

14.1 Structural and Reduced-Form Equations

Before we can study the problems encountered in the estimation of simultaneous equations, we need to introduce a few concepts.

The Nature of Simultaneous Equations Systems

Which came first, the chicken or the egg? This question is impossible to answer satisfactorily because chickens and eggs are *jointly determined*; there is a two-way causal relationship between the variables. The more eggs you have, the more chickens you'll get, but the more chickens you have, the more eggs you'll get.[1] More realistically, the economic world is full of the kind of *feedback effects* and *dual causality* that require the application of simultaneous equations. Besides the supply and demand and simple macroeconomic model examples mentioned previously, we could talk about the dual causality of population size and food supply, the joint determination of wages and prices, or the interaction between foreign exchange rates and international trade and capital flows. In a typical econometric equation:

$$Y_t = \beta_0 + \beta_1 X_{1t} + \beta_2 X_{2t} + \epsilon_t \tag{14.1}$$

a simultaneous system is one in which Y clearly has an effect on at least one of the Xs in addition to the effect that the Xs have on Y.

Such topics are usually modeled by distinguishing between variables that are simultaneously determined (the Ys, called **endogenous variables**) and those that are not (the Xs, called **exogenous variables**):

$$Y_{1t} = \alpha_0 + \alpha_1 Y_{2t} + \alpha_2 X_{1t} + \alpha_3 X_{2t} + \epsilon_{1t} \tag{14.2}$$

$$Y_{2t} = \beta_0 + \beta_1 Y_{1t} + \beta_2 X_{3t} + \beta_3 X_{2t} + \epsilon_{2t} \tag{14.3}$$

---

1. This also depends on how hungry you are, which is a function of how hard you're working, which depends on how many chickens you have to take care of. (Although this chicken/egg example is simultaneous in an annual model, it would not be truly simultaneous in a quarterly or monthly model because of the time lags involved.)

For example, Y_1 and Y_2 might be the quantity and price of chicken (respectively), X_1 the income of the consumers, X_2 the price of beef (beef is a substitute for chicken in both consumption and production), and X_3 the price of chicken feed. With these definitions, Equation 14.2 would characterize the behavior of consumers of chickens and Equation 14.3 the behavior of suppliers of chickens. These behavioral equations are also called *structural equations*. **Structural equations** characterize the underlying economic theory behind each endogenous variable by expressing it in terms of both endogenous and exogenous variables. Researchers must view them as an entire system in order to see all the feedback loops involved. For example, the Ys are jointly determined, so a change in Y_1 will cause a change in Y_2, which will in turn cause Y_1 to change *again*. Contrast this feedback with a change in X_1, which will not eventually loop back and cause X_1 to change again. The αs and the βs in the equation are *structural coefficients,* and hypotheses should be made about their signs just as we did with the regression coefficients of single equations.

Note that a variable is endogenous because it is jointly determined, not just because it appears in both equations. That is, X_2, which is the price of beef but could be another factor beyond our control, is in both equations but is still exogenous in nature because it is not simultaneously determined within the chicken market. In a large general equilibrium model of the entire economy, however, such a price variable would also likely be endogenous. How do you decide whether a particular variable should be endogenous or exogenous? Some variables are almost always exogenous (the weather, for example), but most others can be considered either endogenous or exogenous, depending on the number and characteristics of the other equations in the system. Thus, the distinction between endogenous and exogenous variables usually depends on how the researcher defines the scope of the research project.

Sometimes, lagged endogenous variables appear in simultaneous systems, usually when the equations involved are dynamic models (described in Chapter 12). Be careful! Such lagged endogenous variables are not simultaneously determined in the current time period. They thus have more in common with exogenous variables than with nonlagged endogenous variables. To avoid problems, we'll define the term **predetermined variable** to include all exogenous variables and lagged endogenous variables. "Predetermined" implies that exogenous and lagged endogenous variables are determined outside the system of specified equations or prior to the current period. Endogenous variables that are not lagged are not predetermined, because they are jointly determined by the system in the current time period. Therefore, econometricians tend to speak in terms of endogenous and predetermined variables when discussing simultaneous equations systems.

Let's look at the specification of a simple supply and demand model, say for the "cola" soft-drink industry:

$$Q_{Dt} = \alpha_0 + \alpha_1 P_t + \alpha_2 X_{1t} + \alpha_3 X_{2t} + \epsilon_{Dt} \tag{14.4}$$

$$Q_{St} = \beta_0 + \beta_1 P_t + \beta_2 X_{3t} + \epsilon_{St} \tag{14.5}$$

$$Q_{St} = Q_{Dt} \quad \text{(equilibrium condition)}$$

where: Q_{Dt} = the quantity of cola demanded in time period t

           Q_{St} = the quantity of cola supplied in time period t

           P_t = the price of cola in time period t

           X_{1t} = dollars of advertising for cola in time period t

           X_{2t} = another "demand-side" exogenous variable (e.g., income or the prices or advertising of other drinks)

           X_{3t} = a "supply-side" exogenous variable (e.g., the price of artificial flavors or other factors of production)

           ϵ_t = classical error terms (each equation has its own error term, subscripted "D" and "S" for demand and supply)

In this case, price and quantity are simultaneously determined, but price, one of the endogenous variables, is not on the left side of any of the equations. It's incorrect to assume automatically that the endogenous variables are those that appear on the left side of at least one equation; in this case, we could have just as easily written Equation 14.5 with price on the left side and quantity supplied on the right side, as we did in the chicken example in Equations 14.2 and 14.3. Although the estimated coefficients would be different, the underlying relations would not. Note also that there must be as many equations as there are endogenous variables. In this case, the three endogenous variables are Q_D, Q_S, and P.

What would be the expected signs for the coefficients of the price variables in Equations 14.4 and 14.5? We'd expect price to enter negatively in the demand equation but to enter positively in the supply equation. The higher the price, after all, the less quantity will be demanded, but the more quantity will be supplied. These signs would result in the typical supply and demand diagram that we're all used to. Look at Equations 14.4 and 14.5 again, and note that they would be identical except for the different predetermined variables. What would happen if we accidentally put a supply-side predetermined variable in the demand equation or vice versa? We'd have a very difficult time identifying which equation was which, and the expected signs for the coefficients of the endogenous variable P would become ambiguous. As a result, we must take care when specifying the structural equations in a system.

Simultaneous Systems Violate Classical Assumption III

Recall from Chapter 4 that Classical Assumption III states that the error term and each explanatory variable must be uncorrelated with each other. If there is such a correlation, then the OLS regression estimation program is likely to attribute to the explanatory variable variations in the dependent variable that are actually being caused by variations in the error term. The result will be biased estimates.

To see why simultaneous equations violate the assumption of independence between the error term and the explanatory variables, look again at a simultaneous system, Equations 14.2 and 14.3 (repeated with directional errors):

$$\uparrow \qquad\qquad \uparrow \qquad\qquad\qquad\qquad \uparrow$$
$$Y_{1t} = \alpha_0 + \alpha_1 Y_{2t} + \alpha_2 X_{1t} + \alpha_3 X_{2t} + \epsilon_{1t} \qquad (14.2)$$

$$\uparrow \qquad\qquad \uparrow$$
$$Y_{2t} = \beta_0 + \beta_1 Y_{1t} + \beta_2 X_{3t} + \beta_3 X_{2t} + \epsilon_{2t} \qquad (14.3)$$

Let's work through the system and see what happens when one of the error terms increases, holding everything else in the equations constant:

1. If ϵ_1 increases in a particular time period, Y_1 will also increase due to Equation 14.2.
2. If Y_1 increases, Y_2 will also rise[2] due to Equation 14.3.
3. But if Y_2 increases in Equation 14.3, it also increases in Equation 14.2 where it is an explanatory variable.

Thus, an increase in the error term of an equation causes an increase in an explanatory variable in the same equation: If ϵ_1 increases, Y_1 increases, and then Y_2 increases, violating the assumption of independence between the error term and the explanatory variables.

For a visual understanding of this, take a look at Figure 14.1 on page 416. If the error term in the demand equation increases, then the demand curve will shift from D to D', and both price and quantity will increase. Thus an increase in the error term will be correlated with an increase in an independent variable. We've violated Classical Assumption III!

---

2. This assumes that β_1 is positive. If β_1 is negative, Y_2 will decrease and there will be a negative correlation between ϵ_1 and Y_2, but this negative correlation will still violate Classical Assumption III. Also note that both Equations 14.2 and 14.3 could have Y_{1t} on the left side; if two variables are jointly determined, it doesn't matter which variable is considered dependent and which explanatory, because they are actually mutually dependent. We used this kind of simultaneous system in the cola model portrayed in Equations 14.4 and 14.5.

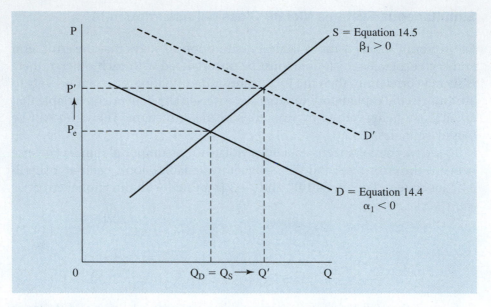

Figure 14.1 Supply and Demand Simultaneous Equations

An example of simultaneous equations that jointly determine two endogenous variables is the supply and demand for a product. In this case, Equation 14.4, the downward-sloping demand function, and Equation 14.5, the upward-sloping supply function, intersect at the equilibrium price and quantity for this market.

This is not an isolated result that depends on the particular equations involved. Instead, this result works for other error terms, equations, and simultaneous systems. All that is required for the violation of Classical Assumption III is that there be endogenous variables that are jointly determined in a system of simultaneous equations.

Reduced-Form Equations

An alternative way of expressing a simultaneous equations system is through the use of **reduced-form equations**, equations that express a particular endogenous variable solely in terms of an error term and all the predetermined (exogenous plus lagged endogenous) variables in the simultaneous system.

The reduced-form equations for the structural Equations 14.2 and 14.3 would thus be:

$$Y_{1t} = \pi_0 + \pi_1 X_{1t} + \pi_2 X_{2t} + \pi_3 X_{3t} + v_{1t} \tag{14.6}$$

$$Y_{2t} = \pi_4 + \pi_5 X_{1t} + \pi_6 X_{2t} + \pi_7 X_{3t} + v_{2t} \tag{14.7}$$

where the vs are stochastic error terms and the πs are called *reduced-form coefficients* because they are the coefficients of the predetermined variables in the reduced-form equations. Where do these reduced-form equations come from? If you substitute Equation 14.3 into Equation 14.2, solve for Y_1, and then regroup terms, you'll get Equation 14.6.

Note that each reduced-form equation includes only one endogenous variable (the dependent variable) and that each equation has exactly the same set of predetermined variables. The reduced-form coefficients, such as π_1 and π_5, are known as **impact multipliers** because they measure the impact on the endogenous variable of a one-unit increase in the value of the predetermined variable, after allowing for the feedback effects from the entire simultaneous system.

There are at least three reasons for using reduced-form equations:

1. Since the reduced-form equations have no inherent simultaneity, they do not violate Classical Assumption III. Therefore, they can be estimated with OLS without encountering the problems discussed in this chapter.

2. The interpretation of the reduced-form coefficients as impact multipliers means that they have economic meaning and useful applications of their own. For example, if you wanted to compare a government spending increase with a tax cut in terms of the per-dollar impact in the first year, estimates of the impact multipliers (reduced-form coefficients or πs) would allow such a comparison.

3. Perhaps most importantly, reduced-form equations play a crucial role in the estimation technique most frequently used for simultaneous equations. This technique, Two-Stage Least Squares, will be explained in Section 14.3.

To conclude, let's return to the cola supply and demand model and specify the reduced-form equations for that model. (To test yourself, flip back to Equations 14.4 and 14.5 and see if you can get the right answer before going on.) Since the equilibrium condition forces Q_D to be equal to Q_S, we need only two reduced-form equations:

$$Q_t = \pi_0 + \pi_1 X_{1t} + \pi_2 X_{2t} + \pi_3 X_{3t} + v_{1t} \qquad (14.8)$$

$$P_t = \pi_4 + \pi_5 X_{1t} + \pi_6 X_{2t} + \pi_7 X_{3t} + v_{2t} \qquad (14.9)$$

Even though P never appears on the left side of a structural equation, it's an endogenous variable and should be treated as such.

14.2 The Bias of Ordinary Least Squares

The first six Classical Assumptions must be met for OLS estimates to be BLUE; when an assumption is violated, we must determine which of the properties no longer holds. It turns out that applying OLS directly to the structural equations of a simultaneous system produces biased and inconsistent estimates of the coefficients. Such bias is called simultaneous equations bias or simultaneity bias.

Understanding Simultaneity Bias

Simultaneity bias refers to the fact that in a simultaneous system, the expected values of the OLS-estimated structural coefficients ($\hat{\beta}$s) are not equal to the true βs. We are therefore faced with the problem that in a simultaneous system:

$$E(\hat{\beta}) \neq \beta \tag{14.10}$$

Why does this simultaneity bias exist? Recall from Section 14.1 that in simultaneous equations systems, the error terms (the ϵs) tend to be correlated with the endogenous variables (the Ys) whenever the Ys appear as explanatory variables. Let's follow through what this correlation means (assuming positive coefficients for simplicity) in typical structural equations like 14.11 and 14.12:

$$Y_{1t} = \beta_0 + \beta_1 Y_{2t} + \beta_2 X_t + \epsilon_{1t} \tag{14.11}$$

$$Y_{2t} = \alpha_0 + \alpha_1 Y_{1t} + \alpha_2 Z_t + \epsilon_{2t} \tag{14.12}$$

Since we cannot observe the error term (ϵ_1) and don't know when ϵ_{1t} is above average, it will appear as if every time Y_1 is above average, Y_2 is also above average (as long as α_1 is positive). As a result, the OLS estimation program will tend to attribute increases in Y_1 caused by the error term ϵ_1 to Y_2, thus typically overestimating β_1. This overestimation is simultaneity bias. If the error term is abnormally negative, Y_{1t} will be less than it would have been otherwise, causing Y_{2t} to be less than it would have been otherwise, and the computer program will attribute the decrease in Y_1 to Y_2, once again causing us to overestimate β_1 (that is, induce upward bias).

Recall that the causation between Y_1 and Y_2 runs in both directions because the two variables are interdependent. As a result, β_1, when estimated by OLS, can no longer be interpreted as the impact of Y_2 on Y_1, holding X constant. Instead, $\hat{\beta}_1$ now measures some mix of the effects of the two endogenous variables on each other! In addition, consider β_2. It's supposed to be the effect of X on Y_1 holding Y_2 constant, but how can we expect Y_2 to be held constant when a change in Y_1 takes place? As a result, there is potential bias in all the estimated coefficients in a simultaneous system.

What does this bias look like? It's possible to derive an equation for the expected value of the regression coefficients in a simultaneous system that is estimated by OLS. This equation shows that as long as the error term and any of the explanatory variables in the equation are correlated, then the coefficient estimates will be biased and inconsistent. In addition, it also shows that the bias will have the same sign as the correlation between the error term and the endogenous variable that appears as an explanatory variable in that error term's equation. Since that correlation is often positive in economic and business examples, the bias often will be positive, although the direction of the bias in any given situation will depend on the specific details of the structural equations and the model's underlying theory.

This does not mean that every coefficient from a simultaneous system estimated with OLS will be a bad approximation of the true population coefficient. However, it's vital to consider an alternative to OLS whenever simultaneous equations systems are being estimated. Before we investigate the alternative estimation technique most frequently used (Two-Stage Least Squares), let's look at an example of simultaneity bias.

An Example of Simultaneity Bias

To show how the application of OLS to simultaneous equations estimation causes bias, we used a Monte Carlo experiment[3] to generate an example of such biased estimates. Since it's impossible to know whether any bias exists unless you also know the true βs, we arbitrarily picked a set of coefficients to be considered "true." We then stochastically generated data sets based on these "true" coefficients, and obtained repeated OLS estimates of these coefficients from the generated data sets. The expected value of these estimates turned out to be quite different from the true coefficient values, thus exemplifying the bias in OLS estimates of coefficients in simultaneous systems.

---

3. *Monte Carlo* experiments are computer-generated simulations that typically follow seven steps: 1. Assume a "true" model with specific coefficient values and an error term distribution. 2. Select values for the independent variables. 3. Select an estimating technique (usually OLS). 4. Create various samples of the dependent variable, using the assumed model, by randomly generating error terms from the assumed distribution; often, the number of samples created runs into the thousands. 5. Compute the estimates of the βs from the various samples using the estimating technique. 6. Summarize and evaluate the results. 7. Consider sensitivity analyses using different values, distributions, or estimating techniques.

We used a supply and demand model as the basis for our example:

$$Q_t = \beta_0 + \beta_1 P_t + \beta_2 X_t + \epsilon_{Dt} \tag{14.13}$$

$$Q_t = \alpha_0 + \alpha_1 P_t + \alpha_2 Z_t + \epsilon_{St} \tag{14.14}$$

where: Q_t = the quantity demanded and supplied in time period t
P_t = the price in time period t
X_t = a "demand-side" exogenous variable, such as income
Z_t = a "supply-side" exogenous variable, such as weather
ϵ_t = classical error terms (different for each equation)

The first step was to choose a set of true coefficient values that corresponded to our expectations for this model:

$$\beta_1 = -1 \qquad \beta_2 = +1 \qquad \alpha_1 = +1 \qquad \alpha_2 = +1$$

In other words, we have a negative relationship between price and quantity demanded, a positive relationship between price and quantity supplied, and positive relationships between the exogenous variables and their respective dependent variables.

The next step was to randomly generate a number of data sets based on the true values. This also meant specifying some other characteristics of the data[4] before generating the different data sets (5,000 in this case).

The final step was to apply OLS to the generated data sets and to calculate the estimated coefficients of the demand equation (14.13). (Similar results were obtained for the supply equation.) The arithmetic means of the results for the 5,000 regressions were:

$$\hat{Q}_{Dt} = \hat{\beta}_0 - 0.37 P_t + 1.84 X_t \tag{14.15}$$

In other words, the expected value of $\hat{\beta}_1$ should have been -1.00, but instead it was roughly -0.37; the expected value of $\hat{\beta}_2$ should have been $+1.00$, but instead it was around 1.84:

$$E(\hat{\beta}_1) \approx -0.37 \neq -1.00$$

$$E(\hat{\beta}_2) \approx 1.84 \neq 1.00$$

This is simultaneity bias! As the diagram of the sampling distributions of the $\hat{\beta}$s in Figure 14.2 shows, the OLS estimates of β_1 were almost never very close to -1.00, and the OLS estimates of β_2 were distributed over a wide range of values.

---

4. Other assumptions included a normal distribution for the error term, $\beta_0 = 0$, $\alpha_0 = 0$, $\sigma_S^2 = 3$, $\sigma_D^2 = 2$, $r_{xz}^2 = 0.4$, and $N = 20$. In addition, we assumed that the error terms of the two equations were not correlated.

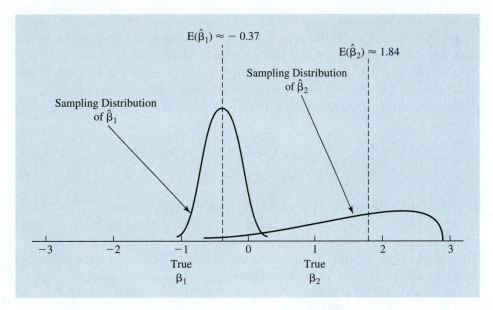

Figure 14.2 Sampling Distributions Showing Simultaneity Bias of OLS Estimates

In the experiment in Section 14.2, simultaneity bias is evident in the distribution of the estimates of β_1, which had a mean value of -0.37 compared with a true value of -1.00, and in the estimates of β_2, which had a mean value of 1.84 compared with a true value of 1.00.

14.3 Two-Stage Least Squares (2SLS)

How can we get rid of (or at least reduce) simultaneity bias? There are a number of estimation techniques that help mitigate simultaneity bias, but the most frequently used alternative to OLS is called Two-Stage Least Squares (2SLS).

Since OLS encounters bias in the estimation of simultaneous equations mainly because such equations violate Classical Assumption III, one solution to the problem is to try to avoid violating that assumption. The first step in doing this is to find a variable that is:

1. highly correlated with the endogenous variable, and

2. uncorrelated with the error term.

Such a variable is called an **instrumental variable**; it is highly correlated with the endogenous variable, but is uncorrelated with the error term. More generally, *instrumental variables (IV) regression* is a method of avoiding the violation of Classical Assumption III by producing predicted values of endogenous variables that can be substituted for the endogenous variables where they appear on the right-hand side of structural equations. These predicted values typically are produced by running an OLS equation to explain the endogenous variable as a function of one or more instrumental variables.

To see how this works, take a look at Equation 14.16 in the following system:

$$Y_{1t} = \beta_0 + \beta_1 Y_{2t} + \beta_2 X_{1t} + \epsilon_{1t} \tag{14.16}$$

$$Y_{2t} = \alpha_0 + \alpha_1 Y_{1t} + \alpha_2 X_{2t} + \epsilon_{2t} \tag{14.17}$$

If we could find a variable (or variables) highly correlated with Y_{2t} but uncorrelated with ϵ_{1t}, then we could produce a predicted value of Y_{2t} by running an OLS regression with Y_{2t} as a function of the instrumental variable(s). The fitted value $\hat{Y}_{2t}$ will be uncorrelated with ϵ_{1t} (because it was produced using variables that are uncorrelated with ϵ_{1t}), so if we substitute $\hat{Y}_{2t}$ for Y_{2t} on the right side of Equation 14.16, then we'll no longer violate Classical Assumption III.

This approach avoids the violation of Classical Assumption III, but it doesn't give us any insight into where to find appropriate instrumental variables (sometimes called instruments). How do we systematically find variables that are highly correlated with the endogenous variable but uncorrelated with the error term? For simultaneous equations systems, there's a straightforward answer. We use Two-Stage Least Squares.

What Is Two-Stage Least Squares?

Two-Stage Least Squares (2SLS) is a method of avoiding simultaneity bias by systematically creating variables to replace the endogenous variables where they appear as explanatory variables in simultaneous equations systems. The simplest form of 2SLS does this by running an OLS regression on the reduced form of every right-side endogenous variable and then using the $\hat{Y}$ (or fitted value) from the reduced-form estimated equation in place of the endogenous variable where it appears on the right side of a structural equation.

Why does 2SLS do this? Every predetermined variable in the simultaneous system is a candidate to be an instrumental variable for every endogenous variable, but if we choose only one instrumental variable, then we'll be throwing away information. To avoid this, 2SLS uses a linear combination of *all* the predetermined variables. We form this linear combination by running a regression for a given endogenous variable as a function of all the predetermined variables in the reduced-form equation to generate a predicted value of the endogenous variable. Thus the 2SLS two-step estimation procedure is:

> **STAGE ONE:** *Run OLS on the reduced-form equations for each of the endogenous variables that appear as explanatory variables in the structural equations in the system.*

Since the predetermined (exogenous plus lagged endogenous) variables are uncorrelated with the reduced-form error term, the OLS estimates of the reduced-form coefficients (the $\hat{\pi}$s) are unbiased. These $\hat{\pi}$s can then be used to calculate estimates of the endogenous variables:

$$\hat{Y}_{1t} = \hat{\pi}_0 + \hat{\pi}_1 X_{1t} + \hat{\pi}_2 X_{2t} \tag{14.18}$$

$$\hat{Y}_{2t} = \hat{\pi}_3 + \hat{\pi}_4 X_{1t} + \hat{\pi}_5 X_{2t} \tag{14.19}$$

These $\hat{Y}$s then are used in place of the Ys on the right-hand side of the structural equations.

> **STAGE TWO:** *Substitute the reduced form $\hat{Y}$s for the Ys that appear on the right side (only) of the structural equations, and then estimate these revised structural equations.*

That is, stage two consists of estimating the following equations with OLS:

$$Y_{1t} = \beta_0 + \beta_1 \hat{Y}_{2t} + \beta_2 X_{1t} + u_{1t} \tag{14.20}$$

$$Y_{2t} = \alpha_0 + \alpha_1 \hat{Y}_{1t} + \alpha_2 X_{2t} + u_{2t} \tag{14.21}$$

Note that the dependent variables are still the original endogenous variables and that the substitutions are only for the endogenous variables where they appear on the right-hand side of the structural equations. This procedure produces consistent estimates of the coefficients of the structural equations.

Be careful! If second-stage equations such as Equations 14.20 and 14.21 are estimated with OLS, the $SE(\hat{\beta})$s will be incorrect, so be sure to use your computer's 2SLS estimation procedure.

This description of 2SLS can be generalized to any number of simultaneous structural equations. Each reduced-form equation has as explanatory variables every predetermined variable in the entire system of equations. The OLS estimates of the reduced-form equations are used to compute the estimated values of all the endogenous variables that appear as explanatory variables in the structural equations. After substituting these fitted values for the original values of the endogenous independent variables, OLS is applied to each stochastic equation in the set of structural equations.

The Properties of Two-Stage Least Squares

1. *2SLS estimates still are biased.* The expected value of a $\hat{\beta}$ produced by 2SLS is not equal to the true β, but the expected bias due to 2SLS usually is smaller than the expected bias due to OLS. One cause of the 2SLS bias is any remaining correlation between the $\hat{Y}$s produced by the first-stage reduced-form regressions and the ϵs. As the sample size gets larger, the 2SLS bias falls, but it is always non-zero in a finite sample.

   To illustrate these properties,[5] let's return to the Monte Carlo example of Section 14.2. If we estimate the equation with 2SLS, we get a mean $\hat{\beta}_1$ of roughly -1.25. This isn't equal to the true β_1 of -1.00, but it's much closer than the OLS mean $\hat{\beta}_1$ of around -0.37. If we then expand the number of observations in each sample from 20 to 50 and re-estimate the equation with 2SLS for the 5,000 samples, the mean of the sampling distribution of $\hat{\beta}_1$ moves to -1.06, which is even closer to the true value of -1.00.

2. *If the fit of the reduced-form equation is poor, then 2SLS will not rid the equation of bias.* Recall that an instrumental variable is supposed to be highly correlated with the endogenous variable. To the extent that the fit of the reduced-form equation is poor,[6] then the instrumental variables aren't highly correlated with the original endogenous variable, and there is no reason to expect 2SLS to be effective. As the fit of the reduced-form equation increases, the usefulness of 2SLS will increase.

3. *2SLS estimates have increased variances and $SE(\hat{\beta})s$.* While 2SLS does an excellent job of reducing the amount of bias in the $\hat{\beta}$s, there's a price to pay for this reduced bias. This price is that 2SLS estimates tend to have higher variances and $SE(\hat{\beta})$s than do OLS estimates of the same equations.

---

5. Under certain circumstances, for example, if only one instrument is used to produce the predicted values of the endogenous variable, then the population mean of the instrumental variable estimator is undefined, and the bias is not defined.

6. See J. Stock and M. Yogo, "Testing for Weak Instruments in Linear IV Regression," in D.W.K. Andrews, *Identification and Inference for Econometric Models* (New York: Cambridge University Press, 2005), pp. 80–108. They develop a test of the fit of the reduced-form equation that is a version of the F–test, not $\overline{R}^2$. A rough rule of thumb is that F should be greater than 10.

On balance, then, 2SLS will almost always be a better estimator of the coefficients of a simultaneous system than OLS will be. The major exception to this general rule is when the fit of the reduced-form equation in question is poor.

An Example of Two-Stage Least Squares

Let's work through an example of 2SLS, a naive linear Keynesian macroeconomic model of the U.S. economy. We'll specify the following system:

$$Y_t = CO_t + I_t + G_t + NX_t \tag{14.22}$$

$$CO_t = \beta_0 + \beta_1 YD_t + \beta_2 CO_{t-1} + \epsilon_{1t} \tag{14.23}$$

$$YD_t = Y_t - T_t \tag{14.24}$$

$$I_t = \beta_3 + \beta_4 Y_t + \beta_5 r_{t-1} + \epsilon_{2t} \tag{14.25}$$

where:
- Y_t = Gross Domestic Product (GDP) in year t
- CO_t = total personal consumption in year t
- I_t = total gross private domestic investment in year t
- G_t = government purchases of goods and services in year t
- NX_t = net exports of goods and services (exports minus imports) in year t
- T_t = taxes (actually equal to taxes, depreciation, corporate profits, government transfers, and other adjustments necessary to convert GDP to disposable income) in year t
- r_t = the interest rate in year t
- YD_t = disposable income in year t

All variables are in real terms (measured in billions of 2000 dollars) except the interest rate variable, which is measured in nominal percent. The data for this example are from 1976 through 2007 and are presented in Table 14.1.

Equations 14.22 through 14.25 are the structural equations of the system, but only Equations 14.23 and 14.25 are stochastic (behavioral) and need to be estimated. The other two are not stochastic, as can be determined by the lack of an error term in the equations.

Stop for a second and look at the system. Which variables are endogenous? Which are predetermined? The endogenous variables are those that are jointly determined by the system, namely, Y_t, CO_t, YD_t, and I_t. To see why these four variables are simultaneously determined, note that if you change one of them and follow this change through the system, the change will get back to the original causal variable. For instance, if I_t goes up for some reason, that will cause Y_t to go up (through Equation 14.22), which will feed right back into I_t again (through Equation 14.25). They're simultaneously determined.

Table 14.1 Data for the Small Macromodel

YEAR	Y	CO	I	G	YD	r
1975	NA	2876.9	NA	NA	NA	8.83
1976	4540.9	3035.5	544.7	1031.9	3432.2	8.43
1977	4750.5	3164.1	627.0	1043.3	3552.9	8.02
1978	5015.0	3303.1	702.6	1074.0	3718.8	8.73
1979	5173.4	3383.4	725.0	1094.1	3811.2	9.63
1980	5161.7	3374.1	645.3	1115.4	3857.7	11.94
1981	5291.7	3422.2	704.9	1125.6	3960.0	14.17
1982	5189.3	3470.3	606.0	1145.4	4044.9	13.79
1983	5423.8	3668.6	662.5	1187.3	4177.7	12.04
1984	5813.6	3863.3	857.7	1227.0	4494.1	12.71
1985	6053.7	4064.0	849.7	1312.5	4645.2	11.37
1986	6263.6	4228.9	843.9	1392.5	4791.0	9.02
1987	6475.1	4369.8	870.0	1426.7	4874.5	9.38
1988	6742.7	4546.9	890.5	1445.1	5082.6	9.71
1989	6981.4	4675.0	926.2	1482.5	5224.8	9.26
1990	7112.5	4770.3	895.1	1530.0	5324.2	9.32
1991	7100.5	4778.4	822.2	1547.2	5351.7	8.77
1992	7336.6	4934.8	889.0	1555.3	5536.3	8.14
1993	7532.7	5099.8	968.3	1541.1	5594.2	7.22
1994	7835.5	5290.7	1099.6	1541.3	5746.4	7.96
1995	8031.7	5433.5	1134.0	1549.7	5905.7	7.59
1996	8328.9	5619.4	1234.3	1564.9	6080.9	7.37
1997	8703.5	5831.8	1387.7	1594.0	6295.8	7.26
1998	9066.9	6125.8	1524.1	1624.4	6663.9	6.53
1999	9470.3	6438.6	1642.6	1686.9	6861.3	7.04
2000	9817.0	6739.4	1735.5	1721.6	7194.0	7.62
2001	9890.7	6910.4	1598.4	1780.3	7333.3	7.08
2002	10048.8	7099.3	1557.1	1858.8	7562.2	6.49
2003	10301.0	7295.3	1613.1	1904.8	7729.9	5.67
2004	10675.8	7561.4	1770.2	1931.8	8008.9	5.63
2005	10989.5	7791.7	1873.5	1939.0	8121.4	5.24
2006	11294.8	8029.0	1912.5	1971.2	8407.0	5.59
2007	11523.9	8252.8	1809.7	2012.1	8644.0	5.56

Source: *The Economic Report of the President, 2009*. Note that T and NX can be calculated using Equations 14.22 and 14.24.

Datafile = MACRO14

What about interest rates? Is r_t an endogenous variable? The surprising answer is that, strictly speaking, r_t is *not* endogenous in this system because r_{t-1} (not r_t) appears in the investment equation. Thus, there is no simultaneous feedback through the interest rate in this simple model.[7]

Given this answer, which are the predetermined variables? The predetermined variables are G_t, NX_t, T_t, CO_{t-1}, and r_{t-1}. To sum, the simultaneous system has four structural equations, four endogenous variables, and five predetermined variables.

What is the economic content of the stochastic structural equations? The consumption function, Equation 14.23, is a dynamic model consumption function of the kind we analyzed in Chapter 12. We discussed this exact equation in Section 12.2, going so far as to estimate Equation 14.23 with OLS on data from Table 14.1, and the reader is encouraged to reread that analysis.

The investment function, Equation 14.25, includes simplified multiplier and cost of capital components. The multiplier term β_4 measures the stimulus to investment that is generated by an increase in GDP. In a Keynesian model, β_4 thus would be expected to be positive. On the other hand, the higher the cost of capital, the less investment we'd expect to be undertaken (holding multiplier effects constant), mainly because the expected rate of return on marginal capital investments is no longer sufficient to cover the higher cost of capital. Thus β_5 is expected to be negative. It takes time to plan and start up investment projects, though, so the interest rate is lagged one year.[8]

Stage One: Even though there are four endogenous variables, only two of them appear on the right-hand side of stochastic equations, so only two reduced-form equations need to be estimated to apply 2SLS. These reduced-form equations are estimated automatically by all 2SLS computer estimation programs, but it's instructive to take a look at one anyway:

$$\widehat{YD}_t = -258.55 + 0.78G_t - 0.37NX_t + 0.52T_t + 0.67CO_{t-1} + 37.63r_{t-1}$$
$$(0.22) \quad (0.16) \quad (0.14) \quad (0.09) \quad\quad (9.14)$$
$$t = \quad 3.49 \quad -2.30 \quad\quad 3.68 \quad 7.60 \quad\quad\quad 4.12$$
$$(14.26)$$

---

7. Although this sentence is technically correct, it overstates the case. In particular, there are a couple of circumstances in which an econometrician might want to consider r_{t-1} to be part of the simultaneous system for theoretical reasons. For our naive Keynesian model with a lagged interest rate effect, however, the equation is not in the simultaneous system.

8. This investment equation is a simplified mix of the accelerator and the neoclassical theories of the investment function. The former emphasizes that changes in the level of output are the key determinant of investment, and the latter emphasizes that user cost of capital (the opportunity cost that the firm incurs as a consequence of owning an asset) is the key.

Note that we don't test any hypotheses on reduced forms, nor do we consider dropping a variable[9] that is statistically and theoretically irrelevant. The whole purpose of stage one of 2SLS is not to generate meaningful reduced-form estimated equations but rather to generate $\hat{Y}$s to use as substitutes for endogenous variables in the second stage. To do that, we calculate the $\hat{Y}_t$s and $\widehat{YD}_t$s for all 32 observations by plugging the actual values of all 5 predetermined variables into estimated reduced-form equations like Equation 14.26.

Stage Two: We then substitute these $\hat{Y}_t$s and $\widehat{YD}_t$s for the endogenous variables where they appear on the right sides of Equations 14.23 and 14.25. For example, the $\widehat{YD}_t$ from Equation 14.26 would be substituted into Equation 14.23, resulting in:

$$CO_t = \beta_0 + \beta_1 \widehat{YD}_t + \beta_2 CO_{t-1} + \epsilon_{1t} \tag{14.27}$$

If we estimate Equation 14.27 and the other second-stage equation given the data in Table 14.1, we obtain the following 2SLS[10] results:

$$\widehat{CO}_t = -209.06 + 0.37\widehat{YD}_t + 0.66CO_{t-1} \tag{14.28}$$
$$(0.13) \quad (0.14)$$
$$2.73 \quad 4.84$$
$$N = 32 \quad \overline{R}^2 = .999 \quad DW = 0.83$$

$$\hat{I}_t = -261.48 + 0.19\hat{Y}_t - 9.55r_{t-1} \tag{14.29}$$
$$(0.01) \quad (11.20)$$
$$15.82 \quad -0.85$$
$$N = 32 \quad \overline{R}^2 = .956 \quad DW = 0.47$$

---

9. Our recommendation to use every predetermined variable in the simultaneous system as an instrumental variable in the first stage of 2SLS is a simplification that we think is appropriate given the level of this text. Experienced econometricians will test each potential instrumental variable to measure the extent to which the variable is highly correlated with the endogenous variable and uncorrelated with the error term. Only those variables that meet these criteria should then be used as valid instruments in the first stage. For an approachable discussion of the topic of checking instrument validity, see James Stock and Mark Watson, *Introduction to Econometrics* (Boston: Pearson, 2015), pp. 442–448.

10. The 2SLS estimates in Equations 14.28 and 14.29 are correct, but if you were to estimate those equations with OLS (using $\hat{Y}$s and $\widehat{YD}$s generated as in Equation 14.26) you would obtain the same coefficient estimates but a different set of estimates of the standard errors (and t-scores). This difference comes about because running OLS on the second stage alone ignores the fact that the first stage was run at all. To get accurate estimated standard errors and t-scores, the estimation should be done with a 2SLS program.

If we had estimated these equations with OLS alone instead of with 2SLS, we would have obtained:

$$\widehat{CO}_t = -266.65 + 0.46YD_t + 0.56CO_{t-1} \qquad (14.30)$$
$$\phantom{\widehat{CO}_t = -266.65 + } (0.10) \quad\; (0.10)$$
$$\phantom{\widehat{CO}_t = -266.65 + } 4.70 \qquad 5.66$$
$$N = 32 \qquad \overline{R}^2 = .999 \qquad DW = 0.77$$

$$\hat{I}_t = -267.16 + 0.19Y_t - 9.26r_{t-1} \qquad (14.31)$$
$$\phantom{\hat{I}_t = -267.16 + } (0.01) \; (11.19)$$
$$\phantom{\hat{I}_t = -267.16 + } 15.87 \;\; -0.83$$
$$N = 32 \qquad \overline{R}^2 = .956 \qquad DW = 0.47$$

Let's compare the OLS and 2SLS results. At first glance, there doesn't seem to be much difference between them. If OLS is biased, how could this occur? When the fit of the stage-one reduced-form equations is excellent, as in Equation 14.26, then Y and $\hat{Y}$ are virtually identical, and the second stage of 2SLS is quite similar to the OLS estimate.

Also, take a look at the Durbin–Watson statistics. DW is well below the d_L of 1.31 (one-sided 5-percent significance, $N = 32$, $K = 2$) in all the equations despite DW's bias toward 2 in the consumption equation (because it's a dynamic model). Consequently, positive serial correlation is likely to exist in the residuals of both equations. Applying GLS to the two 2SLS-estimated equations is tricky, however, especially because, as mentioned in Section 12.3, serial correlation causes bias in an equation with a lagged dependent variable, as in the consumption function.

Finally, what about nonstationarity? We learned in Chapter 12 that time-series models like these have the potential to be spurious in the face of nonstationarity. Are any of these regressions spurious? Well, as you can guess from looking at the data, quite a few of the series in this model are, indeed, nonstationary. Luckily, the interest rate is stationary. However, it turns out that the consumption function is reasonably cointegrated, so Equations 14.28 and 14.30 probably can stand as estimated. Unfortunately, the investment equation suffers from nonstationarity that almost surely results in an inflated t-score for GDP and a low t-score for r_{t-1} (because r_{t-1} is stationary when all the other variables in the equation are nonstationary). Given the tools covered so far in this text, however, there is little we can do to improve the situation.

These caveats aside, this model has provided us with a complete example of the use of 2SLS to estimate a simultaneous system. However, the application of 2SLS requires that the equation being estimated be "identified," so before we can conclude our study of simultaneous equations, we need to address the problem of identification.

14.4 The Identification Problem

Two-Stage Least Squares cannot be applied to an equation unless that equation is *identified*. Before estimating any equation in a simultaneous system, you therefore must address the identification problem. Once an equation is found to be identified, then it can be estimated with 2SLS, but if an equation is not identified (*underidentified*), then 2SLS cannot be used no matter how large the sample. Such underidentified equations can be estimated with OLS, but OLS estimates of underidentified equations are difficult to interpret. It's important to point out that an equation being identified (and therefore capable of being estimated with 2SLS) does not ensure that the resulting 2SLS estimates will be good ones. The question being asked is not how good the 2SLS estimates will be but whether the 2SLS estimates can be obtained at all.

What Is the Identification Problem?

Identification is a precondition for the application of 2SLS to equations in simultaneous systems; a structural equation is identified only when enough of the system's predetermined variables are omitted from the equation in question to allow that equation to be distinguished from all the others in the system. Note that one equation in a simultaneous system might be identified and another might not.

How can we have equations that we cannot identify? To see how, let's consider a supply and demand simultaneous system in which only price and quantity are specified:

$$Q_{Dt} = \alpha_0 + \alpha_1 P_t + \epsilon_{Dt} \quad \text{(demand)} \tag{14.32}$$

$$Q_{St} = \beta_0 + \beta_1 P_t + \epsilon_{St} \quad \text{(supply)} \tag{14.33}$$

where: $\qquad Q_{Dt} = Q_{St}$

Although we've labeled one equation as the demand equation and the other as the supply equation, the computer will not be able to identify them from the data because the right-side and the left-side variables are exactly the same in both equations; without some predetermined variables included to differentiate these two equations, it would be impossible to distinguish supply from demand.

What if we added a predetermined variable like weather (W) to the supply equation for an agricultural product? Then, Equation 14.33 would become:

$$Q_{St} = \beta_0 + \beta_1 P_t + \beta_2 W_t + \epsilon_{St} \tag{14.34}$$

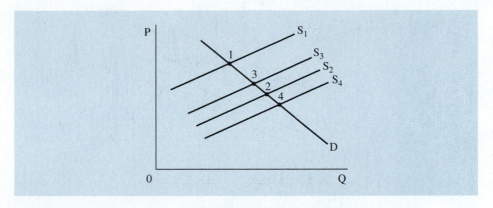

Figure 14.3 A Shifting Supply Curve Allows the Identification of the Demand Curve

If the supply curve shifts but the demand curve does not, then we move along the demand curve, which allows us to identify and estimate the demand curve (but not the supply curve).

In such a circumstance, every time W changed, the supply curve would shift, but the demand curve would not, so that eventually we would be able to collect a good picture of what the demand curve looked like.

Figure 14.3 demonstrates this. Given four different values of W, we get four different supply curves, each of which intersects with the constant demand curve at a different equilibrium price and quantity (intersections 1–4). These equilibria are the data that we would be able to observe in the real world and are all that we could feed into the computer. As a result, we would be able to identify the demand curve because we left out at least one predetermined variable. When this predetermined variable changed, but the demand curve didn't, the supply curve shifted so that quantity demanded moved along the demand curve and we gathered enough information to estimate the coefficients of the demand curve. The supply curve, on the other hand, remains as much a mystery as ever because its shifts give us no clue whatsoever about its shape. In essence, the demand curve was identified by the predetermined variable that was included in the system but excluded from the demand equation. The supply curve is not identified because there is no such excluded predetermined variable for it.

Even if we added W to the demand curve as well (which wouldn't make sense from a theoretical point of view), that would not identify the supply curve. In fact, if we had W in both equations, the two would be identical again, and although both would shift when W changed, those shifts would

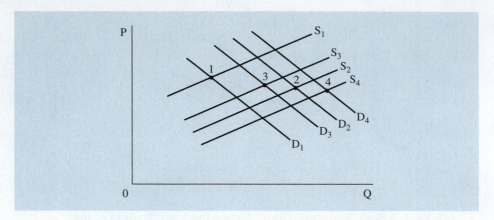

Figure 14.4 If Both the Supply Curve and the Demand Curve Shift, Neither Curve Is Identified

If both the supply curve and the demand curve shift in response to the same variable, then we move from one equilibrium to another, and the resulting data points identify neither curve. To allow such an identification, at least one predetermined variable must cause one curve to shift while allowing the other to remain constant.

give us no information about either curve! As illustrated in Figure 14.4, the observed equilibrium prices and quantities would be almost random inter- sections describing neither the demand nor the supply curve. That is, the shifts in the supply curve are the same as before, but now the demand curve also shifts with W. In this case, it's not possible to identify either the demand curve or the supply curve.

The way to identify both curves is to have at least one predetermined vari- able in each equation that is not in the other, as in:

$$Q_{Dt} = \alpha_0 + \alpha_1 P_t + \alpha_2 X_t + \epsilon_{Dt} \tag{14.35}$$

$$Q_{St} = \beta_0 + \beta_1 P_t + \beta_2 W_t + \epsilon_{St} \tag{14.36}$$

Now when W changes, the supply curve shifts, and we can identify the demand curves from the data on equilibrium prices and quantities. When X changes, the demand curve shifts, and we can identify the supply curve from the data.

To sum, identification is a precondition for the application of 2SLS to equations in simultaneous systems. A structural equation is identified only when the predetermined variables are arranged within the system so as to allow us to use the observed equilibrium points to distinguish the shape of the equation in question. Most systems are quite a bit more complicated than the previous ones, however, so econometricians need a general method by which to determine whether equations are identified. The method typically used is the *order condition* of identification.

The Order Condition of Identification

The **order condition** is a systematic method of determining whether a particular equation in a simultaneous system has the potential to be identified. If an equation can meet the order condition, then it is identified in all but a very small number of cases. We thus say that the order condition is a necessary but not sufficient condition of identification.[11]

What is the order condition? Recall that we have used the phrases *endogenous* and *predetermined* to refer to the two kinds of variables in a simultaneous system. Endogenous variables are those that are jointly determined in the system in the current time period. Predetermined variables are exogenous variables plus any lagged endogenous variables that might be in the model. For each equation in the system, we need to determine:

1. The number of predetermined (exogenous plus lagged endogenous) variables in the entire simultaneous system.
2. The number of slope coefficients estimated in the equation in question.

THE ORDER CONDITION: *A necessary condition for an equation to be identified is that the number of predetermined (exogenous plus lagged endogenous) variables in the system be greater than or equal to the number of slope coefficients in the equation of interest.*

In equation form, a structural equation meets the order condition if:

The number of predetermined variables ≥ The number of slope coefficients
(in the simultaneous system)   (in the equation)

---

11. A sufficient condition for an equation to be identified is called the *rank condition*, but most researchers examine just the order condition before estimating an equation with 2SLS. These researchers let the computer estimation procedure tell them whether the rank condition has been met (by its ability to apply 2SLS to the equation). Those interested in the rank condition are encouraged to consult an advanced econometrics text.

Two Examples of the Application of the Order Condition

Let's apply the order condition to some of the simultaneous equations systems encountered in this chapter. For example, consider once again the cola supply and demand model of Section 14.1:

$$Q_{Dt} = \alpha_0 + \alpha_1 P_t + \alpha_2 X_{1t} + \alpha_3 X_{2t} + \epsilon_{Dt} \tag{14.37}$$

$$Q_{St} = \beta_0 + \beta_1 P_t + \beta_2 X_{3t} + \epsilon_{St} \tag{14.38}$$

$$Q_{St} = Q_{Dt} \tag{14.39}$$

Equation 14.37 is identified by the order condition because the number of predetermined variables in the system (three, X_1, X_2, and X_3) is equal to the number of slope coefficients in the equation (three: α_1, α_2, and α_3). This particular result (equality) implies that Equation 14.37 is *exactly identified* by the order condition. Equation 14.38 is also identified by the order condition because there are still three predetermined variables in the system, but there are only two slope coefficients in the equation; this condition implies that Equation 14.38 is *overidentified*. 2SLS can be applied to equations that are identified (which includes exactly identified and overidentified), but not to equations that are underidentified.

A more complicated example is the small macroeconomic model of Section 14.3:

$$Y_t = CO_t + I_t + G_t + NX_t \tag{14.22}$$

$$CO_t = \beta_0 + \beta_1 YD_t + \beta_2 CO_{t-1} + \epsilon_{1t} \tag{14.23}$$

$$YD_t = Y_t - T_t \tag{14.24}$$

$$I_t = \beta_3 + \beta_4 Y_t + \beta_5 r_{t-1} + \epsilon_{2t} \tag{14.25}$$

As we've noted, there are five predetermined variables (exogenous plus lagged endogenous) in this system (G_t, NX_t, T_t, CO_{t-1}, and r_{t-1}). Equation 14.23 has two slope coefficients (β_1 and β_2), so this equation is overidentified ($5 > 2$) and meets the order condition of identification. As the reader can verify, Equation 14.25 also turns out to be overidentified. Since the 2SLS computer program did indeed come up with estimates of the βs in the model, we knew this already. Note that Equations 14.22 and 14.24 are identities and are not estimated, so we're not concerned with their identification properties.

14.5 Summary

1. Most economic and business models are inherently simultaneous because of the dual causality, feedback loops, or joint determination of particular variables. These simultaneously determined variables are called endogenous, and nonsimultaneously determined variables are called exogenous.

2. A structural equation characterizes the theory underlying a particular variable and is the kind of equation we have used to date in this text. A reduced-form equation expresses a particular endogenous variable solely in terms of an error term and all the predetermined (exogenous and lagged endogenous) variables in the simultaneous system.

3. Simultaneous equations models violate Classical Assumption III that the error term is uncorrelated with the explanatory variables. This occurs because of the feedback effects of the endogenous variables. For example, an unusually high observation of an equation's error term works through the simultaneous system and eventually causes a high (with positive coefficients) value for the endogenous variables that appear as explanatory variables in the equation in question, thus violating Classical Assumption III.

4. If OLS is applied to the coefficients of a simultaneous system, the resulting estimates are biased and inconsistent. This occurs mainly because of the violation of Classical Assumption III; the OLS regression package attributes to explanatory variables changes in the dependent variable actually caused by the error term (with which the explanatory variables are correlated).

5. Two-Stage Least Squares is a method of estimating simultaneous equations systems. It works by systematically using the reduced-form equations of the system to create substitutes for the endogenous variables that are independent of the error terms. It then estimates the structural equations of the system with these substitutes replacing the endogenous variables where they appear as explanatory variables.

6. Two-Stage Least Squares estimates are consistent but biased. Luckily, the expected bias due to 2SLS usually is smaller than the expected bias due to OLS. If the fit of the reduced-form equations is poor, then 2SLS will not work very well.

7. 2SLS cannot be applied to an equation that's not identified. A necessary (but not sufficient) requirement for identification is the order condition, which requires that the number of predetermined variables in the system be greater than or equal to the number of slope coefficients in the equation of interest. Sufficiency usually is determined by the ability of 2SLS to estimate the coefficients.

EXERCISES

(The answers to the even-numbered exercises are in Appendix A.)

1. Write the meaning of each of the following terms without referring to the book (or your notes), and compare your definition with the version in the text for each.
   a. endogenous variables (p. 412)
   b. exogenous variables (p. 412)
   c. identification (p. 430)
   d. impact multipliers (p. 417)
   e. instrumental variable (p. 421)
   f. order condition (p. 433)
   g. predetermined variable (p. 413)
   h. reduced-form equations (p. 416)
   i. simultaneity bias (p. 418)
   j. structural equations (p. 413)
   k. Two-Stage Least Squares (2SLS) (p. 422)

2. Section 14.1 works through Equations 14.2 and 14.3 to show the violation of Classical Assumption III by an unexpected increase in ϵ_1. Show the violation of Classical Assumption III by working through the following examples:
   a. a decrease in ϵ_2 in Equation 14.3
   b. an increase in ϵ_D in Equation 14.4
   c. an increase in ϵ_1 in Equation 14.23

3. The word *recursive* is used to describe an equation that has an impact on a simultaneous system without any feedback from the system to the equation. Which of the equations in the following systems are simultaneous, and which are recursive? Be sure to specify which variables are endogenous and which are predetermined:

a. $Y_{1t} = \beta_0 + \beta_1 Y_{2t} + \beta_2 X_{1t} + \beta_3 X_{2t-1} + \epsilon_{1t}$

  $Y_{2t} = \alpha_0 + \alpha_1 Y_{3t} + \alpha_2 Y_{1t} + \alpha_3 X_{4t} + \epsilon_{2t}$

  $Y_{3t} = \Omega_0 + \Omega_1 X_{2t} + \Omega_2 X_{1t-1} + \Omega_3 X_{4t-1} + \epsilon_{3t}$

b. $Z_t = \beta_0 + \beta_1 X_t + \beta_2 Y_t + \beta_3 H_t + \epsilon_{1t}$

  $X_t = \alpha_0 + \alpha_1 Z_t + \alpha_2 P_{t-1} + \epsilon_{2t}$

  $H_t = \Omega_0 + \Omega_1 X_{2t} + \Omega_2 B_t + \Omega_3 CS_t + \Omega_4 D_t + \epsilon_{3t}$

c. $Y_{1t} = \beta_0 + \beta_1 Y_{2t} + \beta_2 X_{1t} + \beta_3 X_{2t} + \epsilon_{1t}$

  $Y_{2t} = \alpha_0 + \alpha_1 Y_{3t} + \alpha_2 X_{5t} + \epsilon_{2t}$

4. Determine the identification properties of the following equations. In particular, be sure to note the number of predetermined variables in the system, the number of slope coefficients in the equation, and whether the equation is underidentified, overidentified, or exactly identified.
   a. Equations 14.2–14.3
   b. Equations 14.13–14.14
   c. part a of Exercise 3 (assume all equations are stochastic)
   d. part b of Exercise 3 (assume all equations are stochastic)

5. As an exercise to gain familiarity with the 2SLS program on your computer, take the data provided for the simple Keynesian model in Section 14.3, and:
   a. Estimate the investment function with OLS.
   b. Estimate the reduced form for Y with OLS.
   c. Substitute the $\hat{Y}$ from your reduced form into the investment function and run the second stage yourself with OLS.
   d. Estimate the investment function with your computer's 2SLS program (if there is one) and compare the results with those obtained in part c.

6. Suppose that a fad for oats (resulting from the announcement of the health benefits of oat bran) has made you toy with the idea of becoming a broker in the oat market. Before spending your money, you decide to build a simple model of supply and demand (identical to those in Sections 14.1 and 14.2) of the market for oats:

$$Q_{Dt} = \beta_0 + \beta_1 P_t + \beta_2 YD_t + \epsilon_{Dt}$$
$$Q_{St} = \alpha_0 + \alpha_1 P_t + \alpha_2 W_t + \epsilon_{St}$$
$$Q_{Dt} = Q_{St}$$

where: Q_{Dt} = the quantity of oats demanded in time period t
Q_{St} = the quantity of oats supplied in time period t
P_t = the price of oats in time period t
W_t = average oat-farmer wages in time period t
YD_t = disposable income in time period t

a. You notice that no left-hand-side variable appears on the right side of either of your stochastic simultaneous equations. Does this mean that OLS estimation will encounter no simultaneity bias? Why or why not?

b. You expect that when P_t goes up, Q_{Dt} will fall. Does this mean that if you encounter simultaneity bias in the demand equation, it will be negative instead of the positive bias we typically associate with OLS estimation of simultaneous equations? Explain your answer.

c. Carefully outline how you would apply 2SLS to this system. How many equations (including reduced forms) would you have to estimate? Specify precisely which variables would be in each equation.

d. Given the following hypothetical data,[12] estimate OLS and 2SLS versions of your oat supply and demand equations.

e. Compare your OLS and 2SLS estimates. How do they compare with your prior expectations? Which equation do you prefer? Why?

Year	Q	P	W	YD
1	50	10	100	15
2	54	12	102	12
3	65	9	105	11
4	84	15	107	17
5	75	14	110	19
6	85	15	111	30
7	90	16	111	28
8	60	14	113	25
9	40	17	117	23
10	70	19	120	35

Datafile = OATS14

---

12. These data are from the excellent course materials that Professors Bruce Gensemer and James Keeler prepared to supplement the use of this text at Kenyon College.

7. Simultaneous equations make sense in cross-sectional as well as time-series applications. For example, James Ragan[13] examined the effects of unemployment insurance (hereafter UI) eligibility standards on unemployment rates and the rate at which workers quit their jobs. Ragan used a pooled data set that contained observations from a number of different states from four different years (requirements for UI eligibility differ by state). His results are as follows (*t*-scores in parentheses):

$$\widehat{QU_i} = 7.00 + 0.089UR_i - 0.063UN_i - 2.83RE_i - 0.032MX_i$$
$$\quad\quad\quad (0.10) \quad (-0.63) \quad (-1.98) \quad (-0.73)$$

$$\quad\quad + 0.003IL_i - 0.25QM_i + \cdots$$
$$\quad\quad (0.01) \quad (-0.52)$$

$$\widehat{UR_i} = -0.54 + 0.44QU_i + 0.13UN_i + 0.049MX_i$$
$$\quad\quad\quad (1.01) \quad (3.29) \quad (1.71)$$

$$\quad\quad + 0.56IL_i + 0.63QM_i + \cdots$$
$$\quad\quad (2.03) \quad (2.05)$$

where: QU_i = the quit rate (quits per 100 employees) in the *i*th state
UR_i = the unemployment rate in the *i*th state
UN_i = union membership as a percentage of nonagricultural employment in the *i*th state
RE_i = average hourly earnings in the *i*th state relative to the average hourly earnings for the United States
IL_i = dummy variable equal to 1 if workers in the *i*th state are eligible for UI if they are forced to quit a job because of illness, 0 otherwise
QM_i = dummy variable equal to 1 if the *i*th state maintains full UI benefits for the quitter (rather than lowering benefits), 0 otherwise
MX_i = maximum weekly UI benefits relative to average hourly earnings in the *i*th state

a. Hypothesize the expected signs for the coefficients of each of the explanatory variables in the system. Use economic theory to justify your answers. Which estimated coefficients are different from your expectations?

---

13. James F. Ragan, Jr., "The Voluntary Leaver Provisions of Unemployment Insurance and Their Effect on Quit and Unemployment Rates," *Southern Economic Journal*, Vol. 15, No. 1, pp. 135–146.

b. Ragan felt that these two equations would encounter simultaneity bias if they were estimated with OLS. Do you agree? Explain your answer. (*Hint:* Start by deciding which variables are endogenous and why.)

c. The actual equations included a number of variables not documented earlier, but the only predetermined variable in the system that was included in the QU equation but not the UR equation was RE. What does this information tell you about the identification properties of the QU equation? The UR equation?

d. What are the implications of the lack of significance of the endogenous variables where they appear on the right-hand side of the equations?

e. What, if any, policy recommendations do these results suggest?

(14.6) Appendix: Errors in the Variables

Until now, we have implicitly assumed that our data were measured accurately. That is, although the stochastic error term was defined as including measurement error, we never explicitly discussed what the existence of such measurement error did to the coefficient estimates. Unfortunately, in the real world, errors of measurement are common. Mismeasurement might result from the data being based on a sample, as are almost all national aggregate statistics, or simply because the data were reported incorrectly. Whatever the cause, these **errors in the variables** are mistakes in the measurement of the dependent variable and/or one or more of the independent variables that are large enough to have potential impacts on the estimation of the coefficients. Such errors in the variables might be better called "measurement errors in the data." We will tackle this subject by first examining errors in the dependent variable and then moving on to look at the more serious problem of errors in an independent variable. We assume a single equation model. The reason we have included this topic here is that errors in explanatory variables give rise to biased OLS estimates very similar to simultaneity bias.

Measurement Errors in the Data for the Dependent Variable

Suppose that the true regression model is

$$Y_i = \beta_0 + \beta_1 X_i + \epsilon_i \tag{14.40}$$

and further suppose that the dependent variable, Y_i, is measured incorrectly, so that Y_i^* is observed instead of Y_i, where

$$Y_i^* = Y_i + v_i \tag{14.41}$$

and where v_i is an error of measurement that has all the properties of a classical error term. What does this mismeasurement do to the estimation of Equation 14.40?

To see what happens when $Y_i^* = Y_i + v_i$, let's add v_i to both sides of Equation 14.40, obtaining

$$Y_i + v_i = \beta_0 + \beta_1 X_i + \epsilon_i + v_i \tag{14.42}$$

which is the same as

$$Y_i^* = \beta_0 + \beta_1 X_i + \epsilon_i^* \tag{14.43}$$

where $\epsilon_i^* = (\epsilon_i + v_i)$. That is, we estimate Equation 14.43 when in reality we want to estimate Equation 14.40. Take another look at Equation 14.43. When v_i changes, both the dependent variable and the error term ϵ_i^* move together. This is no cause for alarm, however, since the dependent variable is always correlated with the error term. Although the extra movement will increase the variability of Y and therefore be likely to decrease the overall statistical fit of the equation, an error of measurement in the dependent variable does not cause any bias in the estimates of the βs.

Measurement Errors in the Data for an Independent Variable

This is not the case when the mismeasurement is in the data for one or more of the independent variables. Unfortunately, such errors in an independent variable cause bias that is quite similar in nature (and in remedy) to simultaneity bias. To see this, once again suppose that the true regression model is Equation 14.40:

$$Y_i = \beta_0 + \beta_1 X_i + \epsilon_i \tag{14.40}$$

But now suppose that the independent variable, X_i, is measured incorrectly, so that X_i^* is observed instead of X_i, where

$$X_i^* = X_i + u_i \tag{14.44}$$

where u_i is an error of measurement like v_i in Equation 14.41. To see what this mismeasurement does to the estimation of Equation 14.40, let's solve Equation 14.44 for X_i (obtaining $X_i = X_i^* - u_i$) and substitute X_i back into Equation 14.40, giving us:

$$Y_i = \beta_0 + \beta_1 (X_i^* - u_i) + \epsilon_i \tag{14.45}$$

which can be rewritten as:

$$Y_i = \beta_0 + \beta_1 X_i^* + (\epsilon_i - \beta_1 u_i) \tag{14.46}$$

or

$$Y_i = \beta_0 + \beta_1 X_i^* + \epsilon_i^{**} \tag{14.47}$$

where $\epsilon_i^{**} = (\epsilon_i - \beta_1 u_i)$. In this case, we estimate Equation 14.47 when we should be trying to estimate Equation 14.40. Notice what happens to Equation 14.47 when u_i changes, however. When u_i changes, the stochastic error term ϵ_i^{**} and the independent variable X_i^* move in opposite directions; they are correlated! Such a correlation is a direct violation of Classical Assumption III in a way that is remarkably similar to the violation (described in Section 14.1) of the same assumption in simultaneous equations. Not surprisingly, this violation causes the same problem, bias, for errors-in-the-variables models that it causes for simultaneous equations. That is, because of the measurement error in the independent variable, the OLS estimates of the coefficients of Equation 14.47 are *biased* and *inconsistent*. Interestingly, the estimated coefficient β_1 is biased toward zero. This is because if β_1 is negative, ϵ^{**} will be positively correlated with X^*, creating upward bias, while if β_1 is positive, ϵ^{**} will be negatively correlated with X^*, creating downward bias.[14]

In order to rid an equation of the bias caused by measurement errors in the data for one or more of the independent variables, it's logical to use the instrumental variables (IV) approach of Section 14.3. However, the IV approach is only rarely applied to errors in the variables problems for two reasons. First, while we may suspect that there are measurement errors, it's unusual to be sure that they exist. Second, even if we know that there are errors, it's difficult to find an instrumental variable that is both highly correlated with X and uncorrelated with ϵ. In fact, X^* often is about as good an instrument as we can find, so no action is taken. If the mismeasurement in X is known to be large, of course, some remedy is required.

To sum, an error of measurement in one or more of the independent variables will cause the error term of Equation 14.47 to be correlated with the mismeasured independent variable, causing bias that's similar to simultaneity bias.[15]

---

14. See William H. Greene, *Econometric Analysis* (Upper Saddle River, NJ: Prentice Hall, 1999), pp. 375–381.

15. If measurement errors exist in the data for the dependent variable and one or more of the independent variables, then both decreased overall statistical fit and bias in the estimated coefficients will result. Indeed, a famous econometrician, Zvi Griliches, warned that errors in the data coming from their measurement, usually computed from samples or estimates, imply that the fancier estimating techniques should be avoided because they are more sensitive to data errors than is OLS. See Zvi Griliches, "Data and Econometricians—the Uneasy Alliance," *American Economic Review*, Vol. 75, No. 2, p. 199. See also, B. D. McCullough and H. D. Vinod, "The Numerical Reliability of Econometric Software," *Journal of Economic Literature*, Vol. 37, pp. 633–665.

Chapter 15

Forecasting

15.1 What Is Forecasting?

15.2 More Complex Forecasting Problems

15.3 ARIMA Models

15.4 Summary and Exercises

Of the uses of econometrics outlined in Chapter 1, we have discussed forecasting the least. Accurate forecasting is vital to successful planning, so it's the primary application of many business and governmental uses of econometrics. For example, manufacturing firms need sales forecasts, banks need interest rate forecasts, and governments need unemployment and inflation rate forecasts.

To many business and government leaders, the words *econometrics* and *forecasting* mean the same thing. Such a simplification gives econometrics a bad name because many econometricians overestimate their ability to produce accurate forecasts, resulting in unrealistic claims and unhappy clients. Some of their clients would probably applaud the nineteenth century New York law (luckily unenforced but apparently also unrepealed) that provides that persons "pretending to forecast the future" shall be liable to a $250 fine and/or six months in prison.[1] Although many econometricians might wish that such consultants would call themselves "futurists" or "soothsayers," it's impossible to ignore the importance of econometrics in forecasting in today's world.

The ways in which the prediction of future events is accomplished are quite varied. At one extreme, some forecasters use models with thousands of

---

1. Section 899 of the N.Y. State Criminal Code: the law does not apply to "ecclesiastical bodies acting in good faith and without personal fees."

equations.[2] At the other extreme, quite accurate forecasts can be created with nothing more than a good imagination and a healthy dose of self-confidence.

Unfortunately, it's unrealistic to think we can cover even a small portion of the topic of forecasting in one short chapter. Indeed, there are a number of excellent books and journals on this subject alone.[3] Instead, this chapter is meant to be a brief introduction to the use of econometrics in forecasting. We will begin by using simple linear equations and then move on to investigate a few more complex forecasting situations. The chapter concludes with an introduction to a technique, called ARIMA, that calculates forecasts entirely from past movements of the dependent variable without the use of any independent variables at all. ARIMA is almost universally used as a benchmark forecast, so it's important to understand even though it's not based on economic theory.

15.1 What Is Forecasting?

In general, forecasting is the act of predicting the future; in econometrics, **forecasting** is the estimation of the expected value of a dependent variable for observations that are outside the sample data set. In most forecasts, the values being predicted are for time periods in the future, but cross-sectional predictions of values for countries or people not in the sample are also common. To simplify terminology, the words prediction and forecast will be used interchangeably in this chapter. (Some authors limit the use of the word forecast to out-of-sample prediction for a time series.)

We've already encountered an example of a forecasting equation. Think back to the weight/height example of Section 1.4 and recall that the purpose of that model was to guess the weight of a male customer based on his height. In that example, the first step in building a forecast was to estimate Equation 1.19:

$$\text{Estimated weight} = 103.40 + 6.38 \cdot \text{Height (inches over five feet)} \quad (1.19)$$

That is, we estimated that a customer's weight on average equaled a base of 103.40 pounds plus 6.38 pounds for each inch over 5 feet. To actually make

---

2. For an interesting comparison of such models, see Ray C. Fair and Robert J. Shiller, "Comparing Information in Forecasts from Econometric Models," *American Economic Review*, Vol. 80, No. 3, pp. 375–389.

3. See, for example, G. Elliott, C. W. J. Granger, and A. G. Timmermann, *Handbook of Economic Forecasting* (Oxford, UK: North-Holland Elsevier, 2006), and N. Carnot, V. Koen, and B. Tissot, *Economic Forecasting* (Basingstoke, UK: Palgrave MacMillan, 2005).

the prediction, all we had to do was to substitute the height of the individual whose weight we were trying to predict into the estimated equation. For a male who is 6'1" tall, for example, we'd calculate:

$$\text{Predicted weight} = 103.40 + 6.38 \cdot (13 \text{ inches over five feet}) \quad (15.1)$$

or

$$103.40 + 82.90 = 186.3 \text{ pounds}$$

The weight-guessing equation is a specific example of using a single linear equation to predict or forecast. Our use of such an equation to make a forecast can be summarized into two steps:

1. *Specify and estimate an equation that has as its dependent variable the item that we wish to forecast.* We obtain a forecasting equation by specifying and estimating an equation for the variable we want to predict:

$$\hat{Y}_t = \hat{\beta}_0 + \hat{\beta}_1 X_{1t} + \hat{\beta}_2 X_{2t} \quad (t = 1, 2, \ldots, T) \quad (15.2)$$

Such specification and estimation have been the topics of the first 14 chapters of this book. The use of $(t = 1, 2, \ldots, T)$ to denote the sample size is fairly standard for time-series forecasts (t stands for "time").

2. *Obtain values for each of the independent variables for the observations for which we want a forecast and substitute them into our forecasting equation.* To calculate a forecast with Equation 15.2, this would mean finding values for period $T + 1$ for X_1 and X_2 and substituting them into the equation:

$$\hat{Y}_{T+1} = \hat{\beta}_0 + \hat{\beta}_1 X_{1T+1} + \hat{\beta}_2 X_{2T+1} \quad (15.3)$$

What is the meaning of this $\hat{Y}_{T+1}$? It is a prediction of the value that Y will take in observation $T + 1$ (outside the sample) based upon our values of X_{1T+1} and X_{2T+1} and based upon the particular specification and estimation that produced Equation 15.2.

To understand these steps more clearly, let's look at two applications of this forecasting approach:

Forecasting Chicken Consumption: Let's return to the chicken demand model, Equation 9.14 on page 288, to see how well that equation forecasts aggregate per capita chicken consumption:

$$\hat{Y}_t = 27.7 - 0.11 PC_t + 0.03 PB_t + 0.23 YD_t \quad (9.14)$$
$$\phantom{\hat{Y}_t = 27.7} (0.03) \quad (0.02) \quad (0.01)$$
$$\phantom{\hat{Y}_t = 27.7} t = -3.38 \quad +1.86 \quad +15.7$$
$$\bar{R}^2 = .9904 \quad N = 29 \text{ (annual 1974–2002)} \quad DW = 0.99$$

where: Y   = pounds of chicken consumption per capita
          PC and PB = the prices of chicken and beef, respectively,
                        per pound
          YD   = per capita U.S. disposable income

To make these forecasts as realistic as possible, we held out the last three available years from the data set used to estimate Equation 9.14. We'll thus be able to compare the equation's forecasts with what actually happened. To forecast with the model, we first obtain values for the three independent variables and then substitute them into Equation 9.14. For 2003, PC = 34.1, PB = 374.6, and YD = 280.2, giving us:

$$\hat{Y}_{2003} = 27.7 - 0.11(34.1) + 0.03(374.6) + 0.23(280.2) = 99.63 \quad (15.4)$$

Continuing on through 2005, we end up with:[4]

Year	Forecast	Actual	Percent Error
2003	99.63	95.63	4.2
2004	105.06	98.58	6.6
2005	107.44	100.60	6.8

How does the model do? Well, forecasting accuracy, like beauty, is in the eye of the beholder, and there are many ways to answer the question.[5] The simplest method is to take the mean of the percentage errors (in absolute value), an approach called, not surprisingly, the **mean absolute percentage error (MAPE)** method. The MAPE for our forecast is 5.9 percent.

The most popular alternative method of evaluating forecast accuracy is the **root mean square error criterion (RMSE)**, which is calculated by squaring the forecasting error for each time period, averaging these squared amounts, and then taking the square root of this average. One advantage of the RMSE is that it penalizes large errors because the errors are squared before they're added together. For the chicken demand forecasts, the RMSE of our forecast is 5.97 pounds (or 6 percent).

---

4. The rest of the actual values are PC: 2004 = 24.8, 2005 = 26.8; PB: 2004 = 406.5, 2005 = 409.1; YD: 2004 = 295.17, 2005 = 306.16. Many software packages, including Stata and EViews, have forecasting modules that will allow you to calculate forecasts using equations like Equation 15.4 automatically. If you use that module, you'll note that the forecasts differ slightly because we rounded the coefficient estimates.

5. For a summary of seven different methods of measuring forecasting accuracy, see Peter Kennedy, *A Guide to Econometrics* (Malden, MA: Blackwell, 2008), pp. 334–335.

As you can see in Figure 15.1, it really doesn't matter which method you use, because the unconditional forecasts generated by Equation 9.14 track quite well with reality. We missed by around 6 percent.

Forecasting Stock Prices: Some students react to the previous example by wanting to build a model to forecast stock prices and make a killing on the stock market. "If we could predict the price of a stock three years from now to within six percent," they reason, "we'd know which stocks to buy."

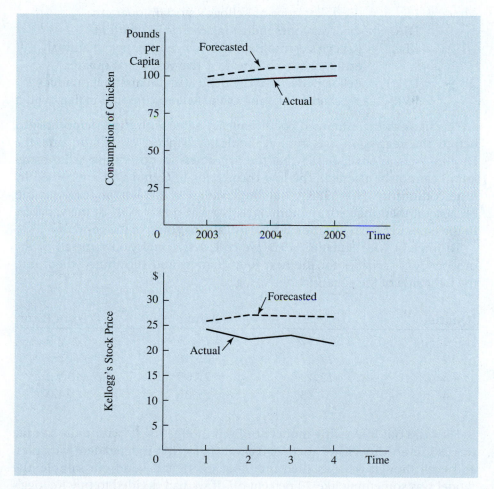

Figure 15.1 Forecasting Examples

In the chicken consumption example, the equation's forecast errors averaged around 6 percent. For the stock price model, even actual values for the independent variables and an excellent fit within the sample could not produce an accurate forecast.

To see how such a forecast might work, let's look at a simplified model of the quarterly price of a particular individual stock, that of the Kellogg Company (maker of breakfast cereals and other products):

$$\widehat{PK}_t = -7.80 + 0.0096DJA_t + 2.68KEG_t + 16.18DIV_t + 4.84BVPS_t$$
$$(0.0024) \quad (2.83) \quad (22.70) \quad (1.47)$$
$$t = 3.91 \quad\quad 0.95 \quad\quad 0.71 \quad\quad 3.29$$
$$\overline{R}^2 = .95 \quad N = 35 \quad DW = 1.88 \quad\quad\quad (15.5)$$

where: PK_t = the dollar price of Kellogg's stock in quarter t
   DJA_t = the Dow Jones industrial average in quarter t
   KEG_t = Kellogg's earnings growth (percent change in annual earnings over the previous five years) that quarter
   DIV_t = Kellogg's declared dividends (in dollars) that quarter
   $BVPS_t$ = per-share book value of the Kellogg corporation that quarter

The signs of the estimated coefficients all agree with those hypothesized before the regression was run, $\overline{R}^2$ indicates a good overall fit, and the Durbin–Watson test indicates that the hypothesis of no positive serial correlation cannot be rejected. The low t-scores for KEG and DIV are caused by multicollinearity ($r = .985$), but both variables are left in the equation because of their theoretical importance. Note also that most of the variables in the equation are nonstationary, surely causing some of the good fit.

To forecast with Equation 15.5, we collected actual values for all of the independent variables for the next four quarters and substituted them into the right side of the equation, obtaining:

Quarter	Forecast	Actual	Percent Error
1	$26.32	$24.38	8.0
2	27.37	22.38	22.3
3	27.19	23.00	18.2
4	27.13	21.88	24.0

How did our forecasting model do? Even though the $\overline{R}^2$ within the sample was .95, even though we used actual values for the independent variables, and even though we forecasted only four quarters beyond our sample, the model was something like 20 percent off. If we had decided to buy Kellogg's stock based on our forecast, we'd have *lost* money! Since other attempts to forecast stock prices have also encountered difficulties, this doesn't seem like a reasonable use for econometric forecasting.

The poor performance of forecasting in the stock market can be explained by an economic theory called the efficient markets hypothesis, which suggests that accurate predictions of stock prices are practically impossible. The efficient markets hypothesis theorizes that "security prices fully reflect all available information."[6] Thus, forecasting stock prices becomes a game of chance to the extent that markets are efficient and current prices reflect the available information. Although an investor who has inside information (or who perhaps invents a superior forecasting approach) has an opportunity to create better than average stock price forecasts, the use of insider information is illegal in most equity markets.

15.2 More Complex Forecasting Problems

The forecasts generated in the previous section are quite simple, however, and most actual forecasting involves one or more additional questions. For example:

1. *Unknown Xs:* It's unrealistic to expect to know the values for the independent variables outside the sample. For instance, we'll almost never know what the Dow Jones industrial average will be in the future when we are making forecasts of the price of a given stock, and yet we assumed that knowledge when making our Kellogg price forecasts. What happens when we don't know the values of the independent variables for the forecast period?

2. *Serial Correlation:* If there is serial correlation involved, the forecasting equation may be estimated with GLS. How should predictions be adjusted when forecasting equations are estimated with GLS?

3. *Confidence Intervals:* All the previous forecasts were single values, but such single values are almost never exactly right. Wouldn't it be more helpful if we forecasted an interval within which we were confident that the actual value would fall a certain percentage of the time? How can we develop these confidence intervals?

4. *Simultaneous Equations Models:* As you saw in Chapter 14, many economic and business equations are part of simultaneous models. How can we use an independent variable to forecast a dependent variable when we know that a change in the value of the dependent variable will change, in turn, the value of the independent variable that we used to make the forecast?

Even a few questions like these should be enough to convince you that forecasting is more complex than is implied by Section 15.1.

---

6. http://www.morningstar.com/InvGlossary, 10/20/15. For more, see Burton Malkiel, *A Random Walk down Wall Street* (London: W. W. Norton, 2007).

Conditional Forecasting (Unknown X Values for the Forecast Period)

A forecast in which all values of the independent variables are known with certainty can be called an **unconditional forecast**, but, as mentioned previously, the situations in which one can make such unconditional forecasts are rare. More likely, we will have to make a **conditional forecast**, for which actual values of one or more of the independent variables are *not* known. We are forced to obtain forecasts for the independent variables before we can use our equation to forecast the dependent variable, which makes our forecast of Y conditional on our forecast of the Xs.

One key to an accurate conditional forecast is accurate forecasting of the independent variables. If the forecasts of the independent variables are unbiased, then using a conditional forecast will not introduce bias into the forecast of the dependent variable in a linear model. Anything but a perfect forecast of the independent variables will contain some amount of forecast error, however, and so the expected error variance associated with conditional forecasting will be larger than that associated with unconditional forecasting. Thus, one should try to find unbiased, minimum variance forecasts of the independent variables when using conditional forecasting.

To get good forecasts of the independent variables, take the forecastability of potential independent variables into consideration when making specification choices. For instance, when deciding which of two redundant variables should be included in an equation to be used for forecasting, you should choose the one that is easier to forecast accurately. When you can, you should choose an independent variable that is regularly forecasted by someone else (an econometric forecasting firm, for example) so that you don't have to forecast X yourself.

The careful selection of independent variables can sometimes help you avoid the need for conditional forecasting in the first place. This opportunity can arise when the dependent variable can be expressed as a function of leading indicators. A **leading indicator** is an independent variable whose movements anticipate movements in the dependent variable. The best known leading indicator, the Index of Leading Economic Indicators, is produced each month.

For instance, the impact of interest rates on investment typically is not felt until two or three quarters after interest rates have changed. To see this, let's look at the investment function of the small macroeconomic model of Section 14.3:

$$I_t = \beta_0 + \beta_1 Y_t + \beta_2 r_{t-1} + \epsilon_t \qquad (15.6)$$

where I equals gross investment, Y equals GDP, and r equals the interest rate. In this equation, actual values of r can be used to help forecast I_{T+1}. Note, however, that to predict I_{T+2}, we need to forecast r_{T+1}. Thus, leading indicators like r help us avoid conditional forecasting for only a time period or two. For long-range predictions, a conditional forecast is usually necessary.

Forecasting with Serially Correlated Error Terms

Recall from Chapter 9 that pure first-order serial correlation implies that the current observation of the error term ϵ_t is affected by the previous error term and an autocorrelation coefficient, ρ:

$$\epsilon_t = \rho\epsilon_{t-1} + u_t$$

where u_t is a non–serially correlated error term. Also recall that when serial correlation is severe, one remedy is to run Generalized Least Squares (GLS) as noted in Equation 9.21:

$$Y_t - \rho Y_{t-1} = \beta_0(1 - \rho) + \beta_1(X_{1t} - \rho X_{1t-1}) + u_t \qquad (9.21)$$

Unfortunately, whenever the use of GLS is required to rid an equation of pure first-order serial correlation, the procedures used to forecast with that equation become a bit more complex. To see why this is necessary, note that if Equation 9.21 is estimated, the dependent variable will be:

$$Y_t^* = Y_t - \hat{\rho} Y_{t-1} \qquad (15.7)$$

Thus, if a GLS equation is used for forecasting, it will produce predictions of Y_{T+1}^* rather than of Y_{T+1}. Such predictions thus will be of the wrong variable.

If forecasts are to be made with a GLS equation, Equation 9.21 should first be solved for Y_t before forecasting is attempted:

$$Y_t = \rho Y_{t-1} + \beta_0(1 - \rho) + \beta_1(X_t - \rho X_{t-1}) + u_t \qquad (15.8)$$

We now can forecast with Equation 15.8 as we would with any other equation. If we substitute $T + 1$ for t (to forecast time period $T + 1$) and insert estimates for the coefficients, ρs and Xs into the right side of the equation, we obtain:

$$\hat{Y}_{T+1} = \hat{\rho} Y_T + \hat{\beta}_0(1 - \hat{\rho}) + \hat{\beta}_1(\hat{X}_{T+1} - \hat{\rho} X_T) \qquad (15.9)$$

Equation 15.9 thus should be used for forecasting when an equation has been estimated with GLS to correct for serial correlation.[7]

---

7. If $\hat{\rho}$ is less than 0.3, many researchers prefer to use the OLS forecast plus $\hat{\rho}$ times the lagged residual as their forecast instead of the GLS forecast from Equation 15.9.

We now turn to an example of such forecasting with serially correlated error terms. In particular, recall from Chapter 9 that the Durbin–Watson statistic of the chicken demand equation used as an example in Section 15.1 was 0.99, indicating significant positive first-order serial correlation. As a result, we estimated the chicken demand equation with GLS, obtaining Equation 9.25:

$$\hat{Y}_t = 28.5 - 0.08PC_t + 0.016PB_t + 0.24YD_t \qquad (9.25)$$
$$\phantom{\hat{Y}_t = 28.5 -} (0.04) \quad\;\; (0.021) \quad\;\;\; (0.02)$$
$$\phantom{\hat{Y}_t =} t = \quad -2.13 \quad\;\; +0.74 \quad\;\;\; +13.12$$
$$\phantom{\hat{Y}_t =} \overline{R}^2 = .963 \qquad N = 29 \qquad \hat{\rho} = 0.56$$

Since Equation 9.25 was estimated with GLS, Y is actually Y_t^*, which equals $Y_t - \hat{\rho}Y_{t-1}$, PC_t is actually PC_t^*, which equals $PC_t - \hat{\rho}PC_{t-1}$, and so on. Thus, to forecast with Equation 9.25, we have to convert it to the form of Equation 15.9, or:

$$\hat{Y}_{T+1} = 0.56Y_T + 28.5(1 - 0.56) - 0.08(PC_{T+1} - 0.56PC_T) \quad (15.10)$$
$$+ 0.016(PB_{T+1} - 0.56PB_T) + 0.24(YD_{T+1} - 0.56YD_T)$$

Substituting the actual values for the independent variables into Equation 15.10, we obtain:

Year	Forecast	Actual	Percent Error
2003	97.57	95.63	2.0
2004	101.02	98.58	2.5
2005	102.38	100.60	1.8

The MAPE of the GLS forecasts is 2.1 percent, far better than that of the OLS forecasts. In general, GLS usually will provide superior forecasting performance to OLS in the presence of serial correlation.

Forecasting Confidence Intervals

Until now, the emphasis in this text has been on obtaining point (or single-value) estimates. This has been true whether we have been estimating coefficient values or estimating forecasts. Recall, though, that a point estimate is only one of a whole range of such estimates that could have been obtained from different samples (for coefficient estimates) or different independent variable values or coefficients (for forecasts). The usefulness of such point estimates is improved if we can also generate some idea of the variability of our forecasts. The measure of variability typically used is the *confidence interval*, which was defined in Section 5.5 as the range of values that contains the true value of the item being estimated a specified percentage of the time. This is the easiest way to warn forecast users that a sampling distribution exists.

Suppose you are trying to decide how many hot dogs to order for your city's Fourth of July fireworks show and the best point forecast is that you'll sell 24,000 hot dogs. How many hot dogs should you order? If you order 24,000, you're likely to run out about half the time! A point forecast is usually an estimate of the mean of the distribution of possible sales figures; you will sell more than 24,000 about as frequently as you will sell less than 24,000. It would be easier to decide how many dogs to order if you also had a confidence interval that told you the range within which hot dog sales would fall 95 percent of the time. The usefulness of the 24,000 hot dog forecast changes dramatically depending on the confidence interval; an interval of 22,000 to 26,000 would pin down the likely sales, but an interval of 4,000 to 44,000 would leave you virtually in the dark about what to do.

The decision as to how many hot dogs to order would also depend on the costs of ordering the wrong number. These costs may not be the same per hot dog for overestimates as they are for underestimates. For example, if you don't order enough, then you lose the entire retail price of the hot dog minus the wholesale price of the dog (and bun) because your other costs, like hiring employees and building hot dog stands, are essentially fixed. On the other hand, if you order too many, you lose the wholesale cost of the dog and bun minus whatever salvage price you might be able to get for day-old buns, etc. As a result, the right number to order would depend on your profit margin and the importance of nonreturnable inputs in your total cost picture.

The same techniques we use to test hypotheses can also be adapted to create confidence intervals. Given a point forecast, $\hat{Y}_{T+1}$, all we need to generate a confidence interval around that forecast are t_c, the critical *t*-value (for the desired level of confidence), and S_F, the estimated standard error of the forecast:

$$\text{Confidence interval} = \hat{Y}_{T+1} \pm S_F t_c \qquad (15.11)$$

or, equivalently,

$$\hat{Y}_{T+1} - S_F t_c \leq Y_{T+1} \leq \hat{Y}_{T+1} + S_F t_c \qquad (15.12)$$

The critical *t*-value, t_c, can be found in Statistical Table B-1 (for a two-tailed test with $T - K - 1$ degrees of freedom). The standard error of the forecast, S_F, for an equation with just one independent variable, equals the square root of the forecast error variance:

$$S_F = \sqrt{s^2 \left[1 + 1/T + (\hat{X}_{T+1} - \overline{X})^2 \middle/ \sum_{t=1}^{T} (X_t - \overline{X})^2 \right]} \qquad (15.13)$$

where s^2 = the estimated variance of the error term
$\quad\quad\quad T$ = the number of observations in the sample
$\quad\quad\quad \hat{X}_{T+1}$ = the forecasted value of the single independent variable
$\quad\quad\quad \overline{X}$ = the arithmetic mean of the observed Xs in the sample

Note that Equation 15.13 implies that the forecast error variance decreases the larger the sample is, the more X varies within the sample, and the closer $\hat{X}$ is to its within-sample mean. An important implication is that the farther the X used to forecast Y is from the within-sample mean of the Xs, the wider the confidence interval around the $\hat{Y}$ is going to be. This can be seen in Figure 15.2, in which the confidence interval actually gets wider as $\hat{X}_{T+1}$ is farther from $\overline{X}$. Since forecasting outside the sample range is common, researchers should be aware of this phenomenon. Also note that Equation 15.13 is for unconditional forecasting. If there is any forecast error in $\hat{X}_{T+1}$, then the confidence interval is larger and more complicated to calculate. Finally, Equation 15.13 should not be used in conjunction with HC standard errors.

As mentioned, Equation 15.13 assumes that there is only one independent variable. The equation to be used with more than one variable is similar but more complicated. Equation 15.13 is valid whether Y_t is in the sample period or outside the sample period, but it applies only to point forecasts of individual Y_ts. If a confidence interval for the expected value of Y, $E(Y_t)$, is desired, then the correct equation to use is:

$$S_F^* = \sqrt{s^2 [1/T + (\hat{X}_{T+1} - \overline{X})^2 / \sum (X_t - \overline{X})^2]} \qquad (15.14)$$

Forecasting with Simultaneous Equations Systems

As you learned in Chapter 14, most economic and business models are actually simultaneous in nature; for example, the investment equation used in Section 15.2 was estimated with 2SLS as a part of our simultaneous macromodel in Chapter 14. Since GDP is one of the independent variables in the investment equation, when investment rises, so will GDP, causing a feedback effect that is not captured if we just forecast with a single equation. How should forecasting be done in the context of a simultaneous model? There are two approaches to answering this question, depending on whether there

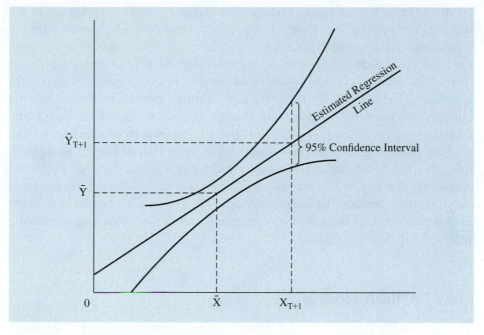

Figure 15.2 A Confidence Interval for $\hat{Y}_{T+1}$

A 95 percent confidence interval for $\hat{Y}_{T+1}$ includes the range of values within which the actual Y_{T+1} will fall 95 percent of the time. Note that the confidence interval widens as X_{T+1} differs more from its within-sample mean, $\bar{X}$.

are lagged endogenous variables on the right side of any of the equations in the system.

If there are no lagged endogenous variables in the system, then the reduced-form equation for the particular endogenous variable can be used for forecasting because it represents the simultaneous solution of the system for the endogenous variable being forecasted. Since the reduced-form equation is the endogenous variable expressed entirely in terms of the predetermined variables in the system, it allows the forecasting of the endogenous variable without any feedback or simultaneity impacts. This result explains why some researchers forecast potentially simultaneous dependent variables with single equations that appear to combine supply-side and demand-side predetermined variables; they are actually using modified reduced-form equations to make their forecasts.

If there are lagged endogenous variables in the system, then the approach must be altered to take into account the dynamic interaction caused by the lagged endogenous variables. For simple models, this sometimes can be done by substituting for the lagged endogenous variables where they appear in the reduced-form equations. If such a manipulation is difficult, however, then a technique called simulation analysis can be used. *Simulation* involves forecasting for the first postsample period by using the reduced-form equations to forecast all endogenous variables where they appear in the reduced-form equations. The forecast for the second postsample period, however, uses the endogenous variable *forecasts* from the last period as lagged values for any endogenous variables that have one-period lags while continuing to use sample values for endogenous variables that have lags of two or more periods. This process continues until all forecasting is done with reduced-form equations that use as data for lagged endogenous variables the forecasts from previous time periods. Although such dynamic analyses are beyond the scope of this chapter, they're important to remember when considering forecasting with a simultaneous system.[8]

15.3 ARIMA Models

The forecasting techniques of the previous two sections are applications of familiar regression models. We use linear regression equations to forecast the dependent variable by plugging likely values of the independent variables into the estimated equations and calculating a predicted value of Y; this bases the prediction of the dependent variable on the independent variables (and on their estimated coefficients).

ARIMA (the name will be explained shortly) is an increasingly popular forecasting technique that completely ignores independent variables in making forecasts. **ARIMA** is a highly refined curve-fitting device that uses current and past values of the dependent variable to produce often accurate short-term forecasts of that variable. While a traditional econometric model attempts to describe and estimate a variable's underlying structure (like a consumption function or a money demand function), an ARIMA model takes these structures as "black boxes" and simply analyzes the correlation pattern of a variable's movements over time in order to forecast it. Examples of such ARIMA forecasts are stock market price predictions created by brokerage analysts based entirely on past patterns of the movement of the stock price.

---

8. For more on this topic, see Chapters 12–14 in Robert S. Pindyck and Daniel L. Rubinfeld, *Econometric Models and Economic Forecasts* (New York: McGraw-Hill, 1998).

Any forecasting technique that ignores independent variables also essentially ignores all potential underlying theories except those that hypothesize repeating patterns in the variable under study. Since we have emphasized the advantages of developing the theoretical underpinnings of particular equations before estimating them, why would we advocate using ARIMA? The answer is that the use of ARIMA is appropriate when little or nothing is known about the dependent variable being forecasted, when the independent variables known to be important really cannot be forecasted effectively, or when all that is needed is a one- or two-period forecast. In these cases, ARIMA has the potential to provide short-term forecasts that are superior to more theoretically satisfying regression models. ARIMA models are particularly well suited to forecast a system that has not undergone a profound structural change within the sample or forecasting period. In such a situation, a naïve ARIMA model often can beat a moderately sophisticated econometric model in terms of forecasting outside the sample and has come close to the performance of state-of-the-art macro models in terms of forecasting key macro variables.[9] In addition, ARIMA can sometimes produce better explanations of the residuals from an existing regression equation (in particular, one with known omitted variables or other problems). This introduction to ARIMA is intentionally brief; a more complete coverage of the topic can be obtained from a number of other sources.[10]

The ARIMA approach combines two different specifications (called *processes*) into one equation. The first specification is an *autoregressive* process (hence the AR in ARIMA), and the second specification is a *moving average* (hence the MA).

An **autoregressive process** expresses a dependent variable Y_t as a function of past values of the dependent variable. This is similar to the serial correlation error term function of Chapter 9 and to the dynamic model of Chapter 12. If we have p different lagged values of Y, the equation is often referred to as a "pth-order" autoregressive process.

A **moving-average process** expresses a dependent variable Y_t as a function of past values of the error term. Such a function is a moving average of past error term observations that can be added to the mean of Y to obtain a moving average of past values of Y. If we used q past values of ϵ, we'd call it a qth-order moving-average process.

---

9. Charles R. Nelson, "The *Ex Ante* Prediction Performance of the St. Louis and FRB-MIT-PENN Econometric Models and Some Results of Composite Predictors," *Journal of Money, Credit and Banking*, Vol. 7, No. 1, pp. 1–32.

10. See, for example, Chapters 15–19 in Robert S. Pindyck and Daniel L. Rubinfeld, *Econometric Models and Economic Forecasts* (New York: McGraw-Hill, 1998).

To create an ARIMA model, we begin with an econometric equation with no independent variables ($Y_t = \beta_0 + \epsilon_t$) and add to it both the autoregressive and moving-average processes:

$$\overbrace{Y_t = \beta_0 + \theta_1 Y_{t-1} + \theta_2 Y_{t-2} + \cdots + \theta_p Y_{t-p} + \epsilon_t}^{\text{autoregressive process}}$$
$$\underbrace{+\ \phi_1 \epsilon_{t-1} + \phi_2 \epsilon_{t-2} + \cdots + \phi_q \epsilon_{t-q}}_{\text{moving-average process}} \tag{15.15}$$

where the θs and the ϕs are the coefficients of the autoregressive and moving-average processes, respectively, and p and q are the number of past values used of Y and ϵ, respectively.

Before this equation can be applied to a time series, however, it must be ensured that the time series is *stationary*, as defined in Section 12.5. If a series is nonstationary, then steps must be taken to convert the series into a stationary one before the ARIMA technique can be applied. For example, a nonstationary series can often be converted into a stationary one by taking the first difference of the variable in question:

$$Y_t^* = \Delta Y_t = Y_t - Y_{t-1} \tag{15.16}$$

If the first differences do not produce a stationary series, then first differences of this first-differenced series can be taken.[11] The resulting series is a second-difference transformation:

$$Y_t^{**} = \Delta Y_t^* = Y_t^* - Y_{t-1}^* = \Delta Y_t - \Delta Y_{t-1} \tag{15.17}$$

In general, successive differences are taken until the series is stationary. The number of differences required to be taken before a series becomes stationary is denoted with the letter d. For example, suppose that GDP is increasing by a fairly consistent amount each year. A plot of GDP with respect to time would depict a nonstationary series, but a plot of the first differences of GDP might depict a fairly stationary series. In such a case, d would be equal to 1 because one first difference was necessary to convert the nonstationary series into a stationary one.

The dependent variable in Equation 15.15 must be stationary, so the Y in that equation may be Y, Y^*, or even Y^{**}, depending on the variable in question.[12]

---

11. For variables that are growing in percentage terms rather than absolute amounts, it often makes sense to take logs before taking first differences.

12. If Y in Equation 15.15 is Y^*, then β_0 represents the coefficient of the linear trend in the original series, and if Y is Y^{**}, then β_0 represents the coefficient of the second-difference trend in the original series. In such cases—for example, Equation 15.19—it's not always necessary that β_0 be in the model.

If a forecast of Y^* or Y^{**} is made, then it must be converted back into Y terms before its use; for example, if $d = 1$, then

$$\hat{Y}_{T+1} = Y_T + \hat{Y}^*_{T+1} \qquad (15.18)$$

This conversion process is similar to integration in mathematics, so the "I" in ARIMA stands for "integrated." ARIMA thus stands for *AutoRegressive Integrated Moving Average*. (If the original series is stationary and d therefore equals 0, this is sometimes shortened to ARMA.)

As a shorthand, an ARIMA model with p, d, and q specified is usually denoted as ARIMA (p,d,q) with the specific integers chosen inserted for p, d, and q, as in ARIMA (2,1,1). ARIMA (2,1,1) would indicate a model with two autoregressive terms, one first difference, and one moving-average term:

$$\text{ARIMA}(2,1,1)\colon Y^*_t = \beta_0 + \theta_1 Y^*_{t-1} + \theta_2 Y^*_{t-2} + \epsilon_t + \phi_1\epsilon_{t-1} \qquad (15.19)$$

where $Y^*_t = Y_t - Y_{t-1}$.

It's remarkable how very small values of p and q can model extremely rich dynamics.

15.4 Summary

1. Forecasting is the estimation of the expected value of a dependent variable for observations that are not part of the sample data set. Forecasts are generated (via regressions) by estimating an equation for the dependent variable to be forecasted, and substituting values for each of the independent variables (for the observations to be forecasted) into the equation.

2. An excellent fit within the sample period for a forecasting equation does not guarantee that the equation will forecast well outside the sample period.

3. A forecast in which all the values of the independent variables are known with certainty is called an unconditional forecast, but if one or more of the independent variables have to be forecasted, it is a conditional forecast. Conditional forecasting introduces no bias into the prediction of Y (as long as the X forecasts are unbiased), but increased forecast error variance is unavoidable with conditional forecasting.

4. If the coefficients of an equation have been estimated with GLS (to correct for pure first-order serial correlation), then the forecasting equation is:

$$\hat{Y}_{T+1} = \hat{\rho} Y_T + \hat{\beta}_0 (1 - \hat{\rho}) + \hat{\beta}_1 (\hat{X}_{T+1} - \hat{\rho} X_T)$$

where ρ is the autocorrelation coefficient rho.

5. Forecasts are often more useful if they are accompanied by a confidence interval, which is a range within which the actual value of the dependent variable should fall a given percentage of the time (the level of confidence). This is:

$$\hat{Y}_{T+1} \pm S_F t_c$$

where S_F is the estimated standard error of the forecast and t_c is the critical two-tailed *t*-value for the desired level of confidence.

6. ARIMA is a highly refined curve-fitting technique that uses current and past values of the dependent variable (and only the dependent variable) to produce often accurate short-term forecasts of that variable. The first step in using ARIMA is to make the dependent variable series stationary by taking d first differences until the resulting transformed variable has a constant mean and variance. The ARIMA(p,d,q) approach then combines an autoregressive process (with $\theta_1 Y_{t-1}$ terms) of order p with a moving-average process (with $\phi_1 \epsilon_{t-1}$ terms) of order q to explain the *d*th differenced dependent variable.

EXERCISES

(The answers to the even-numbered exercises are in Appendix A.)

1. Write the meaning of each of the following terms without referring to the book (or your notes), and compare your definition with the version in the text for each.
   a. ARIMA (p. 456)
   b. autoregressive process (p. 457)
   c. conditional forecast (p. 450)
   d. forecasting (p. 444)
   e. leading indicator (p. 450)
   f. MAPE (p. 446)
   g. moving-average process (p. 457)
   h. RMSE (p. 446)
   i. unconditional forecast (p. 450)

2. Calculate the following unconditional forecasts:
   a. the median price (PR) of a new single-family house in 2014, given the fact that the U.S. GDP in 2014 was roughly $17,400 billion and the following equation:

   $$PR_t = 12,928 + 17.08 GDP_t$$

   b. the expected level of check volume at three possible future sites for new Woody's restaurants, given Equation 3.4 and the following data. If you could only build one new eatery, in which of these three sites would you build (all else equal)?

Site	Competition	Population	Income
Richburgh	6	58,000	38,000
Nowheresville	1	14,000	27,000
Slick City	9	190,000	15,000

3. To understand the difficulty of conditional forecasting, use Equation 1.19 to forecast the weights of the next three males you see, using your *estimates* of their heights. (Ask for actual values after finishing.)

4. Some of the most interesting applications of econometric forecasting are in the political arena. Examples of regression analysis in politics range from part-time marketing consultants who help local candidates decide how best to use their advertising dollars to a fairly rich professional literature on U.S. presidential elections.[13]

   In 2008, Haynes and Stone[14] added to this literature with an article that specified (among others) the following equation:

   $$VOTE_i = \beta_0 + \beta_1 P_i + \beta_2 (DUR^*P)_i + \beta_3 (DOW^*P)_i + \beta_4 (GROWTH^*P)_i \\ + \beta_5 (INFLATION^*P)_i + \beta_6 (ARMY^*P)_i + \beta_7 (SPEND^*P)_i + \epsilon_i$$

   (15.20)

---

13. See, particularly, the work of Ray Fair: "The Effect of Economic Events on Votes for President," *Review of Economics and Statistics*, Vol. 60, pp. 159–173, and "Econometrics and Presidential Elections," *Journal of Economic Perspectives*, Vol. 10, pp. 89–102.

14. Stephen Haynes and Joe Stone, "A Disaggregate Approach to Economic Models of Voting in U.S. Presidential Elections: Forecasts of the 2008 Election," *Economics Bulletin*, Vol. 4, No. 28 (2008), pp. 1–11.

where: $VOTE_i$ = the Democratic share of the popular two-party presidential vote

          P_i = 1 if the incumbent is a Democrat and −1 if the incumbent is a Republican

          DUR_i = the number of consecutive terms the incumbent party has held the presidency

          DOW_i = the annual rate of change in the Dow Jones Industrial Average between January and October of the election year

          $GROWTH_i$ = the annual percent growth of real per capita GDP in the second and third quarters of the election year

          $INFLATION_i$ = the absolute value of the annualized inflation rate in the two-year period prior to the election

          $ARMY_i$ = the annualized percent change of the proportion of the population in the armed forces in the two-year period prior to the election

          $SPEND_i$ = the annualized percentage change in the proportion of government spending devoted to national security in the two-year period prior to the election

a. What kind of variable is P? Is it a dummy variable? If not, what is it?

b. The authors specified their equation as a series of interaction variables between P and the other variables of interest. Look at the equation carefully. Why do you think that these interaction variables were required?

c. Using the data[15] in Table 15.1 (datafile = ELECTION15) estimate Equation 15.20 for the years 1916–1996.

d. Create and test appropriate hypotheses on the coefficients of your estimated equation at the 5-percent level. Do any of the coefficients have unexpected signs? Which ones?

e. Create unconditional forecasts for the years 2000 and 2004 and compare your forecasts with the actual figures in Table 15.1. How did you do?

---

15. These data are from Haynes and Stone, ibid., p. 10, but similar tables are available from a variety of sources, including: fairmodel.econ.yale.edu/vote2008/pres.txt.

f. The authors wrote their article before the 2008 election. Create an unconditional forecast for that election using the data in Table 15.1. Who did the model predict would win? How did the model do?

Table 15.1 Data for the Presidential Election Exercise

YEAR	VOTE	P	DUR	DOW	GROWTH	INFLATION	ARMY	SPEND
1916	51.682	1	1	12.00	6.38	7.73	2.33	4.04
1920	36.119	1	2	−23.50	−6.14	8.01	−107.60	11.24
1924	41.756	−1	1	6.00	−2.16	0.62	−3.38	−23.05
1928	41.240	−1	2	31.30	−0.63	0.81	−0.48	10.15
1932	59.140	−1	3	−25.00	−13.98	10.01	−2.97	−37.56
1936	62.458	1	1	24.90	13.41	1.36	7.60	28.86
1940	54.999	1	2	−12.90	6.97	0.53	16.79	8.33
1944	53.774	1	3	9.00	6.88	1.98	53.10	17.16
1948	52.370	1	4	6.30	3.77	10.39	−38.82	−86.56
1952	44.595	1	5	−1.80	−0.34	2.66	43.89	71.59
1956	42.240	−1	1	2.40	−0.69	3.59	−9.93	−14.34
1960	50.090	−1	2	−13.90	−1.92	2.16	−4.10	−8.44
1964	61.344	1	1	15.80	2.38	1.73	−3.68	−5.88
1968	49.596	1	2	10.00	4.00	3.94	0.06	6.28
1972	38.210	−1	1	5.40	5.05	5.17	−11.91	−19.71
1976	51.050	−1	2	3.00	0.78	7.64	−2.56	−20.15
1980	44.697	1	1	12.40	−5.69	8.99	−1.37	−0.44
1984	40.830	−1	1	−6.90	2.69	3.68	−0.22	7.38
1988	46.070	−1	2	12.60	2.43	3.30	−1.58	−1.09
1992	53.455	−1	3	−0.90	1.34	3.15	−7.33	−10.11
1996	54.736	1	1	24.54	3.08	1.95	−5.62	−12.67
2000	50.265	1	2	−5.02	2.95	1.80	−2.00	1.83
2004	48.586	−1	1	−8.01	3.49	2.50	−0.51	14.91
2008	?	−1	2	30.70	2.10	3.70	−0.87	0.41

Source: Stephen Haynes and Joe Stone, "A Disaggregate Approach to Economic Models of Voting in U.S. Presidential Elections: Forecasts of the 2008 Election," *Economics Bulletin*, Vol. 4, No. 8 (2008), p. 10.

Datafile = ELECTION15

5. Suppose you have been given two different ARIMA $(1,0,0)$ fitted time-series models of the variable Y_t:

$$\text{Model A: } Y_t = 15.0 + 0.5Y_{t-1} + \epsilon_t$$
$$\text{Model T: } Y_t = 45.0 - 0.5Y_{t-1} + \epsilon_t$$

where ϵ_t is a normally distributed error term with mean 0 and standard deviation equal to 1.

a. The final observation in the sample (time period 06) is $Y_{06} = 31$. Determine forecasts for periods 07, 08, and 09 for both models.

b. Suppose you now find out that the actual Y_{07} was equal to 33. Revise your forecasts for periods 08 and 09 to take the new information into account.

c. Based on the fitted time series and your two forecasts, which model (model A or model T) do you expect to exhibit smoother behavior? Explain your reasoning.

Chapter 16

Experimental and Panel Data

16.1 Experimental Methods in Economics

16.2 Panel Data

16.3 Fixed versus Random Effects

16.4 Summary and Exercises

This chapter is a brief introduction to experimental data and panel data. The first section is devoted to experimental methods in economics.[1] The experimental approach is important because it offers a possible way for regression analysis to provide evidence of causality. If one group is exposed to a particular policy (like an increased tax or a decreased price) and a control group isn't, then any meaningful difference between the behavior of the two groups is evidence that the policy caused that difference. Such experiments already are standard procedure in some areas of research, for example the testing of the safety and effectiveness of new medicines by the U.S. Food and Drug Administration.

The remainder of the chapter focuses on panel data. As mentioned in Chapter 11, panel data are formed when cross-sectional and time-series data sets are combined to create a single data set. Although some researchers use panel data to increase their sample size, the main reason for working with panel data is to provide an insight into analytical questions that can't be answered by using time-series or cross-sectional data alone.

---

1. We use this awkward phrase to avoid confusion with the already existing field of experimental economics. Experimental economists run actual laboratory experiments on human subjects. By offering real-world incentives (usually money), experimental economists can reproduce supply and demand equilibria, test economic theories, and study market phenomena that otherwise are difficult to observe. For accessible examples and innovative applications of random experiments to economic questions, see Uri Gneezy and John List, *The Why Axis* (London: Random House Books, 2014).

16.1 Experimental Methods in Economics

Any good statistician knows that correlation doesn't prove causality, but understanding causality is important if we're going to assess the effectiveness of economic policies, the profitability of business practices, or the value of not-for-profit programs. To try to solve this problem, some econometricians have imported experimental techniques from medicine and psychology. Can experimental methods provide evidence of causality in economics?

Random Assignment Experiments

When medical researchers want to examine the effect of a new drug, they use an experimental design called *random assignment*. You're probably familiar with random assignment experiments because medical research studies are in the news virtually every week. The experiment generally proceeds as follows. First, a sample of subjects is chosen or recruited, and then they are randomly assigned to one of two groups—the control group or the treatment group. The **treatment group** receives the medicine that is being tested, and the **control group** receives a harmless, ineffective placebo. Similar experiments are possible in economics. To test whether a job training program has an impact on earnings, for example, the treatment group would receive the training and the control group wouldn't. If the treatment and control groups are chosen randomly, then such experiments are called **random assignment experiments**.

It's not hard to see why some researchers refer to random assignment as the gold standard in terms of establishing causality. Randomization helps ensure that any difference in the outcome between the control and the treatment group is causal and that the difference in outcome was caused by the treatment and not merely correlated with the treatment. The subjects' random assignment to the groups should be enough to guarantee that the only *systematic* reason for observed differences between the treatment and control groups is the treatment. Any other differences are the chance consequence of the random assignment. For example, the random assignment may result in more males in one group than in the other, or one of the subjects may die for a reason that is unrelated to the disease or treatment being studied. With reasonably sized samples, such random fluctuations will most likely balance out so that, on average, the two groups are similar except that one group receives the treatment and the other doesn't. The larger the sample, the more likely it is that random fluctuations will balance out.

Factors other than the treatment that may affect the outcome are put in the error term, and the resulting equation is:

$$OUTCOME_i = \beta_0 + \beta_1 TREATMENT_i + \epsilon_i \qquad (16.1)$$

where: $OUTCOME_i$ = a measure of the desired outcome in the ith individual

$TREATMENT_i$ = a dummy variable equal to 1 for individuals in the treatment group and 0 for individuals in the control group

β_1 is often called the *differences estimator* because it measures the difference between the average outcome for the treatment group and the average outcome for the control group. If the estimated value of β_1 is substantially different from zero in the direction predicted by theory, then we have evidence that the treatment did indeed cause the outcome to move in the expected direction.

However, random assignment can't always control for all other possible factors, and we may be able to identify some of these factors and add them to our equation. In our job training example, suppose that random assignment, by chance, results in one group having more males and being slightly older than the other group. If gender and age matter in determining earnings, then we can control for the different composition of the two groups by including gender and age in our regression equation:

$$OUTCOME_i = \beta_0 + \beta_1 TREATMENT_i + \beta_2 X_{1i} + \beta_3 X_{2i} + \epsilon_i \qquad (16.2)$$

where X_1 is a dummy variable for the individual's gender and X_2 is the individual's age.

Our recommendation is to use Equation 16.2 rather than Equation 16.1 if important additional factors are observable. After all, if the estimates of β_1 in the two equations are quite similar, then the choice doesn't matter. However, if the estimates differ, then we have evidence that random assignment did not control for other factors by evenly distributing these factors between the treatment and control groups. If that's the case, then including these other factors (as in Equation 16.2) is likely to provide a better estimate of the difference caused by the treatment.

Unfortunately, random assignment experiments are not common in economics because they're subject to problems that typically do not plague medical experiments. For example:

1. *Non-Random Samples.* Many subjects in economic experiments are volunteers, and samples of volunteers often aren't random. Not everyone is willing to volunteer, some potential subjects are willing to participate if they're in the treatment group but not if they're in the control group, and

some volunteers change their mind and drop out during the experiment. Unsurprisingly, the characteristics of a volunteer sample are not necessarily representative of the population. Suppose, for example, that our research question is whether financial incentives for student achievement actually increase test scores. The professors and students who are willing to participate in this experiment may not be representative of the overall population and, as a result, our conclusions may not apply to everyone.

2. *Unobservable Heterogeneity.* In Equation 16.2, we added observable factors to the equation to avoid omitted variable bias, but not all omitted factors in economics are observable. This "unobservable omitted variable" problem is called *unobserved heterogeneity.* Of course, if we can truly randomize the treatment, then this problem goes away because treatment is uncorrelated with the unobservables.[2]

3. *The Hawthorne Effect.* Human subjects typically know that they're being studied, and they usually know whether they're in the treatment group or the control group. The fact that human subjects know that they're being observed sometimes can change their behavior, and this change in behavior could clearly change the results of the experiment. For example, workers at the Western Electric Company's Hawthorne Works plant were once put in a special room where researchers could study their productivity under controlled conditions. In one study, the lights were dimmed and the workers seemed to work harder, mainly because they knew that the researchers were watching to see if they worked harder! The fact that people behave differently when they know they are being watched is now called the *Hawthorne Effect.*

4. *Impossible Experiments.* It's often impossible (or unethical) to run a random assignment experiment in economics. Think about how difficult it would be to use a random assignment experiment to study the impact of marriage on earnings. On average, married men earn more than single men even after accounting for observable differences in factors such as education and work experience. Unfortunately, there are a number of potential sources of unobservable heterogeneity, such as the possibility that women are more likely to marry men whom they judge to have high future earnings. A random assignment experiment might be able to sort these issues out, but imagine what such an experiment would entail. You'd have to randomly assign some men to marry and others to stay single! As you can see, this experiment, just like many other random assignment experiments in economics, simply isn't feasible.

---

2. With thanks to David Philips.

Natural Experiments

If random assignment experiments aren't always feasible in economics, what's a good alternative? One approach is to use data from *natural experiments* to try to get at issues of causality. **Natural experiments** (or *quasi-experiments*) are similar to random assignment experiments except that observations fall into treatment and control groups "naturally" (because of an exogenous event) instead of being randomly assigned by the researcher. This approach requires finding natural events or policy changes that can be analyzed as if they were treatments in a random assignment experiment. As long as the natural event is exogenous (for example, not under the control of either of the groups), it turns out that a natural experiment can come very close to mimicking a random assignment experiment. The key is to find naturally occurring events that mimic a random assignment experiment.

For instance, in 1992, New Jersey increased its minimum wage substantially, while Pennsylvania kept its minimum wage constant. This led some economists to expect a decrease in employment at New Jersey fast-food restaurants (and other businesses that paid workers the minimum wage). In a famous study, Card and Krueger compared fast-food restaurants in New Jersey (the "treatment group") with similar restaurants in nearby parts of Pennsylvania (the "control group") and found no indication that the rise in the minimum wage reduced employment.[3] Their study was a natural experiment!

A strict approach to natural experiments would seem to require that one find equivalents of "treatment" and "control" groups that have no systematic differences except for the treatment variable and other factors that can be observed and added to the equation. However, in economics, the treatment and control groups seem quite likely to have started off with different levels of the outcome measure. In addition, unobserved heterogeneity or nonrandom samples could result in the groups having different outcome measures. If the outcomes don't start off equal, then comparing outcomes after the treatment won't give us a true measure of the impact of the treatment. To understand why this is a problem, suppose that you were studying the impact of job training on income, and further suppose that your treatment group was earning an average of $30,000 per year while the control group was earning an average of $29,000 before the treatment. If the treatment group ended up earning $1,000 more than the control group after the treatment, would

---

3. David Card and Alan Krueger, "Minimum Wages and Employment: A Case Study of the Fast-Food Industry in New Jersey and Pennsylvania," *American Economic Review*, Vol. 84, No. 4, pp. 772–793.

this be convincing evidence that the treatment had a positive causal effect on income? Of course not!

To get around this problem, economists who run natural experiments don't compare outcomes between the treatment and control groups. Instead, they compare the changes in the outcomes. Using this approach, we compare the change in the treatment group caused by the treatment with any change in the control group. The resulting "difference in differences" measures the impact of the treatment on the outcome in the natural experiment.

In a regression equation, the appropriate dependent variable in such a natural experiment thus is the difference in the outcome measure, not the outcome level we used in Equation 16.2. If we make this adjustment in Equation 16.2, we get:

$$\Delta OUTCOME_i = \beta_0 + \beta_1 TREATMENT_i + \beta_2 X_{1i} + \beta_3 X_{2i} + \epsilon_i \quad (16.3)$$

where $\Delta OUTCOME_i$ is defined as the outcome after the treatment minus the outcome before the treatment for the ith observation. β_1 is called the **difference-in-differences** estimator, and it measures the difference between the change in the treatment group and the change in the control group, holding constant X_1 and X_2. If the estimate of β_1 is statistically significantly different from zero in the expected direction, then we have evidence that the treatment caused this change.

In essence, the difference-in-differences estimator uses the change in the control group as a measure of what would have happened to the treatment group if there hadn't been a treatment. The validity of this approach thus depends on the assumption that the changes in the outcome would have been the same in both the treatment and control group had there been no treatment.

Be careful, however. Because the dependent variable has changed in Equation 16.3 from what it was in Equation 16.2, we also should change our interpretation of the independent variables and their coefficients. β_2 now measures the impact of a one-unit increase in X_1 on the *change* in the outcome (holding constant the other independent variables), not the level of the outcome. In addition, we should choose independent variables for Equation 16.3 keeping in mind that the dependent variable now is a difference.[4]

---

4. In addition, there's evidence that the $SE(\hat{\beta})$s are underestimated and need to be corrected when difference-in-difference models are estimated with OLS. See M. Bertrand, A. Diamond, and J. Hainmueller, "Synthetic Control Methods for Comparative Case Studies: Estimating the Effect of California's Tobacco Control Program," *Journal of the American Statistical Association*, Vol. 105, pp. 113–132.

One final note. It's important to think through the appropriate "before" and "after" time frames when you're collecting data for a natural experiment. Data on the control and treatment groups should come from a time period far enough in advance of the policy change (treatment) that you are not picking up any anticipatory effects of the intended policy change. For example, if a company announces that it's going to increase prices in the future, many people will buy the product just before the price increase takes effect in order to save money. As a result, data collected just before the price increase will overstate the true "before" quantity. Similarly, "after" data need to be collected a reasonable amount of time after the policy change in order to allow individuals and firms to adjust to the change.

An Example of a Natural Experiment

Let's take a look at an example of a natural experiment. In 1997, ARCO, one of the largest petroleum refiners and gasoline retailers in the world, acquired the Thrifty Oil Company, by far the biggest independent chain of gas stations in Southern California.[5] Economists and consumers were concerned that the acquisition would reduce competition and therefore allow ARCO to increase prices.

This topic has the potential to be a good natural experiment, as the gas stations can be split into a treatment group (gas stations that competed with each other before the merger) and a control group (gas stations that didn't compete with each other before the merger). To measure the impact of the merger on gasoline prices, a researcher would compare the difference in prices between the treatment and control groups before the acquisition with the price difference after the acquisition.

The treatment group consisted of ARCO gas stations that had a competing Thrifty station within a one-mile radius, and the control group was made up of ARCO gas stations that didn't compete directly with a Thrifty station. Data were collected on a station-by-station basis, and gasoline prices before the acquisition were compared to those afterward.

Before the acquisition, prices in the treatment group were, on average, two to three cents lower than in the control group, which makes sense because the ARCO gas stations had to compete with the nearby Thrifty gas stations. After the acquisition, however, the treatment group prices were two to three cents *higher* than those in the control group!

---

5. This example is drawn from Justine Hastings, "Vertical Relationships and Competition in Retail Gasoline Markets: Empirical Evidence from Contract Changes in Southern California," *American Economic Review,* March 2004, pp. 317–328.

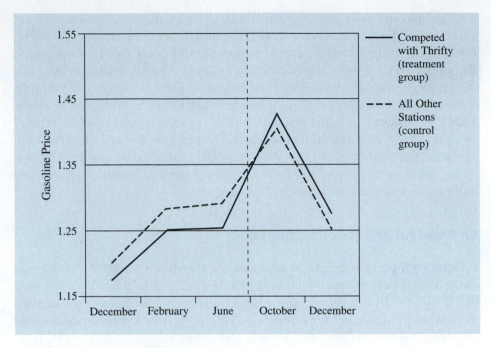

Figure 16.1 Treatment and Control Groups for Los Angeles

Gasoline prices in the treatment group were lower than those in the control group before the acquisition and higher afterward.

Take a look at Figure 16.1, which illustrates these results for Los Angeles. As can be seen, prices in the treatment group were lower than in the control group before the acquisition and were higher afterward. In essence, prices at ARCO gas stations that competed with Thrifty gas stations rose dramatically after ARCO acquired Thrifty.

Does this constitute evidence that the acquisition reduced gasoline price competition in Southern California? Take another look at Figure 16.1 and compare the slopes of the two lines. The price trends in the treatment and control groups are virtually parallel in other time periods, suggesting that these results do indeed provide preliminary evidence that the elimination of an independent competitor raised market prices by 4 to 6 cents.[6]

---

6. Ibid., p. 323. Because Prof. Hastings had data from five time periods instead of just two, she didn't estimate her equation using the difference-in-differences model of this section. Instead, she used the fixed-effects estimation technique to be described in Section 16.2.

16.2 Panel Data

Let's think for a second about the data in the ARCO gasoline price example of the previous section. Is it a time-series data set? Is it a cross-sectional data set? Well, the data set includes gasoline prices from five different months, so it clearly has a time-series component. However, the data set also includes prices for hundreds of individual gas stations for each month, so it clearly has a cross-sectional component. Because it has both time-series and cross-sectional dimensions, it's neither time-series nor cross-sectional; it's a *panel data set*!

What Are Panel Data?

Panel (or *longitudinal*) data combine time-series and cross-sectional data in a very specific way. **Panel data** include observations on the same variables from the same cross-sectional sample from two or more *different* time periods. For example, if you surveyed 200 students when they graduated from your school and then administered the same questionnaire to the same individuals five years later, you would have created a panel data set.

Not every data set that combines time-series and cross-sectional data meets this definition. In particular, if different variables are observed in the different time periods or if the data are drawn from different samples in the different time periods, then the data are not considered to be panel data.[7]

Some panel data sets are created by large-scale, long-term longitudinal surveys, for instance the 1979 National Longitudinal Survey of Youth (NLSY). Available through the Bureau of Labor Statistics, the NLSY has followed a cohort of 12,686 men and women who were 14 to 22 years old in 1979. These individuals were surveyed annually from 1979 through 1994 and have been surveyed every other year since then.[8] Quite obviously, a panel data set of this many individuals collected over such a long time period provides an

---

7. Instead, we refer to these data sets as "pooled cross sections across time." An example of pooled cross sections across time would be if you administered a survey to 200 graduating seniors from the class of 2009 and combined the results of this survey with the results of a survey of 200 graduating seniors from the class of 2004. The combined data set is not a panel data set because the sample changed as the time period changed. Equations can be estimated with pooled cross sections across time data by using a variant of the difference-in-differences estimator of the previous section. For more, see Jeff Wooldridge, *Introductory Econometrics* (Mason, OH: South-Western, 2009), pp. 445–455.

8. http://www.bls.gov/nls/nlsy79.htm.

extremely rich source of labor force data. Other well-known longitudinal surveys include the U.S. Panel Survey of Income Dynamics (PSID), the British Household Panel Data Survey, and the Canadian National Public Health Survey.

Why use panel data? As mentioned earlier, panel data certainly will increase sample sizes, but a second advantage of panel data is to provide insight into analytical questions that can't be answered by using time-series or cross-sectional data alone. For example, panel data can help policymakers design programs aimed at reducing unemployment by allowing researchers to determine whether the same people are unemployed year after year or whether different individuals are unemployed in different years.[9] A final advantage of using panel data is that it often allows researchers to avoid omitted variable problems that otherwise would cause bias in cross-sectional studies. We'll come back to this topic soon.

There are four different kinds of variables that we encounter when we use panel data. First, we have variables that can differ between individuals but don't change over time, such as gender, ethnicity, and race. Second, we have variables that change over time but are the same for all individuals in a given time period, such as the retail price index and the national unemployment rate. Third, we have variables that vary both over time and between individuals, such as income and marital status. Fourth, we have trend variables that vary in predictable ways such as an individual's age.

To estimate an equation using panel data, it's crucial that the data be in the right format because regression packages like Stata and EViews need to identify which observations belong to which time periods and which cross-sectional entities. Unfortunately different software programs have different format requirements for panel data. Stata, for example, requires that a panel data set include a date counter and an id number counter, but it doesn't require that the data be in any particular order. Many other programs, however, require the data to be in a specific order, typically by grouping all the observations from one cross-sectional entity together before moving on to another cross-sectional entity. As a result, it's important to check to make sure that your data format matches what is required by your regression program.

Finally, the use of panel data requires a slight expansion of our notation. In the past we've used the subscript i to indicate the observation number in a cross-sectional data set, so Y_i indicated Y for the *i*th cross-sectional observation. Similarly, we've used the subscript t to indicate the observation number

---

9. Peter Kennedy, *A Guide to Econometrics* (Malden, MA: Blackwell, 2008), p. 282.

in a time-series data set, so Y_t indicated Y for the tth time-series observation. In a panel data set, however, variables will have both a cross-sectional and a time-series component, so we'll use *both* subscripts. As a result, Y_{it} indicates Y for the ith cross-sectional and tth time-series observation. This notation expansion also applies to independent variables and error terms.

The Fixed Effects Model

What's the best way to estimate panel data equations? The two main approaches[10] are the fixed effects model discussed in this section and the random effects model featured in the next section.

The **fixed effects model** estimates panel data equations by including enough dummy variables to allow each cross-sectional entity (like a state or country) and each time period to have a different intercept:

$$Y_{it} = \beta_0 + \beta_1 X_{it} + \alpha_2 EF_2 + \cdots + \alpha_N EF_N + \rho_2 TF_2 + \cdots + \rho_T TF_T + \epsilon_{it} \quad (16.4)$$

where: EF_i = N − 1 Entity Fixed Effects dummies, equal to 1 for the ith entity and 0 otherwise

TF_t = T − 1 Time Fixed Effects dummies, equal to 1 for the tth period and 0 otherwise

βs, α_is, and ρ_ts = regression coefficients to be estimated

ϵ = a classical error term

As you'd expect with a panel data set, Y, X, and ϵ have two subscripts. Although there is only one X in Equation 16.4, the model can be generalized to any number of independent variables.

Why do we need something as complicated as Equation 16.4? To answer, let's begin by taking a look at the problems that would arise if we estimated our model without accounting for the fact that our observations are from a panel data set. Our equation would look like this:

$$Y_{it} = \beta_0 + \beta_1 X_{it} + V_{it} \quad (16.5)$$

That looks pretty familiar, except that you're probably thinking, "Where did that weird looking big V_{it} come from?" It's the error term, and you're right, it *is* weird looking.

---

10. Other methods of estimating panel data equations include *the differencing model* (the subject of Exercise 6) and *the demeaned model* (in which the mean of Y is subtracted from each observation of Y, the mean of X is subtracted from each observation of X, and the regression is run on these "demeaned" variables).

To understand V, remember that because we're dealing with panel data, we have observations from several, maybe many, entities and from several, maybe many, time periods. Just about everyone would agree that no two states are exactly alike. They have different cultures, histories, and institutions. It's easy to imagine that those differences might lead to different outcomes in all sorts of things we might want to explain. Our Y_{it} could be income, health, or crime, for instance.

It's also easy to see that things like a state's history and culture are pretty constant from year to year. They might be hard to measure, but we know that they don't change, and we know that they make each state different from all the others. It is very likely that these unchanging and unmeasured differences are correlated with X, but Equation 16.5 doesn't include them, so they are omitted variables.

And that's a problem, right? In Chapter 6 we learned that omitting a relevant variable from a model forces much of its influence into the error term. And that partly explains the weird error term V in Equation 16.5. But there's more. Remember that we're dealing with panel data. Not only have we combined several cross sections, but we've also combined some time series! That means we have even more potential omitted variables. Why is that?

Well, it's entirely possible that during each time period, certain things affect all the entities, but that those common influences change from period to period. Suppose you're investigating annual traffic fatalities in states over a period of many years. If the federal government raises or lowers the maximum highway speed limit, it affects traffic fatalities in all states. Similarly, changing social norms affect traffic fatalities over time. Attitudes about seat belts, for instance, could play a big role. People didn't always buckle up without thinking! If you doubt this, ask your grandparents how many of them used seatbelts back when they were kids.

With the omitted entity characteristics and the omitted time characteristics, the error term in Equation 16.5 can be broken down into three components:

$$V_{it} = \epsilon_{it} + a_i + z_t$$

where ϵ_{it} is a classical error term, a_i refers to the entity characteristics omitted from the equation, and z_t refers to the time characteristics omitted from the equation. If a_i and z_t are correlated with X_{it}, we're going to have a problem because we will have violated Classical Assumption III. Our estimate of β_1 will be biased.

As we learned in Chapter 6, the solution in theory is simple. Just include the omitted variables in the model, and the omitted variable bias will disappear. But the omitted variables often are unobservable. And even if we could see them, we might not be able to measure them. For instance, if the entities are states, the unobserved characteristics could be such things as culture or history. How in the world would we ever discover what they are, much less measure them?

As it happens, we already have something in our econometric toolbox that can solve the problem—dummy variables! By including dummy variables for every entity (EF_i) but one, we can control for those unobservable but unchanging entity effects. We call them entity fixed effects. And by including dummy variables for every time period (TF_t) but one, we can control for time fixed effects. These entity and time fixed effects will no longer be omitted variables because they will be represented by the dummy variables. Including the dummies transforms V into ϵ and transforms Equation 16.5 into the basic fixed effects model, Equation 16.4:

$$Y_{it} = \beta_0 + \beta_1 X_{it} + \alpha_2 EF_2 + \cdots + \alpha_N EF_N + \rho_2 TF_2 + \cdots + \rho_T TF_T + \epsilon_{it} \quad (16.4)$$

The major advantage of the fixed effects model is that it avoids bias due to omitted variables that don't change over time (like geography) or that change over time equally for all entities (like the federal speed limit). What we're in essence doing is allowing each entity's intercept and each time period's intercept to vary around the omitted condition baseline (when all the fixed effect dummies equal zero). And the beauty of it is that we don't even have to know exactly what things go into the entity and time fixed effects. The dummy variables include them all!

The fixed effects model has some drawbacks, however. Degrees of freedom for fixed effects models tend to be low because we lose one degree of freedom for every dummy variable (the EFs and the TFs) in the equation. For example, if the panel contains 50 states and two years, we lose 50 degrees of freedom by using 49 state dummies and one year dummy. Another potential pitfall is that no substantive explanatory variables that vary across entities, but do not vary over time within each entity, can be used because they would create perfect multicollinearity.

Luckily, these drawbacks are minor when compared to the advantages of the fixed effects model, so our recommendation is that readers of this text use the fixed effects model whenever they estimate panel data models.

An Example of Fixed Effects Estimation

Let's take a look at a simple application of the fixed effects model. Suppose that you're interested in the relationship between the death penalty and the murder rate, and you collect data on the murder rate in the 50 states.

If you were to estimate a cross-sectional model (Table 16.1) of the annual murder rate as a function of, say, the number of convicted murderers who were executed in the previous three years, you'd end up with:

$$\widehat{MRDRTE_i} = 6.20 + 0.90EXEC_i \qquad (16.6)$$
$$(0.22)$$
$$t = 4.09$$
$$N = 50 \text{ (states in 1990)} \qquad \overline{R}^2 = .24$$

where: $MRDRTE_i$ = the number of murders per 100,000 people in the *i*th state in 1990

$EXEC_i$ = the number of executions in the *i*th state in 1987–89

In a cross-sectional model for 1990, the murder rate appears to increase with the number of executions, quite probably because of omitted variable bias or because of simultaneity. This result implies that the more executions there are, the more murders there are! Such a result is completely counter to our

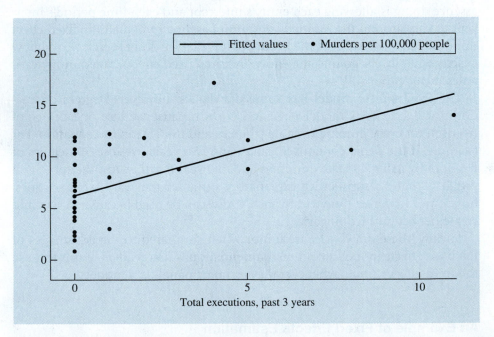

Figure 16.2 In a Single-Year Cross-Sectional Model, the Murder Rate Appears to Increase with Executions

In a cross-sectional model for 1990, the murder rate appears to increase with the number of executions.

Table 16.1 Data for the Murder Example

OBS	STATE	YEAR	MRDRTE	EXEC	TF$_{93}$
1	AL	90	11.6	5	0
2	AL	93	11.6	2	1
3	AK	90	7.5	0	0
4	AK	93	9	0	1
5	AZ	90	7.7	0	0
6	AZ	93	8.6	3	1
7	AR	90	10.3	2	0
8	AR	93	10.2	2	1
9	CA	90	11.9	0	0
10	CA	93	13.1	2	1
11	CO	90	4.2	0	0
12	CO	93	5.8	0	1
13	CT	90	5.1	0	0
14	CT	93	6.3	0	1
15	DE	90	5	0	0
16	DE	93	5	0	1
17	FL	90	10.7	8	0
18	FL	93	8.9	7	1
19	GA	90	11.8	2	0
20	GA	93	11.4	3	1
21	HI	90	4	0	0
22	HI	93	3.8	0	1
23	ID	90	2.7	0	0
24	ID	93	2.9	0	1
25	IL	90	10.3	0	0
26	IL	93	11.4	0	1
27	IN	90	6.2	0	0
28	IN	93	7.5	0	1
29	IA	90	1.9	0	0
30	IA	93	2.3	0	1
31	KS	90	4	0	0
32	KS	93	6.4	0	1
33	KY	90	7.2	0	0
34	KY	93	6.6	0	1
35	LA	90	17.2	4	0
36	LA	93	20.3	2	1
37	ME	90	2.4	0	0
38	ME	93	1.6	0	1
39	MD	90	11.5	0	0
40	MD	93	12.7	0	1
41	MA	90	4	0	0
42	MA	93	3.9	0	1
43	MI	90	10.4	0	0

(*continued*)

Table 16.1 (*continued*)

OBS	STATE	YEAR	MRDRTE	EXEC	TF$_{93}$
44	MI	93	9.8	0	1
45	MN	90	2.7	0	0
46	MN	93	3.4	0	1
47	MS	90	12.2	1	0
48	MS	93	13.5	0	1
49	MO	90	8.8	5	0
50	MO	93	11.3	6	1
51	MT	90	4.9	0	0
52	MT	93	3	0	1
53	NE	90	2.7	0	0
54	NE	93	3.9	0	1
55	NV	90	9.7	3	0
56	NV	93	10.4	0	1
57	NH	90	1.9	0	0
58	NH	93	2	0	1
59	NJ	90	5.6	0	0
60	NJ	93	5.3	0	1
61	NM	90	9.2	0	0
62	NM	93	8	0	1
63	NY	90	14.5	0	0
64	NY	93	13.3	0	1
65	NC	90	10.7	0	0
66	NC	93	11.3	2	1
67	ND	90	0.8	0	0
68	ND	93	1.7	0	1
69	OH	90	6.1	0	0
70	OH	93	6	0	1
71	OK	90	8	1	0
72	OK	93	8.4	2	1
73	OR	90	3.8	0	0
74	OR	93	4.6	0	1
75	PA	90	6.7	0	0
76	PA	93	6.8	0	1
77	RI	90	4.8	0	0
78	RI	93	3.9	0	1
79	SC	90	11.2	1	0
80	SC	93	10.3	1	1
81	SD	90	2	0	0
82	SD	93	3.4	0	1
83	TN	90	10.5	0	0
84	TN	93	10.2	0	1
85	TX	90	14.1	11	0
86	TX	93	11.9	34	1

(*continued*)

Table 16.1 (*continued*)

OBS	STATE	YEAR	MRDRTE	EXEC	TF$_{93}$
87	UT	90	3	1	0
88	UT	93	3.1	1	1
89	VT	90	2.3	0	0
90	VT	93	3.6	0	1
91	VA	90	8.8	3	0
92	VA	93	8.3	11	1
93	WA	90	4.9	0	0
94	WA	93	5.2	1	1
95	WV	90	5.7	0	0
96	WV	93	6.9	0	1
97	WI	90	4.6	0	0
98	WI	93	4.4	0	1
99	WY	90	4.9	0	0
100	WY	93	3.4	1	1

Source: U.S. Department of Justice, FBI *Annual*, www.deathpenaltyinfo.org/execution

Datafile = MURDER16

expectations. To make things worse, it's not a fluke. If we collect data from another year, 1993, and estimate a single-time-period regression on the 1993 data set, we also get a positive slope.

However, if we combine the two cross-sectional data sets to create the panel data set in Table 16.1, we can estimate a fixed effects model, using the fixed effects model of Equation 16.4, adjusted to account for 50 states (with Alabama as the omitted condition) and two time periods (with 1990 as the omitted condition):

$$MRDRTE_{it} = \beta_0 + \beta_1 EXEC_{it} + \alpha_2 EF_2 + \cdots + \alpha_{50} EF_{50} + \rho_2 TF_{93} + \epsilon_{it} \quad (16.7)$$

If we now estimate Equation 16.7 with the data from Table 16.1, we obtain:

$$\widehat{MRDRTE}_{it} = 7.15 - 0.104 EXEC_{it} + 0.35 TF_{93} \quad (16.8)$$
$$(0.04) \qquad\qquad (0.16)$$
$$t = \qquad -2.38 \qquad\quad +2.23$$
$$N = 100 \qquad\qquad \bar{R}^2 = .96$$

As can be seen in Equation 16.8 and Figure 16.3, a fixed effects model estimated on panel data from 1990 and 1993 results in a significant negative estimated slope for the relationship between the murder rate and the number

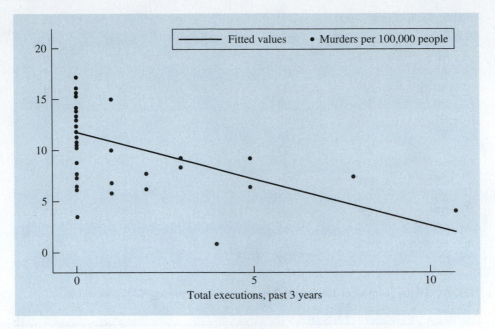

Figure 16.3 In a Panel Data Model, the Murder Rate Decreases with Executions

If we use the fixed effects model to estimate panel data from 1990 and 1993, the murder rate decreases with the number of executions, as you'd expect.

of executions.[11] This example illustrates how the omitted variable bias arising from unobserved heterogeneity can be mitigated with panel data and the fixed effects model. When the dataset is expanded to include another year, you're in essence looking at each state and comparing the state to itself over time.

Note that we included TF_{93}, a year fixed effect variable, in Equation 16.8. A year fixed effect captures any impact that altered the level of executions across the country for a given year. For example, if the Supreme Court declared a moratorium on a type of execution in that year, we would see a decline in executions across states that used that type of execution during the year for reasons unrelated to the relation between murders and executions for each state.[12]

---

11. This example was kept simple to illustrate the value of panel data and to show how to apply the fixed effects model to panel data, so no inferences about the death penalty should be drawn from it. The correct specification surely includes a number of other variables. In addition, the state of Texas plays too large a role in determining the coefficients in this sample, in part because many states didn't allow capital punishment between 1987 and 1993.

12. With thanks to Doug Steigerwald.

You might have noticed the big increase in $\overline{R}^2$ between Equations 16.7 and 16.8. The increase comes from the addition of all the dummy variables for state and time fixed effects. So why don't the coefficients of the state dummies appear in Equation 16.8? Unless the entity fixed effects are the main focus of the research, the coefficients usually are omitted from the results to save space. Some large panel data sets have hundreds or even thousands of entity fixed effects!

In our example, we used only two time periods, but the fixed effects model can be extended to many more time periods. Fixed effects estimation is a standard statistical routine in most econometric software packages, making it particularly accessible for researchers. Notice that we report an intercept. Depending upon which software program you use to estimate the fixed effects model, you may or may not be provided with an intercept estimate.

16.3 Fixed versus Random Effects

The fixed effects model does a good job of estimating panel data equations, and it also helps avoid omitted variable bias due to unobservable heterogeneity. As a result, the fixed effects model is the panel data estimation procedure that we recommend to most readers of this text.

However, if you read the panel data literature, you'll find that many experienced researchers use an advanced panel data method called the *random effects model*. Although we don't suggest that beginning researchers use the random effects model, we think that it's important to have a general understanding of that model.

The Random Effects Model

An alternative to the fixed effects model is called the random effects model. While the fixed effects model is based on the assumption that each cross-sectional unit has its own intercept, the **random effects model** is based on the assumption that the intercept for each cross-sectional unit is drawn from a distribution that is centered around a mean intercept. Thus each intercept is a random draw from an "intercept distribution" and therefore is independent of the error term for any particular observation.

The random effects model has several clear advantages over the fixed effects model. In particular, a random effects model will have quite a few more degrees of freedom than a fixed effects model, because rather than estimating an intercept for virtually every cross-sectional unit, all we need to do is to estimate the parameters that describe the distribution of the intercepts. Another nice property is that you can estimate coefficients for explanatory variables that are constant over time (like race or gender). However, the random effects estimator has a major disadvantage in that it requires us to assume that the unobserved impact of the omitted variables is uncorrelated with the independent variables, the Xs, if we're going to avoid omitted variable bias.

Choosing Between Fixed and Random Effects

How do researchers decide whether to use the fixed effects model or the random effects model? One key is the nature of the relationship between a_i and the Xs. If they're likely to be correlated, then it makes sense to use the fixed effects model, as that sweeps away the a_i and the potential omitted variable bias.[13]

Many researchers use the *Hausman test*, which is well beyond the scope of this text, to see whether there is correlation between a_i and X. Essentially, this procedure tests to see whether the regression coefficients under the fixed effects and random effects models are statistically different from each other.[14] If they are different, then the fixed effects model is preferred even though it uses up many more degrees of freedom. If the coefficients aren't different, then researchers either use the random effects model (in order to conserve degrees of freedom) or provide estimates of both the fixed effects and random effects models.

(16.4) Summary

1. Random assignment experiments are considered the gold standard when it comes to establishing a causal effect from treatment to outcome. A randomly chosen treatment group is exposed to a treatment while a control group isn't, and we test to see if the outcome is significantly different between the two groups. Unfortunately, such experiments aren't feasible in many areas of economics.

---

13. For an excellent explanation of the choice between fixed and random effects, see Peter Kennedy, *A Guide to Econometrics* (Malden, MA: Blackwell, 2008), pp. 284–292.

14. For an illustration of the Hausman test, see E. DiCioccio and P. Wunnava, "Working and Educated Women: Culprits of a European Kinder-Crisis," *Eastern Economic Journal*, April 2008, pp. 213–222.

2. Natural experiments can be used to provide evidence of causality in economics if a naturally occurring event (or a policy change) can be found that mimics a random assignment treatment. If the event causes the mean of the outcome for the treatment group to change substantially more than the mean of the outcome for the control group does, then we have evidence that the treatment was a causal factor in the outcome.

3. Equations involving data from natural experiments can be estimated with a difference-in-differences model, which compares the difference between the change in the treatment group and the change in the control group.

4. Panel data combine time-series and cross-sectional data by including observations on the same variables from the same cross-sectional sample from two or more time periods. Panel data often are produced by large, multi-year survey projects and provide a rich source of material for econometric analysis.

5. Equations involving panel data can be estimated using the fixed effects model and a more advanced technique, the random effects model.

EXERCISES

(The answers to the even-numbered questions are in Appendix A.)

1. Write the meaning of each of the following terms without referring to the book (or your notes), and then compare your definition with the version in the text for each.
    a. control group (p. 466)
    b. difference-in-differences (p. 470)
    c. fixed effects model (p. 475)
    d. natural experiments (p. 469)
    e. panel data (p. 473)
    f. random assignment experiments (p. 466)
    g. random effects model (p. 483)
    h. treatment group (p. 466)

2. Fifteen years ago, the town of Easton decided to increase its annual spending on education so that its high school graduates would be able to earn higher wages. Now Easton has asked you to evaluate the effectiveness of the spending increase. Their data show that before

the spending increase, the average annual salary of recent high school graduates was $25,000 and that now that average salary has risen to $28,500. Fortunately for your analysis, a neighboring community (Allentown) did not change its annual spending on education. Fifteen years ago, recent Allentown high school graduates earned an average of $22,500, and now that average is $23,750.

a. Use a difference-in-differences estimator to determine whether Easton's spending increase caused the wages of their high school graduates to increase.

b. What underlying assumption do you have to make in order for your estimate to be valid? What might cause your underlying assumption to be invalid?

c. This data set contains only two observations. Even if the underlying assumption in part b is met, how much confidence can you have in conclusions based on two observations?

3. The discussion of random assignment experiments in Section 16.1 includes models both with (Equation 16.2) and without (Equation 16.1) two additional observable factors (X_1 and X_2). In contrast, the discussion of natural experiments in Section 16.1 jumped immediately to Equation 16.3 below (which includes these factors) without discussing an equation similar to Equation 16.1.

$$\Delta \text{OUTCOME}_i = \beta_0 + \beta_1 \text{TREATMENT}_i + \beta_2 X_{1i} + \beta_3 X_{2i} + \epsilon_i \quad (16.3)$$

Was this a mistake? What reasons are there for thinking that a natural experiment is more likely to benefit from the inclusion of additional observable factors than is a random assignment experiment? Explain.

4. In 2003, ten states increased the taxes they placed on cigarettes. Because taxes increase the price of cigarettes, we'd expect that a tax increase would reduce the consumption of cigarettes. In Table 16.2, we present cross-sections of state level data on cigarette consumption for the years 2000 and 2006. Forty-four states plus the District of Columbia are listed here, with those states that did not have a tax increase in 2003 listed first.

a. Would you consider this to be a random assignment experiment data set, a natural experiment data set, or a panel data set? Explain.

b. Depending on your answer to part a, use the appropriate estimation technique to determine the impact of the cigarette tax increase on the consumption of cigarettes.

c. Do these results conform with your expectations? If they don't, what problems do you see with this research design?

Table 16.2 Cigarette Consumption by State

State	Tax	2000	2006
Alabama	0	25.3	23.2
Arizona	0	18.6	18.2
Alaska	0	25	24
Arkansas	0	25.2	23.7
Colorado	0	20.1	17.9
Connecticut	0	20	17
Delaware	0	23	21.7
Hawaii	0	19.7	17.5
Illinois	0	22.3	20.5
Indiana	0	27	24.1
Iowa	0	23.3	21.4
Kentucky	0	30.5	28.5
Louisiana	0	24.1	23.4
Maine	0	23.8	20.9
Maryland	0	20.6	17.7
Massachusetts	0	20	17.8
Michigan	0	24.2	22.4
Minnesota	0	19.8	18.3
Montana	0	18.9	18.9
Nebraska	0	21.4	18.7
New Hampshire	0	25.4	18.7
New Jersey	0	21	18
New York	0	21.6	18.2
North Carolina	0	26.1	22.1
Ohio	0	26.3	22.4
Oklahoma	0	23.3	25.1
Oregon	0	20.8	18.5
Pennsylvania	0	24.3	21.5
Rhode Island	0	23.5	19.2
Tennessee	0	25.7	22.6
Texas	0	22	17.9
Utah	0	12.9	9.8
Virginia	0	21.5	19.3
Washington	0	20.7	17.1
Wisconsin	0	24.1	20.8
Washington, DC	1	20.9	17.9
Georgia	1	23.6	19.9
Idaho	1	22.4	16.8
Kansas	1	21.1	20
Nevada	1	29.1	22.2
New Mexico	1	23.6	20.1
South Dakota	1	22	20.3
Vermont	1	21.5	18
West Virginia	1	26.1	25.7
Wyoming	1	23.8	21.6

Datafile = CIGI6

5. Suppose that you're interested in the effect of price on the demand for a "salon" haircut and that you collect the following data for four U.S. cities for 2003:

Location	Year	Average Price	Per Capita Quantity
New York	2003	$75	2
Boston	2003	$50	1
Washington, DC	2003	$60	1.5
Philadelphia	2003	$55	0.8

and for 2008:

Location	Year	Average Price	Per Capita Quantity
New York	2008	$85	1.8
Boston	2008	$48	1.1
Washington, DC	2008	$65	1.4
Philadelphia	2008	$60	0.7

a. Estimate a cross-sectional OLS regression of per capita quantity as a function of average price for 2003. Is the slope positive or negative? Does that meet your expectations?

b. Now estimate a cross-sectional regression on the data for 2008. How is the result different?

c. Now estimate a fixed effects model on the combined data and compare your results with parts a and b.

d. What's your conclusion? Which model offers the best approach to answering your question?

6. A simple alternative to the fixed effects model is called the *differencing model*, in which all the variables and the error term are expressed as differences. For a panel data set with two time periods, the estimating equation would be:

$$\Delta Y_i = \beta_0 + \beta_1 \Delta X_i + \Delta \epsilon_i$$

where: $\Delta Y_i = Y_{2i} - Y_{1i}$, $\Delta X_i = X_{2i} - X_{1i}$, and $\Delta \epsilon_i = \epsilon_{2i} - \epsilon_{1i}$.

a. Using the data in Exercise 5, estimate a differencing model for the price of salon haircuts.

b. Now compare your answer in part a to your answer for part c of Exercise 5. What do you notice? What does this tell you about the relationship between the differencing model and the fixed effects model when there are exactly two time periods?

c. Think about the error term in the differencing model. Which of the Classical Assumptions does $\Delta \epsilon_i$ seem likely to violate? How might you deal with this problem?

β

Appendix A

Answers

Chapter 1

1.2.   Using Stata:
   a. Install and launch the regression software.
   b. Open the datafile. All datafiles can be found in Stata format at www.pearsonhighered.com/studenmund. This particular datafile is "HTWT1."
   c. Run the regression. Type "reg Y X" in the command window. This tells Stata to run a regression using Y as the dependent variable and X as the independent variable. Hit enter and the results will appear in the results window.

   Using EViews:
   a. Install and launch the software.
   b. Open the datafile. All datafiles can be found in EViews format at www.pearsonhighered.com/studenmund. This particular datafile is "HTWT1."
   c. Run the regression. Type "LS Y C X" on the top line, making sure to leave spaces between the variable names. (LS stands for Least Squares and C stands for constant.) Press Enter, and the regression results will appear on your screen.

1–4.   a. The estimated slope coefficient of 3.62 represents the change in the size of a house (in square feet) given a one thousand dollar increase in the price of the house. The estimated intercept of −290 is the value of SIZE when PRICE equals zero. The estimated intercept is negative, but because the estimate includes the constant value of any omitted variables, any measurement errors, and/or an incorrect functional form, we shouldn't attach any importance to the negative sign.
   b. No. All we have shown is that a statistical relationship exists between the price of a house and its size.
   c. The new slope coefficient would be 0.00362 (or 3.62/1000), but nothing else would change.

1–6.   a. 2.29 is the estimated constant term, and it is an estimate of the gift when the alum has no income and no calls were made to that alum. 0.001 is an estimate of the slope coefficient of INCOME, and it tells us how much the gift would be likely to increase when the alum's income increases by a dollar, holding constant the number of calls to that alum. 4.62 is an estimate of the slope coefficient of CALLS, and it tells us how much the gift would be likely to increase if the college made one more call to the alum, holding constant the alum's income. The signs of the estimated slope coefficients are as expected, but we typically do not develop hypotheses involving constant terms.

b. Once we estimate the equation, the left-hand variable now is the estimated value of the dependent variable because the right-hand side of the equation also consists of estimated coefficients (in all but one case multiplied by independent variables).

c. An error term is unobservable and couldn't be included in an *estimated* equation from which we actually calculate a $\hat{Y}$.

d. The right-hand side of the equation would become 2.29 + 1.0INCOME + 4.62CALLS. Nothing has changed except the scale of the coefficient of INCOME.

e. Many good possibilities exist. However, we don't suggest adding "last year's GIFT" (as tempting as that may seem). While the fit would be good, there would be very little analytical content to the result.

1–8.   a. At first glance, the answer is yes, because both coefficients are positive (as we'd expect) and the coefficient of HOT is 59 times the size of the coefficient of EASE (as the article predicted). However, the variable HOT has a maximum value of 5 while the variable EASE has a maximum value of 1, so the two coefficients aren't directly comparable. In addition, there surely are some important variables that have been omitted from this equation, and it's very risky to draw conclusions from regression results when important variables have been left out. We'll address this topic (omitted variable bias) in more detail in Chapter 6.

b. Other possibly important variables include communication skills, knowledge of the field, enthusiasm, organization, etc.

c. Our guess is that the coefficient of HOT would decrease in size quite a bit. The coefficient of EASE already is extremely low, so it might actually go up.

Chapter 2

2-2. a. $\hat{\beta}_1 = -0.55$, $\hat{\beta}_0 = 12.29$
b. $R^2 = .46$, $\overline{R}^2 = .40$
c. Income $= 12.29 - 0.55\,(8) = 7.89$

2-4. a. Yes. The new coefficient represents the impact of HEIGHT on WEIGHT, holding MAIL constant, while the original coefficient did not hold MAIL constant. We'd expect the estimated coefficient to change (at least slightly) because of this new constraint.
b. One weakness of R^2 is that adding a variable will usually decrease (and will never increase) the summed squared residuals no matter how nonsensical the variable is. As a result, adding a nonsensical variable will usually increase (and will never decrease) R^2.
c. $\overline{R}^2$ is adjusted for degrees of freedom and R^2 isn't, so it's completely possible that the two measures could move in opposite directions when a variable is added to an equation.
d. The coefficient is indeed equal to zero in theory, but in any given sample, MAIL may have some random correlation with WEIGHT and therefore may provide some minor explanatory power beyond that provided by HEIGHT. In fact, it's typical to get a nonzero estimated coefficient even for nonsensical variables.

2-6. As we'll learn in future chapters, there's a lot more to getting the best equation than maximizing $\overline{R}^2$. For example, see pp. 55–56.

Chapter 3

3-2. a. D $= 1$ if graduate student and D $= 0$ if undergraduate.
b. Yes; for example, E $=$ how many exercises the student did.
c. If D is defined as in answer a, then its coefficient's sign would be expected to be positive. If D is defined as 0 if graduate student, 1 if undergraduate, then the expected sign would be negative.
d. A coefficient with value of 0.5 indicates that holding constant the other independent variables in the equation, a graduate student would be expected to earn half a grade point higher than an undergraduate. If there were only graduate students or only undergraduates in class, the coefficient of D could not be estimated.
e. With three categories, use two dummies. It doesn't matter which two you pick.

3–4.   If you need help getting started, see the answer to Exercise 1–2.

3–6.   a. All positive except for the coefficient of F_i, which in today's male-dominated movie industry probably has a negative expected sign. The sign of $\hat{\beta}_B$ certainly is unexpected.
    b. Fred, because $\$500,000 < (\$4,000,000 - \$3,027,000)$.
    c. Yes, since $200 \times 15.4 = \$3,080,000 > \$1,200,000$.
    d. Yes, since $\$1,770,000 > \$1,000,000$.
    e. Yes, the unexpected sign of $\hat{\beta}_B$.

Chapter 4

4–2.   a. An additional pound of fertilizer per acre will cause corn yield to increase by 0.10 bushels per acre, holding rainfall constant. An additional inch of rain will increase corn yield by 5.33 bushels per acre, holding fertilizer per acre constant.
    b. No, for a couple of reasons. First, it's hard to imagine *zero* inches of rain falling in an entire year, so this particular intercept has no real-world meaning. More generally, recall that the OLS estimate of the intercept includes the nonzero mean of the error term, so even if rainfall were zero, it wouldn't make sense to attempt to analyze the OLS estimate of the intercept.
    c. No. An unbiased estimator will produce a distribution of estimates that is centered around the true β, but individual estimates can vary widely from that true value. 0.10 is the estimated coefficient for this sample, not for the entire population, so it could be an unbiased estimate.
    d. Not necessarily: 5.33 still could be close to or even equal to the true value. More generally, an estimated coefficient produced by an estimator that is not BLUE still could be accurate. For example, the amount of the bias could be very small, or the variation due to sampling could offset the bias.

4–4.   a. Classical Assumption II.
    b. Classical Assumption VI.
    c. R: A one-unit increase in yesterday's R will result in a 0.1 percent increase in today's Dow Jones average, holding constant the other independent variables in the equation.
    M: The Dow Jones will be 0.017 percent lower on a Monday, holding constant the other independent variables in the equation.

d. Technically, C is not a dummy variable because it can take on three different values. Saunders assumed (at least implicitly) that all levels of cloud cover between 0 percent and 20 percent have the same impact on the Dow and also that all levels of cloud cover between 21 percent and 99 percent have the same impact on the Dow. In addition, by using the same variable to represent both sunny and cloudy days, the equation constrains the impact of 100 percent sunny and 100 percent cloudy to be equal (though in opposite directions).

e. In our opinion, this particular equation does little to support Saunders' conclusion. The poor fit and the constrained specification combine to outweigh the significant coefficients of R_{t-1} and M.

4-6.   a. The coefficient of DIVSEP implies that a divorced or separated individual will drink 2.85 more drinks than otherwise, holding constant the other independent variables in the equation. The coefficient of UNEMP implies that an unemployed individual will drink 14.20 more drinks than otherwise, holding constant the other independent variables in the equation. The signs of the estimated coefficients make sense, but we wouldn't have expected the coefficient of UNEMP to be five times the size of the coefficient of DIVSEP.

b. The coefficient of ADVICE implies that an individual will drink 11.36 more drinks, holding constant the other independent variables in the equation, if a physician advises them to cut back on drinking alcohol. This coefficient certainly has an unexpected sign! Our guess is that DRINKS and ADVICE are simultaneously determined, since a physician is more likely to advise an individual to cut back on their drinking if that individual is drinking quite a bit. As a result, this equation almost surely violates Classical Assumption III. For more, see Chapter 14.

c. We'd expect each sample to produce different estimates of β_{ADVICE}. The entire group of sample means is called a sampling distribution of $\hat{\beta}_s$.

d. The $\hat{\beta}_{ADVICE}$ for this subsample is 8.62, which is a little lower than the coefficient for the entire sample. The other coefficients for this subsample differ even more from the coefficients for the entire sample, and the estimated coefficient of EDUC actually has an unexpected sign. These results are clear evidence of the advantages of large samples.

Chapter 5

5-2.   For all three parts:

	X_1	X_2	X_3
H_0:	$\beta_1 \leq 0$	$\beta_2 \geq 0$	$\beta_3 \geq 0$
H_A:	$\beta_1 > 0$	$\beta_2 < 0$	$\beta_3 < 0$
	$t_1 = 2.1$	$t_2 = 5.6$	$t_3 = -0.1$

a. $t_c = 1.363$. For β_1, we reject H_0, because $|t_1| > 1.363$ and the sign of t_1 is that implied by H_A. For β_2, we cannot reject H_0, even though $|t_2| > 1.363$, because the sign of t_2 does not agree with H_A. For β_3, we cannot reject H_0, even though the sign of t_3 agrees with H_A, because $|t_3| < 1.363$.

b. $t_c = 1.318$. The decisions are identical to those in part a, except that $t_c = 1.318$.

c. $t_c = 3.143$. For β_1, we cannot reject H_0, even though the sign of t_1 is that implied by H_A, because $|t_1| < 3.143$. For β_2 and β_3, the decisions are identical to those in parts a and b, except that $t_c = 3.143$.

5-4.   For β_N: Reject H_0: $\beta \leq 0$, H_A: $\beta > 0$, if $|-4.42| > t_c$ and -4.42 is negative.

For β_P: Reject H_0: $\beta \geq 0$, H_A: $\beta < 0$, if $|4.88| > t_c$ and 4.88 is positive.

For β_I: Reject H_0: $\beta \geq 0$, H_A: $\beta < 0$, if $|2.37| > t_c$ and 2.37 is positive.

a. $t_c = 1.943$; reject the null hypothesis for all three coefficients.

b. $t_c = 1.311$; reject H_0 for all three coefficients.

c. $t_c = 6.965$; cannot reject the null hypothesis for any of the three coefficients.

5-6.   a. For all three, H_0: $\beta \leq 0$, H_A: $\beta > 0$, and the critical 5-percent, one-sided t-value for 24 degrees of freedom is 1.711. For LOT, we can reject H_0 because $|+7.0| > 1.711$ and $+7.0$ is positive. For BED, we cannot reject H_0 because $|+1.0| < 1.711$ even though $+1.0$ is positive. For BEACH, we can reject H_0 because $|+10.0| > 1.711$ and $+10.0$ is positive.

b. H_0: $\beta \geq 0$, H_A: $\beta < 0$, and the critical 10-percent, one-sided t-value for 24 degrees of freedom is 1.318, so we reject H_0 because $|-2.0| > 1.318$ and -2.0 is negative.

    c. $H_0: \beta = 0$, $H_A: \beta \neq 0$, and the critical 5-percent, two-sided t-value for 24 degrees of freedom is 2.064, so we cannot reject H_0 because $|-1.0| < 2.064$. Note that we don't check the sign because the test is two-sided and both signs are in the alternative hypothesis.

    d. The main concern is the possibility that BED and/or FIRE may be irrelevant.

    e. Given that we weren't sure what sign to expect for the coefficient of FIRE, the insignificant coefficient for BED is the most worrisome.

    f. Unless you've read Chapter 6, this will be a difficult question to answer. The most likely answer is that BED doesn't belong in the equation if LOT also is in it. Beach houses on large lots tend to have more bedrooms than beach houses on small lots.

5–8.   a. NEW: $H_0: \beta \leq 0$, $H_A: \beta > 0$. Reject H_0 since $|5.34| > 1.658$ and $+5.34$ has the sign of H_A.

        SCRATCH: $H_0: \beta \geq 0$, $H_A: \beta < 0$. Reject H_0 since $|-4.00| > 1.658$ and -4.00 has the sign of H_A.

    b. BIDRS: $H_0: \beta \leq 0$, $H_A: \beta > 0$.   Cannot   reject H_0 since $|1.23| < 2.358$ even though $+1.23$ has the sign of H_A.

    c. Some econometricians might drop BIDRS from the equation because of its low t-score, but we'd be inclined to keep the variable. The theory is strong, and the estimated coefficient is in the expected direction. As we'll see in Chapter 6, consistently dropping variables with low t-scores will result in coefficient bias.

    d. Most good variables are attributes of the iPod, but attributes of the auction of that iPod (like the length of time of the auction or whether there was a "buy it now" option available) also make sense.

    e. Reject H_0 (that all three slope coefficients equal zero) because 55.09 is larger than 2.68, the 5-percent critical F-value with 3 and 120 degrees of freedom.

Chapter 6

6–2.   a.

	W_i	T_i	C_i	L_i
H_0:	$\beta_1 \leq 0$	$\beta_2 \leq 0$	$\beta_3 \leq 0$	$\beta_4 \leq 0$
H_A:	$\beta_1 > 0$	$\beta_2 > 0$	$\beta_3 > 0$	$\beta_4 > 0$
	$t_W = 4$	$t_T = 3$	$t_C = 2$	$t_L = 0.95$
	$t_c = 1.697$	$t_c = 1.697$	$t_c = 1.697$	$t_c = 1.697$

For the first three coefficients, we can reject the null hypothesis, because the absolute value of t_k is greater than t_c and the sign of t_k is that specified in H_A. For L, however, we cannot reject the null hypothesis, even though the sign is as expected, because the absolute value of t_L is less than 1.697.

b. Almost any equation potentially could have an omitted variable, and this one is no exception. In addition, L_i might be an irrelevant variable. Finally, the coefficient of C seems far too large, suggesting at least one omitted variable. C appears to be acting as a proxy for other luxury options or the general quality of the car.

c. *Theory:* Bigger engines cost more, so the variable's place in the equation seems theoretically sound. However, sedans with large engines tend to weigh more, so perhaps the two variables are measuring more or less the same thing.

t-Test: The variable's estimated coefficient is insignificant in the expected direction.

$\bar{R}^2$: The overall fit of the equation (adjusted for degrees of freedom) improves when the variable is dropped from the equation.

Bias: When the variable is dropped from the equation, the estimated coefficients remain virtually unchanged.

The last three criteria are evidence in favor of dropping L_i and the theoretical argument for keeping it isn't overwhelming, so we prefer Model T. However, a researcher who firmly believed in the theoretical importance of engine size would pick Model A.

6–4.   Expected bias $= (\beta_{\text{omitted}}) \cdot \hat{\alpha}_1$

a. Expected bias $= (-) \cdot (+) = (-) =$ negative bias. (This assumes that peanut butter is a normal good.)

b. $(+) \cdot (+) = (+) =$ positive bias; this bias will be potentially large since age and experience are highly correlated.

c. $(+) \cdot (+) = (+) =$ positive bias.

d. $(-) \cdot (0) = 0 =$ no bias; it may seem as though it rains more on the weekends, but there is no relationship between the two.

6–6.   a. $X_1 =$ either dummy variable
$X_2 =$ either dummy variable
$X_3 =$ Parents' educational background
$X_4 =$ Iowa Test score

b. We have two variables for which we expect positive coefficients (Iowa score and Parents' education) and two positive estimated coefficients ($\hat{\beta}_3$ and $\hat{\beta}_4$), so we'd certainly expect X_3 and X_4 to be those two variables. Choosing between the two is difficult, but we certainly expect the Iowa test score to be more significant. Next, we have two variables for which we expect a zero coefficient (the dummies) and two estimated coefficients ($\hat{\beta}_1$ and $\hat{\beta}_2$) that are not significantly different from zero, so we'd certainly expect X_1 and X_2 to be the dummies. There is no evidence to allow us to distinguish which dummy is X_1 and which is X_2. (If you expected negative signs for the coefficients of the two dummies, note that the presence of the Iowa test score variable in the equation should control for any bias in multiple-choice tests against females and students of color.)

c.

Coefficient:	β_D	β_D	β_{PE}	β_{IT}
Hypoth. sign:	0	0	+	+
t-value:	−1.0	−0.25	+2.0	+12.0
$t_c = 2.093$ (5-percent two-sided with 19 d.f.)	do not reject	do not reject		
$t_c = 1.729$ (5-percent one-sided with 19 d.f.)			reject	reject

d. As you can see, we used a one-sided test for those coefficients for which we had a specific prior expectation but a two-sided test around zero for those coefficients for which we did not.

6–8. a. i. The coefficient of CV is −0.19 with a SE($\hat{\beta}$) of 0.23. The $\overline{R}^2$ is .773, and the rest of the equation is extremely similar to Equation 5.15 except that the coefficient of CVN falls to −0.48 with a t-score of −1.86.

ii. The coefficient of N is 0.00054 with a SE($\hat{\beta}$) of 0.063. The $\overline{R}^2$ is .766, and the rest of the equation is identical (for all intents and purposes) to Equation 5.15.

b. *Theory:* P is a price ratio, and while it's possible that a price ratio would be a function of the size of a market or a country, it's not at all obvious that either variable would add anything since CVN is already in the equation.

t-score: Both t-scores are insignificant.

$\overline{R}^2$: $\overline{R}^2$ falls when either variable is added.

bias: None of the coefficients change at all when N is added, so it clearly is irrelevant. The omission of CV does change the coefficient of CVN somewhat, making it likely that CV is redundant since CVN is in the equation.

c. Since CVN = f[CV/N], it would make little theoretical sense to include all three variables in an equation, even though technically you don't violate Classical Assumption VI by doing so.

d. It's good econometric practice to report all estimated equations in a research report, especially those that were undertaken for specification choice or sensitivity analysis.

Chapter 7

7-2. a. Semilog right; as income increases, the sales of shoes will increase, but at a declining rate.

b. Linear (intercept dummy).

c. Semilog right or linear are both justifiable.

d. Double-log; some researchers prefer the inverse form mentioned in footnote 4 on page 197.

e. Quadratic function; to show diminishing returns to scale.

7-4. a. To avoid confusion with β, let's use αs as the coefficients.

Coefficient	α_{BETA}	α_{EARN}	α_{DIV}
Hypothesized sign:	−	+	+
Calculated t-score:	−1.99	1.44	3.33
$t_c = 1.671$ (5% level), so:	sig.	insig.	sig.

b. It's unusual to have a lagged variable in a cross-sectional model, but in this equation all the variables are for 1996–2000 except for BETA, which is for 1958–1994 and therefore is indeed lagged. Fair assumed that the risk characteristics of companies don't change rapidly over time and stated that "five observations per company is not enough to get trustworthy estimates." (p. 17)

c. We don't believe that any of Fair's variables are potentially irrelevant, because the theory behind each variable is exceptionally strong. Some students will think that EARN might be irrelevant because its coefficient has a low t-score, but we disagree with this concern because earnings growth is one of the most important determinants of stock prices. A student who drops EARN should conclude, based on the four specification criteria, that the variable belongs in the equation, because three of the four criteria support keeping EARN in the equation, and the t-score is close to being significant in the expected direction.

d. The functional form is a semi-log left, which is indeed appropriate on a theoretical basis and also because two of the independent variables are expressed as percentages.

e. This optional question is intentionally difficult. EARN and DIV both include negative values, so it might seem impossible to run the regression. However, since the negative values are extremely small, one possible way to estimate the equation is to set all the negative values equal to $+0.01$, obtaining:

$$\widehat{LNPE} = 3.23 - 0.19LNBETA + 0.071LNEARN + 0.098LNDIV$$
$$(0.11) \qquad\qquad (0.035) \qquad\qquad (0.028)$$
$$t = -1.69 \qquad\qquad 2.02 \qquad\qquad 3.49$$
$$N = 65 \qquad\qquad \overline{R}^2 = .23$$

However, these results, while completely reasonable, shed very little light on whether to use a double-log functional form, because we urge researchers to focus on theory, and not fit, to choose their functional forms. We think that Fair's choice of a semi-log left is supported by the literature and by the fact that two of the independent variables are expressed in percentage growth terms.

7–6. a. polynomial (second-degree, with a negative expected coefficient for age and a positive expected coefficient for age squared)
 b. double-log (We would not quibble with those who chose a linear form to avoid the constant elasticity properties of a double-log.)
 c. semilog (lnX)
 d. linear (All intercept dummies have a linear functional relationship with the dependent variable by definition.)

7–8. a.

Coefficient	β_B	β_S	β_D
Hypothesized sign:	+	+	−
Calculated t-score:	−0.08	1.85	−1.29
$t_c = 1.682$, so:	insig.	sig.	insig.

The insignificance of $\hat{\beta}_B$ could be caused by an omitted variable, but it's likely that the interaction variable has "soaked up" the entire effect of beer consumption. Although we cannot reject the null hypothesis for $\hat{\beta}_D$, we see no reason to consider D to be an irrelevant variable because of its sound theory and reasonable statistics.

 b. The interaction variable is a measure of whether the impact of beer drinking on traffic fatalities rises as the altitude of the city rises. For each unit increase in the multiple of B and A, F rises by 0.011, holding constant all the other independent variables in the equation. Thus, the size of the coefficient has no real intuitive meaning in and of itself.

c. $H_0: \beta_{BA} \leq 0$
    $H_A: \beta_{BA} > 0$
    Reject H_0 because $|+4.05| > t_c = 1.682$ and 4.05 is positive and thus matches the sign implied by H_A.

d. Although there is no ironclad rule (as there is with slope dummies) most econometricians include both interaction-term components as independent variables. The major reason for this practice is to avoid the possibility that an interaction term's coefficient might be significant only because it is picking up the effect of the omitted interaction-term component.

e. The exception to this general practice occurs when there is no reason to expect the interaction-term component to have any theoretical validity on its own. We prefer Equation 7.22 to 7.23 because we don't believe that altitude typically would be included as an independent variable in a highway fatality equation. Of our other three specification criteria, only the increase in $\overline{R}^2$ supports considering A to be a relevant variable. However, even moderate theoretical support for the inclusion of A on its own would result in our preferring Equation 7.23.

Chapter 8

8–2.   a.

	EMP$_i$	UNITS$_i$	LANG$_i$	EXP$_i$
H_0	$\beta_1 \leq 0$	$\beta_2 \leq 0$	$\beta_3 \leq 0$	$\beta_4 \leq 0$
H_A	$\beta_1 > 0$	$\beta_2 > 0$	$\beta_3 > 0$	$\beta_4 > 0$
	$t_{EM} = -.098$	$t_U = 2.39$	$t_L = 2.08$	$t_{EX} = 4.97$
	$t_c = 1.725$	$t_c = 1.725$	$t_c = 1.725$	$t_c = 1.725$

For the last three coefficients, we can reject H_0, because the absolute value of t_k is greater than t_c and the sign of t_k is that specified in H_A. For EMP, however, we cannot reject H_0, because the sign of the coefficient is unexpected and because the absolute value of t_{EM} is less than 1.725.

b. The functional form is semilog left (or semilog lnY). Semilog left is an appropriate functional form for an equation with salary as the dependent variable, because salaries often increase in percentage terms when an independent variable (like experience) increases by one unit.

c. There's a chance that an omitted variable is pulling down the coefficient of EMP, but it's more likely that EMP and EXP are redundant (because in essence they measure the same thing) and are causing multicollinearity.

d. This lends support to our opinion that EMP_i and EXP_i are redundant.

e. If we knew that this particular school district didn't give credit for teaching experience elsewhere, then it would make sense to drop EXP. Without that specific knowledge, however, we'd drop EMP because EXP includes EMP.

f. *Theory:* EMP clearly has a theoretically strong impact on salary, but EMP and EXP are redundant, so we should keep only one.

t-Test: The variable's estimated coefficient is insignificant in the unexpected direction.

$\overline{R}^2$: The overall fit of the equation (adjusted for degrees of freedom) improves when the variable is dropped from the equation.

Bias: The exercise gives *t*-scores only, but if you work backward, you can calculate the $SE(\hat{\beta})$s. If you do this, you'll find that the coefficient of EXP does indeed change by more than a standard error when EMP is dropped from the equation. This is exactly what you'd expect to happen when a redundant variable is dropped from an equation; the coefficient of the remaining redundant variable will adjust to pick up the effect of both variables.

Thus even though it might appear that two of the specification criteria support keeping EMP in the equation, in actuality all four support the conclusion that they're redundant and that EMP should be removed. As a result, we have a strong preference for Equation 8.22 over Equation 8.21.

8-4.   Dominant variables are likely in a and d. In a, the number of games won should equal the number of games played (which is a constant) minus the number of games lost. In d, the number of autos produced should equal four times the number of tires bought (if no spare is sold with the cars or five if a spare is included).

8–6.   a. Coefficient:

	β_M	β_B	β_A	β_S
Hypoth. sign:	+	+	+	+
t-value:	5.0	1.0	−1.0	2.5
$t_c = 1.645$	reject	do not	do not	reject
(5% one-sided		reject	reject	
with infinite d.f.)				

b. The insignificant *t*-scores of the coefficients of A and B could have been caused by omitted variables, irrelevance, or multicollinearity (a good choice, since that's the topic of this chapter). Since many MBA students are in their 20s, the collinearity between A and B must be fairly spectacular (Stanford gave us no clues). In addition, experienced econometricians would be concerned that the dependent variable is "truncated" because it can't be higher than 4.0. This implies that the equation should have been estimated by a technique (similar to those we cover in Chapter 13) that is unfortunately beyond the scope of this text.

c. It's probably a good idea, since the improvement in GPA caused by extra maturity may eventually be offset by a worsening in GPA due to separation from an academic environment.

d. We believe in making just one change at a time to best analyze the impact of each change on the estimated regression. Thus, our first choice would be to drop either A or B (we'd prefer to drop A, but on theoretical grounds, not as a result of the unexpected sign). Switching to a polynomial *before* dropping one of the redundant variables will only make things worse, in our opinion.

Chapter 8

Hints for the SAT Interactive Regression Learning Exercise

1. Severe multicollinearity between APMATH and APENG is the only possible problem in this regression. You should switch to the AP linear combination immediately.

2. An omitted variable is a distinct possibility, but be sure to choose the one to add on the basis of theory.

3. Either an omitted or irrelevant variable is a possibility. In this case, theory seems more important than any mild statistical insignificance.

4. On balance, this is a reasonable regression. We see no reason to worry about theoretically sound variables that have slightly insignificant coefficients with expected signs. We're concerned that the coefficient of GEND seems larger in absolute size than those reported in the literature, but none of the specification alternatives seems remotely likely to remedy this problem.

5. An omitted variable is a possibility, but there are no signs of bias and this is a fairly reasonable equation already.

6. We'd prefer not to add PREP (since many students take prep courses because they did poorly on their first shots at the SAT) or

RACE (because of its redundancy with ESL and the lack of real diversity at Arcadia High). If you make a specification change, be sure to evaluate the change with our four specification criteria.

7. Either an omitted or irrelevant variable is a possibility, although GEND seems theoretically and statistically strong.

8. The unexpected sign makes us concerned with the possibility that an omitted variable is causing bias or that PREP is irrelevant. If PREP is relevant, what omission could have caused this result? How strong is the theory behind PREP?

9. This is a case of imperfect multicollinearity. Even though the VIFs are only between 3.8 and 4.0, the definitions of ESL and RACE (and the high simple correlation coefficient between them) make them seem like redundant variables. Remember to use theory (and not statistical fit) to decide which one to drop.

10. An omitted variable or irrelevant variable is a possibility, but there are no signs of bias and this is a fairly reasonable equation already.

11. Despite the switch to the AP linear combination, we still have an unexpected sign, so we're still concerned with the possibility that an omitted variable is causing bias or that PREP is irrelevant. If PREP is relevant, what omission could have caused this result? How strong is the theory behind PREP?

12. All of the choices would improve this equation except switching to the AP linear combination. If you make a specification change, be sure to evaluate the change with our four specification criteria.

13. To get to this result, you had to have made at least three suspect specification decisions, and you're running the risk of bias due to a sequential specification search. Our advice is to stop, take a break, review Chapters 6–8, and then try this interactive exercise again.

14. We'd prefer not to add PREP (since many students take prep courses because they did poorly on their first shots at the SAT) or ESL (because of its redundancy with RACE and the lack of real diversity at Arcadia High). If you make a specification change, be sure to evaluate the change with our four specification criteria.

15. Unless you drop one of the redundant variables, you're going to continue to have severe multicollinearity.

16. From theory and from the results, it seems as if the decision to switch to the AP linear combination was a waste of a regression run. Even if there were severe collinearity between APMATH and APENG (which there isn't), the original coefficients are

significant enough in the expected direction to suggest taking no action to offset any multicollinearity.

17. On reflection, PREP probably should not have been chosen in the first place. Many students take prep courses only because they did poorly on their first shots at the SAT or because they anticipate doing poorly. Thus, even if the PREP courses improve SAT scores, which they probably do, the students who think they need to take them were otherwise going to score worse than their colleagues (holding the other variables in the equation constant). The two effects seem likely to offset each other, making PREP an irrelevant variable. If you make a specification change, be sure to evaluate the change with our four specification criteria.

18. Either adding GEND or dropping PREP would be a good choice, and it's hard to choose between the two. If you make a specification change, be sure to evaluate the change with our four specification criteria.

19. On balance, this is a reasonable regression. We'd prefer not to add PREP (since many students take prep courses because they did poorly on their first shots at the SAT), but the theoretical case for ESL (or RACE) seems strong. We're concerned that the coefficient of GEND seems larger in absolute size than those reported in the literature, but none of the specification alternatives seems remotely likely to remedy this problem. If you make a specification change, be sure to evaluate the change with our four specification criteria.

Chapter 9

9–2.   a.

	$\ln Y_t$	PB_t	PRP_t	D_t
H_0	$\beta_1 \leq 0$	$\beta_2 \geq 0$	$\beta_3 \leq 0$	$\beta_4 \geq 0$
H_A	$\beta_1 > 0$	$\beta_2 < 0$	$\beta_3 > 0$	$\beta_4 < 0$
	$t_Y = 6.6$	$t_{PB} = -2.6$	$t_{PRP} = 2.7$	$t_D = -3.17$
	$t_c = 1.714$	$t_c = 1.714$	$t_c = 1.714$	$t_c = 1.714$

We can reject the null hypothesis for all four coefficients because the t-scores all are in the expected direction with absolute values greater than 1.714 (the 5-percent one-sided critical t-value for 23 degrees of freedom).

b. With a 5-percent, one-sided test and $N = 28$, $K = 4$, the critical values are $d_L = 1.10$ and $d_U = 1.75$. Since $d = 0.94 < 1.10$, we can reject the null hypothesis of no positive serial correlation.

c. The probable serial correlation suggests GLS or Newey-West.

d. We prefer the GLS equation to OLS, because we've rid the equation of much of the serial correlation while retaining estimated coefficients that make economic sense. Note that the dependent variables in the two equations are different, so an improved fit is not evidence of a better equation.

9–4.   a. Except for the first and last observations in the sample, the DW test's ability to detect first-order serial correlation is unchanged.

b. GLS can be applied mechanically to correct for serial correlation, but this procedure generally does not make sense; this time's error term is now hypothesized to be a function of *next* time's error term.

c. First-order serial correlation in data that have been entered in reverse chronological order means that this time's observation of the error term is a function of next time's, which would be very unusual. This might occur if decision makers are able to accurately predict and adjust to future random events before they occur (which would be the case in a world of rational expectations and perfect future information).

9–6.   a. Equation 9.29:

Coefficient:	β_1	β_2	β_3
Hypothesized sign:	+	+	+
Calculated *t*-score:	0.76	14.98	1.80
$t_c = 1.721$, so:	insig.	sig.	sig.

Equation 9.30:

Coefficient:	β_1	β_2
Hypothesized sign:	+	+
Calculated *t*-score:	1.44	28.09
$t_c = 1.717$, so:	insig.	sig.

b. The three statistical specification criteria imply that SP is a relevant variable: $\overline{R}^2$ increases when SP is added, SP's coefficient is significantly different from zero, and the estimated coefficient of SY changes by more than one standard error. However, the sign of the coefficient of SP is an issue. Many researchers would expect the sign of $\hat{\beta}_3$ to be negative (an idea supported by the fact that the authors obtained a negative sign for the subset of the sample from 1960 to 1976), but the authors explain a positive sign by stating that the Soviet leadership became "more competitive" after 1977, leading the USSR to increase defense spending as SP increased.

c. For both equations, DW is far below the critical value for a 5-percent one-sided test, so we can reject the null hypothesis of no positive serial correlation. (For Equation 9.29, $0.49 < 1.12$, and for Equation 9.30, $0.43 < 1.21$.) This result raises the possibility that $\hat{\beta}_3$'s t-score might be inflated, making it possible that SP is an irrelevant variable.

d. Such a small improvement in the DW statistic is no evidence whatsoever that the serial correlation is impure.

e. Just as we suspected, running GLS makes $\hat{\beta}_3$ insignificant, resulting in it being even more likely that lnSP is an irrelevant variable.

Chapter 10

10–2.   a. Yes, heteroskedasticity is much more likely when CV is the dependent variable than it is when P is the dependent variable, because the aggregate consumption of pharmaceuticals will vary much more widely by country than will the prices of those pharmaceuticals.

b. *Breusch–Pagan Test:* $NR^2 = 10.91 > 7.81$, so we can reject the null hypothesis of homoskedasticity.
White Test: $NR^2 = 28.62 >$ the critical chi-square value of 15.51, so we can reject the null hypothesis of homoskedasticity. 15.51 is the critical value because there are only eight degrees of freedom because PC is a dummy variable.

c. The HC standard error for N is 0.107; for P it is 0.127; and for PC it is 10.61.

d. $\widehat{lnCV}_i = -8.21 + 1.11lnN_i + 1.46lnP_i + 0.88PC_i$
$$(0.14)(0.44)(0.48)$$
t $=$ 7.94 3.30 1.82
$$N = 32 \overline{R}^2 = .71$$

e. $\widehat{CVN}_i = 10.89 + 1.17GDPN_i - 0.36P_i - 1.95PC_i$
$$(0.13)(0.11)(5.52)$$
t $=$ 9.22 -3.23 -0.35
$$N = 32 \overline{R}^2 = .80$$

where CVN = CV/N and GDPN = GDP/N.

f. Most experienced econometricians use HC standard errors to deal with heteroskedasticity, so the most obvious answer is to choose that approach.

g. Although Classical Assumption V is the focus of this chapter, we also have to worry about violating Classical Assumption III in this situation. If P is a function of CV and if CV is a function of P, then we have a simultaneous system, and the error term is no longer independent of the explanatory variables. For more on this, see Chapter 14.

10-4.   a. $\widehat{CO}_i = 1273.2 + 0.720I_i$

                    (0.044)

             $t = 16.21$ $\overline{R}^2 = .97$

where: CO = average consumption

         I = average income.

b. $NR^2 = 3.00 < 3.84$, so we cannot reject the null hypothesis of homoskedasticity.

c. The White test does not agree with the Breusch–Pagan test result.

d. Most econometricians would consider HC standard errors if the Breusch–Pagan test or White test indicated heteroskedasticity. In this case, however, there's another reason for considering HC standard errors. The ranges of the income brackets are not constant in Ando and Modigliani's dataset, so the variables are means of ranges of differing widths. Thus it would seem reasonable to think that different range widths might produce different variances for the error term, making heteroskedasticity even more likely.

10-6.   a.

Coefficient:	β_P	β_I	β_Q	β_A	β_S	β_T
Hypoth. sign:	−	+	+	+	−	+?
t-value:	−0.97	6.43	3.62	1.93	1.6	−2.85
$t_c = 1.684$ (5-percent one-sided with 40 d.f., closest to 43)	do not reject	reject	reject	reject	do not reject	do not reject

The expected signs for the coefficients of the last two variables are tricky. Our opinion is that having more suburban newspapers should hurt metropolitan newspaper circulation but that the number of television stations is a measure more of the size of a city than of the competition a newspaper faces. By the way, we see Q as a proxy for quality and A as an endogenous variable (note that the authors did indeed estimate the equation with 2SLS, a technique that covered in Chapter 14).

b. Heteroskedasticity seems extremely likely, since larger cities will have larger newspaper circulation, leading to larger error term variances, and it turns out that we can indeed reject the null hypothesis of homoskedasticity.

c. Heteroskedasticity, multicollinearity, and omitted variables all seem likely.

d. While it's tempting to reformulate the equation by making the dependent variable per capita circulation, this probably would lessen the equation's usefulness. Instead, we would try to improve the specification. Reasonable possibilities include attempting to reduce some of the multicollinearity (redundancy) among the independent variables, trying to find a better measure of quality than the number of editorial personnel, and substituting the number of major metropolitan newspaper competitors for S and T.

Chapter 11

Hints for the Housing Price Interactive Exercise

The biggest problem most students have with this interactive exercise is that they run far too many different specifications "just to see" what the results look like. In our opinion, all but one or two of the specification decisions involved in this exercise should be made before the first regression is estimated, so one measure of the quality of your work is the number of different equations you estimated. Typically, the fewer the better.

As to which specification to run, most of the decisions involved are matters of personal choice and experience. Our favorite model on theoretical grounds is:

$$\overset{+}{P_i} = \beta_0 + \overset{+}{\beta_1 S_i} + \overset{-}{\beta_2 N_i} + \overset{-}{\beta_3 A_i} + \overset{+}{\beta_4 A_i^2} + \overset{+}{\beta_5 Y_i} + \overset{+}{\beta_6 CA_i} + \epsilon_i$$

We think that BE and BA are redundant with S. In addition, we can justify both positive and negative coefficients for SP, giving it an ambiguous expected sign, so we'd avoid including it. We would not quibble with someone who preferred a linear functional form for A to our quadratic. In addition, we recognize that CA is quite insignificant for this sample, but we'd retain it, at least in part because it gets quite hot in Monrovia in the summer.

As to interactive variables, the only one we can justify is between S and N. Note, however, that the proper variable is not $S \cdot N$ but instead is $S \cdot (5 - N)$, or something similar, to account for the different expected signs. This variable turns out to improve the fit while being quite collinear (redundant) with N and S.

In none of our specifications did we find evidence of serial correlation or heteroskedasticity, although the latter is certainly a possibility in such cross-sectional data.

Chapter 12

12-2.　a. The double-log functional form doesn't change the fact that this is a dynamic model. As a result, Y and M almost surely are related by a distributed lag.

　　b. In their relationship to M, both Y and R have the same distributed lag pattern over time, since the $\hat{\lambda}$ of 0.60 applies to both. (The equation is in double-log form, so technically the relationships are between the logs of those variables.)

　　c. Serial correlation is always a concern in a dynamic model. Many students will look at the Durbin–Watson statistic of 1.80 and conclude that there is no evidence of positive serial correlation in this equation, but that statistic is biased toward 2 in the presence of a lagged dependent variable. Ideally, we would use the Lagrange Multiplier Serial Correlation Test, but we don't have the data to do so. Durbin's h test, which is beyond the scope of this text, provides evidence that there is indeed serial correlation in the equation. For more, see Robert Raynor, "Testing for Serial Correlation in the Presence of Lagged Dependent Variables," *The Review of Economics and Statistics*, Vol. 75, No. 4, pp. 716–721.

12-4.　$LM = NR^2 = 24 * 0.0056 = 0.134 < 3.84 = $ 5-percent critical chi-square value with one degree of freedom, so we cannot reject the null hypothesis of no serial correlation.

Chapter 13

13-2.　a. *WN:* The log of the odds that a woman has used a recognized form of birth control is 2.03 higher if she doesn't want any more children than it is if she wants more children, holding ME constant.

ME: A one-unit increase in the number of methods of birth control known to a woman increases the log of the odds that she has used a form of birth control by 1.45, holding WN constant.

LPM: If the model were a linear probability model, then each individual slope coefficient would represent the impact of a one-unit increase in the independent variable on the probability that the ith woman had ever used a recognized form of birth control, holding the other independent variable constant.

b. Yes, but we didn't expect $\hat{\beta}_{ME}$ to be more significant than $\hat{\beta}_{WN}$.

c. As we've said before, β_0 has virtually no theoretical significance. See Section 7.1.

d. We'd add one of a number of potentially relevant variables; for instance, the educational level of the ith woman, whether the ith woman lives in a rural area, and so on.

13-4.   a. There are only two women in the sample who are over 65, and both of them are out of the workforce. Because this causes a near singular matrix, most Logit programs, including Stata's, will not be able to estimate this equation.

b. In both models, the coefficient of A is insignificantly different from zero, $\overline{R}^2_p$ falls when A is added, and the other coefficients don't change by a standard error when A is added. As a result, you'd include A in the equation only if you believe it clearly belongs there on the basis of theory.

a. $\hat{D}_i = -0.22 - 0.38M_i - 0.001A_i + 0.09S_i$
$$\qquad\qquad\quad (0.16) \quad (0.007) \quad (0.04)$$
$$\qquad t = -2.43 \qquad -0.14 \qquad 2.42$$
$$\qquad \overline{R}^2 = .29 \qquad N = 30 \qquad \overline{R}^2_p = .806$$

b. $\ln[D_i/(1 - D_i)] = -5.27 - 2.61M_i - 0.01A_i + 0.67S_i$
$$\qquad\qquad\qquad\qquad\quad (1.20) \quad (0.04) \quad (0.32)$$
$$\qquad\qquad\qquad\qquad -2.17 \qquad -0.25 \qquad 2.10$$
$$\qquad\qquad\qquad\qquad\qquad\qquad \overline{R}^2_p = .76$$

Chapter 14

14-2.   a. If ϵ_2 decreases, Y_2 decreases and then Y_1 decreases.

b. If ϵ_D increases, Q_D increases, and then Q_S increases (equilibrium condition) and P_t increases. (Remember that the variables are simultaneously determined, so it doesn't matter which one is on the left-hand side.)

c. If ϵ_1 increases, CO increases, and then Y increases and YD increases.

14–4. a. There are three predetermined variables in the system, and both equations have three slope coefficients, so both equations are exactly identified. (If the model specified that the price of beef was determined jointly with the price and quantity of chicken, then it would not be predetermined, and the equations would be underidentified.)

b. There are two predetermined variables in the system, and both equations have two slope coefficients, so both equations are exactly identified.

c. There are seven predetermined variables in the system, and there are three slope coefficients in both equations, so the first two equations are overidentified. Note that we don't worry about the identification properties of the third equation because it isn't part of the simultaneous system.

d. There are five predetermined variables in the system, and there are three, two, and four slope coefficients in the first, second, and third equations, respectively, so all three equations are overidentified.

14–6. a. OLS estimation will still encounter simultaneity bias because price and quantity are simultaneously determined. Not all endogenous variables will appear on the left-hand side of a structural equation.

b. The direction of the bias depends on the correlation between the error term and the right-hand-side endogenous variable. If the correlation between the error term and price is positive, as it most likely is, then the simultaneity bias will also be positive.

c. Three: stage one: P as a function of YD and W
stage two: Q_D as a function of $\hat{P}$ and YD: Q_S as a function of $\hat{P}$ and W

d. OLS: $\hat{Q}_D = 57.3 - 0.86P + 1.03YD$
$\hat{Q}_S = 167.5 + 3.95P - 1.42W$

2SLS: $\hat{Q}_D = 95.1 - 6.11\hat{P} + 2.71YD$
$\hat{Q}_S = 480.2 + 13.5\hat{P} - 5.50W$

Chapter 15

15–2. a. $310,120.00
b. 117,276; 132,863; 107,287; Nowheresville

15-4.   a. P isn't a dummy variable. Instead, it's a variable whose main function is to be multiplied by other variables so that the sign of the resulting interaction variable changes depending on the incumbent's party.

b. The interaction variables were required because the dependent variable measures the percentage of votes won by the Democrats, but the independent variables measure items that support (or damage) public support for the incumbent party. For example, if a Democrat is in office in a time of high growth, that growth should increase the share of votes won by Democrats, so a positive sign makes sense. However, if a Republican is in office in a time of high growth, the growth should decrease the share of votes won by the Democrats, so a negative sign makes sense. Multiplying GROWTH by $+1$ if the incumbent is a Democrat and -1 if the incumbent is a Republican (by using P) is a way of accomplishing this goal.

c.
$$\widehat{VOTE} = 48.70 + 8.183P - 1.845DUR*P + 0.087DOW*P + 0.535GROWTH*P$$
$$\phantom{\widehat{VOTE} = 48.70 + }(2.396)\ (0.843)(0.070)(0.197)$$
$$t = 3.42-2.191.252.71$$
$$-0.762INFLATION*P + 0.040ARMY*P - 0.078SPEND*P$$
$$(0.363)(0.034)(0.036)$$
$$-2.101.15-2.18$$
$$N = 21 \quad \overline{R}^2 = .77 \quad DW = 2.20$$

d. The coefficient of DUR*P is negative, while the coefficient of ARMY*P is positive, both opposite of their expected signs. The coefficients of the other interactive terms have the expected signs. We can reject the null hypotheses for P (assuming a positive expected sign), GROWTH*P, INFLATION*P, and SPEND*P. We cannot reject for DUR*P, DOW*P, and ARMY*P.

e. Plugging the actual values for 2000 into the equation, we get a forecast of 52.740, which is 2.475 percentage points higher than the actual 50.265. For 2004, we get a forecast of 44.280, which is 4.306 percentage points below the actual 48.586.

f. To do this, we should estimate Equation 15.20 with data through 2004, producing:

$$\widehat{VOTE} = 48.76 + 7.340P - 1.659DUR*P + 0.116DOW*P + 0.496GROWTH*P$$
$$\phantom{\widehat{VOTE} = 48.76 +}(2.208)(0.812)(0.064)(0.189)$$
$$t = 3.32-2.041.802.63$$
$$-0.727INFLATION*P + 0.039ARMY*P - 0.081SPEND*P$$
$$(0.342)(0.034)(0.034)$$
$$-2.131.14-2.36$$
$$N = 23 \qquad \overline{R}^2 = .75 \qquad DW = 2.23$$

Plugging the actual values for 2008 into this equation, we get a forecast of 42.892, surprisingly below the share that Barack Obama actually earned.

Chapter 16

16–2.   a. $\Delta OUTCOME_{Easton} = 28{,}500 - 25{,}000 = 3{,}500$
$\Delta OUTCOME_{Allentown} = 23{,}750 - 22{,}500 = 1{,}250$

b. We must assume that the changes in the outcome would have been the same in both the treatment and control group (had there been no treatment) in order for this estimation to be valid. However, there was a $2,500 disparity between the average incomes prior to the treatment, so there most likely are several differences between the two groups.

c. Even if the underlying assumption in part b is met, we should be cautious when interpreting our conclusions. A data set with only two observations is absurdly small and is unlikely to provide accurate results except by chance.

16–4.   a. This is a natural experiment dataset that also happens to be a panel dataset because it contains observations on the same variable from the same cross-sectional sample from two different time periods.

b. The appropriate technique is the difference-in-differences estimator, resulting in:

$$\widehat{\Delta SMOKE} = -2.43 - 0.73 TAX$$
$$(0.57)$$
$$t = \quad -1.29$$
$$N = 45 \quad \overline{R}^2 = .015$$

c. The estimated coefficient is almost significant in the expected direction, but the fit is terrible. Most experienced researchers won't be surprised by this result, because of the design of the research. In particular, it seems extremely optimistic to expect to explain cigarette consumption by state using a dummy for whether the cigarette tax rate increased as the only independent variable. Variables other than tax rates certainly play a role, as does the fact that some states increased cigarette taxes by substantially more than did others, and yet that information is lost if you limit yourself to a dummy variable, since it tells you only whether taxes increased, not the amount by which they increased.

16–6. a. $\widehat{\Delta Q} = 0.039 - 0.025\Delta P$
$$(0.002)$$
$$t = \quad -12.33$$
$$N = 4 \quad \overline{R}^2 = .98$$

b. Fixed effects and differencing produce identical results for the coefficient and standard error on the price variable. The fixed effect approach, however, produces estimates for coefficients on time and entity dummy variables. The adjusted R-squared will also differ. But since the variables of interest should be the same in the differencing and fixed effect approaches, the identical results for the price variable produced by the two methods is reassuring. They produce identical answers.

c. The error term in the differencing model certainly appears to be defined in such a way as to be serially correlated.

Appendix B

Statistical Tables

The following tables present the critical values of various statistics used primarily for hypothesis testing. The primary applications of each statistic are explained and illustrated. The tables are:

Table B-1: The *t*-Distribution

The *t*-distribution is used in regression analysis to test whether an estimated slope coefficient (say, $\hat{\beta}_k$) is significantly different from a hypothesized value (such as β_{H_0}). The *t*-statistic is computed as:

$$t_k = (\hat{\beta}_k - \beta_{H_0})/\text{SE}(\hat{\beta}_k)$$

where $\hat{\beta}_k$ is the estimated slope coefficient and $\text{SE}(\hat{\beta}_k)$ is the estimated standard error of $\hat{\beta}_k$. To test the one-sided hypothesis:

$$H_0\colon \beta_k \leq \beta_{H_0}$$
$$H_A\colon \beta_k > \beta_{H_0}$$

the computed *t*-value is compared with a critical *t*-value t_c, found in the *t*-table on the opposite page in the column with the desired level of significance for a one-sided test (usually 5 percent) and the row with $N - K - 1$ degrees of freedom, where N is the number of observations and K is the number of explanatory variables. If $|t_k| > t_c$ and if t_k has the sign implied by the alternative hypothesis, then reject H_0; otherwise, do not reject H_0. In most econometric applications, β_{H_0} is zero and most computer regression programs will calculate t_k for $\beta_{H_0} = 0$. For example, for a 5-percent one-sided test with 15 degrees of freedom, $t_c = 1.753$, so any positive t_k larger than 1.753 would lead us to reject H_0 and declare that $\hat{\beta}_k$ is statistically significant in the hypothesized direction at the 5-percent level.

For a two-sided test, $H_0\colon \beta_k = \beta_{H_0}$ and $H_A\colon \beta_k \neq \beta_{H_0}$, the procedure is identical except that the column corresponding to the two-sided level of significance is used. For example, for a 5-percent two-sided test with 15 degrees of freedom, $t_c = 2.131$, so any t_k larger in absolute value than 2.131 would lead us to reject H_0 and declare that $\hat{\beta}_k$ is significantly different from β_{H_0} at the 5-percent level of significance. For more on the *t*-test, see Chapter 5.

Table B-1 Critical Values of the *t*-Distribution

Degrees of Freedom	Level of Significance				
	One-Sided: 10% Two-Sided: 20%	5% 10%	2.5% 5%	1% 2%	0.5% 1%
1	3.078	6.314	12.706	31.821	63.657
2	1.886	2.920	4.303	6.965	9.925
3	1.638	2.353	3.182	4.541	5.841
4	1.533	2.132	2.776	3.747	4.604
5	1.476	2.015	2.571	3.365	4.032
6	1.440	1.943	2.447	3.143	3.707
7	1.415	1.895	2.365	2.998	3.499
8	1.397	1.860	2.306	2.896	3.355
9	1.383	1.833	2.262	2.821	3.250
10	1.372	1.812	2.228	2.764	3.169
11	1.363	1.796	2.201	2.718	3.106
12	1.356	1.782	2.179	2.681	3.055
13	1.350	1.771	2.160	2.650	3.012
14	1.345	1.761	2.145	2.624	2.977
15	1.341	1.753	2.131	2.602	2.947
16	1.337	1.746	2.120	2.583	2.921
17	1.333	1.740	2.110	2.567	2.898
18	1.330	1.734	2.101	2.552	2.878
19	1.328	1.729	2.093	2.539	2.861
20	1.325	1.725	2.086	2.528	2.845
21	1.323	1.721	2.080	2.518	2.831
22	1.321	1.717	2.074	2.508	2.819
23	1.319	1.714	2.069	2.500	2.807
24	1.318	1.711	2.064	2.492	2.797
25	1.316	1.708	2.060	2.485	2.787
26	1.315	1.706	2.056	2.479	2.779
27	1.314	1.703	2.052	2.473	2.771
28	1.313	1.701	2.048	2.467	2.763
29	1.311	1.699	2.045	2.462	2.756
30	1.310	1.697	2.042	2.457	2.750
40	1.303	1.684	2.021	2.423	2.704
60	1.296	1.671	2.000	2.390	2.660
120	1.289	1.658	1.980	2.358	2.617
(Normal)					
∞	1.282	1.645	1.960	2.326	2.576

Source: Reprinted from Table IV in Sir Ronald A. Fisher, *Statistical Methods for Research Workers,* 14th ed. (copyright © 1970, University of Adelaide) with permission of Hafner, a division of the Macmillan Publishing Company, Inc.

Table B-2: The *F*-Distribution

The *F*-distribution is used in regression analysis to deal with a null hypothesis that contains multiple hypotheses or a single hypothesis about a group of coefficients. To test the most typical joint hypothesis (a test of the overall significance of the regression):

$$H_0: \beta_1 = \beta_2 = \cdots = \beta_K = 0$$
$$H_A: H_0 \text{ is not true}$$

the computed *F*-value is compared with a critical *F*-value, found in one of the two tables that follow. The *F*-statistic has two types of degrees of freedom, one for the numerator (columns) and one for the denominator (rows). For the null and alternative hypotheses above, there are K numerator (the number of restrictions implied by the null hypothesis) and $N - K - 1$ denominator degrees of freedom, where N is the number of observations and K is the number of explanatory variables in the equation. This particular *F*-statistic is printed out by most computer regression programs. For example, if K = 5 and N = 30, there are 5 numerator and 24 denominator degrees of freedom, and the critical *F*-value for a 5-percent level of significance (Table B-2) is 2.62. A computed *F*-value greater than 2.62 would lead us to reject the null hypothesis and declare that the equation is statistically significant at the 5-percent level. For more on the *F*-test, see Section 5.6.

Table B-2 Critical Values of the F-Statistic: 5-Percent Level of Significance

		v_1 = Degrees of Freedom for Numerator										
	1	**2**	**3**	**4**	**5**	**6**	**7**	**8**	**10**	**12**	**20**	**∞**
1	161	200	216	225	230	234	237	239	242	244	248	254
2	18.5	19.0	19.2	19.2	19.3	19.3	19.4	19.4	19.4	19.4	19.4	19.5
3	10.1	9.55	9.28	9.12	9.01	8.94	8.89	8.85	8.79	8.74	8.66	8.53
4	7.71	6.94	6.59	6.39	6.26	6.16	6.09	6.04	5.96	5.91	5.80	5.63
5	6.61	5.79	5.41	5.19	5.05	4.95	4.88	4.82	4.74	4.68	4.56	4.36
6	5.99	5.14	4.76	4.53	4.39	4.28	4.21	4.15	4.06	4.00	3.87	3.67
7	5.59	4.74	4.35	4.12	3.97	3.87	3.79	3.73	3.64	3.57	3.44	3.23
8	5.32	4.46	4.07	3.84	3.69	3.58	3.50	3.44	3.35	3.28	3.15	2.93
9	5.12	4.26	3.86	3.63	3.48	3.37	3.29	3.23	3.14	3.07	2.94	2.71
10	4.96	4.10	3.71	3.48	3.33	3.22	3.14	3.07	2.98	2.91	2.77	2.54
11	4.84	3.98	3.59	3.36	3.20	3.09	3.01	2.95	2.85	2.79	2.65	2.40
12	4.75	3.89	3.49	3.26	3.11	3.00	2.91	2.85	2.75	2.69	2.54	2.30
13	4.67	3.81	3.41	3.18	3.03	2.92	2.83	2.77	2.67	2.60	2.46	2.21
14	4.60	3.74	3.34	3.11	2.96	2.85	2.76	2.70	2.60	2.53	2.39	2.13
15	4.54	3.68	3.29	3.06	2.90	2.79	2.71	2.64	2.54	2.48	2.33	2.07
16	4.49	3.63	3.24	3.01	2.85	2.74	2.66	2.59	2.49	2.42	2.28	2.01
17	4.45	3.59	3.20	2.96	2.81	2.70	2.61	2.55	2.45	2.38	2.23	1.96
18	4.41	3.55	3.16	2.93	2.77	2.66	2.58	2.51	2.41	2.34	2.19	1.92
19	4.38	3.52	3.13	2.90	2.74	2.63	2.54	2.48	2.38	2.31	2.16	1.88
20	4.35	3.49	3.10	2.87	2.71	2.60	2.51	2.45	2.35	2.28	2.12	1.84
21	4.32	3.47	3.07	2.84	2.68	2.57	2.49	2.42	2.32	2.25	2.10	1.81
22	4.30	3.44	3.05	2.82	2.66	2.55	2.46	2.40	2.30	2.23	2.07	1.78
23	4.28	3.42	3.03	2.80	2.64	2.53	2.44	2.37	2.27	2.20	2.05	1.76
24	4.26	3.40	3.01	2.78	2.62	2.51	2.42	2.36	2.25	2.18	2.03	1.73
25	4.24	3.39	2.99	2.76	2.60	2.49	2.40	2.34	2.24	2.16	2.01	1.71
30	4.17	3.32	2.92	2.69	2.53	2.42	2.33	2.27	2.16	2.09	1.93	1.62
40	4.08	3.23	2.84	2.61	2.45	2.34	2.25	2.18	2.08	2.00	1.84	1.51
60	4.00	3.15	2.76	2.53	2.37	2.25	2.17	2.10	1.99	1.92	1.75	1.39
120	3.92	3.07	2.68	2.45	2.29	2.18	2.09	2.02	1.91	1.83	1.66	1.25
∞	3.84	3.00	2.60	2.37	2.21	2.10	2.01	1.94	1.83	1.75	1.57	1.00

v_2 = Degrees of Freedom for Denominator

Table B-3: The *F*-Distribution

The *F*-distribution is used in regression analysis to deal with a null hypothesis that contains multiple hypotheses or a single hypothesis about a group of coefficients. To test the most typical joint hypothesis (a test of the overall significance of the regression):

$$H_0: \beta_1 = \beta_2 = \cdots = \beta_K = 0$$
$$H_A: H_0 \text{ is not true}$$

the computed *F*-value is compared with a critical *F*-value, found in Tables B-2 and B-3. The *F*-statistic has two types of degrees of freedom, one for the numerator (columns) and one for the denominator (rows). For the null and alternative hypotheses above, there are K numerator (the number of restrictions implied by the null hypothesis) and $N - K - 1$ denominator degrees of freedom, where N is the number of observations and K is the number of explanatory variables in the equation. This particular *F*-statistic is printed out by most computer regression programs. For example, if K = 5 and N = 30, there are 5 numerator and 24 denominator degrees of freedom, and the critical *F*-value for a 1-percent level of significance (Table B-3) is 3.90. A computed *F*-value greater than 3.90 would lead us to reject the null hypothesis and declare that the equation is statistically significant at the 1-percent level. For more on the *F*-test, see Section 5.6.

Table B-3 Critical Values of the *F*-Statistic: 1-Percent Level of Significance

	v_1 = Degrees of Freedom for Numerator											
	1	2	3	4	5	6	7	8	10	12	20	∞
1	4052	5000	5403	5625	5764	5859	5928	5982	6056	6106	6209	6366
2	98.5	99.0	99.2	99.2	99.3	99.3	99.4	99.4	99.4	99.4	99.4	99.5
3	34.1	30.8	29.5	28.7	28.2	27.9	27.7	27.5	27.2	27.1	26.7	26.1
4	21.2	18.0	16.7	16.0	15.5	15.2	15.0	14.8	14.5	14.4	14.0	13.5
5	16.3	13.3	12.1	11.4	11.0	10.7	10.5	10.3	10.1	9.89	9.55	9.02
6	13.7	10.9	9.78	9.15	8.75	8.47	8.26	8.10	7.87	7.72	7.40	6.88
7	12.2	9.55	8.45	7.85	7.46	7.19	6.99	6.84	6.62	6.47	6.16	5.65
8	11.3	8.65	7.59	7.01	6.63	6.37	6.18	6.03	5.81	5.67	5.36	4.86
9	10.6	8.02	6.99	6.42	6.06	5.80	5.61	5.47	5.26	5.11	4.81	4.31
10	10.0	7.56	6.55	5.99	5.64	5.39	5.20	5.06	4.85	4.71	4.41	3.91
11	9.65	7.21	6.22	5.67	5.32	5.07	4.89	4.74	4.54	4.40	4.10	3.60
12	9.33	6.93	5.95	5.41	5.06	4.82	4.64	4.50	4.30	4.16	3.86	3.36
13	9.07	6.70	5.74	5.21	4.86	4.62	4.44	4.30	4.10	3.96	3.66	3.17
14	8.86	6.51	5.56	5.04	4.70	4.46	4.28	4.14	3.94	3.80	3.51	3.00
15	8.68	6.36	5.42	4.89	4.56	4.32	4.14	4.00	3.80	3.67	3.37	2.87
16	8.53	6.23	5.29	4.77	4.44	4.20	4.03	3.89	3.69	3.55	3.26	2.75
17	8.40	6.11	5.19	4.67	4.34	4.10	3.93	3.79	3.59	3.46	3.16	2.65
18	8.29	6.01	5.09	4.58	4.25	4.01	3.84	3.71	3.51	3.37	3.08	2.57
19	8.19	5.93	5.01	4.50	4.17	3.94	3.77	3.63	3.43	3.30	3.00	2.49
20	8.10	5.85	4.94	4.43	4.10	3.87	3.70	3.56	3.37	3.23	2.94	2.42
21	8.02	5.78	4.87	4.37	4.04	3.81	3.64	3.51	3.31	3.17	2.88	2.36
22	7.95	5.72	4.82	4.31	3.99	3.76	3.59	3.45	3.26	3.12	2.83	2.31
23	7.88	5.66	4.76	4.26	3.94	3.71	3.54	3.41	3.21	3.07	2.78	2.26
24	7.82	5.61	4.72	4.22	3.90	3.67	3.50	3.36	3.17	3.03	2.74	2.21
25	7.77	5.57	4.68	4.18	3.86	3.63	3.46	3.32	3.13	2.99	2.70	2.17
30	7.56	5.39	4.51	4.02	3.70	3.47	3.30	3.17	2.98	2.84	2.55	2.01
40	7.31	5.18	4.31	3.83	3.51	3.29	3.12	2.99	2.80	2.66	2.37	1.80
60	7.08	4.98	4.13	3.65	3.34	3.12	2.95	2.82	2.63	2.50	2.20	1.60
120	6.85	4.79	3.95	3.48	3.17	2.96	2.79	2.66	2.47	2.34	2.03	1.38
∞	6.63	4.61	3.78	3.32	3.02	2.80	2.64	2.51	2.32	2.18	1.88	1.00

v_2 = Degrees of Freedom for Denominator

Table B-4: The Durbin–Watson Statistic

The Durbin–Watson statistic is used to test for first-order serial correlation in the residuals. First-order serial correlation is characterized by $\epsilon_t = \rho\epsilon_{t-1} + u_t$, where ϵ_t is the error term found in the regression equation and u_t is a classical (not serially correlated) error term. Since $\rho = 0$ implies no serial correlation, and since most economic and business models imply positive serial correlation if any pure serial correlation exists, the typical hypotheses are:

$$H_0: \rho \leq 0$$

$$H_A: \rho > 0$$

To test the null hypothesis of no positive serial correlation, the Durbin–Watson statistic must be compared to two different critical d-values, d_L and d_U found in Table B-4, depending on the level of significance, the number of explanatory variables (K) and the number of observations (N). For example, with 2 explanatory variables and 30 observations, the 5-percent one-tailed critical values are $d_L = 1.28$ and $d_U = 1.57$, so any computed Durbin–Watson statistic less than 1.28 would lead to the rejection of the null hypothesis. For computed DW d-values between 1.28 and 1.57, the test is inconclusive, and for values greater than 1.57, we can say that there is no evidence of positive serial correlation at the 5-percent level. These ranges are illustrated in the following diagram:

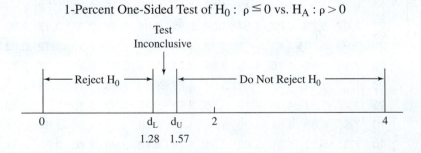

1-Percent One-Sided Test of H_0 : $\rho \leq 0$ vs. H_A : $\rho > 0$

Two-sided tests are done similarly, with $4 - d_U$ and $4 - d_L$ being the critical DW d-values between 2 and 4.

Table B-4 Critical Values of the Durbin–Watson Test Statistics d_L and d_U: 5-Percent One-Sided Level of Significance (10-Percent Two-Sided Level of Significance)

N	K = 1		K = 2		K = 3		K = 4		K = 5		K = 6		K = 7	
	d_L	d_U	d_L	d_U	d_L	d_U	d_L	d_U	d_L	d_U	d_L	d_U	d_L	d_U
15	1.08	1.36	0.95	1.54	0.81	1.75	0.69	1.97	0.56	2.21	0.45	2.47	0.34	2.73
16	1.11	1.37	0.98	1.54	0.86	1.73	0.73	1.93	0.62	2.15	0.50	2.39	0.40	2.62
17	1.13	1.38	1.02	1.54	0.90	1.71	0.78	1.90	0.66	2.10	0.55	2.32	0.45	2.54
18	1.16	1.39	1.05	1.53	0.93	1.69	0.82	1.87	0.71	2.06	0.60	2.26	0.50	2.46
19	1.18	1.40	1.07	1.53	0.97	1.68	0.86	1.85	0.75	2.02	0.65	2.21	0.55	2.40
20	1.20	1.41	1.10	1.54	1.00	1.68	0.89	1.83	0.79	1.99	0.69	2.16	0.60	2.34
21	1.22	1.42	1.13	1.54	1.03	1.67	0.93	1.81	0.83	1.96	0.73	2.12	0.64	2.29
22	1.24	1.43	1.15	1.54	1.05	1.66	0.96	1.80	0.86	1.94	0.77	2.09	0.68	2.25
23	1.26	1.44	1.17	1.54	1.08	1.66	0.99	1.79	0.90	1.92	0.80	2.06	0.72	2.21
24	1.27	1.45	1.19	1.55	1.10	1.66	1.01	1.78	0.93	1.90	0.84	2.04	0.75	2.17
25	1.29	1.45	1.21	1.55	1.12	1.66	1.04	1.77	0.95	1.89	0.87	2.01	0.78	2.14
26	1.30	1.46	1.22	1.55	1.14	1.65	1.06	1.76	0.98	1.88	0.90	1.99	0.82	2.12
27	1.32	1.47	1.24	1.56	1.16	1.65	1.08	1.76	1.00	1.86	0.93	1.97	0.85	2.09
28	1.33	1.48	1.26	1.56	1.18	1.65	1.10	1.75	1.03	1.85	0.95	1.96	0.87	2.07
29	1.34	1.48	1.27	1.56	1.20	1.65	1.12	1.74	1.05	1.84	0.98	1.94	0.90	2.05
30	1.35	1.49	1.28	1.57	1.21	1.65	1.14	1.74	1.07	1.83	1.00	1.93	0.93	2.03
31	1.36	1.50	1.30	1.57	1.23	1.65	1.16	1.74	1.09	1.83	1.02	1.92	0.95	2.02
32	1.37	1.50	1.31	1.57	1.24	1.65	1.18	1.73	1.11	1.82	1.04	1.91	0.97	2.00
33	1.38	1.51	1.32	1.58	1.26	1.65	1.19	1.73	1.13	1.81	1.06	1.90	0.99	1.99
34	1.39	1.51	1.33	1.58	1.27	1.65	1.21	1.73	1.14	1.81	1.08	1.89	1.02	1.98
35	1.40	1.52	1.34	1.58	1.28	1.65	1.22	1.73	1.16	1.80	1.10	1.88	1.03	1.97
36	1.41	1.52	1.35	1.59	1.30	1.65	1.24	1.73	1.18	1.80	1.11	1.88	1.05	1.96
37	1.42	1.53	1.36	1.59	1.31	1.66	1.25	1.72	1.19	1.80	1.13	1.87	1.07	1.95
38	1.43	1.54	1.37	1.59	1.32	1.66	1.26	1.72	1.20	1.79	1.15	1.86	1.09	1.94
39	1.43	1.54	1.38	1.60	1.33	1.66	1.27	1.72	1.22	1.79	1.16	1.86	1.10	1.93
40	1.44	1.54	1.39	1.60	1.34	1.66	1.29	1.72	1.23	1.79	1.18	1.85	1.12	1.93
45	1.48	1.57	1.43	1.62	1.38	1.67	1.34	1.72	1.29	1.78	1.24	1.84	1.19	1.90
50	1.50	1.59	1.46	1.63	1.42	1.67	1.38	1.72	1.34	1.77	1.29	1.82	1.25	1.88
55	1.53	1.60	1.49	1.64	1.45	1.68	1.41	1.72	1.37	1.77	1.33	1.81	1.29	1.86
60	1.55	1.62	1.51	1.65	1.48	1.69	1.44	1.73	1.41	1.77	1.37	1.81	1.34	1.85
65	1.57	1.63	1.54	1.66	1.50	1.70	1.47	1.73	1.44	1.77	1.40	1.81	1.37	1.84
70	1.58	1.64	1.55	1.67	1.53	1.70	1.49	1.74	1.46	1.77	1.43	1.80	1.40	1.84
75	1.60	1.65	1.57	1.68	1.54	1.71	1.52	1.74	1.49	1.77	1.46	1.80	1.43	1.83
80	1.61	1.66	1.59	1.69	1.56	1.72	1.53	1.74	1.51	1.77	1.48	1.80	1.45	1.83
85	1.62	1.67	1.60	1.70	1.58	1.72	1.55	1.75	1.53	1.77	1.50	1.80	1.47	1.83
90	1.63	1.68	1.61	1.70	1.59	1.73	1.57	1.75	1.54	1.78	1.52	1.80	1.49	1.83
95	1.64	1.69	1.62	1.71	1.60	1.73	1.58	1.75	1.56	1.78	1.54	1.80	1.51	1.83
100	1.65	1.69	1.63	1.72	1.61	1.74	1.59	1.76	1.57	1.78	1.55	1.80	1.53	1.83

Source: N. E. Savin and Kenneth J. White, "The Durbin–Watson Test for Serial Correlation with Extreme Sample Sizes or Many Regressors," *Econometrica*, November 1977, p. 1994. Reprinted with permission.

Note: N = number of observations, K = number of explanatory variables excluding the constant term. We assume that the equation contains a constant term and no lagged dependent variables.

Table B-5: The Normal Distribution

The normal distribution is usually assumed for the error term in a regression equation. Table B-5 indicates the probability that a randomly drawn number from the standardized normal distribution (mean = 0 and variance = 1) will be greater than or equal to the number identified in the side tabs, called Z. For a normally distributed variable ϵ with mean μ and variance σ^2, $Z = (\epsilon - \mu)/\sigma$. The row tab gives Z to the first decimal place, and the column tab adds the second decimal place of Z.

Table B-5 The Normal Distribution

z	.00	.01	.02	.03	.04	.05	.06	.07	.08	.09
0.0	.5000	.4960	.4920	.4880	.4840	.4801	.4761	.4721	.4681	.4641
0.1	.4602	.4562	.4522	.4483	.4443	.4404	.4364	.4325	.4286	.4247
0.2	.4207	.4168	.4129	.4090	.4052	.4013	.3974	.3936	.3897	.3859
0.3	.3821	.3783	.3745	.3707	.3669	.3632	.3594	.3557	.3520	.3483
0.4	.3446	.3409	.3372	.3336	.3300	.3264	.3228	.3192	.3156	.3121
0.5	.3085	.3050	.3015	.2981	.2946	.2912	.2877	.2843	.2810	.2776
0.6	.2743	.2709	.2676	.2643	.2611	.2578	.2546	.2514	.2483	.2451
0.7	.2420	.2389	.2358	.2327	.2296	.2266	.2236	.2206	.2177	.2148
0.8	.2119	.2090	.2061	.2033	.2005	.1977	.1949	.1922	.1894	.1867
0.9	.1841	.1814	.1788	.1762	.1736	.1711	.1685	.1660	.1635	.1611
1.0	.1587	.1562	.1539	.1515	.1492	.1469	.1446	.1423	.1401	.1379
1.1	.1357	.1335	.1314	.1292	.1271	.1251	.1230	.1210	.1190	.1170
1.2	.1151	.1131	.1112	.1093	.1075	.1056	.1038	.1020	.1003	.0985
1.3	.0968	.0951	.0934	.0918	.0901	.0885	.0869	.0853	.0838	.0823
1.4	.0808	.0793	.0778	.0764	.0749	.0735	.0721	.0708	.0694	.0681
1.5	.0668	.0655	.0643	.0630	.0618	.0606	.0594	.0582	.0571	.0559
1.6	.0548	.0537	.0526	.0516	.0505	.0495	.0485	.0475	.0465	.0455
1.7	.0446	.0436	.0427	.0418	.0409	.0401	.0392	.0384	.0375	.0367
1.8	.0359	.0351	.0344	.0336	.0329	.0322	.0314	.0307	.0301	.0294
1.9	.0287	.0281	.0274	.0268	.0262	.0256	.0250	.0244	.0239	.0233
2.0	.0228	.0222	.0217	.0212	.0207	.0202	.0197	.0192	.0188	.0183
2.1	.0179	.0174	.0170	.0166	.0162	.0158	.0154	.0150	.0146	.0143
2.2	.0139	.0136	.0132	.0129	.0125	.0122	.0119	.0116	.0113	.0110
2.3	.0107	.0104	.0102	.0099	.0096	.0094	.0091	.0089	.0087	.0084
2.4	.0082	.0080	.0078	.0075	.0073	.0071	.0069	.0068	.0066	.0064
2.5	.0062	.0060	.0059	.0057	.0055	.0054	.0052	.0051	.0049	.0048
2.6	.0047	.0045	.0044	.0043	.0041	.0040	.0039	.0038	.0037	.0036
2.7	.0035	.0034	.0033	.0032	.0031	.0030	.0029	.0028	.0027	.0026
2.8	.0026	.0025	.0024	.0023	.0023	.0022	.0021	.0020	.0020	.0019
2.9	.0019	.0018	.0018	.0017	.0016	.0016	.0015	.0015	.0014	.0014
3.0	.0013	.0013	.0013	.0012	.0012	.0011	.0011	.0011	.0011	.0010

Source: Based on *Biometrika Tables for Statisticians,* Vol. 1, 3rd ed., 1966, with the permission of the *Biometrika* trustees.

Note: The table plots the cumulative probability $Z > z$.

Table B-6: The Chi-Square Distribution

The chi-square distribution describes the distribution of the estimate of the variance of the error term. It is useful in a number of tests, including the White test of Section 10.3 and the Lagrange Multiplier Serial Correlation Test of Section 9.4. The rows represent degrees of freedom, and the columns denote the probability that a number drawn randomly from the chi-square distribution will be greater than or equal to the number shown in the body of the table. For example, the probability is 10 percent that a number drawn randomly from any chi-square distribution will be greater than or equal to 22.3 for 15 degrees of freedom.

To run a White test for heteroskedasticity, calculate NR^2, where N is the sample size and R^2 is the coefficient of determination (unadjusted R^2) from Equation 10.9. (This equation has as its dependent variable the squared residual of the equation to be tested and has as its independent variables the independent variables of the equation to be tested plus the squares and cross-products of these independent variables.)

The test statistic NR^2 has a chi-square distribution with degrees of freedom equal to the number of slope coefficients in Equation 10.9. If NR^2 is larger than the critical chi-square value found in Statistical Table B-6, then we reject the null hypothesis and conclude that it's likely that we have heteroskedasticity. If NR^2 is less than the critical chi-square value, then we cannot reject the null hypothesis of homoskedasticity.

Table B-6 The Chi-Square Distribution

Degrees of Freedom	Level of Significance (Probability of a Value at Least as Large as the Table Entry)			
	10%	5%	2.5%	1%
1	2.71	3.84	5.02	6.63
2	4.61	5.99	7.38	9.21
3	6.25	7.81	9.35	11.34
4	7.78	9.49	11.14	13.28
5	9.24	11.07	12.83	15.09
6	10.64	12.59	14.45	16.81
7	12.02	14.07	16.01	18.48
8	13.36	15.51	17.53	20.1
9	14.68	16.92	19.02	21.7
10	15.99	18.31	20.5	23.2
11	17.28	19.68	21.9	24.7
12	18.55	21.0	23.3	26.2
13	19.81	22.4	24.7	27.7
14	21.1	23.7	26.1	29.1
15	22.3	25.0	27.5	30.6
16	23.5	26.3	28.8	32.0
17	24.8	27.6	30.2	33.4
18	26.0	28.9	31.5	34.8
19	27.2	30.1	32.9	36.2
20	28.4	31.4	34.2	37.6

Source: Based on *Biometrika Tables for Statisticians*, Vol. 1, 3rd ed., 1966, with the permission of the *Biometrika* trustees.

Note: The table plots the cumulative probability Z > z.

INDEX

NOTE: Page numbers in *italics* refer to figures and tables; footnotes are indicated by "n" following the page number.